Improving Healthcare
Through Advocacy

Improving Healthcare Through Advocacy

A Guide for the Health and Helping Professions

Bruce S. Jansson

WILEY

John Wiley & Sons, Inc.

Library of Congress Cataloging-in-Publication Data:

Jansson, Bruce S.
   Improving healthcare through advocacy: A guide for the health and helping professions/Bruce S. Jansson.
      p.; cm.
   Includes bibliographical references and index.
   ISBN 978-0-470-50529-8 (paper: alk. paper); 978-1-118-04414-8 (ePub); 978-1-118-04415-5 (ePDF); 978-1-118-04416-2 (eMobi)
   1. Patient advocacy—United States.   I. Title.   [DNLM: 1. Patient Advocacy—United States.   2. Patient Rights—United States. W 85.4 J35a 2011]
   R727.45.J36 2011
   610—dc22   2010019082

To Lisa Gebo, who taught us how to be skilled
advocates as she battled breast cancer

Contents

Preface

THE GOAL

For the millions of people who navigate the American healthcare system, there are seven common problems they often encounter:

1. They cannot finance their care.
2. They receive care that does not meet widely accepted standards.
3. They encounter violations of their ethical rights.
4. They receive care that is not culturally competent.
5. They fail to receive needed preventive services.
6. They fail to receive appropriate care for their mental health.
7. They do not receive care that links their healthcare to the communities where they live.

Despite these deficiencies, existing health literature and textbooks fail to discuss sufficiently *how* health professionals can become advocates for people with these problems—whether at the case or patient level, or at the policy level. *Improving Healthcare Through Advocacy* provides the first, detailed, hands-on, step-by step, case advocacy framework (see Chapters 3 and 4), as well as a companion policy advocacy framework (see Chapter 12). Each of these frameworks identifies specific tasks of advocates as they provide advocacy interventions, whether at the case or policy levels. Each describes value-clarifying, analytic, influence-wielding, and interactional skills.

Case and policy advocates campaign on behalf of patients or health consumers—or empower them so they can be their own advocates—so that they receive the services, benefits, and rights that they are currently being denied. Advocacy is a highly skilled intervention that often requires the use of influence, assertiveness, and negotiation skills.

Chapters 5 through 11 utilize 118 specific scenarios to describe situations where health consumers often need case advocacy with respect to the seven problems identified previously. Some examples of these scenarios include: *Scenario 5.1: Advocacy to Enhance Consumer's Informed Consent* (in Chapter 5, which discusses health consumers' or patients' ethical rights), *Scenario 6.1: Advocacy to Help Consumers Learn About Evidence-Based Care* (in Chapter 6, which discusses health consumers' or patients' right to quality care), and *Scenario 8.1: Advocacy to Help Consumers Identify Personal At-Risk Factors* (in Chapter 8, which discusses preventive services).

The book also provides many vignettes authored by health professionals or patients themselves. These brief scenarios illustrate how professionals engage in advocacy and why patients or health consumers often need them.

The case and policy frameworks are embedded in their respective policy and regulatory contexts because advocates cannot protect the rights of consumers if they are not informed about the myriad laws and regulations that entitle health consumers and patients to specific rights, benefits, and services. These include HIPAA; Medicare, Medicaid, and S/CHIP, the Americans with Disabilities Act, and the Patient Protection and Affordable Care Act of 2010.

Advocacy is also discussed in its organizational context. Advocates often encounter resistance and negative repercussions from their advocacy. I discuss strategies for minimizing these repercussions. Time pressures also can often make advocacy difficult—this book seeks to identify ways healthcare workers can triage patients to determine who most needs advocacy. It includes discussion of how clinics and hospitals can discourage, as well as promote, use of advocacy—and provides strategies for how readers might team with other health professionals to create institutions that welcome and encourage advocacy.

Advocacy is on the upswing in the health services industry due to the prominence of consumerism and evidence-based practice. Some of the most prominent health systems and institutions that promote advocacy across the nation are identified.

Patients and health consumers often need policy advocacy because their care is hindered by defective policies and procedures in organizational, community, and government settings. I discuss how policy advocates can work to make their clinics and hospitals more receptive to advocacy. (Chapter 13 provides exploratory data that suggest health professionals are more likely to engage in advocacy when it is supported by specific organizational mission, culture, and working arrangements.)

FOR WHOM?

In theory, this book is intended for social workers, nurses, public health staff, and residents (who I sometimes call "frontline staff") because they have more contact with health consumers and patients than many physicians. In practice, this book is intended for *every* health professional because all of them see patients and health consumers whose needs are not currently met by the health system.

Improving Healthcare Through Advocacy can be used in the classroom where its combination of policy, regulations, advocacy interventions, and specific scenarios provide ideal teaching tools. The book's advocacy frameworks and scenarios can be used for role plays and classroom simulations. Its 118 scenarios describe real-life situations confronted by many patients and health consumers who clearly need the help of an advocate. It can be used in continuing education settings because many health professionals must augment their education in order to learn how to provide advocacy interventions.

Consider this book, then, as a bottom-up approach for improving healthcare that complements and supplements top-down policies such as statutes, regulations, and evidence-based medicine. It makes the case that health professionals have an ethical imperative to provide advocacy—and it offers a hands-on methodology for providing it.

ADDED VALUE

Online materials accompany specific chapters in this book at clearly marked places. You may access these materials at www.wiley.com/go/jansson. Also, readers may wish to visit the web site that I am currently establishing for brief updates relevant to this book: http://www.janspan.org.

ACKNOWLEDGMENTS

I am grateful to have received assistance from many people. Helpful comments on the manuscript were given to me by Gary Rosenberg, Ph.D., Director of the Division of Social Work & Behavioral Science at Mount Sinai Hospital in New York City; Laura Weil, M.A. Director of the Health Advocacy Program at Sarah Lawrence College; Kimberly Campbell, ACSW, LCSW, Department of Social Work, Ball State University; Iris C. Freeman, M.S.W, Public Policy Consultant with Advocacy Strategy, Minneapolis, MN and Associate Director of the Center for Elder Justice and Policy at the William Mitchell College of Law, St. Paul, MN; Cassandra J. Bowers, Ph.D., School of Social Work, Wayne State University; and Ann W. Banchoff, M.S.W., M.P.H., Program Director of the Office of Community Health of the School of Medicine of Stanford University.

I greatly benefited, as well, from feedback on early drafts from three health professionals: Julie Anne Miller, M.S.W., Director of the Department of Social Work at Huntington Hospital; Charles Mulley, RN, Care Coordinator at Huntington Hospital; and Carlos Sosa, MSW, Clinical Professor at the USC School of Social Worker and Department of Social Work at Huntington Hospital.

I was greatly assisted in researching this book by the late Jennifer Paek, M.S.W., who tragically died before this book came into print. I benefited from her considerable experience in hospital social work and her commitment to vulnerable populations. She collected some of this book's vignettes. She documented that existing health literature has often exhorted health professionals to engage in case and policy advocacy, but failed to provide them with a hands-on advocacy framework. She tracked down many citations.

Min Ah Kim, M.S.W., and a doctoral student at the University of Southern California School of Social Work, located many citations in this book, particularly in Chapters 10 and 11, as well as helped to develop schematic figures. Erica Lizano, M.S.W, M.P.H, and a doctoral student at the University of Southern California School of Social Work, infused her knowledge of organizational behavior into Chapter 13, which she coauthored with me. Dr. Dennis Kao, Assistant Professor at the School of Social Work at the University of Houston, coauthored Chapter 7 with me. His considerable experience in advocacy with persons from different racial and ethnic groups proved indispensable.

I am indebted to Professor Sarah-Jane Dodd at the School of Social Work at Hunter College for developing and analyzing exploratory data that I cite in Chapter 13 that suggests that the hospital context powerfully influences the extent that social workers and nurses engage in advocacy. Professionals who work in settings that emphasize collaboration, team practice, and multidisciplinary training sessions are far more likely to engage in case and policy advocacy than other professionals.

I am obliged to many students in a graduate health-policy course at the School of Social Work of the University of Southern California, particularly the class of spring 2009, who gave me useful suggestions about this emerging book. Nadya Hernandez and Shunae Dyce contributed vignettes at the ends of Chapters 3 and 5, respectively. Thanks to Gina Frierman-Hunt for her fact-checking and location of citations as this book neared completion.

This book is dedicated to the late Lisa Gebo who, at the end of Chapter 4, contributed a moving personal account of her use of advocacy to battle breast cancer.

Embedding Advocacy in the U.S. Health System

I discuss a bottom-up approach to reforming the American health system in this book, which is to be used in tandem with top-down approaches such as those enacted by the Patient Protection and Affordable Care Act of 2010 as amended by Congress. Health professionals and consumers ultimately decide who gets served and with what benefits and services, even if high-level policies shape these choices—and they must take the initiative to correct ill-advised healthcare choices and policies through the use of advocacy.

I argue in this book that health professionals and consumers often must engage in advocacy to increase the odds that consumers will receive quality services, as well as preventive services, protection of their ethical rights, access to services, culturally-competent services, attention to stress and mental-health issues, and linkages to community resources. I cite extensive research that documents that millions of Americans don't receive these services and benefits.

Advocacy has received insufficient attention in existing health literature, whether the literature of physicians, social workers, psychologists, public health staff, nurses, occupational therapists, or physical therapists. I argue that these professionals have an ethical duty to advocate for specific patients or consumers when they don't receive needed services and access to care—or to provide patients or consumers with the skills and knowledge to advocate for themselves.

I argue that case management and navigation services, while important, do not give sufficient attention to advocacy. They focus on coordinating care and helping patients and consumers navigate the health maze, but they do not usually provide advocacy.

Many health professionals and consumers won't engage in advocacy, however, if they don't learn how to provide it. It requires them to develop specific advocacy skills. This book provides the first framework that links advocacy for individual patients or consumers (case or patient advocacy) with advocacy for groups of patients or consumers (policy advocacy). It identifies specific skills needed by advocates in sufficient detail that they can develop a practice of advocacy in their work.

I link these advocacy practice skills to specific situations or scenarios that many advocates confront in their actual work. I identify and discuss 118 scenarios that often call out for advocacy when patients or consumers don't receive ethical or quality care, when they don't receive culturally competent care, when they can't afford their health services, when specific mental or substance-abuse problems are unaddressed, and when their care is not linked to their communities. I provide many vignettes in this book that demonstrate how health professionals and consumers provide effective advocacy in specific situations.

Health professionals need to create work environments that encourage advocacy. I argue in this chapter, as well as in Chapter 13, that advocacy is often an underground activity that is not encouraged in many hospitals and clinics. Health professionals need to engage in advocacy to create institutions that promote advocacy to improve healthcare in their settings.

Health professionals and consumers, too, need to change high-level policies in clinics, hospitals, communities, or the government that are inimical to quality healthcare. They shouldn't be content to delegate policy advocacy to public officials or to interest groups, but should actively participate in making them.

I hope this book fills a gap in existing health literature. I hope it encourages health educators and health professionals to provide courses and workshops on advocacy. I hope it encourages health professionals and consumers to engage in advocacy whenever they believe that it improves healthcare.

SEVEN PROBLEMS COMMONLY ENCOUNTERED BY HEALTHCARE CONSUMERS

Millions of people encounter seven problems when seeking help from their healthcare providers:

1. They often cannot finance their medical care, including millions of Americans who lack health insurance, persons who are underinsured, persons whose insurance claims are denied—problems that will be alleviated but not eliminated by the health legislation enacted by the Congress and President Barack Obama in March 2010.
2. They often receive medical care that does not meet widely accepted standards, such as the roughly 50% of consumers who do not receive evidence-based medicine for specific health conditions like depression, asthma, and early-stage chronic diseases.
3. They often experience violations of ethical rights, such as insufficient or inaccurate information to allow consumers to make informed choices about their care and breeches of confidentiality.
4. They often receive medical care that is not culturally relevant to them, including services not consonant with their culture, lack of adequate translation services, and lack of sufficient representation of ethnic and racial groups on medical staffs.

5. They often receive insufficient preventive care for specific health conditions, including chronic diseases or ones linked to environmental factors.
6. They often possess excessive levels of anxiety, depression, and other mental conditions that remain unaddressed.
7. Their healthcare often fails to link them with health-related programs and services in their communities.

Many persons possess a combination of two or more of these seven problems. Consider, for example, a woman who fails to receive preventive care (problem #1) because she cannot afford it (problem #2) or an immigrant who lacks sufficient information to give informed consent to a treatment (problem #1) because he lacks adequate translation services (problem #2). Both of them could suffer adverse health consequences if their multiple problems are not addressed. I discuss throughout this book how the Patient Protection and Affordable Care Act of 2010 as amended by the Congress will address many of these seven problems, but its effect will be considerably delayed because many of its provisions are not implemented until 2014 and subsequent years. It is historic legislation that has the potential to improve healthcare for tens of millions of consumers, but only if its provisions are implemented effectively when they take effect from 2010 to 2021. I argue that consumers will need to engage in advocacy, often with the help of specific healthcare professionals, *even* when this legislation is fully implemented because of deep-seated problems in the American healthcare system.

ADVOCACY

Healthcare patients or consumers often need help in addressing these seven problems. Some of them can advocate for themselves, such as persons who seek second opinions, contest adverse decisions by insurance companies, or request preventive services. Many other persons need assistance, however, from healthcare professionals because these people lack sufficient knowledge about the health system, are intimidated by it, lack time to seek redress, fear retaliation, or lack encouragement from family members and friends.

Healthcare professionals need a hands-on framework to help them provide advocacy on two levels. They need to help specific consumers obtain services and rights that would (likely) not otherwise be given to them and that would advance their personal well-being. I call this "case advocacy." Also, they need this advocacy framework to help healthcare professionals change dysfunctional policies in their institutions, communities, and the broader society that often create the need for case advocacy in the first place (I call this "policy advocacy.") I argue that healthcare professionals and consumers can't provide advocacy effectively if they don't develop competencies in specific skills needed for effective advocacy. I identify and discuss these skills with extensive use of vignettes provided by health advocates.

This book provides a framework called the Consumer Advocacy and Navigational Model (CAN), which links four levels or kinds of services provided by healthcare professionals: traditional services, navigation and case-management services, case (or

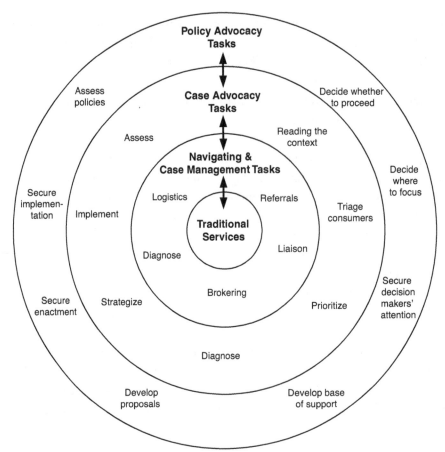

Figure 1.1   Consumer Advocacy and Navigational (CAN) Model

patient) advocacy, and policy advocacy (see Figure 1.1). (See case advocacy and policy advocacy frameworks, respectively, in Chapters 3 and 12).

The innermost circle of Figure 1.1 depicts services that healthcare professionals have traditionally emphasized. Physicians provide care for specific health conditions with diagnostic tests, treatments, and medications. Social workers and nurses devote considerable time, for example, to discharge planning and bedside implementation of physicians' prescribed treatments—even though many leaders in both fields have expanded their roles significantly. Occupational therapists and physical therapists provide services to help patients engage in daily and occupational tasks. Speech and language pathologists help patients regain speech in the wake of strokes and other neurological injuries. Psychologists and social workers engage in counseling. Residents provide general and specialized kinds of medical care.

The next circle in Figure 1.1 depicts tasks commonly associated with patient navigation and case management that respectively help consumers navigate the health system and plan, as well as orchestrate, their services. Although theorists who have developed these models of care sometimes discuss advocacy as part of them, they usually give case advocacy and policy advocacy secondary attention—or ignore them alto-gether. (See discussion of the marginalized status of case and policy advocacy in the online document at the end of this chapter.) The tasks commonly associated with case-management or navigational models *are* important and need to be undertaken, but they do not sufficiently discuss advocacy interventions.

I often use the word "consumers" throughout this book rather than the words "patients" or "clients" to emphasize that case advocates and policy advocates often possess different perspectives than healthcare professionals who operate in the two innermost circles of Figure 1.1. They focus *not* on planning and implementing treatment plans, but in helping people obtain services and rights not likely to be given to them—or in reforming dysfunctional policies in specific institutions and communities, as well as the broader society. Advocates sometimes help people obtain services and benefits to which they are legally entitled under existing statutes and regulations. They sometimes help people obtain ethical rights that many ethicists contend should be honored. They initiate or participate in efforts to reform existing statutes, regulations, and programs. If the term "patients" is widely used to describe persons who are diagnosed and treated for specific illnesses, the term "consumers" describes persons who exercise their rights or choices in a health system that sometimes denies or withholds them—whether through self-advocacy or with the help of healthcare professionals. It builds on the consumer-rights movement that has helped persons secure quality products at affordable prices for the past several decades. It builds upon publications that use the word "consumers," such as Dean Halverson's book *Healthcare Tsunami: The Wave of Consumerism that Will Change U.S. Business* (2008). It is consonant with the movement toward patient-oriented care that currently exists in many hospitals and clinics as is discussed in Chapter 13. Readers who prefer the terms *patients, persons, clients,* or other terms need only substitute those terms for *consumers* throughout this book, while understanding why I use the word consumers. Nomenclature also differs among fields. Nursing literature often discusses "patient advocacy," for example, rather than using the term "case advocacy."

I sometimes use the generic term, "healthcare professionals," to describe persons who can and should provide case and policy-advocacy interventions, that is, *any* professional who works in the healthcare system. I sometimes use the term "frontline staff" because these people are well situated to provide advocacy. They see consumers when they enter and use health systems, as well as when they are discharged from these systems or in their community settings. Social workers, nurses, psychologists, public health staff, speech and language pathologists, occupational therapists, and physical therapists fall within this rubric. I place residents in the ranks of frontline staff because they, too, see consumers for longer and more frequent times than do many physicians. Frontline staff is uniquely positioned to provide advocacy even as I contend that physicians, hospital adminis-trators, and other hospital staff should also engage in case and policy advocacy.

Healthcare professionals wear, in effect, two hats. They plan and implement tradi-tional services when terms like "patients" or "clients" are often used. When they switch into advocacy mode, whether at case or policy levels, they view the persons with whom they work as persons with rights, entitlements, and needs that should be honored. They help them obtain services, resources, ethical care, quality of care, preventive care, culturally competent care, and noninsular care *that they might not otherwise obtain.* They stand beside them. They help them question or challenge existing arrangements. They sometimes take risks as they help consumers—such as encountering anger from other professionals, administrators, or healthcare staff. They often help consumers obtain skills to advocate for themselves, but realize that some consumers need help from healthcare professionals to engage in advocacy, such as people who are traumatized or incapacitated by their medical conditions, those intimidated by the health system or specific professionals, or those who lack sufficient information.

Consumers, too, wear these two hats. They sometimes obtain diagnostic information, select treatment strategies, obtain preventive services, and adhere to physicians' recommendations. This "hat" conforms to what is normally described as the "patient role" although many experts prefer to use the term "consumer" even for this role because it is, they think, more empowering and less restrictive. Consumers wear another hat when they question the health system. They may wish to obtain further information to allow them to have informed consent. They may want second opinions. They may want to insist on specific entitlements, such as translation services if they have limited English proficiency (LEP). They may want to delay specific procedures. They may wish to consider using different medications. They may wish to change medical providers. They may want to consult the Internet to gain further knowledge about a specific health condition.

Frontline people do not actually prescribe medical treatments and medications to consumers, but they often observe their consequences on the consumer's well-being, psychology, family relationships, and finances. They sometimes find them to be confused or disturbed by their medical care. They sometimes discover that they have unanswered questions or doubts about their medical care. They sometimes find that their medical care has deviated from existing rules and regulations. They have an ethical duty to engage in advocacy in these circumstances, such as by helping consumers obtain information and ask questions.

SCENARIOS AND VIGNETTES

Healthcare professionals and consumers experience specific issues and problems as they give and receive services—which I call "scenarios." They describe situations where consumers confront unresolved ethical issues, wonder if they are receiving evidence-based care, believe they do not receive culturally competent services, fail to receive preventive services, cannot afford their care, possess mental distress that is not addressed by their care, and receive healthcare that is not linked to their communities. Each scenario provides a narrative that describes an issue or is confronted by consumers as they encounter one of the seven problems described earlier. Each scenario is often linked to specific policies, regulations, and protocols in health institutions and the broader society. These scenarios serve as alerts for healthcare professionals to provide case advocacy when consumers' needs, entitlements, and ethical rights are not met by the health system. I provide 118 of these scenarios in Chapters 5 through 14, whether in the book (95 of them) or its online component (23 of them). (I discuss at the end of each chapter how to access the scenarios.) Some examples of these scenarios drawn from Chapters 5 through 14 include:

- Scenario 5.1: Advocacy to Enhance Consumers' Informed Consent (Chapter 5 which discusses consumers' ethical rights)
- Scenario 6.1: Advocacy to Help Consumers Learn About Evidence-Based Care Relevant to Their Healthcare (Chapter 6 which discusses consumers' right to quality services)
- Scenario 7.2: Advocacy to Help Consumers Obtain Translation Services (Chapter 7 which discusses consumers' right to culturally competent care)
- Scenario 8.1: Advocacy to Help Consumers Identify Personal At-Risk Factors (Chapter 8 which discusses consumers' right to preventive services)
- Scenario 9.3: Advocacy to Help Uninsured Consumers Obtain Coverage (Chapter 9 which discusses consumers' right to affordable services)
- Scenario 10.10: Advocacy to Help Consumers Manage Stress That Accompanies Physical Illness (Chapter 10 which discusses consumers right to mental-health services)
- Scenario 11.1: Advocacy for Consumers Needing Community Referrals (Chapter 11 which discusses consumers' right to receive healthcare linked to their communities)

This book also presents vignettes contributed by healthcare professionals to illustrate how they provide advocacy. They describe advocacy interventions that are used by many healthcare professionals.

The scenarios and vignettes are embedded in the "policy and regulatory thicket" that envelops the U.S. health system, which is highly regulated by myriad statutes and regulations in federal, state, and local jurisdictions, accrediting authorities, and courts, as well as rules and procedures of specific health organizations. Healthcare professionals can provide effective advocacy only if they possess knowledge of this thicket, which is described as it is relevant to the seven problems of consumers in Chapters 5 through 11.

Health professionals and consumers should often engage in policy advocacy when they observe recurring scenarios or ones that are particularly harmful to consumers. Assume, for example, that a healthcare professional observed that homeless persons were frequently discharged from her hospital even when their underlying medical conditions had not been stabilized and even when a receiving agency or service had not been located. She might engage in policy advocacy by bringing this recurring scenario to the attention of hospital administrators, as well as other health professionals.

RESURGENCE OF INTEREST IN CASE AND POLICY ADVOCACY

Case advocacy and policy advocacy have often been discussed by theorists and practitioners in the literature of healthcare professions in preceding historical eras. (For fuller discussion, see online materials described at the end of this chapter.) Professionals have often been urged to provide these interventions to persons using the health system or to change defective policies that impede or prevent consumers from receiving needed services and resources.

Curiously, however, these theorists and practitioners have failed to provide specific frameworks to help healthcare professionals provide advocacy. I found no framework, for example, that discussed how professionals engage in case advocacy in existing literature—and the author pioneered a policy advocacy framework in prior books (Jansson, 1984, 2011). This book uniquely links the case- and policy-advocacy frameworks by discussing how healthcare professionals, as well as consumers, can use both kinds of advocacy singly and in tandem. This book fills this vacuum in existing literature by providing hands-on advocacy frameworks, as well as scenarios and vignettes that illustrate advocacy interventions.

A resurgence of case advocacy and policy advocacy is underway. Some writers have viewed case advocacy through the lenses of empowerment, seeing it not primarily as a managerial function, but as a way to help persons obtain services and rights that might otherwise be denied them by an unresponsive health system (Klein & Cnaan, 1995; Seal, 2007). Smith and Mason (1995) proposed a formal advocacy structure for the Caribbean American population in New York City to provide them with information about services and to help them gain access to them. Cox (2007) views advocacy as needed in bureaucratic systems to create policy and system-level changes. She desires, as well, a strengths-based perspective, including support groups, to help grandparent-headed families obtain services. Although still marginalizing its role, Hepworth, Rooney, and Larsen (2002) briefly discusses case advocacy as one of many tasks that social workers undertake in direct services—and links it to policy advocacy.

Some leaders in nursing view link health advocacy as necessary to uphold patient rights (Thacker, 2008). Nurse educators, such as A. Davis and Konishi (2007) seek greater nurse advocacy with physicians and other professional personnel. Earp, French, and Gilkey (2008) contend that U.S. nurses increasingly use case advocacy but call it "patient advocacy." They link it to protecting consumers' self-determination, educating and advising them that they can take part in decision making, and "interceding" for patients with others, including family members and physicians, so that patients' wishes are honored (Gilkey, Earp, & French, 2008, p. 6).

Case and policy advocacy have been widely supported among healthcare personnel and advocates who work in end-of-life and palliative care areas. Patients often need help in obtaining fuller communication with health providers about their preferences, the "spiritual and cultural dimensions" of their care, and adequate pain management (Institute of Medicine [IOM], 2003).

Partly following leadership of AIDS activists in the late 1980s and 1990s, a resurgence of advocacy has occurred with respect to specific diseases, such as breast cancer and diabetes (Gilkey et al., 2008.). Case and policy advocates want greater public education, communication of care options, financing of care, and research for these and other diseases (Davenport-Ennis, Cover, Ades, & Stovall, 2002).

Advocacy to help patients gain access to alternative medicine has increased in recent decades. Advocates have sought greater communication among physicians, nurses, and patients about alternative-care options like acupuncture, medication, yoga, and use of herbs. They have fought to allow practitioners of alternative medicine to practice in hospitals. They have sought financing for it by private insurance plans, HMOs, and government programs. They have sought greater federal financing for research on the efficacy of alternative medicine.

The federal government has belatedly shown greater interest in financing research on case advocacy partly spurred by an IOM report (2000) that documented the sheer amount of medical error in the U.S. health system—possibly leading to between 44,000 and 98,000 unnecessary deaths each year. These astonishing figures are more than the number of persons killed during the Vietnam War or from annual deaths from automobile accidents. They make the ethical case for case and policy advocacy even more persuasive. Hospitals and clinics not only need case advocates to come to the aid of specific consumers to prevent medical errors and to help its victims and their families, but to establish safer systems of healthcare. The IOM (2000) contended that between 380,000 and 450,000 preventable adverse drug events take place in hospitals each year. Other scientific research questions overmedication of children and adolescents, the elderly, and persons with such chronic diseases as obesity.

Some graduate-level courses are devoted to advocacy—and even some specialized advocacy programs such as the Health Advocacy Program at Sarah Lawrence College, the Center for Patient Partnerships at the University of Wisconsin-Madison, and the Patient Advocacy Program at Stanford University (Hurst, Gaines, Grob, Weil, & Davis, 2008).

Some hospitals have implemented advocacy programs. Some of them hire "patient representatives" who are assigned to patients to help them use services and to attend to their complaints (Gilkey et al., 2008). Some hire health advocates. Some hire case or care managers who include advocacy in their work. Most hospitals have compliance officers, as well as risk-management departments whose officials sometimes engage in case- and policy-advocacy.

Interest in advocacy has been stimulated as well by background policy developments. As many employers curtail or limit health insurance for their employees because of the recession that began in 2008, the inequities of the U.S. health system become even more apparent, such as the lack of insurance for roughly 47 million Americans and the roughly 40 million Americans who are underinsured. Many insurance companies have capriciously denied coverage for specific health conditions of consumers. These problems will be partly corrected by federal legislation enacted by the Patient Protection and

Affordable Care Act passed by Congress as amended by the Healthcare and Education Reconciliation Act in March 2010 even though it will take years to become fully implemented. (Chapters 2, 5, 6, 8, 9, 10, 11 and 14 discuss this legislation more fully and refer to it by the first title for brevity in these various chapters.)

An increasing body of outcomes-based research has led to renewed interest in evidence-based medicine (EBM) during the past decade. Researchers have discovered that roughly 50% of Americans do not receive evidence-based medicine for such common ailments as asthma and depression. Millions of Americans do not receive state-of-art care for chronic diseases. (IOM, 2008; McGlynn et al., 2003).

Americans have become increasingly aware that the rights of many consumers have been violated by health providers. Some managed-care plans, for example, issued "gag orders" to their physicians to impede referrals to specialists. Some physicians routed patients to facilities that they owned or chose treatments that increased their profits—allowing conflicts of interest to influence their medical decisions.

Advocacy from attorneys and community-based advocacy organizations can be helpful to consumers, but it is not a substitute for advocacy from healthcare professionals, consumers, and consumers working in tandem with healthcare professionals. It is often limited to health-coverage or technical violations of statutes and regulations by providers—rather than the full range of seven problems that consumers often confront.

The enactment of the Patient Protection and Affordable Care Act in March 2010 as amended by Congress illustrates the resurgence of health advocacy. Many smaller health initiatives were enacted in preceding decades, but none equaled the magnitude of this Act, which will cover roughly 32 million uninsured persons, fund a wide array of health-prevention programs, and prohibit insurance companies from withdrawing or withholding coverage to consumers with preexisting conditions. It will greatly increase the size of the Medicaid program. Many health advocates contributed to its enactment. Many health advocates will need to be certain that its provisions are implemented in a timely and effective way during the coming decade.

ADVOCACY FROM OUTSIDE THE HEALTH SYSTEM

Private attorneys have provided advocacy for healthcare consumers for many decades. They have initiated malpractice suits—or threatened suits on behalf of specific consumers. They have brought suits against, or threatened suits, against insurance companies. They have often been involved in suits that allege that providers infringed on their rights, such as withholding information, proceeding with surgical procedures without obtaining informed consent, or divulging confidential information.

Public interest attorneys have litigated extensively against local, state, and public governments on behalf of specific consumers or groups of consumers. In Los Angeles County, for example, attorneys from the Western Center on Poverty and Law, as well as the American Civil Liberties Union, have questioned decisions by Los Angeles County to curtail services, close facilities, privatize facilities, or raise consumer fees.

An array of not-for-profit and for-profit organizations have arisen during the past decade in many jurisdictions that provide advocacy to patients, particularly with respect to insurance claims. Some of them handle hundreds of thousands of inquiries, often brokering decisions among providers, consumers, and insurance companies with re- markable success in overturning denials of insurance claims.

Many states have departments that oversee facets of the health system, such as ones that have jurisdiction over insurance plans, managed-care plans, hospital services, and public systems of healthcare. These departments often have hotlines that consumers can access when they want information or want to complain about specific services or fees.

ADVOCACY AS AN UNDERGROUND ACTIVITY

Advocacy remains an underground activity in many healthcare settings. I discovered that many frontline staff provide advocacy on frequent occasions when I collected vignettes about advocacy with the assistance of doctoral student Jennifer Paek. I was surprised by the number and quality of vignettes that they provided. Frontline staff reported that they frequently engage in advocacy, such as a nurse who said: "I engage in case advocacy on a daily basis often on many occasions." I discuss data gathered in a survey in Chapter 13 that documents that social workers and nurses frequently engage in advocacy with respect to ethical issues of consumers (Jansson & Dodd, 2002; Dodd, Jansson, Brown-Saltzman, Shirk, & Wunch, 2004). They engage in it, I hypothesize, because they see so many consumers who possess one or more of the seven problems I have identified in this book— and realize that they might suffer harm if they did not receive assistance.

This book aims to bring case and policy advocacy into the daylight. I provide frameworks for engaging in them. I discuss why it is often needed by consumers for ethical and evidence-based reasons. I argue in Chapter 13 that it should be a recognized and respected activity in clinics and hospitals as is true in such health systems as the Mayo Clinic, the Geisinger Health System, City of Hope Hospital, and a national network of hospitals that use the Planetree model.

ADVOCACY AS AN ETHICAL IMPERATIVE

Healthcare professionals do not usually receive pay increases, promotions, or re- cognition from engaging in case or policy advocacy. Advocacy usually is not included in their job descriptions. Some of them are censored or punished for engaging in case advocacy *even when they only seek to improve the well-being of specific consumers through responsible actions.* The fear of being censored or punished for advocacy often deters frontline staff from engaging in it—even when this fear is not warranted.

Nor is it surprising that advocacy often ruffles feathers because advocates often question the status quo. Advocates who help consumers obtain second opinions regarding diagnostic tests or treatments may antagonize those physicians who view such advice as a criticism of their work. Policy advocates who seek to change existing policies and protocols within their health organizations may be criticized by officials who support existing policies.

Other barriers exist. It takes time to engage in advocacy when frontline people are hard-pressed by their existing duties—particularly when advocates help persons with particularly difficult problems. Advocates often face adverse odds. They sometimes cannot help consumers for pragmatic reasons, such as when their insurance policies do not cover specific health problems that they possess. They sometimes lose races against the clock when they help people who are nearing death, such as help them make choices about their medical care, complete their wills, or meet with relatives and friends.

Policy advocates sometimes fail to obtain reforms of protocols, budgets, and statutes because of opposition from specific officials, interest groups, and lobbyists. The challenges facing policy advocates were dramatically illustrated by the failure of the American Nurses Association, the National Association of Social Workers, and the American Public Health Association to obtain a "public option" in the Patient Protection and Affordable Care Act of 2010 because of opposition from insurance companies and others—a publicly financed and organized insurance plan that would have competed against private insurance plans and possibly lowered the cost of premiums.

Most advocates are willing to take risks and to devote time to case and policy advocacy even when they confront adverse odds and sometimes do not succeed.

A PHILOSOPHICAL PREMISE

Traditional models of healthcare emphasized its hierarchy extending from physicians at its apex and descending to an array of staff who assumed somewhat subordinate roles. The term *ancillary staff*, often applied to social workers, occupational therapy (OT) and physical therapy (PT) staff, and speech pathologists, describes this subordinate role. Even residents have often been placed in relatively subordinate roles in many hospitals, as have many nurses.

Alternatively, healthcare can be viewed as a partnership between many professions. In this view, consumers "belong" to a health team that includes members of many professions where no one is "ancillary." All members of the team need sophisticated knowledge of consumers' health needs to be able to be advocates for them. They need to know a lot about policies and institutions in the broader society. They need to be knowledgeable about such diverse topics as evidence-based medicine, second opinions, translation services, civil rights, health financing, medical errors, prevention, and court rulings.

It is the ethical obligation of healthcare professionals, in this view, to engage in case advocacy even when not specifically invited by other medical staff to participate. They are ethically obligated, as well, to engage in policy advocacy when they discover that many consumers need case advocacy because they encounter defective policies that are obstacles to the care that they need. They must engage in this work with diplomacy and with due respect to other medical staff, always making it clear by their demeanor, actions, and language that they want to advance the well-being of consumers.

AN OUTLINE OF THIS BOOK

I analyze the evolution of the U.S. health system in Chapter 2 to better understand why many of its consumers experience one or more of the seven problems. I provide a framework for case (or patient) advocacy in Chapter 3 that identifies eight tasks that advocates must undertake. It places advocacy in specific institutional, community, and policy contexts. It discusses how advocates identify contextual factors that assist their advocacies and that impede it.

I discuss four advocacy skills that frontline staff needs when engaging in case advocacy, including developing and using influence, engaging in ethical reasoning, using such interactional skills as communication, conflict management, and group skills; and using analytic skills in Chapter 4.

I emphasize case advocacy for consumers in Chapters 5 through 11 where I discuss policies and regulations germane to the seven problems, discuss some evidence-based research relevant to them, and present 118 scenarios that case advocates and consumers sometimes confront when they experience these seven problems. I provide some vignettes that illustrate the need for case advocacy, as well as the use of case advocacy by healthcare professionals or specific consumers.

I provide a policy-advocacy framework in Chapter 12 that describes eight tasks that advocates undertake when they seek to change specific policies in organizational, community, and government settings.

I discuss policy advocacy in organizational settings in Chapter 13. I relate evidence that frontline staff engages in case advocacy frequently with respect to one of the seven issues confronting healthcare consumers: protection of their ethical rights. This data suggests that case advocacy is integral to the work of many frontline staff even if it is often not sufficiently recognized and encouraged. I discovered, too, that frontline people want to do considerably more case advocacy with respect to consumers' ethical issues. I discuss strategies for embedding case advocacy in clinics and hospitals so that it becomes a recognized and integral part of the practice of healthcare professionals.

Policy advocacy in community and government settings is discussed in Chapter 14. I relate some promising reforms that policy advocates have achieved and are currently seeking to enact in local, state, and federal venues. Healthcare professionals can play an important role in troubleshooting the implementation of the Patient Protection and Affordable Care Act of 2010.

ONLINE MATERIALS RELEVANT TO THIS CHAPTER

Read an overview of the marginalized status of case advocacy in professional literature in social work, nursing, and medicine from 1940 to the present under the heading, "The Marginalizing of Case Advocacy in Professional Literature." Access these materials by going to the web site of John Wiley & Sons at www.wiley.com/go/jansson.

2

How the U.S. Health System Contributes to Consumers' Seven Problems

Healthcare professionals may not understand why U.S. healthcare consumers need advocacy interventions unless they understand how its evolution was shaped by seven factors, including: (1) the poor law tradition; (2) emphasis on technology; (3) entrepreneurialism; (4) insufficient emphasis on prevention; (5) lack of diversity in medical personnel; (6) uneven acceptance of a biopsychosocial framework; (7) medical silos and insular care (see Figure 2.1). These seven factors, in turn, contributed to the development of an American health system that led to the seven problems of consumers that I discussed in Chapter 1. (Readers who want a fuller discussion of the historical evolution of the U.S. health system can access it in the online materials that accompany this book at the end of this chapter.)

THE POOR LAW TRADITION

Americans brought the poor law tradition from England to the United States even in the 17th century—a tradition that required them to establish a safety net for destitute persons, such as by allowing them to stay in Spartan poor houses when they had no other method of supporting themselves (Jansson, 2008). This tradition saved many persons from starvation, but it also stigmatized them by placing them in harsh surroundings. Many Americans assumed they were impoverished not because of adverse economic and other conditions, but because of their poor character.

Americans extended this poor law tradition to medical care by placing persons who could not afford medical care in poor houses—and then later in municipal and county hospitals that became their medical descendents. Rather than creating universal health insurance, Americans continued the poor law tradition when they created Medicaid as a means-tested program to provide coverage to Welfare recipients and destitute elderly

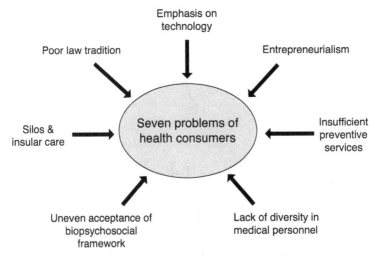

Figure 2.1   Systemic Causes of Consumers' Seven Problems

persons even though they gave them the right to select private providers. Many contemporary public hospitals and clinics often impose long waits and means tests on their consumers—unlike privately insured consumers who are more likely to obtain expedited services and who do not have to face the stigma of means tests (Starr, 1982).

You can view the huge population of medically uninsured persons from World War II onward as descendents, too, of the poor law tradition. These persons often gravitated to public hospitals and clinics when they used medical services unless they had the luck to obtain charitable care from private providers. Rather than protesting their condition, many persons lacking health insurance were *ashamed* of their condition—much like many users of poor law institutions were marginalized in prior centuries. Most Americans assumed that *all* working people received coverage from their employers—overlooking the fact that many employers did not fund their insurance premiums (Hacker, 2002; R. Stevens & Stevens, 1974).

As I discuss in Chapters 6, 8, 9 and 14, the Patient Protection and Affordable Care Act of 2010 as amended by related legislation enacted by the Congress and President Barack Obama in March 2010 extends coverage to roughly 32 million Americans—reducing the number of uninsured consumers to roughly 15 million persons by 2019. Many of these newly covered consumers will join the Medicaid and the State Children's Health Insurance Program (SCHIP)—means-tested programs. Others will receive healthcare from their employers or directly from health insurance exchanges enacted by the various states in 2014.

Advocates in the U.S. health system often have to help consumers obtain coverage (see Chapter 9). They have to help low-income consumers who come disproportionately from racial and ethnic populations receive culturally competent care (see Chapter 7). They have to help low-income persons receive community-based care (see Chapter 11).

EMPHASIS ON TECHNOLOGY

The U.S. health system employs more technology than any health system in the world (G. Anderson, Hussey, Frogner, & Waters, 2005; G. Anderson & Frogner, 2008). This emphasis on technology provides many benefits to U.S. consumers who often receive state-of-art care. It also poses issues that advocates must address. I discuss how technology poses ethical issues, such as whether consumers have given informed consent to treatments with adverse side effects (see Chapter 5). Consumers often need to obtain second opinions (see Chapters 5 and 6), as well as determine what side effects they may experience from technology as in Chapter 6. Consumers with terminal conditions have to decide whether and to what degree to try to extend their lives with use of technology (see Chapters 5 and 6). Some low-income consumers may have coverage that does not give them access to some technology as compared to more affluent persons (see Chapters 5 and 9).

ENTREPRENEURIALISM

The U.S. health system has emphasized entrepreneurialism since its inception (Starr, 1982). Even as large government medical programs like Medicare and Medicaid, and PPOs; managed-care plans with salaried physicians; public regulations like HIPAA have emerged, Americans' competitive and entrepreneurial health system has remained intact. Insurance companies compete with one another for the business of employers. Pharmaceutical, medical-device, and other medical corporations compete with one another for the allegiance of physicians and consumers. Physicians gravitate to high-paying medical specialties where they compete with one another for consumers in such areas as cardiology, neurology, obstetrics, oncology, and urology. Hospitals compete with one another for consumers' business—sometimes even advertising to patients who use competing hospitals in their geographic areas. Providers, insurance companies, and health plans advertise extensively to consumers through direct mail, the Internet, and the mass media (Hacker, 2002).

Entrepreneurialism has positive features, such as giving consumers choice in selecting providers, but it also has caused many problems. Consumers are often subjected to false or deceptive advertising (see Chapters 5 and 6). Some insurance companies, hospitals, and physicians have shunned patients with complex health problems (see Chapter 9)—a practice that could be greatly reduced by insurance regulations in the Obama health plan of 2010. Because hospitals and physicians often locate their practices in relatively affluent areas rather than in areas with low-income populations or where many consumers are Medicaid enrollees, advocates must often help them get access to health services (see Chapters 6, 7, and 9).

INSUFFICIENT EMPHASIS ON PREVENTION

The U.S. health system often gives insufficient attention to preventive services for many reasons. Insurance companies, Medicare, and Medicaid have often not funded preventive services. U.S. consumers disproportionately use specialists rather than primary-care physicians as compared to health systems in other industrialized nations. Americans often make lifestyle choices that contribute to illness and chronic diseases, such as diets with high-fat content and sedentary lifestyles. I discuss how advocates can help consumers get preventive care in Chapter 8. The Patient Protection and Affordable Care Act of 2010 will fund many new preventive programs.

LACK OF DIVERSITY IN MEDICAL PERSONNEL

The United States has been a polyglot of ethnic and racial groups from its inception—whether from the forced immigration of slaves, indigenous Native Americans and Hispanics, or voluntary immigration from most nations of the world (Preston, 2007; Purnell & Paulanka, 2008). No health system in the world has confronted the challenge of dealing with dozens of languages and dialects and diverse cultural norms.

The U.S. health system has had to relate also to populations that view it with fear or indifference. Many African Americans view the health system as actively conspiring against their population after dire experiences with oppressive medical systems in the South and the infamous Tuskegee experiment that denied medical assistance to black men with syphilis to gain information about the disease. Many Latinos came from rural areas in other nations or in the United States that had virtually no formal medical system (Jansson, 2008).

The U.S. health system has navigated this diverse landscape with mixed results. It has made considerable progress in bringing women into the medical profession to go along with their numbers in nursing and social work professions even if they disproportionately practice internal medicine and pediatrics. The system still lags in hiring persons of color, particularly in the ranks of physicians. It fails to give many consumers adequate translation services or to give physicians and other health staff sufficient training to communicate across cultures (Weissman et al., 2005).

The nation has made remarkable progress in lengthening life spans and improving public health in the twentieth century. Despite this progress, health disparities remain unacceptably high in the United States when comparing Caucasians with specific racial groups and when comparing the top fifth of persons in the economic distribution with persons in the bottom fifth. Although the health of members of the bottom fifth has improved in the past four decades, it hasn't improved sufficiently to redress the gap between it and the Caucasian population whose health has also improved during this time span (Kawachi, Daniels, & Robinson, 2005; Satcher et al., 2005).

Many theorists have discussed why health disparities have been so persistent in the United States as compared to other nations like Great Britain (Barr, 2008). Some implicate different levels of access and inequities in treatment. Others emphasize the extraordinary level of economic inequality in the United States when combined with relatively Spartan safety-net programs that marginalize U.S. low-income populations and expose them to hardships.

I mentioned earlier that persons of color are underrepresented among physicians as well as other medical personnel. Some medical personnel, too, are reluctant to refer consumers to practitioners of alternative medicine, such as acupuncturists, chiropractors, and persons who help consumers surmount stress through yoga and other strategies (Pagan & Pauly, 2005). I discuss in Chapter 7 how advocates can help consumers obtain culturally competent care.

UNEVEN ACCEPTANCE OF A BIOPSYCHOSOCIAL FRAMEWORK

I have mentioned that many health personnel emphasize the use of technology in healthcare, but sometimes risk not giving sufficient attention to other factors such as the mental distress of many consumers; family, economic, and social factors; and community factors. Advocates can play an important role by using a biopsychosocial framework to address multiple needs of consumers (Gehlert, 2006a). Advocates can help identify consumers who have mental distress. They can help them obtain mental health services. They can identify family, economic, and social factors that contribute to their health problems and can help consumers address them or find help for them. They can link consumers to community-based agencies. I discuss these advocacy strategies in Chapters 10 and 11. In Chapter 13, I relate how advocates can work to embed case advocacy in the health system so that health organizations welcome contributions from a variety of professionals.

MEDICAL SILOS AND INSULAR CARE

The U.S. health system is often insulated from community-based agencies as well as communities where consumers reside (Beal, 2005; Markel & Golden, 2005). Considerable research implicates economic realities, such as poverty, in creating health disparities, but medical providers assume virtually no role in advocating for better living conditions for low-income consumers. They often are not connected to public health programs in the community that work to educate consumers or prevent an array of diseases such as HIV/AIDS, STDs, and TB or to enhance birth control. Patients are often not linked to community-based agencies that might help them when they are discharged from hospitals.

Medical silos exist within the U.S. health system. Specialists often do not confer with one another as they help consumers with multiple health problems (Lawrence, 2003; Wartman, 2006). Oncologists often do not refer consumers to hospice or to palliative care. Primary-care physicians do not usually follow their patients when they enter hospitals.

Medical silos are accentuated by the profit-driven and entrepreneurial nature of the U.S. medical system, which often places providers in competition with one another for revenues. It is exacerbated, too, by the domination of U.S. healthcare by specialists who often focus on specific health problems to the detriment of broader perspectives.

The insularity of medical care is illustrated, as well, by the paucity of health services in many schools, jails, public housing, and nursing homes where consumers live or reside. As one example, the largest public school in Los Angeles in a low-income area recently had only a single nurse for thousands of students. Many prisons possess inadequate health staff leading to the unnecessary spread of HIV and insufficient attention to inmates' mental issues.

The United States possesses a relatively dense network of nongovernment organizations (NGOs) in the health system as compared to many nations. It includes not-for-profit associations devoted to education and advocacy with respect to specific diseases, such as the American Diabetes Association and the American Cancer Association. It includes support groups, sometimes in liaison with specific hospitals and clinics, which provide emotional support and assistance to consumers with specific diseases, like diabetes, cancer, and substance abuse (Katz, 1990). Many consumers receive free or low-cost medical equipment from an array of charitable organizations, which include community-based hospice organizations.

This network has been supplemented by the Internet in recent decades, providing consumers with a huge reservoir of information, data, and resources relevant to their health issues.

Americans have long made extensive use of advocates outside the health system. Health attorneys do not just obtain financial awards for alleged malpractice, but contest decisions like the denial of benefits from specific insurance companies. Public interest attorneys frequently litigate against local officials, the federal government, insurance companies, or specific providers when they believe their policies or treatment of specific consumers are illegal or harm them. Large not-for-profit and for-profit organizations have emerged during the past decades to provide advocacy to consumers, such as helping them navigate the complex medical system, obtain second opinions, locate resources, contest denials of insurance coverage, or contest specific treatment advice from providers.

These informal adjuncts are integral to the work of case and policy advocacy of frontline staff in the health system. They often refer consumers to them so that they can provide case advocacy. They sometimes accompany consumers to support groups when they fear they might otherwise not use them. They sometimes encourage consumers to determine if they can obtain redress for medical errors and denial of coverage by referring them to attorneys. Advocates need skills in steering consumers toward informal adjuncts that will provide them with accurate information.

Chapter 11 discusses how advocates can help consumers surmount medical silos and insular healthcare. The Patient Protection and Affordable Care Act of 2010 will strengthen community-based care.

FROM HISTORY TO CASE AND POLICY ADVOCACY

Knowledge of the evolution of the U.S. health system helps us to understand why many U.S. consumers need case and policy advocacy with respect to the seven problems commonly experienced by consumers. Many consumers cannot afford medical care because Americans created a health system primarily from private insurance provided by those employers who were willing to fund it—leaving others in the lurch. The technological training of many specialists has not given them skills to communicate adequately with consumers, making it difficult for them to give consumers sufficient information that they receive their ethical right to informed consent. Many consumers receive poor-quality care because of over-provision of medications, diagnostic tests, and surgical procedures that are heavily reimbursed by private and government insurance programs to the detriment of less invasive care. Many consumers receive culturally irrelevant care because the medical profession has only recently made significant strides in including persons of color and persons who speak foreign languages in its ranks. Many consumers receive insufficient preventive care because the U.S. health system places undue emphasis on medical specialties as compared with primary care, and reimburses it at low levels. Insular care derives from the technological nature of care in the United States, which places little emphasis on establishing links between hospitals and clinics with an array of NGOs. Emphasis on physiological interventions means that many consumers do not receive sufficient attention to their mental problems, such as many Latinas with breast cancer who suffer from debilitating depression that is often not diagnosed or treated.

The Patient Protection and Affordable Care Act of 2010 will mitigate some of the problems encountered by healthcare consumers, but, as I discuss in subsequent chapters, it will only partially address some of them and not address others at all. Healthcare professionals have an ethical duty to engage in policy advocacy to address systemic factors that cause or exacerbate consumers' seven problems (see Chapters 12 through 14). Advocates will need to represent the needs of low-income and relatively powerless consumers to be certain that their needs are sufficiently addressed during the implementation of the Patient Protection and Affordable Care Act by the various states, as well as by the federal government.

History and policy help us understand why U.S. consumers often need advocacy, but they do not tell us how to do it. I provide a case-advocacy framework in Chapters 3 and 4, and discuss how health professionals and consumers can use it to help consumers avert the seven problems discussed in Chapters 5 through 11. I provide a policy advocacy framework in Chapter 12 and discuss how it can be used by health professionals and consumers to correct defective policies in organizational, community, and government settings. I argue that case advocacy should be linked with policy advocacy in the practice of healthcare professionals, particularly because they frequently confront scenarios at the patient or consumer level that are inimical to their well-being.

ONLINE MATERIALS RELEVANT TO THIS CHAPTER

Read about the historical evolution of the American health system, titled "Why American Health Consumers Often Need Advocacy: A Historical Analysis" in the online materials that accompany this chapter. Access these materials by going to the web site of John Wiley & Sons at www.wiley.com/go/jansson.

3

An Advocacy Practice Framework

Tasks, Skills, and Actions

Considerable health and professional literature urges health professionals and consumers to engage in advocacy at both case and policy levels. It usually fails, however, to discuss *how* they should provide these interventions, such as the specific tasks they need to undertake and the skills that they need. I provide the first detailed framework for case advocacy in existing literature in this chapter—and link it to a framework for policy advocacy in Chapter 12. This framework can be used in any health or health-related setting including clinics, hospitals, convalescent homes, or nursing homes. It can be used by professionals in community-based agencies. In Chapter 4, I discuss four skills that advocates need when they implement this framework.

In Chapters 5 through 11, I use this framework to discuss how health professionals and consumers engage in advocacy with respect to the seven problems that consumers often confront.

I link case advocacy to policy advocacy in this chapter while discussing policy advocacy in more detail in Chapters 12 through 14.

BRIEF OVERVIEW OF CASE-ADVOCACY INTERVENTIONS

Case advocacy is not an administrative or service-delivery function, but an activity to help consumers contest, improve, or rethink decisions that have been made about their care. Case advocates question the status quo. They work for specific consumers. They provide simple and time-limited interventions—or multifaceted ones that take considerable time.

Case advocates can decide to empower consumers to become their own advocates—giving them suggestions, coaching, information, and help in using the Internet. They may decide to partner with them by dividing advocacy tasks with them. They may implement an advocacy strategy unilaterally, such as when helping comatose consumers or consumers with limited cognitive abilities obtain needed services.

Case advocates engage in advocacy within specific hospitals or clinics, but also in communities, such as when they help specific consumers obtain living arrangements that are conducive to their well-being or when they help teenagers return to their regular schools rather than special schools after they have given birth. Case advocates may help some consumers connect to case advocates outside of the health system by referring them to public interest attorneys, private attorneys, or advocacy organizations.

EIGHT CASE-ADVOCACY TASKS

Case advocates engage in eight tasks (see Figure 3.1). They read the context. They triage consumers to decide which of them would benefit from case advocacy. They prioritize which persons most need their case-advocacy assistance. They diagnose why specific consumers need case advocacy. They strategize to develop a planned case-advocacy intervention. They implement case advocacy with specific consumers. They assess case-advocacy outcomes to decide whether they have successfully completed case advocacy with a specific consumer—or whether they need to continue it with the same or a different strategy.

Advocates determine, as well, whether to progress from case advocacy to policy advocacy.

TASK #1: READING THE CONTEXT

Advocacy always takes place in a context, which is called the "policy/organizational thicket" in Figure 3.1. I use the word "thicket" because the healthcare system is highly regulated from many sources, subject to complex funding, and exists in a competitive

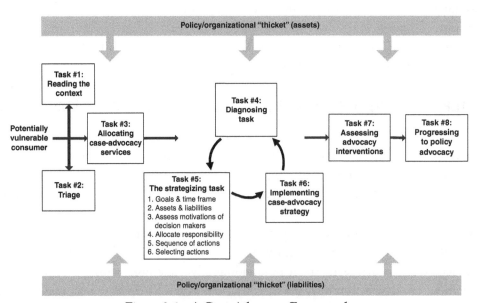

Figure 3.1   A Case Advocacy Framework

medical marketplace. Many policies, procedures, and protocols also exist within specific hospitals and clinics.

This thicket includes assets that facilitate the work of advocates in specific situations and liabilities that impede it. Advocates need a strategic view of the organizations where they work so that they can identify (or find) assets that will facilitate their case advocacy with specific consumers, while not neglecting those contextual liabilities that will make it more difficult. For example, persons with insurance policies that exclude specific services or require considerable out-of-pocket payments may not be able to surmount them when an advocate seeks to help them contend with their health costs (a liability). An advocate who wishes to help an uninsured patient *not* be transferred from a private to a public hospital before she is medically stabilized can cite federal regulations that prohibit such transfers (an asset).

The thicket contains many "streams" that flow into and through the healthcare system from *external* sources. Each of these streams may contain assets or liabilities for advocates in specific situations. They include:

- Court rulings that require health staff to take certain actions and to avoid other actions, such as ones concerning when it is possible to withdraw food, medications, and/or hydration from a dying person
- Statutes (or legislation) that require specific actions, services, or accountability by health organizations and their staff, such as a Medicaid requirement that state Medicaid programs provide five essential services
- Civil rights legislation that mandate that health providers not violate specific rights of specific populations, such as requirements for ease of movement by persons with disabilities as required by the Americans with Disabilities Act (ADA)
- Flows of revenues to health providers from private insurance companies, employers, Medicare, Medicaid, and SCHIP
- Potential sanctions or adverse publicity that specific health organizations might confront, such as from low scores on measures of the quality of their services and patient satisfaction from research by external bodies such as Medicare or state authorities
- Competition from other health plans, hospitals or clinics
- Accreditation standards from such organizations as the Joint Commission on Accreditation of Healthcare Organizations (JCAHO, now called "The Joint Commission") that identify specific service requirements for staff, as well as many other standards to safeguard consumers' well-being
- Regulations of specific local, state, and federal departments, such as ones that establish certain patient rights within managed-care organizations
- Regulations of insurance companies of specific local, state, and federal departments
- Legal litigation and inquiries of public interest attorneys and private attorneys

- Monitoring and oversight of public clinics and clinics in the jurisdictions of health and related departments in cities and counties
- Monitoring and oversight of public health departments and clinics that provide services to promote sanitation, avert the spread of diseases, provide diagnostic tests for specific diseases including HIV/AIDS, STDs, and TB, and provide pre- and postnatal services
- External advocacy groups that help consumers contest denials of resources from insurance companies and other programs such as Medicare, as well as many support groups
- Resources and regulations of publicly funded programs to which consumers may be able to receive assistance, including Medicare, Medicaid, and SCHIP
- Specific research findings in professional literature or from private or governmental sources
- Policies and procedures of community-based agencies
- Evidence-based medicine that draws on empirical research

This thicket includes many streams from internal sources that can also be assets or liabilities in specific instances of case advocacy, including:

- Budgets and their relative surpluses or deficits in specific health settings
- Mission statements that state the priorities and goals of a provider
- Organizational culture as it favors specific activities while discouraging others—including case advocacy and policy advocacy
- Specific units that engage in advocacy or advocacy-related work, such as departments of compliance, risk management departments, bioethics committees, institutional review boards (IRBs), patient representatives or advocates, social work departments, care managers, and financial departments
- Specific officials, administrators, professionals, or staff who have expertise and clout in specific areas, such as hospice, ICUs, NICUs, ERs, and trauma units
- Rules or protocols established within a specific health organization

These internal factors can also be assets or liabilities in specific case-advocacy situations. Healthcare professionals can move forward specific ethical problems or issues, for example, to a hospital's Bio-Ethics Committee and ask for its advice (an asset). Budget deficits may lead to cuts in services that can bring cuts in specific programs needed to provide services to specific consumers (a liability).

Gaining Knowledge to Be an Effective Advocate

It is challenging to be informed about these contextual factors. Advocates need to understand, for example, key provisions of the Health Insurance Portability and Accountability Act of 1996 (HIPAA) as they affect their advocacy work with a consumer who believes the confidentiality of her medical information has been breached. A healthcare professional needs to know what hotlines exist to help consumers with specific information.

I discuss specific contextual factors that are germane to consumers' seven health problems throughout this book, such as those relating to consumers' ethical rights (Chapter 5), the quality of consumers' health services (Chapter 6), the extent consumers' services are culturally competent (Chapter 7), the preventive services of consumers (Chapter 8), the affordability of consumers' health services (Chapter 9), the extent health services address consumers' mental and substance-abuse problems (Chapter 10), and the extent to which consumers receive community-based services (Chapter 11). Evidence-based medicine is discussed in Chapters 5 through 14 as it is relevant to the seven core problems that many consumers confront in the health system.

Advocates have to update their knowledge to be effective. Laws and regulations frequently change. New and revised evidence-based medicine frequently emerges. Ethical standards change. They need to update their knowledge about resources in their health organizations. They need to expand and change their networks as new administrators and professionals are hired.

I place Internet sites at strategic places in this book to facilitate this updating process with reputations for accuracy. These include web sites of governmental agencies, advocacy groups, and self-help groups.

TASK #2: TRIAGE

Healthcare professionals should identify potential advocacy situations as they interact with consumers in the advocacy triage task. Professionals must ask themselves whether specific consumers might suffer harm if they did not provide them with case advocacy. I discuss specific warning signs that should alert healthcare professionals to possible harm, whether specific consumers possess or can develop skills to engage in self-advocacy, and whether consumers' problems are likely to be redressed by staff in the health system without their assistance.

Membership in a Vulnerable Population

All healthcare consumers are at risk of experiencing the seven problems, regardless of their social class, ethnicity, or race. Healthcare staff need to be particularly attentive, however, to the advocacy needs of an array of vulnerable populations because they often possess a higher risk of encountering these problems.

Vulnerable populations include consumers whose predisposing or intrinsic characteristics often expose them to one or more of the seven problems (R. Anderson, 1995). They include consumers with distinctive racial or ethnic characteristics, including African Americans, Latinos/as, Asian Americans and Native Americans, as well as specific immigrant populations from the Middle East, Africa, Eastern Europe, Russia, and

Asia. They include documented and undocumented immigrants, as well as persons with uncertain immigration status. They include women. They include consumers in different age groups, such as children and adolescents, as well as elderly persons. They include consumers with specific sexual orientations including the LGBT population. They include consumers with stigmatized health conditions, including persons with HIV/AIDS/STDs; and victims and perpetrators of family violence and rape. They include consumers with stigmatized forms of mental illness, such as schizophrenia and clinical depression. They include consumers with addictions. They include consumers with eating disorders. They include consumers with reduced mental capacity including persons with dementia, Alzheimer's disease, and developmental disabilities.

Vulnerable populations include people with enabling factors that often expose them to one or more of the seven problems (Anderson, 1995). They include consumers who lack medical insurance or who are underinsured, and those with relatively low levels of education. They include rural and inner-city consumers who live in areas with shortages of medical services. They include consumers with limited-English proficiency (LEP). They include low-income consumers.

Vulnerable populations include ones whose need (or degree-of-sickness) often exposes them to one or more of the seven problems (Anderson, 1995). They include consumers with chronic diseases including COPD, congestive heart failure, heart disease, arthritis, degenerative muscle diseases such as muscular dystrophy, cerebral palsy, and genetic disorders such as Lou Gehrig's disease and Huntington's disease. They include consumers with life-threatening diseases including some kinds of cancer and chronic diseases.

Many consumers belong to two or more of these vulnerable populations, such as African Americans with an advanced chronic disease or consumers with limited education who possess dementia.

Consumers With High-Threshold Problems

Consumers particularly need case advocacy when any of the seven core problems reach a high threshold that endangers their well-being or their ethical rights. Some consumers may experience relatively minor violations of their ethical rights, for example, such as a consumer not receiving a specific food item—as compared with major ethical infringements such as not receiving informed consent for a specific medical treatment. Some affluent consumers may be irritated by out-of-pocket costs that they believe to be unwarranted, but other consumers may have financial problems that cause them to drop out of services, or use them irregularly, when they have a life-threatening condition. Remember, however, that ethical issues that seem low-threshold may be important to specific consumers (Daley, 2001).

Healthcare professionals should consider case advocacy when any of these or the remaining seven problems reach a high threshold and threaten consumers' well-being. I discuss how they use one or more kinds of information to gauge whether consumers possess specific problems and their thresholds. As discussed in Chapters 5 through 11, these include:

- Information from specific consumers
- Care divergent with evidence-based findings
- Care divergent with ethical standards including informed consent
- Notations in medical records
- Direct observations
- Feedback from other professionals
- Feedback from family members

Consumers With Multiple Problems

Many consumers are plagued by more than one of the seven core problems. Advocates should often engage in case advocacy with consumers with two or more of these problems. Some consumers possess multiple, interacting problems that, together, place them in jeopardy—but receive care for only one of them. Consumers who are obese, diabetic, depressed, and lack insurance are likely to need case advocacy to develop strategies for obtaining multifaceted care and for their multiple problems, as well as their financial problems.

Consumers Not Receiving Any, Partial, or Delayed Care

Some consumers do not receive any care for a specific health condition. Perhaps they encounter barriers to using healthcare, such as lack of insurance or funds to pay out-of-pocket costs. Perhaps they lack transportation to health settings. Perhaps they lack child care so they cannot use health services on a regular basis. Perhaps they drop out from services or do not adhere to recommended treatments or medications, even when nonadherence could prove harmful or life threatening.

Health staff may discover some consumers who do not seek healthcare because they have preconceptions that may deter them from using it. Specific African American males may believe, for example, that persons with cancer are doomed or possess negative views of the medical profession—views that lead them not to seek care for prostate cancer. Some consumers may refrain from seeking care for a stigmatized condition in their ethnic or racial group, another reference group, or in the broader community. Persons of color sometimes do not seek attention for HIV/AIDS, for example, because it is stigmatized in their communities.

Consumers may be seen by health providers, but find their treatments to be excessively delayed. They may be caught in long lines particularly in public clinics and hospitals even when they possess serious health conditions. They may be unable to obtain care from specific primary-care physicians or specialists due to long waits.

Consumers With Overlooked Problems

Many consumers receive assistance for a presenting problem, but find other problems to be unaddressed by medical staff. A disabled person may receive care for her physical limitations, but not attention for her anxiety or depression. A consumer may receive heart bypass surgery but not receive help with cognitive problems in its wake.

Consumers Caught in a Revolving Door

Health staff often encounter consumers who repeatedly return to an ER, outpatient clinic, or hospital. A considerable portion of medical services is devoted to the "worried well," that is, to persons who do not have serious health problems, but who want reassurance, attention, or companionship from healthcare providers. Other consumers come to specific health facilities repeatedly for the same condition, such as alcoholism, substance abuse, or attempted suicide. Advocates may need to help them receive preventive, counseling, or other services to address causes of this repetition.

Consumers Enmeshed in Destructive Relationships

Health staff may engage in case advocacy when they observe or detect family members or other persons who sabotage the healthcare or the ethical rights of a specific consumer. Existing laws require them to inform authorities, for example, when specific consumers, such as women, children, or elderly persons, are subject to violent acts from family members or other persons.

Consumers in Physical or Psychological Jeopardy

Health staff may fear that specific consumers will die or suffer grievous physical injury if they do not receive case advocacy. A nurse in a public clinic in the Bronx in New York City took it upon herself, for example, to locate consumers who had recently received biopsies revealing aggressive and advanced cancer, but had not returned for follow-up visits. She persuaded many of them to return for treatment that they might otherwise have not received—and possibly saved some of their lives (Perez-Pena, 2005).

Consumers Unable to Self-Advocate

Health staff often decide that specific consumers are able to advocate for themselves because they are highly skilled at navigating the healthcare system and have read about their conditions or searched the Internet diligently. They may already have received a second opinion from experts and already received advice from other persons who have experienced their condition. They are appropriately assertive, skilled communicators, and persistent. They keep records. They know about emerging treatments and tests.

They are not traumatized by adverse diagnoses. Healthcare professionals may decide that these persons are able to advocate for themselves with no or minimal assistance from them. They should prioritize case advocacy for consumers who lack these skills and knowledge, particularly when they possess serious problems that could threaten their well-being and their ethical rights.

Consumers Unlikely to Receive Case Advocacy From Others

Some consumers have supportive families and friends who help them self-advocate or become surrogate advocates when they lack the skills, knowledge, or ability to advocate for themselves. Healthcare professionals need to consider providing advocacy when consumers do not have these supports.

In the case of comatose persons, persons with limited cognitive function, or persons under sedation or heavy medication, healthcare professionals should often obtain the concurrence of family members or friends before engaging in case advocacy.

Consumers Bewildered by the Medical System

Health organizations are complex institutions with multiple professions, administrative staff, internal units, and linkages with myriad external organizations. Their staff uses complicated jargon. It is not surprising that many consumers find it difficult to understand them or to navigate within them, particularly when they have complex or serious medical conditions and when they contend with medical jargon. Many providers are not good communicators.

Skilled case advocates can better decide who needs case advocacy by viewing these institutions from the bottom up so they view them like consumers do. They can bring simple improvements to their care, such as scheduling visits by hospital staff, so that consumers do not lose their privacy when professionals flow through their rooms at nonstop and unpredictable intervals. They can interpret hospital procedures to them, help them locate places, facilitate family members' visits, and learn to detect consumers' confusion and angst.

Consumers Who Endanger Themselves

Case advocates usually focus on factors that preclude consumers from receiving needed services or that violate their rights. In some cases, however, they provide "reverse advocacy" that focuses on consumers' self-destructive behaviors like smoking, substance abuse, lack of exercise, or poor diet. They may have received little assistance from physicians and other medical staff who do not want to antagonize or confront them—but this avoidance may prove harmful to those consumers who proceed unchallenged by their caregivers.

Case advocates can point consumers in new directions tactfully. They can ask, for example, whether anyone has informed them of support groups, Internet sites, or counseling assistance that might prove helpful in reducing their smoking, excessive use of alcohol, or other self-destructive behaviors. They can ask if they have received data that examines their health prognosis if they do not curtail or eliminate specific destructive behaviors.

TASK #3: ALLOCATING CASE ADVOCACY SERVICES

Even when triaging suggests that specific consumers possess at-risk indicators for case advocacy, healthcare professionals cannot always provide it for legitimate reasons. They sometimes can find advocacy shortcuts, as well.

Competing Tasks

Healthcare professionals often encounter daunting workloads when their regular work is combined with paperwork and other bureaucratic requirements. The urgency of their regular work may sometimes trump case advocacy because case advocacy takes time, particularly in complex situations.

Unlikely Positive Outcomes

Healthcare professionals sometimes decide that positive outcomes are highly unlikely in specific instances. Perhaps they have attempted case advocacy on prior occasions with a particular consumer with no success, or a consumer does not want case advocacy, or they cannot gain access to specific consumers who might otherwise benefit from it.

Likely Repercussions

Case advocates often question the status quo, such as the failure of medical staff to obtain informed consent, follow evidence-based practices, or attend to consumers' depression or anxiety. They may decide in some situation that they will encounter excessive risk when injecting themselves into some situations that could jeopardize their ability to engage in case advocacy in future situations. Perhaps particular physicians or other medical staff would view case advocacy as an attack on their competence or integrity no matter how diplomatic they might be. Perhaps they fear inciting anger or complaints from the spouses, relatives, and friends of specific consumers who do not agree that their family member has received poor or inadequate services or has had their rights violated—or who insulate a family member from others.

Dangers of Rationalization

Healthcare professionals need to beware, however, of using rationalizations to refrain from engaging in case advocacy, such as deciding they do not have time to do it or that they might experience adverse repercussions. They need to remember that they have an ethical obligation to increase consumers' well-being and to protect their ethical rights even when it is inconvenient or expedient not to engage in it. They may also wrongly conclude that they will suffer repercussions or wrongly decide that case advocacy takes a lot of time.

Alternatives to Direct Provision of Case Advocacy: Shortcuts

Healthcare professionals should also realize that they can use legitimate shortcuts and avoidance even in those situations where they cannot devote much time to case advocacy or fear repercussion. They can try to convince other healthcare professionals to provide case advocacy to a particular consumer—what I call "advocacy punting." These staff may have more time in particular situations, more expertise relevant to a specific consumer, or "better standing" with a particular physician or other members of the health staff—and they may be better able to fit case advocacy into their workloads at a particular moment.

They may also diminish the likelihood of adverse repercussions to themselves by empowering specific consumers to self-advocate. Consumers possess considerable power in case-advocacy situations based on their right to self-determination and their ability to seek another provider if they are dissatisfied with their current medical service. Case advocates can empower consumers by referring them to the Internet, educating them, coaching them, and engaging in role plays with them (see Chapter 4).

Other shortcuts exist. A health professional may insert a notation in the medical record to alert other medical staff to a consumer's wishes, such as writing that a consumer does not want heroic treatment when faced with a terminal condition. She may describe a consumer's dissatisfaction with some aspect of her care in the medical record, such as noting that he wants additional information about a particular procedure or about other treatment options.

TASK #4: DIAGNOSING TASK

Before they can devise case-advocacy strategy, healthcare professionals need to diagnose why consumers' needs have not been adequately addressed by the health system or why their ethical rights have been violated. They can develop sensible case-advocacy strategy only when they have made this determination.

Developing Narratives

Advocates often need to develop narratives of specific transactions between consumers and medical staff to be able to diagnose specific situations that include a chronology of events, the participants, motives or beliefs, the nature of communications, and key actions (Steiner, 2005). To construct a narrative, advocates rely on the same sources of evidence commonly used in medical settings: information from specific consumers, medical records, direct observations, feedback from other professionals, and feedback from family members. Advocates can sometimes draw on their prior experiences in a specific health setting when constructing their narratives. Assume, for example, that a frontline professional has had prior experiences with a specific oncologist who has often not informed terminally ill consumers about palliative care or hospice programs. While she needs to double check its accuracy, she can attach particular weight to feedback from a terminally ill consumer that he did not receive this information from this urologist.

Advocates should understand some challenges in constructing accurate narratives. They cannot assume that reports or perceptions of specific participants are necessarily accurate. A physician may report in the medical record, for example, that he had an extended discussion with a consumer where he covered the plusses and minuses of specific treatment options. The actual discussion may have been relatively brief and may have only covered treatment options tangentially because the physician was already committed to a specific diagnosis and course of treatment.

Consumers, too, may exaggerate, distort, or even falsify events and communications. When given serious diagnoses, for example, some consumers may be sufficiently traumatized that they cannot process information accurately, so they may wrongly believe they were given (or not given) specific information. They may misinterpret communications from specific physicians because they do not understand their medical terms or come from a different cultural background. A few consumers may even deliberately falsify information to advance their claims for workmen's compensation or to lay the groundwork for malpractice litigation.

Medical records are often useful to establish a chronology of key events. Here, too, however, information may be absent or insufficient. Because most hospitals do not yet have electronic records, key information may be missing from medical records, such as transactions of consumers with caregivers outside of a specific unit or department—or from a primary-care physician in a community clinic or an outpatient department.

The narrative should lead to an informed opinion about why a specific consumer needs case advocacy. Here are some recurring causes:

- Prejudice
- Narrow mind-sets
- Flawed transactions and communications between specific consumers and specific medical staff
- Poor ethical reasoning
- Inadequate use of evidence-based medicine
- Bureaucratic and organizational malfunctioning
- Flawed policies and procedures
- Causation by multiple factors

Prejudice

Advocates need to be alert to prejudicial treatment of specific consumers in the healthcare system—overt prejudice as well as more subtle forms. They need skills not only in recognizing when prejudicial treatment exists, but in helping individual consumers surmount it.

Prejudice Against Specific Vulnerable Populations

I have identified numerous vulnerable populations in this chapter. Specific physicians or other medical staff may harbor prejudice against any of these groups. Overt prejudice, such as exclusion of specific persons from clinics or hospitals, has been greatly reduced by enactment of federal and state civil rights laws. Considerable evidence suggests, however, that more subtle forms of prejudice exist (Institute of Medicine [IOM], 2003). Medical staff can make some persons wait for longer periods of service than others. They can discourage them from using specific services, such as not encouraging lesbian women to use fertility services on grounds that they would not be "good parents." They can initiate certain diagnostic tests or surgeries for some people but not for others, such as when women do not receive specific treatments for heart disease as compared with men or when persons with schizophrenia are not given certain tests unless they request them. Medical staff sometimes relate differently to specific kinds of persons. A physician may be relatively upbeat with persons in the early stages of cancer, but not with persons in later stages.

One form of exclusion is commonplace: refusal to serve persons lacking health insurance when they do not possess urgent medical conditions. Some medical staff would deny that such refusal represents "prejudice" because it is based on the inability of specific consumers to finance their healthcare. Yet many hospitals possess charitable funds and medical staff that often can donate their services. Were medical staff to deny service disproportionately to specific kinds of uninsured persons, such as persons of color, prejudice would clearly exist.

Prejudice also exists when medical staff blames some consumers for their medical conditions. Perhaps they treat consumers with clinical obesity or substance abuse harshly, or they imply that certain kinds of consumers are responsible for their illness, such as cancer or heart disease. Perhaps they state or imply that certain kinds of consumers are unlikely to make medical progress or to recover.

Harsh attitudes toward certain kinds of persons can shape the actions and communications of medical staff in other ways. Perhaps they establish follow-up appointments with some consumers but not others, or they send reminder notices to some consumers but not others. Perhaps they make some consumers wait longer than others. Perhaps they deny treatments to some consumers but not others, or they do not even tell some consumers about their treatment options.

Prejudice also exists when medical staff allows nonmedical facts to shape their interactions with consumers. Perhaps a physician implies that a low-income person on

Medicaid and welfare does not "deserve" medical care to the extent a working person does. Perhaps she implies or states that a consumer with a prison record will not adhere to recommended treatments.

Responding Negatively to Consumers' Behaviors

Some medical staff may be biased against consumers who are not "good" patients. Some consumers are, for example, excessively compliant and noncommunicative, not asking important questions, not seeking alternatives, and not educating themselves about their health condition. Unless their providers take the time to elicit their ideas and level of information, they often do not receive full explanations. Frontline staff may engage them in discussions that empower them to become fuller participants in their care.

Other consumers are hostile even when given no apparent reason—whether because they have had prior negative experiences, believe they know more than medical staff, or have difficulty relating to authority figures. They may elicit hostile or noncommunicative relations with medical staff, which may make them even more hostile.

Some consumers may be habitual users of medical care even when they have no urgent medical condition. As they view their lengthy medical charts, medical staff may sometimes assume they have no serious medical problems and deal with them in perfunctory fashion.

Health providers should not let bothersome actions and behaviors distract them from the ethical goal of offering a person optimal care.

Narrow Mind-Sets

Healthcare is sometimes compromised by excessively narrow perspectives of providers. Here are some examples.

Technological Narrowness

Many physicians rely excessively on technological remedies. They may not refer patients with mood disorders or other mental conditions for counseling—or simply give them medications without referring them to mental health experts. They may not consider implications of specific surgeries or medications for consumers' employability or lifestyles. They may not warn consumers of side effects of specific treatments that might have led them not to agree to them.

Excessive Specialization

Many providers cannot see beyond the confines of their practices and specialties. Older persons may see an array of specialists, for example, who treat them for separate conditions, but who are unaware that others have given them medications that adversely interact with ones that they have prescribed. Specialists often do not communicate with consumers' primary physicians, who often do not follow their care even when they receive surgery and other treatments in hospitals. Many of them do not refer consumers with mental problems to psychiatrists, psychologists, or social workers.

Insularity

Health staff often have little knowledge of community-based agencies and professionals even when consumers would benefit from mental health services, job-training services, alternative medicine, welfare programs, child-care services, schools, rehabilitation services, services for seniors, services for disabled persons, independent-living programs, and physical therapy programs—to name only a few of them. When many consumers leave hospitals, they receive scant follow-up from hospital-based personnel—even to see if they have adhered to medications and other treatments.

Flawed Transactions and Communications

Personal interactions between providers and consumers sometimes place consumers at risk of poor care and violation of their rights.

Inadequate Communication

Consumers often do not receive sufficient information from providers to enable them to make intelligent choices as in the case of a physician who only briefly discusses specific surgeries, medications, and tests. They often receive information that they cannot understand because it uses terms and concepts beyond their grasp. Persons with limited English proficiency (LEP) often cannot understand English sufficiently to comprehend medical options discussed with them.

Providers cannot communicate effectively if they lack the ability to listen to consumers sufficiently. Many physicians talk to patients from a distance with their hands on door knobs, failing even to enter their hospital rooms and to sit next to their beds—even as they discuss complex medical options.

Some providers do not sufficiently empathize with consumers. They may not realize that they do not understand information that has been given to them or feel comfortable with the advice that they are receiving.

Poor Ethical Reasoning

Poor ethical reasoning sometimes leads providers to make decisions that compromise the care of consumers as is discussed in more detail in Chapter 5.

Lack of Ethical Reasoning Skills

Although many healthcare professionals receive training in ethics, others possess inadequate ethical reasoning skills. They may believe they have given consumers sufficient information that they can make informed choices, even when they have not.

They may believe they have protected confidential information, only to divulge it to family members and others without seeking the consumer's permission. They may believe that they have honored the ethical value of honesty only to have failed to tell consumers about likely side effects of treatments and medications.

Many healthcare professionals are not comfortable about discussing end-of-life issues with consumers, partly because medical culture sometimes emphasizes curing consumers of specific medical ailments rather than also helping them to deal with life-ending conditions. Many of them do not refer consumers to palliative care or to hospice—and some persist in providing heroic treatments to ones who have signed documents saying they do not (see Chapter 5).

Conflicts of Interest

I have discussed the entrepreneurial nature of the U.S. medical system where physicians, hospitals, and clinics often compete with one another for revenues from insurance companies, employers, and consumers. Wishing to increase their revenues, some providers resort to unethical behavior. Physicians may wish to increase their revenues by providing unnecessary or ill-advised treatments, tests, or prescriptions. Or they may not fully inform consumers about treatment options. Managed-care plans may wish *not* to give consumers meritorious medical procedures to avoid specific expenses. Physicians may have an economic interest in specific facilities, such as convalescent hospitals or nursing homes but refer their patients to it without disclosing their conflict of interest.

Inadequate Use of Evidence-Based Medicine

I discuss evidence-based medicine throughout this text. Consumers cannot assume that their providers use it, as is discussed in more detail in Chapter 6.

Lack of Knowledge of Relevant Research

Some providers are unaware of recent empirical data that suggests that specific consumers would likely benefit from specific medical strategies. Despite in-service training and continuing education, many health providers are not current with existing research (IOM, 2008).

Unwillingness to Consider New Approaches

Some providers may be aware of specific evidence-based medicine findings (EBM) pertinent to the care of specific consumers, but do not want to change their customary approach. Berwick (2003) contends that "innovators" constitute a relatively small portion of the workforces of most organizations with many other staff not implementing innovations until months or years later.

Misinterpretation of Research

Medical professionals sometimes interpret medical research incorrectly (see Chapter 6). Perhaps they think it is more definitive than it is. Perhaps they do not realize that it applies to a specific population, but is untested with other populations.

Bureaucratic and Organizational Malfunctioning

Health professionals deliver healthcare services in relatively complex organizational settings. These settings not only possess bureaucratic structures, but also rules, protocols, budgets, and cultures that profoundly influence their provision of health services. Consumers, too, must navigate these bureaucracies, which often appear confusing to them. Advocates need to be alert to negative impacts of organizations upon health services, particularly as they lead to medical errors and lack of team practice.

Failure to Follow a Preferred Sequence of Events

Medical error can often be reduced if providers follow a specific sequence of actions when treating consumers—particularly in such settings as ICUs and NICUs. Medical injuries and deaths have been dramatically reduced in ICUs that follow these treatment regimens compulsively (Gawande, 2010). Many consumers still fail to receive such care, partly because of resistance from medical staff who believe that they possess expertise that does not require such standardization of medical practice.

Many consumers are placed in jeopardy from medical oversights (IOM, 2000). A patient may not have been given a test, medication, or treatment at the correct time—or at all. A consumer may receive the wrong test result or even the wrong surgical procedure. Pharmacists may not have been able to read a physicians' handwriting, leading to an incorrect medication. Nurses may fail to give proper medications.

Lack of Team Practice

Many consumers with chronic diseases, substance abuse problems, and serious mental problems benefit from team practice that couples medical assistance, "talking therapies," and other professionals such as physical therapists, nutrition experts, and occupational therapists. Many elderly persons benefit from team practice. Many barriers frustrate team practice, however. Insurance companies and health plans often do not fund it. Some physicians do not want to share their patients—or their medical information—with other professionals. Many health systems have not implemented medical records that are shared by health staff across different departments or between primary-care physicians and specialists.

Flawed Policies and Procedures

Health systems have many policies and procedures, including ones established in response to public statutes and regulations, court rulings, and accreditation standards.

Others are established within clinics and hospitals to facilitate their work. Advocates often help health professionals, as well as consumers, know about or understand some of these policies and procedures, particularly when they impact consumers' well-being.

Lack of Knowledge

Consumers sometimes suffer violations of their rights or nonoptimal care because specific health professionals lack knowledge of specific regulations, protocols, and standards. Perhaps providers did not participate in briefings or in-service training. Perhaps they received inaccurate information from other staff. Perhaps they are unaware of specific accreditation standards. Perhaps they possess a mistaken view that their professional status makes them not subject to policies and procedures. Perhaps they are not aware of specific court rulings and public regulations, such as those concerning discharge policies, rights of consumers, and important provisions of the Patient Protection and Affordable Care Act of 2010 as amended by the Congress.

Lack of Policy Guidance

Policies and procedures may not even exist in some situations, such as ones that require health staff to make referrals when encountering consumers with specific health conditions, such as mental trauma. Policies and procedures can be excessively vague, rigid, and misdirected so that medical staff lack sufficient guidance. Advocates have to be attentive to these shortcomings in existing policy if they pose dangers to specific consumers. They also need to move from case advocacy to policy advocacy to clarify existing policies or to develop new ones.

Causation by Multiple Factors

Many factors, operating in tandem, often compromise the care of specific patients or lead to violation of their ethical rights. Perhaps a consumer is subject to prejudice, receives inadequate communication, and runs into bureaucratic snafus. The work of case advocates is often made more complex as the number of causal factors increases.

TASK #5: THE STRATEGIZING TASK

Healthcare professionals can accomplish the strategizing task by dividing it into six steps, including setting goals and time frames, identifying assets and liabilities, assessing motivations of decision makers, allocating responsibility, developing a sequence of actions, and developing specific actions.

Step #1. Establishing a Goal and Time Frame

Case advocacy requires the development of a goal, a subgoal, and a time frame. Goals that contain these three components become actionable ones that can be monitored to see if consumers have actually achieved them. The goals can be illustrated by using the seven core problems that consumers often confront in the health system:

- *Overarching goal:* Surmount a financing problem as it adversely affects a consumer's medical care. *Subgoal:* Gain eligibility to Medicaid to allow financing of specific tests, medications, or procedures. *Time frame:* Obtain eligibility within two weeks and receive charitable care in the interim.
- *Overarching goal:* Surmount a possible threat to a consumer's quality of care. *Subgoal:* Help a consumer obtain a second opinion. *Time frame:* Obtain it within three weeks so the consumer can better decide what course to take.
- *Overarching goal:* Obtain specific preventive services. *Subgoal:* Have a diabetic consumer receive a consultation from a nutrition consultant. *Time frame:* Obtain it within one month.
- *Overarching goal:* Obtain culturally relevant care. *Subgoal:* Obtain the services of a certificated translator in Vietnamese. *Time frame:* Obtain the translator within one hour.
- *Overarching goal:* Obtain an appointment to relevant health-related resources outside a specific hospital or clinic. *Subgoal:* Obtain an appointment at a local Welfare office to make applications for food stamps and to obtain information for filing for an Earned Income Tax Credit (EITC). *Time frame:* Obtain the appointment within two days.
- *Overarching goal:* Address excessive anxiety, depression, or other mental issues. *Subgoal:* Have a suicidal consumer at the ER get an appointment with a mental health provider at a mental health agency. *Time frame:* Obtain it within three days with the use of medications in the interim as well as daily phone calls.
- *Overarching goal:* Protect ethical rights of a consumer. *Subgoal:* Obtain separate consultations for a consumer for palliative care and hospice. *Time frame:* Obtain two consultations within 5 hours.
- Establishing goals, subgoals, and time frames for consumers with interacting problems that include two or more of these seven core issues. Health staff may decide to accomplish two or more goals in the same time frame, such as helping a consumer surmount a financial issue *and* obtain quality services—both within two weeks. They may decide to accomplish these two goals sequentially, beginning with one of them and progressing to another after the first one has been achieved.

Step #2. Identifying Assets and Liabilities

It is sometimes useful to make a list of assets and liabilities in the policy/organizational thicket—and their locations outside or within the site of a case-advocacy intervention. Assume, for example, that a case advocate wants to help a consumer get into a smoking cessation program, but finds that none exists in the hospital. Also assume that the consumer is uninsured and Latino—and has early-stage emphysema. Also assume that

Table 3.1   Evaluating the Context

	Assets	Liabilities
External	1. Evidence-based research 2. State-subsidized clinics at community sites	1. No referral system in place
Internal	1. Other physicians have referred persons to smoking-cessation programs 2. Accreditation standards require referrals for persons with lung disease	1. Consumer's physician hasn't made referrals in the past

the physician who has treated him has made no effort to get him into such a program. Assets and liabilities are summarized in Table 3.1.

Even with her limited information, the case advocate finds that the context contains both favorable and unfavorable factors—suggesting that a positive outcome is possible. Clinics do exist. Other physicians in the hospitals have referred consumers to them. State subsidies do exist. Empirical evidence supportive of smoking cessation is strong.

She needs, however, to offset or minimize these liabilities. This physician has not made prior referrals. She believes that this patient is less likely to join a smoking cessation program if the physician does not refer him to it, because he told her that, "My smoking must not be that important because my physician did not discuss it with me."

She realizes, too, that she does not know some important facts. Do culturally competent and accessible services exist for this consumer? Does a smoking cessation clinic exist near this consumer's home? Does it have evening or weekend hours and a short wait list? Would he have out-of-pocket costs?

Step #3. Assessing Motivations of Decision Makers

Case advocates' effectiveness often hinges on their abilities to assess the motivations of specific decision makers. Did they take specific actions because they were not familiar with specific regulations and statutes? Did they make honest mistakes? Did they place organizational matters ahead of consumers' interests, such as cutting costs or obtaining reimbursements? Did they misunderstand specific consumers? Were they not familiar with specific ethical norms? Did their personal beliefs, such as wanting to extend all possible medical assistance to a terminally ill consumer, lead them to overlook the consumer's views and wishes? Case advocates need to factor into their strategies ways to address these motivations effectively so that they increase the chances that they will change directions and take different actions to enhance consumers' well-being.

Step #4. Allocating Responsibility

Healthcare professionals must decide who takes responsibility for an advocacy intervention. Different possibilities exist.

Healthcare professionals can become the prime movers in a case advocacy intervention, such as with comatose consumers, ones with limited cognitive function, ones with serious mental disorders, or ones overwhelmed by their health condition or by external realities. Some consumers may expect them to be the prime mover.

Healthcare professionals can empower consumers so that they advocate for themselves. They provide consumers with knowledge about resources, health conditions, treatment options, and relevant research, whether by giving them written materials or by helping them to use the Internet if they do not already have sufficient Internet skills. They may coach them, such as helping them develop questions to ask medical staff. They may help them to be appropriately assertive, giving them suggestions about how to ask questions or communicate with medical staff to increase the likelihood of successful outcomes. They may engage in role plays with them where they assume the role of the medical staff.

Even when empowering consumers, healthcare professionals may wish to keep in touch with specific consumers to see if they have taken key actions. They may discover, for example, that a consumer fails to follow through with specific actions or becomes intimidated by medical staff. Perhaps other life events intrude so that they cannot become self-advocates.

Healthcare professionals can partner with consumers, as well as other medical staff in a team arrangement. They can decide who does what and by when—and select someone to be the lead person who keeps track of progress. In partnering arrangements, a lead person should often be identified who can keep track of the implementation of the strategy—and troubleshoot when key actions are not taken.

Healthcare professionals can initiate a team approach where a number of professionals and family members participate in an action system. Perhaps a nurse works with a consumer to obtain an appointment for a second opinion *as* a social worker helps him get an appointment in a community-based agency *as* the consumer agrees to adhere to specific medications and to keep the appointments. Perhaps progress on these three actions is monitored online, by telephone, or through a case conference to be held at a specified time. Considerable research suggests that persons with chronic diseases need to be helped by a team to obtain a full range of interventions not available to them under solo practice. Diabetics need, for example, help in monitoring their weight, healthy lifestyles, monitoring of insulin, occupational therapy, counseling, and participation in support groups—help that can only be provided by a team.

Healthcare professionals can shift their roles as events unfold. Perhaps they believed they had to be the prime mover, but discover that a family member or friend wishes to take more responsibility. Perhaps they discover that a consumer who had wanted to take responsibility for self-advocacy wants some assistance.

Step #5. Developing a Sequence of Actions

Case advocates plan a tentative sequence of communications, fact finding, contacts, and meetings at the outset of their work—with some contingencies included in it. In the case of the Latino with lung disease who will not join a smoking-cessation clinic unless his physician "prescribes" it and signs a referral form to a specific smoking cessation clinic, she decides to implement the following sequence of actions:

- She will conduct some research for the consumer, such as finding a smoking cessation clinic near his residence that has evening and weekend hours, provides free services, and has Spanish-speaking staff.
- She asks the consumer to take this information to his physician and ask for a medical referral to this clinic—and to let her know if he has received it.
- *Contingency.* If he does not receive the referral, she will work with the physician's nurse to get the referral from another physician in the clinic that serves consumers with lung disease.
- She asks the consumer to get an appointment at the clinic—telling him to see a specific Spanish-speaking staff person who she has contacted by telephone—and she asks him to leave a message on her cell phone whether he kept his appointment.
- *Contingency:* She will place in his medical record a notation that he failed to keep his appointment if she learns this from the clinic staff person—and suggest further discussions with him about how his smoking could greatly increase the pace of his lung disease.

Different kinds of sequences exist. The simplest of them involves a single action by a case advocate who helps a person who lacks skills or ability to self-advocate. Perhaps she asks a physician to make a medical referral for counseling that she can present to a hospital-based psychiatrist. A more complex sequence of action takes place when a case advocate empowers a consumer to get this referral from his physician. The case advocate works with the consumer at two points in time: coaching him to get the referral from his physician and coaching him to get an appointment with the psychiatrist. An even more complex sequence of action occurs when the case advocate initiates a team approach that involves a physician, a social worker, a psychologist, and an occupational therapist. Assume the social worker assumes the lead role in helping a consumer with serious mental illness. She initiates a case conference to help a consumer receive medications (from the physician), counseling (from the psychologist), and job readiness and job search skills (the occupational therapist). She monitors the consumer's progress and orchestrates another case conference in three months.

Sequences also vary by the extent they include contingencies and question marks. Contingencies take place when case advocates anticipate two (or more) possible courses of action depending on the outcome of a particular meeting or event as illustrated by the referral to a smoking cessation program where two contingencies were identified. Question marks can be placed on a sequence of actions where the case advocate does not know what specific actions might be needed after a certain point in the sequence. Perhaps a consumer will have numerous options—and the case advocate does not know what they will be until an interview, case conference, diagnosis, or medical procedure is complete.

Step #6. Selecting Specific Actions

Healthcare professionals possess a smorgasbord of actions they can take during their case advocacy.

Using Technology

Healthcare professionals can use technology to facilitate case advocacy in several ways. They can use spreadsheets to identify the goals, subgoals, and timelines of an advocacy intervention. They can select specific activities, as well as who does them and by when. If they evolve a team approach where different persons agree to perform specific actions, they can enter them into the spreadsheet and record when they are completed. They can e-mail spreadsheets that show what activities have been accomplished and which ones have not.

For simpler advocacy plans, they can resort to e-mail between the lead person and those consumers with Internet access.

Empowering Consumers

Case advocates can empower consumers in many ways. They can show them Internet sources that may be useful to them—and give them some instruction about how to distinguish between accurate and inaccurate information.

Case advocates can refer consumers to support groups that meet within a hospital or clinic or that hold meetings in community-based organizations, schools, and religious organizations. The members of support groups, who have often been treated for specific health-related conditions, often give consumers invaluable information as well as emotional support. They often encourage members to be appropriately assertive.

They can direct consumers to reliable sources of data about specific institutions and physicians on the Internet at sites of public agencies that evaluate and rate their services. They can discover whether particular physicians, hospitals, or clinics have been cited for poor services—or have lost their accreditation.

Advocates can help consumers develop a list of questions *before* they see providers. They might ask about treatment options and side effects that could accompany them. They might evaluate medical staff by asking how many times they have performed a specific surgery and what outcomes they have achieved. They might ask whether a physician performs the delicate part of complex surgeries or a resident or intern.

They can inform consumers that they are entitled to their medical records, as well as scans, and tell them how to obtain them. They can help consumers develop a log of their medical transactions as they encounter specific illnesses like cancer that may include test results, appointments, medications, and diagnostic tests like scans.

Case advocates can give consumers hotlines, as well as names of advocacy groups outside their hospitals or clinics, to help them contest decisions by insurance companies or managed-care plans about the coverage and financing of specific medical procedures, tests, and medications.

Case advocates can empower specific consumers by coaching them to prepare for specific encounters with medical staff. They can encourage them to be appropriately assertive. They can give them a list of specific questions they might wish to ask. They can encourage them to have a spouse, family member, or friend accompany them.

Arranging Case and Family Conferences

Health staff and specific consumers might wish to arrange a case conference with medical staff and specific attendees. They might wish to hold a conference with a consumer and members of her family. They might accompany a consumer to a site outside of a hospital or clinic to help them obtain access to a program that might otherwise exclude them, such as an independent-living program or a retirement home. They might plan an informational meeting to allow consumers to understand specific programs that they might wish to use or join.

Case conferences are important to case advocates if they help them receive services or help them avoid violation of their ethical rights. If a family member does not agree with the wishes of a consumer—or with written documents or wishes of a consumer who is no longer competent—the case advocate can work with other family members to honor her wishes. If a retirement facility is disinclined to admit an elderly person because of his medical condition, a case advocate can work with him in a case conference with officials from the facility to reverse this decision. Case conferences with physicians and other medical staff can allow a consumer to clarify treatment options—or allow a consumer to decide whether he wants to use that provider or to seek another one.

Making Institutional Contacts

Hospitals and clinics are complex organizations with administrators, highly placed physicians and nurses, experts, compliance officers, and risk managers who may be relevant to specific issues of consumers. They also have important committees, such as ethics committees and Institutional Review Boards (IRBs) that respectively oversee ethical issues and research. Relatively few consumers even know that these persons, departments, and committees exist, what powers they possess, how to access them, and how they might be useful to them. Some frontline people are not aware of them.

Healthcare professionals can approach these officials and professionals on behalf of specific consumers, such as gaining important information from them or helping consumers gain access to specific programs. Or they can direct consumers to approach them to ask specific questions about their healthcare (see Chapter 4).

Planning Meetings with Hospital Staff or Administrators

Case advocates often help persons who are dissatisfied with their healthcare or want more information, whether because they believe they have been denied benefits or services, have been treated unfairly or inappropriately, or have received poor services—and who wish to meet with persons who can listen and respond to them. Case advocates may arrange meetings between these consumers and authority figures in the hospital or clinic, such as an administrator, the medical chief of a department, an official from the risk management or compliance departments.

These events allow consumers to tell their stories to these authority figures. They may want to ventilate. They may want an apology if they believe they were victims of medical error. They may want some redress or they may want assurances that the hospital or clinic will change the way it has dealt with consumers with similar problems. They may want information.

Many health institutions are not forthcoming with consumers when they have committed medical errors, such as giving someone incorrect medication, making mistakes during surgeries, giving consumers inaccurate or the wrong diagnostic tests, or failing to diagnose their conditions accurately. Considerable research suggests that denial of medical errors harms not only the institution by increasing malpractice lawsuits, but often has a devastating impact on consumers and their families (Delbanco & Bell, 2007). Healthcare professionals can route consumers to appropriate authorities in a hospital or clinic to ascertain if an error was made—and then to discover what happened—and to obtain redress if an error did occur.

Case advocates need to decide with consumers what role they should play in such meetings. Should they attend and act as mediators or supporters? Should they not attend, focusing, instead, on coaching consumers so that they ask important questions and have realistic expectations? Should they suggest that another person, such as a family member, accompany them?

Obtaining and Using Medical Records

Healthcare professionals engage in case advocacy, as well, when they place information in medical records in ways that increase the odds that consumers' preferences and needs will be honored or addressed. A speech pathologist would sometimes place consumers' wishes about not wanting heroic measures at end of life in capitalized letters. They can use urgent or strong language, such as "the patient *expressed in the strongest terms that she did not want. . . .* "

Locating External Advocates

Some consumers will believe that they cannot seek redress unless they use external advocates, whether advocacy groups, government personnel who regulate and oversee healthcare in a specific jurisdiction, private attorneys, or public-interest attorneys such as ones in legal aid organizations.

Many advocacy organizations engage in case advocacy for specific consumers. Some of them mediate among insurance companies, medical administrators, and consumers to solve specific reimbursement or coverage issues—often successfully. Others request that specific consumers gain services or resources to which they are entitled, such as translation services, equipment funded by Medicare for older persons, and referrals to home health agencies before they are discharged.

Other advocacy organizations seek to educate consumers about services and resources that they can obtain on discharge, such as support groups for persons with breast cancer, diabetes, and many other health conditions. They sometimes visit consumers in hospitals before they are discharged.

Many health organizations possess internal arbitration mechanisms so that aggrieved consumers can seek redress without taking legal action. Many managed-care organizations require enrollees to sign agreements that require them to use arbitration rather than courts to seek redress.

Many private attorneys represent consumers. They may threaten or take legal action against specific medical staff or specific hospitals or clinics, insurance companies, health plans, and managed-care organizations. Public interest attorneys often represent persons who lack the resources to obtain private attorneys.

Making Referrals

Consumers often need timely appointments with specialists and other medical staff, but they sometimes cannot get them when they are overbooked or have to wait for long periods. Low-income consumers are particularly disadvantaged, sometimes waiting for months just to be seen by specialists.

Case advocates become involved in referrals when they believe that consumers will not otherwise receive them. They can coach consumers to call for appointments on repeated occasions, often early in the morning, in hopes of getting an appointment through a cancellation. They can find nurses or other health staff who have contacts with appointment nurses for physicians. They can suggest that consumers ask primary-care physicians to call for appointments on an expedited basis.

Some consumers do not keep appointments even when they have serious health problems. Case advocates may sometimes e-mail or phone specific consumers to increase the odds that they keep the appointment—and then help them, or urge them, to reschedule them if they miss them.

Finding Resources

Consumers often need to obtain eligibility to specific programs, like Medicare, Medicaid, and SCHIP. Case advocates not only inform consumers of these programs and their guidelines, but help them prevent adverse decisions, such as denial of eligibility or coverage.

Some health staff know about specific community-based programs that are relevant to specific consumers that they would probably not access without case advocacy assistance. A woman who has been subjected to physical harm from a spouse may need help, for example, in finding a shelter that protects her from further harm. Persons with serious mental- or substance abuse problems may need to be linked to specific community resources.

Using Intermediaries

Health staff often decides to contact intermediaries during their case advocacy, such as their supervisors, highly placed nurses, administrators, or physicians. These intermediaries often have more clout than frontline staff, as well as information and resources that may be helpful to specific consumers. Perhaps a consumer needs a referral to palliative care or hospice—and frontline staff knows that a specific nurse has oversight responsibilities for these programs. This nurse can easily initiate an action system for the consumer, such as having personnel from these programs visit the consumer soon after she calls them.

Intermediaries are often positioned to discuss specific cases with their physicians. Perhaps a consumer is dissatisfied with a particular surgeon to whom he was referred by his managed-care plan to learn the results of a biopsy that shows that he has cancer. He finds that the surgeon fails to answer questions that he poses to her adequately or correctly—and is evasive when he asks how often she has performed this surgery and with what outcomes. If no one helps this consumer to find another surgeon, he may leave the health plan altogether—or refrain from getting surgery when it may promote his well-being. A case advocate might refer this consumer to the medical chief of oncology or urology in the health plan who could, in turn, establish an appointment with another surgeon.

Honoring Consumers' Wishes

Consumers often find that some of their wishes are not honored or are marginalized by healthcare staff. Assume, for example, that a consumer wants to use nontraditional medicine to ease chronic pain, but finds that her physician responds sarcastically to her wish, saying, "No credible evidence supports its effectiveness, so just take this medication." Healthcare professionals can affirm the consumer's wish to seek help from an acupuncturist, if only by saying, "Try it and then decide if it helps you," or by saying, "Some interesting research is now being conducted on this strategy with persons with chronic pain," or providing an NIH web site that gives her information about current research on alternative medicine.

Some physicians may question whether other health staff possess the competence, or even the right, to affirm consumer wishes that conflict with medical advice. Were these staff to give medical advice that suggests consumers should resort to specific remedies or medications, they would probably exceed their authority—although this example suggests that the boundary between advising and affirming is often not clear. Had a social worker said, "I know persons with your condition who use acupuncture who say they have benefited from it, so why not try it?" she would possibly have crossed the boundary.

Citing Regulations, Protocols, and Ethical Guidelines

When case advocates observe apparent violations of regulations or court rulings by other professionals, such as a specific court ruling that requires that consumers give their "informed consent" to a medical treatment, case advocates can take several actions. They can remind or inform persons about these regulations or court rulings. They can ask, "Are we following guidelines that mandate us to . . . ?" Or, "Have we heard what course of treatment the patient desires?" They can discuss possible penalties that providers can encounter if they violate specific regulations. They can report violations to an intermediary, such as an administrator or a high-level nurse. They can report them to a relevant department, such as the compliance or risk management departments. They can inform consumers where they can find specific regulations.

Steering Consumers

Healthcare professionals sometimes steer consumers to specific medical personnel and programs because they believe they offer outstanding services. They make favorable comments about these personnel or programs, or refer consumers to them.

Obtaining Mandates from Physicians and Other Medical Staff

Healthcare professionals sometimes observe actions or behaviors of medical staff that lead them to believe that specific consumers are not receiving optimal or ethical care. These professionals may find it difficult to intrude, however, because they have not been involved in their services—and are not their physicians.

To gain entrée, a healthcare professional can ask the physician for permission to talk with the consumer or join a case conference. They can ask for permission to continue to help in any way that they can. They can talk to consumers *after* their physicians have left the room, listen to them, and engage in case advocacy if they believe that this is warranted.

TASK #6: IMPLEMENTING CASE-ADVOCACY STRATEGY

A case advocate may develop a brilliant strategy, but it will fail if it is implemented without skill. Chapter 4 shows how case advocates need analytic, interactional, influence-using, and value clarifying skills to make it more likely that their case advocacy will be effective.

TASK #7: ASSESSING ADVOCACY INTERVENTIONS

Case advocates assess specific advocacy interventions to determine their relative success in improving healthcare for specific consumers. If they were not successful, they may provide another advocacy intervention, possibly relying on a different strategy.

TASK #8: PROGRESSING TO POLICY ADVOCACY

Case advocates progress to policy advocacy when they conclude that many consumers need case advocacy because fundamental flaws in existing policies, procedures, statutes, budgets, and protocols make it necessary. Lack of universal health coverage causes many consumers not to be able to use healthcare, for example, because they cannot finance it. Insufficient funding of preventive services, such as the physical exams by primary-care physicians, *causes* them to be undersupplied in the health system. See Chapters 12 through 14 for a discussion about ways to progress from case advocacy to policy advocacy.

CASE ADVOCACY FOR A VERY SICK CHILD

Vignette 3.1 is an extended example of case advocacy geared to improving the quality of care for a consumer and to link our discussion to the advocacy framework in this chapter.

Vignette 3.1 Seeking Quality Care for a Very Sick Child

By Nadya Hernandez

Children's Hospital Los Angeles (CHLA) was founded in 1901 and is a leading international pediatric hospital in the Hollywood area of Southern California. Children's Hospital Los Angeles serves children and adolescents from birth through 20 years of age. The mission statement for CHLA is "To make a world of difference in the lives of children, adolescents, and their families by integrating medical care, education and research to provide the highest quality care and service to our diverse community" (childrenshospitalla.org). Striving to meet this mission, CHLA takes a multidisciplinary approach to provide high-quality care to patients and their families. This includes advocacy on behalf of the patient by the multidisciplinary team as well as often by the patient and the patient's family. What follows is a narrative of case advocacy associated with a patient and the family. Since the population treated at CHLA is pediatrics, the client is viewed to be the patient and their family. All identifying information has been altered to provide anonymity.

　　This case narrative illustrates obstacles imposed by health insurance on individuals with chronic illness having access to quality healthcare. Uninsured and underinsured individuals are unable to receive adequate healthcare. For individuals who have a chronic illness in addition, this lack of access is even more detrimental to their health.

　　Max Garcia is an 8-year-old Mexican-American boy who lives in Henderson, Nevada, with his mother, maternal grandmother and a 4-year-old sister. Ms. Garcia is a single mother, who is originally from Los Angeles. Per Ms. Garcia, she relocated her family to Nevada because of the high living expenses in Los Angeles.

(continued)

(*continued*)

Ms. Garcia is unemployed and is currently a student with ambitions for a career as a licensed vocational nurse. Ms. Garcia receives Temporary Assistance for Needy Families (TANF) in addition to Special Supplemental Nutrition Program for Women, Infants, and Children (WIC). The family is currently enrolled in and receives medical insurance through Medicaid. The Garcia family identifies as Catholic as well as having a strong belief and faith in their religion. Max is currently attending the third grade at a local public elementary school. His mother describes Max as social, active, and particularly interested in sports. Max has reached all appropriate milestones and has no cognitive delays or special needs.

Max began to present with headaches and Ms. Garcia immediately made an appointment with a local pediatric clinic. The pediatrician examined Max and found the headaches to be related to eyestrain from homework. Two months later, Max's headaches had increased and he also presented with vomiting and weight loss. Max's pediatrician felt that he might have a food allergy and created a modified diet for gentle digestion. Shortly after, Max's headaches and vomiting increased drastically, and Max was brought to a hospital's emergency department by his mother. The hospital ordered a CT scan of Max's abdomen and the results were found to be negative. Feeling that there must be something else going on with her son, Max's mother insisted that more tests be given. She requested that the physician petition Medicaid for approval of a CT scan of Max's entire body. Medicaid denied this request, but agreed to approve a CT scan of Max's head due to the headaches. The test results found a tumor in Max's brain. Frustrated with the delays in Max's diagnosis, Ms. Garcia contacted Candlelighters Childhood Cancer Foundation (CCCF) for support. CCCF is a national organization that provides families of children with cancer information, support, and advocacy (candlelighters.org). Ms. Garcia was provided a caseworker who sent a referral on behalf of Ms. Garcia to Children's Hospital Los Angeles. An oncologist of CHLA that specializes in brain tumors accepted the referral and organized a multi-disciplinary meeting that included the nurse practitioner, child life specialist, social worker, and social work intern of the brain tumor team. The oncologist was concerned with Max's delay of diagnosis, treatment, and Ms. Garcia's frustration with the care her son had received. The team agreed to provide as much support to the Garcia family as possible.

The social worker contacted Ms. Garcia's case manager at CCCF to initiate contact and collaboration. The social work intern contacted Ms. Garcia to introduce herself and the role of social work, as well as to assess the family's needs, build rapport, and provide support. Through the assessment, the social work intern found that Ms. Garcia was frustrated and angry with her son's treatment so far and hopeful that they would receive better care at CHLA. Ms. Garcia stated that she requested a referral to CHLA because she felt that her son would receive

(continued)

the best treatment and care. After assessing the family's needs, it was found that Ms. Garcia would need assistance with transportation, lodging, a stipend for travel expenses, a meal stipend, and additional financial support. Ms. Garcia reported that she felt calmer and more confidence for her son's care after speaking with the social work intern. The social work intern then contacted Ms. Garcia's caseworker at CCCF to collaborate on meeting the Garcia family's needs. CCCF agreed to provide financial support for lodging, transportation, and a meal stipend. The social work intern agreed to secure lodging for the Garcia family through Ronald McDonald House, a charitable organization located close to CHLA that provides lodging for pediatric patients and their families. In addition, applications were submitted to the National Children's Cancer Association and for Supplemental Security Insurance on behalf of the Garcia family to assist them with additional financial support.

The Garcia family was successfully able to meet the brain tumor oncology team at CHLA and received a consultation and treatment plan. Max Garcia was diagnosed with Stage IV posterior fossa ependymoma, an aggressive form of brain cancer that at a stage IV is considered the most high-risk stage. Max's treatment plan consisted of surgery and a combination of chemotherapy and radiation. The oncology team felt that this level of high risk required immediate action, however insurance barriers created a delay. The financial counselor for the oncology team reported that the Garcia family's insurance, Nevada's Medicaid, had approved for the consultation but not for the treatment. The primary oncologist of the brain tumor team submitted a claim for approval, which was granted by Medicaid. However, medication was not. The oncologist submitted a claim for approval, which was rejected by Medicaid until the surgery was completed first. Realizing that there would be another obstacle by Medicaid and the importance that Max's treatment in regard to medications would not be delayed; the brain tumor team's nurse practitioner and social worker submitted a request for CHLA's Telethon Funds. This CHLA resource offers emergency financial assistance by the hospital made possible by a variety of donations. The Garcia family was approved and CHLA agreed to pay for the necessary medications until Medicaid approved the claim.

Prior to Max's treatment, a child life specialist met with Max and his mother to discuss the treatment and work with Max at an age-appropriate level. Max had many fears and misconceptions that the child life specialist was able to address and normalize for Max. The social work intern also met with Ms. Garcia and Max prior to treatment to assess the family's understanding and feelings toward the hospitalization. The social work intern found that Ms. Garcia was anxious and nervous about her son's surgery. The social work intern explored her feelings and normalized them as well as provided psychosocial education regarding how parents may feel after their child's diagnosis. The social work intern felt that a conference with the oncologist and surgeon would be helpful to clarify and to address any of

(continued)

(*continued*)

Ms. Garcia's concerns and organized a conference. Knowing that Ms. Garcia was Catholic and had a strong faith in her religion, the social work intern submitted a referral to CHLA's spiritual care services to provide additional emotional and spiritual support for the family. A referral was also submitted to Padres Contra Cancer (Parents Against Cancer). Padres Contra Cancer is a nonprofit, Latino-based organization that offers emotional support through education, support groups, and counseling (Padres Contra Cancer, 2008). A social worker from this organization met with the family to offer support as well. Max's surgery was successful and thereafter, he began a combination of chemotherapy and radiation.

After several months of treatment, the oncologist felt that a bone marrow transplant was needed for further improvement of Max's high-risk cancer. Bone marrow transplants are considered for high-risk cancer as a final stage of the patient's therapy. Research from the National Marrow Donor Program Network shows that one-year patient survival rates are 42.2% (Loyola University Health System, 2004). At CHLA, bone marrow transplants are a standard part of treatment for high-risk cancer in patients. As the Garcia family prepared for the final step of treatment, they were met with yet another obstacle from their insurance provider. Medicaid denied approval for the procedure on the premise that it was an experimental treatment and therefore not covered in its policies. The oncologist resubmitted the claim, with a justification for the treatment. Medicaid denied the treatment again. The brain tumor team: the oncologist, social worker, and nurse practitioner along with Ms. Garcia each submitted a letter requesting an appeal by Medicaid. Medicaid agreed to review the resubmitted claim for the transplant. Unfortunately, during this delayed time period, Max's tumor reoccurred aggressively and he died before the decision from Medicaid's review was finalized.

Learning Exercise

I use this example of case advocacy to review the case advocacy tasks in Figure 3.1, including reading the context, triaging, allocating advocacy services, diagnosing why a consumer needs advocacy, strategizing, implementing strategy, and assessing strategy.

Advocacy Practice: Reading the Context

Ms. Garcia encountered many liabilities. She had received poor medical care from a physician who misdiagnosed Max's medical condition. She found difficulty from the outset in securing authorization from Medicaid for important medical tests. Medicaid would prove to be a major obstacle for financing Max's care throughout this case. Ms. Garcia may have sought primary care for her son's health condition belatedly because Medicaid enrollees often have inadequate primary care because of low reimbursements of physicians for it. Ms. Garcia was a persistent and resilient advocate for Max even when faced with poor medical care—and was a key asset in this situation.

It was not apparent at the outset of this case, but an array of external supports existed for Ms. Garcia. The Candlelighters Childhood Cancer Foundation (CCCF) referred her to Children's Hospital Los Angeles (CHLA). Once she was there, other groups helped her, including the Ronald McDonald House and the National Children's Cancer Association.

Her most important asset would prove to the CHLA—a world-class hospital with a culture that supported team-based advocacy.

Advocacy Practice: Triaging

CHLA staff quickly realized that Ms. Garcia and Max needed their advocacy assistance. She was a member of a vulnerable population. She received Medicaid in the State of Nevada—and would require advocacy to secure needed financing from them. As a child, Max could not self-advocate and was wholly dependent on his mother and other advocates for his well-being. Max's aggressive cancer meant that he needed advocacy to surmount any barrier to rapid treatment.

Advocacy Practice: Allocating Advocacy Services

Advocacy came to Ms. Garcia in several stages and ways. She self-advocated at the outset by persisting in getting a new diagnosis for Max after an initial diagnosis implicated only a food allergy and then abdominal problems. Not only did she persist in seeking care, but she asked that an ER physician seek approval for a CT scan of his entire body—finally getting Medicaid (with a physician's help) to approve a CT scan of his head. She located CCCF—and then received advocacy from them, including a referral to CHLA after a workup by their social workers. The brain tumor multiprofessional team at CHLA gave her yet a new round of advocacy on many fronts. *This case illustrates how case advocacy often occurs sequentially for consumers—and from many sources.* Had she not received this chain of advocacy over an extended period, Max would likely not have gotten to CHLA and would not have received prompt care for his condition.

Advocacy Practice: Diagnosing Why a Consumer Needs Advocacy

Ms. Garcia and Max had clearly been enmeshed in a system of inferior healthcare in Nevada.

Advocacy Practice: Strategizing

The brain tumor team at CHLA set in motion advocacy on multiple fronts when Ms. Garcia and Max came to them. The life-threatening nature of his illness required them to establish an urgent timeline for their advocacy efforts with the paramount goal of offsetting or addressing economic, social, and logistical barriers to prompt surgery and medication, as well as a bone marrow transplant that might save Max's life. The team included a financial planner, nurse practitioner, social worker, social work intern, and child life specialist who *each* engaged in case advocacy. They had to attend to the family's lodging and financing needs by getting help from Ronald McDonald House, as well as funding from CCCF. They provided counseling themselves as well as through the pastoral program of CHLA to help Ms. Garcia and Max deal with the harsh realities that they confronted and the courage to go through with the invasive medical procedures that his condition demanded. They linked Ms. Garcia to the National Children's Cancer Association as well as Supplementary Security Income (SSI). They repeatedly advocated for Max with Nevada Medicaid authorities—and found backup resources to cover medication costs and radiation when they refused to fund them immediately. *This case illustrates how advocacy often becomes a team affair with contributions from each of its members.* It also illustrates how case advocacy is much easier in hospitals that encourage, expect it, and work collaboratively to achieve it, as we will discuss in Chapter 13.

Advocacy Practice: Implementing Strategy

The team members implemented their multipronged advocacy with skill and dispatch. They worked around the Nevada Medicaid authorities so that they could not delay Max's care. This case illustrates how controversy sometimes exists about EBM. Physicians at CHLA clearly believed that bone marrow transplants were highly effective with children like Max. Yet Nevada Medicaid officials viewed bone marrow transplants for Max as merely "experimental." Only after considerable advocacy were they willing to reconsider their decision not to fund this procedure.

Advocacy Practice: Assessing Strategy

The ultimate reward for the team would have been to have seen Max survive this ordeal. Their work was nonetheless remarkably successful in getting Max outstanding medical interventions—and not letting financial barriers intrude.

SUMMARY

An advocacy practice framework (see Figure 3.1) must provide the following:

- Place advocacy practice in its contextual setting because it never occurs in a vacuum.
- Identify key tasks that advocacy practitioners must undertake, whether they are case or policy advocates.

- Identify fundamental skills that advocacy practitioners should possess to be effective advocates.
- Link case advocacy with policy advocacy.

I have discussed the eight case-advocacy tasks in the advocacy practice framework in this chapter. Chapter 4 discusses how to implement case advocacy by using the four core skills needed by case advocates.

4

Case Advocacy Skills

Case advocacy and policy advocacy are practice interventions that require specific skills. To accomplish the tasks in the Case Advocacy Framework presented in Figure 3.1 (see Chapter 3) effectively, healthcare professionals need four skills: value clarifying, analytic, influence-using, and interactional ones. Value clarifying skills describe the ability to recognize ethical dilemmas and to reach ethical conclusions. Analytic skills are used to understand policies and regulations, as well as to identify alternative options and make rational choices when devising case-advocacy strategy. They are used to locate research relevant to specific health problems or to prevention. Influence-using skills help health staff to develop and employ influence resources. Interactional skills describe the ability to communicate, negotiate, and maneuver within families and groups. Advocates also need personal attributes that facilitate their involvement in case and policy advocacy. These four skills are needed to implement the tasks in Figure 3.1.

FOUR SKILLS FOR READING THE ADVOCACY CONTEXT (TASK #1)

Case advocates use value-clarifying skills when they identify contextual factors grounded in ethics, such as regulations or protocols established to protect consumers' rights or to advance the quality of the services that they provide. An advocate who protects consumers' confidentiality will become versed in HIPAA regulations, understand regulations that govern when and how hospitals discharge patients, and understand relevant Joint Commission accreditation standards. Professionals who are committed to giving consumers choices during end-of-life care become versed in Medicare and other regulations that require professionals to give consumers information about end-of-life options.

Value-clarifying skills sensitize and alert health staff, as well, to contextual factors that work against a consumer's well-being. Perhaps a hospital's culture gives excessive leeway to providers that are not current with evidence-based medicine; fails to implement some accreditation standards; or allows conflicts of interest to jeopardize patient well-being. Perhaps private insurers fail to cover preventive care sufficiently. Perhaps application forms for Medicaid are so complex that many eligible consumers are not enrolled.

Healthcare professionals use analytic skills to understand existing rules and regulations, as well as other contextual factors. They use them to locate assets and liabilities in the context. They use them to locate research that analyzes what medical and related interventions are effective with specific kinds of consumers and specific kinds of medical and related conditions.

Healthcare professionals need influence-using skills to identify assets and liabilities that are relevant to specific case-advocacy interventions and to understand power realities that are relevant to a specific case-advocacy strategy. They might decide in some situations that liabilities preclude a successful outcome, while deciding in other cases that sufficient assets exist to make a positive outcome possible or likely.

Healthcare professionals need interactional skills to join networks that can keep them informed about contextual and power realities in specific hospitals or clinics.

FOUR SKILLS FOR CASE-ADVOCACY TRIAGE (TASK #2)

Healthcare professionals use value-clarifying skills when they triage consumers to determine if they need case advocacy. When determining which consumers most need it, for example, they often select members of vulnerable populations—a choice that reflects their commitment to social justice and equity.

Healthcare professionals use analytic skills when they gauge which consumers most need case advocacy in the triaging task, such as gauging the seriousness of their problems. They might examine existing policies, for example, to ascertain if a consumer's rights have been seriously violated under existing regulations or court rulings. They might examine research literature to ascertain whether a specific consumer's care deviated from evidence-based medicine. They might analyze the medical records of specific consumers to help them decide if they need a case-advocacy intervention.

Healthcare professionals use influence-using skills when trying to convince other professionals, such as their supervisors or professional peers, that a particular consumer needs a case-advocacy intervention. Perhaps a social worker uses her expertise. Perhaps she seeks corroboration from another professional. Perhaps she warns her supervisor that a consumer could bring a legal suit against the hospital and its staff if specific complaints or violations of ethics are not addressed.

Healthcare professionals use interactional skills during the triaging of consumers to ascertain which of them need case-advocacy interventions. They develop listening skills to discover whether specific consumers believe they have not received adequate services or have had their rights violated by health staff. They receive information about specific consumers from networks they have joined. A social worker might learn from a nurse, for example, that a specific consumer has not been informed about hospice or palliative care—and then decide to engage in case advocacy with him.

FOUR SKILLS FOR ALLOCATING CASE-ADVOCACY SERVICES (TASK #3)

Healthcare professionals use value-clarifying skills when they decide to engage in case advocacy when they have heavy workloads. They use them to decide when to proceed if they believe they will face personal risks if they engage in case advocacy in specific situations, such as retaliation from other professionals. They use analytic skills when they estimate the time needed to complete an advocacy intervention with a specific consumer—a calculation that helps them to determine whether to proceed in light of their other work demands. They use influence-using skills when they try to convince their supervisors that a specific case-advocacy intervention is meritorious—or when persuading other health staff to take the lead. They use interactional skills when they schedule a meeting with several professionals to examine the merit of case advocacy for a specific consumer.

FOUR SKILLS FOR THE DIAGNOSING TASK (TASK #4)

Healthcare professionals use value-clarifying skills when diagnosing why a specific consumer needs case advocacy. Values make them sensitive to unfair, inappropriate, or unprofessional actions by specific providers. They sensitize them to power disparities. Values make them want to aid consumers who have received care that is not consonant with evidence-based medicine or that violates their rights.

Healthcare professionals use analytic skills when they diagnose why specific consumers need case advocacy in the first place. Did they receive inadequate services because their provider lacked requisite skills, made honest mistakes, was insensitive to a consumer's culture or gender—or because of bureaucratic barriers, or other reasons?

Professionals use influence-using skills to understand power realities that might have compromised services for specific consumers. Perhaps a physician was unable to listen to her patient, creating a power imbalance. Perhaps a consumer's actions or communications were viewed as offensive by a physician and influenced her medical judgments adversely. Perhaps hospital administrators failed to assert their authority sufficiently by not organizing in-service trainings to educate staff about key regulations and accrediting standards.

Healthcare professionals use interactional skills to communicate with consumers and other professionals to gain information to diagnose why specific consumers are not receiving optimal care or have had their rights violated.

FOUR SKILLS FOR THE STRATEGIZING TASK (TASK #5)

Healthcare professionals use value-clarifying skills when they compare alternative strategies and select among them. In some cases, for example, their values motivate them to select ones that require considerable time or that expose them to possible repercussions—and they make these choices because their values commit them to enhancing a consumer's well-being. Their values often motivate them to empower consumers to be able to self-advocate effectively.

Healthcare professionals use analytic skills when they identify several case-advocacy strategies and select the one that they believe will be effective with specific consumers. They use them to develop goals, subgoals, and timelines, and to develop specific actions that will allow them to achieve these goals.

Healthcare professionals use influence-using skills at many points during case advocacy. They sometimes use "soft power" to persuade other staff to correct errors in their services to specific consumers, such as low-key communications. They sometimes use "hard power," such as strong language or warnings. They sometimes work through intermediaries when they can use their power resources to rectify errors.

Healthcare professionals use interactional skills, such as group-work skills during case conferences, team meetings, and family meetings. Assume, for example, that a family conference is held to develop a plan for helping an elderly consumer with early-stage dementia stay in her home for an extended period as she fervently wishes. A social worker might lead this discussion and help the family develop a promising strategy, using her knowledge of group dynamics to foster a positive outcome in a timely way.

FOUR SKILLS FOR THE IMPLEMENTING TASK (TASK # 6)

Case advocates use value-clarifying skills when they expend considerable time in implementing a case-advocacy strategy even when they encounter obstacles and experience repercussions. They use analytic skills when they monitor and evaluate their case-advocacy strategy whether their strategy is successful—and select alternative ones if it is not.

Advocates use influence-using skills at many points during the implementation of strategy. They have to persuade other medical staff to take actions they would not otherwise have selected, such as improving services to a specific consumer. They have to decide which of their influence resources to use in specific situations, such as expertise, incentives, or warnings. They often use influence to convince others to participate in their case advocacy, such as high-level administrators or nurses, in their case advocacy. When empowering consumers to self-advocate, they teach them how to develop and use their own influence resources.

Case advocates use interactional skills when they communicate, bargain, negotiate, or organize meetings during the implementation of case advocacy strategy. They use them when they coach or educate consumers to empower them so that they are equipped to engage in self-advocacy.

FOUR SKILLS FOR THE ASSESSING TASK (TASK #7)

Frontline staff primarily use analytic skills to determine if a case-advocacy intervention has been successful as they compare the results with goals established at the outset. They cannot evaluate an intervention, however, without using interactional skills to secure views from consumers and medical staff, influence-using skills to seek changes in policies, protocols, and procedures that led a consumer to need case advocacy in the first place, and value-clarifying skills when they decide whether to invest more time and resources in a specific intervention even when it was not successful.

FOUR SKILLS FOR THE PROGRESSION TASK (TASK #8)

Health staff use value-clarifying skills when they move beyond case advocacy to policy advocacy because they want to change policies and procedures that led consumers to need case advocacy in the first place. Assume that a social worker finds that many diabetic consumers have not received assistance from a nutritional expert in a hospital or clinic. She could decide that this is a systemic problem that can only be corrected by changing protocols or policies in this setting. Operating from the value premise that healthcare professionals must work to improve consumers' well-being and drawing on extensive research that demonstrates that diabetic persons need assistance from nutritional experts to manage their diets, she develops a policy advocacy intervention in her health organization. She works to create a protocol that requires all diabetics to be referred to a nutritional expert—and possibly even to add more of them to the medical staff. Her values lead her, as well, to engage in policy advocacy even when confronting such obstacles as professionals' resistances to regulations and budget realities.

Tasks and skills needed for policy advocacy are discussed in Chapters 12 through 14.

TWO SKILLS IN MORE DETAIL

I have argued that healthcare professionals, as well as consumers, need four skills to be effective case advocates. I discuss influence-using and communication skills in more detail in this chapter. Value-clarifying (or ethical) skills and analytic skills are covered in more detail in Chapters 5 and 6.

THE NATURE OF INFLUENCE

Persons exercise "influence" when they try to make others take specific actions or make specific communications that they would not otherwise consider. Influence is exercised in transactional relationships where person X (let us call her Mary) exercises specific influence resources that persuade person Y (let us call him Joe) to take actions or deliver communications that Joe would not otherwise have considered. (Had Joe made this decision already, Mary would not have exercised influence.)

Here is a simple example to illustrate the transactional nature of influence. Consider "expertise" to be an influence resource such as citing a finding from evidence-based medicine that seems applicable to a specific medical encounter. Mary must first believe she possesses expertise. She must then exercise her expertise with Joe, who must believe

Figure 4.1   Direct Power Transactions

Mary does possess it and who decides to change his actions or communications in ways that Mary suggests. Were any of these conditions not present, the effective use of influence depicted in Figure 4.1 would not occur.

This scenario can be illustrated with a social worker who interacts with an obese consumer who is receiving only medications from her physician to treat her condition. Assume that the social worker has read a recent research finding that many obese consumers can benefit from a combination of medications and behavioral counseling. She talks with the physician about including behavioral counseling in the treatment plan. He accedes to this request because he respects the social worker's expertise—and makes a referral to a staff psychologist. The social worker must not only use an influence resource (expertise) with the physician, but must communicate it in a style that brings a positive response. Had she made her request to the physician belligerently, he might have responded negatively to her suggestion. In this case, then, the social worker used two kinds of influence: expertise coupled with effective communication.

Case advocates sometimes use their influence resources through intermediaries. Assume that the social worker had decided that the consumer's physician would be unlikely to respond favorably to her use of expertise, possibly because she doubted that he would believe that she possessed relevant expertise or because he would believe she exceeded her role in suggesting that the consumer might benefit from behavioral counseling. The social worker might decide, then, to consult a health educator (call her Rebecca, see Figure 4.2) on the hospital's staff about the case and ask her to recommend to the physician that he consider referring the consumer to a staff psychologist for behavioral counseling. If the physician responds affirmatively, the

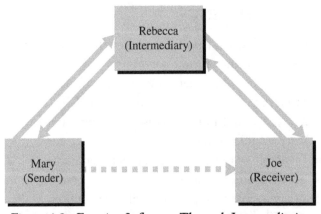

Figure 4.2   Exerting Influence Through Intermediaries

intermediary would have used influence effectively because the physician probably would not have made this referral otherwise.

EMPOWERING CONSUMERS

Healthcare professionals sometimes choose not to use their personal influence resources in a case-advocacy intervention, but to help specific consumers develop and use their influence resources. By giving them information and helping them develop their own influence resources, frontline staff enhances consumers' strengths and skills rather than dealing with them paternalistically. As they develop their abilities to interact with health staff confidently, they are better able to improve their healthcare on future occasions, as well.

Consumers become the intermediary in Figure 4.2 in this scenario. They receive information, access to information through the Internet, and coaching from health staff (Mary in Figure 4.2) to develop and learn how to use specific influence resources—and then use these influence resources to obtain better care or to protect their ethical rights in interactions with medical staff (or Joe in Figure 4.2).

Healthcare professionals can choose an empowerment approach, as well, for practical reasons. They may find it less time-consuming to coach and educate consumers to negotiate their health services with health staff—an important consideration because they often are preoccupied with their other duties.

Healthcare professionals can also choose an empowerment approach for political reasons. Consumers already possess influence resources. Except when courts declare them to be incompetent, consumers are sovereign in the health system. They possess the right to choose their own treatments, to reject medical advice, and to seek new or altered treatments—even if they cannot make a physician provide services that are medically futile. Consumers have the right to leave the care of a particular healthcare professional or health organization and to select other ones. Consumers have an ethical and legal right to sufficient information that they can give informed consent to specific medical recommendations.

Only consumers ultimately decide, moreover, whether they wish to tolerate specific side effects from medical interventions. They can ask physicians to reconsider, change, or terminate specific treatments on the basis of them.

Consumers can sue providers—or demand an administrative tribunal to respond to their complaints in the case of some managed-care plans.

In many situations, then, consumers have greater influence resources than health staff with physicians who possess the exclusive legal power to diagnose patients, propose treatments, and provide surgery. They can question their decisions, ask for more information, and change providers if they are not satisfied—assuming they realize they possess this power and are sufficiently assertive to use it.

Despite these advantages over healthcare professionals, however, many consumers do not use their influence resources at all—or skillfully. Many of them are socialized to think that "doctor always knows what's best." Others are fearful of medical staff, whether because of prior adverse experiences or for cultural reasons.

A Variety of Influence Resources

Case advocates can draw on an array of influence resources:

- Networking
- Using influence in interpersonal exchanges
- Using ethical arguments
- Using medical culture
- Employing power dependency
- Taking initiative and responsibility
- Developing a positive track record
- Using process skills
- Managing conflict
- Using intermediaries
- Bypassing specific professionals
- Navigating regulations
- Gaining entrée
- Interpreting a professional role
- Using Appropriate assertiveness
- Designing communication strategy
- Using group skills
- Affirming collective self-interest
- Using peer pressure
- Using influence resources in tandem and sequentially

Networking

A network is the number and range of supportive relationships a person possesses (Matthews, 1988). Networks are important to case advocates in several ways. Individuals with broad networks develop early-information systems through which they learn about issues, problems, and trends relevant to their work, and they have many sources of advice as they develop policies and strategies.

There are many kinds of networks (Jansson, 2008). *Lateral networks* consist of relationships with colleagues; *vertical* and *subordinate networks* consist, respectively, of persons who are superior to and beneath a person in an organization's hierarchy. People have *heterogeneous networks* when they have supportive relationships with others in a range of positions both within and outside their work. A social worker in a hospital has a heterogeneous network, for example, when it includes members of different units or departments and different professions. Some relationships in networks are short-term, perhaps fashioned in response to a specific problem, while others are long-standing.

Strategies that help expand a person's networks include enhancing visibility, seeking inclusion in decision-making bodies, cultivating mentors, obtaining access to informal groups, and developing links with social movements. Networks provide frontline staff with information about the culture and operations of a health organization. It provides them with persons who can serve as intermediaries in case advocacy. It gives them an opening to myriad services scattered throughout the organization. It provides them with information about procedures and protocols, and gives them access to persons with particular power, such as administrators and top professionals. It provides them with purveyors of advice about what works and does not work when engaging in case advocacy with specific kinds of consumers.

Networks often include administrators, physicians, nurses, OT/PT staff, residents, social workers, and external stakeholders.

Administrative Staff

Administrators often possess considerable influence in health organizations because they allow them to survive in a competitive medical marketplace.

Private health organizations have Boards of Trustees or Governing Boards that oversee their operations. Public health organizations are governed by health authorities or by elected officials such as the County Board of Supervisors in Los Angeles County. These boards, authorities, or elected officials are ultimately responsible for the operations of the health units. They want their health organizations to run efficiently, to avoid deficits, to be regularly reaccredited, and to offer quality services. They want them to compete effectively with other providers—or at least maintain sufficient revenues from consumers, government, or private donors to fund operations. They want to avoid scandals and consumer law suits, such as malpractice.

CEOs, presidents, or directors preside over specific health organizations at the pleasure of governing boards, authorities, or elected officials. They are responsible not only for establishing high-level policies in conjunction with the board, but developing strategic plans that identify future directions. CEOs often have assistant administrators or chief operating officers. Most of them are not physicians, but possess master's degrees in hospital administration or related fields.

These top officials oversee other administrators who operate as high-level staff to facilitate effective operations. The compliance administrator is charged with making the hospital conform to Joint Commission accreditation requirements, federal Medicare and Medicaid regulations, state and local regulations, and an array of court rulings. The risk-management administrator is charged with decreasing medical errors in the organization and, as a byproduct, malpractice or other litigation—and often seeks to increase the extent to which medical services conform to evidence-based medicine. A marketing administrator seeks to advance the ability of the organization to retain and increase its current clientele and revenues. A grants administrator seeks to increase private donations, foundation grants, and government grants. The director of the finance department is charged with developing and implementing budgets and making recommendations to retain the fiscal viability of a health organization. The legal department not only litigates for the organization—or contracts with external attorneys—but works to make hospital operations compliant with existing legal and regulatory requirements. A medical director oversees medical programs and medical staff.

These officials, as well as their aides, are sources of information about regulations, statutes, and fiscal issues relevant to case advocacy. They can be accessed directly or through supervisors of social work, nursing, and other departments.

Physicians

Physicians receive the MD when they graduate from accredited medical schools in the United States—and are usually the most powerful professional group within health organizations. They also include graduates of foreign medical schools who often must take specific exams to be able to legally practice in the United States. Their power derives from their importance to health organizations. They alone can perform surgeries, make diagnoses, prescribe prescription drugs, admit patients, and discharge patients. They bring revenues to health organizations, whether by bringing patients to hospitals from their community practices or attracting patients because of their positive reputations.

It is not surprising, then, that they assume major roles in designing services, obtaining needed diagnostic equipment, and ensuring that health organizations maintain services at a level that is consonant with accreditation standards. They provide major inputs to budgets of the overall organization, as well as specific units within it.

Physicians, in turn, have their own status hierarchy. Board-certified physicians occupy the top position because they have passed specific exams and have the experience to make them experts in such specialties as neurology, oncology, internal medicine, and surgery. Physicians who engage in postgraduate education—often called *residents*—are next down the hierarchy. They perform clinical work in specific specialties under the supervision of senior physicians, often lasting three years or longer in a specific hospital as they gain knowledge and experience needed to eventually become board-certified. Some physicians receive fellowships, as well as doctorates in related fields, that prepare them for medical research. Medical students occupy a lower niche, often engaging in considerable clinical work in the last two years of medical schools as they rotate between different specialties. Medical students work under the close supervision of physicians.

Specialists in surgery or the treatment of specific diseases often have greater prestige and have higher incomes than primary care, or internal medicine, physicians. A serious shortage of primary-care physicians exists for this reason, particularly in low-income areas—leading to serious shortages of preventive care and early detection of diseases. Most primary-care physicians do not visit hospitalized patients—leaving their care to specialists and interns although some health plans are experimenting with expanding their role to include care to hospitalized patients.

Physicians can only practice in specific hospitals if they receive "privileges" from physicians who already practice in them. Physicians with privileges in specific hospitals vote to determine who will occupy such positions as president or chief of staff, vice president or chief of staff elect, and secretary. The president presides over regular meetings of the medical staff, "and is, *ex officio*, a member of medical staff committees." The vice president serves in his absence and the secretary keeps minutes and handles correspondence. The medical staff establishes committees to monitor and improve the quality of services, as well as an executive committee to coordinate activities and policies of the various departments and a credentials committee to review applications for appointment and reappointment to all staff categories. The joint conference committee links physicians and hospital administrators. Other committees include a medical education committee and a program committee. Specific physicians hold quasi-administrative posts in their specific specialties, such as the lead physician in a urology unit.

Many physicians are not salaried employees of hospitals, but bring patients to them as "admitting physicians." Those admitting physicians who bring many patients to their hospitals are powerful because hospitals depend on them for their revenues. Physicians who work for managed-care organizations like Kaiser Permanente are salaried although they often receive bonuses based on revenues of the overall organization. Other titles are given to physicians including consulting physicians (who advise other physicians), courtesy physicians (who have honorary positions), and provisional physicians (who work on a temporary basis).

This medical governance system makes important decisions about services and budgets. Advocates who want changes to the policies, protocols, and budgets of their organizations often need buy-in from one or more physicians. They should realize, too, that they can work cooperatively with many kinds of physicians and at different levels of this medical hierarchy.

Many social workers and nurses discover, too, that they often work collaboratively with residents. They are often more cognizant of key problems in health institutions because they see hospitalized consumers on a daily basis and more intensively than many admitting or staff physicians who often only make brief visits to them. I include residents in the ranks of frontline staff in this book.

Nurses

As the largest healthcare occupation, registered nurses held about 2.5 million jobs in 2006. Hospitals employ the majority of registered nurses (or RNs) with 59% of them. Other industries also employ them with 8% of their jobs in offices of physicians, 5% in home healthcare services, 5% in nursing care facilities, 4% in employment services, and 3% in outpatient care centers. About 21% of RNs work part time.

The term "registered nurse" is reserved for nurses who have passed national licensing exams and met specific supervised clinical experience requirements. In all states, the

District of Columbia, and U.S. territories, students must graduate from an approved nursing program and pass a national licensing examination, known as the NCLEX-RN, in order to obtain a nursing license. Nurses may be licensed in more than one state, either by examination or by the endorsement of a license issued by another state. The Nurse Licensure Compact Agreement allows a nurse who is licensed and permanently resides in one of the member states to practice in the other member states without obtaining additional licensure. They come from three kinds of educational programs: a bachelor's of science degree in nursing (BSN) from colleges or universities, an associate degree in nursing (ASN) often from a community college, and a diploma from an approved nursing program that is not part of a university or community college. Further training or education can qualify nurses to work in specialty areas, and may help improve advancement opportunities. Licensed graduates of any of the three types of educational programs usually qualify for entry-level positions.

Many RNs with an ADN or diploma later enter bachelor's programs to prepare for a broader scope of nursing practice. Often, they can find an entry-level position and then take advantage of tuition reimbursement benefits to work toward a BSN by completing an RN-to-BSN program. Some career paths are open only to nurses with a bachelor's or master's degree. A bachelor's degree often is necessary for administrative positions and is a prerequisite for admission to graduate nursing programs in research, consulting, and teaching, and all four advanced practice nursing specialties—clinical nurse specialists, nurse anesthetists, nurse-midwives, and nurse practitioners. Individuals who complete a bachelor's degree receive more training in areas such as communication, leadership, and critical thinking, all of which are becoming more important as nursing care becomes more complex. Additionally, bachelor's degree programs offer more clinical experience in nonhospital settings. Education beyond a bachelor's degree can also help students looking to enter certain fields or increase advancement opportunities.

RNs, regardless of specialty or work setting, treat patients, educate patients and the public about various medical conditions, and provide advice and emotional support to patients' family members. RNs record patients' medical histories and symptoms, manage pain, help perform diagnostic tests and analyze results, operate medical machinery, administer treatment and medications, and help with patient follow-up and rehabilitation. RNs teach patients and their families how to manage their illness or injury, explaining post-treatment home care needs; diet, nutrition, and exercise programs; and self-administration of medication and physical therapy. Some RNs work to promote general health by educating the public on warning signs and symptoms of disease. RNs also might run general health screenings or immunization clinics, blood drives, and public seminars on various conditions.

When caring for patients, RNs establish a plan of care or contribute to an existing plan. Plans may include numerous activities, such as administering medication, including careful checking of dosages and avoiding interactions; starting, maintaining, and discontinuing intravenous (IV) lines for fluid, medication, blood, and blood products; administering therapies and treatments; observing the patient and recording those observations; and consulting with physicians and other healthcare clinicians.

Nurses have other titles. Some nurses have doctoral degrees in nursing, which prepares them for specialty work as well as administrative work and research. Clinical nurse specialists and nurse practitioners possess master's degrees in nursing and increasingly hold administrative and clinical nursing positions. Licensed practical nurses (LPNs) are the lowest level of nurse and have completed 12 to 18 months of training without an undergraduate degree. Associate degree programs are two-year programs that include nursing theory and undergraduate courses in sciences and liberal arts, are usually offered by junior or community colleges and prepare persons for entry-level nursing positions. Nurse aides/assistants, orderlies, and attendants (often collectively referred to as "aides") perform bedside and housekeeping tasks. They include licensed vocational nurses (LVNs) and certified nursing assistants (CNAs). Some RNs provide direction to licensed practical nurses and nursing aides regarding patient care. RNs with advanced educational preparation and training may perform diagnostic and therapeutic procedures and may have prescriptive authority.

RNs can specialize in one or more areas of patient care. Some specialize in a work setting or type of treatment, including ambulatory care nurses, critical care nurses who often work in critical or intensive care hospital units, emergency or trauma nurses who work in hospital or stand-alone emergency departments, holistic nurses provide care such as acupuncture, massage and aroma therapy, and biofeedback, home health nurses who provide at-home nursing care for patients; hospice and palliative care nurses, long-term care nurses who provide healthcare services on a recurring basis to patients with chronic physical or mental disorders often in long-term care or skilled nursing facilities, and psychiatric-mental health nurses, rehabilitation nurses care for patients with temporary and permanent disabilities.

RNs specializing in a particular disease, ailment, or healthcare condition are employed in virtually all work settings, including physicians' offices, outpatient treatment facilities, home healthcare agencies, and hospitals. They include addictions nurses, developmental disabilities nurses, HIV/AIDS nurses, and oncology nurses.

RNs specializing in treatment of a particular organ or body system usually are employed in hospital specialty or critical care units, specialty clinics, and outpatient care facilities. They include cardiovascular nurses, dermatology nurses that treat patients with disorders of the skin, such as skin cancer and gynecology nurses, nephrology nurses care for patients with kidney disease, neuroscience nurses, and many other specialties.

RNs specializing by population provide preventive and acute care for newborns (neonatology), children and adolescents (pediatrics), adults, and the elderly (gerontology). RNs also may provide basic healthcare to patients outside of healthcare settings in such venues as including correctional facilities, schools, summer camps, and the military.

Some RNs choose to become advanced practice nurses, who work independently or in collaboration with physicians, including clinical nurse specialists who provide direct patient care and expert consultations in one of many nursing specialties, such as psychiatric-mental health; nurse-midwives; family practice, adult practice, women's health, pediatrics, acute care, geriatrics, neonatology, and mental health. Advanced practice nurses can prescribe medications in all states and in the District of Columbia.

Some nurses have jobs that require little or no direct patient care, but need an active RN license including case managers, forensics nurses, infection control nurses, and nurse administrators, nurse educators, and nurse informaticists who manage and communicate nursing data and information.

Case advocates in health systems need to know about the many kinds of nurses because they often help them. They provide invaluable information because they exist in every niche of the health system and with many kinds of consumers. They sometimes take the lead in case advocacy. They have skills that go beyond traditional nurse roles that had sometimes made them subservient to MDs. One model of nursing practice seeks a "restructuring of nursing roles on the basis of education, experience, and competence," which gives nurses multiple skills including advocacy, case management, involvement in ethical issues, and managerial roles (Hamric, Spross, Hanson, & Spross, 1996). Nurses use an ecological framework.

Social Workers

Most social workers in healthcare possess MSW degrees as compared to BSW degrees, although social workers with BSWs often work in nursing homes. Unlike nurses with their many specializations, social workers often work across many inpatient and outpatient units of hospitals, as well as ERs and ICUs. They obtain most of their clientele from MD referrals although they can also engage in case finding.

Social workers often possess relatively broad competencies flowing from their use of ecological models of care. They provide personal counseling and family counseling; staff support groups; manage discharge planning; make referrals to community agencies; engage in case advocacy; and participate in ethical deliberations with MDs, patients, and families.

Social workers are both hindered and helped by their lack of nurses' technical medical training. They cannot participate in case conferences or discussions with MDs about some technical medical issues because they lack this training. Yet their roles *outside* the medical hierarchy also emancipate them by giving them an external perspective and role that allows them to see human, family, and ethical dimensions of care. They do not have to focus on implementing physicians' medical orders because they fall outside their expertise and job descriptions. Some research suggests that social workers may be more likely to initiate or join deliberations about ethical issues than nurses in several urban hospitals (Dodd & Jansson, 2004; Jansson & Dodd, 2002).

Social workers benefit from the fact that most in health settings have master's degrees (MSWs) as compared to undergraduate degrees (BSWs). They benefit, too, from their multiple competencies, as well as their ability to work with such populations as children, adults, and elderly persons.

Both nurses and social workers need to be appropriately assertive to avoid being marginalized in health settings—whether being relegated merely to the role of implementing physicians' treatments (nurses) or to the role of discharge planning (social workers). Members of both professions should engage in advocacy.

Speech and Language Pathologists, Occupational Therapists, and Physical Therapists

Speech and language pathologists, occupational therapists, and physical therapists provide critical services to consumers. Speech and language pathologists, who usually have master's degrees in accredited programs, have traditionally focused on diagnosing persons with swallowing disorders, such as elderly persons with impeded swallowing abilities in the wake of strokes and cancer. They help persons with neurological trauma to communicate. They diagnose neurological causes of incompetence.

Occupational therapists traditionally focus on helping consumers with disabilities or recovering from medical procedures to regain physical and mental skills to reenter the workforce after leaving hospitals. They now provide a wide range of services geared to stress reduction, healthy diets, healthy lifestyles, and coping skills based on an empowerment model.

Physical therapists help patients regain physical skills, such as the ability to walk, in the wake of medical procedures and as patients experience disabilities stemming from strokes and physical trauma. They help consumers develop healthy lifestyles that include physical activity.

Internal Units

Hospitals possess many inpatient service units, often including oncology, pediatric, general surgery, dermatology, neurology, cardiology, and others. They contain intensive care units that are reserved for persons with life-threatening conditions, including the Neonatal Intensive Care Unit (NICU) and the Intensive Care Unit (ICU). They often possess an Emergency Department (ED) ostensibly to serve persons with urgent conditions, but usually serve many other persons with nonurgent conditions who use it as a substitute for outpatient care. Some hospitals have trauma units that serve medically stabilized persons with serious health conditions, such as victims of automobile accidents or persons who have suffered trauma from falls.

Many hospitals possess an array of outpatient clinics. Some of them provide primary-care medical services, while others specialize in outpatient care for persons with specific medical ailments like diabetes, hypertension, and cancer.

Case advocates benefit from networking with staff in these different hospital units. They can expedite referrals for specific consumers, gain specific information, and help consumers obtain second opinions.

External Stakeholders

Every health organization is linked to other institutions—whether cooperatively, competitively, or marginally. Some are viewed as posing possible risks. Organizations with cooperative links include those that send or receive patients on a regular basis, including home health organizations, convalescent homes, nursing homes, retirement homes, solo and group MD practices, pharmacies, social agencies, and employers. Health organizations may contract with other providers for specific services, such as managed-care plans that contract with mental health organizations to care for some of their enrollees who need inpatient care. Public health agencies often have close links to hospitals and clinics, referring consumers with STDs, TB, and infectious diseases to them.

Health organizations often depend on specific employers for their patients or their enrollees in the case of managed-care organizations. They often give discounted fees to consumers who come from these employers.

Health organizations also have competitive relationships with other ones. They compete for clientele, physicians, residents, and consumers. They may try to lure patients from them by direct advertising. They may purchase health facilities in the geographic area of another health organization.

They have marginal relationships with many other community institutions. Many physician groups that do not attend patients in specific hospitals are only marginally related to them. Many community agencies that do not have a health mission, such as job-training programs, have few relationships with hospitals. I argue in Chapter 11 that some of these marginal relationships should be converted into active and cooperative ones, such as with schools, community mental health agencies, and public health agencies.

Health organizations have guarded or defensive relationships with many federal, state, and local regulators and accrediting agencies. They need their technical advice on many occasions, but they also fear adverse publicity and penalties if they do not meet their standards or lose their accreditation such as from the Joint Commission.

These external links are important to case advocates. Cooperative organizations often accept referrals on an expedited basis from health staff, as well as provide helpful information. They participate in grants written by health staff for augmented services.

Using Influence in Interpersonal Exchanges

Case advocates sometimes exert influence in interpersonal transactions that draw on expertise, coercion, rewards, charisma, and authority as influence resources. Case advocates demonstrate expertise by displaying their personal credentials and knowledge, as well as citing evidence-based medicine from professional literature or technical information gleaned from reliable Internet sources such as the web sites of federal health agencies such as the National Institutes of Health (NIH) or the National Cancer Institute (NCI). They must demonstrate their expertise tactfully so that other health personnel do not see them as intruding on their turf.

When using reward power, case advocates promise or provide rewards, incentives, or inducements. A case advocate can praise a physician who helps a specific consumer. She can promise to "go the extra mile" at a later point in time when he wants special services for a consumer. She can offer a quid pro quo, saying that she will help him at a later point in time in return for assistance to this consumer. Frontline staff can sometimes co-opt other professionals into their case advocacy by asking them how they would recommend improving services for a dissatisfied consumer.

Charismatic power derives from personal qualities of leadership, moral authority, and persuasiveness and is used to stimulate others to follow their wishes. Case advocates who possess these intangible qualities may find it easier to convince others to modify or improve services for specific consumers. Perhaps a case advocate becomes widely admired for "putting patients first." Perhaps she is viewed as a "team player" who takes on extra work to help a specific unit.

Case advocates use coercive influence when they threaten penalties or retributions that they might suffer from outside regulators, courts, or internal administrators and supervisors. Someone who witnessed flagrant violations of HIPAA regulations, for example, could argue that the offending person might eventually face court action from a consumer if the violations continue. Case advocates can sometimes use implied threats, such as suggesting that a specific consumer might protest to management if she fails to receive better or more ethical services or that a specific unit may be docked in a forthcoming reaccreditation. They can cite adverse implications of consumer dissatisfaction for patient satisfaction surveys that are widely used to rate hospitals—as well as the possible migration of specific consumers to other health plans. They can point to reputational losses that could occur to a specific professional or work unit if specific lapses in patient care continue.

The power of authority stems from one's position in an organization's hierarchy. Frontline staff usually cannot use this kind of power because they are not in high positions, but they can augment their authority by holding leadership positions in their departments or in specific units. They can persuade administrators and highly placed professionals to serve as intermediaries in specific case advocacy interventions.

Case advocates use influence in interpersonal exchanges most effectively when they tailor it to specific persons and situations. A specific professional may respond to expertise, for example, but not to coercion. He may respond to information that a specific kind of service violates specific external regulations, such as HIPAA, but not to ethical arguments. Other professionals may respond to other influence resources.

Using Ethical Arguments

Healthcare professionals often increase their traction in specific situations by using ethical arguments. As is discussed in more detail in Chapter 5, they can use specific ethical first principles such as honesty, self-determination, confidentiality, fairness, and conflict of interest. Any of these ethical principles can be invoked by stating or implying that specific services, statements, or actions have violated one of these ethical principles. A case advocate can assert that a patient has not been given sufficient information about available medical options to treat her condition—a violation of self-determination. Or he can assert that she has been given lesser or different services than a male patient with a similar condition—a violation of fairness. Or he can assert that a patient's medical information has become known to other persons without the patient's consent—a violation of confidentiality. Or he can assert that she has not been given accurate information, such as possible side effects or other complications that might ensure from a particular treatment—a violation of honesty.

It is difficult for health staff to confront physicians on grounds their conflicts of interest jeopardize the quality of their services—even when this might be true. A surgeon might not consider nonsurgical options, for example, because they do not enhance his personal revenues. A physician might refer patients to a convalescent home that he partly or entirely owns. It may make sense to gain information from trusted persons in a network to decide how to approach these situations. Perhaps this information could be presented by a supervisor to a hospital administrator or, in rare cases, to an external regulator because medical staff are not supposed to allow undisclosed conflicts of interest to jeopardize the quality of their services.

Case advocates sometimes assert that multiple ethical violations exist, such as a patient not given accurate information and not given sufficient information and not given quality services.

Case advocates can also use the ethical argument that they seek to advance the well-being of specific consumers—often called *beneficence* by ethicists. They can cite evidence-based research that documents that a consumer may benefit from specific medical or sociopsycho interventions other than ones currently being considered. Social workers are particularly well positioned to cite this research when it bears on their own competence, such as research that shows that counseling improves health outcomes of specific kinds of consumers.

Case advocates who use ethical arguments often gain influence by placing issues on a moral high ground. They need to realize, however, that ethicists often disagree about specific issues.

Using Medical Culture

Health staff can portray their work as flowing from concern about the well-being of specific consumers as required by the Hippocratic Oath as well as medical ethics. They can acknowledge that they do not have the skills to provide medical treatment, but can attend to many other needs of consumers that will also enhance their well-being. Case advocates can often gain the good will of physicians and administrators by acknowledging their good intentions at the outset. They may say, for example, "I've seen on many occasions how you go the extra mile for many patients . . . and now I have another situation that requires this."

They can achieve these goals by their demeanor, their words, and their track record over an extended period of time. They can use plural nouns to describe their work, such as, "I bring this case to your attention so that *we* can provide the best services possible." Or, "I bring this case to your attention so that *we* won't have a dissatisfied patient." Or, "My professional expertise in family interactions as a social worker makes me think that *we* will prevent family conflict if *we* hold a family conference." They can make clear that they want to make constructive improvements to patient services in a multiprofessional context.

Employing Power-Dependence

Adherents of power-dependence theory suggest that others view us as credible when they depend on us (Jansson & Simmons, 1985; Jansson & Simmons, 1986). Consider the social work units in two hospitals. The unit in Hospital 1 contents itself with providing crisis intervention services to patients, whereas the unit in Hospital 2 fills several functions besides traditional counseling, including discharge planning, financial counseling for patients, providing social services to rape victims, serving as intermediaries between the hospital and the state's department of children's services in suspected cases of child abuse and neglect, operating a substance abuse clinic, and providing home-based services to frail, older persons. Depending on social work staff for these services, top decision makers in Hospital 2 cannot imagine how their hospital would function without this unit. By contrast, top decision makers in Hospital 1 hardly know that the social work unit exists, much less that it is vital to the hospital. According to power-dependence theory, decision makers are more likely to heed suggestions of the director or other staff of the expansive social work unit at Hospital 2 than at Hospital 1 (Jansson & Simmons, 1985).

Power-dependence theory suggests, then, that case advocates can increase their stature by assuming multiple functions beyond their narrow job descriptions. As the director of a social work unit once said to me, "I might even consider washing windows!" These expanded functions serve several purposes; they make high-level administrators feel beholden to these units—and make them come to believe they cannot function without them.

Power-dependence theory suggests, too, that firing line staff gain influence as they take burdensome and irksome tasks from other professionals. Many physicians do not *want* to spend much time with consumers attending to their anxiety or depression, helping them negotiate with family members, or doing follow-up work with them around adherence, the family living situation, or myriad other details. They not only concede these tasks to others, but are more likely to cooperate with their future case-advocacy interventions.

Taking the Initiative and Responsibility

Case advocates also can enhance their credibility by taking the initiative to suggest enhancements in consumers' healthcare. Initiators often gain influence by the mere fact that they took the first step. If they also take responsibility for the intervention that they initiated, they also gain influence because they do not obligate others to engage in additional tasks.

Developing a Positive Track Record

Advocates gain influence when they have positive reputations that are based on first- or secondhand observations and reports that demonstrate that they are competent and trustworthy. Word spreads fast that specific frontline staff can be counted on to do what they promise.

Using Process Skills

Case advocacy takes place in the give-and-take of deliberations, which are characterized by their tenor, tempo, and scope of conflict. The tenor is the level of conflict; the tempo is the timing, pace, and duration of deliberations; and the scope of conflict is the number and kind of people who participate in them. Case advocates use process power when they influence the tenor, tempo, or scope of conflict of deliberations in order to get a specific proposal enacted (Schattscheider, 1980).

I can also usefully contrast win-lose interactions with win-win interactions. In win-lose politics, each side in the contest believes that it loses each time the other side wins and therefore wants to contest every point. In win-win interactions, the two sides believe they will both emerge with benefits, such as a satisfied consumer or a positive achievement. Case advocates can instill a win-win atmosphere by their use of language, such as using the pronoun "we," finding common goals such as wanting to improve the care of a particular patient, and lowering conflict by making concessions to the other party.

Timing is another kind of influence resource. The timing of a disputed proposal often favors a specific side. If someone introduces a proposal at an inopportune moment, its chances may be imperiled, no matter how skillful its defenders or how great its merits. Case advocates may decide in specific situations to wait until the course of events becomes clearer before they advocate for specific consumers.

Managing Conflict

Individuals can influence the level of conflict. People who wish to intensify discord, for example, can use emotion-laden words; refer to conflicts in the fundamental values at stake; enlarge the scope of conflict by publicizing the issue; or clearly state that they do not want amicable resolution: "We plan to fight to the finish," or, "We will accept no significant changes in our proposal (Froman, 1967). People who believe that conflict will be detrimental to their cause will try to diminish conflict, for example, by emphasizing a proposal's technical features, identifying the common interests of all the parties, and discouraging the participation of those who will raise the level of conflict.

The ability to shape the level of conflict is an important influence resource. Conflict is sometimes advantageous such as when it allows a case advocate to gain the attention of another professional and to dramatize an issue. It can also create nonproductive animosity and anger and inhibit collaboration needed to address consumers' problems.

Healthcare professionals sometimes become mediators where they assume a neutral or arbitrating role between contending parties. They may help conflicting parties to state their views, establish ground rules, highlight commonalities, and find constructive solutions.

Using Intermediaries

I have already mentioned how healthcare professionals can use intermediaries in their case-advocacy interventions. Perhaps a head nurse in a specific unit can better initiate discussion about a specific consumer with a physician with whom she has worked for many years. Perhaps an administrator can discuss specific confidentiality regulations or reaccreditation standards with a physician than with a specific social worker.

Bypassing Specific Professionals

Professionals can bypass specific professionals by referring consumers to other professionals. Assume, for example, that an oncologist fails to inform a terminally ill person about hospice or palliative care options. A social worker could bypass the oncologist by referring a patient to staff in these programs—or could ask them to contact the patient directly. The social worker could ask family members to accompany a consumer to a nearby hospice program to gain information about it.

Navigating Regulations

Rules are meant to be honored, such as HIPAA regulations and hundreds of other regulations such as ones in statutes, hospital protocols, and accreditation standards. Intentional violation of regulations sometimes results in penalties or court action. Case advocates increase their influence as they are informed about specific regulations and protocols so that they can invoke them in specific situations

Regulations are also meant to be bent or even disregarded in certain cases to promote consumers' well-being. Assume that a disoriented elderly patient does not want to be discharged as quickly as Medicare and hospital policies dictate even though no narrow medical rationale exists for her not to be discharged by noon on a specific day. An advocate might decide that this patient could be harmed psychologically if she is discharged with possible consequences for her medical condition. She could cite the patient's distress as a rationale. She could contend that existing agencies or the place of residence where the patient might be discharged would render her unable to manage her distress effectively. The advocate could inform the elderly patient that she has the right to appeal the discharge order.

Gaining Entrée

Health staff often depend on referrals from physicians to gain entrée to specific cases. Physicians often refer consumers to social workers, for example, only when they need discharge planning or need referrals to community-based agencies. Case finding becomes, then, a source of influence because it allows them to obtain entrée to consumers who they would not otherwise see—and to situations where they can become case advocates.

They can gain entrée in several ways. If they establish networks with other health staff, they can often receive information that specific consumers not only need their assistance, but case advocacy. A nurse may inform a social worker, for example, that a specific consumer is immobilized by depression concerning her serious medical condition or the medical condition of her spouse. Or they can connect to specific consumers through reading their medical records, by observing them, or by initiating discussions with them. They can talk with a resident about a case—and then initiate a discussion with the patient. They can offer to attend a family conference. Some states, such as California, have legal provisions in their Health and Welfare Codes that give social workers access to patients *even* if physicians do not refer them, although this must be exercised with tact.

Interpreting a Professional Role

Many physicians do not understand the roles and skills of frontline staff, ascribing to them such limited roles as discharge planning (social workers) or administering bedside medications (nurses). Frontline staff gain influence resources as they help physicians understand their multifaceted roles. They can "market" their competencies in various ways, including by participating in in-service training sessions, participating in rounds, contributing to medical records, case finding, and distributing written information about their competencies. They educate physicians about their capabilities when they engage in case advocacy.

Using Appropriate Assertiveness

To use influence effectively, people must first decide that they possess influence resources, that they can use them successfully, and that they want to use them. The word assertiveness describes this proclivity to test the waters, rather than to be excessively fatalistic.

Assertiveness is undermined, however, by two dispositions. The first is a victim mentality that disposes people to believe that others will conspire to defeat their preferences (Kanter, 1977). A director of a hospital's social work department might believe, for example, that the nurses and physicians will systematically oppose any proposals by social workers—and therefore not initiate any of them. The second is fatalism about using influence in a more general sense on the mistaken belief that only high-level persons or powerful interests can wield influence successfully. Both the victim mentality and fatalism create self-fulfilling prophecies that restricts assertive behaviors by predisposing persons not to initiate change.

I can make a distinction between appropriate and inappropriate assertiveness. Health staff who are appropriately assertive exercise influence in situations and in ways that will not compromise their ability to engage in case advocacy in the future. They do not burn bridges with others by alienating them unnecessarily, such as by being heavy-handed or intruding into situations where they cannot be effective. Yet they do not want to be so cautious that they remain on the sidelines, not even engaging in case advocacy for fear of antagonizing others.

Case advocates sometimes encounter persons who seek to intimidate them from engaging in case advocacy whether by threatening them, demeaning them, or using offensive language toward them. They need skills in *not* being intimidated when consumers' well-being is at stake. They can avoid personalizing conflict with intimidators by interpreting their professional rationale for engaging in case advocacy with specific consumers. They may need to seek help from intermediaries, such as supervisors, if they confront persons who chronically seek to intimidate them in ways that prevent them from acting professionally.

Designing Communication Strategy

Healthcare professionals enhance their influence when they communicate skillfully with different audiences and in different situations. With audiences that regard themselves as experts, such as many physicians, a case advocate has to be careful not to be excessively directive in suggesting a remedy to a consumer's problem. She might ask a physician why he thinks this consumer is perplexed about treatment options and then ask him how he would propose addressing the situation. She might pose several options, while asking which one he prefers.

With audiences that view themselves as hostile to a specific case advocate, she might state her objective in terms that create commonalities with them. She might say that she merely wants to help this consumer feel better about his healthcare as she serves as his case advocate. She would want to appear low key and reasonable. She might offer to help in any way that she can.

The tone of communications is important in medical settings where power disparities often exist. Healthcare professionals do not have to be excessively deferential, but must be respectful and open to differing viewpoints. When they encounter hostility from other professionals, they avoid personalizing it by returning to the goal of improving services for consumers or honoring their ethical rights.

Using Group Skills

Healthcare professionals need group skills to help consumers in group settings where key decisions are made about their care. These groups include meetings of professionals, meetings between professionals and consumers, and meetings of specific consumers and their family members, partners, and friends. They also include support groups that are often staffed by social workers and nurses and that often provide information and case advocacy for their members.

Healthcare professionals need skills to carry several roles in these various groups. They can be leaders in some of them, including preparing agendas, facilitating discussion, summarizing decisions, and helping to implement them. They can be facilitators who help a group make progress in discussing issues, hearing different viewpoints, and making decisions. They can act as resource persons as they present technical information needed by group members to reach conclusions. They can be mediators who serve as honest brokers to help members resolve conflict. They help groups establish ground rules that allow group members to respect one another (Jansson, 2011).

Group skills can be viewed as influence resources because they allow a case advocate to shape group process to improve services and the ethical treatment of specific consumers. Assume, for example, that family members do not agree with their parent's decision to forego heroic treatment after being diagnosed as terminally ill. A case advocate would use her group skills to help the family honor their parent's ethical right to self-determination while trying to preserve a positive relationship between them and their parent.

Affirming Shared Collective Interests

Case advocates can cite shared collective interests to improve the care of consumers. They can argue that improvements in care will improve the reputation of the health organization, will avert litigation, will result in higher patient satisfaction, and will help the institution secure reaccreditation. They can help the institution avert bad publicity, such as when the mass media report that some hospitals release homeless persons to the streets with disregard for the well-being.

Using Peer Pressure

Case advocates can sometimes use peer pressure to help consumers, while realizing that this strategy can place physicians and other health providers on the defensive. They can remark to health staff in one unit that other units in the hospital have introduced specific innovations that might be useful to it. They can cite specific Joint Commission accrediting standards to imply that a specific unit or professional is at odds with them in their professional practice.

Using Influence Resources in Tandem and Sequentially

Effective case advocates view their influence resources like artists view their palette. They can use them singly or in tandem. They can experiment with one kind of influence resource and shift to another if necessary. They can use a carrot (reward power) or a stick (coercive power) in specific situations—or both of them. They can use a specific kind of communication and switch to another if it does not work.

EMPOWERMENT (CONTINUED)

I have discussed a variety of influence resources that can help case advocates help consumers obtain better services and ethical treatment. Now I discuss how they can help consumers develop and use their influence resources.

Healthcare professionals must often give consumers confidence to act in their own behalf or in the interest of a spouse or relative when they cannot self-advocate. They can instill confidence by informing consumers that they have the right to informed consent, confidentiality, and honest and correct information. These rights, they can be told, derive from ethics as well as regulations and court decisions. They should exercise them when they feel uneasy about specific transactions with providers; they should feel free to ask questions, seek additional information, and obtain a second opinion before proceeding further.

They can instill confidence, as well, by engaging in role plays with consumers where they play the role of physicians or consumers. Or they can state the kinds of questions consumers might ask. They can coach them about specific questions, such as asking a physician why she ruled out a specific option and what she thinks about alternative treatment strategies.

It is useful to consider empowerment options when consumers are at critical junctures in their care. Perhaps they do not have a troublesome health condition but want to engage in prevention because they fear they might develop it because of their family history. Perhaps they have undiagnosed health conditions, but want to explore how to proceed even when physicians have not identified why they feel sick. Perhaps they have received a diagnosis that is troubling to them and want to know how to proceed. Perhaps they are receiving treatment, but have side effects that bother them—or want to explore other treatment options.

Empowering Consumers Prior to Possessing Troublesome Health Conditions

Chapter 8 deals with the underfunding and underproviding of preventive services in the U.S. health system. Consumers should seek information about their risk factors for specific health conditions, such as environmental factors, family history, ethnicity or race, personal health history, social class and level of education, life style factors, diet, weight, age, and (increasingly) genetic information. They should develop a personal strategy for offsetting or negating the effects of these risk factors in a collaborative process with healthcare providers that can also include physical therapists, nutritional consultants, sleep consultants, geneticists, and practitioners of alternative medicine. Prevention requires a team of physicians and others who help consumers develop and implement sensible preventive strategies.

Empowering Consumers With Undiagnosed Health Conditions

Many consumers possess undiagnosed health conditions. They may not have symptoms, but obtain test results that suggest that they may possess a health condition. Or they may have symptoms but not definitive test results.

This is a frustrating period for many consumers because they want to know what is ailing them and why—but do not have definitive information. Some medical conditions are *never* diagnosed because of their rarity or the lack of agreement among healthcare providers about them.

Case advocates should encourage consumers to be full participants in the health process at this point. They should view test results, including scans. They should ask for alternative explanations of their health condition. They should inquire why test results are not definitive. They should obtain second opinions. They should gain access to their medical records. They should start a medical diary that contains test results, dates of medical examinations, and self-reports of their symptoms.

Empowering Consumers With Diagnosed Health Conditions

Even when consumers receive test results that confirm a diagnosis, such as cancer, congestive heart failure, diabetes, or myriad other conditions, they should realize that they are only at the start of a medical journey that can take them in many directions. At each stage in this journey, they should ask whether their test results are definitive and what they mean. It is no time to be timid because their future hangs in the balance, particularly with serious health conditions.

When consumers receive test results and a diagnosis, they should already have prepared questions for the physician who presents them—often based on research that they have already done. They can find books written for general audiences, such as *Guide to Surviving Prostate Cancer* that are written in digestible form by experts (Walsh, 2001). These questions should probe whether they need to be treated and when, whether the test results and diagnosis appear definitive, how advanced the disease appears to be, and what treatment options exist. They should examine current controversies in medical science about whether, when, and how to treat the medical condition, such as with surgery, medication, radiation, and other strategies.

Consumers should think along with their physician rather than merely receiving information for several reasons. Some physicians are trained in a single methodology for treating specific conditions when several methodologies exist and when definitive research is lacking on their efficacy. Many physicians are not skilled at communication, so they will not give patients the full spectrum of information they need to be empowered to make decisions. Patients should often expect to be confused because medical science is often unclear or conflicted even if some physicians gloss over these realities.

When deciding who they might consider for specific medical procedures, consumers should always ask specific questions that can often be obtained from experts such as Dr. Patrick Walsh (2001) who counsels consumers searching for surgeons for prostate cancer to ask: Where were you trained and are you board-certified in urology (avoid ones who are not board-certified and favor ones trained in respected settings), how many operations do you do a week (preferably several times a week), how many operations have you done in your career (preferably hundreds or far more), do you collect data on your outcomes including longevity and side effects (avoid ones who do not and who cannot tell you what they are), is your medical institution closely connected to a medical school (preferably yes), do you keep up with the latest research (avoid ones who do not), do you keep up with the latest surgical procedures for avoiding side effects like incontinence and impotence (avoid ones who do not), and do you operate on nearly every person who has prostate cancer (avoid ones who do because some men with advanced cancer shouldn't have surgery)?

It may seem uncomfortable to ask these questions, but Walsh and other experts counsel consumers to remember that, "*You don't want a surgeon who's 'pretty good'* at removing the prostate . . . There are no second chances here; this is a one-shot operation . . . (the only one) you will ever receive in your life." (Walsh, 2001, pp. 214–216).

Many physicians are reluctant to discuss prognosis with consumers, so consumers should seek accurate information so they know what they face. Prognoses are usually given in probabilities, such as a 50% chance of recurrence in the next three years or an average life expectancy of five years.

Empowering Consumers in the Posttreatment Period

When recovering from a medical procedure for a serious health condition, all consumers face a roller coaster as they face ongoing medical tests and interactions with medical providers, as well as chemotherapy, radiation, and other treatments. Consumers will want to be assured that they receive accurate and sufficient information about their medical options; that their providers use evidence-based practice, and that they are true partners with their providers. See Vignette 4.1, written by Lisa Gebo, a highly skilled self-advocate, for discussion of empowerment strategies in the wake of surgery for serious breast cancer.

Vignette 4.1 Metastatic Breast Cancer and Consumer Self-Advocacy: Lessons Learned and Miles to Go

by Lisa Gebo

From 0 to 60 mph in Seconds Flat: On receiving an Initial Stage-IV Breast Cancer Diagnosis

Life in the Fast Lane

In the fall of 2005, I was in my late forties and I was tooling along at high speed in my publishing career. My main role as an executive acquiring editor for a major textbook company was to research and meet visionary authors and to negotiate publishing agreements with them on behalf of the company. I worked with a very successful group and I loved mentoring newer colleagues. To achieve our annual goals, we all worked long hours and traveled a lot. As a result of my own work efforts, I was often very stressed and tired, didn't eat well or exercise enough, and I wished I had more time to spend with my husband and family. At the same time, I was energized by new ideas and I felt grateful for the stimulation and autonomy that my position afforded me. Conflicted, I felt that the increasing job demands were not good for my health or my personal relationships, yet I couldn't seem to step out of the driver's seat.

What Is That Knocking Under the Hood?

While fastidious about my annual spring mammograms and other health check-ups, I'd had ongoing problems for a number of years in my right breast. It began when I felt a lump in the upper outer quadrant of that breast in 1998. I saw my gynecologist immediately and she referred me to the only surgeon who was in my HMO plan at the time. After examining me, the surgeon conducted a fine needle biopsy. While he later informed me that the results showed no malignancy, the surgeon recommended that I have the "fibrous growth" removed. At the time, I didn't think to ask for a copy of the pathology report from the fine needle biopsy, nor did I request a copy of the surgeon's biopsy report. Unfortunately, the surgical stitches opened while I was on a business trip in Chicago. I saw the surgeon when I got home from Chicago and he asked if I wanted to have plastic surgery to address the inevitable scarring. I was not eager to have more surgery, so I elected to let the wound heal naturally. While it eventually healed, a broad scar remained. The scarring also made my annual mammograms more challenging to read. Therefore, when I then began to have problems with pain and persistent cysts in that same breast, my breast care center doctors began conducting sonograms following my annual mammograms to rule out anything "troublesome." I was told by my doctors that this combination of annual mammograms with follow-up sonograms represented the best standard of care for someone with my presenting concerns. And, since all of these tests were consistently not indicative of cancer according to my local breast care center, I just kept moving along.

In June 2005, I felt increased tenderness in the right breast, this time in the lower outer quadrant, so I returned to my gynecologist who sent me to the breast care center yet again. I had had my annual mammogram/sonogram earlier that year and it had shown no malignancies. Still, based on my concerns, the radiologist at the breast care center conducted another sonogram and found what she called another collection of cysts. The doctor informed me that I had especially dense breasts and that she suspected that the pain I was having was associated with perimenopause. I asked about a needle biopsy and the doctor said that while she could certainly do one, she did not recommend it as she felt it was not necessary. Why go through the pain and potential risk of infection when there was no need? Asserting there was no apparent malignancy, she did recommend that I return in 4 months for another ultrasound. I returned sooner, in September 2005, as I was becoming more concerned about the pain I was feeling. Again, a sonogram was conducted and the images continued to generate no serious concerns in the doctor's view. What I was feeling was now deemed an "old cluster of cysts." The doctor suggested that I watch and wait until my next annual mammogram.

In October 2005, I received an appealing job offer from another prestigious publishing company. It was a difficult decision as I had worked at my current publishing house for 15 years. However, the allure of signing professional books with a long-established company combined with the opportunity to work from home was just too appealing to turn away. A good change of lanes it seemed . . . but there were more changes and unforeseen collisions to come.

Driving Lesson, Part One: Learning to Listen to Your Own Intuition

At my 2006 annual mammogram, the technician entered the exam room after the test with a concerned look on her face. A "spiculated mass" had been identified in the mammogram and this was confirmed in the sonogram that followed immediately. Like a curling fractal arm, I could see the spiculation extending from a dark mass into my breast tissue. This time, the radiologist suggested that we conduct a core needle biopsy on the spot, and I readily agreed. The very next day I was told that a cancerous tumor had indeed developed in the right breast and that it had to be removed as soon as possible. At the same time, I was assured that we had caught this breast cancer very early and I was encouraged to pursue a lumpectomy and radiation.

At this point, a new level of lucidity and questioning flooded my mind: Given the fibrous growth and subsequent, long history of cysts that I'd experienced, had this breast cancer perhaps been in my body longer than the doctors suspected?

(continued)

(*continued*)

Had it been hiding deep behind the innocuous cysts and dense tissue? If so, why had the breast cancer not been discovered earlier during my persistent visits for mammogram/sonogram tests? And, if this breast cancer had been so stealthy and had evaded identification via those "standard of care" tests, perhaps it was not such an "early identification" after all? I began to think long and hard about a mastectomy followed by a "let's see from there" approach, instead of the lumpectomy followed by radiation approach that my doctors were advising. While the doctors insisted that lumpectomy and radiation in early-stage breast cancer is the intervention of choice, I decided to start listening more carefully to my own inner voice, my intuition. After all, mammogram and sonogram—the other recommended standards of care—had, at least in my case and in my view, not served me well. To my doctors' dismay, I elected mastectomy with concurrent reconstruction.

Driving Lesson, Part Two: When Doctors Learn to Listen

When I awoke from surgery, I sensed from reading the nurses and doctors' nonverbal behavior that my intuition had guided me appropriately. When the surgeon finally told me that 14 out of 20 lymph nodes had had cancer in them, and that a second tumor had been found in the removed breast tissue, we all knew that the cancer was far more advanced than the doctors had originally suspected. And then, later, when I inadvertently ran into one of my other doctors while gingerly navigating about the hospital halls trailing my PCA morphine pump, her sad eyes and even sadder statement hit me hard, "Lisa, you were right. The breast cancer was more advanced than any of us could ever have imagined. You'll need to see the oncologist again and more scans will be needed to assess how far the breast cancer has traveled." This frank and direct doctor then said, "You kept coming back to us, Lisa, yet with the existing technologies, in your case, we were unable to find the problem. This is a perfect example of how we need to better listen to our patients."

Who's at the Wheel? Letting Go of Blame and Shame

What *could* we have done differently? My immediate reaction to the advanced status of my disease was anger—both at my doctors and at myself. Why was the breast cancer not detected on any of the mammograms and sonograms? Had it just suddenly appeared out of the blue? Why had I not insisted on another needle biopsy sooner? I had seen the doctors every time I felt concern despite my busy work schedule over all those years . . . Why had the standard of care tests perhaps let me down? (According to the helpful web site created by Breast Cancer Action, "mammograms do not always detect breast cancer" and in day-to-day practice, mammograms can miss more than a quarter of all tumors." *From Mammography Screening and New Technologies, 6.4.08, C2000-2008, Breast Cancer Action at* http://bcaction.org/index.php?page=mammography-and-new-tech.

Would we ever really know when the cancer had first appeared?

In response to these questions, the head of the breast care center agreed to meet with me and she carefully walked me through all my films dating back to 1998. From those records, it appeared that the cancer was either not there earlier or it was completely undetectable until 2006. While I appreciated this doctor's time, I was not satisfied, so I went about getting copies of my own films and other historical reports. In the case of the 1998 surgery, the doctor's office staff had to go to their cellar to pull the old archived files. My husband and I were disconcerted to read in the pathology report from that very first fine needle biopsy from 1998 that "atypia" had been found in the sample. While the subsequent biopsy had revealed no cancer, could the surgeon have missed some early abnormal cells? We'll never know. We then took the breast center films and surgery samples from my mastectomy to a well-known university hospital more than 2 hours from our home. After reviewing the films and specimens, their experts concurred that quite possibly the breast cancer may have eluded the standard of care technology. The grade II tumors were not indolent, nor were they highly aggressive. Had I been tested and been positive for the BRCA I or II breast cancer gene, insurance would have paid for an MRI that may have caught the cancer sooner. However, women with difficult, very dense breasts with a history of cysts did not qualify for insurance reimbursement for MRI. I asked myself, "Why did the doctors assume I would not wish to pay for my own MRI?" (At this writing, Assembly Bill 2234 has been proposed in California whereby MRI would be required for screening and diagnosis of breast cancer for women with a variety of qualifying conditions, including "heterogeneously or extremely dense breast tissue on mammography," but to date, the bill has not passed. Insurance companies and some doctors continue to argue that the potential false positives and cost of MRIs do not warrant this extra screening. After witnessing the thousands of dollars that my treatment has cost us, (and more so, our insurance), I ask myself, "Wouldn't qualified MRI screening save insurance companies more money in the long run?" Why did they not tell me about the development of gene profiling? What other options were not shared with me? Although these questions initially provoked anger, my husband and I determined that while perhaps flawed, the thinking of our doctors had been done in good faith. We needed to address the immediate situation at hand, and for us, anger and self-blame was not helpful. Instead, we decided to be well-informed self-advocates going forward, in a shared and concerted effort to prolong my life.

Taking a Different Highway

Following my mastectomy, I had scans of my heart, brain, viscera, and bones. Fortunately, the brain, liver, and lungs were clear. However, multiple sites in my bones showed metastasis. This confirmed that the stage of this breast cancer was

(*continued*)

(continued)

not early Stage I but rather advanced Stage IV, currently incurable. I could consider this a terminal disease or a recurrent one. I have elected the latter perspective.

Moving on in Self-Advocacy: Living With Stage IV Breast Cancer

Directions and Choices

Because my disease was not diagnosed until it was at Stage IV, and because the tumors were ER/PR positive/Her2neu negative (essentially, reactive to hormones), the current Zeitgeist prompted my oncologists, (both local and second and third opinion university doctors) to recommend hormonal treatment as a primary intervention. My initial response was, "What, no chemo?! Have you given up on me completely?" I even went so far as to note to my (now beloved) local oncologist that I felt he was significantly less interested in me as a patient now that he realized he could not cure me or have me participate in his Stage 3 study. Fortunately, the man is both honest and wise and we have since developed a trusting and respectful relationship. He took my desperate comment in and after a long pause, admitted that in fact, unintentionally, he had pulled back when he found out how advanced my disease was. Still, he promised to partner with me to do all that we could to delay disease progression and prolong my life. He also promised to always be straightforward with me and help me control my pain. Moreover, he explained in exquisite detail why hormone treatment would be a good first direction in staving off the cancer. Not only was there good data about these drugs with my kind of tumor with progression to bone, but holding off on chemotherapy at that point would keep my options open for more trials when it absolutely became necessary to take chemotherapy. In order to establish a baseline, entry into many studies around new chemotherapies requires that participants have not yet taken any other chemotherapeutic drugs.

So, based on several doctors' assessments, I elected to begin hormone treatment. Because I was still premenopausal, we first tried Tamoxifen. However, it made me ache in my bones and joints and I felt very depressed. The depression may well have been due to my diagnosis so I also began seeing a therapist—with my husband. Still, I wanted to get off the Tamoxifen. The next class of hormone drugs to take then would be aromatase inhibitors. However, these are only available to and effective with postmenopausal women. Therefore, in order to suppress my estrogen levels, we tried Lupron injections. When this did not work, I had an oophorectomy. Without ovaries, I was able to begin Arimidex. This hormone blocker worked for about a year . . . but then my tumor markers began to rise significantly. We switched to Aromacin and then to Faslodex injections but still the numbers rose. A subsequent scan revealed that the breast cancer had progressed to the lining of my left lung. I began having more and more difficulty breathing, and weekly, for a month, I had to go to our local hospital to have a needle pushed through my back so that fluid could be drained from the pleura. It was now time to consider chemotherapy.

Shifting Gears: Beginning a Clinical Trial

During the time that I was on the aromatase inhibitors, my husband was concurrently researching clinical trials. Every morning, he would get online and check the latest outcomes and newest announcements. We had both been impressed with the study director at one of the university hospitals in our state who had provided a second opinion at my initial diagnosis. I therefore maintained an e-mail relationship with her. I would let her know about each milestone or setback in my treatment, and to my amazement, she would usually get back to me very quickly with her opinion. While I had often cursed e-mail in the past, I am very grateful for this mode of communication now. When she heard of the progression to my lungs, she invited me to participate in one of her appropriate studies.

As it turns out, the university doctor's study was very promising and I was a qualified candidate. Moreover, I was randomized into the very arm of the study that would have been my first choice. That is, Arm A represented a new and promising drug, Ixempra, administered three times a month with one week off, combined with two weeks with Avastin. Arm B combined Ixempra and Avastin but with higher doses on a less frequent schedule. Arm C combined Avastin with Taxol, a more known drug. We had read in other study outcomes that hitting the cancer with lower doses more frequently over a longer period of time had been effective. While there was no guarantee that this would be the case with this study, the logic appealed to us. At the time, Avastin was off-label (not approved by the FDA for advanced breast cancer, and therefore not reimbursable by insurance), so we would have had to pay dearly for it if I received it locally. However, Avastin was proving very effective in the fast shrinking of tumors, and if possible, I wanted to get rid of the growths that were causing the pleural effusion and fluid build-up in my lungs as soon as possible. The study sponsors were providing both the Ixempra and the Avastin for free. The new drug, Ixempra, is a taxane-like medication but with some promising benefits. While we did not relish the 2-hour drive with overnights three times a month, and while the experimental nature of this Phase II trial and its alarming consent form (listing all the possible side effects) frightened us, we decided to go for it.

Passengers You Didn't Even Know Were There With You

Getting into the study was a whirlwind. Scans had to be taken, blood had to be drawn, and opinions from local doctors had to be obtained. Then there was the practical concern of the dogs and cats. Who would feed them and let them in and

(continued)

(*continued*)

out of the house when we overnighted in the city? And what about all those hotel bills and the rising price of gas? This is where reaching out and asking for help has been a humbling and amazing experience. Friends stayed up for hours one night with me and my husband, reviewing the consent form line by line, helping us get over our fears. Friends and family from afar sent cards, books, humorous CDs, music, and other treats. My book group friends quickly organized a schedule and have been caring for our pets while we are away ever since I began the study eight months ago. One of our friends has a studio apartment in the city for work and because she travels so much and is seldom there, we stay at her place most of the time when we need to overnight. Free acupuncture, hypnosis, and invitations to mountain cabins and meditation retreats have been offered like flowers. After some research, we learned that our health insurance has additional coverage for cancer patients that provides for enhanced coverage when being treated by an approved "Center of Excellence." This service also pays for gas and provides a daily stipend for meals. Friends and family have faithfully continued to post encouraging notes on our CaringBridge web site. Work colleagues have without complaint taken over the projects I left when I stopped working and I hear from them often with wonderful stories about the books that are coming out soon. Nurses and other cancer patients in the study have shared precious time, stories, and care. Friends I have made through our local cancer support group and my volunteer work with hospice have shared fears, tears, hope, and loss with me. Having Stage IV cancer is nothing to write home about, but it has shown me how big our community of true friends and family is, and how many people occupy our hearts.

The Road From Here

After two treatments with the study drugs, my pleural effusion went away. After six months, the tumors in my pleura have gone away, barring a few tiny spots. The disease in bone is still diffuse throughout, but less intense. Side effects have included fatigue, nausea, worsening neuropathy, loss of hair and fingernails, headache, high blood pressure, weight gain (steroids are used to avert allergic reaction), and vision changes. My husband and I are tired but hopeful. Our lives have been disrupted and forever changed. We don't know how long the study drugs will work or when my red and white blood cell counts will require a break. A cure will perhaps come in our lifetimes. Or, a new drug, equally effective, is or will become available if my participation in the current study is ended because of disease progression. If an effective drug is not found at that time, I will likely die, (if some other act of fate doesn't intervene before that, of course). Still, I feel fortunate. And I am less afraid. I believe this comfort comes in large part from learning to be a self-advocate as it relates to my ongoing healthcare. My thoughts for you? Don't hesitate to ask questions and insist on getting what you need, learn from my experience and that of others, advocate for improvements in our healthcare system, and live each day as fully as possible.

Lessons Learned: A Suggested Driver's Guide for Women With Advanced Breast Cancer

- Take a partner or friend with you to the oncologist or any doctor visit and ask this person to take detailed notes. Or, ask the doctor's permission to tape record your appointments.
- Prepare good questions before seeing your doctors and bring a list of all symptoms and current medications that you are taking.
- Maintain a written, up-to-the-minute medical history—a log of all appointments and interventions. It is incredible how quickly you can forget what test was done on what day. Keeping a detailed log helps with health insurance questions and if necessary, your application for social security disability.
- Don't be afraid to ask questions or challenge your doctor or get second and third opinions. This is your life. Partner with the doctor(s) you respect the most.
- A good nurse is a best friend. Cultivate that relationship.
- Don't be shy about checking the labels on all drugs that are to be administered during chemotherapy—before the infusion begins. Better to provide one more set of eyes to the drug check than suffer the effects of a mistake.
- If you are feeling depressed, do not hesitate to seek help. Therapy has helped me tremendously to cope with this disease and to sort out lifetime and end-of-life concerns that I needed to process.
- Investigate clinical trials. The National Cancer Institute posts updates about recent trial outcomes at http://www.cancer.gov/clinicaltrials/breast-cancer-updates.
- If you find doctors who will engage in e-mail with you, try to keep your e-mail brief and number your questions. I have long been notorious for long e-mails so this is a challenge for me. However, I get more helpful responses when I keep my e-mail concise and focused.
- Keep a personal journal to process your experience. If you need to keep family and friends apprised of health updates but are overwhelmed by visits, telephone calls, and e-mail, consider setting up a caringbridge site at http://www.caringbridge.org. There, for free, you can maintain a journal of personal updates, read your guest entries, post photos, and provide links to your circle of friends and family about relevant information.
- Eat healthy foods, drink lots of water, and get plenty of sleep and exercise. Don't be afraid to ask for an anti-anxiety medication like Ativan or Xanax if cancer medications or anxiety keep you awake. I have found meditation,

(continued)

(*continued*)

visualizations, acupuncture, gentle massage, breath-work, and yoga to be very helpful in alleviating both physical and emotional pain.

- Get copies of all pathology reports, lab reports, blood test reports, doctor reports, and all films and keep a library of same at home. Medical staff should be able to make you a CD of your films if you ask.
- Do not hesitate to challenge insurance claim denials. In my experience, denials are often the result of "clerical errors" and persistence pays off, literally. I have also found that providers may give you more time to pay bills if you keep them apprised of your efforts and the status of claims. If you don't have the energy to push back or maintain these records, ask someone for help with this onerous but necessary paperwork.
- If you have not completed a will, with durable power of health directives, please consider doing it now.
- A decision to continue to work depends on your doctor's recommendation as well as your own emotional and financial needs. Medical insurance continuance may also be a factor although HIPAA law requires that persons with preexisting conditions may not be denied insurance (although that same insurance may be exorbitant). I continued to work because I loved my new job, I was able to work at home, and it helped me think about other things besides my health. However, when the disease spread from my bones to my lungs, the doctors urged me to stop work so that I could focus exclusively on my health. Participating in a study, while very positive overall, has in fact taken a great deal of time and focus, and the side effects have not been insignificant, so for me, going on disability was a good decision at that point. Clearly, when to stop work is not only the doctor's decision, but yours as well.
- Check out reliable web sites created by breast cancer advocacy groups. There are a number of them. I have found Breast Cancer Action at http:// bcaction.org to be especially helpful. There, you will find a wealth of information including, for example, practical guidance, suggested readings, myths debunked, and latest research.
- Don't let people make you blame yourself for having this disease. We may have a great deal to learn about the mind-body connection and our thoughts and attitudes may well contribute to our health. However, there is a fine line between believing in positive thinking and believing that one can completely control the unknown.
- Be kind to yourself and let yourself feel what you feel. There will be good and bad days—just like before your diagnosis.
- Boundaries: Share what you want to with friends and family. No more and no less. But if you can, try to ask for and accept help. It may really help you, and it will definitely help those who love you and perhaps feel otherwise powerless in the face of this challenge.

- Consider volunteer work if you feel well enough. Working with hospice has helped me to face my own fear of death while moving the focus off myself for a while. Sitting with dying persons or helping their loved ones with grief has helped me to have greater perspective on this universal process.
- No avoiding it—this experience is painful. However, it is also an opportunity to learn and grow and feel and connect even more deeply. There will be some pleasant surprises mixed in with living with this most unwelcome disease. Family and friends, both new and old, can reveal themselves in new, profound, and life-changing ways.

Epilogue

As this book goes to production, I have an opportunity to update this case. After a year in the study, chemo-caused neuropathy forced us to lower the dose. Within months, my cancer progressed to my liver and I had to stop my participation in the study. Since the disease in my bones had also gotten worse, I received a month of radiation to my hip. The pain there is now gone. I looked into other viable studies but the still severe neuropathy caused me to not qualify. So, for now, I am in local treatment with a new chemotherapy. We'll know after another cycle if the drug is working on the liver lesion. I recently learned that our local breast care center is using MRI more readily than it had been when I was first diagnosed, and this represents progress. Also, I am participating in a focus group at my local oncologist's office next week to brainstorm with providers and other consumers about ways to continually improve the treatment experience. This book represents a huge step toward better consumer advocacy and for that, I thank the author, the other contributors, and the publisher from the bottom of my heart.

Learning Exercise

Discuss how this case illustrates *skilled* case advocacy by analyzing:

- Influence resources that she used.
- Her relative assertiveness and persistence.
- How she undertook the various case advocacy tasks in Figure 3.1 (Chapter 3).
- Her ease at asking physicians tough questions.
- Her use of analytic skills.
- Her skill in using communication.

Author's Note: Lisa Gebo lost her battle with breast cancer in June 2010 after her long struggle with the disease. Both consumers and health professionals can learn about advocacy from her inspiring account. I have dedicated this book to her.

ADVOCACY WITH RESPECT TO SEVEN CONSUMER PROBLEMS

We have provided an advocacy practice framework, discussed eight tasks that case advocates often confront, and discussed some skills they need to implement these tasks. We now progress to case-advocacy situations, which health professionals often confront when they encounter consumers with the seven problems discussed in Chapter 1, before discussing policy advocacy in Chapters 11 through 14. Advocacy is discussed for:

- Securing ethical care in Chapter 5
- Obtaining quality care in Chapter 6
- Obtaining culturally competent services in Chapter 7
- Obtaining preventive care in Chapter 8
- Obtaining help in financing healthcare in Chapter 9
- Obtaining help with mental distress in Chapter 10
- Obtaining noninsular or community-based care in Chapter 11
- Reforming policies in Chapters 12 through 14 through use of policy advocacy

5

Advocacy to Protect Consumers' Ethical Rights

C onsumers have a right to healthcare that promotes both their well-being and their ethical rights. I discuss specific ethical rights of consumers in the context of different styles of ethical reasoning, and how health providers and consumers often confront ethical dilemmas, in addition to and how they can use ethical reasoning to resolve them. I relate 19 scenarios that case advocates confront as they work to protect consumers' ethical rights. (Seven of them can be viewed online as indicated at this chapter's end.)

PROMOTING ETHICAL CONDUCT IN HEALTHCARE

When people think of medical science, they often focus on specific medical interventions geared to detecting, preventing, and treating illness, such as chemotherapy, surgery, and diagnostic tests.

Medical science has achieved remarkable breakthroughs in recent decades. Yet the health enterprise also includes the realm of virtuous, moral, or ethical conduct. (I use these terms interchangeably because philosophers offer different definitions of them.) It is not enough to cure disease or prevent illness (medical science) because providers must also relate to consumers in a virtuous, moral, or ethical way. I use a different vocabulary in the ethical and medical realms. If I use pragmatic words like "works," "does not work," "is theoretically sound or promising," and "has no basis in theory" in the scientific realm, I use words like "right," "wrong," "good," "bad," "ought," "should," and "should not" in the moral realm. If medical science explains and solves, the ethical realm establishes *normative prescriptions about virtuous or moral or ethical conduct between providers and consumers.*

Ethics is integral to healthcare for many reasons. Although healthcare offers medical interventions to consumers, only consumers can ultimately decide if they want them. They can reject treatments even when they are viewed as meritorious by their care givers, including medical care based on evidence-based medicine (EBM). As determined by many court rulings, accreditation standards, regulations, and laws, consumers are masters of their personal realm unless they are minors or have been declared by courts unable to make decisions for themselves. Ethics sometimes trumps EBM since competent consumers can choose to decline treatment recommendations that are supported by science.

Healthcare must be infused with ethical conduct by providers, moreover, because treatments often have side effects. When they prescribe chemotherapy to cancer patients, for example, physicians do not experience side effects, but consumers do. Some treatments, such as many forms of surgery, even carry some risk of death or permanent injury. Only consumers can decide if the benefits of specific treatments warrant these side effects.

Consumers have the power to risk death rather than to accept treatment. Consumers who have terminal illnesses, for example, can forego treatment even when physicians tell them that this decision will likely lead to their demise. They can make this decision for many reasons. They may decide that projected treatments will diminish the quality of their lives excessively. They may believe "their time has come." They may not want to burden their spouses or children. Providers can try to persuade them not to forego treatment, but this decision rests with them if they are competent to make decisions.

Ethical providers, then, must honor consumers' rights to self-determination. They must provide accurate and timely information so consumers can make intelligent decisions. They should not manipulate or coerce consumers into decisions. They should not overstate the likely benefits of specific medical procedures or understate their possible side effects.

Providers must act ethically, as well, because they develop and store consumers' medical information in medical records, professional notes, and recollections from conversations with them. This information may include data about stigmatized life habits, like alcoholism and substance abuse. It may include information about mental issues or problems. It may include information about serious diseases, and also information about consumers' propensities to have serious diseases based on family history and genetic information. Providers who violate this confidentiality can exact considerable harm on consumers. They can endanger their jobs, harm a consumer's self-image, and harm their relationships with those persons who receive the information.

Healthcare must also be infused with ethics because it depends on scientific experimentation with human subjects to develop clinical guidelines based on EBM. Animal studies are useful, but evidence for EBM must come primarily from human subjects. Consumers can make intelligent decisions about whether to participate in specific scientific experiments only if they are given accurate and timely information about the possible risks and benefits that they might encounter. Two unfortunate historical incidents demonstrate the dangers of forced or manipulated involvement in scientific experiments by unwilling or uninformed consumers. In Nazi Germany, officials forced some Jews in concentration camps to participate in medical experiments that often maimed or killed them. In the United States, health personnel deprived African

Americans in the South of medications to treat their syphilis in order to study the progression of the disease. Providers ought to gain full and informed consent from consumers before they enter these scientific experiments, such as clinical trials, funded research projects, or small-scale experiments.

Providers must realize that clinical guidelines based on EBM are not a panacea. They often do not even exist for some health problems. Even when they do exist, they do not offer a fail-safe solution for all consumers. Many consumers do not benefit from treatments based on guidelines even if they are effective for a majority of persons in specific clinical trials. Some kinds of consumers are often not included in the clinical trials or medical research that led to the development of the guidelines, such as persons of color, women, or persons with co-morbidities. Some consumers may not want the side effects of specific treatments even when supported by EBM.

Providers need to realize, as well, that culture, familial experiences, history, and personal experiences powerfully shape consumers' health preferences. Many consumers use alternative medicine, for example, even when it is not supported by EBM—whether as their major approach to dealing with a health condition or as an adjunct to it. Cultural, personal, and religious beliefs shape how persons approach end of life, whether they favor abortion, and many other health decisions.

Healthcare requires ethical behavior, as well, because power differentials exist between consumers and providers that can easily tip the balance toward providers absent ethical rules of conduct. Physicians possess greater technical expertise than most consumers because of their training and experience. They occupy high status within U.S. society. They are highly educated. They are disproportionately male and Caucasian even with recent strides in diversifying their ranks. If they do not act with considerable restraint, they can easily impose decisions on consumers, particularly ones who are intimidated by their expertise or status for cultural, economic, or educational reasons. Consumers who are traumatized by adverse diagnoses about their health conditions are particularly susceptible to unethical behavior by health staff because their fears may lead them to accept medical recommendations without fully understanding them or considering alternatives.

Many physicians and health administrators confront ethical issues because of the entrepreneurial nature of the U.S. health system that presents them with conflicts of interest. Providers who receive fee-for-service reimbursement often benefit financially as they provide diagnostic tests, medications, and treatments to consumers. Unless they act with restraint, they risk subordinating patient care to personal profit. Physicians with financial stakes in nursing homes, convalescent homes, optometry and pharmacy businesses, outpatient surgery centers, scanning centers, or other components of the health system should not refer consumers to them without disclosing their conflicts of interest. They should not favor specific medications, medical devices, and diagnostic tests in their care of patients because they received gifts from the corporations that manufacture them. The Patient Protection and Affordable Care Act of 2010 as amended by the Congress requires disclosures of financial relationships among health entities, including physicians, hospitals, pharmacists, pharmaceutical companies, and distributors of drugs, devices, and supplies in 2013.

Physicians and administrators in managed-care plans encounter their own conflicts between financial considerations and consumers well-being. Because these plans are financed by flat monthly payments from employers, their income increases as they do not provide costly services to their enrollees. When some of these plans instructed their primary-care physicians to curtail referrals to specialists to cut their costs, a public outcry led some states to enact laws that prohibited "gag orders."

Many critics contend that the U.S. health system is built on an uncertain ethical foundation that violates the ethical principle of social justice (Barr, 2008). Is it ethical, they ask, to not provide health coverage to tens of millions of Americans while the majority of Americans receive it? Does medical bankruptcy, experienced by millions of American per year, advance their well-being? Does the United States violate the ethical norm of social justice by failing to reform its health system to equalize coverage and access among its residents?

The Patient Protection and Affordable Care Act of 2010 represents a major step toward social justice in the American health system. It prevents insurance companies from canceling health policies of sick consumers, as well as denying coverage to children with preexisting conditions. It prohibits insurance companies from setting lifetime limits on insurance policies beginning in 2010—and to phase out lifetime limits on insurance policies issued or renewed after September 23, 2010. It removes insurance company barriers to receiving emergency care. As we discuss in Chapter 9, by 2014, it will vastly expand coverage for roughly 32 million Americans who are currently uninsured.

As we also discuss in Chapter 9, the legislation will vastly increase eligibility for Medicaid throughout the nation, as well as for the SCHIP program for children. These changes are critical to the ethical principle of social justice because Medicaid and SCHIP programs are disproportionately used by low income persons and families, Hispanics, and persons of color.

Even the Patient Protection and Affordable Care Act of 2010 will only extend insurance coverage to 32 million consumers, however, leaving roughly 15 million uninsured by 2019—and many of its insurance provisions do not take effect until 2014.

When the United States selected employers to fund health insurance for most Americans rather than developing universal health insurance, it created ethical issues for hospitals, clinics, and physicians. Many of them rely on private insurance to fund their operations, so they have an economic incentive not to serve uninsured or underinsured persons or to give them inferior service in violation of the ethical duty not to discriminate against persons for financial reasons. Many hospitals, clinics, and physicians do not serve enrollees in government programs like Medicaid and Medicare because they reimburse them at lower levels than private insurance companies (Stevens & Stevens, 1974).

Ethical conduct is needed also by consumers. They should not bully healthcare professionals into specific treatment decisions without entering into respectful discussions with them. They should not expect them to give them treatments that are medically futile, such as specific medications, surgeries, or diagnostic tests that are not effective. They should not threaten them verbally or physically. They should not seek false or misleading diagnoses in order to receive workmen's compensation or other financial awards.

THE POLICY AND REGULATORY THICKET
FOR PROMOTING ETHICAL CONDUCT

A policy and regulatory thicket has emerged to promote ethical conduct in the healthcare system. Advocates need to understand its major elements not only to inform themselves about consumers' ethical rights, but to be effective advocates when their rights are violated.

I often discuss ethics in this chapter as a process of decision making by healthcare professionals and consumers who make ethical choices after considering different options. While this is often the case, we should remember that public laws and regulations, when they exist, often *require* healthcare professionals and consumers to follow specific guidelines or risk penalties, litigation, and loss of accreditation if they fail to do so. Claiming ignorance of these statutes and regulations, whether in courts or in interactions with public officials, is often not a valid defense.

Accreditation Standards

An entire chapter of the Joint Commission accreditation standards for hospitals is devoted to "rights and responsibilities of the individual" (Joint Commission, 2009a). It asks hospitals to develop written policies on patient rights and to disseminate them to consumers, including their right to refuse care, treatment, and services in accordance with law and regulation. It requires patients be given informed consent. It requires that patients be informed about advance directives including their right to forgo or withdraw life-sustaining treatment and to withhold resuscitative services. It identifies patients' rights to participate in care decisions and to be treated in a dignified and respectful manner. It discusses patients' rights to privacy including their rights to decline being filmed or recorded. It requires that patients receive caring treatment, including knowing the names of physicians or other practitioners who care for them. It discusses patients' rights to participate in end-of-life decisions. It says that consumers have the right to receive information in a manner that they understand, because "communication is a cornerstone of patient safety and quality care," including the right to translation services and communication with visual and hearing impairments, children, and persons with cognitive impairments. It asks hospitals to respect consumers' cultural and personal beliefs and preferences—as well as their right to religious and other spiritual services. It asks hospitals to allow consumers access to information disclosures of their health information. It requires hospitals to "put its respect for the patient's rights into action by showing its support of these rights in the ways that staff and caregivers interact with the patient and involve him or her in care, treatment, and services" (Joint Commission, 2009a). It asks hospitals to involve surrogate decision makers when consumers are unable to make their own decisions. It asks them to involve consumers' families in making health decisions to the extent permitted by specific patients or surrogates. It requires hospitals to inform consumers or their surrogates of unanticipated outcomes of care, treatment, and services. It asks hospitals to respect consumers' rights during research, investigation, and clinical trials. It requires hospitals to give consumers copies of some of its policies, including ones about informed consent and advanced directives.

These accreditation standards ask hospitals to develop measures to determine the extent they implement many of these policies, whether through documentation (such as in medical records) or consumer surveys. The accrediting team grades the hospital as achieving insufficient compliance, partial compliance, or satisfactory compliance with many of these ethical standards. It can recommend loss of accreditation or probationary status for hospitals that violate ethical standards—a decision that could lead to loss of Medicare and Medicaid funding and make it difficult to attract qualified staff.

Statutes and Constitutions

Many state and federal statutes establish ethical requirements for healthcare staff. The Civil Rights Act of 1964 was enacted, for example, to end the practice of excluding persons of color from hospitals—a common practice in the South where African Americans were often limited to small segregated hospitals. Even after segregation was outlawed in hospitals by this legislation, many Southern hospitals continued to exclude African Americans until federal Medicare officials threatened to cut Medicare revenues from them in the wake of Medicare's enactment in 1965.

Specific provisions in state and federal constitutions are cited by courts as recognizing consumers' rights to self-determination. The 14th amendment to the federal constitution states a right to privacy, for example, that is used by consumers to protect their right to informed consent (T. Stein, 2004). Many state constitutions require local jurisdictions to protect the health of local residents.

I discuss the Health Information and Portability and Accountability Act of 1996 (HIPAA) in this chapter as it establishes procedures for protecting the confidentiality of consumers' health information.

Federal programs to provide coverage to consumers have advanced the ethical principle of social justice including Medicare, Medicaid, and the Children's Health Insurance Program (CHIP). Many seniors, low-income persons, and children in relatively low-income families would have had to rely on local charitable programs had these reforms not been enacted. Even with their enactment, however, roughly 47 million Americans were uninsured in 2009. The enactment of the Patient Protection and Affordable Care Act will advance social justice by infusing new resources into community clinics, subsidizing insurance premiums of many low- and moderate-income persons, and subsidized insurance pools of states for consumers with high-risk medical conditions. It will not allow private insurance companies to not cover consumers with preexisting medical conditions or to establish life-long limits on coverage even in 2010 and to devote most of their resources to patient care rather than overhead. It will give incentives to primary-care physicians and general surgeons who practice in underserved areas.

Regulations

Many state and federal regulations protect consumers' ethical rights. They cover such diverse topics as determining when medical interventions can be terminated for dying persons, determining who may give consent, advance healthcare directives, safeguards for consumers who participate in research on human subjects, and privacy rights. Regulations have the force of law: medical staff that violates them can be subject to fines and criminal sanctions.

Court Rulings and Litigation

Litigation in the health field is extensive and varied and profoundly influences providers' actions. The U.S. Supreme Court, as well as lower courts, have ruled on such diverse topics as the right of a state to enact legislation allowing physicians to prescribe lethal drugs to terminally ill patients and allow the use of medical marijuana for patients in pain, women's right to abort a fetus, and the right of physicians to discontinue medical care for comatose patients.

The right of self-determination lies at the heart of medical care and is manifested in the legal right to "consent" for competent persons. Physicians and health providers must obtain "informed consent" for complex medical procedures, such as many forms of surgery. Physicians who provide care to specific patients are responsible for obtaining their informed consent. When consent is not provided, physicians may be subject to charges of battery, which is defined legally as an intentional touching of a person in a harmful or offensive manner without his or her consent (CHA, 2008, p. 1.1). They may be subject to charges of malpractice of they fail to inform patients of the nature of their proposed treatment and its possible risks and benefits, as well as treatment alternatives (CHA, 2008, p. 1.1). While hospitals are not responsible for securing the patient's informed consent, they need consent for routine procedures, such as blood tests and nursing services. Therefore, patients give their consent by signing forms at the point of admission (CHA, 2008, p. 1.2). Hospitals can be held liable for certain breaches of confidentiality, as we discuss later.

Specific exemptions release providers from some legal requirements. State laws may release physicians from the need to gain consent, for example, when unconscious consumers receive emergency care, absent evidence that the patient would have refused the treatment for religious reasons or personal reasons (CHA, 2008, p. 1.2).

Regulating Professionals' Conduct

Physicians are licensed and regulated by state boards or commissions. They have the right to place physicians on probation or to prohibit them from practicing medicine if they violate specific ethical standards, such as engaging in fraudulent behavior, using drugs, battery, malpractice, or sexually abusing their patients. Critics contend that these boards and commissions discipline relatively few physicians. Nurses, social workers, and other healthcare professionals are licensed and regulated by state boards or commissions, as well. They can also be placed on probation or excluded from practice for ethical violations.

Every profession has a code of conduct that specifies ethical behaviors, including ones of physicians, social workers, and nurses.

Medical staff monitors and regulates their peers in hospitals and clinics as required by Joint Commission accrediting standards. They determine if they have appropriate credentials and competencies; determine if they provide effective patient care; and decide if their "behaviors . . . reflect a commitment to continuous professional development, ethical practice, an understanding and sensitivity to diversity, and a responsible attitude toward their patients, their profession, and society" (Joint Commission, 2009a). Ethical malfeasance can be grounds for not giving privileges to practice in a specific hospital and for withdrawing or limiting them subsequently.

Organizational Policies

The Joint Commission requires hospitals to have written policies with respect to ethical issues that are discussed in its standards—and to distribute them to patients. Medical professionals are expected to have read them and to be informed about them.

Patient Bill of Rights

With the shift from fee-for-service to managed-care plans that are financed by monthly flat payments, many consumers complained that the plans restricted their access to specialists, gave physicians economic incentives to restrict specialists' care, and required enrollees to sign agreements accepting arbitration from internal boards rather than resorting to courts. A national patient bill of rights was defeated in the Congress in 2001, but some states have enacted them for hospitals, managed-care plans, nursing homes, and mental healthcare. The American Hospital Association (AHA) has also promulgated a patient bill of rights. It often requires humane and dignified treatment, forbids transferring patients when they refuse a certain kind or level of treatment, and requires medical professionals to treat persons with HIV/AIDS (T. Stein, 2004).

In the wake of the enactment of the Patient Protection and Affordable Care Act of 2010, President Barack Obama issued a Patient's Bill of Rights that included:

- Prohibiting insurance companies from cancelling consumers' policies if they become sick, effective in 2010
- Stopping insurance companies from denying coverage to children with preexisting conditions, effective in 2010 and extended to all Americans in 2014
- Prohibiting lifetime limits on insurance coverage issued or renewed after September 23, 2010
- Phasing out annual dollar limits on coverage from 2010 to 2013
- Allowing consumers to designate any participating primary care doctor as their provider—and allowing women to see an OB-GYN without referral
- Removing insurance company barriers to receiving emergency care and not allowing them to charge consumers more when they are out of the network that contains a specific emergency room (Obama, 2010)

Regulations of Health Insurance Companies

States regulate health insurance companies, such as prohibiting deceptive advertising, requiring coverage for specific health conditions, and following regulations that prescribe how rapidly they can increase their premiums. The federal government enacted legislation in 2008 that required them to treat mental health conditions on a par with physical conditions. As mentioned earlier, the Patient Protection and Affordable Care Act, enacted in March 2010, promulgated many federal regulations over private insurance companies, such as prohibiting them from denying coverage for preexisting conditions.

Bioethics Committees and Institutional Review Boards (IRBs)

Hospitals and clinics are required by the Joint Commission to have bioethics committees that are accessible to staff members and consumers who want advice or decisions with respect to specific ethical issues. These bioethics committees are required to include staff from different disciplines such as nurses and social workers.

The federal government and the Joint Commission require hospitals and clinics to use Institutional Review Boards (IRBs) to examine inquiries from researchers who wish to conduct research on their premises. IRBs can reject proposed research if they determine they will harm consumers or other staff members, breech confidentiality, fail to provide subjects adequate methods of gaining their informed consents, or fail to meet other standards.

OBTAINING SKILLS IN ETHICAL REASONING AT THE CASE LEVEL

Policies, regulations, and accrediting standards provide legal and official guidelines for ethical behavior, but they do not provide healthcare professionals with skills in ethical reasoning that can help them deal with specific situations. Healthcare professionals need skill in recognizing ethical issues and dilemmas and in ethical reasoning.

Recognizing Ethical Issues and Ethical Dilemmas

Healthcare staff undertakes many issues when helping consumers. Many of them are practical or logistical in nature, such as helping someone get an appointment or attending to their specific needs in a routine manner. Many of these issues are resolved expeditiously. Ethical issues arise when normative issues arise when words like "ought," "should," and "duty" are used. A social worker might decide, for example, that she ought to provide a consumer with more information so that he can make an intelligent choice among different treatments. She links this decision unconsciously to her underlying moral or ethical standards when she thinks, "It is my (ethical) duty to provide this information." Most professionals recognize ethical issues at a gut level because they are viewed as linked to moral standards that have been internalized from upbringing, religious beliefs, or ethical studies.

Many ethical decisions are made speedily because they do not involve competing ethical or moral standards. When a social worker gives a consumer correct information about some facet of her care, she does not usually agonize about this decision because she is used to subscribing to the ethical norm of honesty. Physicians typically give consumers correct diagnostic information without even wondering whether they should give them incorrect information.

It is more difficult to make ethical choices, however, when health staff encounter ethical dilemmas that involve competing ethical duties. Assume, for example, that health staff deliberate about whether to accede to a woman's request to withdraw treatment from a baby that was delivered at 23 weeks on grounds that he is likely to have enduring physical or mental problems because of his prematurity. They want to honor her self-determination (ethical duty #1), but they do not want to kill the baby (ethical duty #2). They decide to take this issue to the hospital's ethics committee to help them resolve this ethical dilemma. The field of bioethics has emerged to give us tools for recognizing and resolving ethical dilemmas.

Developing Ethical Reasoning Skills

Ethical reasoning allows engagement in ethical discourse with others. It helps health staff to identify important factual and ethical considerations. It allows them to analyze an ethical situation with different styles of ethical reasoning. It allows healthcare professionals to identify alternative solutions. It gives ways to reach ethical conclusions even if others may reach different ones.

The Utilitarian Approach

The utilitarian approach to ethical reasoning focuses on judging alternative solutions to an ethical issue or dilemma by focusing on their outcomes (Beauchamp & Childress, 1994). It asks health staff to:

- Develop specific measures of well-being for a population or a specific consumer, such as increasing survival rates of persons with specific medical conditions, preventing specific diseases, slowing the progression of specific diseases, curtailing obesity, curtailing high blood pressure, improving a person's mental well-being—or some combination of these or other outcomes.
- Identify several strategies for achieving these outcomes with specific consumers or populations.
- Measure one or more positive outcomes of each of these alternatives, such as the likelihood they will cut consumers' deaths, diseases, or injuries.
- Measure one or more negative outcomes of each of these alternatives, such as their cost, or their risks.
- Select the action or policy that is, on balance, preferable when its likely positives and costs are considered in tandem.

This utilitarian approach is favored by many philosophers because it focuses on outcomes. It is congruent with scientific research because positive and negative outcomes associated with specific options require empirical data.

We can understand, then, how philosopher Peter Singer reasoned about medical decisions for premature infants, including ones born before 23 weeks of gestation (Singer, 2007). He focused on two outcomes: the well-being of the infants and the cost to society of providing them with healthcare and other social services in succeeding years. He identified three alternatives: Allow these infants born before or at 23 weeks to survive with all possible medical interventions, withhold medical treatment from them, or allow parents to decide whether to withhold treatment *after* they are apprised of the grim medical facts *and* having hospitals discourage treatment. (No babies born before 26 weeks survived without entering a neo-natal intensive care unit.) He selected the third alternative. Parents should be informed, he argued, that few babies born at less than 23 weeks survived, but that their survival rates increased from 29% to 65% between 23 weeks and 25 weeks. Parents should be informed, he argued, that two-thirds of infants born at 23 weeks have some form of functional disabilities when they reach 2 to 3 years of age—and one-third of these assessed survivors have a severe disability. Infants born at 25 weeks have much better outcomes, with only one-third of them possessing functional disabilities and 13% with a severe disability when born at 25 weeks (Singer, 2007).

Vignette 5.1

Social workers often help families make difficult decisions with respect to premature infants. Philosopher Peter Singer emphasizes physiological outcomes of these premature infants, such as disabilities and death, but fails to consider the potential emotional and marital stress often experienced by parents caring for those infants who survive. They must surmount, as well, economic burdens including medical costs and lost time from work.

Learning Exercise

- Identify an array of outcomes that Singer might also have considered.
- Discuss whether and to what extent social, economic, and familial stress should be considered.
- How important are these outcomes as compared to physiological ones and survival rates of premature infants?
- View the legal considerations health professionals must ponder in Chapter 10.

When he presented these ideas to a workshop in Australia, all participants agreed with this recommendation, including a consensus that babies born at 26 weeks should receive all necessary medical interventions to survive. In the United States, by contrast, fewer citizens agree with withholding medical treatment to babies born at 23 weeks of gestation. They are often told that medical treatment is futile, when, in fact, active treatment can prolong life, but with a high probability of disability (Singer, 2007, p. 10). In Singer's view, parents and health staff should engage in discussion of these realities and make decisions after they have considered the three options.

Persons who use utilitarian ethics sometimes cannot agree how to prioritize different outcomes. They may want clinical guidelines to advance physical health, such as effective medications for specific kinds of cancer (outcome #1), but want to keep costs within some limits (outcome #2). Although these two outcomes can be merged into a single measure, known as *cost-effectiveness*, debates still occur about how much money society should be willing to spend on medical interventions with limited success in curing disease or extending lives.

Many recommendations of utilitarian ethicists are less controversial. They support evidence-based medicine because it provides evidence that specific treatments are likely to improve the health of persons with specific health conditions. They support public health measures that are supported by empirical evidence, such as screenings for breast cancer for women over a specific age or requirements that motorcyclists use helmets to avert brain damage in the event of accidents.

The First-Principle or Deontological Approach

Ethicists who use a first-principle approach contend that utilitarian ethicists some-times risk violating widely held ethical principles (Beauchamp & Childress, 1994). They argue, for example, that consumers' rights to self-determination should often trump health outcomes even in the case of evidence-based medicine. Physicians may rightly inform specific patients that their health will be improved by using a treatment that has been demonstrated to be effective in empirical research, but their certitude may sometimes lead them to give consumers inadequate opportunity to give their consent to it.

A first-principle approach places less emphasis on medical outcomes than on honoring widely accepted ethical principles. These ethicists:

- Identify relevant first ethical principles that are relevant to the ethical issue or dilemma (discussed later).
- Identify two or more options for addressing an ethical issue or dilemma.
- Decide which of these first principles are relevant to these options.
- Select the option that does not conflict with the first principles.

First-principle ethicists draw on religions and philosophers like Immanuel Kant to identify widely accepted first principles as well as popular culture. These principles include preservation of life (or not killing), honesty, confidentiality, self-determination, privacy, fairness, due process, and the right to hold and express personal opinions. They also include the ethical principle of social justice, which stipulates that specific groups of consumers, such as low-income persons, persons of color, women, or other vulnerable populations, not receive poorer access to healthcare—or poorer quality of services— than the broader population. Each of these first principles is vital to health systems. If consumers feared that they would lose their lives because of medical interventions, they would avoid them. If they believed physicians and other health staff falsified information or did not honestly inform them of their options, they would not view them as credible. If they discovered that health staff paid little attention to their views and even sought to ignore or over-rule them, they would not trust them. If persons not central to their medical care were allowed to intrude on them and to view them in their rooms, they would feel they had lost their privacy. If they believed that health staff gave them inferior services as compared to other people, they would view the health system as unfair. If they believed that their complaints about their services were not carefully investigated, they would see themselves as deprived of due process. If they believed the staff of a hospital or clinic frowned on free expression of their views, they would feel stifled and ignored.

These first ethical principles have existed for centuries. They are enshrined in the Bible, the Koran, and the teachings of Buddha. They describe how people want to be treated by others as described by the Golden Rule: "Do unto others as you would have them do unto you." They exist in the text of Joint Commission accreditation standards. Many of them are supported by specific regulations, statutes, and court rulings.

Ethical reasoning based on first principles has the merit of bringing time-honored moral considerations to the foreground. It is a useful supplement—and sometimes antidote—to utilitarian ethics. Its proponents contend that medical interventions and clinical trials to advance consumers' physical well-being should not sacrifice their ethical well-being. Consumers' informed consents always takes precedence unless courts have determined they are incompetent to make medical decisions—and spouses and family members, even then, must usually give their informed consent as medical proxies. *Consumers have the right to forego treatments even when they are strongly supported by clinical guidelines based on EBM.*

First-principle ethics has drawbacks of its own, however. Its users find it difficult to make ethical choices in situations where the first principles conflict with one another. Assume, for example, that a consumer wants a physician to prescribe lethal medications so she does not have to endure pain. In this case, "not killing" conflicts with "self-determination." It is difficult to decide what weight to give to each first principle in these circumstances—as illustrated by high levels of conflict over ballot measures in some states about whether to legalize physicians' participations in euthanasia.

It is sometimes difficult, as well, to define first principles, as well as their gradations. Persons who believe that abortion is not a wrongful taking of life disagree with pro-life persons about whether and when fetuses are "living persons." Persons sometimes disagree about when "white lies" or omitting information constitute dishonesty. Are physicians justified in "shading the truth" to give consumers greater hope than they would otherwise have?

Advocates of utilitarian ethics contend that advocates of first-principle ethics give too little attention to measurable health outcomes. Are not first principles too fuzzy a basis for ethics, they ask, even though first ethics often include the ethical principle of "beneficence" (or consumer well-being), which does focus on health outcomes (Veatch, 1981)?

The Relativist Approach

Some ethicists contend that ethical choices are often made not through ethical reasoning, but by following norms that exist in everyday culture, as well as to advance the economic and political interests of specific persons or groups (Mackie, 1977). They point to shifts in popular culture: If many Americans accepted placing suspected criminals on public display in the colonial era, most Americans would now see this practice as unethical. If some physicians favored use of frontal lobotomies for some mentally ill persons in the 1940s and 1950s, as well as not fully informing them of risks of this procedure, all of them would now view these practices as unethical.

Relativism has currency among some bioethicists in the health system, as well, because of the importance of culture to health choices. Christian Scientists and Seventh

Day Adventists often decline specific medical services that most consumers would use even when informed these decisions might harm their physical well-being. Many consumers like alternative medicine even when informed that some of its treatments have not been scientifically tested or found to be harmful. Relativists ask:

- What cultural norms do specific consumers possess that shape their views of what is right and wrong?
- Does self-interest often shape ethical choices?
- Do providers risk imposing their ethical views on specific consumers?

Relativism helps people understand how ethical choices can be influenced by culture and self-interest, but it can lead to the nihilistic conclusion that shared ethical norms do not exist or that people cannot find ways to engage in ethical deliberations that cut across self-interest and culture. Courts have sometimes ruled, for example, that Seventh Day Adventists must provide medical care to children when their lives hang in the balance.

Practical Considerations

Ethical choices are often influenced by practical considerations. I have already discussed, for example, how many costly medical procedures produce marginal results—leading some ethicists to contend that they ought to be shelved because of the runaway costs of the U.S. medical system *even* if many persons want them. Some medical interventions that might enhance consumers' health are difficult to implement, such as routine home visits that were once used extensively in the U.S. health system. Some legislators reject policy options that they view as ethically meritorious, such as universal health coverage, because they fear that vested political and economic interests will defeat them.

Special Medical and Legal Considerations

Some ethical decisions in the health system are contingent on medical and legal considerations. If a court of law determines that someone is "incompetent" to make decisions, for example, health staff is justified in not honoring their ethical right to self-determination while relying, instead, on surrogate decision makers like spouses or family members (T. Stein, 2004). Social workers cannot keep conversations with consumers confidential when they inform them that they intend to harm or kill someone else because regulations, court rulings, and laws require them to divulge this information to the police and the intended victim. Laws and regulations also shape how health workers respond to allegations of family violence and rape, as well as to some mental conditions.

Merging Different Approaches to Ethical Reasoning

Rather than relying on a single approach, bioethicists can sometimes fuse different ones in a combined method (Jansson, 2011). They can ask, for example, whether a specific medical intervention would advance people's well-being (a utilitarian approach) and whether it can be combined with informed consent (a deontological approach) and whether it is acceptable to a consumer from a specific culture (a relativist approach) and whether it is feasible on cost or other grounds (a practical consideration).

If these different methods of ethical reasoning converge to a single choice, you can then be more certain that you have made a correct choice. If the different methods diverge to different choices, you must decide how to reconcile them, such as by giving greater weight to one of the methods or by finding an ethical option that is acceptable to many of them.

Developing an Ethical-Reasoning Matrix

We can use an ethical-reasoning matrix to facilitate the discovery of solutions to ethical dilemmas whether you use a utilitarian, first-principle, or combined method of ethical reasoning (Francoeur, 1983). (See Vignette 5.2.)

Step #1: Identifying Options

Realizing that he faced an ethical dilemma, the physician identified three options: not informing the woman about her diagnosis (the husband's wish), informing her about her diagnosis with the husband present, or asking the woman if she would like to know the diagnosis without her husband being present and informing her if she asked him to do so.

Vignette 5.2 An Ethical Dilemma Confronted by Health Staff

A woman, age 73, had neurological and cognitive tests to find the cause of her memory lapses. Her husband, an international medical expert, suspected she might be diagnosed with Alzheimer's disease because her mother had had this disease. The husband requested the physician *not* disclose the diagnosis to her if it was Alzheimer's disease on grounds it would cause her extraordinary mental suffering as she recalled her mother's many years of suffering from this disease. He informed the physician that he would accompany her to the appointment.

The physician soon learned that the medical expert's wife did have Alzheimer's disease as best he could determine. She had never discussed Alzheimer's disease with him prior to the diagnosis.

The physician realized that he confronted an ethical dilemma. He didn't want to harm the woman by giving her adverse news. He didn't want to ignore the husband's views, yet he also wanted to honor the woman's right to self-determination by giving her information about the diagnosis.

Step #2: Selecting and Weighing Criteria

He identified two criteria to be used to determine the relative merit of the three options:

1. The first ethical principle of self-determination, which requires informed consent unless the woman is incompetent.
2. The utilitarian goal of advancing the physical and mental well-being of the woman.

He also had to weigh the criteria to determine their relative priority in his ethical reasoning. He decided to give each of them a score or weight so that they equaled 1 when added together. He gave the first criterion a score of 0.6 and the second one a score of 0.4.

Creating an Ethical Reasoning Matrix

He created an ethical reasoning matrix with the two criteria placed at the top of the table with their weights, respectively, of 0.6 and 0.4—and the three options on each of the table's rows as seen in Table 5.1 (Francoeur, 1983). He then proceeded to score each option by each criterion using a simple procedure. In the upper left-hand corner of each cell, he gave each option a score from 1 to 10 with respect to each criterion. He decided, for example, that "only telling the husband" the diagnosis of Alzheimer's disease scored poorly with respect to self-determination, meriting a score of only 1. (He had already determined that she was cognitively able to make choices because he had diagnosed her as having early-stage Alzheimer's disease.) He decided that "telling the wife (her diagnosis) by herself" scored well with respect to self-determination, meriting a score of 10. He gave the option of "telling them together" a midrange score of 6 because he feared that the husband might undermine his wife's ethical right to self-determination if he was present by interfering with the physician's ability to communicate with her.

He used the same strategy for ranking each of the options by the criterion of promoting the wife's well-being. He believed that "only telling the husband" did

Table 5.1   Ethical Reasoning Matrix

Options	Self-determination (0.6)	Woman's well-being (0.4)	Total
Only tell the husband	1	1	
	0.6	0.4	1.0
Tell the wife by herself first, and both if she consents	10	9	
	6.0	3.6	9.6
Tell them both together	6	8	
	3.6	3.2	6.8

not advance her well-being, giving it only a score of 1 because he doubted she could deal with her illness if she did not know she had it, such as making plans for her life or her treatments. He believed "telling the wife by herself" and "telling them both together" would both advance her well-being, giving them respectively scores of 9 and 8.

With each option ranked by each criterion in the upper left-hand corner of each cell, he then made a simple calculation to adjust these scores by the weight of each criterion. He multiplied the score in the upper left-hand corner of each cell by the weight of the criterion above it—and placed that score in the lower right-hand corner of each cell. He then added the scores for each option in the lower right portion of each cell to determine a total score for each option on the far right of the table. The option of talking with the wife by herself received the highest score (9.6) and was, he believed, the best ethical choice in this situation. The worst ethical option, he decided, was "only telling the husband" because it scored poorly on both criteria, receiving a score of only 1. He gave the remaining option of "telling them both together" a midrange score of 6.8.

He decided that he would tell the husband that he would meet with the wife by herself when they came for the appointment. With the husband absent, he asked her if she wanted to know her diagnosis. When she said, "yes," he told her that she had early-stage Alzheimer's disease. He discussed the nature of the disease and how its progress could often be slowed with available treatments. He was hopeful, he said, that she would have a considerable period when she could have good quality of life. He answered some questions that she asked him. After she affirmed she wanted her husband to know the diagnosis, he called him into the room and informed him that he had told his wife her diagnosis of early Alzheimer's disease because she had wanted this information. He then proceeded to discuss the nature of the disease, as well as alternative treatments, with both of them.

When reviewing this ethical decision-making matrix, it is important to dwell not on the details of the scoring rules, but on the style of analytic reasoning. Other approaches to scoring could easily have been used to rank the criteria and the various options and to compute the final scores. When using an analytic style of reasoning, the ethics decision maker breaks the selection process into a series of sequential steps that eventually lead to an overall score for specific options.

Using an ethical decision-making matrix like Table 5.1 does not necessarily eliminate conflict among bioethicists, because they might disagree about the criteria selected and the weights given to them. They might wish to consider different or additional options. They might use different ways to calculate scores.

Dealing With Trade-Offs

The second option ranked higher than the other options on each of the criteria in this case. In many cases, however, the option with the highest score ranks lower on some of the criteria than other options *even though it receives the best overall score*. Under these circumstances, the physician would have had to select an option that had clear flaws, but that was nonetheless better than other options. This problem often exists with respect to ethical decisions at end of life. Assume, for example, that bioethicists ponder whether to withdraw hydration and food from a comatose person who had requested this approach in an advance directive. This option would score high with respect to the ethical criterion of self-determination, but lower with respect to the ethical criterion of not killing. Conversely, the option of continuing hydration and food would score poorly with respect to self-determination but higher with respect to not killing. They might decide that the first option was, on balance, preferable to the second option.

NINETEEN SCENARIOS ENCOUNTERED BY CASE ADVOCATES

I now discuss 19 scenarios encountered by case advocates (the first 12 of them are presented in this book and the remaining 7 can be accessed online as discussed at the end of this chapter).

Scenario 5.1: Advocacy to Enhance Informed Consent

Consumers must be informed and give their consent to exercise their ethical right to self-determination. In a ruling in 1990, the U.S. Supreme Court affirmed that consumers have a right under common law not to be touched by another person without legal justification or permission from the person touched. Medical providers cannot treat patients without their consent except in emergencies or under court order when, for example, patients are minors or incompetent (T. Stein, 2004).

Consumers need to be informed about their health conditions, treatment alternatives, clinical guidelines, and possible risks and benefits of specific treatments. Consumers need to hear this information about proposed treatments in language they can understand, not in complex terms and medical jargon. They need time to engage in discussions about proposed treatments, where they can pose questions prior to giving consent (CHA, 2008, p. 1.5). Some physicians have patients sign informed-consent forms that contain medical information that consumers can understand. Notations on the hospital medical record often describe these discussions and verify that the patient gave informed consent (CHA, 2008, p. 1.6). Only physicians can obtain informed consent. Hospital personnel can answer questions posed to them by patients about their treatment, but should contact their physicians "to allow him or her to assure that the patient indeed gave informed consent to the procedure" (CHA, 2008, p. 1.6). Consent has to be "freely given" rather than coerced or made under duress.

Consumers need providers, moreover, who do not manipulate them toward specific diagnosis, surgical, medication, or rehabilitation options. Medical manipulation takes place when providers understate the risks and overstate the benefits of specific medical interventions that they favor while overstating the risks and understating the benefits of alternative approaches. It occurs when providers do not acknowledge that a consensus does not exist when this is the case.

Providers need to discuss probabilities with consumers of risks and benefits for persons at the same stage and severity of their health conditions as well as states of general health *if* these probabilities have been reliably established by researchers. Consumers need to know the risk of death or injury, as well as the specific side effects they might suffer, from specific medical interventions.

Courts determine whether consumers gave their informed consent by using one of two standards. What information would a reasonable practitioner have provided under these circumstances? What information did the patient need to know to make an intelligent decision (Stein, 2004)?

Consumers should often talk with others who have had the same medical interventions. They should access reliable Internet sites, such as ones maintained by federal agencies and respected advocacy sites. They should obtain second opinions for many medical interventions.

Consumers need to select not only their treatments and diagnostic tests, but their providers through a process of informed consent. They need to gauge the experience, skills, and reputation of specific providers to gain confidence to use them, as well as the health outcomes they achieved from specific kinds of medical interventions.

Vignette 5.3 presents a scenario where a professor failed to receive sufficient information about impending surgery.

Vignette 5.3 A Professor Facing Back Surgery Without Adequate Information

A professor had encountered severe back pain for several years. When he obtained scans from a surgeon at a prominent medical school, he was informed that nine vertebrae had to be fused in a complex surgery that would require a lengthy hospital stay, as well as prolonged rehabilitation. He was not informed of alternative approaches or encouraged to obtain a second opinion. He knew this physician had been mentored at one of the nation's best medical schools and hospitals.

Alarmed by the predicted length of the hospital stay and rehabilitation, as well as the proposed surgery's complexity, he sought a second opinion from another experienced and recognized surgeon. After reviewing the scans, this surgeon told him that he could probably remedy the back pain by surgery that focused on two specific areas. He predicted that he would only need a short stay in the hospital and relatively brief rehabilitation.

(continued)

When the professor informed the second surgeon of the treatment recommendation of the first surgeon, he told him he was surprised to hear that the first surgeon had not informed him that he would face a 5% chance of not surviving the lengthy surgery—and would face a 15% chance of paralysis. When he asked the second surgeon why the first surgeon had suggested this invasive strategy, he surmised that he was following the lead of his mentor who had pioneered this intervention and who had used the procedure on many patients who required less invasive strategies with fewer side effects and less risk in his opinion.

Learning Exercise

- Under what circumstances should consumer obtain second opinions?
- What ethical errors do you think the first surgeon made?

Consumers should consent only after they have received sufficient information and had time to process it. They should carefully review information on consent forms to be certain that they have been informed, well in advance, of relevant side effects, risks, and benefits. They should request these consent forms well in advance of scheduled medical interventions so they are not given to them at the last moment as they await surgery or other medical interventions.

Exceptions to informed consent exist. Persons deemed competent can refuse transfusions, for example, but courts often order them when patients are pregnant or are parents, using the doctrine of *parens patriae* to order transfusions for children. Courts often overrule parents who claim religious convictions to refuse life-saving treatments for children. Yet some rulings uphold parents' rights to refuse life-saving treatments for their children (T. Stein, 2004).

Advocates should help consumers consider some of these questions:

- Has a consumer been properly informed in terms of substantive information about a recommended medical intervention, including its risks and benefits?
- Has a consumer been given relevant probabilities?
- Has a consumer been given sufficient time to process this information?
- Has a consumer been encouraged to obtain information about alternative treatments from different sources?
- Has the consumer asked to receive consent forms well in advance of the intervention if this is feasible?
- Do specific consumers believe they have received adequate information to be informed and to give their consent?
- Are specific consumers confident they have selected professionals in whom they have confidence to provide specific services?

Scenario 5.2: Advocacy for the Right to Refuse Treatment

The right to refuse treatment is the corollary to the right to informed consent—even, according to the Supreme Court of New Jersey, if this decision results in death unless the person is found to be incompetent (T. Stein, 2004).

Advocates should help consumers consider the following:

- Do consumers realize they have the right to refuse treatment even if this decision could cause them harm in the view of medical experts?

Scenario 5.3: Advocacy to Determine Competence

Consumers can only give their informed consent in a credible manner if they possess sufficient cognitive skills to make rational choices in general. (Courts determine someone is incompetent when he or she is unable to make any major decisions, as compared to a determination that healthcare professionals make that someone merely lacks the capacity to make a specific decision, such as to consent to an MRI.). Persons who sometimes lack sufficient levels of cognitive skills include some persons with dementia, Alzheimer's disease, Parkinson's disease, victims of strokes, persons with some forms of brain injuries such as from automobile accidents, veterans with brain injuries, developmentally disabled persons, children, and persons with mental conditions like schizophrenia, bipolar disorder, and depression. Impairment in decision making exists among some outpatient cancer patients, particularly people with cognitive impairment. It is relatively common among persons living in nursing homes and intensive care units (Applebaum, 2007). It exists among some sedated persons and persons with specific physiological problems like fever, uremia, and sedation. Children can make some decisions, but not others according to legal rulings.

It can't be presumed, however, that anyone is not competent to give informed consent; indeed, the law presumes a person is competent until otherwise proven *even if they are members of groups commonly assumed to be incompetent* (T. Stein, 2004). Many persons are temporarily incompetent, but become competent as their mental and physical health changes with time or with medical treatments.

Consumers can be considered incompetent only after courts make this decision, often relying on tests given them by medical experts that assess consumers' abilities to communicate choices, understand relevant information, appreciate the situations and their consequences, and reason about treatment options. Physicians and health staff often find published question sets with good face validity helpful even though they often do not produce consistent findings. In many cases, physicians do not use these structured approaches, but rely on their professional judgments even though research demonstrates that these judgments often are not reliable or valid. In one study, physicians correctly identified only one-fourth of the 48% of medical inpatients with acute conditions found to be incompetent to consent to treatment with physicians (T. Stein, 2004, p. 1835).

Decisions about competence are sometimes made by courts, but healthcare professionals often do not resort to court decisions when assessing the ability of consumers to make specific decisions because "resorting to judicial review in every case of suspected impairment of capacity would probably bring both the medical and legal systems to a halt" (Applebaum, 2008).

Physicians have an incentive to analyze patients' competences because they can be held liable if they offer treatments to persons incompetent to give their informed consent without consulting spouses, partners, or family members (Applebaum, 2007, p. 1834).

Advocates need to consider the following:

- Do specific consumers possess the four key abilities recognized by courts for determining competence?
- Should courts be asked to assess whether a specific consumer is incompetent rather than relying on healthcare professionals' judgments about their capacity to make specific decisions?
- Are certain persons prematurely or falsely deemed to be incompetent because of their membership in a group widely viewed as incompetent?
- Is a consumer, once deemed incompetent by a court, still incompetent?
- Is health staff aware that they could be liable for not obtaining informed consent if they give medical interventions to persons who are competent?
- Have spouses, partners, or family members been used as proxies when specific consumers have been deemed to be incompetent by the courts?
- Should specific consumers or family members contest specific competency determinations by healthcare professionals regarding the capacity of specific persons to make specific decisions?

Scenario 5.4: Advocacy to Complete Advance Directives

An advance directive "is a written instruction in which a person outlines the health or mental health services that may be provided to him or her in the event that he or she becomes incompetent" (T. Stein, 2004). They include living wills, where persons state their health preferences, and durable power of attorney, where they state who will serve as surrogates for them, which remains in effect even when courts appoint surrogates for them. (Some power-of-attorney forms also ask consumers to state their health preferences.) They specify whether and when they would favor use of passive measures to hasten death, including such options as withdrawing resuscitation aids, withdrawing hydration and/or food, not using feeding tubes, and not using nonpalliative forms of surgery. They may also specify if persons want to donate their bodies for medical training. Considerable variations exist between states: New York State does not accept living wills, but accepts healthcare proxies, while California accepts both. Different states use different terms to describe healthcare proxies.

Even though Medicare and Medicaid, as well as Joint Commission Accreditation Standards, require health providers to give consumers advance directive forms at point of admission as mandated by the Patient Self-Determination Act of 1990, as well as to offer them counseling, many consumers have not completed them by the time they are deemed incompetent by courts (H. Lynch, Mathes, & Sawicki, 2008). Forms that have been completed may not be locatable by medical personnel when they are needed for decision making or lack sufficient detail to provide medical guidance in specific situations.

It is challenging to counsel persons about advance directives before they encounter medical issues that require these kinds of choices. They often appear as abstractions when they are relatively healthy—particularly if they are not aware of hardships encountered by many persons who remain alive after they are competent. Many of them do not realize that medical technology can keep persons alive even for decades after they become comatose.

It is difficult to counsel them, as well, because skilled counseling takes considerable time to complete. It requires health staff to educate consumers about end-of-life situations. It requires them to bring up difficult, even threatening, subjects at times when they are traumatized by impending surgeries or other medical procedures. It requires skill in informing them about myriad options for hastening death. It also requires health staff to help consumers revisit this subject as they age or as their medical condition changes.

Advance directives are not a panacea, because they sometimes are not honored (see Vignette 5.4).

Vignette 5.4 Who Will Uphold Patient Rights?

As a case manager, we are often the eyes and ears not only for insurance companies, but also for spokespersons for patients, when the latter lack the capacity to make medical decisions. Mary had been in the hospital for weeks. The nurse reported that Mary had specifically stated that she did not want dialysis or life-sustaining measures if her health worsened. Yet Mary was on dialysis.

Mary had been transferred through institutions far from her home in San Diego. Her caseworker was still in San Diego and called me yesterday morning. The caseworker, Joanne, sounded flabbergasted: "She's on dialysis?!? But there were documents with her that specified that she should not be on dialysis or having all these extreme life-sustaining measures. I've been her worker for over five years. I haven't been able to get there, but I'm coming this week and we'll settle this." Joanne was understandably angry on behalf of her client, Mary. Mary's wishes had been blatantly disrespected despite the voices of case advocates who had attempted to bring attention to Mary's wishes and how her current level of care contradicted those desires.

(continued)

Joanne, the caseworker arrived. Furious, she had already put motions into action to obtain a court order to stop the heroic measures that were artificially keeping Mary alive against her will and her previously stated desires. Joanne received her court order and came directly to the hospital with it. Joanne and I stood in the room as the nurse stopped the dialysis and ventilator, which were supporting Mary's weak last moments of existence. Just then, the doctor who had been opposing Mary's wishes and who was adamant about keeping Mary alive walked in, equally angry and demanding that the heroic measures continue. We observed as Joanne, Mary's case advocate, showed the physician the court order and assured him that Mary's wishes and needs were being met, by being allowed to pass with dignity as she had wanted. The physician was angry, but finally left as Mary died.

Learning Exercise

- Could this horrible "end-game" have been avoided by preventive strategies?
- Should this case be taken to the risk manager or bioethics committee to see if it represents systemic problems in this hospital with honoring advance directives?

Advocates should help consumers consider some of the following questions and Internet sites.

- Are specific consumers knowledgeable about end-of-life realities that confront many consumers, such as life extension when quality of life has eroded?
- Are specific consumers knowledgeable about important choices they can make to hasten death when quality of life has eroded?
- Can specific consumers name persons who can make choices for them under these circumstances?
- Have specific consumers received advance-directive forms, whether living wills or durable-power-of-attorney forms, discussed them, completed them, and filed them in accessible places?
- Direct consumers to the National Hospice and Palliative Care Organization web site called Caring Connections at www.caringinfo.org that offers links to advance directives for every state.

Scenario 5.5: Advocacy to Secure Guardians

Persons deemed incompetent to make specific medical decisions are often given guardians by courts if physicians, spouses, family members, or others ask for this designation. Courts are often reluctant to name guardians except when specific persons are severely impaired by a "life-threatening disability" because they do not want to deprive consumers of liberty capriciously. In one case, a court refused to appoint a guardian for an 85-year-old woman because she was shown only to have mildly impaired cognitive skills (T. Stein, 2004). Another court refused to appoint a guardian for a woman in her late seventies who refused surgery for a gangrenous foot even though this decision would result in her death because it found that she had compelling reasons for not wanting this surgery, such as not being a burden on her children, her unhappiness since her husband's death, her belief the surgery would not cure her, her desire not to be an invalid, and her awareness that her decision could cause her to die. They also gave credence to a social worker's testimony that she was a rational person who only occasionally tuned out others when she disagreed with them (T. Stein, 2004).

The state is likely to appoint guardians to compel treatment when it wishes to prolong life, protect children or others from emotional and financial problems following a parent's death, prevent suicide, and maintain the ethical integrity of hospitals and physicians in caring for people under their care (T. Stein, 2004).

It should not be assumed that consumers who have been declared incompetent by courts, cannot make medical decisions (see Vignette 5.5).

Vignette 5.5 A Consumer With Schizophrenia Decides Against Chemotherapy

Sam had been afflicted with schizophrenia for decades. He had been involuntarily institutionalized on several occasions decades ago, but had remained in halfway houses or with his parents thereafter. A court named his parents as his conservators (a term similar to "guardian" that is used for persons with mental health and substance abuse problems), deeming him unable to handle his own finances. He occasionally sold his art in a local gallery—and shopped for his aging parents who gave him a weekly allowance. When they died, conservatorship was transferred to his surviving brothers. He was informed when he was 62 years of age that he had terminal lung cancer, probably caused by his chronic smoking. His physician pressured him to begin chemotherapy by giving him an appointment with the nurse in charge of the hospital's chemotherapy unit. She urged him to begin chemotherapy the next morning.

Sam readily assented to visiting the administrator of a local hospice organization the same day when a relative suggested it. After hearing about its services, Sam informed her, as well as the nurse in the chemotherapy unit, that he would decide by the next morning whether to undergo chemotherapy or enroll in the hospice program.

Saying he had voluntarily taken medications for his schizophrenia for decades and did not want more of them, Sam announced the next morning that he would enroll in hospice rather than beginning chemotherapy. He died six months later

(continued)

under the care of hospice accepting only palliative care with himself, his brothers, and his physician believing he had made the correct choice. No one chose to contest his decision by appealing Sam's decision to a court. Only his psychiatrist criticized the decision, seeing it as one more example of the medical system (in his view) denying needed treatment to schizophrenic persons.

Learning Exercise

- Why would some health staff assume that Sam could not make this decision?
- Could this have become a contested situation—and how could an advocate have sought to prevent this outcome?

Advocates should help consumers consider whether:

- Spouses, family members, or health providers should seek a court-appointed guardian to protect the interests of a possibly incompetent person.
- Specific consumers who have guardians can nonetheless make important medical decisions.

Scenario 5.6: Advocacy to Identify and Work with Surrogates

Surrogates "stand in the place of others and speak for the persons they represent" for the purpose of making their medical decisions (T. Stein, 2004). They can be named by competent persons who want others to make their medical decisions. They can be named by courts who select specific persons to be surrogates, such as guardians they have already selected—or new guardians for persons not previously found to be incompetent by them. They can be used by healthcare professionals in ERs and ICUs when spouses, relatives, or partners are comatose, unconscious, or unable to communicate decisions (N. Davis et al., 2003).

Persons who complete advance directives usually name someone to be their surrogate in the event they cannot make their own medical decisions at some future point, even decades away. They often name a succession of persons, such as a spouse or partner and then a child if the spouse has died or is unable to serve this function. Surrogates often follow the instructions of persons who name them in advance directives, particularly when advance directives contain sufficient detail to be useful, such as instructions not to insert feeding tubes if they are unable to swallow, to withhold ventilation aids if they cannot breathe, to withhold hydration and nutrition if they are comatose, and to not resuscitate if they are terminally ill. Healthcare professionals often have to help resolve family bedside conflicts (Schwartz, 2005).

Surrogates often make health decisions as outlined in advance directives without controversy. In other cases, complexities arise. Surrogates may lack sufficient guidance from advance directives because they are not sufficiently detailed or do not describe the specific medical situation confronted by persons in their care. Persons in their care may have left no advance directives. Advance directives sometimes cannot be located when they are needed such as when paramedics come to places of residence to help persons who are unconscious, only not to find advance directives that state that they did not want to be resuscitated. Advance directives are sometimes not attached to medical records in hospitals so they are not discovered in time to direct the medical care of persons who made them—a possibility that is greatly decreased if physicians place do-not-resuscitate orders in their medical records. Residents who care for specific consumers on weekends or during evening hours are sometimes not familiar with the wishes of specific consumers.

Surrogates' wishes can be contested in court or out of court by relatives, children, partners, and friends not named as their surrogates. Surrogates' wishes can be overturned by courts, as well, if they rule that they seek to withhold treatments that could result in harm or death for persons who did not express their preferences at earlier points in their lives—or who desired not to have their lives ended prematurely. Surrogates' decisions can be contested, as well, when they are alleged to make decisions that advance their financial interests. Conflicts can sometimes be resolved through group meetings facilitated by health staff.

When consumers have not left advance directives, surrogates must often resort to recollections of communications of persons left to their care with themselves or with other persons such as comments by someone in their care who stated that she did not want to be resuscitated if she became comatose.

Law suits sometimes take place. Some relatives may question recollections of a surrogate of conversations with a person in their care. They may question whether the stated wishes of a person in an advance directive are legal in their state, such as by withholding hydration or food or not inserting feeding tubes. A relative may contend that a surrogate has a conflict of interest, such as wanting someone in their care to die so that they can inherit money. Physicians and hospitals sometimes bring suit against surrogates who insist on medically futile treatments for comatose patients.

Lawsuits have led to rulings in different jurisdictions and in the Supreme Court—sometimes with contradictory results. When the father of Karen Quinlan asked a New Jersey Court in 1976 to appoint him as surrogate for his daughter who had been in a persistent vegetative state for a year and to remove a respirator, the State argued it had a compelling interest to keep her alive. The Supreme Court rejected the State's argument on grounds that she would have had the right to refuse treatment had she been competent. It found that "her interest in resisting the bodily intrusion required to sustain her life, coupled with no possibility of recovery, made her interests superior to any that the State could advance" even though she had not left written instructions (T. Stein, 2004). The New Jersey Supreme Court ruled in 1985 that incompetent persons' wishes could be determined by oral communications. The U.S. Supreme Court ruled in 1990 that a hospital did not have to withhold treatment from Nancy

Cruzan, who was in a persistent vegetative state after an automobile accident, even when her parents made this request. It ruled that Missouri had no obligation to accept her parents as surrogates and that Nancy had never made her wishes known prior to the accident.

Surrogates and family members sometimes confront or sue physicians who ignore specific advance directives that ask them not to resuscitate, not to insert feeding tubes, to withdraw ventilation-assisting devices, or to withhold hydration.

Advocates should help consumers consider some of the following:

- Develop strategies to mediate conflicts between surrogates and family members.
- Make certain that advance directives are attached to medical records and are kept in accessible places of homes so that paramedics see them.
- Work with surrogates to see that advance directives are implemented by physicians.

Scenario 5.7: Advocacy for Parents With Premature Births or Disabled Infants

Social workers often assume pivotal roles in helping a parent or parents decide whether to use extraordinary medical measures often needed for premature infants to survive, such as using services provided by Neonatal Intensive Care Units (NICUs). Their decisions take place in the context of federal and state regulations. The U.S. Department of Health and Human Services (HHS) decided in 1982 to limit the right of parents of premature children to allow them to die when it declared that the Vocational Rehabilitation Act (VRA) disallowed withholding of medical care from newborns with severe physical or emotional impairments after an infant with Down's syndrome died when its parents would not consent to surgery (T. Stein, 2004). The Department of Health and Human Services (DHHS) ordered local child welfare departments to intercede in these cases. The U.S. Supreme Court subsequently ruled that DHHS lacked authority to regulate treatments for infants with disabilities, but Congress subsequently amended the Child Abuse Prevention and Treatment Act to require states to investigate reports of medical neglect defined as withholding medically indicated treatment from disabled infants with life-threatening conditions (T. Stein, 2004, p. 331).

Many ethicists contend, however, that decisions about medical treatment with premature infants before 26 weeks of gestation should be made through discussions between parents and health staff, with social workers assuming pivotal roles. Parents' views about hastened death of infants need to be examined, as well as the financial, mental, and other impacts of caring for disabled infants in the home. Parents should be informed about the probability that their babies will survive as well as the probability of disabilities when they reach age 2 and beyond.

Advocates should help consumers consider some of the following questions and internet sites:

- Have parents of infants born before 26 weeks of gestation been informed of the probability of specific disabilities that their children will encounter in coming years?
- Have these parents been informed of financial, medical, and mental-health challenges in raising disabled children?
- Have these parents been informed of an array of medical options so they can make informed choices?
- March of Dimes web site at www.marchofdimes.com offers information about premature birth and birth defects. The Hospital for Sick Children, located in Toronto, has a web site, www.aboutkidshealth.ca, that provides excellent resources for parents of disabled and premature babies.

Scenario 5.8: Advocacy for Children

Parents usually have the right to make medical decisions for their children, but government can intervene when its officials determine that their decisions may endanger their safety under the *parens patriae* authority. A petition can be filed by a department of social services, a hospital, a child's attorney, or a child's guardian to ask the court to exercise this authority by ordering medical treatment (T. Stein, 2004).

Parents can also be cited under civil law for medical neglect under state laws relevant to child abuse and neglect. Parents may fail to provide medical care for religious reasons, ignorance, poverty, or a desire to protect their children from side effects from medical treatments. Reports are investigated by child welfare staff and can lead to court appointment of a guardian *ad litem* to make decisions in the child's interests.

Courts must decide the probability that a recommended medical procedure will be effective, will have serious side effects, and will enhance a child's survival or well-being. They consider the children's views when they are old enough to state them. They consider parents' rights to make decisions for their children. Courts can side with parents or order medical treatments. They can place children in foster care. They can transfer legal custody to the state with government officials making medical decisions.

Criminal charges can be lodged against a parent or caregiver for failure to provide medical care. Courts have a higher burden of proof with criminal charges than with civil charges, having to show that defendants intended to harm the child, caused harm through their actions, and committed "gross negligence" (T. Stein, 2004).

The U.S. Supreme Court has ruled several times that parents cannot withhold medical care from children on the basis of their religious beliefs when clear evidence exists that the child will be harmed without treatment.

All states specify age 18 as the date when a minor is emancipated and received many of the rights of adults, including the right to make medical decisions. Minors have certain rights, however, including a constitutional right to terminate a pregnancy even if some laws require parent notification, parental consent, or judicial bypass (T. Stein, 2004). Some states allow minors to become emancipated before age 18 when they marry, become pregnant, enlist in the military, are judged competent by courts to manage their affairs, and after they voluntarily leave their homes. Some children are emancipated when they refuse to visit with a parent after a divorce or are "rude, disrespectful, and disobedient" (T. Stein, 2004, p. 334). Physicians can treat children without parental consent when they experience medical emergencies and when society's best interest is served by treating them, such as when they have a sexually transmitted disease, are pregnant, or seek care for mental or substance abuse conditions. Surrogates of children who haven't reached age 18 can withdraw treatment if they are in a persistent vegetative state according to a court in Michigan (T. Stein, 2004).

Advocates should help consumers consider:

- When can children make and not make decisions about their medical care?
- How blurred lines exist when deciding when children can or cannot make decisions.
- How and when withholding of medical care for children is "neglect."

Scenario 5.9: Advocacy for Passive Measures for Hastening Death

Courts make a distinction between suicide and measures used to hasten death as someone approaches end of life. If suicide is often viewed as an illegal act to terminate life, measures to hasten death for persons with terminal health conditions or untreatable pain are widely viewed as legitimate choices for competent persons or their surrogates such as expressed in an advance directive.

Death is often hastened informally during the latter stages of terminal illness by two measures: escalating use of pain medications like morphine and withdrawal of antibiotics. Physicians often prescribe morphine to address consumers' mounting pain in end-stage cancer and other diseases. They prescribe increasing amounts because the drug becomes ineffective if dosages remain constant—but it eventually kills consumers when it is given at high levels. Many terminally ill consumers contract pneumonia in the latter stages of their lives that can be cured only with antibiotics—only to face new bouts of pneumonia and antibiotics in a never-ending cycle because they have compromised immune systems. Withdrawal of antibiotics leads some of these patients to succumb from pneumonia.

These means of hastening deaths at end of life often evolve through interactions among family members, nurses, and physicians with respect to patients who are often incompetent. Family members often negotiate with nurses who are charged with altering morphine levels as persons near death.

Oregon and Washington have both enacted so-called euthanasia laws—and these laws will appear on the ballots of other states. The U.S. Supreme Court defers to the states to make their own decisions about euthanasia (Greenhouse, 2005). They establish detailed requirements that must be met, however, before euthanasia provisions can be used.

Consumers sometimes make their wishes known nonverbally (see Vignette 5.6).

👍 Vignette 5.6 Advocacy With a Family by a Social Worker

In my role as a medical social worker, I often am called to resolve "mysterious" medical conflicts. Several years ago, I was requested to speak with an elderly black gentleman who had curiously, obstinately, been sitting on the side of his hospital bed for three days. The frustrated nurse said, "I don't even know why he's in the hospital! The patient has been refusing all treatment and refusing to even lie down and sleep for three days." My initial question to myself was, "Three days, what took them so long to call a social worker?"

When I entered the patient's room, he was surrounded by family: his wife, more than one of his children, nieces, even a grandchild or two. The family was trying to engage the patient into talking with them. They were also trying to get him to lie down and "rest." The gentleman refused all their efforts, remained silent as he sat upright, hung on to the side of the mattress, and stared at the wall. I greeted his family and introduced myself to the patient first and then his family. I then knelt in front of the patient and looked into the ill proud elderly gentleman's eyes. In his eyes, I recognized what I had seen so many times before, the look of a person who knew they were about to pass on.

For the next few minutes, I quietly spoke with Mr. Russell (name has been changed to preserve his privacy) about his family and his "favorite things." He smiled when he pointed his wife out and told me he loved his wife's cooking. I asked what his favorite foods were that his wife made, he responded, "Homegrown green beans and homemade peach pie." His wife excitedly said that she had some of each of those foods in the freezer and would bring them for him. Other family members said he could not have peach pie because it contained too much sugar and he was diabetic. The patient and I continued to have a quiet conversation, the only words he had spoken in three days. I asked Mr. Russell what he "wanted" and he responded, "Don't leave me. I want to go home." Mrs. Russell couldn't believe her ears and said, "You are the first person he has talked to." The rest of the family said, "He can't go home, he has to start dialysis today. He has to take his medicine and get his breathing treatments. He has to stay in the hospital." Again the patient implored, "Don't leave me," and grabbed my hands.

I knew then that I needed to speak with his family and determine how to give Mr. Russell what he had been wanting, waiting for for three days. He wanted to go home to die. He wanted to die surrounded with familiar voices, sounds, smells, and tastes. I asked his permission to speak with his "lovely wife." He again asked that I not leave him. I think he was afraid I wouldn't come back if I left the room and he would feel "alone" again, though he was surrounded by family in his hospital room. I promised him I would return quickly. He agreed. I asked his wife to step out of the room with me. Once outside, I asked her if she knew what was happening, what it was that her husband and I both knew. As her eyes welled with tears, she nodded

(continued)

"yes" and then I said, "You know he is dying, don't you?" She said, "Yes," as she let the tears she'd been holding back stream down her face. She revealed that her husband was a retired minister and that he had a very strong faith. She added that he was ready to go join his Maker. This revelation made everything even more clear. Mr. Russell was a religious man who had made peace with and accepted that it was his time to die. I told Mrs. Russell that her husband's bedside protest was likely out of fear that he would die in his sleep in the hospital and never see, hear, or feel home again. Mr. Russell had decided he did not want to die surrounded by strangers. I asked, "Is it possible for your husband to die at home? Can you let him die surrounded by his favorite things?" She responded that it would be possible, that it is what he would want. We discussed the essentials of a viable discharge plan: How much time would the family need to prepare? What kind of family support is in place? What equipment would be helpful to make sure Mr. Russell is comfortable? Mrs. Russell and I discussed the plan with her family and it was determined that if Mr. Russell wanted to go home and he consented to the plans, he would go home in the morning. He agreed on the condition that a family member stay with him all night. In addition, I promised I would be present in the morning to help him go home. Mr. Russell went home in the morning accompanied by his wife and several other family members, and others awaited his arrival.

Three weeks later, as I was getting ready for work, I suddenly remembered the quiet proud elderly retired minister and his family. The memory of his situation three weeks earlier stayed on my mind as I traveled into the hospital. As soon as I arrived in my office, I pulled out his case file and placed a follow-up phone call and left a message on their answering machine. Several hours later, as I went on with my work, I received a call from Mrs. Russell. She said, "It is so interesting that you called, my husband died this morning. When you called, I was at the mortuary making the arrangements." She then thanked me and said, "Mr. Russell spoke often of you over the last few weeks. He said you were the only one who listened to him. I want you to know he spent three wonderful weeks at home. He was surrounded by family, with his grandchildren running all around him. We put his hospital bed in the living room so he could be a part of every day. He ate homegrown green beans and his favorite homemade peach pie. Only a bite or two sometimes, but he had whatever he wanted. I want to thank you for everything you did for us. If it wasn't for you, my husband and I wouldn't have the memories of those wonderful last days."

Learning Exercise

- How did the social worker facilitate resolution?
- Does this vignette illustrate flaws in case-finding by social workers in this hospital—and how might that be corrected?

(continued)

(*continued*)

Advocates should help consumers consider:

- Have they developed advance directives that are readily available?
- Are spouses, partners, and family members aware that death can be hastened at end of life through escalating doses of morphine and termination of antibiotics—and do they wish to intercede with health staff so that they are used?
- Is hastened death congruent with other instructions in an advance directive or with views of the person nearing death?
- Do persons in care of the patient want counseling as they make these decisions or in their aftermath?

Scenario 5.10: Advocating to Preserve Confidentiality

Even when they do not possess specific fears about disclosure, consumers have the right to determine when, where, and to whom to divulge some or all of their medical information because it is their property. They often have legitimate reasons not to have their health information disclosed to others, such as losing employment or promotions, straining or severing relations with other persons, damaging their reputations, triggering family conflict over possible inheritance, or being embarrassed.

It is often difficult to protect medical information. Health staff may leave health information on telephone message machines, only to have them accessed by others. They may leave health records in public places in waiting rooms or other locations. They may allow excessive access to medical records. They may allow health staff to access electronic records when they lack permission—or lack sufficient safeguards to prevent outsiders from gaining access to them. Health staff may discuss medical information about specific consumers in public venues, such as elevators and cafeterias. Persons posing as relatives may illicitly seek their medical information. (See Vignette 5.7.)

Health staff sometimes experience dilemmas when dealing with consumers' spouses and relatives, particularly ones who have caregiver roles. If they are not familiar with medications, recommended diet, prognoses, likely side effects, and other health matters, they sometimes cannot provide effective home care. Yet some consumers will not authorize the release of this information to them and will not give it to them. Health providers are not allowed under current regulations to provide it to them unless these consumers authorize it. In some cases, physicians and other health staff might discuss why specific consumers might consider authorizing it, while realizing that the final decisions rest with them.

Concerned that medical information was not sufficiently protected, Congress enacted the Health Information Portability and Accountability Act of 1996 (HIPAA) (Annas,

✍ Vignette 5.7 The Case of Farrah Fawcett

Farrah Fawcett, a widely known movie star, developed a serious malignancy and underwent many medical treatments over an extended time period at one of the nation's leading hospitals. She discovered that personal health information appeared in the mass media on successive occasions. When she registered her displeasure with high-level hospital administrators, they seemed indifferent to her plight, even saying they had a duty to protect their personnel when she asked them to investigate the matter. She was deeply troubled by public disclosure of her private information. She decided to take matters into her own hands after she discovered that these disclosures took place shortly after specific appointments. By analyzing who had access to her medical information at specific times just before illicit disclosures were made, she and the hospital staff were able to pinpoint who had made them. The hospital fired an employee who was discovered to have received cash from a mass-media outlet and vowed to tighten procedures for gaining access to medical records.

Learning Exercise

- Surmise why hospital staff were indifferent to her plight.
- Does this vignette illustrate that some consumers have more power than others—but was her notoriety a mixed blessing?

2003). Most states have enacted confidentiality laws of their own, which may conflict with HIPAA.

HIPAA protects individually identifiable health information, which it calls "protected health information (PHI)[,] without written authorization from the patient or the patient's personal representative" (CHA, 2008, p. 16.4). It protects this information in transmission or maintenance in any form or medium. It defines it to include "any information, oral or recorded, relating to the health of an individual, the healthcare provided to an individual, or payment for healthcare provided to an individual" (CHA, 2008, p. 16.4). It applies to health providers and to health plans.

Providers must obtain authorizations from consumers to release their PHI in advance and in plain language (CHA, 2008, p. 16.5). Either the patient or someone authorized by the law to act on the patient's behalf must sign and date an authorization (CHA, 2008, p. 16.5). The information to be disclosed must be described. The authorization must name specific persons or entities that can receive the information. The authorization must include a date or event after which the authorization expires. It must indicate the patient's right to revoke the authorization. Authorization must meet some other requirements, as well (CHA, 2008, pp. 16.6 and 16.7).

Patients are allowed to make disclosures to family members and close personal friends verbally under HIPAA although not under some state laws (CHA, 2008, p. 16.6). HIPAA requires providers to give a copy of each authorization to patients or their representatives.

HIPAA allows some exceptions to its protections of PHI that involve specific activities of a covered entity, such as using it to assess the quality of their services through outcome evaluations, to provide case management and care coordination services, to conduct training programs, and to resolve internal grievancesas well as during many other specific activities (CHA, 2008, p. 16.11). Psychotherapy notes can be used by providers' training programs for students, trainees, or practitioners for the purpose of improving their helping skills in various kinds of counseling. HIPAA sometimes allows release of information with respect to victims of abuse, neglect, or domestic violence; disclosures for judicial and administrative hearings; and disclosures to law enforcement when sought by courts or judicial officers. Health staff should consult legal officials in their health organization or their supervisors when using information without the patient's authorization.

Concern about violation of confidentiality has increased with the advent of electronic medical records. Less than 20% of health plans used them in 2009, but most experts believe their use will greatly increase. Critics fear that these records could be breached by hackers, as well as by some health staff. Supporters of electronic medical records believe that technology could safeguard them and bring other advantages, such as enhancing case management and monitoring the effectiveness of services.

HIPAA has been widely praised by advocates of confidentiality. Critics wonder if the extraordinary paperwork needed to implement it is excessively costly (Kilbridge, 2003). It mandates fines and other legal sanctions for medical staff who breech confidentiality.

Advocates should help consumers consider some of the following:

- Have you decided what parts of your data you want shared—and with whom?
- What fears do you have about disclosure of your data? And to whom?
- Have you informed your provider about your authorizations of PHI?
- If you have reason to think your data has wrongly been used, have you contacted your physician—or registered an official complaint with the risk manager or other hospital staff charged with implementing HIPAA?

Scenario 5.11: Advocating for Consumers With Institutional Review Boards (IRBs) and Bioethics Committees

Federal agencies require researchers to obtain approval from hospitals' and clinics' IRBs before collecting data for the projects that they fund—and most organizations require approvals from IRBs for *any* research no matter its source of funding. Advocates can discuss concerns about patient safety or informed consent with IRBs.

Hospital staff can bring ethical issues to bioethics committees. See Vignette 5.8 where a physician sought advice from the bioethics committee and received latitude for issuing a Do Not Resuscitate (DNR) to an elderly woman.

Vignette 5.8 Case Advocacy: Bioethics and End-of-Life Vulnerability

Several years ago as an ethics resident, I received my introduction to the work of clinical bioethics with a case that remains with me today. It has proven to be enlightening in many different ways. One day my supervisor called me into her office to tell me that a doctor referred a case to the ethics committee. I was familiar with this case because I had attended ICU rounds earlier that morning. The doctor's referral requested that the ethics committee "determine code status." My supervisor then asked me to do a workup on the case and draft a consult report.

Ms. J, the patient, was an 88-year-old who was admitted for shortness of breath. She lived at a nursing home and did not have any family or friends. An administrator at the nursing home was her only social contact; state law, however, precluded this administrator from functioning as her decision maker. This patient also lacked any decisional capacity: she was intubated and sedated, and her history indicated advanced dementia. She did not have an advance directive. Because of several co-morbidities and serious diagnoses, her condition was worsening; the doctors felt that there was nothing more they could do to benefit her. However, the primary physician on the case, the one who requested the consult, was uncomfortable writing a DNR order. This doctor feared that the patient would have to endure a traumatic resuscitation effort before she died: to her, Ms. J would experience indignity in the very last moments of her life.

Looking back, two ideas strike me now in retrospect. On the one hand, Ms. J was extremely vulnerable. She had no voice, no advocate. She was at risk for experiencing, or undergoing, a mechanized and technological death beyond her control. She would likely die alone, away from home, and at the end of what many describe as a harsh form of treatment, especially for the frail elderly. Although she retained the right to refuse medical treatment, she could not exercise that right, and there was no one who could speak on her behalf. On the other hand, the doctor was also vulnerable. The physician felt trapped; she was uncertain about what she *as a doctor* was to do in the case. She had been trained to heal and to cure. Letting go brought with it many questions. It conjured up feelings of failure; and it evoked concerns about her duties as a physician. That is, what could she legally do without getting in trouble? Above all, the question—What *should* she do?—cast a shadow over the whole case.

In the consult report, the ethics committee stated that the bioethics consultation service does not establish code status: it cannot and should not write DNR orders. Such an action would be an invasion of bioethics into the physician-patient

(continued)

(*continued*)

relationship. However, the committee did recommend that a DNR order was within the range of morally and legally acceptable alternatives given the conditions of the case (not all of which are reported here).

The next day, I followed up on the case and discovered that Ms. J had died. Her empty bed was, and is, a constant reminder for me of how profound and important bioethics is. It humbles me to think that I had a role to play in Ms. J's last hours. Perhaps the kind of case advocacy in this bioethics consult was not just for Ms. J— to advocate for treating her with dignity at the end of her life. Rather, the advocacy here was to give a forum and a voice to the ethical concerns of those who cared for Ms. J as well as to protect Ms. J's dignity.

Learning Exercise

- Why did the physician not make the DNR decision herself?
- Did the bioethics committee establish appropriate limits on its own power?
- Can consumers access IRBs and bioethics committees?
- Can frontline staff bring ethical issues to bioethics committees?

Scenario 5.12: Advocacy to Link Consumers to Hospice

Hospice originated in England to give community-based care to terminally ill persons to allow them to die with dignity rather than in hospital settings. Emphasis was placed on care that emphasized comfort rather than cure provided by interdisciplinary teams of social workers, nurses, and other health staff; interactions with family, friends, and spiritual advisors; and efforts to make terms with approaching death in a home or community setting.

It migrated to the United States in the 1970s when a growing number of community-based hospice organizations were formed that relied heavily on volunteers. It has been bolstered by such theoreticians as Elizabeth Kubler-Ross (1979) and Susan Block (2002) who have developed psychosocial and existential approaches to helping persons cope with the dying process (Henig, 2005).

Hospice gained momentum in the United States when Medicare initiated reimbursement of hospice fees in 1982—partly for altruistic reasons and partly to save money by replacing reimbursements for medical procedures with flat payments to hospices for routine home care, continuous home care, general inpatient care, and inpatient respite care. It stipulated that enrollees had to be diagnosed as having a life expectancy of less than 6 months to qualify for the benefit—and had to agree not to seek heroic medical treatments during their stay in hospice. Many private insurance companies agreed to fund hospice for nonelderly persons with terminal conditions, such as victims of accidents, cancer, and other terminal conditions in succeeding years. If only 1,000 persons enrolled in hospice in 1975, more than 700,000 used it in 2000 (Last Acts, 2002).

Hospice played a role in decreasing the percentage of Americans who die in hospitals by 17% from 1990 to 2000, but it still failed to cover many persons. Only 23% of persons who die are enrolled in hospice—and 50% of Americans died in hospitals as compared to 85% of them who said they would prefer to die at home (Kuehn, 2007). Considerably fewer persons of color use hospice than Caucasians for cultural reasons and because providers do not inform them of it sufficiently (Gatrad, 2008; Koffman & Higginson, 2001; Sczezepura, 2004). Many physicians still do not inform terminally ill persons about hospice or do so belatedly. Experts agree that patients need to be enrolled in it for at least 60 days to gain pain and symptom management, as well as psychological and spiritual support, but the average length of hospice stays declined from 70 days in 1983 to 36 days in 2002 (Last Acts, 2002).

Many persons have questioned the requirement that only terminally ill consumers can gain access to hospice (Henig, 2005). This policy favors persons with cancer over persons with chronic health conditions because physicians are less able to predict life expectancy with the latter group. Medicare officials have tried to educate physicians so that persons with chronic conditions *can* be admitted to hospice, even when physicians are uncertain how long they will live. They can also admit patients who they are not certain will live less than 6 months because Medicare officials realize that it is difficult to predict life expectancy with precision.

Attending physicians are key to gaining access to hospice because they submit a statement declaring a patient to be terminally ill. Patients do not have to have cancer or DNR codes. They do not have to be homebound. They *can* receive care in inpatient units and skilled nursing facilities (SNFs) if their physicians explain why such care is reasonable and why they can't get necessary care in outpatient or community settings. Consumers sign up for the Medicare hospice benefit for an initial period of 90 days— and need to be recertified by the hospice physician, not by their admitting physician— for an additional 90 days and for an *unlimited* number of subsequent 60-day periods. Some persons are asked to leave hospice if their health condition improves, but they can appeal this decision to Medicare, even getting an expedited appeal.

The Medicare hospice benefit should be distinguished from the Medicare Home Health benefit, which is available on a short-term basis when Medicare enrollees leave hospitals. They can receive, for example, physical therapy services as a Home Health benefit as long as they continue to improve. The Home Health benefit does not, however, provide comprehensive services for an extended period unlike the hospice benefit.

Hospice is an optional program under state Medicaid programs. Medicaid hospice programs must meet the same standards as Medicare programs even if they sometimes provide more limited services than hospices funded by Medicare. Persons receiving Medicaid-reimbursed care in a nursing facility can receive the Medicare hospice benefit, as well as Medicaid-reimbursed personal care aides.

Medicare hospice benefits are subject to periodic cuts. After the Centers on Medicare and Medicaid Services (CMS) proposed to cut payments by more than 1% by 2010, the stimulus program of the Obama Administration placed a one-year moratorium on cuts in February 2009.

Medicare has recently become more permissive about hospice enrollees receiving palliative surgery, as well as chemotherapy, radiation, feed tubes, blood transfusions, and resuscitation. They can call 911 when they believe they have a medical emergency, but many of these persons are taken to an ER and often to an ICU (Henig, 2005).

Advocates should help consumers consider some of the following suggestions and Internet sites:

- Consumers can ask their physicians to enroll them in hospice if they are diagnosed as having less than 6 months of life expectancy.
- They are eligible even if they are less than 65 years of age, have chronic conditions rather than cancer, and are not homebound.
- They can receive hospice as in- or outpatients, as well as in SNFs.
- They can stay in hospice for two periods of 90 days, as well as unlimited subsequent 60-day periods—and then they can appeal providers' decisions to terminate their hospice benefits.
- They can select a different hospice provider *once* during their hospice tenure.
- They can decide to exit hospice at any time.
- They can receive hospice under state Medicaid programs if their state has this benefit—or through private insurance if they are not eligible for Medicare.
- Refer consumers to www.medicareadvocacy.org for specific details about hospice care for Medicare recipients, or to National Hospice and Palliative Care Organization web site at www.caringinfo.org for general information.

Online Materials Relevant to This Chapter

Six Additional Scenarios Can Be Accessed Online by Going to the web site of John Wiley & Sons (www.wiley.com/go/jansson)

Scenario 5.13: Advocacy for Women Who Decide Whether to Abort Fetuses

Scenario 5.14: Advocacy for Active Measures to Hasten Death

Scenario 5.15: Advocacy to Enhance Honesty in Healthcare

Scenario 5.16: Advocacy to Enhance Consumers' Privacy Rights

Scenario 5.17: Advocacy for Consumers' Rights to View Their Rights

Scenario 5.18: Advocacy for Consumers' Rights to Dignified and Respectful Care

Scenario 5.19: Advocacy for Managing and Negotiating Pain

SUMMARY

I have discussed an array of ethical issues that often require case advocacy in healthcare. Vignette 5.10 shows how a social work intern helped a person of color obtain ethical care.

Vignette 5.10 Using Case Advocacy to Help Consumers Obtain Their Ethical Rights

by Shunae Dyce

Malinda, an African-American 87-year-old patient with end-stage COPD (Chronic Obstructive Pulmonary Disease) lives at home and is able to make it to doctor's appointments by relying on her 60-year-old daughter, Sara, to drive her. Malinda is insured through Medicare and has increasingly become weaker and somewhat confused; she has now been diagnosed as having dementia. The doctor recommends to Sara that she return her mother home, hire a caregiver, and the hospital will send out a nurse periodically to evaluate Malinda. Sara does not really know what to do: she does not feel that she has the money to hire a caregiver, and how can she care for her mother with dementia? The doctor was in such a hurry to get to his next patient that Sara did not have the time to ask specific questions nor to assimilate what she just heard. One day while at work, Sara overhears a co-worker's conversation. This person's mother also had a recent dementia diagnosis: "My mother was given the option to go to assisted living and live on the Alzheimer's unit or to remain at home and receive hospice care where she would have a doctor, nurse, home health aide, chaplain, and social worker working together to provide her care." Sara was shocked to hear this, wondering why her mother's doctor hadn't given her this information. Was it the color of her skin? Did her doctor feel that culturally she would shy away from hospice because she viewed it as usurping the care-giving role commonly given to families in the African-American community?

Other Factors

Malinda and Sara should have received additional information from their healthcare provider. Sara should have received some guidance about how to coordinate her mother's services. She should have received counseling to help her cope with the diagnosis of dementia for her mother. The physician seemed unaware of research that demonstrates that visits from a nurse and social worker for elderly persons recently discharged from a hospital reduces the chances of that patient returning to the ER or to a hospital based on a fall or other malady.

(continued)

(continued)

Historically, African Americans have not utilized hospice services because of their lack of knowledge about it and also the perception of healthcare providers toward this group. Malinda belongs to a vulnerable group in that culturally she is not perceived as wanting to receive particular services. Perhaps this physician believed she had sufficient supportive care from her family. Perhaps he believed that she did not need organized care to help her because she held religious views that led her to believe that God would allow her to heal and recover in a kind of denial of impending death (Reese, Ahern, Nair, O'Faire, & Warren, 1999, p. 551). A multidisciplinary team should have assessed this family's religious preferences as they influenced end-of-life preferences, possibly including Malinda's pastor, with whom she had a long-term and trusting relationship, as well as the hospital's chaplain.

Participants in Case Advocacy

The participants in this advocacy effort include Sara and the hospital's social worker. Since Malinda cannot advocate for herself, it falls to Sara to carry out what she knows her mother would have desired. The hospital social worker encourages and educates Sara on completing an advance directive. She, too, wonders why Malinda and Sara did not receive more information, concluding that the physicians acted unethically by not giving them sufficient information to exercise their self-determination.

Hospitals in general are becoming more accepting toward palliative care with hospice units and home healthcare, partly because of the growing unmet needs of aging and dying persons, as well as research. An article entitled, "Hospitals embrace palliative care," Kuehn (2007, p. 1) argues that unmet needs of aging and dying persons has given rise to palliative care in hospitals. The doctor also failed to do an assessment of the patient's capacity to make informed decisions. Although he diagnosed her with dementia, he did not use state-of-art research instruments to make this diagnosis or call experts in neurological functioning into the case (Applebaum, 2007).

Social workers have multiple kinds of power, including expert power. The social worker's expertise on aging, developmental theory, and family dynamics is vital in advocacy efforts for the family. Another source of power is legitimate power, the social worker's effectiveness in past advocacy efforts as well as their position and influence will gain the approval of other disciplines within the hospital. The patient's power derives from her enrollment in Medicare and her family member, Sara, who serves as her advocate. Sara's power derives from her growing knowledge of hospice and hospital rules, as well as her knowledge of her mother's wishes.

The goals in this case are to:

- Present the mishandling of this case to the bioethics committee within the hospital.

(continued)

- Have Malinda and Sara receive information about hospice.
- Appropriate the necessary resources to further aid with care.

The expected outcomes of advocacy goals are:

- To ensure that future patient care is thoroughly assessed.
- To have Malinda and Sara make an informed decision about hospice and receive hospice care within their home.
- To prevent burnout of family caregivers by supplementing them with hospice services.

Advocacy Strategy

The specific targets of these advocacy interventions will be hospital administrators, the bioethics committee and other family members. Hospital administrators oversee the hospital's procedures and policies and are responsible for enhancing ethical behavior. They are also educators to enhance hospitals' values and mission. They evaluate hospital staff. The social worker hoped administrators would not only evaluate the actions of this physician but use this case to develop reforms in the hospital.

Bioethics committees focus on the dignity and worth of each individual and seek to uphold this value within the hospital setting through education and advocacy. They work to enhance such values as self-determination and fairness.

The social worker wants to assess if there are other concerned family members besides Sara. Could they, she wondered, provide emotional support for Sara during the care of her mother and participate in making key decisions about her care? Could they help Sara with practical tasks?

Important case advocacy interventions for this case include empowerment through education, communication, and confrontation. The social worker has given Sara several dementia web sites to educate Sara about dementia. She helps Sara determine how she can obtain the Durable Power of Attorney for her mother's healthcare—and to get a better sense of her mother's wishes.

Communication is important here, in both the role of the social worker and the daughter. The social worker will need to communicate to hospital administration, the bioethics committee, and the doctor who handled the case. She hopes that the physician will acknowledge that he handled the case poorly after the bioethics committee agreed that it is unethical to simply send a patient home after giving her a diagnosis of dementia. She hopes to organize a meeting between the physician and Sara so that they can move forward.

Another advocate in this case who has not been mentioned is that of the nurse who evaluated the patient visiting that day. Nurses can be great advocates for

(continued)

(*continued*)

end-of-life care. The social worker later learned that the nurse was concerned about Malinda's declining health and trusted that the doctor would have recommended hospice that day. Nurses' roles in advocacy are that of protecting the patient, listening to the patient's voice, moral and ethical decision making, and promoting patient well being (Thacker, 2008, p. 176). The barriers that nurses face in advocacy efforts stem from the physician, the patient's family, and fear and lack of communication (p. 179). Therefore, it is imperative to allocate advocacy tasks to various individuals within the medical system.

The social worker has the responsibility of setting up several meetings. The first meeting is with a hospital administrator to hear the narrative of this case as well as what this implies for the hospital in future treatments. The responsibility of the nurse will be to communicate her observations on the day of Malinda's visit. It is through this education that the daughter was able to clearly articulate in the meeting with the administrator what information she should have received on the day of her visit. The administrator, who was impressed by her knowledge and moved by this family member's concern as well as the support of other family members, apologized to Sara for the hospital's oversight. The social worker facilitated as a mediator in the meeting with the administrator; the goal was not to attack the administrator but to put a face with the complaint of one of the hospital's patients. The outcome of this meeting proved successful, the administrator guaranteed future training for all doctors in thoroughly assessing the patients no matter what the time frame allowed and to have each patient followed up by a social worker if they were not able to meet this standard. This training would be mandatory for all facility doctors.

The second meeting is with the bioethics committee to discuss ethical issues associated with this case. The bioethics committee was open to hearing about the case during one of their monthly meetings. The social worker gave a synopsis of the visit and then had Sara explain what she learned and the services she knew she ought to receive. The bioethics committee was able to validate the feelings and thoughts of Sara and agreed to write an affidavit to support the need for training about ethical issues associated with end-of-life issues.

The third meeting took place among the physician, the nurse, Sara, and Malinda. The social worker again served as mediator and clearly outlined that this was in no means an attack of either work ethic or intentions of the staff; however, there was a clear error that needed to be rectified and addressed. The doctor and nurse apologized. The physician agreed that he had failed sufficiently to diagnose Malinda's neurological problems and would evaluate her for hospice at her next visit unless the family wanted another physician. He felt that he should have been more sensitive to Sara who had just heard that her mother was showing signs of dementia. The doctor offered to be on Malinda's hospice team if the family chose to go with hospice services.

(*continued*)

Implementation

Implementation was simple yet skillful. The social worker facilitated as a mediator, educator, and advocate. Malinda received a recommendation for hospice from her physician. A primary physician was selected to head her hospice team that Malinda and Sara respected.

This and other cases led the health plan to ensure that elderly patients have a regular primary care physician so that patients do not have to continually explain their symptoms and what is going on with them at each visit. This can be extremely difficult for the aging population as their memory and physical bodies start to decline. Examination of the patient's chart is not enough; a conversation has to be conducted with either the patient or the patient's family/conservator. Strides were made to inform patients and their families about hospice at an earlier point in their care rather than waiting until the last moment. Myths have to be dispelled, such as the widespread belief in the African-American community that hospice usurps the role of families rather than partnering with them and helping ease some of their burdens when helping persons in end-of-life care (Gazelle, 2007, p. 321). This misunderstanding of hospice is what I believe has led to the underutilization of its services.

Suggested Learning Exercises

Discuss some what-if scenarios if this case had any of the following events from the vantage point of the advocate.

- An oncologist committed to using all possible medications and medical procedures.
- Family conflict over the option of ceasing heroic treatments.
- Shifts in the views of the patient as he or she progresses toward death.
- Problems financing hospice through the patient's insurance.
- Paramedics transport the person to the ER when someone dials 911, exposing the patient to procedures he or she did not want.
- Conflict over the use of clinical trials (the person uses a clinical trial that is not effective).
- Conflict over the use of morphine as the patient nears death.
- Mediating conflicts within a family.

MOVING FROM CASE-ADVOCACY SCENARIOS TO BROADER POLICY ISSUES

To better understand how case advocacy should sometimes lead to policy advocacy, discuss some rules, protocols, budgets, court rulings, and statutes that are germane to one of the following 19 ethical scenarios that are discussed in this chapter, whether within specific organizations, communities, public programs, or legislatures in local, state, or federal jurisdictions. (Some scenarios relevant to the ethical principle of social justice are in Chapters 6 and 9.)

Scenarios in this book:

- Advocacy to Enhance Informed Consent
- Advocacy for the Right to Refuse Treatment
- Advocacy to Determine Competence
- Advocacy to Complete Advance Directives
- Advocacy to Secure Guardians
- Advocacy to Identify and Work With Surrogates
- Advocacy for Parents With Premature Births or Disabled Infants
- Advocacy for Children
- Advocacy for Passive Measures for Hastening Death
- Advocacy to Preserve Confidentiality
- Advocacy for Consumers With IRBs and Bioethics Committees
- Advocacy to Link Consumers to Hospice

Scenarios that are online:

- Advocacy for Women Who Decide Whether to Abort Fetuses
- Advocacy for Active Measures to Hasten Death
- Advocacy to Enhance Honesty in Healthcare
- Advocacy to Enhance Consumers' Privacy Rights
- Advocacy for Consumers' Rights to View Their Rights
- Advocacy for Consumers' Rights to Dignified and Respectful Care
- Advocacy for Managing and Negotiating Pain

ONLINE MATERIALS RELEVANT TO THIS CHAPTER

To access the seven scenarios that are online (Scenarios 5.13 through 5.19), please go to the website of John Wiley & Sons at www.wiley.com/go/jansson.

Advocacy to Improve Consumers' Quality of Care

This chapter discusses strategies for helping consumers obtain healthcare that addresses major diseases and illnesses that they confront. It discusses why the U.S. health system often fails to provide quality care for such diseases as diabetes, cancer, and heart disease, as well as some strategies that have emerged to improve it. It identifies 17 scenarios that consumers often confront as they seek quality healthcare. It provides specific questions that advocates can provide consumers to help them obtain better healthcare during these scenarios.

A DEFINITION OF "QUALITY HEALTHCARE"

This chapter analyzes physiological dimensions of quality care, such as the extent the U.S health system adequately addresses such health conditions as cancer, diabetes, and heart disease. I focus on the use of medical interventions in promoting quality of care for specific physiological problems, but it is important to note that physiological well-being is also linked to many of the other dimensions of quality healthcare that are discussed in Chapters 6 through 11. The availability of highly skilled surgeons may come to naught, for example, if consumers cannot afford their services or have to wait months to get an appointment—or have to discontinue care for financial reasons (see Chapter 9). Consumers may obtain state-of-art care for advanced diabetes, but might have avoided this condition had they received sufficient preventive care (see Chapter 8). Consumers may fail to take needed medications because they do not understand instructions from a provider who fails to provide culturally relevant services (see Chapter 7). They may receive world-class surgery, but receive no attention for mental disorders that emanate from their illness or other sources (see Chapter 10).

Healthcare is often measured in physiological terms as it cures specific diseases, manages chronic diseases, and extends life expectancies. Physiological measures are important but a healthcare system measured only in these terms would be remiss on many counts. Healthcare systems should also promote ethical care such as advancing consumers' self-determination, giving them truthful information, preserving confidentiality, treating them fairly, and advancing social justice. They should not only cure diseases and manage chronic diseases, but prevent acute and chronic diseases in the first place. They should be accessible to consumers so that they can receive timely and affordable care. They should provide culturally relevant services. They should address consumers' social and mental needs. They should link consumers to an array of community resources and services.

Providers cannot achieve these dimensions of quality care, however, without enhancing consumers' positive perceptions of their care on both rational and emotional levels. Rational perceptions concern the "what" of the service experience such as the correctness of diagnoses and the quality of technical work such as surgeries. If consumers do not believe their health staff are confident, empathetic, humane, personal, forthright, respectful, and thorough, they are not likely to be satisfied with their service (Berry & Seltman, 2008). Emotional perceptions concern the "how" of the service experience. Does the setting appear inviting, warm, supportive, and connected to nature, as well as uncrowded, using natural light, and muting noise? Are human interactions with staff suffused with civility, thoughtfulness, commitment, and resourcefulness (Barry & Seltman, 2008)? Consumers with positive rational and emotional perceptions are more likely to respond favorably to medical staff and their recommendations, as well as become partners in the health process.

Providers should be accountable for achieving each of these dimensions of quality care by the use of data, whether by showing they use evidence-based medicine, achieve positive outcomes when their services are compared to other providers, achieve high scores in accreditation visits, or receive positive ratings by consumers in satisfaction surveys.

Providers should strive to improve the quality of their care along these various dimensions. They should troubleshoot their services to see where they may be deficient. They should be open to criticism from consumers. They should welcome case advocacy from any of their staff. They should empower consumers to become active partners in their care. They should initiate projects to improve services, such as by collecting data to find flaws in existing services. They should work collectively to improve services, such as through in-service training and innovative programs. They should create a culture of quality (Dlugacz, Restifo, & Greenwood, 2004).

GENERAL CRITICISMS OF THE SUCCESS OF U.S. HEALTHCARE IN ADDRESSING PHYSIOLOGICAL ILLNESSES

Many critics contend that Americans often receive suboptimal healthcare. They point to data that suggests that the United States does not fare well in international comparisons in life expectancy and infant mortality even as the United States spends a far greater percentage of its GDP on healthcare than Great Britain, Sweden, France, or Japan.

Other criticisms of the success of the U.S. health system in redressing physiological problems have emerged. The Institute of Medicine has estimated that between 44,000 and 98,000 Americans die in hospitals each year from medical errors—and between 3% and 11% of hospital admissions are attributable to adverse drug effects (ADEs) from outpatient prescriptions (Institute of Medicine, 2000). These include injuries or deaths from ADEs, injuries from falls not caused by patients' diseases, illness resulting from a diagnostic procedure or any form of therapy, failure to administer treatment regimens properly, malnutrition, patient abuse or rape, faulty equipment, dehydration, and sepsis. About 1.18 million patient safety incidents occurred among the 39 million hospitalizations in the Medicare population during 2001 through 2003 (Health Grades Inc., 2005).

Considerable evidence suggests, as well, that wide variations in the quality of healthcare exist. Consumers who use physicians who have performed many surgeries, on specific organs, have better outcomes than ones who have performed few of them and consumers who use hospitals that are connected to medical schools often have better outcomes than other ones (IOM, 2001).

Persons of color are often less likely than Caucasians to receive gold-standard medical care. Even when adjusting for socioeconomic status (SES), health insurance, and clinical status, Caucasians are more likely than blacks to receive many specific medical procedures. African-American Medicare patients are less likely than whites to receive common procedures funded by Medicare, and African Americans who presented themselves in ERs with acute chest pain were less likely to be admitted or triaged into the coronary care unit (Council on Ethical and Judicial Affairs, 1990; IOM, 2003; McBean & Gornick 1994). African Americans were found to receive the poorest quality of care for congestive heart failure, acute myocardial infarction (AMI), pneumonia, or stroke, were less likely than Caucasians to undergo angioplasty and bypass surgery even after accounting for patient refusals of treatment, and were less likely to receive thrombolysis for AMI even after controlling for patient demographics, co-morbidity, and hospital characteristics and received poorer care for coronary heart disease (Fincher et al., 2004; IOM, 2003; Kahn, 1994; Pashos et al., 1994; Taylor, 1998). Caucasian male internists are more likely to give psychogenic diagnoses to African Americans with chest pain than to Caucasians (McKinlay, Potter, & Feldman, 1996). Physicians spend less office time with Hispanic patients than Caucasians (Hooper, Comstock, Goodwin, & Goodwin, 1982). Physicians often have more negative perceptions of African-American patients than Caucasian patients including likelihood of adherence, propensity to engage in risk behaviors, low intelligence, uncooperativeness, and anger (Van Ryn & Burke, 2000; Finucane & Carrese, 1990; Gregory, Wells, & Leake, 1987; Van Ryan & Burke, 2000). Summarizing considerable research, Beach et al. (2006) contend that provider behaviors and practice patterns contribute to health disparities—and that African Americans and other minority patients often receive differential care than Caucasians (Cooper-Patrick et al., 1999).

Women often do not respond to specific medications or medical procedures that are effective respectively with males and younger persons (Wartik, 2002). They sometimes do not receive state-of-art care as compared to males, such as for diagnosing myocardial infarctions (Willingham & Kilpatrick, 2005). African-American women are less likely to receive some needed health interventions than Caucasian women (Schulman et al., 1999). Medical care is often insensitive to many needs of older women (Mayo, Nasmith, & Tannenbaum, 2003). Older women often receive contradictory and uncoordinated care (Lawrence, 2003).

THE POLICY AND REGULATORY THICKET AS IT PERTAINS TO QUALITY OF CARE

Many policies and regulations are geared toward measuring the extent health providers give consumers healthcare that meets specific medical standards. Advocates need to have knowledge of them because they may have to invoke them to improve the care of specific consumers. These include evidence-based medicine (EBM), evaluations of services of specific providers that are conducted internally or by external authorities such as Medicare officials, public release of these evaluations to the media and the public, documentation of the number and kind of adverse events in specific hospitals and clinics, developing incentives to providers, accreditation standards, electronic records linked to EBM, litigation by private and public-interest attorneys, regulations by the Food and Drug Administration (FDA), and the use of purchasing power by the federal government, employers, and private insurance companies.

Evidence-Based Medicine (EBM)

EBM has emerged as another strategy for improving medical practice. Medical decisions are often made by professionals who relied on their intuition, advice from their mentors, or medical traditions. It is hardly surprising that wide variations exist in medical practice when each professional determines what works best. Remarkable variations exist in different regions of the nation, for example, in medical practice, even when faced with identical information from biopsies, such as the extent physicians surgically remove men's prostate gland, perform radical mastectomies, and use surgical interventions for soreness in joints (Halvorsen, 2007; Lefton, 2008).

EBM has emerged as an antidote for extensive reliance on nonscientific rationales for medical interventions. The Agency for Healthcare Research and Quality (AHRQ) was established in 1997 to promote EBM as a tool for using scientific standards of evidence to discover what clinical practices were most effective in preventing and treating specific medical problems, using such outcome measures as mortality and morbidity rates, numbers of infections, numbers of readmissions, adverse drug events, and costs (Lefton, 2008). The National Guideline Clearinghouse, which is supported by the AHRQ, now supports almost 2,200 guidelines. The volume of medical research has greatly increased with more than 500,000 articles indexed by MEDLINE annually in recent years (IOM, 2008). Many organizations establish clinical guidelines and recommendations, including the AHRQ, the American Heart Association, the American College of Physicians, the American Diabetic Association, the American Society of Clinical Oncology, and the National Heart, Lung, and Blood Institute. Many other organizations synthesize evidence collected by medical scientists, including the AHRQ, the Blue Cross and Blue Shield Association Technology Evaluation Center, the Cochrane Collaboration, the ECRI Institute, and Hayes Inc. (IOM, 2008).

EBM has led to identification of scores of widely used health interventions that have been found to be ineffective or harmful. These include radiation therapy for acne, autologous bone marrow transplant with high-dose chemotherapy for advanced breast cancer, routine episiotomy for birth, hydralazine for chronic heart failure, and spinal manipulation to treat migraine headaches. EBM has identified many effective interventions, including use of the medication, statins, to prevent heart disease and stroke; stents for some forms of heart disease; the medication gleevac for some forms of cancer; tamoxifin for some women with breast cancer; and an array of treatments for various kinds of childhood cancer (IOM, 2008). Such medical advances appear almost daily in the national media.

Medicare has promoted EBM, as well. It used retrospective reviews of medical charts in the 1970s and 1980s to evaluate the quality of care given to Medicare enrollees in specific regions through physicians who worked for Peer Review Organizations (PROs)—but changed their roles from punishing substandard providers to encouraging EBM when it implemented the Health Care Quality Improvement Program in 1993 (M. Cooper, 1999).

EBMs utilizes scientific research to determine what works best and for whom. In the ideal world, its advocates contend, virtually every important medical decision should be based on rigorous scientific findings that include:

- Precise definition of a medical regimen that is to be tested so that experimental subjects receive it and not something else—such as a medication, a surgical procedure, a medical device, a specific behavioral or counseling intervention—or a multifaceted intervention that includes two or more interventions, such as a program that combines medication and behavioral interventions to help clinically obese persons lose weight.
- Careful definition of medical outcomes that are to be measured, such as rates of mortality, rates of relapses or setbacks, and rates of specific medical complications.
- Dividing subjects with specific medical conditions randomly into control groups, which receive little care or different kinds of care, and experimental groups, which receive the medical regimen that is being tested.
- Determining whether subjects who receive a specific medical regimen experience side-effects—and measuring their likelihood and severity.

- Implementation of the experiment over a specified period of time in a careful way that follows established scientific procedures.
- Deciding if, and to what extent, the medical outcomes of the experimental group surpass ones of the control group with use of statistics.

Findings from EBM have emerged in recent decades with respect to many medical interventions to address such diseases as cancer, heart disease, lung disease, and diabetes. Others have emerged that identify effective strategies for preventing specific diseases or slowing their progress.

EBM has not transformed U.S. medical practice to the extent its adherents had hoped, however, for several reasons (Timmermans & Mauck, 2005). Specific research findings are sometimes disputed by other researchers on methodological criticisms of specific studies. In many cases, for example, researchers do not use control groups because they cannot find sufficient numbers of consumers who want no or even different kinds of treatment from the experimental group. They often perform quasi experimental studies under these circumstances, giving members of the control group some modified version of the medical intervention—a strategy not usually as rigorous as a truly experimental design. Sometimes technical arguments take place about sample size and sample attrition as some subjects leave the experiment due to withdrawal or death. Some experiments are prematurely aborted because researchers decide that the medical intervention appears to be sufficiently helpful to members of the experimental group that they must ethically provide it to members of the control group—or that they must stop the experiment because early findings suggest that members of the experimental group are harmed by the intervention. Critics can argue in either case that experiments were prematurely aborted. Critics can argue, as well, that experiments have been contaminated by nonuniform provision of the medical intervention that is being tested or by giving it to some members of the control group.

Controversy exists, too, about definitions and timelines of researchers. Assume, for example, that one set of researchers deems a medical intervention to cure prostate cancer to be a success when the PSA score (a blood test) of subjects does not go above 2.0 within two years of the procedure. Another set of researchers uses far more stringent standards: They deem the intervention to be successful only if the men's PSA scores do not exceed 0.1 within 5 years. These two sets of researchers could reach divergent evaluations of the same medical intervention partly because they use these different definitions and timelines (Walsh, 2001). Evaluations of specific medical interventions can be markedly influenced, too, by the standard used to include or exclude patients from trials. Evaluations that exclude persons with relatively advanced disease may reach more favorable evaluations than ones that include them.

Critics of specific experiments often contend, moreover, that researchers often use samples that did not include specific kinds of persons, such as women, persons of color, children, or older persons—or persons co-morbidities (IOM, 2008). They contend that clinical successes with study populations cannot be assumed to be effective with excluded populations—and can point to many instances where this has been true. Women and children respond in different ways to some medications, for example, than men just as medical interventions that are successful with younger adults may not be successful with older persons.

EBM sometimes is an uncertain guide to physicians, moreover, because it rarely results in medical successes for all members of an experimental group. Researchers often deem an experiment to have been successful when differences in outcomes in control and experimental groups are statistically significant—even when considerable numbers of persons in experimental groups are not helped by the intervention. Results often are not stated in terms that many physicians desire, such as the number of patients who need to be treated to prevent a single event, such as a heart attack (IOM, 2008). It is understandable, then, that some physicians are not convinced that EBM can supplant their professional judgments even when presented with scientific studies.

Critics of EBM sometimes argue, as well, that researchers often fail to identify a sufficient array of outcome measures. A specific kind of chemotherapy might extend cancer patients lives by three months, for example, but with serious side effects such as nausea, headaches, insomnia, and loss of energy.

Some EBM findings have been questioned because specific medical researchers have served as consultants for the medical corporations that have produced the substances or devices that they test. Only recently have many medical journals required authors to disclose conflicts of interest (IOM, 2008; Steinbrook, 2005).

Other factors have limited EBM's impact on medical practice. Many physicians pride themselves on their professional autonomy making them reluctant to follow guidelines (Berwick, 2003). Many of them are unwilling to modify their traditional practices. Consumers sometimes pressure them to provide them with specific treatments that are not supported by EBM, such as giving them antibiotics when they have the flu even though they are ineffective with this ailment. Administrators and high-level physicians often do not monitor medical staff to ascertain if they use guidelines derived from EBM—or fail to sanction them if they do not.

Recent surveys of physicians' practices suggest that many of them do not use EBM. A study from the RAND Institute discovered that roughly half of physicians in a national sample failed to use EBM findings to treat patients with asthma and depression—and even more of them failed to use an array of preventive measures (Adams et al., 2003). Researchers reached similar conclusions when surveying providers for Medicaid enrollees in a broad of hospitals and examining ambulatory care for children (Mangione-Smith et al., 2007).

The Patient Protection and Affordable Care Act of 2010 as amended by the Congress will advance quality of care through several provisions. It will create an Innovation Center in the Centers for Medicare and Medicaid Services (CMS) in 2011, as well as develop a national quality improvement strategy to improve the delivery of healthcare services, and advance patient health outcomes. It will establish a national Medicare pilot program to develop and evaluate a bundled payment for acute inpatient hospital services, physician services, outpatient services, and post-acute-care services for specific episodes of care. It will establish in 2012 a hospital Value-Based Purchasing Program (VBP) to give hospitals financial incentives to improve the quality of their care. (Hospitals will be required to report publicly the extent to which they deal effectively with heart attacks, heart failure, pneumonia, surgical care, and healthcare associated infections, as well as the extent to which patients are satisfied with their care.) The legislation seeks to pay physicians (by 2015) based on the quality of their services rendered rather than on volume; doctors who provide higher value care will be reimbursed at higher levels than those who provide lower quality care. The federal government already maintains a method of comparing the quality of care in hospitals in local areas at its Hospital-Compare website; an overview of the provisions of the Patient Protection and Affordable Care Act of 2010 also exists at this site (see www.HealthCare.gov).

This legislation provides incentives, by 2012, for "Accountable Care Organizations," which are medical groups that allow physicians to better coordinate patient care, improve its quality, prevent disease and illness, and reduce unnecessary hospitalizations. Effective January 1, 2012, these organizations can recoup some of the funds they have helped to save.

This legislation aims, as well, to increase the cost-effectiveness of the American health system in several ways. It requires movement toward standardized billing procedures to cut paperwork costs. Beginning in 2012, it requires the adoption of electronic records to cut paperwork costs, as well as to reduce medical errors due to the failure of physicians to share information with one another. We have discussed the national pilot program, to begin in 2013, to encourage hospitals, doctors, and providers to accept reimbursement for a flat rate for "bundled" care to reduce fragmentation of services in the current health system.

The legislation requires health plans to participate in State Exchanges, which will market insurance plans to the general public by 2014. These health plans are to be accredited on their performance; the quality measures are yet to be developed. It requires health plans to report the proportion of their premium dollars spent on clinical services, quality, and other costs by the end of 2010—and requires them by January 1, 2011, to return rebates to enrollees if they spend less than 85% of their premium costs on clinical services and quality for large plans, and 80% for plans for individuals and small groups (for an overview of the Patient Protection and Affordable Care Act, go to the web site of the Kaiser Family Foundation and locate publication #8061 at www.kff.org).

Following Fixed Procedures

Researchers have discovered that medical errors substantially decline in intensive care units when staff follows checklists when providing specific medical treatments. In intensive care units (ICUs), for example, staff provides mechanical ventilators, insert tracheotomy tubes, conduct dialysis, use aortic balloon pumps, feed patients through tubes, provide direct infusions into the blood stream, and care for open wounds—providing 178 individual actions per day. If they use checklists for these procedures, death rates plummet by as much as 66% in ICUs (Gawande, 2010).

Many researchers have discovered, as well, that medical staff is more likely to provide effective services when they provide them on many occasions partly because they follow certain procedures automatically and perfect their skills (Walsh, 2001.)

Evaluations of Medical Practice by Clinics, Hospitals, and Health Plans

Medical records are reviewed by the Joint Commission on Accreditation of Healthcare Organizations (JCAHO) accreditation teams, as well as internal review teams to examine practice decisions of health staff. Medical records are an essential record of health services in hospitals and clinics. Each one should contain the initial history and physical examination of consumers; significant medical conditions and surgeries; reports of diagnostic tests; progress reports; consultations; and referrals. It should contain consent forms and documentation of discussions that led to informed consent. Each entry should be accompanied by a signature. Medical records should not contain erasures; blaming of others; inflammatory or prejudiced descriptions of patients since medical records are used by other staff and can be used in court proceedings (Olshinski, 1999). As the data bases of clinics, hospitals, and health plans have improved, they can monitor the health services of their physicians and health staff. This capability will be increased further as electronic records become more widely used from the minority of hospitals that used them in 2010.

Patient satisfaction surveys are often used to evaluate healthcare and for marketing purposes. Many health plans carefully monitor, as well, how many consumers choose to exit them and often query them about the reasons for this action so that they can use the information to improve consumer satisfaction with their services.

Public Disclosure of Evaluations of Medical Practice

Evaluations of specific physicians, clinics, and hospitals have increasingly been released to the public by state departments of public health, Medicare, state Medicaid programs, and state departments of health. These have included results of patient satisfaction surveys, overall mortality rates, mortality rates for specific kinds of cancer and heart disease, and rates of complications after specific kinds of surgery. They have evaluated the extent specific managed-care plans provide preventive services. They evaluate the extent specific providers use outdated equipment or equipment that is not properly maintained.

The impact of these evaluations on providers has been increased by coverage in the mass media, as well as public access to them on the Internet. It is too soon to tell whether public disclosure of health outcomes will markedly increase the effectiveness of health services in the United States. On the negative side, many consumers do not read this information. Others do not change their health utilization because loyalty to specific physicians or hospitals. On the positive side, poor evaluations can promote improvements in care as specific providers improve their services to retain or gain consumers and to improve their well-being.

Preventing and Collecting Information About Adverse Events

Risk managers in hospitals and clinics require staff members to report "incidents" or "occurrences" that are "events which occur that are not consistent with normal operating procedures" (Olshinksi, 1999). Each of them can harm consumers, staff, or the institution and are tracked to find trends and to find remedies. They are not punitive measures, but used to improve patient services after they have been investigated.

Some states require health providers to report "adverse events" that cause consumers to develop serious disabilities while under their care. Under state legislation in 2007, for example, California defines adverse events as ones that limit patients' major life activities or loss of bodily functions if they last more than seven days or are present at the time of discharge from an inpatient health facility (CHA, 2008, pp. 20.15, 20.16). Adverse events include surgeries performed on the wrong body parts or on the wrong patient; a surgical procedure to which the consumer had not given informed consent; and certain deaths of otherwise healthy patients after surgery. They include some patient deaths or serious disabilities from contaminated drugs, devices, or biological agents; some patient deaths or serious disabilities associated with patients' disappearance for more than 4 hours; some patient suicides or attempted suicides after admission to a health facility while under its care, unless specific patients were admitted for self-inflicted wounds (CHA, 2008, p. 20.16). They include some medication errors and infusions of incompatible blood products. They include some maternal deaths or serious disabilities associated with low-risk pregnancies. They include some patient deaths or serious disabilities from environmental events, including burns, falls, use of restraints or bedrails, and administration of contaminated oxygen or other gasses (CHA, 2008, p. 20.16). They require reports of care by persons working at a facility or on its grounds. Hospitals and clinics that do not report adverse events are subject to fines in California (CHA, 2008, p. 20.18).

The State of California requires its Department of Public Health to make reports of substantiated adverse events, as well as outcomes of inspections and investigations, accessible to consumers (including on its web site) by 2015. Medicare, too, collects information about adverse events.

Changing Incentives

It was assumed by many economists that overtreatment would diminish were the nation to move from fee-for-service reimbursement to ones that gave physicians a flat sum for each patient they treated, as in managed-care plans or HMOs because the revenues of these plans rose as they did not overtreat patients. They assumed, too, that managed-care plans would provide more preventive services than physicians reimbursed on a fee-for-service basis because they would increase their revenues as many of their enrollees did not develop preventable illnesses like some forms of diabetes.

Had these economists been correct, the rate of increase in health costs would have substantially declined in the past two decades as the number and percentage of Americans in managed-care systems substantially. Data is, however, decidedly mixed. Some health plans, such as Kaiser Permanente, do have lower per person costs than physicians reimbursed on a fee-for-service basis. The discrepancies are not that large, however, partly because U.S. physicians and patients use expensive medical procedures, diagnostic tests, and medications no matter the mode of reimbursement. Some health plans fear, as well, that some enrollees will exit them if they do not provide expensive services that consumers want *even* when they are not supported by EBM.

Some funders of healthcare, such as Medicare officials, some insurance companies, and HMOs, have begun to reimburse physicians who follow specific EBM findings or who provide preventive care at higher levels than other ones, such as by giving them annual bonuses.

Accreditation Standards

Most hospitals and clinics are reaccredited by the Joint Commission on Accreditation of Healthcare Organizations, commonly called *The Joint Commission*, every three years and are subject to random surveys by it. (Some states accredit hospitals instead of the JCAHO or accredit them in tandem with them.) The Joint Commission is a non-governmental not-for-profit organization whose officials have developed many standards for healthcare that focused until recently on the "inputs" to medical services, such as credentials of health staff, medical record documentation, and safety for employees and patients. Only accredited hospitals can receive Medicare and Medicaid because of a provision in the Medicare Act of 1965. Unaccredited hospitals often find it difficult to attract medical staff and to receive funds from some managed-care plans. The Joint Commission conducts its evaluations by interviewing high-level officials and high-level medical staff, as well as staff in specific units and departments, examine medical records, and examine service statistics. They write an overall summary that discusses both strengths and weaknesses of services in a specific institution. They can come to various conclusions. They can reaccredit the institution, give it a provisional or probationary accreditation pending specific improvements, or not accredit it. Specific institutions can appeal adverse decisions, often leading to another inspection.

The Joint Commission was not vested with the power to measure or evaluate quality, but began in the late 1980s to develop a set of indicators that measured rates of mortality and other medical outcomes in specific hospitals, calling this initiative ORYX (M. Cooper, 1999). It aimed to compare health outcomes in different hospitals retrospectively, such as measuring rates of mortality, but has had to surmount different definitions of it in different institutions with some defining it as death in 24 hours, 72 hours, 7 days, or 30 days after a medical procedure. Evaluations of specific hospitals need to be adjusted, as well, for the severity of health problems in them so that ones with a disproportionate share of severely ill persons are not penalized (M. Cooper, 1999). The Joint Commission also seeks performance improvement where hospitals use data to continuously upgrade their services to improve outcomes (M. Cooper, 1999).

Other federal, state, and private agencies monitor services. The Joint Commission also accredits psychiatric facilities, long-term care organizations, alcohol and substance abuse programs, community mental health centers, home care associations, ambulatory health centers, laboratories, and home care organizations. The Health Services and Resource Administration (HRSA) provides grants to many free-standing clinics that serve low-income and uninsured populations and offers them technical services to upgrade their services. States monitor services provided by Medicaid.

Managed-care organizations are mostly accredited by the private National Committee on Quality Assurance (NCQA), which recently evaluated more than 300 managed-care plans covering more than 37 million lives (M. Cooper, 1999). Like the JCAHO, it has moved toward evaluating health services, such as determining the extent that they provide specific preventive measures like mammograms, Pap smears, and smoking-cessation counseling.

Accreditation standards enforce ethical standards. Accreditation teams check medical records, for example, to ascertain if a hospital's health staff has notified patients that they can fill out advanced directives prior to or after admittance should they be incompetent to express their preferences at a subsequent point. They ascertain if health staff has followed relevant state and federal guidelines.

Critics of the Joint Commission contend that it is overly permissive because roughly 99% of inspected hospitals are accredited. They argue that its governing board is dominated by representatives of the industries it inspects. It notifies hospitals in advance of the timing of inspections (http://en.wikipedia.org/wiki/Joint_Commission). It does not accredit or monitor outpatient care of patients using private doctors. Yet it powerfully shapes health services by inspecting them in considerable detail, including emergency management, human resources, information management, medication management, patient safety, nursing, and transplant safety. Advocates should have working knowledge of the sections that cover provision of care, treatment, and services, as well as medical and other records that document them.

Advocates can help consumers obtain information about accreditation by reading the Joint Commission's Accreditation Standards. They can help them discover how particular institutions fared during recent reaccreditation visits.

Electronic Medical Records and Other Forms of Emerging Technology

Although only a small portion of hospitals had implemented electronic medical records by 2009, the administration of Barack Obama included substantial funds in its stimulus package to help fund technology that would promote their use. Electronic medical records have the potential to allow monitoring of medical practice to see if they follow EBM findings, to upgrade physicians' knowledge, and to reward physicians who follow it.

Electronic records may also allow physicians and other health practitioners to *track* the medical care of specific consumers as they move through the health system. Logistical problems with traditional hand-written medical records often prevent them from being transferred from specific physicians and units to other physicians and units—meaning that physicians often do not possess complete information about specific consumers. Electronic records may be particularly easy to implement in managed-care plans that include primary and specialty care placed under one roof so that they include information from primary-care physicians as well as specialists.

Electronic records also allow physicians, nurses, pharmacists, and other health providers to diminish medical errors that stem from undecipherable handwritten notes. Some consumers receive incorrect medications, for example, because nurses and pharmacists cannot read handwritten notes of physicians.

Electronic records are not panaceas, however. They require large up-front installation costs. Some physicians prefer handwritten medical notes. It may be easier for some persons to breech confidentiality by making unauthorized use of medical records. Advocates can help consumers ask providers questions about where information about their healthcare is kept, such as whether it is transmitted from their primary-care physician to specialists and vice versa, whether records are kept in one place about their diagnostic tests so they do not duplicate them, and whether prior scans are stored electronically so current providers can access them.

Consumer Litigation

Consumers sometimes take matters into their own hands when they believe that they have been provided medical care that diverges from accepted norms, particularly if they believe they have suffered injuries because of subpar care. Millions of them have engaged private attorneys in past decades to litigate such issues as alleged malpractice or violation of their ethical rights. They have often sued hospitals, as well, when they have believed they lacked sufficient quality controls in their procedures, hiring of staff, in-service training, and monitoring of the quality of care provided within them. Consumers have often litigated against pharmaceutical companies when they believed they failed to disclose potential side effects of medications or adverse drug inter-actions—or when they overstated likely benefits from them. Consumers have sued manufacturers of medical devices that they believed malfunctioned due to faulty manufacturing or inadequate testing.

The extent of consumer litigation is considerable, but should not be exaggerated. Some experts argue that its elimination would only modestly cut health costs. Con-sumers have directed their litigation against a relatively small number of physicians who are often the recipients of multiple suits. These physicians disproportionately practice in such disciplines as OB/GYN and plastic surgery.

Some public officials have tried to discourage litigation of consumers against physicians and hospitals on grounds that it is often frivolous in nature or seeks huge awards not merited by consumers' alleged injuries. Some states have placed limits on the size of allowable malpractice awards, such as $250,000 in California. Many managed-care plans require enrollees to sign agreements when they enter their plans where they agree to forego litigation through the courts and to rely, instead, on the findings of internal administrative boards and the awards they suggests that are often limited to a specific ceiling. If many providers, the AMA, and corporations that make medical devices and medications often support policies that limit litigation by consumers, many attorneys and consumer rights group often oppose such policies.

It is difficult to ascertain whether consumer litigation improves or decreases the overall quality of medical services. It prods physicians to be attentive to their patients lest they expose themselves to litigation, but it encourages defensive medicine by inducing some physicians to overtest and overtreat some consumers to avert litigation. Advocates cannot counsel consumers about litigation against their hospitals or clinics because they would face a conflict of interest because they work for them. If they believe that staff of these institutions engage in questionable medical procedures, they should advise high-level administrators and, in rare instances, engage in whistle blowing by divulging information to local, state, or federal officials if they cannot obtain redress otherwise or believe they will face personal repercussions.

Medical personnel do not have a conflict of interest, however, when giving consumers information about possible litigation against manufacturers of defective medical devices and pharmaceuticals. These may include class action suits. They can help consumers by helping them discover possible class action suits against specific medical corporations that manufacture specific medical devices and pharmaceuticals and by helping them know where to lodge complaints against specific health providers by contacting relevant agencies in their state.

Approvals for Medical Devices and Medications from the Federal Government

The Food and Drug Administration (FDA) is charged with approving new pharmaceuticals and medical devices for specific medical conditions after they have been subjected to clinical trials and other evaluations. These evaluations have averted many injuries and deaths when unsafe products have been removed from the market.

Many problems exist in processes used by the FDA to determine if medical innovations are safe and effective, which I discuss later. Other problems exist in the existing regulatory system. The federal government does not regulate new surgical techniques that require no public approval such as when a surgeon passes on a surgical innovation to other surgeons (R. Jansson, 2003).

No federal agency has the power, moreover, to determine if specific innovations are cost-effective; that is, deliver sufficient improvements to health outcomes to merit their cost. Let us compare two hypothetical cases. Assume a medication increases life expectancy for specific kinds of cancer in terminally ill patients for an average of 30 days at a cost of $100,000. Assume another medication extends lives of persons with another form of cancer for 6 months at an average cost of $50,000. The second medication is more cost-effective than the first one, but both medications would likely be approved by the FDA. Why not, some experts contend, grant approval only for the second drug?

Unlike the British government, the FDA possesses the authority to approve new medications that are effective, but cannot currently disapprove them if they are not cost-effective, so it would likely approve both the first and second medications. Nor can it determine the cost-effectiveness of many other innovations, including scanning machines, diagnostic tests, and specific surgical techniques. Top advisors of President Barack Obama proposed strengthening federal research to examine the cost-effectiveness of treatments, which has been included in the Patient Protection and Affordability Act of 2010.

Case advocates also deal with issues of cost-effectiveness at the level of specific consumers. They need to help consumers ask questions to their providers to decide whether to undertake specific treatments, medications, or diagnostic tests that may provide relatively few benefits as compared to their costs. They need to help them inquire whether new technology is covered by Medicare, private insurances, or managed-care plans—and, if not, whether their out-of-pocket costs are merited by its likely benefits. They need to help them ask whether the benefits of new technology are sufficient to outweigh their possible side effects

Using Federal and Private Purchasing Power to Protect Consumers

Medicare uses its funding authority to determine which medications, devices, and diagnostic tests are used by physicians. It decides which of them to fund and which ones not to fund based on evaluations conducted by the FDA, other governmental agencies, and university-based research. Medicare officials usually decline to provide Medicare coverage for medical innovations deemed to be merely experimental. Many private health plans and insurance companies, as well as Medicaid, follow Medicare's example.

This policy has sometimes led to problems for consumers who engage in clinical trials. Consumers who receive Medicare coverage for a specific medication during a clinical trial often cannot get continued coverage for it until the FDA approves it after all stages of the clinical trial have been completed. They must often stop the medication when their participation in a clinical trial ends and revert to another one that does not help them.

Employers often funded coverage for their employees without evaluating the cost or quality of the care that they received. They increasingly monitor their care, however, because they realize that workers' productivity is enhanced when they receive quality care. They also realize that their profit margins are diminished if their employees receive inefficient care, such as excessive numbers of surgeries and medications. Employers often develop Preferred Provider Organizations (PPOs) where they select the providers that their employees will use based on their cost or cost-effectiveness in providing services. Some employers develop even greater control over their employees' healthcare by themselves insuring them—sometimes adding some health programs at the job site.

Advocates can help consumers determine what medications and devices are covered by Medicare and whether specific private insurance carriers or Medicaid cover specific medications and devices once Medicare has approved them.

Risk Managers

Risk-manager administrators are troubleshooters who try to prevent and to manage incidents and adverse events in hospitals and clinics—not only to decrease litigation against their institutions and staff, but to improve patient care. They monitor ratios of staff to patients so that sufficient staff exists to provide quality services even during cutbacks. They monitor the credentials and competencies of staff. They monitor physician extenders such as nurse practitioners and physician assistants (Olshinski, 1999). They monitor contracts with other organizations with whom they exchange patients. They also handle complaints from consumers, who often want "a serious respond to his complaint, immediate action, compensation for his inconvenience, a solution to the problem so others don't confront it . . . and most importantly, a complaining patient wants to be heard (Olshinski, 1999). Consumers are most likely to complain when they are treated harshly, not heard, not treated fairly, or kept in the dark regarding their treatment (Olshinski, 1999). Consumers whose complaints are ignored are likely to exit the institution or health plan—and to urge others to follow suit. Risk managers often initiate investigations that include examining the medical record, interviewing staff, interviewing family members and the consumer, and consulting with legal and financial staff. Resolution may include apologies and financial compensation if the institution and its staff are at fault.

Advocates should gain familiarity with the location and roles of risk managers, seek advice about specific patient quality issues from them or through their supervisors, and inform consumers how they register complaints.

Government Regulations

State and federal governments have established many regulations germane to quality of care. California has enacted regulations, for example, that establish a maximum ratio of nurses to patients of nurses. Many states prohibit managed-care plans from issuing "gag orders" that instruct primary-care physicians *not* to refer consumers to specialists under certain circumstances. Some states accredit hospitals or share this duty with Joint Commission. State agencies often investigate consumer complaints against hospitals, clinics, and managed-care plans.

Advocates should gain familiarity with specific state and federal regulations that govern consumer care in their facilities, know how to refer consumers to specific web sites that discuss them, and know hotlines or other methods that consumers can use to contact relevant agencies.

FIFTEEN SCENARIOS ENCOUNTERED BY CONSUMERS WITH RESPECT TO QUALITY OF CARE

Case advocates can help consumers navigate 17 scenarios relevant to obtaining quality healthcare, including two scenarios in the online materials relevant to this chapter with instructions for accessing them at the end of this chapter. I discuss each of them in turn.

Scenario 6.1: Advocacy for Consumers with Respect to EBM

Consumers should engage in discussions with their physicians or other health providers about medical research that is germane to their health condition and their treatment options. If EBM findings exist that are relevant to them, they should discuss them and make an informed decision whether to proceed with treatment that accords with them. If their healthcare providers inform them that they wish to use an approach not supported by EBM, they should be told *why* they are rejecting it, particularly when they possess a serious, even life-threatening health condition. Physicians may say, for example, that they have documented success in dealing with specific health conditions using another approach—or may question the validity of specific EBM findings.

These discussions often do not take place. Perhaps physicians believe consumers cannot understand technical research findings. Perhaps they do not believe they have the skills and training to provide care that is supported by EBM. Perhaps they disagree with specific EBM findings, but do not want to engage consumers in discussion as to why this might be the case. They may dismiss specific EBM findings without explaining why this is the case.

Some physicians may not want to admit that EBM findings do not exist with respect to treating a specific health condition or that conflicting findings exist—possibly because they do not want to erode consumers' confidences. They may believe that consumers will be so confused by honest acknowledgment of the lack of scientific certainty that they will not agree to any treatment. They may overstate the medical urgency of the situation by implying or stating that specific consumers will suffer harm if they do not proceed at once even if this assertion is not supported by existing science. They may attack reputations of physicians and medical researchers who support approaches different from ones that they use. They may respond to honest questions with irritation or dismissively.

Consumers often find it difficult, too, to understand the seriousness of their medical conditions because many physicians are not comfortable about discussing medical prognosis with their patients. Perhaps they do not like to deal with dying and death in the case of persons with terminal health conditions. Perhaps they believe specific consumers will be traumatized by poor prognoses. If patients cannot understand where they are headed, however, and with what probability, how can they make medical plans and life plans?

Advocates should help consumers enter these discussions with specific questions that they pose to medical staff to allow them to gain:

- Sufficient information so that they can give informed consent to treatment plans.
- Confidence and trust in the physicians who will implement these plans.
- A treatment plan based on EBM findings if they apply to them and their condition.
- Information about the severity of their conditions and their prognoses stated in probability terms—and how physicians have tailored their remedies to these realities.
- Reasons why specific EBM findings are rejected by specific physicians.
- The National Institutes of Health at www.nih.gov offers a wealth of information on health topics that is based on research results published in peer-reviewed, scientific literature.

Scenario 6.2: Advocacy for Consumers with Respect to Evaluating Physicians' Outcomes

Consumers should want data about medical outcomes that specific physicians have achieved with persons with their medical condition (Walsh, 2001). They should ask to what extent have consumers been free of symptoms after specific medical procedures and for what length of time? They should inquire about the extent consumers have experienced specific side effects and with what severity. They should inquire about how many times physicians have provided specific health procedures.

Advocates should help consumers develop a list of questions that may include:

- What is the track record of a physician in using it?
- What alternative treatments exist and why does the physician not use them?
- Why does the physician reject a watch-and-wait strategy?
- What guideposts will be used to ascertain if the treatment is effective?
- Is the treatment covered by consumers' insurances?

Scenario 6.3: Advocacy to Help Consumers with Respect to Selecting Quality Providers

Consumers not only select specific physicians, but clinics and hospitals where they work. These clinics and hospitals are crucial to consumers for many reasons. They decrease the likelihood of medical errors and misjudgments when they possess a culture that prizes excellence. They monitor the quality of medical care, reward excellence, hire out-standing staff, foster team practice, and provide consumers with amenities like superior food. They provide nursing, social work, psychology, occupational-therapy (OT), and physical therapy (PT) staff who are often important to medical outcomes.

Considerable research indicates, as well, that institutional affiliations with medical schools often promote quality care because faculty and medical students foster critical analysis and evaluation of existing services. These institutions may be more likely to support medical care that is congruent with EBM findings because their staff often engages in research.

Consumers can obtain considerable information about specific hospitals from online data from Medicare and from state agencies. These may include data about health outcomes from specific kinds of surgeries, whether an institution is accredited and patient satisfaction. They should examine the institution's medical roster to ascertain if it contains graduates of respected medical schools and the extent its medical staff are board certified.

Advocates should help consumers develop lists of questions that include information regarding:

- The reputation of specific health institutions in the medical community as attested by the caliber of its medical staff.
- Whether specific health institutions possess affiliations with medical schools.
- Whether the organizational culture prizes excellence.
- Evaluations about medical outcomes and patient satisfaction from federal and state sources.
- Whether the institution is accredited and whether it has had recent difficulties in obtaining reaccreditations.

An excellent resource for consumers is "Your guide to choosing quality healthcare" from the Agency for Healthcare Research and Quality www.ahrq.gov/consumer/qualguid.pdf. Quality of the care of specific hospitals can be obtained at www.HealthCare.gov.

Scenario 6.4: Advocacy to Help Consumers with Respect to Second Opinions

Some consumers wrongly believe that they are offending the physician who gave them their first opinion when they receive a second opinion—and are less likely to seek one if they have a trusting relationship with their physician (Thom, Hall, & Pawlson, 2004). If they receive second opinions about purchases of cars and appliances, however, why not get them about more important matters such as life-threatening or serious health conditions? Many surgeries, such as removal of a tumor or organ, are provided only once in a consumer's lifetime—meaning that these procedures cannot be redone if they are performed poorly. Capable healthcare professionals are not threatened by second opinions—and will welcome them as ways to encourage helpful discussion about how best to address a specific medical condition. Second opinions can reduce surgery rates by prompting decisions to postpone or forego decisions (Martin, 1982). Researchers in Massachusetts discovered, after it had enacted a mandatory second opinion rule, that Medicaid costs dropped significantly in its wake (Martin, 1982). One study discovered, however, that five of every six patients who obtained second opinions had the first recommendation confirmed—but 85% of the remaining patients decided not to have the operation (Groopman, 2000). Many private insurers pay the entire cost of second opinions, while others pay only a part of their costs.

Many consumers obtain use the internet to check their physicians' advice (Chapple et al., 2004). They also use it to gain experiential advice from other patients and make anonymous private inquiries.

Consumers may need help in finding medical staff who can give them second opinions. They should consider obtaining them from different hospitals or clinics so that they obtain independent opinions. They should seek them from staff in respected medical institutions, such as ones with medical school affiliations and with positive online evaluations from Medicare and state authorities.

Advocates should help consumers develop and use the same list of questions for their first opinion that they prepared for their second opinion. It may be easier for consumers who are enrolled in preferred provider organizations (PPO) to obtain second opinions than members of managed-care plans. If PPO subscribers can select from a relatively large list of independent physicians and institutions, members of managed-care plans must often use in-house medical staff for second opinions unless their plans allow enrollees to get outside second opinions and will even fund them.

Advocates can help consumers determine if they need second opinions by asking:

- Do they possess health conditions that are sufficiently complex that physicians may disagree about how to diagnose them?
- Are potential treatments sufficiently difficult that consumers need to find specific physicians with a proven track record in providing them?
- Are potential treatments associated with sufficient side effects or other risks that consumers want assurance that a specific physician has skills to avert them?
- Should consumers seek other sources of information from public data sources, other physicians, or consumers who have used specific physicians?

Scenario 6.5: Advocacy to for Help Consumers With Respect to Finding Information Germane to Quality-of-Care Issues

Most consumers realize that the Internet is a vast repository of medical information about specific medical conditions, specific health institutions, and specific physicians. They know, as well, that it contains information from persons with divergent perspectives, including from medical researchers, practitioners of alternative medicine, and patients. Many of them do not understand how to find this information from a broad range of sources that include the Internet, journals, mass media, and books.

The Internet has become the major resources for many consumers, but they often need help in discriminating between excellent and inferior sites. They also need skills in detecting overall perspectives or points of view that are incorporated in some sites. They should realize upfront, as well, that some consumers become overwhelmed by the sheer quantity of information on the Internet.

Advocates can help them *begin* with sites with reputations for accuracy, starting with search engines maintained by respected federal sites, such as the National Library of Medicine. They can use sites maintained by an array of federal agencies, including the National Institutes of Health (NIH), the National Cancer Institute (NCI), and other federal institutes dealing with an array of diseases.

They can then proceed to an array of sites maintained by respected private groups that provide useful information such as WEBMD.

They can then proceed to sites maintained by advocacy groups with expertise in specific diseases or in medical problems confronted by specific populations such as women, persons with disabilities, and populations of color. They can usually find these sites by using such search engines maintained by Google, Yahoo, or Microsoft. Some of these sites maintain chat sites that allow specific consumers to discuss their health condition with other persons—or to observe discussions of other consumers.

They can then proceed to sites that offer perspectives that deviate from medical orthodoxy. They can examine sites of practitioners of alternative medicine. They can examine blogs of specific patients who possess their medical condition.

They should realize, as well, that medical journals and books often contain information relevant to their health condition. They can access articles in journals that cover a range of medical conditions, such as the *Journal of the American Medical Association*, the *New England Journal of Medicine*, and *Lancet*, but specialized journals in specific areas like diabetes, heart disease, and urology. Medical encyclopedias can easily be found in most bookstores.

Many books provide invaluable insights. Some of them are written by persons who have dealt with specific health conditions, such as cancer survivors who give useful information to other consumers with this health condition. Some of them are written by physicians for popular audiences, such as books on prostate cancer (Walsh, 2001).

Diligent consumers should begin reading materials soon after they learn that they have a specific health condition. They should use this information to refine the list of questions that they wish to pose to their physicians.

Advocates should help consumers identify search sites for information about their health conditions, including from:

- Internet sites, including ones maintained by government agencies, private medical groups, and advocacy groups. National Institutes of Health information

web site at http://health.nih.gov/ has links to information about many diseases and treatments
- Journal articles
- Books
- Consumers who have received treatment for their health condition

Scenario 6.6: Advocacy to Help Consumers Who Cannot Decide How to Proceed With Treatments

Consumers sometimes become overwhelmed by medical terminology, the gravity of their situations, divergent opinions in the medical community, the sheer amount of information on the Internet, and divergent advice from physicians giving first and second opinions. It often does not matter if they cannot decide what to do for extended periods if they possess a health condition that experts believe to be relatively benign, but they could place themselves in jeopardy if experts believe it is serious and fast-moving such as an aggressive cancer.

Consumers sometimes become overwhelmed because they misinterpret the extent of danger that their health conditions pose for them, particularly when they have such health conditions widely viewed as likely to lead to their death or incapacitation, such as cancer. It is useful to discuss with them how considerable numbers of persons do survive for extended periods even when they have advanced Stage 3 or Stage 4 cancer. It sounds grim at first glance, but someone who has a 30% chance of surviving five years or longer has a good chance at additional years of life to deepen relations with family members and friends, work on prioritized projects, and have many valuable experiences.

It may be helpful to discuss their health condition with some other persons who have or do possess it, such as members of support groups. They can ask how other persons, faced with a similar medical condition, made difficult choices. A prime example is the program "Breast Friends Forever," which is often offered through hospitals. Breast Friends Forever links survivors of breast cancer with newly diagnosed consumers to offer information and support. Nurse care managers often serve as advocates with cancer patients.

It is important, too, to explore with consumers the dangers of mental distress when they cannot decide whether or when to proceed with additional medical care such as surgery, radiation, or chemotherapy. If EBM suggests that additional care has significant potential for arresting or slowing the progression of a health condition, commencement of that care can empower consumers because they believe they are not standing still and are taking matters into their own hands—even if unknowns will always exist.

Mental distress from not taking action can also be ameliorated by obtaining scientific evidence that "watchful waiting" is viewed as a valid option by recognized experts. If consumers have biopsy results that suggest they are not at a threshold that suggests imminent harm or that suggest that their health condition, such as cancer, does not appear to be aggressive, they can view their "indecisions" as a valid choice.

Advocates can help them develop questions to physicians that obtain information about:

- The extent that treatments will become less effective in curing it, or slowing its progress, if treatment does not begin soon.
- Evidence about whether their biological markers suggest that "watchful waiting" might become harmful.
- How they can deal with mental distress that emanates from *not* taking action.
- How they can find consumers who faced a similar dilemma to see how they dealt with it.

Scenario 6.7: Advocacy to Help Consumers Decide Whether to Participate in Clinical Trials

Many consumers discover that established treatment interventions, such as specific kinds of chemotherapy, do not help them at all—or lose their effectiveness as their health conditions progress. They can apply for a clinical trial where they receive study or experimental medications for a specific period under the medical supervision of a physician. (These medications do not become "treatments" until they are approved by the Food and Drug Administration.) Consumers' participation is entirely voluntary and they can withdraw at any time. They should not feel pressured to enter a trial.

Clinical trials are divided into three stages. Stage 1 clinical trials test the safety of specific substances and devices. Stage 2 trials test the efficacy of specific medications at different levels of doses. Stage 3 trials, often longer in duration and with larger samples, test efficacy at the chosen level of dosage between patients who do and do not receive them. Medicare funds these trials subject to consumers gaining access to them through specific nonfinancial eligibility procedures.

Many patients are reluctant to enter clinical trials because they view them as desperate, and usually ineffective, measures. They often view Stage 1 trials that test merely the safety of specific treatments, not their effectiveness, as unlikely to help them. They fear, as well, adverse side effects. They may be more willing to enter Stage 2 and Stage 3 trials because treatments are relatively safe and focused on measuring efficacy, although many of them also have adverse side effects. Nor are these reservations ill-considered because some medications that emerge from Stage 3 trials are approved by the FDA. Some physicians counsel some of their patients with advanced diseases that lack effective treatments not to "chase clinical trials," but to accept palliative care and enjoy whatever quality time that they have left. Moreover, some clinical trials are interrupted because researchers cannot find sufficient numbers of enrollees (Editorial, *New York Times,* 2010).

Other reasons for caution exist. Physicians who are reimbursed to administer clinical trials and to administer its medications sometimes have an economic incentive to persuade patients to join them. Consumers are often not given sufficient information to make an informed decision, such as possible side effects. Even when specific treatments are helpful to consumers, they may not be able to continue them when they have received all of the treatments in a specific clinical trial.

Even if many clinical trials do not cure specific health conditions, a positive case exists for participating in them. Some effective treatments *do* emerge from clinical trials as attested by the fact that many current treatments emerged from clinical trials. A few clinical trials are halted because tested treatments prove so effective that the FDA approves them before they have run their course. Some persons with terminal conditions participate in specific clinical trials to contribute to the development of new treatments, even if they do not benefit from them.

Medical treatments in some clinical trials may delay the progression of a medical condition even if they do not cure it, giving patients and families more time to come to grips with their medical condition and to make plans if the enrollee does not survive.

Enrollees who qualify for specific clinical trials agree to follow specific medical regimens. They have to qualify for financing from Medicare or other sources. They sometimes have to foot costs of traveling to the site of a clinical trial, as well as lodging costs unless they can receive financial assistance from specific charities.

Advocates can help consumers locate existing clinical trials by helping them use the National Institutes of Health web site that identifies existing clinical trials http://clinicaltrials.gov, as well as criteria used to determine eligibility for them. Advocates can help consumers develop questions to their physicians that obtain information about:

- Whether and why their current treatments are no longer effective—and whether EBM suggests that other approved alternative treatments, such as FDA approved medications, exist.
- If alternative approved treatments do not exist, whether they should consider exploring specific clinical trials versus receiving care that focuses on giving them quality of life for the remaining duration of their lives.
- What specific clinical trial is most likely to be effective and to not bring side effects that they would find harmful to the quality of their lives.
- What criteria will be used to determine whether and when a consumer may be required to exit a specific clinical trial.
- How to secure a second opinion about a specific clinical trial.
- Whether entry in a specific clinical trial precludes entering additional clinical trials.
- How to enroll in a clinical trial, how to finance it, and where to receive it.
- How to receive financial assistance with lodging and other expenses.
- How to receive help for any injuries that may occur during or after a medical trial.

Scenario 6.8: Advocacy to Help Consumers Who May Have Been Subject to Medical Errors

I have already discussed the sheer number of consumers who have been victimized by medical errors by medical staff, including incorrect medications, surgical mistakes, and inattentiveness to their medical distress. These errors can result in injury or death. They commonly experience stigma, guilt, and anger. Many healthcare workers believe that medical errors often lead to disruptive behavior by consumers (Tarkan, 2008). They can traumatize survivors and their families who often feel guilty that they did not detect them earlier or somehow contributed to them. A growing body of research indicates that victims of medical errors develop post-traumatic stress and other detrimental mental health symptoms (Azoulay et al., 2005; Delbanco & Bell, 2007; Lautrette, Ciroldi, Ksibi, & Azoulay, 2006). They are demoralizing to health workers.

Many health institutions have failed to admit their staff committed medical errors even after they have been discovered by medical staff or external investigators, such as the coroner's office or others. A culture of silence often exists (Smerd, 2007). They have sometimes tried to cover up these errors, even withholding or destroying information to avert litigation or adverse publicity. Some healthcare professionals do not share their concerns about incorrect medications because they are intimidated by physicians who order them (Tarkan, 2008).

A growing body of research suggests hospital staff should admit errors when they have been committed and apologize to victims and, if they die, to their survivors (Delbanco & Bell, 2007; Gallagher, Waterman, Ebers, Fraser, & Levinson, 2003). (The Sorry Foundation was developed to encourage health providers to be more transparent.) They should provide medical care to diminish the physical harm already experienced by consumers who survived medical errors. They should allow open-ended discussions not limited by time and interruptions.

The Patient Protection and Affordable Care Act of 2010 will penalize hospitals for medical conditions caused by error by cutting their Medicare and Medicaid reimbursements.

Advocates can help consumers or their relatives gain information about:

- How to discover if they, or a relative, has been subject to a medical error.
- How to gain an audience with medical staff and administrators to receive their response to a medical error.
- How to find legal counsel if the health institution has not been forthcoming.
- How to speak up when dissatisfied with a healthcare experience, from a guide at http://assertivepatient.org/.

Scenario 6.9: Advocacy to Help Consumers Use the Health System to Maximum Benefit

Providers often provide care that is effective in detecting and addressing health conditions, but that is compromised or made ineffective when consumers do not cooperate with it by keeping appointments, adhering to medications, or following lifestyle recommendations. Take the case of someone with Chronic Obstructive Pulmonary Disease (COPD) who does not keep regular appointments to monitor its progress, fails to take medications that can slow its progress, and continues to smoke two packs of cigarettes daily. These poor decisions may needlessly subtract years of life from this person's lifespan.

Other consumers jeopardize their health by exiting a clinic or emergency department *before* they are seen by health staff—a decision that jeopardizes their well-being if they possess a serious medical condition.

Several researchers have discovered that many consumers who leave while being seen (LWBS) had conditions that required immediate attention, were hospitalized within a week, or had a deterioration in their condition including 31% respectively with a deterioration of their condition and with development of a serious acute condition (Baker, Stevens, & Brook, 1991; Bindman, Grumbach, Keane, Rauch, & Luce, 1991; F. Bourgeois et al., 2008; Kronfol, Childers, & Caviness, 2006; Tamayo-Sarver, Hinze, Cydulka, & Baker, 2003).

Many patients do not keep appointments even when they have serious health conditions. This practice "disrupts continuity of patient care, delays treatment, and affects the doctor-patient relationship . . . deprives other patients of earlier appointments, reduces the efficiency of health systems, and increases healthcare cost (Chen et al., 2006). Patients who miss appointments are less likely to adhere to prescribed regimens (Haynes, McDonald, & Garg, 2002). Patients with low SES levels are least likely to keep appointments, as are consumers who have poor communication with physicians.

Case advocates should move toward policy advocacy by identifying reforms in their hospitals and clinics, as well as in the broader health system, which could facilitate consumers' behaviors to use medical services to their maximum benefit. Some health systems have had success in cutting LWBS in ERs by giving patients some treatment during their waits, such as ice bags to ease their pain or by asking patients at the conclusion of their appointments if all their questions had been addressed, summarized the services they had been provided, and addressed patient concerns.

Reminder notices substantially increase the extent consumers keep appointments (Chen et al., 2006; Lazebnik & O'Brien et al., 1998).

Patients prematurely exit ERs for many reasons including long waits, overcrowding, patients' lack of insurance, poor treatment by medical staff, or being too sick, tired, or in pain to wait (Arendt, Sadotsky, Weaver, Brent, & Boie, 2003; Hobbs, Kunzman, Tandberg, & Sklar, 2000). African-American and Hispanic patients are more likely to LBWS than Caucasian patients (F. Bourgeois et al., 2008).

The Patient Protection and Affordable Care Act of 2010 will provide subsidies to hospitals to allow them to increase the capacity of their ERs and trauma centers.

Case advocates can help specific patients not LWBS, keep appointments, and adhere to treatments by:

- Triaging them to find ones most likely to be harmed by noncooperation, including asking them if they would rate their health needs as serious in ERs.

- Asking patients who leave ERs prematurely, patients who miss appointments, and patients who do not adhere *why* they make these decisions—and then addressing the causes when possible.
- Offering to expedite services for ones who LBWS.
- Attempting to reach patients who missed appointments, asking why they missed them, and acting as a troubleshooter to help them attend a rescheduled appointment—even seeing if transportation can be arranged by the health system.
- Sending reminders to patients who do not adhere, planning in advance, or seeking assistance from family members.

Scenario 6.10: Advocacy to Help Consumers with Diagnostic Tests

A remarkable array of diagnostic tests have been developed in the past decades, with many additional ones in the technology pipeline. These include *noninvasive* diagnostic tests that include scanning ones like X-Ray, MRI, mammograms, bariatric procedures, and PET images of specific portions of bodies or entire body scans. They include a large array of blood tests. They include sonar devices used to examine fetuses or blockage in carotid arteries. They include routine checks of heart, pulse, blood pressure, and lung function with use of stethoscopes and blood-pressure devices. They include electrical sensors, such as ones that measure electrical currents from the brain. They include tests of DNA from saliva.

Tests include, as well, invasive tests where physicians insert devices into consumers, such as catheters that examine blockages of specific arteries and veins or mini-cameras that take images of organs or blood vessels. They include mini-surgical devices that take specific tissues from consumers such as from intestines or the cervix. Invasive tests also include surgical interventions to obtain tissue that can be biopsied by pathologists.

Diagnostic tests often provide invaluable information. They alert physicians and consumers to the presence of specific health conditions, diagnose their stages of development, and determine their seriousness or aggressiveness.

Some diagnostic tests have negative consequences that need to be understood and evaluated before consumers submit to them. Some of them pose *physiological* risks by exposing consumers to toxic substances or radiation, such as full-body scans, radiation, and injuries from devices inserted into blood vessels or the body cavity. Some of them can cause infections, such as surgeries used to obtain tissue. Some of them impose financial burdens on consumers if they are not covered by insurance or managed-care plans. Physicians sometimes fail to seek needed tests, resulting in delays in proper treatment. Some result in unnecessary or premature surgeries and medications. Take the example of PSA screening from blood samples from males over age 50 that is widely used to detect prostate cancer. Males who have elevated levels when adjusted by age are often advised to agree to a procedure to collect prostate tissue, which is then biopsied by pathologists to determine if cancer exists and its location and likely aggressiveness as measured by the irregularity of the cancer cells. It is difficult to determine, however, the threshold of these findings that indicate that specific consumers will develop life-threatening cancer even if many experts agree that widely diffused cancer that is associated with very high PSA and Gleason scores merits some combination of surgery, radiation, and chemotherapy. Persons with less diffused cancer, lower PSA scores, and lower Gleason scores are at some risk of this cancer spreading, but most die from other health conditions. Relatively few men are willing not to receive surgery, radiation, or chemotherapy when they are told they have cancer, even when informed they are highly unlikely to die from it. Men receiving invasive surgery often develop such side effects as incontinence and impotence.

Screening often fails to help persons even with aggressive cancer because it develops so rapidly that it often is not caught by annual screenings and only after developing into a life-threatening condition.

Many experts contend that full-body scans to asymptomatic persons are more harmful than effective. They expose them to significant radiation while detecting few serious diseases. They often detect "false positives," such as dark spots that lead to invasive surgery to biopsy them, but rarely discover life-threatening cancer.

Some experts believe that asymptomatic persons should avoid many existing diagnostic tests, save for routine ones that examine blood cholesterol and other common indicators. An asymptomatic medical scientist agreed with his primary care physician, for example, not to take a stress test for his heart even though his brother has serious heart disease and his father died from a heart attack on grounds it would trigger invasive diagnostic tests that would likely prove to be unnecessary.

Consumers need to carefully consider, then, whether and when to receive specific diagnostic tests. Physicians and hospitals sometimes do not inform patients of their minuses and dangers, as well as their positives, whether because they are not aware of the minuses or wish to obtain reimbursements for them.

Everyone agrees that routine diagnostic tests performed by primary care physicians are effective, but advocates need to help consumers ask these questions about nonroutine ones:

- Does the test expose consumers to physiological dangers when the probability of detecting serious illness is low?
- What proportions of persons who take specific tests avert serious injury or death because they took the test?
- What are the merits and demerits of taking or not taking specific diagnostic tests?
- What are the merits and demerits of "watchful waiting" in the wake of specific test results versus seeking invasive treatments like surgery, radiation, and chemotherapy?
- Refer consumers to MedLine Plus Information about recommended and nonusual screening tests http://www.nlm.nih.gov/medlineplus/healthscreening.html.

Scenario 6.11: Advocacy to Avert Premature Discharges from Hospitals

Consumers leave hospitals for many reasons and usually at appropriate times. They may no longer need service. They may not be able to find specialized care that they need. They may want to transfer to other institutions, such as when they receive reimbursements for nonemergency care from them.

Consumers may be discharged inappropriately, however. They are sometimes discharged from hospitals even while they are not medically stabilized, such as older persons, persons with trauma, or persons with strokes or heart disease. They may be discharged too quickly because of misdiagnosis. They may be discharged because health staff is under pressure to discharge them when they are uninsured for additional services at their institution. They may be discharged prematurely due to unruly behavior or prejudice among hospital staff.

State and federal laws, as well as legal rulings, place restrictions on premature discharges. After dramatic stories in the mass media in Los Angeles, where some hospitals discharged homeless persons to skid row areas even in their hospital gowns, California enacted legislation that require hospital staff not to discharge them before confirming spaces in specific shelters for them and arranging staff to meet them when they arrive. The Patient Protection and Affordable Care Act of 2010 will penalize hospitals that discharge Medicare and Medicaid consumers to the community only to have to readmit them because their medical conditions have not been adequately address.

The Congress enacted the Emergency Medical Treatment and Active Labor Act (EMTALA) in 1986 to impose civil penalties on hospitals that transfer medically unstabilized patients to other institutions, particularly because many private hospitals had transferred these patients to public hospitals when they were uninsured (M. Cooper, 1999). EMTALA guidelines can be found at: http://www.cms.hhs.gov/manuals/Downloads/som107ap_v_emerg.pdf. Specific payers give enrollees the right to appeal denials of benefits. Medicare enrollees can appeal denials of benefits, as well as determinations that they no longer need hospitalization (California Hospital Association, 2008).

Advocates may sometimes decide that specific consumers need to remain hospitalized for relatively short additional periods for mental reasons. Perhaps they are disoriented or traumatized from a medical procedure. Perhaps they need time to ready themselves for transfer. Perhaps they need more information about their destinations.

Hospital staff must follow specific guidelines for patients who do not want to be discharged, but who no longer need acute care (CHA, 2008, p. 9.21). Hospital staff need to identify possible causes and treat each case differently. They should be certain that they have met existing medical and legal requirements, which are discussed in more detail in Chapter 11. They should follow Medicare's requirements and those of all other payers. They should exhaust all strategies before resorting to available legal remedies (CHA, 2008, 9.21).

Some patients wish to leave hospitals even against their physicians' advice. California law allows them to exit the hospital if they are competent, but their physicians should inform them as to why they believe continued hospitalization is medically needed, the risks of leaving, as well as possible alternative places to secure treatment (CHA, 2008, p. 5.2). I discuss transfers to skilled nursing or intermediate care facilities in more detail in Chapter 11.

Advocates should determine if:

- Informed consent of consumers has been obtained.
- The consumers are medically stabilized.
- Transfer facilities are appropriate and have been alerted.
- The requirements of applicable payers have been followed with respect to a consumer's right to appeal denial of benefits for continued services.
- EMTALA and state regulations have been followed when making transfers.
- Transfer or release of consumers should be delayed for mental-health reasons.
- EMTALA guidelines are available from the Centers for Medicare and Medicaid services web site at http://www.cms.hhs.gov/manuals/Downloads/som107ap_v_emerg.pdf.

Scenario 6.12: Advocacy for Consumers from Vulnerable Populations

I have already discussed how vulnerable populations often do not receive optimal medical care because of prejudice and misperceptions of medical staff—not even considering how lack of access and resources may contribute to such care. Some members of vulnerable populations may wish to find physicians and health staff from their own ethnicity because research suggests they report better healthcare experiences with them (P. Chen, 2008a). Case advocates need to be aware that "because of the power dynamics between physicians and patients, questioning the expertise or skill of an authority figure is particularly fraught for the least empowered members of society (including) members of minority groups, immigrants, and non-native English speakers" (Delbanco & Bell, 2007). Many other groups can be considered "vulnerable" including women; physically challenged persons; persons with stigmatized conditions like HIV/AIDS, obesity, and COPD stemming from smoking; and persons with chronic health conditions. The Patient Protection and Affordable Care Act of 2010 provides resources to community clinics to allow them to help underserved populations, as well as to give insurance to 32 million persons uninsured persons—policies that will greatly improve access to healthcare by vulnerable populations including ones with low- and moderate income. They need to help members of these groups:

- Frame relevant questions about their care.
- Talk with providers about these questions.
- Seek second opinions.

- Gain support from other members of vulnerable populations from support groups or from online sources.
- Learn more about these issues from the UC San Francisco Center for Vulnerable Populations web site at http://www.cvp-sf.com/.

Scenario 6.13: Advocacy for Consumers with Co-Morbidities

Physicians are often ill-equipped to care for persons with co-morbidities that elderly, disabled, and minority consumers often possess. They often see specialists who focus on specific diseases. Most EBM guidelines only address single diseases (Boult et al., 2005). Insurance companies, Medicare, and Medicaid fund services for specific conditions. It is not surprising, then, that many patients with co-morbidities are treated only for a single condition, lack a lead physician who monitors care that they receive from multiple specialists to see if they experience adverse interactions between different medications and treatments, and helps them establish priorities. The Patient Protection and Affordable Care Act of 2010 creates a new Medicaid state plan option that gives federal incentives to providers of home-related services for consumers with two chronic conditions, including care management, care coordination, and health promotion.

Case advocates need to:

- Identify consumers with co-morbidities who are not receiving care for their multiple medical conditions.
- Identify consumers who see several or more specialists who give them different treatments and medications without examining adverse interactions between them.
- Help consumers identify a lead physician who coordinates their care.

Scenario 6.14: Advocacy for Consumers Who Have Received Poor Communication from Providers

A study found that consumers were asked questions in less than half of their outpatient office visits (Alper, Epstein, & Quill, 2004). Poor communication exacerbates LWBS, missed appointments, consumers' inabilities to make important health decisions, medical errors, lack of confidence in providers' decisions, and low satisfaction. Physicians and other health staff need to adopt consumers' perspectives (P. Chen, 2008b). They need to engage in active listening where they obtain consumers' narratives of their illnesses (Steiner, 2005). They need to view relations with consumers as partnerships (Alper, Epstein, & Quill, 2004). They need to use discourse that helps consumers see themselves as equal partners (Sumner, 2001). They need to "roll with resistance," affirm consumer strengths, and summarize treatment recommendations (Beitz, Forcehimes, Levensky & O'Donohue, 2007). They need skills in conveying bad news in ways that do not devastate consumers, yet provide transitions to palliative care. Effective communication is particularly needed with consumers from vulnerable populations (Betancourt, Green, Carillo, & Park, 2005).

Poor communication not only harms quality of care, but leads consumers to exit specific health plans and to abandon specific providers. It is caused by many factors, including lack of sufficient training in it, crowded work schedules, technological bias by some providers, medical elitism, and personality variables. At its worst, it can lead to bullying (see Vignette 6.2).

Vignette 6.2 Case Advocacy That Might Have Averted Bullying

Brooklyn Levine, MSW

We found out that my grandmother had melanoma that had metastasized to her brain in April. She was 89, about to turn 90 in August. The process of discovering the cancer, learning where it had spread to in the body and exploring treatment options happened so quickly that it was difficult for my family to fully process what was going on. The doctors at Maimonedes Hospital in Brooklyn, New York, were aggressive in regard to treatment. I remember a doctor bringing my dad, my aunt, and I into a room in the hospital to "discuss" what was best for my grandmother. He told us that we needed to treat the tumor in her brain with the gamma knife procedure. This is a single-day procedure involving a very high dose of radiation therapy. My first thought was echoed by my dad's statement, "What if we do nothing?" My grandmother hated hospitals, doctors, procedures, and anything else in the realm of medicine. She had once cast her own arm after breaking it from a fall down the stairs. She had only succumbed to going to the hospital when her fingers began to turn black, and that was purely for aesthetic reasons and not for pain management. My dad, my aunt, and I all knew that the worst thing we could do for my grandmother's well-being would be to keep her in the hospital any longer than necessary. But the doctor did not see "doing nothing" as an option. He was more than persistent that she needed to have the surgery in an attempt to manage any pain and to keep her alive longer. My father is a businessman and I have never seen him step down from a negotiation. It seemed peculiar to me that he could not argue with this doctor, that he could not articulate his gut instincts. I suppose that this man's title of "doctor" made all of us feel inferior, that despite knowing nothing about my grandmother he could somehow still know what was best for her. We felt cornered; there was no option but his. My grandma stayed in the hospital longer for the treatment.

My grandma died less than two weeks after the gamma knife procedure. I know we will never know if we made the right decision or not, but I also know that I feel tremendous guilt for not trusting my instincts. I know that not a day goes by in which I don't think about what might have happened if we had just let my

(continued)

grandmother die as she wanted to, without any medical intervention. I think about the pain we put her through because some doctor who knew her from a medical chart had made me believe that he was doing what was best for her and wouldn't give me and my family the room to trust what we knew would be best for her.

Learning Exercise

- How can you determine if consumers have been given real choices?
- Are consumers sometimes intimidated by providers?
- Do consumers sometimes suffer from guilt when they believe they didn't express their views sufficiently?
- Would EBM have supported use of this procedure?

Scenario 6.15: Advocacy to Help Consumers Improve Adherence

A review of 50 years of research on adherence covering 569 studies found that it ranged from 4.6% to 100% with an average of 75.2% (DiMatteo, 2004). Adherence can be improved by engaging consumers in family-based interventions like multifamily discussion groups and collaborative family-oriented primary and tertiary care (McDaniel, Campbell, Hepworth, & Lorenz, 2005; McFarlane, 2002; Weihs, Fisher, & Baird, 2002).

The well-being of consumers with chronic diseases often hinges on adherence to slow their progression and to decrease symptoms, yet adherence is diminished by the complexity of medication and other regimens as well as their side effects. Research implicates familial, psychosocial, and demographic variables causes for nonadherence, although different factors may influence levels of adherence to different parts of treatment regimens (W. Auslander & Freedenthal, 2006). Research implicates substance abuse, depression, and stress, as well as unsupportive relationships with providers, in causing non-adherence to drug cocktails used to treat HIV/AIDS (Chesney, 2003). Models of adherence counseling have been developed that include behavioral and cognitive components that enhance adherence among diabetics and HIV/AIDS that include assessments of family support, family income, family stressors, and family's ability to resolve conflicts (W. Auslander & Freedenthal, 2006). A four-phase adherence counseling strategy includes patient and family assessment, planning the treatment regimen, facilitating behavioral change, and maintain long-term adherence. The assessment phase includes assessing psychological factors including depression, anxiety, eating disorders, and substance use, health beliefs, and adherence history and satisfaction. The planning phase includes promoting a realistic medical regimen in a collaborative process with consumers and physicians. The behavioral-change phase includes helping consumers initiate new behaviors with specific goals and timelines, as well as activating support from family members. The fourth phase seeks to maintain consumers' adherences over extended periods of time including cognitive reframing so that consumers do not view lapses as failures and learn from them (W. Auslander & Freedenthal, 2006).

Advocates can enhance adherence by:

- Helping measure rates of nonadherence among consumers with chronic and life-threatening diseases, as well as consumers at risk of developing specific health conditions like diabetes.
- Developing psychosocial interventions that combine medical and psychosocial components.
- Securing resources and mandates for these interventions.
- Placing these interventions into place.

ONLINE MATERIALS RELEVANT TO THIS CHAPTER

Two additional scenarios can be found online at the web site of John Wiley & Sons at www.wiley.com/go/jansson. These include:

Scenario 16: Advocacy for Consumers With Respect to Personalized Medicine
Scenario 17: Advocacy for Consumers Who Probably Cannot Be Cured

PROGRESSING FROM CASE ADVOCACY TO POLICY ADVOCACY TO ENHANCE QUALITY OF CARE

I have discussed 15 scenarios that case advocates may confront in their work with consumers in this book, as well as two scenarios in the online materials for this chapter.

Select any one of these 17 scenarios confronted by consumers as they seek the quality healthcare that is discussed in this chapter. Switch from case advocacy to policy advocacy by selecting an *internal* factor that impedes quality of care within a specific clinic or hospital, such as a protocol, procedure, internal budget allocations, lack of knowledge or training, prejudice, or organizational culture. Also identify an external factor to a specific clinic or hospital that impedes quality of care in one of the scenarios such as a regulation, policy, reimbursement policies, or budgetary commitments from local, state, or federal governments.

Scenarios in This Book

- Advocacy for Consumers with Respect to EBM
- Advocacy for Consumers with Respect to Evaluating Physicians' Outcomes
- Advocacy to Help Consumers with Respect to Selecting Quality Providers
- Advocacy to Help Consumers with Respect to Second Opinions

- Advocacy to Help Consumers with Respect to Finding Information Germane to Quality-of-Care Issues
- Advocacy to Help Consumers Who Cannot Decide How to Proceed with Treatments
- Advocacy to Help Consumers Decide Whether to Participate in Clinical Trials
- Advocacy to Help Consumers Who May Have Been Subject to Medical Errors
- Advocacy to Help Consumers Use the Health System to Maximum Benefit
- Advocacy to Help Consumers with Diagnostic Tests
- Advocacy to Avert Premature Discharges From Hospitals
- Advocacy for Consumers From Vulnerable Populations
- Advocacy for Consumers with Co-Morbidities
- Advocacy for Consumers Who Have Received Poor Communication From Providers
- Advocacy for Consumers to Improve Adherence

Scenarios Found in Online Materials

- Advocacy to Improve Consumers' Quality of Care
- Advocacy for Consumers Who Cannot Be Cured

Advocacy to Promote Culturally Competent Health Services

COAUTHORED WITH DENNIS KAO, MSW PHD

The United States is currently one of the most diverse countries in the world. This diversity presents tremendous challenges to an already overburdened health system and increases the need for more culturally competent healthcare interventions. As discussed in Chapter 6, one important component of care quality is the extent to which services are being provided in a culturally competent or appropriate manner. This chapter focuses on strategies for helping consumers who may face difficulty finding or getting appropriate services in a healthcare system dominated by a Westernized or Eurocentric medical framework, including consumers with different cultural values, consumers who speak different languages, consumers who may be stigmatized by health providers such as gay and lesbian ones, consumers who prefer alternative medicine, and consumers with low levels of literacy. First, we attempt to define the concept of cultural competence[1] and present a conceptual model on how a case advocate can become more cultural competent. Second, we provide the demographic, medical, and legal rationale for providing cultural competent services. Third, we discuss the policies and regulations that govern cultural competency (and more specifically, linguistic competency) in the healthcare setting. Fourth, we present several common scenarios where cultural conflict may arise and how case advocates can help to address through the use of cultural competent services. Finally, we present ways in which case advocates could promote changes in broader organizational or government policies that would lead to greater cultural competency for their patients.

---

[1] We primarily use the term "cultural competence," which seems to be most widely used in the literature and policy circles. However, we also acknowledge that there may be some disagreement among healthcare professionals and scholars regarding which is the most appropriate terminology. For example, some individuals may prefer other terms, such as "cultural relevance," "cultural sensitivity," and "cultural appropriateness."

Ten scenarios are discussed in this chapter relevant to the cultural competence of consumers' services.

CONCEPTUALIZING CULTURAL COMPETENCY

Cultural competence is a broad concept that draws specific attention to the (sometimes nuanced) differences in the values, beliefs, or other cultural norms between two people with different backgrounds and life experiences. For example, the Office of Minority Health of the U.S. Department of Health and Human Services (Department of Health and Human Services Office of Minority Health, 2005) has defined cultural competency as "a set of congruent behaviors, attitudes, and policies that come together in a system, agency, or among professionals that enables effective work in cross-cultural situations." Unfortunately, how to be culturally competent can be difficult to define or to put into practice. The extent to which services are culturally competent can also be difficult to measure or evaluate. In developing its 2001 *National Standards for Cultural and Linguistically Appropriate Services in Healthcare* (simply referred to as the "CLAS standards"), the DHHS OMH concluded: "There currently is no agreement across healthcare professional specialties on what specifically constitutes individual cultural competence or how it is best measured" (p. xvii).

It begins with the inherent difficulty of defining culture. For example, Richard Brislin (2000) defines culture as the "shared values and concepts among people who most often speak the same language and live in proximately to each other [and] . . . are transmitted for generations, and they provide guidance for everyday behaviors" (p. 4). However, cultural values or concepts can arguably permeate every aspect of a person's life. In the health context, these values and beliefs also influence a person's perception and attitude toward his or her own health. Cultural differences can also complicate or diminish the quality of the interaction a patient or consumer has with healthcare professionals and more broadly, the health system. Theoretically, when there is cultural diversity, there is possibly the need for cultural competency. Of course, this level of need would vary with the extent of these differences and whether the quality of care received by the patient or consumer is compromised.

Language is the one small component of culture that is more straightforward and has garnered much attention. According to the National Center for Cultural Competence, linguistic competence is:

> The capacity of an organization and its personnel to communicate effectively, and convey information in a manner that is easily understood by diverse audiences including persons of limited English proficiency, those who have low literacy skills or are not literate, and individuals with disabilities. Linguistic competency requires organizational and provider capacity to respond effectively to the health literacy needs of populations served. The organization must have policy, structures, practices, procedures, and dedicated resources to support this capacity. (Goode & Jones, 2006)

Language assistance services could include: bilingual staffing; interpreters (in-person, telephone, videoconferencing, or other communication technologies); translated print materials; and community outreach or use of ethnic media in languages other than English.

Language barriers could also impact the healthcare experiences and overall health of individuals who may speak English well but have lower levels of literacy or not be able to use "printed and written information to function in society, to achieve one's goals, and to develop one's knowledge and potential" (Kutner, Greenberg, & Baer, 2006, p. 2). Based on the 2003 National Assessment of Adult Literacy (NAAL), an estimated 14% of U.S. adults (aged 16 years or older) could only accomplish "below basic" literacy tasks, such as obtaining information from a short, simple text (Kutner, Greenberg, Jin, Paulsen, & White, 2006). This includes more than one-third of Hispanics and one-fifth of African Americans. Immigrants also tend to have lower literacy than the U.S.-born population (Warkentien, Clark, & Jacinto, 2009).

It is important to note that even individuals who are relatively well-educated or well-versed in the English language may have difficulties in understanding the complex medical terminology. Therefore, it is reasonable to assume that an even greater segment of our population may lack health literacy, which is defined as "the degree to which individuals have the capacity to obtain, process, and understand basic health information and services needed to make appropriate health decisions" (Institute of Medicine, 2004). In fact, more than a third of the U.S. adult population, or 89 million people, have some difficulty dealing with health information (Kutner, Greenberg, Paulson, & White, 2006). Particularly vulnerable are older adults, minorities, immigrants, low-income populations, and individuals with chronic mental or physical health conditions (National Network of Libraries of Medicine, 2008; Weiss, 2007).

Beyond language issues, however, culture (the need for cultural competence) can be applied to a broad range of different groups and individuals and situations:

- Many minority groups may perceive the healthcare system with distrust or wariness. For example, African Americans and other minorities today may still encounter more subtle forms of discrimination or prejudice, which can still impact their ability to get health services (Institute of Medicine, 2003).
- Migrants who fled their countries to escape persecution, violence, or war and came to the U.S. as refugees may have a general distrust or fear of government— feelings that may flow into how they view the mainstream health system and providers (Segal, 2002).
- Different cultural groups hold shared behavioral norms such as a high respect for authority or fatalistic perspective, as found in many Asian groups, which may run counter to values inherent in the mainstream health system (Segal, 2002).
- Other groups may lack an understanding of U.S. medical practices or because of their tradition or religion, may simply prefer so-called complementary and

alternative medicine (or CAM) therapies, such as natural products, meditation, yoga, and so on (Barnes, Bloom, & Nahin, 2008).

- Other groups of consumers, such as lesbian, gay, bisexual, and transgender (LGBT) people or individuals with disabilities, are often stigmatized in the healthcare system and may encounter insensitive or incompetent healthcare professionals (Rainbow Heights Club, 2009; Stone, 2005).

For all of these groups, case advocacy to promote cultural competency during their encounters or interactions with the health system can assist in ensuring that they receive quality healthcare services.

The reach of culture can be quite broad. I hope to provide the reader with a brief introduction, but I acknowledge that it is an impossible task to cover every facet of culture. Others, such as Galanti (2008), Helman (2007), and Purnell and Paulanka (2008), have devoted entire books to exploring the role of culture in the healthcare setting and can serve as helpful resources to the case advocates interested in delving more into these issues.

WHAT IT MEANS TO BE CULTURALLY COMPETENT: A CONCEPTUAL FRAMEWORK

Adapted from previous literature (e.g., Campinha-Bacote, 2002; Doorenbos & Schim, 2004), we have developed a conceptual model to guide case advocates. It requires case advocates to become culturally competent themselves so they understand when specific consumers do not receive culturally competent services.

Cultural competency can be perceived as a process (or "road"), consisting of five major steps: self-awareness, respect for other cultures, cultural awareness, cultural knowledge, and cultural skills as illustrated in Figure 7.1. This process is an iterative one that is likely to continue throughout a person's career as he or she encounters patients of different cultures. This process is also unique for each person who comes with his or her own background and experiences. It also depends on the particular setting in which the case advocate works (e.g., the extent to which he or she is working with patients of similar or different cultures).

First and foremost, I argue that the case advocate must start by becoming more aware of his or her own cultural beliefs and values. The case advocate needs to be aware of the potential biases or prejudices that may be inherent in one's own cultural values or background. Problems or conflicts involving the lack of cultural competence are always two-way streets in healthcare settings and in everyday life. The potential for conflict exists whenever there are differences in the culture, values, or beliefs, between two parties. Case advocates must recognize that their perceptions of and attitudes toward other people may be heavily influenced and biased by their own cultures.

Second, after understanding their own cultural biases and prejudices, case advocates can begin to respect and become more open to different cultures. The Joint Commission

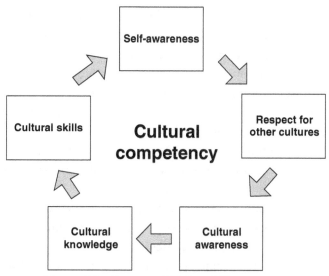

Figure 7.1   Process of Cultural Competency

(2009) mandates culturally competent services in its Accreditation Standards, by declaring that "the hospital respects the patient's cultural and personal values, beliefs, and preferences" (Standard RI.01.01.01, Element 6). This attitude of openness—coupled with the case advocate's own personal awareness—would reflect what Doorenbos and Schim (2004) refer to as "cultural sensitivity."

Third, case advocates must have an awareness of different cultures and the potential roles they can assume in shaping consumers' health. Consumers with different cultures and languages may also face tremendous barriers in accessing the healthcare system in the first place, have difficulty understanding and following the instructions given by physicians or nurses, and possess negative attitudes toward the medical system in general. Case advocates must also recognize that culture can have a significant influence on how consumers may view or even define their illness or condition—perceptions that can affect their decision making regarding the most appropriate treatment or care.

Fourth, case advocates must become knowledgeable of working with patients with different cultures and beliefs and the potential impacts on consumers' health and their medical decision making. Advocates' formal education and training may be helpful, but their ability to acquire cultural knowledge will be shaped by their own experiences and by their willingness to learn. They can begin with their own ethnic background because they already will have some knowledge about how to work effectively with patients of their own ethnicity. For this reason, hospitals and clinics should maintain a diverse staff that is representative of their patient populations. Case advocates need both cultural awareness and knowledge even to identify potential problems experienced by consumers.

Fifth, case advocates need to develop and hone a set of skills to allow them to work with consumers of different cultures and serve as intermediaries between them and the health system in which they work. These skills may be technical in nature, such as proficiency in another language, knowledge of medical terminology, or training in health interpretation. More commonly, more subtle skills would be required when case advocates negotiate or facilitate relationships between consumers and providers who may have difficulty in communicating or interacting because of cultural or linguistic differences. Nursing scholar Mary Ann Jezewski refers to the "culture broker" as one who resolves conflict and solves problems (Jezewski & Sotnik, 2005). In her research exploring this model, she found that the two most common strategies were mediation (i.e., where a person serves as an intermediary when conflict arises) and negotiation (i.e., where a person helps to reach some agreement).

Case advocates continually reflect on this process and seek to improve their self-awareness and awareness of other groups. Most importantly, armed with this awareness, knowledge, and skills, they may play a critical role in recognizing and helping others to recognize situations where specific consumers do not receive culturally competent care. Although no case advocate can be fully knowledgeable about all cultures or subtle nuances in the values or beliefs of each consumer, they can be proficient in understanding consumers' points of view by knowing which questions to ask. Medical anthropologist Geri-Ann Galanti (2008) argues that "culturally competent care is essentially patient-centered care" (p. 2) and proposes the "4 Cs of Culture" model (summarized in Table 7.1).

Case advocates should allow consumers to define their problems in their own terms as shaped by their culture. They need to understand how consumers perceive their problems through their own cultural lenses as a first critical step in diagnosing and bridging cultural gaps between them and the mainstream health system. They need to realize that some consumers can feel powerless when interacting with the mainstream health system.

Table 7.1   The 4 Cs of Culture

	Key questions
CALL	What do you *call* the problem? What do you think is wrong?
CAUSE	What do you think *caused* your problem?
COPE	How do you *cope* with your condition? What have you done to try to make it better? Who else have you been to for treatment?
CONCERNS	What *concerns* do you have regarding the condition? How serious do you think this is? What potential complications do you fear? How does it interfere with your life, or your ability to function? What are your *concerns* regarding the recommended treatment?

Source: Galanti (2008).

THE CASE FOR PROVIDING CULTURALLY COMPETENT SERVICES

In this section, I argue that demographic, medical, and legal factors require health systems, institutions, and providers to develop and incorporate culturally competent health services.

The Demographic Case

The United States has experienced tremendous rates of growth and diversification in the past several decades, much of it driven by immigrants coming from Latin America and Asia. With the exception of American Indians and Alaska Natives, the major racial and ethnic groups have experienced population growth, adding more than 20 million people since 2000. About half of the nation's population growth can be attributed to growth of the Hispanic or Latino population (see Table 7.2). From 2000 to 2007, the Hispanic population grew from 35 to 45 million, a net increase of more than 10 million persons. In terms of percentage change, Asians had a slight edge (30%), making them the fastest-growing racial group. By 2050, it has been projected the Hispanics will represent about 29% of the nation's population, while the percentage of Asians is projected to increase to almost 10% (Passel & Cohn, 2008).

Much of the population growth for the next 40 years will be driven by immigrants and their descendants. In 2007, there were an estimated 38 million immigrants in the United States, about 13% of the total population (U.S. Census Bureau, 2009). By 2050, it has been projected that about one in five Americans will have migrated from another country (Passel & Cohn, 2008). As the past decade has shown us, immigration is no longer confined to a handful of states, which have historically served as key immigrant gateways (Passel & Suro, 2005). Since 1990, the flow of new immigrants has slowed in

Table 7.2   Racial Distribution in the U.S., 2000 to 2007

	Population in 2000	Population in 2007	Population Change	Percent Change
Total	281,421,906	301,621,159	20,199,253	+7.2%
Hispanic or Latino	35,238,481	45,427,437	10,188,956	**+28.9%**
Non-Hispanic				
White	194,514,140	198,553,437	4,039,297	+2.1%
Asian	10,067,813	13,077,192	3,009,379	**+29.9%**
Black or African American	33,707,230	36,657,280	2,950,050	+8.8%
Native Hawaiian & Other Pacific Islander	342,743	401,932	59,189	+17.3%
American Indian & Alaska Native	2,091,206	2,019,204	−72,002	−3.4%
Other or multiple races	5,460,293	5,484,677	24,384	+0.4%

Sources: 2000 U.S. Census; 2007 American Community Survey.

states such as California and New York, while so-called "new growth" states, such as Georgia and Indiana, have seen a continually increasing share of the new immigrants.

These demographic trends have increasingly resulted in a tapestry of cultures and languages. This diversity presents significant challenges for federal, state, and local healthcare systems. In his book *Ethnologue: Languages of the World*, Raymond Gordon (2005) estimated that the United States alone is home to more than 300 different language or dialects. More significantly, health providers are encountering increasing numbers of Limited English proficient (LEP) individuals—or those who speak English less than "very well." In 2007, according to the U.S. Census Bureau, there were approximately 24.5 million LEP persons living in the United States, which represents about 9% of the country's total population. According to a recent national survey of hospitals, about two-thirds of hospitals now encounter LEP patients on either a weekly or daily basis (Hasnain-Wynia, Yonek, Pierce, Kang, & Greising, 2006).

Finally, it is important to note that there are significant subcultural differences within each racial and ethnic population and even within the same families as illustrated by intergenerational differences within each of them. Depending on how long they have lived in the U.S., immigrants may have varying levels of familiarity with U.S. culture and the English language—often referred to as the process of acculturation (Segal, 2002). Compared to their parents, the children of immigrants may be more adapted to the U.S. way of life—and their children will be even more adapted to it.

The Medical Case

Despite tremendous medical advances, health disparities continue to persist in the United States. Racial and ethnic minorities also continue to have less access to healthcare services. For example, between 2000 and 2005, minority groups saw no improvement, or even experienced poorer outcomes, across the majority of healthcare quality and access measures, such as effectiveness, patient safety, timeliness, and patient-centeredness (Agency for Healthcare Research & Quality, 2009). Compared to non-Hispanic white adults, both Hispanic and Asian adults were around two times less likely to receive timely care for an illness or injury. African Americans were more likely to visit but leave the emergency department without being seen, compared to non-Hispanic whites.

Unfortunately, racial discrimination and intolerance remain widespread but now assume more subtle forms. Minorities who face racial discrimination may be less likely or willing to access the healthcare system and tend to exhibit worse health outcomes, such as self-reported health or chronic conditions (J. Williams & Mohammed, 2009). In its 2003 report on racial health disparities, *Unequal Treatment*, the Institute of Medicine argued that experienced racial discrimination (real or perceived) can shape the expectations, attitudes, and behaviors of minority patients toward the healthcare system and health providers. One study found that compared to whites, African Americans tend to have less trust in their healthcare providers (Halbert, Armstrong, Gandy, & Shaker, 2006).

Minority patients who are treated by a doctor of the same race or ethnicity (as in a racially concordant patient-physician relationship) tend to be more satisfied with the services they receive, possibly due to perceived personal or ethnic similarities (Street, O'Malley, Cooper, & Haidet, 2008). Relatively few minority physicians practice in many settings in the United States (Reede, 2003).

Compared to the U.S.-born population, immigrants and their children are less likely to have access to health services (E. Brown, Wyn, Yu, Valenzuela, & Dong, 1999; Huang, Yu, & Ledsky, 2006; Ku & Matani, 2001; Leclere, Jensen, & Biddlecom, 1994). Some qualitative studies suggest that culture may powerfully shape interactions between many immigrant and refugee families and the U.S. health system. Ngo-Metzger et al. (2003) found, for example, that Chinese and Vietnamese immigrants often encountered negative reactions regarding their use of traditional practices and commonly felt disrespected and devalued by their physicians.

The inability to speak or understand English can also lead to less access to health-services and worse health outcomes. LEP persons are less likely to have a usual source of care, utilize fewer preventive services, and tend to be less satisfied with their health services (Carrasquillo, Orav, Brennan, & Burstin, 1999; Ponce, Ku, Cunningham, & Brown, 2006). Consumers' lack of linguistic and cultural competency can also lead to medical errors. In one study of six randomly selected accredited hospitals, for example, Divi and colleagues (2007) found that almost 50% of adverse events with LEP patients resulted in some physical harm (and in some cases, death), compared to only 30% of those with English-speaking patients. The majority of these adverse events involved communication errors, such as questionable documentation, inaccurate or incomplete information, questionable assessment of patient needs, and questionable advice or interpretation

Research demonstrates that access to health services is greatly improved with the provision of language assistance services. Pairing a patient with a language-concordant doctor who speaks the same language as the patient, for example, often leads to better health outcomes and overall patient satisfaction (Green et al., 2005). In the absence of the language-concordant physician, interpreters can facilitate communication between consumers and healthcare professionals, but research demonstrates that use of professionally trained health interpreters, as opposed to "ad hoc" or untrained interpreters that include untrained medical professionals, bilingual staff, and family members, is particularly effective (Flores, 2005; Karliner, Jacobs, Chen, & Mutha, 2007). Use of children as interpreters is strongly discouraged under federal guidelines and raises both ethical and psychological issues.

Persons with low levels of health literacy also face health-related challenges. Evidence strongly shows that health literacy is significantly related to both health and healthcare (N. Berkman, DeWalt, Pignone, Lohr, Lux, & Sutton, 2004). For example, persons with low health literacy are more likely to self-report fair or poor health, compared to those with higher health literacy (Kutner et al., 2006). This health disparity may be linked to their lower level of knowledge about diseases and risk factors, such as smoking, contraception, HIV/AIDS, diabetes, and asthma. It may also be linked to their underuse of preventive services such as mammography. Parents with low literacy may be less able to diagnose health problems of their children. Consumers with low literacy may be less likely to adhere to physicians' recommended treatments (N. Berkman et al., 2004).

Evidence suggests that many groups also face cultural barriers to health services (e.g., Ngo-Metzger, et al., 2003). (This research is mostly qualitative and descriptive in nature given the challenges of measuring culture.) Cultural differences may help to explain, for example, the distrust of Caucasian physicians felt by many minority patients (Santana-Martin & Santana, 2005).

Unfortunately, limited research examines the direct health benefits of cultural competency interventions beyond language assistance services (Anderson, Scrimshaw, Fullilove, Fielding, Normand, and the Task Force on Community Preventive Services, 2003; Beach et al., 2005; Brach & Fraserirector, 2000). L. Anderson et al. (2003) conducted a systematic review of five interventions (bilingual staffing, interpretation, cultural competency trainings, translated educational materials, and culturally specific healthcare settings) and found that there was too little research from which to draw any conclusions. There have been some promising results regarding the use of cultural competency trainings with healthcare professionals. For example, in a literature review conducted by Brach and Fraserirector (2000), the use of cultural competency trainings resulted in self-assessed improvements in communication skills and awareness among health providers. Similarly, Beach et al. (2005) found that there is good evidence that cultural competency training can have a positive effect on the knowledge, attitudes, and skills of healthcare professionals. However, while they also found some evidence of the positive effects of cultural competency trainings on patient satisfaction, there was little evidence as to their effects on treatment adherence and virtually no research addressing direct patient health outcomes.

The Legal Case

Healthcare systems and organizations are subject to a broad array of federal and state policies, as well as standards and guidelines, which deal with different aspects of cultural competence. For example, federal civil rights law requires that federally funded programs to provide meaningful access to LEP consumers; this virtually encompasses all hospitals, clinics, and other healthcare providers (including private physicians). The U.S. Department of Health and Human Services (DHHS) has issued LEP guidance (through its Office of Civil Rights) as well as the CLAS standards (through it Office of Minority Health). There also exists a complex patchwork of state-level policies, with each states passing their own policies dealing with linguistic competence. Accrediting agencies—such as the Joint Commission on the Accreditation of Healthcare Organizations ("Joint Commission") for hospitals and other health organizations and the National Committee for Quality Assurance (NCQA) for health plans—also have standards dealing with cultural and linguistic competence. In the next section, we elaborate more on some of these policies and regulations governing cultural competency, particularly linguistic competency in the health-care setting.

Providers may also be financially liable for damages when failing to provide culturally competent services, particularly language assistance services. For example, in an Oregon court case, the lack of interactive interpretation services resulted in one LEP patient being awarded $350,000 (Carbone, Gorrie, & Oliver, 2003). The plaintiff was working at a construction site and was using a nail gun when a piece of metal struck his eye. At an urgent care center, the examining physician used a telephone interpreter, but the plaintiff was not included in the conversation and never spoke directly to the interpreter. The plaintiff claimed that he had tried to communicate his injury to the physician. According the medical records, the physician had diagnosed the injury as an abrasion to the eye resulting from a wood chip. The plaintiff's injury worsened and surgery was later performed to remove the piece of metal from his eye. However, the plaintiff's eyesight remains impaired.

Medical errors, which may come from the lack of linguistically or culturally competent services, can also result in medical malpractice claims. In addition, in the case of informed consent, physicians or organizations may be liable for damages if they fail to effectively communicate to their patients the available treatment options and potential risks (Perkins, Youdelman, & Wong, 2003). Moreover, when challenged in the courts, this was the case even if a LEP or nonliterate consumer signed the informed consent form, but did not fully understand to what they were signing. For example, Shenker, Wang, Selig, Ng, and Fernandez (2007) found that at one hospital in San Francisco, LEP patients were less likely to have a documented informed consent.

THE POLICY AND REGULATORY THICKET

To date, policies and regulations have been largely focused on addressing language barriers to health services—an important but somewhat narrow aspect of cultural competency. First and foremost, language is protected under the nation's anti-discrimination laws. Title VI of the 1964 Civil Rights Act provides the foundation for these protections:

> No person in the United States shall, on the ground of race, color, or *national origin*, be excluded from participation in, be denied the benefits of, or be subjected to discrimination under any program or activity receiving Federal financial assistance. (42 U.S.C §§ 2000d, italics added for emphasis)

"National origin" has been interpreted in the courts to also include an individual's primary language (Perkins, Youdelman, & Wong, 2003; Perkins & Youdelman, 2008). In other words, no one should be excluded from federally funded programs because of their inability to speak, read, or understand English. In 2000, President Bill Clinton issued Executive Order 13166 (EO 13166),[2] which reinforced the protections afforded to LEP individuals under Title VI and instructed all federal agencies and federally funded programs to provide "meaningful access" to LEP persons. Because most health providers receive some federal funding (e.g., in the form of Medicare or Medicaid), hospitals, clinics, and health providers have a legal obligation to provide linguistically appropriate services to LEP persons.

In response to EO 13166, there has been a tremendous amount of activity. However, the implementation of Title VI regarding LEP persons varies greatly across health providers—due in part to the tremendous flexibility in how organizations can comply with the requirements. In addition, the actual enforcement of Title VI is largely driven by lawsuits or complaints, so the burden really falls on those who are facing discrimination.

The DHHS Office of Civil Rights' LEP Policy Guidance—first published in 2000 under the Clinton administration but later finalized in 2003 under the Bush administration—requires that organizations take "reasonable steps to ensure meaningful access to their programs and activities by LEP persons" (DHHS, 2003, p. 47314). However, health providers are asked to conduct a self-assessment to determine the extent of their obligation to provider language assistance services, based on four factors: (1) number or proportion of LEP persons served or encountered; (2) frequencies with which LEP persons interact with the programs or organization; (3) the nature or importance of the programs or services; and (4) the available resources. Because agencies and organizations are granted tremendous discretion, coupled with a lack of enforcement, there is great variation in the level of accommodation or services LEP persons can expect when they walk into any given health facility. Nonetheless, the DHHS LEP guidance provides some "bottom-lines" (see Figure 7.2), which provide a good starting point for case advocates working with LEP patients.

Adding to the complexity is the multitude of state-level policies governing the linguistic accessibility of healthcare services at the state level. These policies range from the more comprehensive laws (that apply to all healthcare providers or state agencies) to more targeted laws for specific populations (e.g., women, children, seniors, or persons with disabilities) or programs (e.g., training for healthcare professionals, facility licensure, or health interpreter competency) (Youdelman, 2008). There is tremendous variation across the 50 states, ranging from states with more comprehensive approaches, such as California with more than 150 laws pertaining to language access, to states with fewer than 10 laws. Case advocates can find more information about their states' regulations and statutes by referring to several reports by the National Health Law Program at http://www.healthlaw.org (Perkins, Youdelman, & Wong, 2003; Perkins & Youdelman, 2008).

Most statutes, regulations, and litigation focus on provision of translation and interpretation services rather than provision of culturally competent health services.

---

[2] Executive Order 13166 was later reaffirmed under President George W. Bush's administration.

- Federal fund recipients should have written LEP policies.
- Recipients should offer interpreter services at no cost to LEP individuals.
- Recipients should ascertain language needs at the earliest opportunity.
- Recipients should have a system for tracking LEP clients and client needs.
- Recipients should identify a single individual or department that will be responsible for the provision of language services.
- Recipients should identify the most frequently spoken languages in their service area and post notices of the availability of interpreter services in those languages.
- Family and friends of LEP individuals should be asked to interpret only after alterative, no-cost methods have been offered and the patient declines.
- Minors should not be used to translate or interpret.
- Recipients should ensure the availability of interpreters so that healthcare is not denied or unreasonably delayed.
- Interpreters should be qualified, with demonstrated proficiency in both English and the other language, knowledge of specialized terms and concepts, and the ethics of interpreting.
- Telephone translation services should be limited to emergencies, uncommon languages, and situations where there is no competent on-site interpreter available.
- Recipients should identify essential brochures, terms, and notices used by patients and provide written translation into the appropriate languages.
- Recipients should conduct community outreach to immigrant communities, and give notice to community agencies and referral sources about the facility's policies
- Recipients should assure their staff is aware of language policies and procedures and should have cultural sensitivity training programs for their staff.

Figure 7.2   "Bottom-Lines" from the Department of Health and Human Services LEP Guidance

Taken from: Perkins, Youdelman, and Wang (2003).

Aside from the largely symbolic gestures, few government policies exist mandating that health providers and services be culturally competent. The DHHS Office of Minority Health's (2001) CLAS Standards is an exception, because its combination of mandates, recommendations, and suggestions address cultural competence. Although Standards 4 through 7 reflect the current federal requirements regarding linguistic competency, the remaining standards touch on culturally competent care or the necessary organizational supports, but they are either recommendations (Standards 1–3 and 8–13) or suggestions (Standard 14) rather than mandates. Nonetheless, the CLAS Standards provide a useful framework for organizations seeking to improve the way they deliver services to consumers of different cultures.

Accreditation standards may have the greatest influence in how hospitals, clinics, and other healthcare provider organizations actually deliver their services because key accrediting organizations have recently engaged in significant efforts to reexamine and revise their standards regarding culturally competent services. As of this writing, the Joint Commission had released proposed requirements dealing with cultural competency and was in the process of seeking comments with respect to proposed requirements that will go into effect in January 2011 (Joint Commission, 2009b). More information can be obtained from the Joint Commission's web site. Similarly, in March 2010, the National Committee for Quality Assurance (NCQA), a not-for-profit organization that assesses and accredits health organizations and plans, also released its new Multicultural Health Care standards, which applies to health plans. Although its membership is voluntary, NCQA has a tremendous amount of influence in the field and health plans have a vested interest to be affiliated with NCQA. More information can be obtained from the NCQA's web site (http://www.ncqa.org).

The Patient Protection and Affordable Care Act of 2010 as amended by the Congress mandates enhanced collection and reporting of data on race, ethn.icity, gender, primary language, disability status, and underserved rural populations in 2012 to allow the Secretary of Health and Human Services to use this data to help identify and reduce disparities.

TEN SCENARIOS PERTAINING TO CULTURALLY INCOMPETENT SERVICES

The following discussion briefly presents some scenarios that case advocates encounter in their practices. Remember that single solutions or strategies for helping consumers who experience these scenarios do not exist because "while recognizing that there are many similarities among people from the same culture, it is important for healthcare providers to remember that each individual has a unique personal history, belief system, communication style, and health status" (Management Sciences in Health's 2004 web-based *The Provider's Guide to Quality & Culture*). Indeed, the first tip to promoting cultural competency is to recognize individual differences.

Scenario 7.1: Advocacy to Advance Effective Communication With Consumers

Effective communication is critically important to building effective relationships between consumers and physicians. However, health staff face significant challenges when communicating with consumers from different cultural backgrounds. Case advocates should understand that effective communication requires an understanding of cross-cultural differences in both verbal and nonverbal ways of communication (Jezewski & Sotnik, 2005). As a low-context culture, the United States tends to focus on the verbal part of communication (G. Liu, 2005). In contrast, high-context communication cultures emphasize "the physical or social context of the situation and relies heavily on nonverbal cues and identification or understanding shared by the communicators" (p. 79).

Styles of verbal communication may differ between different cultures, including the use of formal versus informal language, directive versus nondirective approaches, the level of conversational formality, and so on. (Galanti, 2008; Jezewski & Sotnik, 2005). Americans, for example, may value more informal conversations while other cultures may see the informality as a sign of disrespect. The use of titles, such as Mr., Mrs., Miss, and Dr., are all important signs of respect in some cultures. A direct manner of asking questions may be viewed as being rude or blunt among consumers from cultures that discourage assertive or aggressive communications. Even asking questions of consumers, like the 4 Cs questions in Table 7.1, may be viewed by some patients as being intrusive or too personal (Galanti, 2008). Greetings in the U.S. also tend to be short and are often simply gestures, such as a handshake at the start of a conversation (Jezewski & Sotnik, 2005). However, not taking the time to greet and engage in small talk may be perceived as a lack of respect or interest by individuals from other cultures, such as consumers from Chinese or Jamaican culture (G. Z. Liu, 2005; D. Miller, 2005). Vignette 7.1 provides a case where communication became a challenge, but also highlights how the communication styles in the same family may differ, such as by members of different generations.

Vignette 7.1 Advocacy to Improve Communication

As I sat with my mother in the crowded tiny clinic waiting room, I wondered why she had made me drive her for 45 minutes to receive medical services at a clinic that appeared dirty and that required a lengthy wait. I finally asked my mother why she had dragged me down to the middle of Los Angeles for her to see a doctor when there were perfectly good clinics and hospitals in the region where we lived. She quickly reminded me that there were few Spanish-speaking doctors and nurses in the hospitals near our home and the costs were much too high for someone with no health coverage. Although my brother and I had frequently played the role of translator when it came to my mother's communication between her and her doctors, she felt the need to speak directly to the doctor to truly convey what she was feeling. She expressed that she was tired of having to communicate her ailments through someone else and believed it was a major reason why she had not received the appropriate medical treatment that she needed. As our wait continued on, we suddenly heard my mother's name being called by the nurse who was admitting clients. We quickly gathered our belongings and made our way toward the nurse. While we maneuvered through the crowd toward the nurse, she began to verify the symptoms that had brought my mother into the clinic out loud in front of the other patients in the waiting room. Upon hearing the information being disclosed, I could see my mother shake her head with a look of embarrassment to confirm the reasons that had brought her into the clinic. She looked around to scan the crowd to see if the other patients had heard. It was clear that everyone had heard what was ailing my mother. Upon approaching the nurse I asked her if she was aware of her responsibility to maintain client confidentially and I openly verbalized my anger at the manner in which she had just violated my mother's privacy. My mother pulled me aside and asked that I stop challenging the nurse's authority as she did not want to upset her. I explained to my mother that I had every intention to file a formal complaint against the woman so that this would never happen to any other individual again. My mother asked that I do no such

(continued)

(*continued*)

thing as she felt it would make it impossible for her to return to this clinic again, which allowed her to pay a fee that was affordable while having access to Spanish-speaking doctors. I respected my mother's wishes and never filed a formal complaint. Upon leaving the clinic that afternoon I left with a sense of helplessness and frustration at my inability to protect my mother's right to adequate, affordable, and culturally competent health services.

Learning Exercise

- How would case advocates have to adapt their approach to a situation like the one in Vignette 7.1?
- How does this vignette demonstrate that case advocates have to begin with wishes of the consumer rather than proceeding without heeding their wishes?

Understanding cross-cultural differences in nonverbal communication styles, such as personal space, hand gestures, body movements, facial expressions, and eye contact is also critical to ensuring effective communication. For example, Asians may avoid eye contact as a sign of respect to their elders or individuals of a higher status, which often includes healthcare professionals. In contrast, American Caucasians often value eye contact because they believe it demonstrates that the listener is interested in what the speaker has to say (Jezewski & Sotnik, 2005). Many Asians are also taught as children not to question or disagree with someone who is of a higher status such as a physician; many Americans may interpret this behavior as demonstrating unresponsiveness or lack of concern. There are other differences: Though Asians seldom interject while offering verbal and non-verbal cues to encourage communication, Caucasians provide head nods and other non-verbal markers. Asians often provide minor delays when responding to questions or points, however, Caucasians often respond quickly. Often Asians will use low-key and indirect forms of communication, while Caucasians might use objective and task-oriented messages (G. Z. Liu, 2005).

Table 7.3   Differences in Communication Styles: Asians and Caucasians

Asians	Caucasians
Speak softly	Speak loudly/quickly
Eye contact avoided when listening or speaking to older or high-status person	Eye contact when listening or speaking
Seldom interject; offer verbal or non-verbal cues to encourage communication	Provide head nods and other nonverbal markers
Mild delay in response time	Quick response
Low-key, indirect communication	Objective, task-oriented communication

Source: G. Z. Liu (2005).

Advocates should:

- Follow the 4Cs in Table 7.1 in a tactful way.
- Be alert to verbal and nonverbal modes of expression.
- Involve consumers in case-advocacy strategy in order not inadvertently to lose their trust.
- Know your own cultural preferences so that you are self-aware as you engage in case advocacy with others.

Scenario 7.2: Advocacy to Obtain Interpretation Services

How your organization deals with LEP consumers should be outlined in your organization's LEP plan. More specifically, what happens when your organization encounters a LEP patient? Different procedures may exist depending on whether your organization has certain language covered by staff. If your organization has language capacity, then there may be procedures for contacting an interpreter or there may be a list of bilingual staff or interpreters who are on call. In cases when your organization does not have coverage for a particular language, you may be asked to utilize a telephone interpretation service.

The first step, of course, is identifying an individual's preferred language if not English. Given the multitude of languages and dialects, this sometimes can be a challenging task, especially if your organization rarely encounters individuals who speak a certain language. In some cases, the consumer may know just enough English to communicate what their preferred language is. There are also helpful tools for language identification. If the consumer is literate in his or his language, you may be able to use so-called language identification postcards or signs that allow the consumer to point to his or her language (see Figure 7.3 for an example). Interpretation telephone services also have prerecorded bilingual messages that will ask consumers to listen to a long list of languages and to push a button when their language comes up. If your organization encounters a certain language group often, it is possible that your reception area will already be set up to accommodate LEP consumers speaking that language such as with a bilingual receptionist and translated signage.

At any hospital or clinic, consumers are entitled to free interpretation and should be informed of this right. Ideally, interpretative services should be arranged beforehand, when the appointment is first set up to avoid unnecessary delays or lengthening the health visit. In some cases, after being informed of their right to an interpreter, consumers may ask if they could have a family member or friend interpret for them. However, it is important for an organization not to depend on patient's family or friends for interpretation. Organizations should not use minor children as interpreters.

Communicating through an interpreter can also be challenging for those healthcare professionals and other staff not accustomed to doing so. The Management Sciences in Health (2004) offers some helpful guidelines:

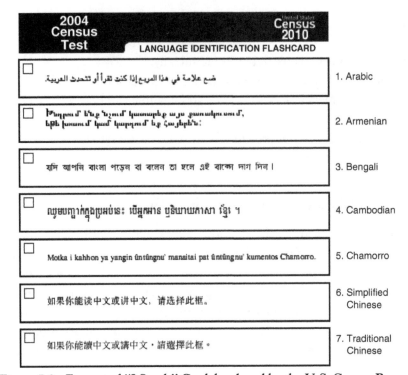

Figure 7.3   Excerpt of "I Speak" Card developed by the U.S. Census Bureau

Source: Federal Interagency Working Group on Limited English Proficiency (http://www.lep.gov).

- Hold a brief pre-interview meeting with the interpreter.
- Establish a good working relationship with the interpreter.
- Plan to allow enough time for the interpreted sessions.
- Do not ask or say anything that you do not want the patient to hear.
- Use carefully chosen words to convey your meaning, and limit the use of gestures.
- Speak in a normal voice, clearly, and not too fast or too loudly.
- Avoid jargon and technical terms.
- Keep your utterances short, pausing to permit the interpretation.
- Ask only one question at a time.
- Expect the interpreter to interrupt when necessary for clarification.
- Expect the interpreter to take notes if things get complicated.
- Be prepared to repeat yourself in different words if your message is not understood.
- Have a brief postinterview meeting with the interpreter.
- Remember that the interpreter is not there (just) to interpret for the patient or to interpret the patient's language.
- Use a seating arrangement in which you, the patient, and the interpreter form the points of a triangle.

In some cases, patients may not feel comfortable with using an interpreter and have "strong reservations about airing family problems to an outsider" (Kim-Rupnow, 2005, p. 129). Therefore, when a patient's family or friend is interpreting, it is important to check whether the messages are clearly understood. You may ask the family member or friend to repeat the message back in English and encourage them to ask for clarification for anything they may not understand.

Scenario 7.3: Advocacy for Persons With Limited Health Literacy

Health literacy continues to be a growing concern as medical tests and treatments become increasingly more complex. More than a third (36%) of U.S. adults have limited health literacy, which could mean they have a poor understanding of medical terminology (e.g., screening, bowel, tumor) or more generally, healthcare concepts (e.g., the proper use of an asthma inhaler) (Weiss, 2007). Given the complexity of medical terminology and health information, even well-educated individuals may have trouble fully understanding everything their physicians are telling them. Some patients with limited health literacy will not "understand when their next appointment was scheduled" (Weiss, 2007, p. 12). More disturbingly, most patients with limited health literacy will "misinterpret warnings on prescription labels" (p. 12) or will not fully understand a Medicaid application.

It may be difficult to identify who has limited health literacy, especially given that such individuals often may feel ashamed and try to hide their limitations (Weiss, 2007). Some key risk factors for limited health literacy include consumers from the following groups: the elderly; low-income consumers; unemployed consumers; consumers with no high school degree; members of minority groups such as African Americans or Latinos; recent immigrants; or consumers with English as a second language.[3] Certain behaviors, such as frequently missed appointments, noncompliance to treatment, or the lack of follow-up with tests or referrals, may also signal a potential situation where the patient has limited health literacy. In many cases, literacy-related questions added to the social history or initial assessment can help to determine a consumer's health literacy. Contrary to what one might think, evidence suggests many healthcare consumers do not mind having their literacy skills assessed (Ryan et al., 2008). Their skills can be assessed in most cases by asking the single question: "How often do you need to have someone help you when you read instructions, pamphlets, or other written material from your doctor or pharmacy?" (Chew, Bradley, & Boyko, 2004; Morris, MacLean, Chew, & Littenberg, 2006). At the very least, you may be able to identify patients who may need some further assistance.

---

[3] LEP persons are included within the broader population of persons with limited health literacy and therefore, many of these strategies would also be applicable to working with LEP patients.

Table 7.4   Strategies to Address the Needs of Patients With Limited Health Literacy

Goal	Examples of Strategies
Making your practice patient-friendly	Exhibit a general attitude of helpfulness. Use clear and easy-to-follow signage. Help patients prepare for visits by asking them to bring all of their medications and a list of any questions. Provide assistance with completing forms. Provide forms in an easy-to-read format and in the patient's language. Review instructions for tests, procedures, etc. Provide directions to referrals. Routinely review important instructions. Provide handouts in an easy-to read format.
Improving interpersonal communication with patients	Slow down. Use plain, nonmedical language. Show or draw pictures. Limit the amount of information provider and repeat. Use the teach-back technique by asking patients to repeat back your instructions. Create a shame-free environment by encouraging questions.
Creating and using patient-friendly written materials	Don't provide too much information or try to cover everything at once. Limit content to what patients really need to know. Use only words that are well-known to those without medical training. Write at or below the 6th grade level, with one- or two-syllable words and short paragraphs. Test the user-friendliness of any created materials with patients. Utilize nonwritten patient education materials, such as graphic illustrations (pictures), audio recordings (tapes or CDs), video recordings, (tapes or DVDs), and computer-assisted materials.

Source: Weiss (2007).

In his guide for physicians, Dr. Barry D. Weiss (2007) offers some helpful strategies for addressing the needs of their patients with limited health literacy (see Table 7.4). These strategies fall under three primary goals: (1) making your practice patient-friendly; (2) improving interpersonal communication with patients; and (3) creating and using patient-friendly written materials. Case advocates can play a critical role in promoting many of these strategies or practices in their health settings.

Advocates can:

- Assess consumers' health literacy often with one or several simple questions.
- Assess whether they do not understand important information essential to their giving informed consent.
- Assess if they understand treatment or prevention recommendations of physicians.
- Create an atmosphere where consumers who lack understanding of key information do not feel belittled or ashamed.
- Develop and use consumer-friendly informational materials.

Scenario 7.4: Advocacy to Promote Culturally Competent Relationships Between Health Staff and Consumers

Differences in cultural values and backgrounds may present significant challenges in developing a successful patient-doctor relationship. For example, there may be cultural differences in how individuals relate to healthcare professionals. In many cultures, it is the norm to respect authority, and therefore, never question a person in authority or of a higher social status. As mentioned before, many consumers may therefore be hesitant to question their physicians, nurses, or social workers, which can be mistakenly perceived as unresponsive or unconcerned. Even if they do not fully understand or agree, they may simply agree with all that is said such as by nodding their heads or answering in the affirmative. Whether intended or not, the relationship between physicians and consumers may become a didactic one. In these cases, it is important to ensure that consumers fully understand what is being said and to encourage consumers to ask questions. For other cultures, it is important for healthcare professionals to develop personal relationships with healthcare consumers as illustrated by "personalismo" in Hispanic or Latino groups (Galanti, 2008).

In some cases, promoting a culturally competent relationship may involve linking consumers with health-care professionals with similar cultural backgrounds. The research literature provides some evidence that consumers from minority groups may be more satisfied with physicians who share their racial or ethnic background (Institute of Medicine, 2003). Effective communication—even if it has been through an interpreter—can also be helpful.

Advocates can:

- Be attentive to the way culture influences the way specific consumers related to healthcare professionals when providing case advocacy.
- Factor information about culture into the way they engage in case advocacy with specific consumers, including the extent they do, or do not, encourage consumers to be assertive.

Scenario 7.5: Advocacy to Develop Consumer Trust

Consumers need to trust physicians to have successful relationships with them—and such relationships lead to better patient adherence to treatment, stronger continuity with providers, and increased use of preventive services (Thom, Hall, & Pawlson, 2004). Many minority groups may view the health system with a significant amount of distrust or apprehension. Strong evidence shows that Africans Americans continue to face discrimination in the healthcare setting (Institute of Medicine, 2003). Refugees who fled persecution or conflict in their home countries, such as those from the Southeast Asian, African, and the Middle Eastern countries, may still have a fear or distrust of governmental or other formal establishments. Because of their precarious situations, undocumented immigrants may also be fearful of going to hospitals or clinics, seeking healthcare only when absolute necessary.

As discussed earlier, the process of cultural competence first involves becoming aware of one's own cultural beliefs and values, which includes how one's cultural background may influence how he or she perceives or interacts with individuals who may be different culturally. Discrimination or prejudice, whether explicit or implicit, still exists today and it would be naive to believe that the health system and its providers are immune to this social context. In its review of the health disparities research, the Institute of Medicine (2003) argues that

> Negative stereotypes about minorities, held explicitly or implicitly by physicians, can contribute to healthcare disparities . . . providers will selectively attend to and recall information that confirms their stereotypes, and will tend to allow such stereotypes to enter into clinical decisions regarding the diagnosis and appropriate course of treatment. (p. 172)

The case advocate can play a critical role in fostering consumer trust. According to Thom, Hall, and Pawlson (2004), the concept of "interpersonal trust" is "the acceptance of a vulnerable situation in which the truster believes that the trustee will act in the truster's best interests" (p. 125) and involves three key attributes of the physician: technical competency (as judged by the patient); interpersonal competency (communication and relationship-building skills); and agency (i.e., acting in the patient's best interests). They recommend a broad range of approaches, such as emphasizing mutual interests, ensuring good communication and patient understanding, sharing information, and accepting personal disclosures in an encouraging and nonjudgmental way. When the lack of trust is a result of cultural differences, the case advocate can play a cultural brokering role in helping to mediate or negotiate these differences.

Advocates can:

- Assume a cultural brokering role to enhance relationships between consumers and providers.

Scenario 7.6: Advocacy for Consumers With Different Cultural Perceptions of Health and Disease

Depending on their worldview, individuals may have very different perceptions of health or more specifically, their particular current problems. Individuals who adhere more to American culture may believe that problems can be solved through the use of science and technology while other cultures may believe that problems are essentially predetermined by fate and thus, cannot be changed by humans (Sotnik & Jezewski, 2005). For example, followers of Buddhism may be more apt to accept their health-related problems, such as a disability, simply as a predestined misfortune. In contrast, a disability may be perceived in Mexican culture as either an act of God or a punishment for one's actions (Santana-Martin & Santana, 2005). This more fatalistic perspective of health may often conflict with the values of many U.S. healthcare professionals.

Beliefs regarding the cause or etiology of certain diseases may also vary greatly across cultures. As Galanti (2008) argues, "most Americans believe that germs cause disease. Not all cultures share that belief, however" (p. 21). For example, many cultures believe that a person gets ill when his or her body is out of balance. In some Asian cultures, this is referred to as "yin" and "yang," which are loosely translated as "hot" and "cold" elements (not temperature), respectively. So, in order to treat someone, the goal would be help them achieve their body balance again—which is usually accomplished through food. In the traditional Hindu culture, a mix of food, minerals, and herbs may be used to restore balance between the three *dosha* (or elements), which relate to the different body functions: air (as in the respiratory system); fire (as in the digestive system); and water (as in the body's moisture). Other categories of disease etiology include: "soul loss" (i.e., when the soul has left a body or has been stolen), "spirit possession" (i.e., when a spirit has taken over a body), "breach of taboo" (i.e., when someone has done something that is culturally forbidden) and "object intrusion" (i.e., when a magical object, often invisible, has entered the body and is said to be causing the illness).

To address these varying cultural views, Galanti (2008) offers two recommendations for healthcare professionals: (1) "The treatment must be appropriate to the cause;" and (2) "We must not let our ethnocentrism blind us to the merits in the beliefs of other cultures" (p. 23). In other words, it is important for healthcare professionals to respect and accommodate different cultural beliefs regarding health and diseases. The extent to which a healthcare professional is able to accommodate a patient's belief regarding a certain condition may determine his or her willingness to follow through and adhere with recommended treatment regimens.

Helman (2007) writes about the importance of treating both illnesses and diseases. A disease is how the medical world may define a certain condition, the concept of illness reflects "the subjective response of an individual and of those around him to his being unwell" (p. 126). Illness reflects both an individual's experience and his or her interpretation or reflections of the meaning of that experience. For example, a patient may have questions such as "Why me?" or "Why now?" or "What have I done to deserve this?" Case advocates can play critical roles in ensuring that these broader questions are addressed with consumers.

Case advocates should also be aware that many cultural groups also have their own folk illnesses. For example, common illnesses in the Hispanic culture include *caída de maollera* (or fallen fontanelle, which may be diagnosed as dehydration), *empacho* (blocked intestine, which may include indigestion, constipation, diarrhea), and *susto* (soul loss, which is caused by a traumatic experience and may include fever, insomnia, depression, and anxiety) (Galanti, 2008).

Finally, it is important to also note that concepts or terms that we tend to use in the U.S. to identify or describe certain diseases or conditions may not exist in some cultures. For example, in their study of Cambodian refugees, J. Jackson and colleagues (1997) found that most Cambodians did not understand the translated expression for hepatitis B: *rauk tlaam* (which means "liver disease"). Moreover, most found the term to be meaningless and when the symptoms of hepatitis B were described to them, identified other terms, such as *khan leuong* ("yellow illness") or *ampeau* ("swollen stomach"). In some cases, certain medical terms may also have different cultural meanings. For example, in their study of Russian émigrés, Dohan and Levintova (2007) found that the term "cancer" is generally perceived as a death sentence. Moreover, telling this to Russian patients may cause them to become depressed and take away their will to live. The providers in their study suggested that the term "tumor" may be more appropriate.

Advocates can:

- Talk with consumers to better understand how they describe and view specific illnesses.
- Engage in cultural brokering in some cases to help U.S. health personnel better understand how consumers from different cultures understand their illnesses—and words or concepts that be useful in discourse with them, as well as words and concepts to avoid.
- Help other health personnel not be condescending to consumers from other cultures who use different words and concepts than are prevalent in Western medicine.
- Use materials written in ways specific to the consumer's culture, such as those listed at the Kalieda Health Libraries Culturally Specific Patient Health Information for Non-English Speakers http://library.kaleidahealth.org/resources/non English.asp.

Scenario 7.7: Advocacy for Including Families in Healthcare

The centrality of the family is an important norm in many cultures, which may be contrary to the U.S. culture where individualism and autonomy is more valued. For example, Santana-Martin and Santana (2005) argue: "possibly the most significant value of Mexicans (and those of most Latino cultures) is the value of *familismo* . . . Family comes first; therefore, if a major decision needs to be made, the immediate and extended family are involved in the process" (p. 171). They suggest that when possible, the family needs to be included in the interview or assessment. Consumers' families should be kept well-informed throughout the entire process. In many cases, family members will also want to be included in the decision-making process although it is important to let consumers determine which family members.

Advocates can:

- Include family members in advocacy strategy if consumers' favor this.

Scenario 7.8: Advocacy to Accommodate Religious and Spiritual Practices

Religion is an important (and often dominant) aspect of a person's culture. The Joint Commission's revised standards require that all hospitals accommodate the patient's right to religious and spiritual practices (Standard RI.01.01.01, EP 9). Unfortunately, as Galanti (2008) argues, "religion is rarely a topic of conversation in hospitals, but religious beliefs and spiritual practices are common sources of conflict and misunderstanding. Patients' exercise of their beliefs can result in amusing or even tragic interference with medical care" (p. 62). Vignette 7.2 provides an example of this conflict.

Vignette 7.2 A Mother's Religious Beliefs Conflict with Medical Science

Author: Frances Nedjat-Haiem, MSW, PhD

A hospital social worker received a referral to speak with a mother of a 3-year-old child who had been hospitalized with fluid on his lungs. The 37-year-old mother, Ayanna,* immigrated to the United States from Ethiopia while pregnant with her third child and gave birth to a baby with Down Syndrome. Baby Nishan* has been in and out of the hospital with multiple medical problems since birth. His mother Ayanna has not been able to care for him because of his extensive physical and emotional problems and placed him in a group home for disabled children since birth. Ayanna's Muslim faith and belief in God has helped her cope with the circumstances of her son.

At this point of the referral, medical staff asked the social worker to assist with obtaining informed consent from the mother for a surgical procedure to remove fluid from the Nishan's lung. Staff stated that Ayanna refused to give consent for this procedure and the child will not survive without it. Ayanna believes that Western medicine has intervened in her son's life from birth and that he would not be suffering today if "those Western doctors had not revived him. They should have just let him die." Ayanna goes on to say that her son would not have experienced such suffering if she had given birth in Ethiopia because they would have allowed him to peacefully die at birth. Ayanna loves her son very much and believes that he is about to die. Ayanna believes that Nishan spoke with her in a dream and told her not to worry about him because he will finally be at peace soon.

Medical staff explain that Ayanna has not been cooperative and, at times, has been verbally combative with staff. Staff explains that she does not understand that her child can survive as long as he receives this surgical procedure. They have consulted the bioethics committee and are planning to override her rights as a

---

* (Names have been altered to protect patient identities)

(*continued*)

(*continued*)

mother to make medical decisions for her child. In addition, they have contacted two security guards who are waiting outside the patient's room in the intensive care unit to restrain her if needed when they take her son to surgery. Ayanna strongly feels that the medical staff does not understand her beliefs and claims that they are prejudiced against her.

In this case, the social worker and the nurse involved in caring for baby Nishan worked together with his mother to evaluate the situation and improve communication between Nishan's mother and medical staff before taking the baby away. The nurse asked Ayanna what would help her feel better about the current situation. Ayanna asked if she could lead a prayer to help her and her son face the current problem. During this prayer Ayanna asked God to help everyone involved in caring for her son to understand her reasons for letting her son go. She hoped that everyone could understand her faith in God and the dream that allowed her to be at peace with the loss of her son. After Ayanna finished her prayer she was more open to listening to the urgency of the medical staff and signed the consent form, which allowed the surgeons to perform the procedure. However, during the surgery, baby Nishan stopped breathing and died.

Complicating this case was the assertion of prejudice and misunderstanding between medical staff and Nishan's mother. Medical staff had neglected to evaluate the mother's cultural and religious beliefs, which increased the intensity of an argument between them. The social worker and nurse together were able to de-escalate the conflict in this difficult case and build rapport with the mother who was obviously distraught over her child's circumstances. Making a connection with the mother eliminated the need to supplant her parental rights to remove the child for surgery. With a connection made before surgery, the social worker was able to provide supportive grief counseling with the mother for the loss of her child.

This vignette illustrates the important role that prayer can play in how one copes with disease or illness. For example, many groups, such as many African Americans, believe strongly in the use of prayer (Purnell & Paulanka, 2008).

Religion—the extent to which it influences a worldview—can also lead to differences in how a patient perceives his or her condition and consequently, preferences and decisions regarding treatment. Moreover, a person's religion may also dictate whether certain medical procedures or medications are acceptable. For example, Jehovah's Witnesses are not allowed to have blood transfusions. Healthcare professionals need to address or provide space for consumers' religious or spiritual needs, which may particularly be heightened during the time when they are ill. In some cases, it may be helpful to involve the patient's key religious figure (minister, pastor, shaman, etc.) (Galanti, 2008).

Advocates can:

- Understand and interpret to others how religious beliefs influence choices and wishes of specific consumers.
- Mediate when religious beliefs conflict with medical science.

Scenario 7.9: Advocacy to Incorporate Complementary and Alternative Medicine (CAM)

The use of CAM therapies has become increasingly more widespread. The National Center for Complementary and Alternative Medicine estimated that about 40% of adults were using some form of alternative therapies in 2007, the most common being nonmineral natural products (e.g., fish oil/omega 3, glucosamine, Echinacea, and flaxseed), deep breathing exercises, meditation, massage therapy, and yoga (Barnes, Bloom, & Nahin, 2008). CAM therapies were used to deal with a broad range of diseases or conditions, such as pain (back, neck, and joint), arthritis, anxiety, high cholesterol, and colds. As discussed above, consumers' uses of CAM is commonly tied to one's cultural perceptions of illness. For many minority groups, traditional medicines or practicies are an inherent part of their culture and traditions.

Case advocates need to promote a safe environment in which any discussions about CAM therapies are welcomed and encouraged. Many consumers may be wary or hesitant about informing their doctors or nurses that they are using CAM therapies. Healthcare professionals who are primarily trained in Western medicine may not be aware of CAM therapies and/or their potential utility, which may lead consumers to think or perceive that their physicians are not open to their use of CAM therapies. In other cases, patients may simply perceive their use of traditional medicines or practices as part of their daily lives (Mehta & McCarthy, 2009). This lack of communication can lead to potentially harmful consequences that may result from mixing herbal medicines and pharmaceutical drugs (Pagán & Pauly, 2005). Lack of communication can also lead to misunderstandings. For example, bruises resulting from the traditional practices of "coining" (where a person's back is rubbed with heated oil and scraped with a coin-like apparatus) or "cupping" (where cups filled with heated air are placed on the skin, creating a suction) may be mistaken as injuries (e.g., signs of abuse) or other diseases (Ngo-Metzger et al., 2003). Both practices are common in Asian cultures as a means to draw the illness out of the body. In the case of cupping, the heated air is believed to draw the "cold" out of the sick person's body.

Case advocates can gain some understanding of the various CAM systems and modalities, and help to educate their health provider colleagues. Certain practices are becoming more standard in the mainstream healthcare system as a way to deal with a broad range of conditions. For example, acupunture—a more than 2,000-year-old practice originating from China—requires national licensing and has been shown to be effective in treating nausea and vomiting, asthma, chronic pain, headaches, fibromyalgia, osteoarthitis, and so on (Mehta & McCarthy, 2009). Some practices, such as yoga, are now covered by insurance companies. Many cultures have their own traditional healers, so it is important to facilitate collaborations between the patient's doctor and traditional healer when possible (Galanti, 2008).

Advocates can:

- Discuss use of CAM with specific consumers in a tactful way to better understand how they view illness and cures.
- Encourage consumers to discuss with their physicians their use of CAM so they can better understand their approach to their illness.
- Recommend resources available from the National Center for Complementary and Alternative Medicine web site at http://nccam.nih.gov/health/.

Scenario 7.10: Advocacy for the Needs and Rights of Vulnerable Populations

This final scenario and discussion serve as a "catch-all" for the broad range of groups that case advocates could encounter. Hypothetically, cultural misunderstandings or insensitivity can affect any group that is in any way different from the mainstream health system, including the disabled, LGBT persons, women, and elderly persons.

In many cultures, the elderly are highly respected, so it is important for healthcare professionals to demonstrate that they respect them.

It is important to create an inclusive and encouraging environment for consumers who are often stigmatized in the broader community. LGBT persons may often feel stigmatized by the mainstream health system, for example. The Rainbow Heights Club (2009) provides five steps to providing culturally competent services to LGBT persons in the mental health setting, which may also be applicable and helpful for the broader health system. These steps are: (1) use inclusive language (e.g., the use of the term "relationship" as opposed to "marriage"); (2) be aware of subtle signals you may be sending; (3) welcome and normalize disclosures about orientation, identity, or relationships; (4) utilize knowledge about consumer sexuality in discharge planning (e.g., including partners in the process); and (5) avoid overpathologizing and underpathologizing specific consumers.

Many consumers with disabilities fear that they will be cast into a dependent role by the medical system rather than empowering them to lead fuller and meaningful lives. Frontline staff may assume critical roles in encouraging them not to become overly dependent on medical systems, or, at least, to develop other dimensions of their lives. Health staff should be sensitive to the terms they wish to apply to their health conditions, such as not using the term "disabled" or "disability" if they find this to be offensive.

Advocates can:

- Link consumers to healthcare professionals with whom they feel comfortable.
- Address nonmedical aspects of consumers' lives, such as how they are coping in their community and home environments.

- Develop advocacy plans that link them to community-based organizations and support groups when this seems advisable.
- Use resources from the Office of Minority Health web site at http://minority health.hhs.gov/ and the Centers for Disease Control and Prevention Life Stages and Specific Populations web site at http://www.cdc.gov/LifeStages/.

POLICY ADVOCACY TO PROMOTE THE CULTURAL COMPETENCY OF THE HEALTH SYSTEM

The legal framework provided by Title VI of the Civil Rights Act provides a strong foundation for case advocates seeking to promote greater cultural competency in their organizations and more broadly, within their local or state health systems. As discussed earlier, the DHHS LEP guidance provides sufficient "bottom-line" requirements that are applicable to any agency or organization receiving federal funding (refer back to Figure 7.2). For example, health provider organizations are required to have an LEP plan or policy, which details how the organization will ensure access to services to LEP consumers. The following is a checklist of key issues that may require broader organizational advocacy:

- Does your organization have an LEP policy that is continually being revisited and updated?
- Has your organization assigned a person whose sole responsibility is to implement the LEP policy and/or to coordinate interpretation services?
- Does your organization keep records of a consumer's preferred language?
- Does your organization typically ask individuals to bring their own interpreters to an appointment?
- Does your organization have dedicated health interpreters who are specifically trained in medical interpretation? How does your organization ensure the skills and quality of its health interpreters (e.g., testing language skills, medical interpretation training)?
- Does your organization continually train staff on its LEP policy and more broadly, cultural competency issues?

Because of its accrediting role, the Joint Commission probably plays a significant role in influencing how hospitals and clinics implement its services and programs. Case advocates should be familiar with the cultural competency standards. Once the Joint Commission finalizes its cultural competency standards (scheduled for January 2011), case advocates can play a critical role in assisting their organizations to comply with these new standards, but more importantly, to adopt procedures and practices that will lead to improved health services for their consumers. Similarly, under the revised NCQA standards, case advocates may play a role in advocating for better services for their consumers with certain health plans.

Beyond simply complying with policies, regulations, or standards, healthcare provider organizations, and, more broadly, health systems, have a vested interest in ensuring the quality and effectiveness of its services. Promoting the cultural competency of its services could help a hospital or clinic to reduce medical errors and malpractice claims, increase patient satisfaction, improve patient comprehension of informed consent for treatment, increase its market share in a continually diversifying population, and potentially decrease medical costs in the long-term (Goode, Dunne, & Bronheim, 2006). For example, by not adequately addressing health-literacy issues, the health system loses an estimated $50 to $73 billion each year (Weiss, 2007).

Like individuals, health provider organizations may also go through the process of cultural competency (refer back to Figure 7.1). Organizations need to also become aware of the extent to which their values (missions, goals, organizational structures, etc.) are aligned with principles of cultural competency and whether as an organization, cultural differences are respected. A National Quality Forum report (NQF, 2009) provides some useful principles for organizations seeking to promote cultural competency (see Figure 7.4).

After gaining self-awareness and respect for other cultures, organizations must move forward to develop its cultural awareness, followed by knowledge and skills. This organizational change or improvements can occur in seven key domains (NQF, 2009):

1. Leadership (e.g., diversity of all levels of leadership, organizational culture and policies).
2. Integration into management systems and operations (e.g., strategic planning, reward systems, and marketing).
3. Communication between consumers and healthcare professionals (e.g., interpreter services, translation, and health literacy strategies).
4. Care delivery and supporting mechanisms (e.g., physical environment, assessment tools, and linkages with alternative medicine providers).

Principle 1: Multilevel approach–Cultural competency should be viewed as a multilevel approach with assessments and interventions needed at the system, provider organization, group, and individual levels.
Principle 2: View as a process and continuum–Cultural competency should be viewed as an ongoing process of organizational transformation in a continuum from early to later stages of development.
Principle 3: Systems approach–Successful implementation of cultural competency initiatives to achieve high-quality, culturally competent care requires an organizational commitment toward a systems approach.
Principle 4: Diversity management–Addressing both organizational and clinical aspects in managing diversity and the needs of both a diverse workforce and patient population are important factors in culturally competent care.
Principle 5: Continuous improvement–Cultural competency should not be viewed as an endpoint but rather organizations should strive for continuous improvement.

Figure 7.4   Guiding Principles for Organizational Cultural Competency

5. Workforce diversity and training (e.g., recruitment, retention, and training).
6. Community engagement (e.g., outreach, community representation in organizational decision making, and community investments).
7. Data collection, public accountability, quality improvement (e.g., collection of patient information, documentation of cross-cultural complaints, and self-assessments of cultural competence).

Again, the process of cultural competency is an iterative one, where the organization conducts ongoing self-evaluation and is continually trying to improve and adapt.

Because primary language is protected under the Civil Rights Act, filing complaints could provide a vehicle for consumers (or organizations) to potentially push a healthcare provider or government agency to more adequately address their needs or the needs of LEP consumers in general. Complaints can be filed by mail, e-mail, or fax to the DHHS Office of Civil Rights (OCR; http://www.hss.gov/ocr), but need to be within 180 days of the alleged violation. The law ensures that the organization cannot retaliate against those who file a complaint (e.g., deny services). In some cases, case advocates may assist a consumer in preparing his or her complaint. However, doing so may be a conflict of interest, because it would require the case advocate to play the role of a "whistleblower" if he or she is currently a staff member of the organization. If a violation is found, the healthcare provider will be given a specific time period to correct the violation (or submit a plan of correction), or risk losing its federal funding.

Depending on where you live, there may also be local or state-level opportunities to advocate for policies or legislation that improves the cultural competency of the health system. For example, the federal government has matching funds available through Medicaid and State Children's Health Insurance Program (SCHIP) that states can draw down and use to directly reimburse for language assistance services, such as the use of an interpreter (Perkins & Youdelman, 2008; Youdelman, 2007). As of 2007, only 14 states are taking advantage of these matching funds and have created mechanisms for providers or interpreters to get directly reimbursed for providing language assistance services.[4] Other states are in the process or investigating or developing such a reimbursement mechanism. Beside funding, there are a broad range of different policies that can be pushed at the state level that would promote the cultural competent health services, including: licensing or funding mandates for hospitals, mandates for managed-care plans, interpreter competency requirements, improvements in state civil rights law, and policies that deal with specific services (e.g., prenatal care, long-term care) or populations (e.g., older adults or children) (Perkins & Youdelman, 2008). For more information on state policy efforts, please refer to the National Health Law Program's web site at http://healthlaw.org.

---

[4] These states include Connecticut, Hawaii, Idaho, Kansas, Maine, Minnesota, Montana, New Hampshire, New York, Utah, Vermont, Virginia, Washington, and Wyoming.

Local county governments may also play a role in addressing the cultural competency of health services provided by hospitals and clinics in their jurisdiction. For example, advocacy eventually led the Los Angeles County Department of Health Services (LAC-DHS, 2003) to form the Cultural and Linguistic Standards Workgroup, which was made up of LAC-DHS staff and community leaders and was charged to develop a set of principles and guidelines. This effort resulted in the development and release of LAC-DHS's *Cultural and Linguistic Competency Standards* in 2003.

MOVING FROM CASE ADVOCACY SCENARIOS TO BROADER POLICY ISSUES

Take any of the scenarios in this chapter and discuss rules, protocols, budgets, court rulings, and statutes that are relevant to one of ten scenarios.

Scenarios in this chapter are:

7.1 Advocacy to Advance Effective Communication With Consumers

7.2 Advocacy to Obtain Interpretation Services

7.3 Advocacy for Persons With Limited Health Literacy

7.4 Advocacy to Promote Culturally Competent Relationships Between Health Staff and Consumers

7.5 Advocacy to Develop Consumer Trust

7.6 Advocacy for Consumers With Different Cultural Perceptions of Health and Disease

7.7 Advocacy for Including Families in Healthcare

7.8 Advocacy to Accommodate Religious and Spiritual Practices

7.9 Advocacy to Incorporate Complementary and Alternative Medicine (CAM)

7.10 Advocacy for the Needs and Rights of Vulnerable Populations

8

Using Advocacy to Promote Prevention in Health

M any critics contend that the U.S. health system fails to provide sufficient preventive services to consumers. This failure, they contend, makes the health system unnecessarily costly and exacts a toll on many consumers who might otherwise have averted serious health conditions such as cancer and heart disease, as well as chronic diseases like diabetes, COPD, obesity, and congestive heart failure. This chapter discusses why the U.S. health system is remiss in providing sufficient preventive care, as well as specific policies, regulations, and services that have emerged with promising potential. I provide 12 scenarios that advocates may encounter when helping consumers obtain preventive care.

The Patient Protection and Affordable Care Act of 2010 as amended by the Congress will have major implications for health prevention. I discuss various barriers to prevention in the United States in this chapter—and then discuss how this legislation proposes to redress them from 2010 to 2020.

DEFINING PREVENTION

Theorists have traditionally distinguished among primary, secondary, and tertiary prevention. Primary prevention aims to prevent the emergence of specific health problems among persons who do not possess them, such as cancer, chronic diseases, and epidemics. Secondary prevention seeks to identify and treat health conditions early in their development to slow their progress or, if possible, to cure them. Tertiary seeks the same goals, but for more advanced health conditions. I illustrate the three levels of prevention with respect to diabetes. If primary prevention aims to help consumers avoid it by exercising and eating low-fat diets, secondary and tertiary prevention seeks to slow its progress by these lifestyle changes, as well as use of medications and other interventions by physicians and alternative medicine (Schild & Sable, 2006).

Prevention aims, then, to help consumers avoid, cure, slow the progress, or mitigate specific health conditions that would otherwise cause harm to them.

Prevention aims, as well, to help consumers suffer from fewer illnesses and live longer lives than would otherwise be the case, as well as compress morbidity into a shorter period near the ends of their lives. Prevention aims, too, to help people avoid debilitating neurological diseases that often occur later in life, such as dementia and Alzheimer's disease.

Prevention is not a panacea. No one can eradicate most illnesses or prolong life beyond some limit. As we do not die from some illnesses, we *will* die of other ones. Some health problems are difficult to prevent. Experts often disagree about best strategies and the cost-effectiveness of specific approaches. Some kinds of prevention carry risks with them.

Some theorists speculate that the human organism evolved in a hunting-and-gathering lifestyle that emphasized exercise, limited food intake, limited quantities of meat, and no dairy products. As anthropologist Richard Wrangham contends, "Once you had communal fires and cooking and a higher-calorie diet, the social world of our ancestors changed" (Dreifus, 2009).

It is often difficult to lose weight, improve diet, increase exercise, stop smoking, stop excessive consumption of alcohol, and stop use of harmful drugs, however. Consumers have to be motivated to change, break habits and develop new behaviors. They have to sustain the new behaviors for an extended period and possibly forever, surmount setbacks, and find physicians, self-help groups, family members, or friends who they trust for advice and support. Consumers have to accomplish all of these tasks to change their lifestyle.

It is difficult to change habits because it requires energy to change learned behaviors that are embedded in the neural patterns of the brain and often lead to repetitious behaviors. Often learned in specific situations, such as occasional smoking with friends, dysfunctional lifestyles often gather steam. They become even harder to curtail when they are supported by physiological addiction, as is often the case with smoking and drugs—or by genetic factors that predispose some consumers to specific habits such as eating, smoking, or use of some drugs (Ball, 2008). Yet people do modify habits, sometimes easily or sometimes after many failed attempts. They can outsmart them in many ways, such as removing ice cream from a refrigerator, substituting fruit for ice cream, avoiding situations that entice or promote bad habits like an ice-cream store, identifying "triggers" for bad habits, practicing new habits, finding rewards for new habits, tapping into their willpower, learning to ignore certain thoughts, remembering that occasional lapses can be corrected, and not succumbing to fatalism (Ravn, 2009).

Some consumers can change bad habits on their own because they are adept at some of these tactics. Others need help from a counselor or program that gives them structure, monitors their progress, comes to their assistance when they slide backward, and rewards them for success. Consumers can find support from family members or friends as they try to change habits.

Insurance companies often do not fund programs that teach wellness behaviors. They do not reimburse physicians for discussing these matters. They do not fund consumers' fees for wellness courses. Lacking sufficient reimbursement for these services, hospitals often do not hire sufficient nutritionists, physical therapists, and occupational therapists. It is often unclear which profession should take the lead in orchestrating lifestyle changes—and some of them are ill-prepared to provide these services.

THREATS TO HEALTH

Imagine a utopian society where everyone exercises, consumes low-fat foods, maintains sensible weight, and does not smoke. Pollution does not exist. No one dies in automobile accidents. Homicides rarely occur. Everyone has sufficient resources and lives in a relatively egalitarian society. Everyone has sufficient access to a healthcare system that emphasizes primary-care services, but also provides world-class specialty services. Assume, as well, that this society never engages in wars.

Even in this utopian society, however, some threats to health would still exist. Some of them would emanate from genetic factors, such as ones predisposing persons to specific diseases such as Huntington's disease. Neurological diseases of aging would likely exist, such as dementia and Alzheimer's disease. Threats to health from nature, such as radiation from the sun, could cause diseases like cancer. The aging process would give elderly persons higher rates of such diseases as cancer—and would eventually bring their demise at some unknown limit. Some of these threats to health could be addressed by the health system, such as helping persons detect illnesses at an early stage or manage them to slow their progression.

Far more threats to health exist in our society than in this utopia. Considerable research implicates environmental threats, such as pollution, toxic chemicals, and radiation; socioeconomic threats such as inequality, poverty, isolation, and poor housing; physical threats such as violence, homicides, unemployment, and accidents from automobile accidents; lifestyle threats such as poor diets, smoking, addictions like alcoholism, lack of exercise, clinical obesity, and insufficient leisure; mental health threats such as depression and psychoses; medical threats such as lack of sufficient access to primary care and health screening; exposure to medical errors, exposure to excessive radiation, excessive surgery, and adverse drug interactions; physiological threats such as high blood pressure or high levels of blood cholesterol or triglycerides; genetic threats that cause or predispose persons to specific health conditions; social threats such as homelessness and lack of good housing. Gender can be viewed as a health threat in several ways. Males live shorter lives than females, possibly due to some combination of genetic factors, as well as their greater disinclination to use the health system than women, as well as more deaths from homicides, work accidents, and military combat. (Women live longer than men even when they hold high-stress jobs.) Many women confront social and economic pressures when marriages end and when they earn lower wages than men—and they sometimes receive inferior treatment from the medical system. Persons of color, particularly African Americans and Native Americans, have lower life expectancies than the general population.

If these various threats contribute to their development, specific chronic diseases often make persons vulnerable to further health problems. A person with emphysema who is confined to a chair is more likely than other persons, for example, to develop health problems associated with lack of exercise. Poorly managed chronic diseases may rapidly develop into life-threatening and disabling conditions as illustrated by diabetes that often leads to loss of eyesight and amputations.

Persons who smoke, lack exercise, are exposed to medical errors, suffer injuries or death from automobile accidents, are clinically obese, are alcoholic, are members of a lower social class, possess chronic diseases, and are members of specific racial groups live shorter lives than other persons. These health threats exact other health tolls on consumers, including days spent in hospitals, number of visits to emergency rooms, absenteeism from work, and illnesses.

PREVENTION GOALS AND STRATEGIES

Consumers who experience these threats are often called *at-risk populations*. I describe the toll associated with specific threats to health, as well as the diseases caused by these threats. If consumers stop smoking, exercise regularly, cut serum cholesterol by 10%, and control blood pressure, the United States would prevent 328,000, 178,000, 133,000, and 68,000 annual deaths for a total of 707,000 lives just from these four health threats (Knight, 2004; Woolf, 1999).

Consumers with combinations of these threats are particularly at risk of developing health problems, such as consumers who both smoke and are alcoholic; consumers who are poor and reside in communities polluted with industrial emissions; and persons who are diabetic and clinically obese. Persons who smoke live 14 years less than persons who do not (Centers for Disease Control and Prevention, 2002a). Deaths attributed to alcohol use shorten lives by 17 to 30 years (Aragon, Lichtensztajn, Katcher, Reiter, & Katz, 2008, CDC, 2004). Persons who are diabetic and those who are severely obese respectively have life expectancies shortened by of 7 years and 8 years to 12 years. Persons who begin with a specific chronic disease are at risk of developing others, such as persons with heart disease and diabetes.

I depict at-risk populations with circles in the larger population. As in Figure 8.1, a multitude of at-risk populations exist—and many of them are linked to other ones as depicted by arrows that link different circles.

Prevention aims, then, to improve the well-being of the general population and to reduce the extra health burden experienced by specific at-risk populations and individuals. It is useful to view prevention as reducing excess illness and death—in other words, illness and death that would not occur if specific health threats were eliminated or mitigated or if consumers were given prompt and effective care for specific health conditions. If healthcare provided to African Americans was equal to that provided to

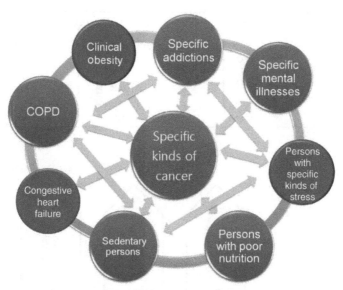

Figure 8.1   Linked At-Risk Populations

whites, the death of 886,202 African Americans would have averted between 1991 and 2000 (Woolf, Johnson, Fryer, Rust, & Satcher, 2004). Imagine the years of life that would be gained if preventive interventions were able to achieve a fraction of these reductions of death for each population of color, as well as each of the populations depicted in Figure 8.1, and each of the linked populations in Figure 8.1.

Considerable progress has already taken place. As the rate of smoking has declined during the past 30 years, for example, the incidence of lung cancer has declined among males since 1975 as have deaths from this disease (Jemal, 2008). Seat belts and front air bags saved nearly 18,000 lives in 2007 alone (National Highway Traffic Safety Administration, 2009). The development of a vaccine given to girls to immunize them from cervical cancer will likely cut deaths from this disease dramatically in coming decades. The death rate from heart disease declined by 56% from 1950 to 1996 due to the decline in smoking, the introduction of medications that reduce unhealthy blood cholesterol and hypertension, and changes in diet that researchers have linked to heart disease (CDC, 1999).

These successes have, however, brought new challenges to the fore. Most people died of infectious diseases, accidents, heart disease, stroke, liver disease, cancer, and senility in 1900—with 25% of deaths emanating from infectious respiratory diseases alone (Guyer, Freedman, Strobino, & Sondik, 2000; Knight, 2004). When life expectancy increased by 56% between 1900 and 2000, people died much later and from different causes including heart disease (29.5% of all deaths) and cancer (22.9% of all deaths). Medical errors, such as adverse drug reactions, became the fifth leading cause of death. Most Americans die in contemporary society, then, from diseases or habits linked to lifestyle—making prevention critical to health today (Hoyert, Freedman, Strobino, & Guyer, 2001; Knight, 2004).

We can conceptualize prevention as a flowchart consisting of primary, secondary, and tertiary strategies that each improve consumers' health over levels that would otherwise

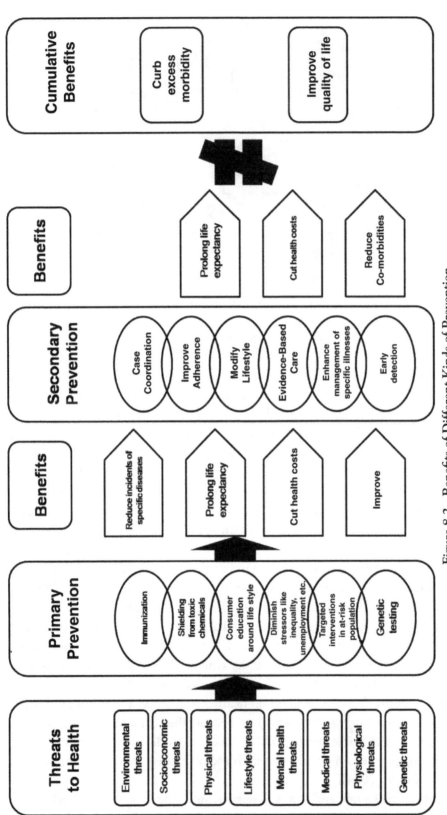

Figure 8.2   Benefits of Different Kinds of Prevention

exist (see Figure 8.2). Some primary-prevention strategies immunize consumers from specific viral and bacterial threats. Some shield consumers from toxic threats from pollution, toxic chemicals, carcinogens, and drugs. Some aim to educate consumers to terminate or reduce threats from unhealthy lifestyles. Some seek to end or diminish social and economic stressors like unemployment, poverty, economic and social inequality, exposure to violence, and discrimination. Some seek to reform the health system, and the way it is financed, so that it provides consumers with health education and so that everyone has roughly equal and adequate access to it. Some favor increased genetic testing so that consumers can seek to prevent specific diseases or health conditions that they might experience.

Primary-prevention strategies include:

- Health education so that consumers can improve their lifestyles whether provided in person or through the media.
- Sufficient access to primary-care clinics and physicians so that consumers receive health education.
- Provision of vaccines with proven effects in averting specific diseases.
- Genetic counseling.
- Counseling to motivate consumers to curtail unhealthy activities and practices.
- Removal of toxic substances from the environment including pollution, exposure to dangerous viruses and bacteria, and food poisoning.
- Providing neighborhoods with health-promoting amenities, such as grocery stores and places to exercise—while decreasing threats to health such as exposure to violence, poor housing.
- Out-stationing health services to locations like schools and jails.
- Removal of health hazards in occupational settings.
- Regulating activities known to produce illness and injury, such as smoking, use of some kinds of drugs, and riding motorcycles or bicycles without using helmets.
- Regulating and enforcing speed limits for motorized vehicles.
- Reducing medical errors through maintaining and enforcing standards of healthcare.
- Labeling foods so consumers can avoid unhealthy contents.
- Reducing social and economic inequality.
- Economic incentives to induce consumers to avoid health-endangering activities such as smoking.
- Fostering safe driving through law enforcement, safety regulations for motorized vehicles, driver training, establishing minimum driving ages, and incorporation of safety standards in highway construction.
- Quarantining of some persons with infectious diseases.
- Using medications that diminish health conditions likely to produce specific diseases, such as statins to prevent high blood cholesterol.

- Genetic counseling that determines the likelihood that consumers will develop specific diseases so that they work to prevent them.
- Helping consumers surmount mental problems that may cause specific health conditions.

Some secondary prevention strategies overlap with primary-prevention ones. Persons in the early stages of specific diseases need, for example health education to give them knowledge about lifestyle modifications that might slow their progress or even cure them. If they are shielded from toxic substances, their diseases may slow or disappear, such as when someone with early-stage asthma moves from a polluted to a nonpolluted area. Genetic testing may help them find medications and other health interventions that will particularly help them. They also benefit from reforms in the health system and how it is financed so that they have sufficient access to healthcare that they can receive early diagnoses and treatment of specific health conditions. They benefit from assistance in managing specific diseases and health conditions to slow their progress, such as learning to use specific medications or medical devices. They need access to screening for specific diseases, such as blood tests and imaging technology to discover health conditions at an early stage.

Tertiary prevention strategies overlap with secondary prevention with respect to health education, lifestyle modifications, genetic testing, reforms in the health system, and assistance in managing specific health conditions. Consumers need access to regular screening to discover when their health conditions have become less or more serious so that medical interventions can be recalibrated.

Secondary- and tertiary-prevention strategies include:

- Slowing the progress of specific health conditions through health education that fosters healthy lifestyles, removal of toxic substances from the environment, reducing social and economic inequality, and promoting health-inducing neighborhoods.
- Using screening and other early-detection strategies to identify consumers with specific health conditions, preferably in their early stages.
- Using imaging technology to catch health conditions at an early stage and to track their development.
- Using blood samples, biopsies, analysis of feces, and other biological products to diagnose health conditions at an early stage.
- Providing medical interventions that slow the progress of specific health conditions.
- Improving access to primary healthcare to help consumers detect health problems early in their development.
- Improving access to medical specialists who can diagnose and treat specific health conditions preferably in their early stages.
- Providing consumers with the means of financing the medical care.
- Helping consumers manage specific diseases to slow their progress.

- Using medical treatments to seek cures of specific diseases, preferably in their early stages.
- Genetic counseling so that consumers can learn what treatments can be tailored to their physiological make-up, as well as which preventive strategies.
- Health education so consumers recognized health symptoms often associated with specific medical conditions so that they can be diagnosed and treated in their early stages.
- Helping consumers surmount mental problems that may exacerbate specific health conditions.
- Providing in-home aides to consumers to help them manage specific health conditions.

Prevention aims to curtail excess deaths and illness at each stage of the prevention cycle so that cumulative gains are made at each stage. If primary prevention aims to prevent many diseases and health conditions from even beginning, secondary, and tertiary prevention aims to cure, slow, or mitigate them as they develop from early- to later stages of development.

WHY U.S. CONSUMERS PARTICULARLY NEED PREVENTION

The United States fares poorly when compared with such nations as Canada, Great Britain (U.K.), and Japan with respect to life expectancy, infant mortality, days annually absent from work, and incidence of major chronic diseases.

These differences in health outcomes in these nations are partly linked to different lifestyle factors. If Americans consume 97 pounds of beef per year, Canadians consume 69 pounds, U.K. residents consume 38 pounds, and the Japanese consume 21.3 pounds (Red Meat Industry Forum, 2007; Department of Agriculture, 2006). Homicides claim 5.2 Americans per 100,000 each year, 1.7 Canadians, 1.4 persons from U.K., and 0.5 Japanese (United Nations Office on Drugs and Crime, 2010). Large differences exist, as well, in injuries from automobile accidents. If 626 Americans per 100,000 are injured in automobile accidents each year persons, only 312 in England persons are injured per year per 100,000 people (Economist, 2009). Americans are more sedentary than residents of these other nations watching 8 hours of television per day as compared with 3 hours in Canada, 3 hours in the U.K., and 3.5 hours in Japan (Ramsay, 2008).

The United States has cut rates of smoking from 40% in the 1970s to 20% in 2007—a remarkable public health gain (Saad, 2008). However, roughly 30% of young people 18 to 24 years old still smoke, along with significant increases in the female population since 1950. About 87% of the 159,000 lung cancer deaths in 2008 were linked to smoking—with 444,000 Americans dying from the effects of tobacco in 2004 (American Cancer Society, 2009).

More than 10 million adults and 3 million children and adolescents suffer from alcoholism and its medical effects, which include brain damage and damage to other organs. It has many social effects, such as causing absenteeism, harming work productivity, causing spousal and child abuse, causing birth defects, and causing a majority of the nation's 55,000 annual fatalities from automobile accidents.

Other addictive drugs, such as cocaine and heroin cause such health problems as heart and respiratory problems, strokes, and premature deaths; 34.2 million Americans reported over age 11 reported having used cocaine in 2004 and 7.8 million reporting have used crack cocaine, which is injected rather than smoked. In 2008, 453,000 persons reported using heroin (Substance Abuse and Mental Health Services Administration, 2009). A large number of artificial or lab-created drugs have emerged in recent decades including PCP and methamphetamine. These drugs not only have medical side effects of various kinds but can lead to sudden death.

Many persons come to emergency rooms because they are inebriated or high. There were 548,000 visits to emergency rooms by cocaine users and 190,000 by heroin users in 2006 (Substance Abuse and Mental Health Services Administration, 2008).

Drugs have had dire effects on low-income areas. A vast network of distributors of these drugs has evolved since the 1960s. Fighting over turf, these distributors have often killed one another—and precipitated wars between rival gangs who have often become enmeshed in the drug trades. U.S. prisons are filled with persons convicted of drug-related offenses, particularly African-American inmates from 18 to 25, which have come to include growing numbers of women.

More persons have chronic diseases such as diabetes in the United States that are closely linked to lifestyle factors than in Canada, the U.K., or Japan. If 10.3% of persons in the United States have diabetes, 9.2% of persons in Canada, 3.6% of persons in the U.K., and 5% of persons in Japan has this disease (International Diabetes Federation, 2010).

Consumers at risk for one chronic disease are often at risk for multiple ones, such as the combination of diabetes and congestive heart disease. People with diabetes are twice as likely to have pneumonia, asthma, and 50% more likely to have COPD than people without diabetes (Ehrlich, Quesenberry, Van Den Eeden, Shan, & Ferrara, 2010).

The United States ranks only 45th in the world in infant mortality (6.2 deaths per 1,000 live births), while Japan ranks fourth (2.8 per 1,000 live births), Canada ranks 35th (5 deaths per 1,000) and U.K. ranks 31st (4.85 deaths per 100 births) (Central Intelligence Agency, 2009). One in eight babies are born prematurely in the United States, partly because many women do not receive sufficient prenatal care (March of Dimes, 2009).

Americans' relatively poor health exists even though it spends far more on health services than any other nation—in 2006 this amounted to 15.3% of United States GDP as compared to 10% in Canada, 8.2% in the U.K., and 8.1% in Japan (World Health Organization, 2009). Many children remain uninsured despite recent legislation.

No one has attempted to estimate the costs that Americans bear because of their burden of excess deaths and injuries, as well as preventable chronic and other diseases. The CDC estimates that 60% of visits to physicians' offices and hospitalization are due to disorders that can be prevented or delayed (CDC, 1998; Knight, 2004). Even in 2002, COPD was estimated to cost the United States $32 billion (Rogers & Shirey, 2002). Estimates for costs of treating diseases associated with smoking were $96 billion in 2009, $116 billion for diabetes in 2007, $147 billion for clinical obesity in 2008, and $475 billion for cardiovascular diseases in 2009. (American Heart Association, 2010; Campaign for Tobacco-Free Kids, 2010; Finkelstein, Trogdon, Cohen, & Dietz, 2009; National Diabetes Information Clearinghouse, 2008). These costs cannot be eliminated because no national prevention strategy can eradicate these chronic diseases, particularly as the life expectancy of Americans increases. Experts agree, however, that the costs could be reduced considerably if prevention became a national priority and if physicians used evidence-based medicine (EBM) to detect, manage, and treat these diseases.

BARRIERS TO PREVENTION

The United States has not implemented more prevention interventions for several reasons, including the power of special interests, the structure and financing of the U.S. health system, U.S. culture, and social and economic inequality.

Special Interests

Corporations have often blocked enactment of important prevention measures by lobbying politicians. Despite extensive research that links smoking to lung cancer, heart disease, emphysema, and many other diseases, tobacco companies and elected officials from areas that grow tobacco successfully fought for decades to stop Congress, as well as state and local legislatures, from regulating their products or restricting smoking. They also defeated legal initiatives by relatives of deceased or injured smokers from obtaining claims against them in court. Owners of restaurants, businesses, and bars often succeeded in blocking local regulations that would bar smoking in them in spite of research that linked secondhand smoke to lung cancer.

Legislation geared to reducing fatalities and injuries from automobiles has been slowed by opposition from U.S. automobile companies that delayed enactment of regulations requiring seat belts and improving crash safety standards. When the federal government developed fuel efficiency standards that promoted the manufacturing of small vehicles, it failed to require companies to make them safer during crashes, leading to many deaths of these owners when they had accidents with larger cars. The United States has failed to invest sufficiently in mass transportation partly because of opposition from automobile companies.

Manufacturers and purveyors of alcoholic beverages have often resisted efforts to place obvious warning labels on them or to curtail the number of bars in neighborhoods with a high concentration of them.

Manufacturers of foods and grocery chains delayed federal regulations that required food labeling. Fast-food chains only belatedly placed charts that displayed the contents of their food in places where consumers could access them—only in some cases to remove them altogether.

The medical industrial complex has succeeded in advertising many of their products directly to consumers through the mass media, even when this practice leads to overuse of some of them. These companies have often encouraged physicians to use their products by having salespeople visit them in their offices and by paying doctors for trips, conventions, and entertainment. Special interests, too, have promoted excessive use of some kinds of preventive services. The United States possesses, for example, 33 scanning devices (such as MRIs and PET scanners) per million persons as compared to only 12 in Canada per million persons—but Canadians live longer lives and have less infant mortality (A. Jackson, 2002).

Corporations have often opposed regulations to combat pollution by toxic chemicals, whether in the air, water, or soil. Only after many years have regulations and programs been initiated by state and federal governments to diminish various kinds of pollution—and only after they exacted a health toll on many consumers. Even now, many toxic waste sites have not been corrected. In places like Fresno County, California, toxic air pollution has led nearly one in three of its children to contract asthma (G. Anderson, 2007).

Chapter 2 discussed how organized medicine fought to circumscribe the role of public health in the U.S. health system, such as divesting its agencies and staff from giving inoculations on grounds that private physicians ought to provide them. Vestiges of this opposition still exist: the U.S. public health system runs on a fiscal shoestring with limited resources.

Many special interests, too, have fought against enactment of universal health insurance system, whether so-called single payer or one that subsidizes uninsured consumers to purchase public or private insurance such as proposed by President Bill Clinton and enacted by Barack Obama. Private insurance companies often feared they would lose revenues. Private physicians and hospitals feared their reimbursements would fall. Pharmaceutical companies feared that they would be subjected to federal price regulations—even as they sold many of their products at far higher prices than to such nations as Canada. The United States finally ratified legislation to greatly expand coverage in March 2010 with enactment of the Patient Protection and Affordable Care Act as amended by Congress, which is discussed in more detail later in this chapter, as well as in remaining chapters of this book.

Medical schools opposed federal regulations that would require them to train fewer specialists and more primary-care physicians when roughly three-fourths of American physicians are specialists as compared to over 60% in the U.K. Health insurance companies, as well as Medicare and Medicaid, reimburse primary-care physicians at far lower rates than specialists.

Powerful political interests have opposed efforts to decrease economic inequality in the United States even though many researchers contend that it causes low-income persons to be sicker and live shorter lives than low income persons in nations with less inequality. They oppose sufficient job training programs, as well as educational programs, to help low-income people improve their economic condition. They oppose enhancements of safety-net programs.

Private insurance companies, Medicare, and Medicaid have often not funded preventive programs well. Provisions in the health legislation enacted by President Obama and the Congress in March 2010 will require them to fund annual physical exams, as well as some other preventive services.

Structure and Financing of the U.S. Health System

These lifestyle differences are coupled with striking differences in access to primary-care physicians. Only 39% of U.S. physicians are primary care and fewer medical students are choosing primary care as a career (Kaiser Family Foundation, 2008b).

Primary-care physicians do not usually follow their patients into hospitals or engage in team practice with specialists. This disjuncture of patient care has profound implications for consumers' well-being. It increases the odds that side effects of surgery, adverse interactions between medications, and adherence to treatment suggestions will not be addressed or followed. When some health plans suggested this policy, they were met with opposition from many specialists.

Many experts hoped that managed-care plans would provide more preventive services than traditional medical arrangements for two reasons: they require consumers to access their plans through gatekeeper primary-care physicians and they have an economic incentive to emphasize prevention since they are funded by capitation rather than fee-for-service payments. Physicians in managed-care plans are no more likely, however, to provide many preventive services than other physicians (Pham, Schrag, Hargraves, & Bach, 2005).

Many uninsured Americans receive less preventive care than insured Americans. They often use ERs for healthcare rather than possessing ongoing relationships with primary-care physicians. They receive less healthcare per year than insured consumers— or $583 per year as compared to $3,915. Even for these services, they self-fund 35% of them as compared with self-funding by insured persons of 17% (Hadley, Holahan, Coughlin, & Miller, 2008). Between 35,000 and 45,000 uninsured persons die unnecessarily each year (Wilper et al., 2009).

American Medical Culture

Specialists possess extraordinary power in the U.S. medical system. They are reimbursed at higher levels than primary-care physicians. They focus on surgical interventions rather than preventive ones.

The residual position of prevention in the U.S. health system is illustrated by the disinclination even of primary-care physicians to prioritize it. Only 19% of these physicians discuss exercise with consumers, 22% discuss diet, and 10% discuss weight reduction. Only 4% encourage consumers to stop smoking, only 14% refer overweight persons to dieticians, and only 1% recommend exercise to overweight persons (CDC, 1998; Knight, 2004). Only 11% of the contact time of primary-care physicians is devoted to disease prevention—or 7 minutes per year on average (Knight, 2004;

Rafferty, 1998). Only 50% of physicians follow the National Cholesterol Education Program guidelines even with patients with high-risk coronary heart disease (Frolkis, Zyzanski, Schwartz, & Suhan, 1998; Knight, 2004). A survey of medical practice discovered that physicians give consumers only 54.9% of recommended preventive care (Knight, 2004; McGlynn et al., 2003).

Physicians sometimes discount the value of some prevention interventions that are ultimately vindicated by research. They have often used surgical interventions to remedy lower back pain, for example, when acupuncture is often more successful, less invasive, and less costly (Ratcliffe, Thomas, MacPherson, & Brazier, 2006).

Paucity of Funded Research and Approved Prevention Interventions

The federal government provides roughly $30 billion for health research by universities and other research centers, principally from the National Institutes of Health (NIH). Most of these resources are devoted, however, to treatment of diseases, with only 3% of national health expenditures devoted to health prevention (Knight, 2004). NIH funds research on alternative medicine but with relatively meager resources.

U.S. Culture

Americans work harder than residents of many other nations except for Japan, taking only 10 days vacation per year as compared to 17 days for Canadians, 24 days in the U.K., and 8 days in Japan (Expedia.com, 2009). Relatively affluent Americans may drive themselves occupationally to excess, but they possess vacation options not available to poorer Americans, such as second homes and resources to fly to vacation destinations. Many low-income Americans, such as single mothers often hold two or more jobs in their effort to earn sufficient resources to meet their survival needs. Some researchers contend that a lack sufficient leisure is detrimental to health (California Newsreel, 2008).

Residents of many other nations may be linked more closely to social networks than Americans partly because they often reside in locations where they were born and raised unlike Americans who are more mobile. Members of many other nations often possess social institutions that promote social networks, such as British pubs. Far more Europeans belong to trade unions than Americans.

Many Americans have a strong appetite for unhealthy foods. Forty-one percent of Americans eat at least once a week in fast-food restaurants. Among 18 to 29 year olds, 59% eat in a fast-food restaurant at least once a week (Pew Research Center, 2006). We have discussed how they consume more meat and dairy products than residents of many nations. Now many Americans have become addicted to television, with adults watching it for 8 hours per week compared to only 3 hours for adults in Canada, 3 hours in the U.K., and 3.5 hours in Japan (Ramsay, 2008). Television, as well as increasing preoccupation with games, texting, and social networks can promote a sedentary life style. The Patient Protection and Affordable Care Act of 2010 as amended by Congress will require disclosures of the nutritional content of food sold by chain restaurants and vending machine companies in 2011.

Occupational Factors

We have discussed how U.S. employers often give their workers few or no vacation hours—and sometimes support a culture that discourages workers from using even these hours. Workplace injuries are often prevented by federal and state regulations that require reducing levels of exposure of workers to toxic chemicals and unsafe equipment and machines, but corporations succeeded in shifting the burden of inspections and penalties from the federal Occupational Safety and Health Administration (OSHA) to state affiliates—and states vary widely in the stringency of their standards and monitoring. Corporations have aggressively lobbied state legislatures to loosen state regulations and to weaken enforcement.

Some corporations, such as the Safeway grocery chain and Microsoft, have implemented workplace programs that promote healthy lifestyles, but most corporations have not or have greatly reduced these programs that they began with great fanfare. Safeway contends it has held its healthcare costs at the same level for four years while other company's costs increase an average of 40% (Hook, 2009). Many corporations do not provide their employees with health insurance or provide meager policies that exclude many health conditions and require large out-of-pocket payments from employees, but federal health reforms enacted by President Obama and the Congress in 2010 will greatly reduce this problem.

The Congress enacted the Consolidated Omnibus Budget Reconciliation Act (COBRA) in 1986 to require employers to allow employees who have left their jobs to retain their health coverage at the rates paid by their former employers for 18 months. The legislation requires these consumers, however, to self-fund these insurance premiums, which places them out of economic reach of many consumers.

Social and Economic Inequality

The poverty rate in the United States is 17% compared to only 10.3% in Canada and 6.4% in Sweden. The child poverty rate in the United States is 22.4% as compared to 15.5% in Canada and 2.6% in Sweden (A. Jackson, 2002). Low-income Americans have access to less generous safety-net programs than residents of many other industrialized nations. Unemployment insurance pays only 14% of workers' prior earnings in the United States, for example, compared with 28% in Canada and far higher levels in Europe. Poor Americans are disproportionately uninsured as compared to counterparts who live in nations with universal healthcare, such as Canada, the U.K., and Japan.

When taken in tandem, these data suggest that low-income Americans are more marginalized economically and educationally than their counterparts in Canada, the

U.K. and Japan. They are poorer, less educated, and lack strong supports from safety-net programs (California Newsreel, 2008). They have lower rates of civic participation with voting rates of only 49.1% as compared to 56.1% in Canada and 83.2% in Sweden (A. Jackson, 2002).

Poverty and race intersect in the United States to cause poor health outcomes. Low-income African Americans have poorer health outcomes than low-income Caucasians (Kawachi, Daniels, & Robinson, 2005). African Americans die sooner, have more illness, are more likely to develop cancer, and are more likely to have chronic diseases. Relatively affluent African Americans have better health than low-income members of their race, but they often have poorer health outcomes than relatively affluent Caucasians (Kawachi, Daniels, & Robinson, 2005).

Some researchers have contended that Latinos appear to have escaped the nexus between race, poverty, and poor health in the so-called Mexican-American paradox. Mexican Americans have a life expectancy of 77 years for men and 83 years for women, for example—and this longevity, they contend, extends even to low-income Mexican Americans (Lee & McConville, 2007). Researchers conjecture that social factors, such as cohesive families and religiosity, as well as diet, may have caused these positive effects. Other researchers argue, however, that sampling errors may account for some of these results. They note that immigrants to the United States have better health than migrants who have resided in the United States for a considerable period, which would suggest that Latinos' health will erode as more of them reside here for longer periods. They also note that Latinos have been plagued by an epidemic of obesity and diabetes that already is eroding these positive health outcomes. If 6.4% of Caucasians are diabetic, 11.1% of Latinos are now afflicted with this disease (Office of Minority Health, 2009). Latinos also suffer from increasing rates of HIV/AIDS and heart disease (Lee & McConville, 2007).

Low-income persons often lack resources to purchase food to meet their needs. Many children in low-income families, for example, rely on school breakfasts and lunches for most of their nutrition. Persons who work two or three jobs often do not have the time or energy to exercise and may be sleep-deprived.

Community Factors

Many people live in communities that do not promote healthy lifestyles. Many low-income neighborhoods lack full-service grocery outlets, forcing residents to rely on small stores that have limited food choices and that charge excessively. Many neighborhoods lack safe places to exercise. Residents are exposed to high levels of violence in some low-income areas. Disproportionate toxic waste and pollution can exist there. Children who live near parks and who have access to public recreational programs are less likely to become obese, though access to these amenities may be limited in lower income areas (Dunton, Kaplan, Wolch, Jerrett, & Reynolds, 2009).

Intrinsic Challenges in Developing Effective Prevention Interventions

Public health researchers identify "at-risk indicators" for specific health problems as illustrated with the example of colon cancer. They try to find at-risk factors that predict who will, and who will not, contract this disease, such as family history, diet, and discovery of benign polyps in the intestine during colonoscopies or other tests. By comparing populations with and without these factors or combinations of them, they identify likely "true positives" who will develop colon cancer and "true negatives" who will not develop it. They may launch clinical trials to ascertain if different daily doses of aspirin lead to reduction in colon cancer in experimental groups as compared to control groups that take placebos.

Unfortunately, the ability to predict who will and will not develop a disease is often not highly accurate except in diseases completely predicted by genetic factors such as rare kinds of breast cancer or Huntington's disease. Some persons with a family history and benign polyps do not develop the disease—becoming "false positives." Still others develop the disease who have no family history and who do not develop polyps—becoming "false negatives." Researchers often cannot distinguish between true and false positives on the one hand and true and false positives on the other hand with complete accuracy.

This inability to make accurate predictions has important implications. Assume, for example, that clinical trials demonstrated that daily ingestion of two aspirins per day reduced the incidence of colon cancer significantly. If physicians recommended this dosage of aspirin for all consumers with family histories and benign polyps, they might help some of them to avoid the disease, but would also subject false positives to side effects from aspirin such as ulcers and strokes. They would also fail to give this remedy to false negatives, depriving them of the opportunity to reduce their risk of colon cancer. If they gave this dosage of aspirin to all of their patients, physicians would risk saddling many of them with ill side effects of aspirin even when they would not contract the disease anyway.

Some geneticists hope that a new era of personalized medicine will emerge where persons' genes will allow predictions as to who will and will not contract specific health conditions. Promising results have emerged, but this technology remains at an early stage of development. Not only do specific genes or combinations of them need to be linked to the development of specific diseases, but consumers must engage in specific preventive strategies to avert these diseases. To return to colon cancer, for example, scientists would need both to prove that specific genes or combinations of them led to the disease with a high degree of probability and to develop effective interventions to greatly reduce this probability that did not have adverse side effects. (Such interventions have not yet been discovered for Huntington's disease, Lou Gehrig's disease, and many other genetically determined diseases, such as breast cancer for women, with specific genes that will cause them to contract it.) Scientists, too, would need to find ways to genetically screen large segments of the population at costs that make this technology feasible.

Prevention becomes more difficult with fast-moving diseases like aggressive cancer. Even annual screenings often prove unable to detect these diseases in time to allow medical science to cure them.

A surprising number of reputed prevention strategies are based on correlation studies rather than gold-standard experimental ones. Experimental research does not exist, for example, to demonstrate that ingestion of red wine cuts heart disease, so medical professionals do not know with precision whether it prevents heart disease or for whom. A considerable time lag often exists between an intervention and improved health outcomes that might stem from a specific diet, physical regimen, herb, genetic interventions, vitamin, health education, proposed vaccine, medication, or surgical intervention. During this time lag, many other factors can intrude to influence health outcomes even if persons assiduously use a preventive strategy. This time lag also makes it difficult to conduct gold-standard experimental studies because it is difficult to retain subjects in their control and experimental groups for long periods.

Prevention Panaceas

Prevention is bedeviled by popular support for specific interventions that researchers have found to be ineffective. The health value of taking many vitamins has been questioned by many researchers, for example, along with many other prevention panaceas including vitamins A, C, and E as well as folic acid even though they are widely used (Preventive Services Task Force, 2003). Scores of articles have touted the life-extending powers of resveratrol, a plant compound in red wine, though scientific evidence based on experimental designs does not exist (Healy, 2009).

Specific medications used for prevention interventions have been found to have sufficiently serious side effects that researchers suggest they be withdrawn from use or used only with great caution and in special circumstances such as Zelnorm, used for irritable bowel syndrome that was found to raise the risk of heart attack and stroke. Zicam, a cold remedy, was found to lead to permanent loss of the sense of smell in some consumers. The cholesterol-lowering statin drug Baycol, was found to cause severe muscle breakdown that resulted in the deaths of 31 people.

Prevention Phobias

Americans often wrongly believe that specific activities or substances will harm their health in a pattern that distracts from actual health needs (Glassner, 1999, 2007). Some Americans had feared that even "plumpness" had adverse health effects when research discovered that such persons live longer than persons who are very thin (Flegal, Graubard, Williamson, & Gail, 2005). Some persons believed that living near electrical transmission lines would harm them when research discovered no ill effects (National Cancer Institute, 2005). Phobias distract attention from real or serious health threats.

Surgical and Medication Replacements for Prevention

Many consumers and physicians may use surgery and medications rather than engaging in prevention. About 145,000 Americans underwent weight-loss surgery in 2005, for example, even though one in five had postoperative complications (Freudenheim, 2005). Many Americans use medications to combat obesity that have serious side effects.

THE POLICY AND REGULATORY THICKET

Many policies and regulations, as well as institutions, have fostered effective preventive strategies in the United States. I touch on several of these in the following pages. I conclude this section with an analysis of the Patient Protection and Affordable Act of 2010.

Network of Federal and State Agencies

A Communicable Disease Center (CDC) was established in Atlanta, Georgia, in 1946 as a branch of the Public Health Service (PHS). Beginning with a focus on tropical diseases like malaria, the center evolved to a disease surveillance program that gained fame by its pivotal role in preventing polio and influenza epidemics in the 1950s, also adding prevention of venereal disease and TB to its mission. It played a key role in the eradication of smallpox and in tracking Legionnaires disease. It changed its name to the Centers for Disease Control in 1981 and then to the Centers for Disease Control and Prevention in 1992.

The CDC has many programs within it such as the National Center for Chronic Disease Prevention and Promotion; the Division for Heart Disease and Stroke; the Division of Cancer Prevention and Control; Diabetes Prevention Program; the National Breast and Cervical Cancer Early Detection Program (B&C); the Office of Public Health Genomics; the Division of Reproductive Health; and the Division of Adolescent and School Health. (Each of these programs has a web site that can be accessed through www.cdc.gov.)

These programs not only conduct research about the incidence of specific diseases, but mobilize coalitions in different states and tribes to promote and fund screening programs that are funded and implemented by states. The CDC often funds screening programs in various states, such as for low-income and uninsured persons who lack access to them. Among its own screening programs, as well as ones funded by Medicare, Medicaid, and states, it hopes to prevent up to 90% of deaths from colorectal cancer by identifying and removing all precancerous polyps (Collins, Marks, & Koplan, 2009). All states have screening and wellness programs in such areas as tobacco use, diabetes, breast and cervical screening, comprehensive cancer control, as well as the Behavioral Risk Factor Surveillance System, which surveys consumers and collects information on health risk behaviors, preventive health practices, and healthcare access primarily related to chronic disease and injury.

The CDC often issues reports geared to mobilizing action, such as *A Public Health Action Plan to Prevent Heart Disease and Stroke*. It helps fund a network of 33 Prevention Research Centers that fund collaborative research of community, academic, and public health partners with use of participatory research that seeks implementation of public health programs, such as the Enhance Fitness program to increase exercise by senior citizens at 300 sites in 26 states. It develops evidence-based prevention strategies, such as a study that found that type 2 diabetes can be prevented or delayed with moderate weight loss, improved nutrition, and greater exercise (Collins, Marks, and Koplan, 2009). It promotes programs, such as the Health Communities Program, that mobilizes action in local communities, including schools, worksites, and healthcare settings, to increase physical activity, improve nutrition, and curtail smoking to prevent chronic diseases. It targets women between ages 50 and 64 who are uninsured or underinsured in its Well-Integrated Screening and Evaluation for Women Across the Nation (WISE-WOMAN) to enhance lifestyle changes, as well as monitoring of blood pressure and cholesterol.

The CDC promotes early detection of public health issues in different states by helping them implement surveys of citizens that probe the extent they have such problems as obesity and specific mental health problems. It has initiated programs to gather data about links between genetics and chronic diseases that can be used in public health campaigns to target prevention programs to consumers at risk of developing them.

The CDC is often plagued, however, by insufficient resources with inadequate programs in such urgent areas as ones that improve nutrition, promote physical activity, and those that address heart disease, stroke, arthritis and oral health (Collins et al., 2008). Its highly successful youth media campaign to increase physical activity of youth between ages 9 and 13 had to be ended after five years because of a lack of funding.

The Department of Health and Human Services (DHHS) has developed many prevention programs not just in its Medicare and Medicaid programs, but many specific divisions and programs. Many public agencies research and promote health prevention, including the U.S. Public Health Service. The National Institutes of Health (NIH), which traces its roots to 1887, contained health-prevention units that focused on tuberculosis and venereal disease before they were transferred to the CDC.

The Center on Medicare and Medicare Services (CMS) currently administers the Medicare and Medicaid Programs. Medicare promotes prevention by covering immunizations; screening for cancer, cardiovascular disease, glaucoma, and diabetes; bone density measurement; and smoking cessation programs. It will cover additional prevention programs under the health legislation enacted by President Barack Obama and the Congress in 2010. Medicaid promotes prevention by covering smoking cessation, preventive health and dental care, prescription drugs, laboratory tests and X-rays, family planning and prenatal care. Coverage and services vary by state.

Officials in specific divisions and programs of DHHS promote prevention by funding research, including the Agency for Healthcare Research and Quality (AHRQ), Office of Disease Prevention and Health Promotion, NIH, and the CDC.

Specific divisions and programs of DHHS develop and provide funding to implement plans that promote prevention. For example, the Centers for Disease Control and Prevention developed *Healthy People 2000*, *Healthy People 2010* and *Healthy People 2020* that respectively established health and prevention goals for specific decades. Many of these goals, such as cancer, diabetes, heart disease, and HIV/AIDS were focused on in both *Healthy People 2000* and 2010. If *Healthy People 2000* also focused on clinical preventive services, surveillance and data systems, and violent and abusive behavior, *Healthy People 2010* focused on vision and hearing, respiratory diseases, medical product safety, and access to quality health services (CDC, 2009a). Surgeon General David Satcher launched an initiative to diminish health disparities in the United States with the 1998 Surgeon General's report, "Tobacco Use Among U.S. Racial/Ethnic Minority Groups" (Satcher et al., 2005).

The Public Health Service (PHS), which was formed in 1798, is administered by the U.S. Surgeon General, who is nominated by the President and confirmed by the U.S. Senate. Some surgeon generals have been particularly effective such as Dr. C. Everett Koop who issued on influential report on the AIDS epidemic in 1986 soon after President Ronald Reagan had decided to commit only $51 million to fighting it even as experts predicted it would kill up to 50,000 persons in a few years. In fact, it killed nearly 200,000 Americans and 336,000 Americans had been diagnosed with AIDS by 1992 alone (Osmond, 2003). He courageously advocated for a greatly enhanced federal role in combating the disease, as well as combating discrimination against its victims.

These programs, divisions, and plans that promote prevention are, unfortunately, a pittance of DHHS's funding of curative health programs. The federal government spends $452 billion for Medicare and $290 billion for Medicaid per year, for example, funds that overwhelmingly are used for the treatment of specific health conditions, surgery, and medications. Although the Medicare payments to primary-care physicians have been increased in recent years, primary-care physicians still earn only about half as much as specialists and the salary gap is increasing (Bodenheimer, 2006).

The federal Agency for Healthcare Quality (AHCQ) oversees and funds considerable research on prevention. It contains the U.S. Prevention Services Task Force that grades specific preventive interventions from "A" to "D" depending on their cost-effectiveness in preventing specific health conditions.

Regulations

Many regulations promote health by placing restrictions on unhealthy practices. Many local jurisdictions ban smoking in public places, which can include restaurants, bars, airplanes, trains, buses, and places of employment. Federal regulations require food labeling on many products that describes grams of saturated fat per serving, as well as salt and sugar. They require fast-food establishments to post the level of these ingredients in their food. Some local jurisdictions ban the use of partially hydrogenated oils in cooking French fries, as well as ending use of trans fats in fast food and other food establishments. I have discussed new regulations established for chain restaurants and vending machine companies established by the Patient Protection and Affordable Care Act of 2010 as amended by Congress.

Federal regulations have placed many restrictions on false advertising by tobacco companies, such as ones that claimed that filters or modifications in ingredients significantly curtailed the health risk of tobacco products. When different states successfully sued tobacco companies for medical costs they incurred for lung cancer and other diseases linked to smoking, tobacco companies made huge monetary settlements with the states, which states used to run public-service advertisements warning residents of health hazards from smoking.

A breakthrough took place in summer 2009 when Congress enacted legislation that defined tobacco as a drug that could be regulated by the Food and Drug Administration (FDA). Armed with this power, the FDA established, expanded, and monitored regulations already in place in some local jurisdictions and states that prohibited smoking advertisements and vending machines near schools, sales to minors, use of billboards to advertise, and tobacco companies' practices of giving away free samples of cigarettes. Forty-three states currently allow employers *not* to hire persons who smoke. Many jurisdictions prohibit smoking in public places or in places at work where others will breathe their secondhand smoke.

Some local jurisdictions have regulated the number of fast-food outlets in specific neighborhoods after public health advocates documented that they were disproportionately located in low-income neighborhoods. Some have placed restrictions on food provided in local schools, requiring lunches with lower fat content and more vegetables. Some have prohibited vending machines in schools that sell soda, as well as candy.

Most states prohibit the sale of alcoholic beverages to minors. Some jurisdictions place limits on the number of bars in specific communities, as well as locations near schools. Many jurisdictions take away driving licenses from persons caught driving while intoxicated (DWI) after several incidents—and may give them prison sentences.

The Occupational Safety and Health Administration (OSHA) establishes specific regulations to protect workers' safety, as well as state chapters that administer them and establish some of their own regulations. It regulates emissions of toxic chemicals within plants, requires the use of safety practices and equipment, and requires employers to monitor hazards and maintain records of workplace injuries and illnesses.

Statutes

Many local jurisdictions had established public health agencies in the early part of the twentieth century or even sooner that helped contain epidemics through quarantining their victims, as well as fostering cleanliness. They detected STDs like syphilis and gonorrhea, TB, and other diseases even if they lacked modern medications to treat some of them. The Social Security Act of 1935 initiated modest federal funding of these agencies as well as the U.S. Public Health Service, headed by the Surgeon General. They expanded their mission to prenatal services. Funded by an array of federal, state, and local grants, public health agencies continue their older functions with additional roles in planning for large-scale epidemics as well as bio-terrorism. They are linked to the CDC.

Medicaid and Medicare greatly increased primary care available to welfare recipients and elderly persons on their enactment in 1965. The Early Periodic Screening, Diagnosis, and Treatment (EPSDT) screening program of Medicaid, while poorly implemented in many states, provided screening to low-income children. Medicaid coverage for prenatal and postnatal healthcare was increased and broadened in the 1980s, as well as obstetrics services for undocumented women. The Women's and Infant Care Program (WIC) was established in 1972 to provide nutrition to low-income pregnant women and their children.

The enactment of the Children's Health Insurance Program (CHIP) in 1997 provided matching federal funds for healthcare of children for low-income families not eligible for Medicaid. Subsequent revisions allow states to include healthcare for their parents. The Patient Protection and Affordable Healthcare Act of 2010 forbids states from cutting eligibility levels for children until 2019.

President Richard Nixon launched a "War on Drugs" in 1973 with the stated purpose of protecting consumers from ill-effects of specific drugs. President Nixon and the Congress enacted the Controlled Substances Act in 1970 that established four schedules of drugs. Schedule 1 included drugs with a high potential for abuse and with no known medical use even when supervised by physicians, including most previously banned drugs. They include opium as well as morphine and heroin, which are made from opium; cocaine, which is made from the leaves of the coca shrub; and marijuana and hashish, which are made from hemp. Schedule 2 included drugs with a high potential for abuse but with currently accepted medical use, including morphine (used for pain) and methadone (used to help alcoholics). Many prescribed medications fall into Schedules 3 and 4, which have less potential for abuse and have widely accepted medical use. Other "designer drugs" have since emerged that are manufactured in home laboratories and elsewhere, including ecstasy and methamphetamines, which have severe side effects and can cause death.

Criminalization of these drugs failed to stop their importation into the United States or their widespread use. If the mafia and other criminal elements distributed them through a black market in the 1940s through the 1960s, gangs became major purveyors of them in succeeding decades, as well as many other distributors and international drug dealers.

Critics of U.S. drug policy contend that it has focused attention on interdiction at the borders as well as detecting and jailing purveyors and users rather than also providing addicted and other drug users with counseling and medical assistance. If the United States spent roughly $36 billion in 2002 on interdiction, prosecution, and incarcerating drug users and purveyors, it has spent only $9 billion in 2002 on drug treatment and prevention programs even though research suggests that treatment, while not a panacea, is often cost-effective (Office of National Drug Control Policy, 2004).

American policies regarding marijuana have been particularly controversial. Many researchers contend that medical harm from this drug is relatively minor when compared to many other illegal drugs—and that the drug helps consumers reduce pain and nausea from cancer, cancer treatments, and some chronic illnesses. Most states criminalize its use, but 14 states allow use of marijuana by consumers if it is prescribed by physicians to prevent pain and nausea. A stalemate existed in 2008 as the President George Bush left office. Federal officials from the Drug Enforcement Agency (DEA) sometimes raided growers and purveyors of marijuana in states that allowed physicians to prescribe it—on grounds that it is a Schedule 1 drug under federal law. Barack Obama's Administration decided not to raid growers and purveyors, but to let states and local governments decide how to regulate them.

Many states have enacted laws and programs that control smoking. Many of them subsidize smoking cessation programs that provide counseling, as well as nicotine orally or through skin patches. They often fund these programs, as well, as public service advertisements that depict health threats from smoking, from awards given by courts to the states when they prevailed in litigation that sought damages from tobacco companies for health costs of states that stemmed from cancer and other illness caused by smoking by their residents.

As mentioned earlier, the federal government received the right to regulate tobacco as a drug in landmark legislation in 2009. The Family Smoking Prevention and Tobacco Control Act authorizes the FDA to regulate the manufacturing, marketing, and sale of tobacco for the first time.

All states have laws that require that children receive specific vaccines commonly including ones for Diphtheria, Tetanus, Pertussis, Hepatitis B, Measles, Mumps, Rubella, polio and chicken pox. Eighteen states allow children not to have immunizations if their parents are philosophically opposed to them. All states except Mississippi, Missouri, and West Virginia allow exemptions to immunization requirements based on religious reasons (National Center for Immunization and Respiratory Diseases, 2008). About 10% of American children are not immunized for many diseases, disproportionately from low-income families, but this poor record should be improved by policies established by the Patient Protection and Affordable Healthcare Act of 2010 as was discussed earlier (CDC, 2009c).

The CDC, in collaboration with the World Health Organization, predicts which seasonal influenza strains are likely to spread to the United States during fall and winter of a succeeding flu season. Following approval by the FDA, pharmaceutical companies manufacture vaccines deemed likely to immunize persons from these flu strains with priority to persons with compromised immune systems and older persons. In 2009 a novel strain of flu, H1N1, commonly known as swine flu, required preparation of a separate vaccine. This strain was of special interest because it posed particular threats to children and pregnant women.

The federal government can require quarantining or isolating persons deemed to be highly infectious, such as with virulent strains of tuberculosis. In 2007, a man with extensively drug-resistant tuberculosis traveled to Europe, where he was informed that he should not travel on an airplane because of the possibility of transmission of the disease. His passport was subjected to a no-fly order, but he flew to Canada anyway and drove across the border to the United States. When he arrived back to the United States, he was subject to a federal order of isolation, the first since 1963 (Swendiman & Jones, 2007).

Accreditation Standards

Accreditation standards of the Joint Commission require that consumers complete a nutritional screening within 24 hours of admission if their conditions require it. They must screen patients for family violence, such as child and elder abuse, as well as partner abuse. They must screen consumers for alcoholism, other substance abuse disorders, as well as emotional and behavioral disorders if they receive psychosocial services for them as well as they receive treatment for them (Joint Commission, 2009a).

Hospitals are required to coordinate consumers' care, treatment, and services. They are required to educate consumers about their health conditions, including persons with chronic diseases who "are becoming increasingly responsible for managing their own health at home." They must tailor this education to consumers' needs and abilities, including their cultural and religious beliefs, emotional barriers, desire and motivation to learn, physical or cognitive limitations, and barriers to communication" (Joint Commission, 2009a).

It is to be lamented that accreditation standards do not specifically discuss health prevention, subsuming it under "clinical services." By hardly mentioning this term, the standards contribute to the failure of the American health system to prioritize prevention.

Insurance Incentives to Promote Prevention

Some health experts have maintained that consumers who engage in healthy lifestyles should be rewarded by insurance companies for these choices. Many insurance companies give lower rates to consumers who do not smoke, for example—and this approach could be extended to consumers who are not obese and who exercise. These incentives are not widely used, however, to promote exercise, healthy diets, or other health-promoting behaviors. Insurance incentives can be criticized, however, because they risk punishing consumers who do not make healthy choices when they suffer from addictions, genetic factors, and emotional factors that make it difficult for them to modify their lifestyle choices. Smokers become, for example, physiologically or psychologically addicted to use of tobacco. Insurance companies that reward persons who exercise or who eat nutritious diets could treat low-income persons inequitably who lack grocery stores that sell nutritious products or who live in neighborhoods where it is not safe or possible to exercise.

Emergence of "Miracle Drugs"

The class of oral medications known as statins have assumed a major role in slowing coronary heart disease and in lowering death rates from it. Even people who retain a diet relatively high in saturated fats still dramatically lower their unhealthy cholesterol (LDL) with promising health outcomes. Other medications have emerged that effectively lower high blood pressure—another risk factor for coronary heart disease. Partly because of these drugs, deaths from heart disease have decreased 56% from 307.4 per 100,000 in 1950 to 134.6 per 100,000 in 1996 (CDC, 1999).

New vaccines that are currently tested in clinical trials may prevent prostate cancer, melanoma, and lymphoma. As discussed earlier, a vaccine is widely given to prepubescent adolescent girls to prevent some kinds of cervical cancer.

Promising Research: Longitudinal Studies, International Comparisons, Comparisons of Natural Populations, and Experimental Studies

It is often difficult to conduct experimental studies of sufficient duration to assess the long-term effects of specific life style behaviors on health because of cost and attrition of study participants. Longitudinal surveys of specific populations over decades have yielded useful information. In a longitudinal survey of nurses, called the Nurses Health Study, researchers discovered that the incidence of stroke in a sample of 72,488 female nurses was reduced by physical activity (Hu et al., 2000; Knight, 2004). A longitudinal study of Harvard graduates, known as the Harvard Alumni Health Study, similarly discovered that graduates who exercised were less likely to have strokes (Knight, 2004; Lee & Paffenbarger, 1998).

Perhaps the most influential longitudinal survey in public health is the so-called Framingham Heart Study, which gathered data from residents of Framingham, Massachusetts, from 1948 to the present. It coined the term "risk factor." It revolutionized knowledge of cardiovascular diseases in 1,200 scientific papers that emerged from it, linking it to smoking, obesity, high cholesterol, high blood pressure. It published a cardiovascular risk calculator in 1998 that estimated a person's chances of developing heart problems within the next decade. It is now focusing on finding biological markers that predict heart disease (Dance, 2009).

Researchers have gathered important information, as well, from surveys of the health of relatively isolated populations with distinctive lifestyles such as Seventh Day Adventists, Jehovah's Witnesses, and Mormons. The relatively long life expectancy of members of these groups, as compared to the general population, appears to be linked to lifestyles, such as not smoking or drinking—and possibly to strong social ties among members of these congregations (Hummer, Ellison, Rogers, Moulton, & Romero, 2004).

International comparisons are often used to identify possible preventive strategies for the United States. Consumers in East Asian nations, for example, consume relatively little meat and dairy products, but greater amounts of rice, seafood, soy, and vegetables than

Americans. Many experts believe that East Asians have less heart disease and cancer—and live longer lives—than Americans partly because of these dietary differences (Marmot & Smith, 1989). Many experts speculate, too, that lesser social and economic inequalities in East Asian, Japanese, and European societies contribute to the greater longevity of their residents as compared to Americans. I have discussed how some experts speculate that Europeans fare better than Americans because they take more vacations, have more leisure time, and have greater social supports (California Newsreel, 2008).

Many researchers cite, as well, the well-documented decline in longevity and morbidity among immigrants the longer they reside in the United States—as well as their descendents who reside in the United States. This research strongly suggests that immigrants' overall health status and longevity declines as they adopt U.S. diets and lifestyles, as well as experience the social inequalities widely experienced by relatively poor Americans (Kim, Van Wye, Kerker, Thorpe, & Frieden, 2006).

Researchers often compare natural populations with one another to determine if specific factors do, or do not, cause specific health conditions. They have asked questions like: do school children who attend schools in close proximity to freeways suffer higher rates of asthma than other school children; do people who live near nuclear power plants suffer higher rates of cancer than people who do not; and do people with intake of specific vitamins avert specific health conditions as compared to persons who do not? Natural populations can be compared before and after the introduction of specific policies, such as asking if death rates of motorcyclists declined after the requirement that they wear helmets.

A growing number of research projects have been developed to determine whether specific interventions succeed in preventing health conditions that rely on the gold standards of empirical research: random controlled projects (RCPs). Researchers have asked questions like: do persons who take specific vitamins avoid specific health problems as compared to a control group; and, do elderly persons who engage in exercise regimens fracture bones from falls with lower frequency than elderly persons who do not?

The Patient Protection and Affordable Care Act of 2010

I have painted a relatively pessimistic view of health prevention in the United States, but the Patient Protection and Affordable Care Act of 2010 as amended by Congress could improve this situation. The media and many commentators have focused on its insurance provisions, while ignoring its many stipulations that promise to increase preventive health measures in the United States (Pear, 2010). The legislation:

- Attacks underfunding of prevention by insurance companies by requiring qualified health plans to provide coverage for specific preventive services marked as "A" or "B" by the U.S. Preventive Services Task Force in the Agency for Healthcare Quality (AHCQ). Beginning in 2010, insurance companies must provide, without cost-sharing with consumers, recommended immunizations; preventive care for infants, children, and adolescents; and screenings for women.

- Increases funding of preventive programs by Medicare and Medicaid including:
  - Expanding Medicare coverage for persons with health conditions caused by environmental hazards (2010).
  - Preventing unwanted children by giving states the option to cover family planning in their Medicaid health programs.
  - Eliminating cost-sharing for Medicare preventive services with "A" or "B" ratings by the U.S. Preventive Service Task Force (2011).
  - Waiving the Medicare deductible for colorectal cancer screening tests (2011).
  - Giving Medicare beneficiaries access to a health-risk assessment and creation of a personalized prevention plan and annual wellness visits by 2011—and providing incentives to Medicare and Medicaid beneficiaries to complete behavior modification programs such as those that seek to reduce obesity.
  - Requiring certain free preventive services under Medicare by 2011, including annual wellness visits and personalized prevention plans for seniors.
  - Increasing Medicaid payments for primary care physicians to levels no less than 100% of Medicare payment rates (beginning in 2013 and 2014).
- Aims to greatly reduce unnecessary deaths of uninsured persons, estimated to be as high as 45,000 persons per year, by extending health coverage to roughly 32 million Americans by 2014.
- Aims to rebuild the primary care workforce by funding scholarships and loan repayments for primary care doctors, nurses, and physician assistants. It allows members of this workforce who locate in underserved or professional shortage areas not to pay taxes on these resources, effective in 2010. It will establish a national health workforce strategy in 2010 by forming a Workforce Advisory Commission. It will establish Teaching Health Centers to provide payments for primary-care residency programs in community-based ambulatory care settings in 2011.
- Allows consumers to select any available participating primary care doctor as their provider, beginning in 2010—and allows women to see an OB-GYN physician without referral.
- Permits employers to offer employees rewards of up to 30%, increasing to 50% if appropriate, of the cost of coverage for participating in a wellness program and meeting certain health-related standards (2014). It will establish state pilot programs in 10 states to offer similar rewards to consumers in wellness programs who purchase individual policies.
- Extends health benefits to millions of low-income persons by vastly expanding eligibility for the CHIP and Medicaid programs (between 2010 and 2014).
- Extends health benefits to millions of workers (as we discuss in Chapter 9) by giving small businesses tax credits to cover a portion of the cost of insuring their employees—and by requiring all Americans to obtain insurance or pay a penalty.

- Establishes a new $15 billion Prevention and Public Health Fund that will invest in proven prevention and public health programs from smoking cessation to combating obesity, with funding beginning in 2010.

Learning Exercise

1. Discuss whether this legislation will markedly decrease morbidity and mortality in the United States during the coming decade.
2. Identify some additional prevention measures that would be effective.

TWELVE SCENARIOS OF CONSUMERS REGARDING PREVENTIVE SERVICES

Twelve scenarios describe situations where consumers may need case advocacy to receive preventive services. Refer back to key provisions of the Patient Protection and Affordable Care Act, enacted by President Barack Obama and the Congress in March 2010 that are discussed earlier in this chapter.

Scenario 8.1: Advocacy to Help Consumers Identify Personal At-Risk Factors

Many consumers do not receive important information about health threats they might confront because many physicians, including primary-care ones, focus on presenting problems, like flu and minor injuries. Consumers need to ask physicians to tell them if they appear to be at risk of developing specific chronic or other diseases based on family histories, results of routine diagnostic tests, and current lifestyles. They should seek an assessment of their lifestyles, including exercise and diet, as well as whether they smoke. This assessment should examine if they are relatively isolated or possess strong positive networks within and outside their families. They should discuss the nature of their work and the extent it is fulfilling. Very few consumers engage in discussions with primary-care physicians on this level so they do not view the larger strategic health situation that they currently encounter—and how it might increase their probability of contracting specific chronic and other illnesses.

Consumers should request a full spectrum of blood tests, including LDL-C ("bad" cholesterol), HDL-C ("good" cholesterol), and triglycerides, as well as any other ones relevant to specific chronic diseases. All adults should have a fasting lipoprotein profile every five years.

Even consumers who appear to be at low risk should ask their physicians if specific tests are appropriate. Assume, for example, that a 65-year-old male had normal blood pressure, weight, and serum cholesterol, but had many close relatives that had died from stroke in the seventies. He could ask his physician whether a sonic test for clogged carotid arteries was appropriate, as well as other preventive measures.

Many experts contend that consumers should have these "wellness interviews" that help them develop their personal health strategic plans. Consumers ought to prepare a list of questions they want discussed to identify at-risk factors. They should prioritize prevention even if their physicians do not—and request their physicians to make health prevention a key part of their discussions with them.

Such interviews are not panaceas. Even consumers with strong family histories of specific diseases often do not develop them. Many consumers who make poor lifestyle choices do not get cancer and other chronic diseases. Experts often disagree about how to prevent specific chronic and other diseases. Many consumers do not change dysfunctional lifestyle habits.

Case advocates should ask consumers:

- Has their physician given them a wellness interview that identifies risk factors they may possess from family history, diagnostic tests, prior medical history, gender, and age?
- Have they established goals and timelines with their physician for improving their at-risk factors?
- Have they identified community-based programs that might help them reach their prevention goals?

Scenario 8.2: Advocacy to Help Consumers Obtain Tests Relevant to Their At-Risk Factors

Consumers should engage in ongoing discussion with health providers about prevention—and advocates should prompt them to make prevention an integral part of their healthcare. They should request charts that compare diagnostic findings from prior periods with their current findings to determine if their overall risk has decreased, remained constant, or improved—or whether new risks have emerged (Knight, 2004).

Considerable evidence suggests that low-income persons have greater risk for many chronic diseases, including coronary heart and cerebrovascular diseases—yet they are least likely to obtain diagnostic information on a regular basis (Barr, 2008).

Case advocates should ask consumers:

- Have they discussed whether their risk factors have become better, remained constant, or become worse?
- Have they discussed specific behavioral, dietary, exercise, or other changes that might improve risk ratings with their physician?
- Have they established new time tables or goals with their physicians as risk factors change?

Scenario 8.3: Advocating for Consumers to Get Chronic Diseases Diagnosed

Many consumers with chronic diseases get chronic diseases diagnosed belatedly or not at all. Many consumers with type 2 diabetes are not diagnosed for at least four to seven years after they contract it—even though it is the sixth most common source of death in the U.S. (Harris, Klein, Welborn, & Knuiman, 1992; Knight, 2004). Delayed diagnosis can have serious effects on consumers, who not only delay their preventive work, but do not benefit from existing treatments that may delay progression. In the case of consumers who progress from HIV status to AIDS, for example, prompt commencement of the so-called cocktail of drugs is critically important to delaying the progression of AIDS (Castilla et al., 2002).

Consumers who have a positive family history, are obese, and do not regularly obtain exercise should ask to be tested for type 2 diabetes. Consumers who have shortness of breath when they exercise, frequently feel faint, have elevated blood pressure, have elevated serum cholesterol and have a family history of heart disease—or some combination of these risk factors—should ask to be tested for heart disease. Consumers cannot assume they will be tested for these diseases unless they take the initiative with their physicians.

Some consumers receive biopsies that show they have cancer or other life-threatening diseases, but do not return for medications and treatment. Every clinic and hospital should have procedures for locating these patients even if they have unstable addresses.

Advocates should ask consumers:

- Have they received definitive information that rules out specific chronic diseases or that suggests they have contracted one of them?
- How advanced is any chronic disease they might possess?
- What treatments might slow the progression of a chronic disease they might possess?
- What lifestyle and other changes might slow its progression?
- Have they identified specific support groups that might help them with a prevention program?

Scenario 8.4: Advocacy for Consumers to Obtain Help in Losing Weight

Vast numbers of Americans believe they are overweight, often selecting innumerable panaceas like the high-protein Scarsdale diet (Tarnower, 1978), the low-fat Pritikin Program (Pritikin, 1979), the fruit-heavy Beverly Hills diet (Mazel, 1981), the Atkins low-carbohydrates, high-fat, and high-protein diet (Atkins, 1992), and the South Beach diet that falls midway between the low-fat, high-carbohydrate recommendations of many nutritionists and the Atkins diet (Agatston, 2003).

Proponents of each of these diets contend that they will allow users to lose weight, but they have often produced poor results, whether because they are intrinsically flawed or because consumers rarely stick with them for protracted periods. Some experts fear that repeated dieting may contribute to weight gain "by molding the mind to be fixated with food" (Mestel, 2003). (The results are, as one psychologist confessed, "It just goes around and around and around—and we're fatter than ever" Mestel, 2003). No one could take comfort when the CDC discovered that the rate of obesity in the United States had leveled at 34.3% of the population in 2007 (72 million persons) for the first time two consecutive years since 1980 (Kaplan & Gellene, 2007). Nor can they take comfort in data that showed a surge in obesity among boomers aged 55 to 64—and that identified states with particularly high rates of obesity including eight Southern states (Neergaard, 2009).

Recent research findings suggest that dieting is more successful with low-caloric diets no matter what macronutrients they emphasize. The researcher's sample was restricted to overweight and obese persons who were motivated to lose weight, were not diabetic, did not have heart disease, and did not take medications. The study tested four diets that varied in their composition of proteins, carbohydrates, or fats—but all of them were low-caloric ones. After two years, enrollees lost, on average, about 9 pounds, while about 15% of enrollees lost about 10% of their weight. Enrollees were offered group sessions with attendance strongly associated with weight loss or 0.45 pounds lost per session attended. It is not known if enrollees will retain their weight loss after two years—nor is it known if less motivated persons, diabetics, persons with heart disease, or persons taking medications would benefit from this regimen (Sacks et al., 2009).

Other researchers have discovered that persons with diabetes are most likely to lose weight if they receive intensive counseling about diet and exercise. They discovered that consumers who followed this regimen lost an average of 8.6% of their weight in a year as compared to only 0.7% for ones who did not receive intensive counseling (Wadden et al., 2009).

Some researchers contend that an exercise program should be integral to any weight-reduction program (Blair, 1993; Knight, 2004). It burns energy that might otherwise promote fat. It may regulate appetite. It may reduce an adverse ratio of waist-to-hip that has been identified by some researchers as a risk factor for coronary heart disease (Blair, 1993; Knight, 2004).

Other recent research findings suggest that "obesity" may need to be redefined from the older standard of having a body-mass index of 30 or more by a mathematical formula of the ratio of weight and height—a formula that identifies as obese a woman who is 5 feet tall and weighs 154 and a 6-foot man who weighs 220 pounds. This research discovered that many persons who have been classified as obese live longer than many persons who have low weight-to-height ratios (Price, Uauy, Breeze, Bulpitt, & Fletcher, 2006).

Some researchers implicate genes in causing obesity so that persons with genetic predisposition find it far more difficult to lose weight than others. Some researchers have discovered that the weight of adopted twins conformed to the weight of their biological parents, not their adoptive parents, suggesting that biological factors, not nurture, influenced their weight. Dr. Jules Hirsch discovered that many dieting obese persons resemble starving people by every metabolic measure such as fantasizing about food, hiding food, binging, and, in some cases, contemplating suicide. He concluded that genetic factors often both cause obesity and make it difficult for some obese persons to diet (Kolata, 2007). Some obese people may therefore be likely not to succeed in meeting desirable weight levels—and may develop poor self image if they are pressured excessively to do so (Burkhauser & Cawley, 2008).

Consumers need to understand, then, that research information has only recently shed light on effective strategies for weight loss. Almost no studies extend beyond one year. They should understand that many panaceas exist, but with uncertain effectiveness. They need to select a course of action that has a greater probability of success than many existing diets by emphasizing caloric intake and by selecting programs with group sessions or counseling as a key feature. They should realize that some persons cannot lose weight easily and that many of them engage in a cycle of weight loss and weight gain.

Advocates should ask consumers:

- Have they been told that they are "obese" or "overweight"?
- Have they been told whether their weight places them at risk of developing specific diseases or health conditions—or aggravating existing ones?
- Are they concerned about their weight primarily for aesthetic reasons?
- Have they been directed to specific weight-loss programs that emphasize low-caloric content, have strong group support and/or counseling components?

Scenario 8.5: Advocacy for Consumers to Engage in Exercise

Consumers engage in different levels of exercise. If activity involves body movement to perform such tasks as walking to automobiles, mowing grass, or cleaning houses, exercise is undertaken to obtain regular, and more demanding body movement, such as walking on a tread mill, using an exercise bicycle, walking, jogging, or swimming. Someone is sedentary if he or she mostly does not engage in activity or exercise, such as a chair-bound person or someone who mostly watches television (Knight, 2004).

A huge body of research links level of exercise to many diseases and health conditions (Knight, 2004). The 1990 Global Burden of Disease Study listed physical inactivity in the top 10 risk factors (Murray & Lopez, 1996). Inactivity has been linked by many researchers to degree of longevity, as well as increasing the odds that persons will contract specific diseases including heart disease, some forms of cancer, hardening of the arteries, type 2 diabetes, osteoporosis, and stroke. It contributes, as well, to such disorders as aging, falls and fractures, hypertension, decreased immunity, mental health, obesity, and muscle loss (sarcopenia).

Exercise can prevent, or diminish, disability among elderly persons. Twenty percent of elderly persons, some researchers contend, have chronic disabilities and 8 percent have mobility problems (V. Freedman, Martin, & Schoeni, 2002; Knight, 2004). These disabilities often lead to their moving from independent status into nursing homes at huge cost to themselves and to the government. Many studies document that exercise programs curtail these disabilities to allow them to perform daily living activities (J. Davis, Ross, Preston, Nevitt, & Wasnick, 1998; Knight, 2004). It reduces incidence of falls (Knight 2004; Wolf, Barnhart, Kutner, & McNeely, 1996). Exercise also prevents or diminishes the prevalence of arthritis and other rheumatic conditions, as well as chronic joint symptoms, which are the leading cause of disability in the U.S. (C. Cooper, Inskip, Croft, Campbell, Smith, McLearn, & Coggan, 1998; Knight, 2004).

Exercise not only prevents specific diseases, but reduces at-risk factors like hypertension (Kelley & Kelley, 2000; Knight, 2004). It can reduce total cholesterol and unhealthy LDL cholesterol, as well as triglycerides, which are at-risk factors for coronary heart disease (Knight, 2004; Kraus, et al., 2002).

Many consumers are relatively sedentary. A 1996 CDC survey found that 60% or more of adults did not report that they achieved the minimum, recommended level of physical activity (CDC, 1996; Knight, 2004). Another survey rated physical activity on four levels: physically inactive, irregularly inactive, regularly active but not intensive, and regularly active and intensive. Six in 10 persons were in the first two categories—and less than one was regularly active and intensive (Casperson & Merritt, 1995; Knight, 2004). The Surgeon General recommends moderate physical activity most days of the week for 30 minutes, but researchers discovered that women of color, women over age 40, and women without college education had the lowest levels of participation (Knight, 2004; Ransdell & Wells, 1998).

Many factors contribute to sedentary life styles. Physical education has been terminated in many schools. Low-income persons often do not have safe places to exercise and cannot afford memberships in fitness centers. Television, mobile phones, and computers consume huge amounts of time. Many Americans do not make room for exercise in their schedules. Many seniors feel uncomfortable exercising and underestimate their ability to engage in it.

Physicians often do not assess levels of exercise in their patients or counsel them about it. The CDC discovered that only 19% of physicians counsel patients about it (CDC, 1995; Knight, 2004). Only 1% of physicians recommended exercise for patients at high risk for chronic heart disease in a study by Frolkis et al., 1998 (Knight, 2004). Physicians are, however, more likely to counsel consumers for exercise when they already have specific health conditions such as heart disease and diabetes—thus favoring secondary over primary prevention (Knight, 2004; Wee, McCarthy, Davis, & Phillips, 1999).

Advocates should ask consumers:

- Whether their physicians have discussed health consequences of not exercising even before they have a chronic disease, particularly in light of their other risk factors—and whether exercise could reduce some risk factors such as high-serum cholesterol or obesity.

- Whether their physicians have discussed health consequences of not exercising when they have a specific health condition or chronic disease.
- Whether exercising could decrease their odds, if they are elderly, of not falling, living independently, and avoiding health conditions.
- Whether their physician has developed exercise goals with them—and monitored their progress—or referred them to a physical or occupational therapist for consultation.
- Whether exercise might help them surmount depression or other mental health problems, as well as help them overcome insomnia.

Scenario 8.6: Advocacy for Consumers to Improve Their Nutrition

Food not only provides energy that powers the human organism, but gives it crucial micronutrients like minerals and vitamins essential to maintain health. Poor nutrition takes several forms: under- or overcaloric intake, intake of harmful foods, or deficiencies of protein and specific micronutrients.

A Food Guide Pyramid is widely used to illustrate a healthy diet. The USDA introduced a new food pyramid in 2005 that emphasizes exercise and eating a variety of foods. The new pyramid is linked to a web site that allows a person to personalize eating recommendations based on age, gender, and amount of exercise. The pyramid also emphasizes eating whole grains daily to improve health (U.S. Department of Agriculture, 2010).

A new diet developed by the American Heart Association to prevent heart disease recommended balancing food intake and exercise. It suggested a diet rich in whole and grain and fiber as well as fruit and vegetables. It also recommended eating fish at least once a week, selecting lean meats, limited use of saturated and trans fats, using skim or low fat milk and dairy products, consuming less sugar and salt and moderate or no use of alcohol (Lichtenstein et al., 2006).

Considerable research links high intake of red meats, processed meats, and dairy products to heart disease and cancer, as well as shorter life expectancy (Brody, 2009). As many as 1 million male deaths and half a million female deaths could be prevented just in one decade if men and women eat less red meat and processed meats. Persons with high meat intake are also less likely than others to exercise, more likely to smoke, and less likely to eat vegetables, fruit and fiber (Brody, 2009).

Many researchers contend that antioxidants, such as vitamins C, E, carotenoids, flavenoids, and selenium neutralize free radicals, which are believed to contribute to aging as well as more than 100 medical conditions (Knight, 2004). Whole grains, fruits and vegetables, and omega-3 fatty acids protect against coronary heart disease. The Mediterranean diet, which emphasizes fish, vegetables, nuts, seeds, olive oil, and wine appears to decrease coronary heart disease significantly, vitamins E, C, A, and flavenoids also appear to decrease coronary heart disease. Folic acid prevents birth defects if given to pregnant women. Iron deficiency erodes immune function and energy. Dietary fiber, such as from vegetables and legumes, lower coronary heart disease as do unsaturated fatty acids, such as fish oil, olive oil, and canola oil.

Some researchers regard cancer as a largely preventable disease citing smoking and nutrition (Bal, 2001; Knight, 2004). Mediterranean diet reduces the incidence of several cancers (de Lorgeril et al., 1994; Knight, 2004). Fatty acids and red meat have been implicated in colorectal and prostate cancers. Persons with diets high in fruits and vegetables have less lung cancer, breast cancer, and prostate cancer. Vitamin D appears protective against prostate cancer. Potassium is protective against heart disease (Sohn, 2009). Trans fats, chemically modified food ingredients that raise LDL, have been linked to heart disease (Lueck & Severson, 2006).

The Nurses Health Study concluded that 91% of type 2 diabetes is preventable, such as by exercise, weight loss, and reduction of fatty saturated fat (Knight, 2004). Other researchers contend that higher dietary fiber, whole grains, and legumes protect against diabetes (Knight, 2004; S. Liu et al., 2000).

Researchers have found that some prevention strategies with wide acceptance have negligible effects or can even be harmful. Widely viewed as preventing colds and cancer, for example, high doses of vitamin C were discovered to have little or no preventive effects—and some researchers believe that large doses of vitamin C promote the growth of some kinds of cancers based on laboratory tests (Walker, 2008). Vitamins C, D, and E, selenium, calcium and folate were found not to prevent prostate cancer (Vastag, 2009). High levels of beta-carotene have been linked to some kinds of cancer (Touvier, Kesse, Clavel-Chapelon, & Boutron-Ruault, 2005). Since lower doses of many of these substances occur naturally in well-rounded diets, many experts recommend multi-vitamin tablets with relatively low doses of an array of substances to meet current daily Dietary Reference Intakes (DRI) (Knight, 2004; Trumbo, Yates, Schlicker, & Poos, 2001).

Many nutritional problems exist in the United States including:

- Malnutrition among low-income persons since roughly 35 million Americans live in households that cannot afford to eat good diets, despite the existence of the Food Stamp program. The Food Stamp program in 2007 averaged only $1.05 per person per meal because it has not been increased for inflation since 1996, though its funding was increased in the Obama Administration to $606 for a family of four per month, an extra $80 a month. Legal immigrants who have lived less than 5 years in the United States, as well as undocumented persons, are ineligible for the program. In 2010, 44% of consumers who qualified for the Food Stamps program did not enroll in it (Zavis & Mutert, 2010).
- Malnutrition among children—or about one-third of the 35 million Americans in households that cannot afford food. Many children rely on school breakfast and school lunch programs for a considerable portion of their daily food intake.
- Malnutrition among elderly persons where 12% reported they did not have enough food, 13% had not eaten for a full day, and 14% reported going hungry

because they could not afford food in an urban county (Knight, 2004; Nelson, Brown, & Lurie, 1998). Malnutrition may be particularly likely if seniors have a current health problem, eat two or less full meals per day, eat few vegetables, fruits, and milk products, imbibe three or more alcoholic drinks on most days, have tooth or mouth problems, have inadequate resources, eat alone, take three or more prescription drugs, lose 10 or more pounds in the past 6 months without trying, or are physically unable to shop (Knight, 2004; Mojon, Budtz-Jorgensen, & Rapin, 2000; S. P. Murphy, Davis, Neuhaus, & Lein, 1990).

- Anorexia (self-starving behavior) and bulimia (food binging coupled with frequent vomiting) among women can lead to emaciation and, in many cases, death. Women are also subject to insufficient iron and calcium.
- Excessive caloric intake leading to persons who are overweight or obese—or roughly one-third of Americans—with possible adverse health consequences for persons at-risk of diabetes, heart disease, some kinds of cancer, arthritis, and liver and gall bladder disease.
- Insufficient caloric intake among elderly persons leading to excess loss of body fat and muscle.
- Insufficient micronutrients for elderly persons, particularly ones who consume less than 1,000 calories per day (Goodwin, 1989; Knight 2004), as well as protein deficiency (Knight, 2004; Sullivan, Sun, & Wells, 1999).
- Insufficient caloric intake among persons with advanced cancer, leading to "wasting away."
- Malnutrition among homeless people because they cannot afford healthy food, have no place to store it, and have no cooking facilities. In addition, staff at food pantries and soup kitchens rarely includes trained dieticians, so diets do not offer all the nutrition that homeless people need (Wiecha, Dwyer, & Dunn-Strohecker, 1991).
- Neglected or abused children who do not receive an adequate diet. They may suffer from significant developmental delays, which may affect them for their entire lives.
- Consumers with food allergies who become malnourished because they cannot afford the restricted diet they need.
- Consumers who live distant from full-service grocery stores and have difficulty getting fresh and healthy food.
- Consumers who live in areas with high concentrations of fast-food outlets and who eat frequently in them.
- Consumers who eat excessive amount of red meat, processed meats, and dairy products.

Many experts cite data from the Framingham Heart Study that documented that diets high in saturated fat are associated with higher rates of coronary heart disease and strokes than diets with low levels—particularly when persons have high natural levels of low density lipoprotein (LDL), as well as low levels of high density or "good" cholesterol (HDL). Exercise and diets that are low in saturated fats can also lower LDL (Knight, 2004; Knopp et al., 1997). Consumers who cannot lower their LDL and elevate their HDL to appropriate levels should take medications such as statins to control levels of cholesterol and medications to control hypertension.

Experts agree that specific populations have special nutritional needs. Premenstrual women need higher levels of iron than men and that women need higher levels of calcium than men to prevent osteoporosis. Children need many micronutrients, as well as sufficient caloric intake to allow them to develop normally. Older persons sometimes need special diets to slow the loss of body fat and muscle. Women need to be screened for anorexia and bulimia.

Malnourished patients experience higher rates of medical complications and mortality, as well as the medical cost of caring for them. One study found that 59% and 48% of medical and surgical patients had a likelihood of malnutrition—and they were respectively 2.6 and 3.4 times as likely to suffer a complication and 3.8 times as likely to die as other patients (Knight, 2004; Reilly, Hull, Albert, Waller, & Bringardener, 1988).

Many physicians do not discuss nutrition with consumers, or less than half of primary care physicians in a survey in Massachusetts—even though some researchers find counseling by physicians to be effective such as when advising low-income persons to eat more fruits and vegetables (Galuska, Will, Serdula, & Ford, 1999; Knight 2004; Wechsler, Levin, & Idelson, 1996).

Case advocates should ask consumers whether physicians have discussed:

- Their overall nutritional intake with them, including their adherence to the updated Pyramid, their caloric intake, and their intake of saturated fat.
- Their risk profiles for specific diseases, as well as their overall risks, makes specific dietary profiles particularly important for them.
- If they should be taking statins or medications to lower blood pressure.
- Where they can receive detailed nutritional counseling to help them address nutritional problems.
- How they can surmount barriers to healthy nutrition, including financial, neighborhood, and familial ones.

Scenario 8.7: Advocacy to Help Consumers Stop Smoking

Smoking contributes to the morbidity and lowered life expectancy more than any other lifestyle factor. It caused about 442,000 premature deaths each year from 1995 to 1999, including 264,000 men and 178,000 women (CDC, 2002a). While the incidence of smoking has decreased from 1965 to 2008 by 51%, it will continue to cause this health toll because of the time lag required to develop cancer and other illnesses from smoking and cumulative effect on specific persons—save for those persons who stopped smoking five years ago who escape a considerable amount of their risk for many kinds of cancer, heart disease, and many other diseases (American Lung Association, 2010). Smoking is particularly prevalent among low-income persons and persons who did not complete high school.

Smoking can be viewed as a chronic disease with complex physiological and psychological components—with less than 10% of smokers succeeding in quitting over the long term until recently (DHHS, 1990). Nicotine is highly addictive—and smokers experience strong withdrawal symptoms when they stop smoking. Only 44% of smokers who had seen a physician in the previous year indicated in a Michigan survey they had ever been advised to quit smoking—and only 30% of young male smokers (Anda, Remington, Sienko, & Davis, 1987; Knight, 2004). The American Heart Association asks healthcare professionals to counsel smoking patients to quit at every office visit and to record how often they smoke with periodic updates. It suggests all clinicians receive training in patient-centered counseling techniques (Knight, 2004; Ockene & Houston, 1997). Relatively few hospitals have clinics to provide this therapy. A combination of counseling, monitoring, and pharmacotherapy are relatively effective—including use of nicotine patches and oral nicotine medications. Roughly 21% of persons who combine counseling with pharmacotherapy quit smoking for extended periods (Fellows, Bush, McAfee, & Dickerson, 2007).

Consumers need strategies not only for their own smoking, but how to avoid secondhand smoke, which has been implicated in causing cancer and other diseases.

Case advocates should ask consumers if their physicians have:

- Discussed smoking with them.
- Monitored their smoking at each appointment.
- Identified places they can obtain help with ending smoking.
- Discussed with them how medication and counseling, together, have greater success than either of them alone.
- Asked them if they are exposed to secondhand smoke in their homes or places of work—and how they might reduce this risk.

Scenario 8.8: Advocacy for Consumers to Receive Vaccines

Many consumers do not receive vaccines even when they are in high-risk groups. For example, only about 60% of elderly people over age 60 receive influenza vaccines even though influenza and pneumonia are the sixth leading cause of death in the United States with 90% of these deaths occurring in this age group (Govaert, Thijs, Masurel, Springer, Diant, & Knotnerus, 1994; Knight, 2004; Sprenger, Mulder, Beyer, Van Strik, & Masurel, 1993). Most older Americans have not received a vaccine for shingles, partly because some insurance companies do not cover it, even though the vaccine will prevent 50% of them from getting this painful condition (CDC, 2009b). Roughly 40% of older

Americans have not received the pneumococcal vaccine to prevent pneumonia that cause 40,000 deaths annually and Medicare costs in excess of $1 billion (CDC, 2010b). Many adults have received booster doses every 10 years for tetanus and diphtheria; hepatitis A and B vaccines for adults with medical, behavioral, occupational, or other indications; or meningococcal vaccines for adults with medical or other indications (CDC, 2002b; Knight, 2004).

The United States also needs to ensure that children receive the full series of all recommended vaccines. Although 92% of young children receive at least one dose of measles vaccine, only 77% received the full combined vaccine series of 4 doses of Diphtheria/Tetanus/Pertussis, 3 doses of polio, 1 of measles/mumps/rubella, 3 of Haemophilus influenzae type b, 3 of Hepatitis B and 1 of Varicella (chickenpox) (CDC, 2010a).

Scenario 8.9: Advocacy for Consumers to Reduce Environmental Stressors

Many consumers reside in homes and communities that pose threats to their health. Homes with insect and rodent infestations or homes in neighborhoods with high levels of pollution can aggravate asthma of children. Elderly and disabled persons are more prone to accidents in homes that are not reengineered to remove barriers to movement through them or to make kitchens and bathrooms more accessible and safe. Neighborhoods with high levels of violence imperil the safety of their residents.

Physicians and other health staff often do not help consumers avoid or mitigate these dangers. They often fail to discuss these realities. They often do not visit consumers after they are discharged. They often do not point consumers to community-based programs, such as ones that inspect for lead-based paint, help consumers modify their living arrangements, or control insects and rodents.

Advocates can:

- Ask whether physicians or other health personnel have talked to them about specific environmental stressors.
- Link consumers to community-based programs that might help them address them.

Scenario 8.10: Advocacy for Pregnant Women and Young Children

Many researchers contend that regular prenatal care cuts rates of premature births, as well as infant mortality (Frick & Lantz, 1999; Krueger & Scholl, 2000). Others have documented that postnatal care, as well as augmented diets from the Women's and Infant Care Program (WIC), foster greater health among young children. Many women and children do not receive these services and augmented diets, however, whether because they do not know about them, believe they are not eligible for them, find them to be inaccessible, or do not understand their importance, particularly in low-income communities.

Advocates should ask pregnant women, as well as women with young children:

- If they have received regular prenatal care.
- If they have used, or intend to use, WIC.

Scenario 8.11: Advocacy for Consumers Considering Nonusual Screening Tests

All consumers need routine screening, such as blood tests and Pap smears. More controversy exists, however, around full-body screens for asymptomatic persons and screening for heart disease among asymptomatic persons. Controversy exists, as well, about PSA screening for men. Some controversy exists, as well, about when men and women should get screened for specific health conditions, like prostate and breast cancer.

Advocates should ask consumers:

- If their physicians have discussed the relative merit of nonroutine screenings including their benefits and risks.

Scenario 8.12: Advocacy for Consumers for Nontraditional Providers

Nontraditional providers can often assume important roles in helping consumers obtain preventive services. Some researchers have discovered that acupuncture eases low back pain, neck pain, chronic idiopathic or tension headache, migraine, and knee osteo-arthritis (Kelly, 2009). Some nontraditional providers help consumers deal with stress that has been implicated in causing some diseases, as well as insomnia, including yoga and meditation. Chiropractors sometimes help consumers avoid surgery for back and joint problems, as well as chronic pain.

Advocates should ask consumers:

- If they have been informed about nontraditional providers.
- If nontraditional providers give service within, or under contract with, their health plan or health facility.
- If they have examined information about the relative effectiveness of specific nontraditional interventions in addressing health problems.

MOVING FROM CASE ADVOCACY TO POLICY ADVOCACY

Take any of the scenarios in this chapter and discuss some rules, budgets, court rulings, and statutes that are germane to one of the following twelve scenarios:

8.1 Advocacy to Help Consumers Identify Personal At-Risk Factors
8.2 Advocacy to Help Consumers Obtain Tests Relevant to Their At-Risk Factors

SUMMARY

Advocates can assume important roles in helping specific consumers obtain preventive services in clinics, hospitals, and communities at a case-advocacy level. They can build upon the prevention provisions of the Patient Protection and Affordable Care Act of 2010 as amended by Congress to create additional policies and resources for prevention.

Using Advocacy to Help Consumers Finance Their Healthcare

Health systems consume vast amounts of resources in all industrialized nations when hospitals, convalescent homes, skilled nursing homes, physicians, nurses, social workers, and many other staff are included, as well as services, medications, and diagnostic tests. Each nation has to decide how to finance them, as well as how to keep their overall costs within acceptable limits.

Our presentation of 20 scenarios that advocates often confront suggests how pervasive difficulties in funding healthcare have been in the United States. (Fifteen of the scenarios are in this book and five are in online materials relevant to this chapter.)

Unlike other industrialized nations that have funded their health systems primarily from central or regional governments, the United States has evolved a complex financing system that includes employers, private insurance companies, all levels of government, consumers, and charitable care funded by physicians, hospitals, and private donors. This complex financing system has yielded inequitable outcomes among insured persons as well as between insured persons and uninsured persons. It results in large out-of-pocket costs for many consumers, sometimes leading to bankruptcy. Poorly insured persons, too, have sometimes suffered excess deaths and illnesses.

The financing of healthcare will greatly change during the 10 years following the enactment of the Patient Protection and Affordable Care Act of 2010 as amended by Congress. I refer to it as "the Obama Plan" for brevity in this chapter. I discuss financing changes anticipated by experts as flowing from this plan even though many provisions will not be implemented until 2014 and beyond. I refer throughout this chapter to the Pre-Obama Plan that refers to how healthcare was financed prior to the plan's enactment and the Post-Obama Plan to refer to anticipated changes. Note that predictions are only best guesses because of uncertainties in mid-2010 about how this statute will be implemented and how its programs will interact with the many parts of the existing health system.

Here is a brief overview of the development of the Obama Plan in the Congress from summer 2009 to its passage in March, 2010. President Barack Obama promised some form of national health insurance when he ran for the presidency. Unlike President Bill Clinton whose plan failed to pass Congress, Obama asked the Congress to develop the plan. Various committees in the House and Senate attempted to negotiate one, but had not succeeded by the August, 2009 recess of Congress.

The plan's chances were greatly improved by the decision of health plans, insurance companies, and pharmaceutical companies to accept health coverage for everyone and to cut health costs rather than to oppose a government plan as during Clinton's effort. Critics wondered, however, if these companies made these concessions merely to gain a seat at the bargaining table because they had concluded that some plan would emerge (Krugman, 2009a). They also wondered if insurance companies mostly wanted to avoid competition from a public insurance plan or even health cooperatives that some legislators favored (Krugman, 2009b). Walmart, the nation's largest private employer, agreed to support a policy to require all Americans to enroll in health insurance (Lazarus, 2009d).

The Obama Plan, considered during the first year of Obama's presidency, did not propose to fundamentally alter the way the U.S. health system was financed. It retained existing private health plans and health insurance by giving employees the right to retain them if they chose. It continued huge corporate tax deductions for employers' health costs. It proposed a new public insurance plan that anyone could use—a plan that would reimburse private physicians and hospitals like existing private insurance plans, Medicare, and Medicaid. It retained Medicare and Medicaid programs. It left the financing of healthcare of immigrants, except for obstetrics services and some public health programs, to states and local governments.

Even though this version of healthcare reform differed markedly from single-payer systems like Canada's, it came under sharp attack from many Congressional moderates and conservatives, as well as health lobbying groups. It appeared by early August 2009 that it would be markedly changed. Many uninsured persons would be covered by Medicaid rather than public or private insurance. It was not certain that a basic package of benefits would even be specified in the legislation.

Yet the legislation proposed striking innovations that were partly modeled on features of a national health proposal offered during Bill Clinton's presidency, as well as the recently enacted universal coverage program of Massachusetts. It required all employers over a certain size to fund health insurance for their employees. It introduced "cooperatives" that would be nongovernmental, but with boards with strong consumer representation as alternatives to private insurance. It proposed new federal subsidies for many small businesses that could not afford insurance premiums for their employees. It required all nonelderly U.S. citizens to select an insurance plan or to enroll in Medicaid.

The federal plan proposed new regulations on private insurance plans, such as not allowing them to refuse coverage to persons with preexisting health conditions, requiring clearer contracts with enrollees, and making it easier for consumers to contest those decisions of insurance companies that they believed to be unfair. The plan hoped to cut the premiums of private insurance companies by making them compete with cooperatives and with Medicaid for enrollees.

The Congress and the Obama Administration proposed, then, both a cautious and a bold initiative. It was cautious because it kept the existing U.S. health system intact with its emphasis on employers' funding health insurance for many employees while expanding Medicaid's size. It continued spreading the costs among employers, the states, the federal government, and consumers. It retained the central role of private insurance companies and private health plans while expanding Medicaid. Yet it boldly proposed to eliminate or greatly reduce the number of people with low insurance coverage, the uninsured, and people needing COBRA in the most sweeping change in the health system in U.S. history.

Critics of the Obama Plan came from relatively conservative and relatively liberal politicians and pundits. Many conservatives used language that had long been used by opponents of universal healthcare. The conservatives argued that the Obama Plan represented a government "takeover" of the health system, in other words, "socialist medicine." They contended the cooperatives would be more costly than ones of private providers. They argued that regulations over private insurance companies would inhibit their ability to lower costs by market competition. Some libertarians believed the government should not require citizens to obtain insurance, join cooperatives, or enlist in Medicaid. They argued that the plan favored "death panels" when it asked the federal government to fund physicians' discussions of advance directives with consumers.

Liberal critics of the plan contended that it did not go far enough in restructuring the U.S. health system. Some liberals wanted a single-payer system like the plans in most industrialized nations because it would eliminate costly marketing and administrative costs of existing private health insurance companies. Some liberals were leery about expanding the role of Medicaid markedly because it is a means-tested or Welfare program. Some believed that U.S. corporations would compete more effectively in national and world markets if they no longer had to pay substantial costs for their employees' health insurance.

In complex political maneuvering between January and early March 2010, the Congress enacted a Senate version of health reform that considerably differed from the House version enacted in late 2009. (The House version was considerably more liberal than the Senate version.) It became apparent that a compromise version could not be fashioned because the Democrats had lost their 60-vote, filibuster-proof edge in the Senate when Republican Scott Brown defeated his Democratic opponent in a race in Massachusetts left vacant by the death of Senator Ted Kennedy. Nancy Pelosi, the Democratic House Speaker, and Obama developed a clever strategy that proved successful. The House approved the Senate version of the legislation—and the Senate then amended it with the House version using the procedure for Reconciliation bills that only required a 50% majority so that it was immune from a Republican filibuster. Health reform consisted, then, of two measures: the Patient Protection and Affordable

Care Act that had been approved by the House (the Senate version), as well as the Healthcare and Education Reconciliation Act (the House version approved by the Senate). I use the summary of this legislation provided by the Kaiser Family Foundation at many points in this and other chapters as accessed at http://healthreform.kff.org on July 10, 2010, as well as a government web site, HealthCare.gov, as accessed on July 11, 2010.

I discuss some features of the American system of financing healthcare that preceded the Obama health plan so that we can better understand the nature and extent of reforms in this plan. These include dividing runaway costs among different entities, buckpassing, seniors' angst, the medical wheel of fortune, and ripple effects.

Pre-Obama Plan

The cost of healthcare exploded during the past five decades in the United States when total health expenditures rose from $27.5 billion in 1960 to $2.3 trillion in 2008—and from 5.2% of GDP in 1960 to 16.2% of GDP in 2008 (Centers for Medicare and Medicaid Services, n.d.). Total per capita cost of healthcare was $7,681 in 2008 (Centers for Medicare and Medicaid Services, n.d.). Many researchers agree that these burgeoning costs derived principally from two sources: medical technology, and the advertising and administrative costs of insurance companies, health plans, and pharmaceutical companies. Providers in the U.S. health system spend far more than their counterparts in Europe, Canada, and Japan on surgical procedures, organ transplants, orthopedic implants, scans, expensive medications, and chemotherapy (G. Anderson & Frogner, 2008). The United States also spends more than these counterparts on healthcare for persons in the last two years of their lives—or at least 25% of Medicare spending in 2000 (Hogan et al., 2000). Roughly 25% of U.S. health costs stem from the marketing and administrative costs of private insurance companies and health plans that advertise their services—not even counting the large marketing and advertising costs of pharmaceutical companies to sell their products to physicians and hospitals, as well as consumers through television advertisements (Kahn, Kronick, Kreger, & Gans, 2005). These costs, too, are considerably lower in many industrialized nations, particularly ones with single-payer or government-dominated systems where little or no advertising exists in the public plan.

The United States devised a financing system that divided or spread these extraordinary costs among many parties as can be seen in Figure 9.1. The federal government split the cost of Medicare with employees and employers who fund roughly half of its hospital costs (Part A)—and with seniors who fund a considerable portion of physicians' costs with monthly premiums along with contributions from general revenues from the federal government (Part B). It split the cost of Medicaid with states (Center for Children and Families, 2008; Kaiser Family Foundation, 2010). Many employers funded private health insurance premiums of employees, but received lucrative tax deductions

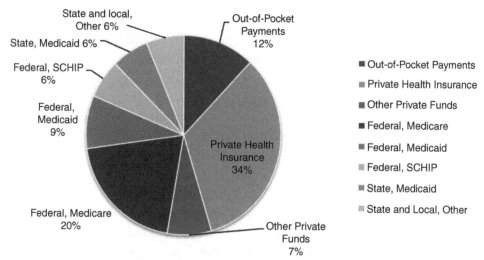

Figure 9.1 Shares of Health Spending

Source: Centers for Medicare & Medicaid Services, U.S. Department of Health & Human Services (n.d.). NHE Web Tables. Retrieved February 9, 2010, from http://www.cms.hhs.gov/NationalHealthExpendData/02_NationalHealth AccountsHistorical.asp.

against corporate income from the federal government. Roughly 59% of American citizens receive health insurance from private employers (DeNavas-Salt, Proctor, & Smith, 2009). Private health insurance companies, as well as Medicare and Medicaid, required consumers to pay such out-of-pocket costs as deductibles, co-payments, and co-insurance. Some uninsured consumers self-funded part or all of their medical costs with the balance coming from Medicaid DSH payments, local or state governments, and charitable funds of clinics and hospitals. State and local governments split the medical costs of many uninsured persons with Medicaid, as well as SCHIP. Costs of un-documented persons were split between Medicaid (obstetrics and some emergency costs), local governments, and state governments. Hospitals and clinics picked up so-called uncompensated care from their own charitable funds and private donors.

The different contributors to U.S. health spending felt considerable economic distress even from their share of health costs because overall spending was so large. Federal officials feared that their large medical costs would make it impossible to reduce the federal deficit, which had ballooned to $1.4 trillion in late 2009 in the wake of expenditures on the economic recovery plan in the first year of the Obama presidency (Congressional Budget Office, 2009). Medicare, Medicaid, the U.S. Department of Veterans Affairs (VA), SCHIP, and the Federal Employees Health Plan consumed 28% of the federal budget in 2008, (Office of Management and Budget, 2010 and Centers for Medicare and Medicaid Services [n.d.]). This number does not count lost tax revenues of the federal government of $240 billion in 2010 from tax deductions it gave corporations for their health expenditures for their employees' healthcare (Urban-Brookings Tax Policy Center, 2009). Federal officials often threaten to cut their share of Medicaid costs, such as by banning use of its funds to train physicians, cutting Medicaid payments to public hospitals, and limiting Medicaid coverage of rehabilitation costs for serious mental illness and other disabilities, as in 2008 (Pear, 2008). State officials fear that they cannot afford the growing costs of Medicaid, which often consumed between 20% and 30% of their budgets—not counting the additional health expenditures on S/CHIP and undocumented residents (Center for Children and Families, 2008). States often cut Medicaid benefits and reimbursements—forcing local providers to pick up these costs or denying services to enrollees. Public hospitals, such as Grady hospital in Atlanta, cannot keep up with their huge numbers of uninsured and underinsured persons, as well as undocumented persons, even when getting special Medicaid subsidies known as disproportionate share funds (DSH). Many private hospitals run in the red or barely break even because so many consumers cannot afford hospital costs, because the Medicaid program often does not reimburse them sufficiently even to cover Medicaid enrollees' hospital costs, and because Medicare often reimburses them only at a break-even level. Most hospitals lose money on their emergency rooms—forcing many of them to close them. Insurance company officials often fear they will be encumbered by costs of enrollees with costly medical conditions or that their profits will be eroded if the rising cost of medical care outstrips their premiums. Officials from managed care plans often fear that flat annual fees paid to them by employers, the federal government, state Medicaid authorities, or consumers will not suffice to cover their costs. Consumers often become bankrupt or destitute because of their health costs, particularly people with no or inadequate coverage or people with costly health conditions.

Spreading costs among many parties have the advantage of insulating each of them from the exclusive burden of these gigantic costs. It created, however, a chaotic system that proved inequitable. Some consumers received excellent coverage and access to world-class services, but others had no or partial coverage that exposed them to financial distress if they developed a serious or chronic health condition.

Post-Obama Plan

U.S. health spending in the wake of Obama's Plan will continue to spread health costs among many entities rather than concentrating them in the federal government as is true in many European nations and Canada. But it will modify expenditures in important ways. It will increase federal spending such as its share of Medicaid costs, tax credits to small employers, subsidies to low- and moderate-income consumers, and expenditures for prevention and demonstration programs, but offset these costs by various taxes and penalties imposed on affluent persons, consumers who choose not to obtain insurance, and employers who choose not to provide insurance to their employees. It will save resources, as well, by instilling more competition into health markets by having states establish insurance exchanges that will sell health policies to consumers and businesses at competitive rates. The Obama Plan will decrease consumers' out-of-pocket costs by requiring that many more of them receive insurance—and by imposing regulations on insurance companies that place limits on consumers' out-of-pocket costs in their insurance plans. It will considerably increase expenditures by states because they will have to expend more on their Medicaid programs after it is greatly expanded in 2014, but these expansion costs will largely be borne by the federal government. It will increase expenditures by many small employers who will have to provide insurance to their employees, but whose costs will be reduced by federal tax credits if they have fewer than 25 employees. It will probably cut profits of insurance companies by requiring them to insure consumers with preexisting conditions, banning lifetime limits on health benefits, and limiting the amount they can spend on marketing and administrative costs as compared to patient-care costs.

The Congressional Budget Office (CBO) estimated in late March 2010 that the Obama Plan would reduce federal deficits by $143 billion from 2010 to 2019 because new federal revenues and savings would exceed new federal costs. The federal government would have to spend new resources to subsidize insurance premiums of many low- and moderate-income consumers, spend more on its federal share of an expanded Medicaid program, fund additional pharmaceutical benefits for Medicare recipients, and spend funds on many new prevention programs. These new expenditures would be offset, however, by funds from excise taxes on high-premium insurance policies, taxes on high-income persons, funds from penalties exacted on employers and individuals choosing not to obtain insurance for their employees or themselves, and cuts in reimbursements to private Medicare Advantage Plans. Some preventive programs and enhanced primary care funded by the federal government may somewhat reduce curative medical costs, although experts disagree about the likelihood and size of these savings. The federal government may reduce some of its long-term health costs by persuading more people to subscribe to long-term care insurance before they retire.

The Obama Plan proposes other ways to cut health spending. It requires health plans and insurance companies to give rebates to consumers if they spend less than 85% of their premium dollars on clinical services, quality, and other costs—a policy certain to cut the extent they use premium dollars for marketing and administrative costs. It exacted discounts from drug companies for Medicare and Medicaid recipients and imposed fees on pharmaceutical companies. It gives incentives for the development of generic drugs. It promotes purchasing strategies of drugs and supplies in Medicare and Medicaid to cut costs. The Obama Plan will not fundamentally change the way Americans spread the cost of healthcare among many entities and populations. It will likely increase the federal share of health costs as it expands Medicaid by 2014, when Americans earning less than 133% of the poverty level (or about $14,000 for individuals and $29,000 for families of four) will be eligible. (The federal government will cover 100% of this expanded Medicaid coverage for the first three years phasing to 90% in years following 2014). It will increase Medicare expenditures by expanding its coverage of medications in phases extending to 2020. It will markedly cut some consumers' costs, particularly consumers with preexisting conditions because they can no longer be denied coverage by private insurance companies in 2010. Small employers' expenditures will rise as they are required to provide health insurance to their employees or to pay the cost of their care to a state pool, often with the help, however, of a significant federal tax credit. Affluent Americans will help fund some of the added federal costs by paying higher taxes on capital gains from their investments, as well as paying higher taxes if their incomes exceed $250,000 for couples. Uninsured individuals will be required to purchase health insurance from private insurance companies or from state pools if their income is too high to qualify for Medicaid.

The United States chose, in other words, to spread the costs of these changes in health coverage to many different entities rather than to fund their healthcare primarily by expenditures of central and/or regional governments like many European nations and Canada. In general, state and federal governments, small employers, affluent Americans, and some uninsured individuals received the largest increases in the new distribution of costs.

BUCK-PASSING

As compared to many other nations where central governments fund most of their medical costs, the United States has created a financing system that encourages "buck-passing" where states, insurance companies, public programs, and the federal government often attempt to pass medical costs onto one another.

Pre-Obama Plan

Distressed by their share of the total cost of the health system, governments, insurance companies, health plans, and corporations often try to shift some of their costs to one another. Federal and state governments jockey over who should foot specific Medicaid and CHIP costs. States often ask the federal government to pay a larger share of their Medicaid costs through a variety of tactics, including seeking special subsidies when they face large deficits such as during the recession of 2007 to 2009. Federal officials, in turn, often ask state governments to return funds that they contend had been used fraudulently or did not conform to Medicaid statutes. Private insurance companies ask Medicare to fund medical bills of their enrollees who receive it so they do not have to fund their medical costs. Private insurance companies often try to reject consumers with costly medical problems or to push them to the public sector. Managed care plans often lobby Congress to obtain higher reimbursements from Medicare and Medicaid— only to be countered by federal authorities who often insist on giving them such low annual fees that many managed-care plans refuse to enroll new members in these programs and may even drop existing ones.

Many health advocates are distressed by the extent that federal and state governments, private insurance plans, and managed-care plans often seek to pass costs onto consumers—leading them to fund about 45% of total medical spending in the United States when out-of-pocket fees, insurance premiums, and payroll deductions are aggregated (see Figure 9.1) (Centers for Medicare & Medicaid Services, U.S.

Department of Health & Human Services, n.d.). Consumers in the United States pay about twice the amount of out-of-pocket healthcare costs as consumers in other developed nations (G. Anderson & Frogner, 2008). Federal officials often increased the monthly premiums that seniors paid for physicians' services in Part B of the Medicare program. They added a pharmaceutical benefit in 2003 that still left many seniors' medication costs unfunded. They continued not to fund podiatry and eyeglasses or the costs of most chronic health conditions for Medicare enrollees.

State officials often cut Medicaid benefits when they face fiscal problems, such as eliminating or curtailing dental care and in-home care for seniors. They often raise consumer fees for specific health services. They often cut reimbursements to hospitals and physicians to such low levels that enrollees find it more difficult to find services. Only massive subsidies to the states from the federal government averted drastic cuts in Medicaid benefits and imposition of greater consumer fees during the recession of 2008 through 2010 when many states developed large deficits.

Employers often saddle consumers with the burden of covering their health costs— and could do so legally because no federal or state law required them to provide health coverage. Many employers provide no health coverage, particularly small companies, often citing their fear that they will go bankrupt or be unable to compete successfully with other corporations if they provide them, even when the federal government offers them considerable tax deductions for funding it. Many companies provide only minimal benefits, such as excluding many medical services and establishing an annual cap on benefits. Others ask employees to pay large out-of-pocket payments for healthcare. Some employers provide health benefits only to full-time employees while giving no benefits or only minimal ones to part-time employees. Other employers drop health coverage abruptly when they face economic downturns, such as during recessions, and some give monies to employees to be placed in "medical savings accounts" to be used for their medical costs—but these funds are usually so minimal that they are quickly exhausted when employees face expensive medical conditions. Some employers cover dependents' health costs generously, but many cover them only modestly or not at all.

Some employers dismiss those employees who they believe would soon encounter costly medical conditions to avoid these costs, as well as to avert increases in premiums from the health insurance company that they use to cover their employees. (Many insurance companies, as well as state workers' compensation programs that fund healthcare for occupational injuries, use experience ratings that adjust their charges to companies based on employees' medical costs.) Some dismiss workers with dependents with costly health problems. They often do not hire or they dismiss older workers partly to avoid their pension and health costs.

Many employers face a catch-22 situation. If they fund relatively generous health benefits for their employees and some or all of their competitors do not, they often fear that these competitors might be able to sell goods or services at lower prices than them. Many employers who fund health benefits also are placed at a competitive disadvantage with foreign competitors that pay no health benefits, such as companies in nations with national health coverage paid by their governments or those in developing nations where few corporations funded health benefits. Employees' health benefits account for $1,525 per car manufactured by General Motors but only $201 per car manufactured by Toyota (Geng, 2005).

Private insurance companies often pass costs onto consumers by using many strategies. They often contend that consumers did not divulge information about prior medical conditions when they had filled out their application forms often years earlier. When consumers respond that their medical providers had not informed them that they had these medical conditions, they often answer that they ought to have known that they had these conditions by examining their own blood and other tests. They often do not reimburse specific surgeries, diagnostic tests, or medications because they are not medically necessary even though their physicians had recommended them. They often refuse to fund costs of emergency care on grounds consumers that do not face a true emergency. Because companies often gave consumers contracts written in fine print and indecipherable language, consumers often do not know what benefits they could receive or what fees they would have to pay. Insurance companies often send bills to consumers for their share of medical care that are so difficult to understand that consumers cannot understand them, much less contest them if they are inaccurate.

Insurance companies often increase their premiums at remarkable rates, markedly raising costs to employers as well as those consumers annually between 1999 and 2008 (Kaiser Family Foundation and Health Research and Education Trust, 2009). In addition, many employees also face large general annual deductibles. In 2009, a deductible of $1,000 or more was required for 22% of workers with health coverage, compared to 10% in 2006 (Kaiser Family Foundation and Health Research and Education Trust, 2009). If the companies often insist that these increases are justified by escalating medical costs, critics often contend they are profit-mongering.

Health-insurance companies engage in aggressive competition for the business of employers. They offer them an array of cost-reducing policies that place even greater burdens on consumers, such as exclusions of specific services and medications, time limits on benefits for specific illnesses, maximum annual payouts, maximum lifetime payouts and high levels of consumer fees that include deductibles, co-payments, and co-insurance.

Consumers often bear the brunt of buck-passing. Roughly 14,000 Americans lost their health insurance every day in 2009 (Center for American Progress, 2009). Data from polls confirms this angst among many consumers. In a 2010 survey in Michigan, 40% of people were very or somewhat worried about losing their health insurance. The level of worry about loss of health insurance was directly linked to their worry about losing their job (Center for Healthcare Research and Transformation, 2010). Americans think that the cost and availability of healthcare is the most urgent health problem in the United States, not AIDS, cancer, diabetes, or any other disease (Harper, 2008).

Many employers prompt their employees to use Preferred Provider Organizations (PPOs) for their healthcare. PPOs required employees to select those physicians, hospitals, and other providers that had agreed to charge discounted prices to employees of specific employers, while allowing them to use other providers only if employees paid a substantial additional fee. This arrangement works well for consumers unless they want specific providers outside this list—whether because they had used them in the past or believed they gave superior services to ones used by their PPO.

Some managed-care plans also pass significant costs to consumers even if such leading ones as Kaiser Permanente keep these costs at a minimal level. They ask them to pay significant fees for physician visits, diagnostic tests, or surgeries. They make it difficult for them to make appointments with physicians, such as by having only a few phone lines for same-day appointments. They fail to refer them promptly to specialists. They fail to inform consumers about their services. They refuse to fund medical care for enrollees who want to use medical providers outside their managed-care plan even when its staff lacks sufficient expertise or competence for specific medical procedures.

Hospitals often try to pass some of their costs onto their patients. They sometimes overcharge for services, tests, medications, and supplies. They sometimes charge consumers for duplicative services, such as specific diagnostic tests, that sometimes occurred because staff in one department often did not realize that patients had received them from another one. Consumers sometimes become enmeshed in conflict between hospitals and private insurance plans when they could not agree who was responsible for specific costs—sometimes leaving the consumer with the costs.

Consumers often face legal jeopardy if they fail to pay medical bills promptly—even when they believed them to be inaccurate or confiscatory. Insurance companies, managed-care plans, physicians, and hospitals often hire collection agents to collect funds they contend are owed to them even while consumers were contesting those charges. Consumers often find their credit ratings to be lowered during these negotiations, sometimes losing assets like cars or homes. More than half of the bankruptcies in the United States are caused by consumers' inabilities to fund their medical expenditures (Warren, 2005).

Single women with children pay a high portion of their budgets for health expenses. They often have no private insurance because their employers do not provide it, yet they must fund their family's health costs. Their former husbands often do not make alimony payments.

Post-Obama Plan

The Obama Plan will greatly decrease buck-passing. Even in 2010, the Plan disallows many practices of private insurance companies that deprived consumers of coverage, including denying care because of preexisting conditions and lifetime limits on benefits. It requires health insurance plans by 2014 to create an essential health benefits package that includes a comprehensive set of services. It places limits on out-of-pocket costs of consumers by 2014—with federal subsidies to low- and moderate-income consumers for the cost of their premiums on a sliding basis as they move from the Federal Poverty Level

(FPL) to 400% of the FPL. (They placed limits on out-of-pocket costs for all other consumers, as well.)

The Obama Plan defines, as well, a division of responsibility between the states and the federal government. The states will organize Health Benefit Exchanges and Small Business Health Options program exchanges through which individuals and small businesses up to 100 employees can purchase coverage in 2014. (Small businesses with less than 25 employees qualified even in 2010 for tax credits for the cost of insuring their employees on a sliding basis.) These exchanges will cut the cost of insurance by allowing these companies and individuals to purchase coverage in a competitive market. The Plan decreases the number of uninsured persons by allowing young people to remain on their parents insurance policies until they are 26—a group that disproportionately had lacked insurance.

The cost of health insurance may be reduced by the creation of Consumer Operated and Oriented Plans (CO-Ops) in 2013. These not-for-profit, member-run health insurance programs in all 50 states and the District of Columbia will compete with private insurance plans.

Both individuals and companies will be penalized if they choose not to secure coverage. Health experts believe that the cost of coverage can be reduced only if all possible consumers participate—especially relatively healthy and young persons.

The Obama Plan proposes a significant expansion of Medicaid in 2014, as we have discussed, but will fund most of the costs of this expansion.

SENIORS' ANGST

Senior citizens have often borne major fiscal challenges in funding their healthcare costs in the United States as they have lost health coverage from employers in the wake of retirement and developed expensive health conditions. As we discussed in preceding chapters, Medicare's benefits do not cover chronic health conditions and many of their medications, not to mention many other costs. It is unclear to what extent the Obama Plan will ease seniors' angst.

Pre-Obama Plan

The budgets of elderly persons are usually hard hit when they move to retirement homes or nursing homes because Medicare and many supplemental insurance policies do not cover these costs. Although long-term care insurance and so-called reverse mortgages may eventually ease seniors' costs of retirement homes and nursing homes, relatively few of them have purchased or used these strategies. Many seniors become medically bankrupted or destitute when they enter nursing homes, whether skilled nursing facilities (SNFs) or intermediary care ones (ICNFs)—or even assisted care settings.

Here, too, great discrepancies exist between relatively affluent and less affluent consumers. The former group can often self-fund retirement homes that have independent-living units, as well as intermediary and skilled care units, by paying an entrance fee, such as $175,000 or more, as well as monthly fees, such as $2,000, from their Social Security payments as well as their personal resources. (Some retirement homes allow residents to purchase their units and sell them or pass them onto others in their wills.) Relatively affluent persons, too, can purchase in-home care for help with daily activities or even around-the-clock care when they become more infirm. Less affluent persons often cannot afford retirement homes or in-home care, so they must often spend down their resources when they become disabled or too ill to become eligible for Medicaid, which funds these amenities for low-income consumers.

When seniors have costly chronic diseases, even relatively affluent ones are often fiscally challenged to the point of selling their homes and exhausting other savings or assets. They quickly discover that Medicare coverage rules are very complicated. Full coverage of hospital stays is only for the first 60 days of hospitalization in any 100 day "benefit period." The consumer must pay part of the cost for day 61 to day 90 during each benefit period, and a larger portion for a maximum 60 "lifetime reserve day" after that. These restrictive policies were intended to shield the Medicare program from funding the high cost of long-term chronic illnesses.

Medicare covers stays in skilled nursing facilities only after a minimum 3-day hospital stay. Care in skilled nursing facilities is covered for a maximum of 100 days after each 3-day hospital stay. The full cost of the skilled nursing stay is covered for 20 days, and the consumer must pay a large portion of the costs for days 21 through 100. Medicare covers physical therapy and some in-home care only as long as their physicians certify that their health continues to improve—in other words, only if there is an acute health problem rather than a chronic one. (Hospitalization, convalescent care, and in-home period is also called a Medicare benefit period.) Once seniors are again hospitalized after recovering from a bout of illness, the time clock begins to run again in a new benefit period identical in length to the prior period. If seniors exceed this time period in the hospital, they have to self-fund remaining care.

Supplemental insurance often helps more affluent seniors with health and in-home costs when Medicare coverage has lapsed. If they are medically unlucky, however, their illness or illnesses persist and require new bouts of hospitalization that leads them eventually to exhaust their supplemental insurance (if they possess it). Once they exhaust both their Medicare and supplemental coverage, they must draw on their personal savings and assets to finance their healthcare until they qualify for Medicaid.

Many elderly persons are traumatized by this depletion of their personal resources. Many of them had assumed that Medicare would cover most of their health expenditures, including ones associated with chronic diseases, cancer, and serious accidents. Many of them had assumed that their savings and assets would remain sufficiently intact for travel, restaurants, and other amenities through their retirement years while leaving them an estate to pass on to their spouses, children, relatives, or charity. A typical couple at the age of age 65 can expect pay healthcare expenses of $260,000 over the remainder of their lives (Webb & Zhivan, 2010). This includes Medicare and insurance premiums, long-term care and other costs.

These grim fiscal realities entice many seniors and some physicians to "game the system."

Physicians use different diagnostic categories to describe illnesses or medical conditions of seniors in different benefit periods to obscure the fact that they are receiving care for a specific chronic health condition like diabetes, COPD, heart disease, stroke, or congestive heart failure. Physicians sometimes certify that their patients' health is improving after a bout of hospitalization so they remain eligible for physical therapy, visiting nurses, and some in-home assistance. Determined to pass resources to their children and others on their forthcoming death, many elderly persons give their resources to their children during the spend-down period before they gain eligibility for Medicaid. This practice was mostly halted when Congress outlawed it by requiring that these resources transfers had to occur at least 60 months before they enrolled in Medicaid.

Post-Obama Plan

The Obama Plan did not fundamentally relieve seniors' angst. Medicare's coverage remained limited to specific time periods so that seniors with chronic or serious illness will have to continue to self-fund care once they exceed them, forcing them to still spend-down their resources until they qualify for Medicaid.

The Obama Plan does, however, greatly increase Medicare's prescription benefit by phasing out the so-called donut hole by 2020. Medicare had not even covered prescription drugs prior to 2003 when the Congress added prescription drugs to Medicare's benefits. This legislation funded prescription drugs up to a certain annual limit, but then did not fund them above that limit until seniors reached a considerably higher level of expenditures for drugs. This so-called "donut hole" proved financially devastating to many seniors.

The Obama Plan will help seniors in other ways. As we discussed in the preceding chapter, it funds annual wellness visits and personalized prevention plans for seniors under Medicare beginning in 2011. To help persons who retire before they are eligible for Medicare and who often are no longer eligible for health insurance funded by employers, the Obama Plan creates a $5 billion program to subsidize employers who continue coverage to retirees between 55 and 65 years of age. These seniors will be able to purchase private health insurance in 2014, when states establish insurance exchanges.

The Obama Plan will create a national, voluntary insurance program for purchasing community living assistance services and supports for long-term care, beginning in 2011 (the CLASS program). This program could greatly expand the number of Americans who do not need to depend on Medicaid to fund long-term care.

Marked reductions in Medicaid eligibility levels by 2014, for individuals and families who fall beneath 133% of federal poverty levels, will make it easier for those seniors who exhaust their savings from medical expenses to enter the Medicaid Program.

A Community First Choice Option allows states to offer home and community based services to disabled persons through Medicaid rather than institutional care in nursing homes (2012). Medicaid will create the "State Balancing Incentive Program" in 2011 to provide enhanced federal matching payments to increase non-institutionally based long-term care services.

THE MEDICAL WHEEL OF FORTUNE

Unlike many other nations where all residents obtain health insurance, the United States has created a medical wheel of fortune where consumers' coverage and health services depend on their group membership. The Obama Plan did not eliminate this wheel of fortune, but made coverage far more equitable.

Pre-Obama Plan and Post-Obama Plan: 13 Groups

The preceding discussion suggests that Americans created a medical wheel of fortune that consists of 13 groups. Let's discuss these groups pre- and post-Obama Plan—while recognizing that we will not know for certain how the Obama Plan will fare as its policies are implemented from 2010 to 2020.

Group 1: Employer-Sponsored Plans With Good Coverage: Pre-Obama Plan

Consumers working for corporations often receive excellent coverage that funds an array of benefits for long periods of time and also requires them to pay minimal out-of-pocket fees even for chronic health conditions. Their dependents usually received generous coverage. They rarely dip into their savings or sell assets to fund their medical care. Many students in higher education have health insurance through their colleges or universities that they fund as part of their fees. Federal employees usually receive their healthcare through the Federal Employee Health Benefits Plan, which offers generous benefits and a wide choice of health plans. Many county and state employees have health coverage through private insurance plans that are funded by local and state governments.

Group 1: Employer-Sponsored Plans With Good Coverage: Post-Obama Plan

The Obama Plan will require all employers to provide an "essential benefits package" by 2014—meaning that all of them will give good coverage. It will tax high-premium benefit packages—so-called Cadillac plans—of companies and individuals.

Group 2: Employer-Sponsored Plans With Moderate Coverage: Pre-Obama Plan

Other employees have mid-range benefits often funded for shorter periods of time with somewhat higher out-of-pocket fees and limited coverage for dependents. Other employees receive even more restricted coverage and must pay higher out-of-pocket fees, such as employees who only have catastrophic coverage or have low annual caps on their coverage.

Group 2: Employer-Sponsored Plans With Moderate Coverage: Post-Obama Plan

Some of these plans will be upgraded by 2014 to meet requirements of the essential benefits package. The Obama Plan will also place limits on out-of-pocket costs of employees.

Group 3: Uninsured Persons: Pre-Obama Plan

Uninsured employees have the bad fortune to work for employers who choose not to fund health insurance for them. If they are fortunate, they remain healthy. Their health can be jeopardized, however, if they develop a medical condition that is not detected because of their lack of regular primary care due to a paucity of physicians and outpatient clinics that serve them, even on a sliding-fee basis. They often use ERs to deal with medical conditions and, if necessary, to be referred to specialists. Unless they receive uncompensated (or charitable) care from a specific hospital, they must use one that receives Medicaid DSH funds or a public hospital funded with local or state resources. Here, too, their coverage depends on the generosity of the locality and state where they live: some jurisdictions, such as Los Angeles County, provide uninsured persons with most of the health benefits given to Medicaid recipients. Many uninsured consumers feel stigmatized by their uninsured status even though most of them are employed—and this stigma can lead them not to seek timely care for specific health conditions. Some employees are offered insurance by their employers, but decline to take it because they do not want to pay fees or costs associated with it. They disproportionately include younger workers, with 30% of young adults aged 19 to 29 lacking insurance because they are unemployed, work for employers who do not offer it, or decline coverage (Kritz, 2009b).

A minority of the uninsured population do not work. They include women who had coverage under their former husbands' policies, but who lose it when they separate from them. They include people applying for, but not having received, disability under Social Security or SSI. They include people whose Medicaid has lapsed even though they still remain eligible. They include children in families that are uninsured or whose insurance policies do not cover dependents. They include people who have exceeded caps on payouts from their private health insurance policies. They include nonelderly people "spending down" their assets to get onto Medicaid. They include people who cannot afford private health insurance because of high premiums due to preexisting health conditions or age. They also include elderly persons who exhaust their Medicare benefits when they possess chronic health conditions, forcing them to divest some or all of their savings and assets. They become uninsured during this "spend-down period" until they are have sufficiently low assets and income to qualify for Medicaid.

Group 3: Uninsured Persons: Post-Obama Plan

The Obama Plan will give coverage to roughly 32 million persons by requiring their employers to cover them, or to pay a penalty, or by expanding eligibility of the Medicaid program. By 2019, about 23 million persons will remain uninsured because they are undocumented or choose to pay penalties rather than purchase coverage or cannot afford private insurance even with various subsidies and out-of-pocket limits that will begin in 2014. States will have the option of creating a Basic Health Plan for uninsured persons with incomes between 133% and 200% of federal poverty standards.

Many persons between age 19 and 26 have traditionally been uninsured, but the Obama Plan requires private insurance companies to provide dependent coverage for them from all individual and group policies beginning in 2010.

Employers will have to pay a penalty if they do not insure their employees. Small employers with 25 employees or less qualify for tax credits on a sliding basis for the cost of insuring their employees. Employers with 100 or fewer employees qualify for insurance policies offered in the state exchanges. Employers with more than 100 employees are required to purchase coverage for their employees in the regular insurance market.

Many uninsured persons currently use public safety-net clinics and hospitals. The Patient Protection and Affordable Care Act of 2010 as amended by Congress will make global capitated payments to safety-net hospitals effective fiscal years 2010 through 2015. Special subsidies to public and not-for-profit hospitals that serve a disproportionate share of uninsured and low-income persons will be markedly reduced by the Act as more of these persons obtain insurance.

To fund insurance for persons with preexisting medical conditions who are currently uninsured, the Act establishes a temporary national high-risk pool effective from July 2010 to January 1, 2014, after which many of them will have purchased health insurance from State Exchanges.

Group 4: Unemployed Persons With COBRA Coverage: Pre-Obama Plan

Unemployed people sometimes qualify for COBRA benefits that they purchase from the insurance company at group rates used by their prior employers if those employers funded health insurance for their employees. These unemployed persons can retain this insurance for 18 months. If they cannot afford this insurance or their prior employer did not provide it, they join the ranks of uninsured people until they find employment with an employer that funds health insurance for them.

Group 4: Unemployed Persons With COBRA Coverage: Post-Obama Plan

COBRA will be far less necessary under the Obama Plan because individuals can purchase their insurance through state exchanges in 2014—or be eligible for the Medicaid program.

Group 5: Individuals' Insurance Plans: Pre-Obama Plan

Some consumers self-fund their insurance often when their employers do not provide it. Consumers usually pay more for this insurance than if it had been funded by employers because they do not qualify for a group rate—and the costs rapidly escalate with the age of consumers, as well as when they have health conditions as determined by a medical examination required by the insurer or managed-care program as part of the application process. Some consumers obtain insurance from special state insurance programs for uninsured consumers at reduced rates, including consumers with medical conditions.

Group 5: Individuals' Insurance Plans: Post-Obama Plan

Individuals will be able to purchase their own insurance through the state-sponsored insurance exchanges in 2014. They will have a mandate to be insured—meaning they will have to pay a penalty if they choose not to purchase insurance. The cost of insurance will often be reduced from current levels due to competition between plans offered by the state exchanges, allowing consumers to choose policies that are relatively inexpensive. Insurance companies will be required to reduce out-of-pocket payments for persons with incomes up to 400% of federal poverty levels. They will have to limit waiting periods for coverage to 90 days. Insurance plans will be required to provide an essential health benefits package that provides a comprehensive set of services. States will have the option to create a basic health plan for uninsured persons with incomes between 133 and 200% of federal poverty levels.

Group 6: Medicaid Enrollees: Pre-Obama Plan

Medicaid recipients receive medical coverage whose generosity depends on the policies of the state where they reside as well as the kind of health systems available to them in a specific community. Most Medicaid recipients are enrolled in public or private managed-care plans. They have coverage for outpatient, inpatient, emergency, medications, and long-term care, but often have relatively spartan coverage for specific services like podiatry and dental care. Most states require them to re-enroll frequently in a difficult process that requires them to complete many forms and bring in extensive documentation. Medicaid recipients often receive delayed care from specialists because relatively few of them are willing to help Medicaid recipients due to ultralow reimbursement rates in many states—even when they have relatively serious health conditions. When they leave welfare rolls for extended periods because of employment, they can usually remain Medicaid recipients for a specified period, but often join the ranks of uninsured or underinsured persons if their employers do not provide generous coverage. Medicaid is a means-tested program for persons regardless of age, including children, nonelderly adults, and elderly adults. Many seniors move to nursing homes that are funded by Medicaid, which vary greatly in their quality. Medicaid has become the largest funder of nursing home care for elderly persons in the United States. Many elderly consumers are "dually eligible" for Medicare and Medicaid, often having their medications and some other benefits funded by Medicare with other medical costs funded by Medicaid.

Group 6: Medicaid Enrollees: Post-Obama Plan

The Medicaid program will be vastly expanded by 2014 as it comes to cover persons earning less than 133% of the federal poverty standard. Any person meeting these income limits can join the Medicaid program, even if they are single or are married without children. Prior to 2014, states establish their own eligibility standards. Medicaid will continue to have large numbers of elderly enrollees who spend-down to its eligibility levels due to medical costs that exceed their Medicare benefits or the benefits of supplemental insurance that they purchase.

Group 7: SCHIP: Pre-Obama Plan

Several medical programs focus on children including the State Children's Health Insurance Program (SCHIP). CHIP, a federal-state program, exists for children in families too affluent to qualify for Medicaid but who reside with uninsured parents. States establish eligibility levels and services.

Group 7: SCHIP: Post-Obama Plan

Many fewer children and their parents will need to use the SCHIP program after 2014 when enrollments in private insurance plans, as well as Medicaid, dramatically increase.

Group 8: Medicare Enrollees: Pre-Obama Plan

Medicare recipients are a diverse group because all persons over age 65 participate in the program with many purchasing supplemental coverage to fill in gaps in Medicare benefits. Other seniors only have Medicare coverage, which makes them vulnerable to large out-of-pocket payments if and when they exhaust their Medicare coverage, such as funding healthcare for chronic diseases and some levels of pharmaceutical costs. Roughly 7 million nonelderly persons with end-stage renal disease have received coverage from Medicare since 1972 when this benefit was added to Medicare.

Group 8: Medicare Enrollees: Post-Obama Plan

Medicare will remain roughly in its current configuration but with additional services, additional pharmaceutical benefits, and expanded community-based services.

Group 9: Retirees and Seniors With Coverage Other Than Medicare: Pre-Obama Plan

Retired public-sector employees often have their own insurance policies. Federal retirees get their health insurance from the Federal Employees Health Benefits Plan. State and local government officials often receive healthcare from publicly funded programs that supplement Medicare. These retirees usually have generous benefits, although some local and state governments, as well as school districts, have cut benefits in response to budget deficits (Halper, 2007).

Group 9: Retirees and Seniors With Coverage Other Than Medicare: Post-Obama Plan

Health benefits for public retirees will remain intact.

Group 10: Self-Funded Long-Term Care: Pre-Obama Plan

Residents of long-term care include relatively affluent Americans who pay for admission to continuing care retirement communities that sometimes include independent living, intermediary care, and skilled care. This elite form of care is accessed by large entrance payments, usually $150,000 or more and monthly payments of several thousand dollars, which are self-funded or partly funded by private long-term care insurance. (Some retirement facilities for affluent Americans allow them to purchase units that can be inherited and sold by family members.) Many seniors receive in-home services, but self-fund help for varying parts of the day or fund it through long-term care insurance that they have purchased.

Group 10: Self-Funded Long-Term Care: Post-Obama Plan

The Obama Plan will establish a national voluntary insurance program for purchasing community living assistance services and supports in 2011, which may provide less expensive options for insuring for retirement. It will establish Medicare "Independence At Home" demonstration projects in 2012.

Group 11: Immigrants: Pre-Obama Plan

Some working immigrants, such as highly skilled engineers with technology firms, secure health insurance from their employers. Many students with green cards receive health-care from the colleges or universities that they attend. Immigrants with temporary H-2A visas, who enter the country only if specific employers request them for time-limited visits, can receive health insurance from their employers, but often do not—requiring them to receive care from ERs. Immigrants with uncertain status and undocumented immigrants often qualify only for emergency care, obstetrics care, or some benefits from public health programs that is funded by local governments, states, or Medicaid. Persons with uncertain immigrant status include persons who are applying for citizenship, such as refugees from other nations, persons seeking amnesty, and some green-card holders who seek citizenship. Undocumented persons have entered the United States illegally. They qualify for medical care for medical emergencies, obstetrical services for childbirth, and public health services such as for preventing tuberculosis and HIV/AIDS, but not for publicly subsidized primary care or other medical services.

I have discussed how immigrants are entitled to emergency care when they have urgent health conditions, including hospitalization. They cannot be transferred from a hospital where they have been admitted until they are stabilized medically. Beyond these basic protections, immigrants' rights to healthcare vary greatly among specific counties, cities, and states. The Personal Responsibility and Work Opportunity Reconciliation Act, also known as the 1996 Welfare Reform Act, which reformed federal welfare programs, disqualified many immigrants from health services, including Medicaid. It prohibited immigrants who entered the United States after August 22, 1996, from receiving most types of public assistance, until the immigrant becomes a citizen. By setting up a five-year waiting period before newly arrived immigrants qualify for many types of federal assistance, it pushed services to immigrants onto state budgets. It was modified in 1997, however, when SCHIP programs were enacted. Some states used state funds to cover immigrant children under SCHIP, or to cover immigrant pregnant women, seniors, and the disabled.

Los Angeles County is an example of a local jurisdiction with relatively liberal policies. It allows access by documented and undocumented immigrants to emergency Medicaid, pregnancy-related Medicaid, minor consent services Medicaid, county mental health services, and services from the Child Health and Disability Program (CHDP) services provided by many free and community clinics. Only "qualified" immigrants can receive regular or full-scope Medicaid, however, such as ones who have become U.S. citizens, green card holders, refugees under federal law, ones granted asylum, people granted withholding of deportation, Cuban and Haitian entrants, persons paroled into the U.S. for at least one year, conditional entrants, victims of trafficking, and some spouses and children who are victims of domestic violence. "Not qualified immigrants" include undocumented immigrants, immigrants with Temporary Protected Status, immigrants who are not deported because they are Permanently Residing Under Color of Law (PRUCOL), persons in the United States on a temporary nonimmigrant visa, and applicants of "U" visa/interim relief. By contrast, immigrants in many other local jurisdictions have considerably fewer health rights.

Many immigrants qualify for SSI who meet its income limit and other requirements including those who have become citizens, already received it prior to August 22, 1996, are a refugee, are a Cuban or Haitian entrant, have received asylum, are a "qualified immigrant" who is a current or veteran U.S. military personnel or lawfully resided in the United States in August 22, 1996, who is blind or disabled, are a spouse or dependent child of one, or are a lawful permanent resident with credit for 40 quarters of work in the United States.

Securing health benefits by immigrants, then, can be a complicated task that hinges on federal, state, and local policies; the specific immigrant subgroup of a consumer; date of initial residence, income, and other factors.

Group 11: Immigrants: Post-Obama Plan

Undocumented immigrants will continue to be ineligible for Medicaid, as well as for clinic and hospital services in many jurisdictions. Documented or legal immigrants will qualify for the Medicaid program, as well as purchasing of private insurance, as well as private insurance from their employers.

Group 12: Disabled Persons: Pre-Obama Plan

Consumers who suffer disabling physical and mental problems qualify for medical care under two major programs: Supplemental Security Income (SSI) and Social Security Disability Insurance (SSDI). SSI was established in 1972 as a means-tested program for persons with disabilities. It is financed and administered by the federal government. Consumers who seek eligibility for SSI not only have to meet its income and resource requirements, but must follow specified procedures to obtain medical evaluations. Eligibility decisions are made by Social Security administration staff. Consumers can appeal these decisions in writing to the Social Security Administration. Appeals must be made within 60 days of receiving a decision. The decision is reconsidered by Social Security Administration staff, and this decision may also be appealed to a hearing with an administrative law judge. Consumers who receive SSI are automatically eligible for Medicaid in their state, including mandatory Medicaid services as well as optional ones selected by their home state.

Consumers with 40 quarters of work can apply for SSDI, which is a federally funded program funded by Social Security. Consumers must follow specified procedures to secure medical examinations and to file their applications, the Social Security Administration Disability Determination Services office making eligibility decisions.

Consumers who apply for SSI and SSDI must often endure long waits before they are admitted to either program, or roughly three to six months for SSI and three to five months for SSDI. SSDI benefits may be given immediately in cases where the disability is obvious, and benefits are retroactive to the date of application if approved. These waits often impose considerable hardship on them. Consumers who are denied eligibility to either program confront additional waits when they choose to appeal these decisions, for sometimes as much as three to six months.

Group 12: Disabled Persons: Post-Obama Plan

The Obama Plan makes no fundamental changes in disability policies. The Obama Plan will fund demonstrations to provide enhanced community-based services for disabled persons.

Group 13: Veterans: Pre-Obama Plan

Established in 1948 to provide medical care for veterans, the VA has become a massive program that currently has more than 8 million veterans enrolled in the VA Healthcare

System. More than 5.7 million of these veterans received treatment at a VA facility in 2009 at an annual cost of roughly $40 billion (U.S. Department of Veterans Affairs, 2010). Through use of evidence-based medicine, electronic records, and procedures to reduce medical error, the VA is widely seen as offering quality health services at relatively low cost. Its services include hospital, ER, and outpatient services in every state. Its reputation was tarnished, however, by poor treatment of some veterans from the Iraq and Afghanistan wars, including ones with mental health, substance abuse, and head trauma problems—as well as poor conditions in some of its hospitals. All veterans are eligible for services from the VA, but many obtain private health insurance and use private providers. There are two healthcare programs for families of veterans, TRICARE and Civilian Health and Medical Program of the Department of Veterans Affairs (CHAMPVA). CHAMPVA serves the spouse or children of veterans who are permanently and totally disabled from a service-connected disability. It also serves the surviving spouse or children of deceased disabled veterans and military members who died in the line of duty (U.S. Department of Veterans Affairs, 2010).

TRICARE provides services to family members and survivors of active duty service members and retirees of the military, including the National Guard and reserves and their families (Military Health System, 2010).

Group 13: Veterans: Post-Obama Plan

Health programs of the VA will remain intact. More veterans may migrate from the VA to private insurance as it becomes more widely available, less expensive, and with enhanced benefits before, during, and after 2014.

The Obama Plan offers additional resources and services to many of the 13 groups. It promises to markedly increase inequities among many of these groups in a striking and historic way. It offers less assistance, however, to undocumented immigrants. Many seniors will still have to spend-down to be eligible for Medicaid. The full effects of the Obama Plan will not be known until it has been fully implemented by 2021.

SOME EFFECTS OF POOR COVERAGE ON HEALTH OUTCOMES

Extent of coverage does not predict medical outcomes with certainty because many factors intrude. Relatively young consumers are likely to be healthy no matter their group membership—so many uninsured persons who do not receive coverage or who refuse coverage from their employers are not medically harmed by their lack of insurance. Consumers with limited education and income are likely to have poorer health than persons with considerable education and income no matter their group membership. Consumers who have chronic diseases are likely to have poorer health than other persons. Recent immigrants are likely to be relatively healthy even though they have no or scant access to the health system. Many low-income and poorly educated Hispanics are healthier than their social class would predict if they were from other ethnic groups, even if they are not recent immigrants.

Financial factors can affect health outcomes in several ways:

- Delayed care when consumers do not initiate recommended care because they fear it will bankrupt them or make them destitute.
- Interrupted care when consumers discontinue care because they fear it will bankrupt them or make them destitute.
- Unavailable care because Medicaid or related health plans reimburse specialists at such low levels that insufficient numbers are available to their enrollees.
- Inadequate primary care because consumers use ERs excessively due to lack of insurance.
- Hostile or shunning actions by health providers because they do not want to serve uninsured or underinsured persons.
- Angst from uncertain or inadequate health coverage.
- Not taking prescription or splitting pills because they cannot afford expensive drugs.

Many of these factors will be minimized by the Obama Plan, but many will still remain for the roughly 15 million persons who will be uninsured in 2019. Lack of sufficient primary care will likely remain a problem because of shortages of primary physicians, physician assistants, and nurse practitioners as 32 million Americans receive insurance in 2014 even after programs to train more of these healthcare professionals are implemented.

RIPPLE EFFECTS OF HEALTH COSTS AND COVERAGE

The American health system has impacted families, business, state governments, and the national economy in many ways in what we call indirect or "ripple effects." These effects may be substantially reduced by the Obama Plan.

Pre-Obama Plan

Finances can bring adverse repercussions for consumers in other ways. Persons who cannot afford their medical care may face social and mental consequences as their medical expenses impoverish them—including mental problems, family violence, suicide, homelessness, substance abuse, and other social problems. These ripple effects may, in turn, exacerbate their health conditions, such as accelerating chronic diseases and cancer.

Consumers often make important economic and employment decisions based on the impact on health coverage rather on other personal and family considerations. They may remain in a job just to keep its health benefits even when they do not like it or are not productive—particularly when they or their dependents have costly health conditions. They may delay retirement to have resources for personal or familial health conditions.

They may decide not to have another or additional children if someone in their family has a costly medical condition. They may delay purchasing a home or other amenities to fund healthcare.

Corporations often make strategic decisions based on the cost of healthcare. They may relocate to developing nations where they do not encounter union pressure to provide it. They may defer research on their products or expansion of their facilities to have resources to fund employees' health coverage.

Consumers' lack of coverage exacts a toll, as well, on the nation's budget deficits. While federal and state governments save funds by passing health costs on to consumers, they ultimately encumber costs when uninsured or underinsured consumers turn to public programs like Medicaid, S/CHIP, and the U.S. Department of Veterans Affairs to finance their healthcare. Failure to fund sufficient preventive care by private insurance companies, Medicaid, and Medicare contributes to overuse of ERs in the United States—a form of care far more expensive than primary care, which is disproportionately financed by Medicaid and Medicare. Many hospitals run in the red because they have so many patients who must rely on uncompensated care.

Reliance on employers to finance healthcare diminishes economic growth in the United States because they must charge higher for goods to fund it, unlike corporations in nations where central governments fund healthcare. Employers often cut wage levels to fund health insurance for their employees (Freudenheim, 2007). Some companies greatly increase their competitive advantages by not covering employees (Freudenheim, 2007).

Reliance on private insurance companies to fund the benefits of the bulk of nonelderly persons in the United States contributes to runaway health costs. Per capita cost of healthcare administration is more than $1,000 per person in the United States compared to $300 in Canada. This includes insurance company overhead, employers' costs to manage health insurance, hospital administration, and other administrative costs (Woolhandler, Campbell, & Himmelstein, 2003). Physicians and hospitals devote vast amounts of time and staff in billing insurance companies— each with different forms and different reimbursement policies. These physicians and hospitals expend about $200 billion a year in appealing incorrect reimbursements from insurance companies, such as not reimbursing physicians correctly for their fees about 14% of the time (Girion, 2008b).

Runaway U.S. health costs divert vast resources from private and government sources to healthcare rather than to other social needs or economic investments. Although these expenditures support the medical industrial complex, which employs many people, they risk depriving other sectors of the economy of needed resources.

Post-Obama Plan

These ripple effects will be greatly reduced by the Obama Plan. Many corporations will still be at a competitive disadvantage with corporations in nations with national health.

Some small businesses may be hard-pressed to fund employees' health premiums even with tax credits from the federal government. Far fewer consumers will need to stay in their jobs for fear of losing insurance. Far fewer consumers and families will be devastated by high health costs.

THE POLICY AND REGULATORY THICKET PROTECTING CONSUMERS WITH RESPECT TO HEALTH COVERAGE

The Obama Plan became part of the policy and regulatory thicket that protected consumers' rights with respect to financing their healthcare, but other policies and regulations predated it.

Policies Protecting Employees from Specific Actions Related to Healthcare

Employers are forbidden to discriminate against consumers with specific kinds of health needs. They cannot refuse to hire or dismiss women because they are pregnant. They have to give employees unpaid leave for specified periods under the Family and Medical Leave Act. They cannot discriminate against disabled persons. They cannot refuse to hire or dismiss persons on the basis of genetic information in many states that have enacted legislation protecting employees. They have to participate in state worker's compensation programs that fund health benefits for persons injured or disabled on the job if employees can demonstrate to state authorities that the injury or disability exists and that it occurred on the job.

Despite these protections for employees, corporations have often been accused of violating these laws. Many employers dismiss older employees, for example—and these employees will find it difficult to bring suit against them because a recent Supreme Court ruling in 2009 held that they had to prove intent on the basis of age. Employers often discriminate against women in the hiring process because they do not want to incur medical costs or leaves due to pregnancy, but women find it difficult to prove this. Many companies offer high-deductible insurance plans to employees even though they discriminate against women because they spend higher out-of-pocket costs than men as a result of more routine medical exams (Associated Press, 2007).

Policies Protecting Consumers from Arbitrary Treatment by Insurance Companies

Insurance companies have traditionally been regulated by insurance commissioners or departments of insurance of the different states. Most insurance companies are for-profit corporations, including Blue Cross and Blue Shield insurance programs that converted from not-for-profit to for-profit status in most states. All states have an elected or appointed insurance commissioner responsible for regulating insurance companies and agents and handling consumer complaints. Most states have some protections for consumers who work for corporations that provide health insurance to them, including requiring clear and complete information describing coverage, an appeals process, and coverage for emergency services when appropriate. The insurance regulations of the Obama Plan will be enforced by these state insurance commissioners, such as prohibitions on excluding persons with preexisting conditions and lifetime limits on coverage. They will enforce requirements that insurance companies expend roughly 80% of their premiums on consumers' health costs rather than spending large portions on advertising and marketing.

Critics note that the Obama Plan does not give states sufficient authority to stem increases in premiums—a deficiency that may be addressed by pending legislation in Congress to bolster states' authorities.

Policies Protecting Consumers From Arbitrary Treatment by Managed-Care Health Plans and Bankruptcies

Managed-care health plans are regulated by state health departments not just for the quality of their health services, but for ethical abuses. These abuses have included so-called "gag orders" where top administrators inform gatekeeper physicians to curtail referrals of consumers to specialists except under strict conditions. These plans have included not funding services for their consumers with physicians outside their plans when they lack physicians or technology needed by them. Some managed-care plans have promised specific benefits to enrollees, then did not provide them. When federal legislation to provide a Medical Bill of Rights to outlaw these abuses failed to pass, some states, such as California and New York, enacted their own legislation.

Policies Protecting Consumers from and during Medical Bankruptcy, a 2009 study, found that 62% of bankruptcies had a medical cause and that bankruptcies linked to medical expenses rose 50% between 2001 and 2007 (Himmelstein, Thorne, Warren, & Woolhandler, 2009). Bills have been introduced in congress (such as the Medical Bankruptcy Fairness Act of 2009) to create protections for people facing bankruptcies due to medical expenses, but none has passed. The Patient Protection and Affordable Care Act should markedly reduce the number of medical bankruptcies by 2014.

Policies Protecting Consumers During Applications for Medicaid and Medicare

States are required by federal legislation to offer fair hearings to consumers who wish to dispute specific service, reimbursement, or eligibility decisions made by Medicaid staff, as well as to give them access to medical transactions and records. Because Medicare is a federal program, appeals about decisions should be directed to your State Health Insurance Assistance Program or the Medicare Beneficiary Ombudsman.

Policies Giving Consumers the Right to Emergency Treatment

Federal laws protect the right of all U.S. residents, including undocumented consumers and other noncitizens, to emergency care when they possess urgent medical problems. These laws also protect them from transfers from a specific hospital to another one before they are medically stabilized.

Policies Protecting Health Benefits for Injured Workers

Each state has workers' compensation programs that fund medical and other costs associated with injuries at places of employment. Consumers must follow specified procedures for making claims, including medical examinations by physicians, as well as for appealing adverse decisions of state officials.

Policies Protecting the Right to Humane Nursing Home Care

Scandalous conditions in many nursing homes have led to state and federal policies to license and regulate them. These policies are discussed in Chapter 6.

Protections for Disabled Persons and Persons With Limited English When Applying for Health Programs

Under federal civil rights laws, as well as the Americans with Disabilities Act (ADA), applicants for public programs are entitled to oral translation services, assistance in reading forms, as well as assistance with filling out forms, as we discussed in Chapter 7. These programs include SSI, Medicaid, SSDI, and SCHIP.

Policies Protecting the Right of Consumers to Mental Healthcare

Federal legislation was enacted in 2007 that required private insurance plans to give mental health problems parity with physical problems. See Chapter 10 for more details.

TWENTY SCENARIOS ENCOUNTERED BY ADVOCATES

Twenty scenarios that advocates may encounter are discussed in this section. Fourteen are in this book and six are in the online materials relevant to this chapter.

Scenario 9.1: Advocacy to Help Consumers Select Health Insurance Policies

Pre-Obama Plan

When employees begin work for a corporation that provides health insurance, they need to research options carefully given cost and services implications. Employees paid an average of $3,826 in out-of-pocket costs (including premiums) in 2009 for health plans offered by employers.

Employers are required by the federal government to offer employees a range of plans. Employees need to review their own health needs and financial situations, as well as whether to retain their current physicians, to decide whether to select a PPO, HMO, high-deductible plan, or other options available to them, as well as whether to seek dental coverage, vision coverage, and disability coverage. Employees may want to participate in programs that might reduce their costs, such as a health-risk appraisal (Kritz, 2009b).

Consumers who are self-employed or who purchase individual policies should weigh seven key elements (Kristof, 2009). In light of consumers' prior usage of the health system, their ages, their finances, their risk tolerances, and their health conditions, they should consider:

- Premium levels that range from $50 to more than $1,000 depending on their age and health, as well as the level of deductibles.
- Deductibles for individuals and entire families, as well as possible separate deductibles for prescriptions. The deductibles increase with age. These are often significant as one family plan suggests, which included a $2,500 deductible for individuals, $5,000 for the family, and $500 for some prescriptions. Managed-care plans often exempt check-ups and vaccinations from deductibles.
- Co-payments, such as $20 to $50 every time a consumer sees a physician.
- Co-insurance, which requires consumers to pay a constant percentage of each physician's or hospital's bill, such as 30%, unless the plan has a cap on such expenditures.
- Lifetime coverage maximum that caps an insurance company's overall cost if a consumer gets cancer or other chronic disease, such as $1 million or higher.
- Limitations and restrictions that specify what services are not covered, such as maternity care or payouts to physicians not in the network.

Advocates can help consumers:

- Learn how to shop online at sites such as www.vimo.com or www.eHealth Insurance.com.
- Find trustworthy insurance agents by ascertaining if they are licensed by their state department of insurance and have no recorded fraud.
- Ascertain if a specific insurance company is licensed by the state with no recorded fraud.
- Fill out applications with great care so that the insurance company cannot claim that they withheld information accidentally or intentionally.
- Refer consumers to National Association of Insurance Commissioners website at www.naic.org that has links to each state's insurance commissioners web site.

Post-Obama Plan

I have discussed how consumers will be afforded many protections against insurance plans—and how greater uniformity in their benefits and costs will occur by 2014.

Scenario 9.2: Advocacy to Help Uninsured Consumers Get Insurance

Pre-Obama Plan

Most states have special state-funded insurance programs for consumers who are not employed and for consumers who are unemployed and have preexisting health conditions. These programs are often underfunded, requiring consumers to experience long waits before they obtain them. The precise benefits and out-of-pocket fees vary among states. Advocates can:

- Help consumers contact their state departments of health to discover how to access these programs.
- Recommend the Georgetown University Health Policy Institute web site that focuses on health insurance at http://www.healthinsuranceinfo.net/.

Post-Obama Plan

I have discussed how uninsured persons will have many additional options by 2014.

Scenario 9.3: Advocacy to Help Consumers Gain Access to Charitable Funds of Hospitals and Clinics

Pre-Obama Plan

Many hospitals and some clinics have charitable funds or are willing to suffer income losses to give free or low-cost care to uninsured persons. These funds vary in size, as well as the policies used to determine how to use them. Advocates can:

- Discover the size of these funds and the policies and personnel that determine how they are used.
- Help specific consumers gain access to these funds by referring them to appropriate officials or by sometimes making a personal inquiry to document why a specific consumer needs them.

Post-Obama Plan

Hospitals and clinics will probably have less demand on their charitable funds during and after 2014 because more of their clientele will be insured, but 23 million Americans will still be uninsured in 2019 according to current estimates.

Scenario 9.4: Advocacy to Help Uninsured Consumers Obtain Medical Services

Pre-Obama Plan

Resources exist in major urban areas for uninsured persons, but they have to look for them, such as ones listed for Los Angeles County on the web site www.healthycity.org (Colker, 2009). Consumers should know:

- They cannot be turned away at ERs with a life-threatening condition, though they can be charged, usually on a sliding-fee scale. If they use the ER of a public hospital, they will probably have waits of eight hours or more and will probably remain at that hospital for continued care.
- Walk-in clinics maintained by a county or city often exist with ability-to-pay care for uninsured consumers that are often listed on a web site, such as www.ladhs.org for Los Angeles County.
- Surgery for nonemergency conditions at public hospitals can require waits of three to five months, such as for gall bladder problems.
- Public systems often will not give physicals or general exams, but these exams can often be covered from federal programs funded by the CDC, such as free breast cancer screenings and Pap tests for eligible women, as well as state-funded breast cancer screenings.
- Free blood pressure readings and other tests are often offered free at local health fairs.
- A national web site (www.helpingpatients.org) helps uninsured persons find programs that offer no- or low-cost medications to the uninsured. Consumers who qualify for free or low-cost care at specific clinics or hospitals often qualify for prescription drugs at no or low cost.
- Government-funded dental services usually cover just emergency work, but some university dental schools provide free or low-cost services, often only for persons who agree to comprehensive ongoing care.
- Mental health services are usually limited to emergency care for uninsured persons who are a danger to themselves or others, but some nonprofit institutions and some private practitioners offer nonemergency therapy on a no-cost or sliding fee basis that can sometimes be located by calling a county or city mental health department through their help lines.

Post-Obama Plan

Uninsured consumers will still need help in gaining access to health services. The considerable federal resources that will be given to community-based clinics from 2011 onward will be an important asset for these consumers who will often turn to them for their primary care. Local safety-net health systems, such as municipal and county hospitals, will remain a key resource for uninsured and undocumented consumers.

Most uninsured persons work for relatively small employers who do not provide them with health insurance. Beginning in 2010, up to 4 million small businesses will be eligible for tax credits to help them provide insurance benefits for their employees. In the first phase of this provision, these companies' tax credits will be worth up to 35% of the employer's contribution to employees' health insurance. Small non-profit organizations may receive up to 25% credit.

Under the Obama Plan, most people who can afford it will be required to obtain basic health insurance coverage or pay a fee to offset the costs of caring for uninsured persons, effective January 1, 2014. Workers meeting certain requirements who cannot afford coverage provided by their employer may take whatever funds their employer might have contributed to their insurance and purchase a more affordable plan in their state's health insurance exchanges (2014).

Scenario 9.5: Advocacy to Help Consumers Gain Access to Medicaid

Pre-Obama Plan

Medicaid has become a massive program rather than just a program that serves poor people. It has 12 million more participants than Medicare. It covers one in five of the nation's children, pays for one-third of all childbirths, covers two-thirds of elderly persons in nursing homes, and pays for half of all states' mental health services (Grogan & Gusmano, 2007).

Although Medicaid began as a program primarily to serve welfare recipients, it has expanded far beyond this restricted group. Medicaid legislation identifies "optional groups" that states may cover, such as working parents up to 250% of the federal poverty level (FPL)—and these optional groups now consume about two-thirds of Medicaid expenditures (Grogan & Gusmano, 2007). Many states have received permission (or waivers) to enable them to raise eligibility levels in return for requiring Medicaid recipients to enroll in managed-care plans that are believed likely to cut health costs as compared to fee-for-service medicine.

Advocates have an important role in moving consumers from ranks of uninsured persons to Medicaid when they are eligible for it. Each state has its own application procedures for its Medicaid program. Consumers must meet specific monthly income and resource tests established by each state—and these income and resource tests are usually complex as is illustrated by the standards of one state (California) that bases eligibility on countable income, which is income left over after deducting certain kinds of income that do not count or subtracting certain kinds of income from gross total monthly income (Los Angeles Coalition to End Hunger and Homelessness, 2008). It does not count income of relatives, friends, or others who cohabit a house with an applicant, allow families to deduct $90 each month for each working adult, up to $175 for child care for each child age 2 and over, court-order child and spousal support, $50 of child support received, educational expenses, business expenses of self-employed persons. It allows consumers to not count the first $240 of earned income plus half the remaining earned income.

It allows persons 65 and older to deduct $20 from their income, another $65 from earned income, half of any remaining earned income, any health insurance premiums paid by the consumer. It has other rules for elderly and disabled persons not getting SSI if they meet strict monthly income levels. It has low-cost Medicaid for working disabled persons if they meet strict monthly standards. It allows some consumers to pay a "Share of Cost" for each month they have a medical expense with Medicaid paying the rest of the bill for covered services in that month. It requires residents to have lived in the state for a specific period before they could gain eligibility to its Medicaid program, but this policy was struck down by the courts—so it now only requires consumers to state that they intend to stay in the state.

Eligible groups of consumers who meet its income and resource tests include persons in SSI and foster care, families within adoption assistance programs, pregnant women, children under age 21, adults 65 and over, persons who are disabled or blind by SSI guidelines, caretaker relatives of minor children under age 21, refugees as defined by federal law, persons in long-term care facilities, persons with tuberculosis unless they are undocumented, and women with breast or cervical cancer. Infants born to women on Medicaid receive Medicaid until the age of one when their parents must complete an annual redetermination form. Medicaid is, in short, a program that meets the health needs of many groups of consumers.

Application procedures often change in specific states according to the whims of specific elected officials or state budget deficits. Benefits can be slashed, eligibility criteria lowered, and forms changed.

Consumers must periodically reestablish their eligibility for Medicaid in each state, but the required interval varies from state to state, such as every three months, six months, or annually. They must also report any changes to their information within a specified period, such as 10 days. Applicants usually visit an eligibility worker at specified sites that must provide translation services and give special assistance to disabled persons who cannot otherwise complete application forms. States vary in required documentation, but often require identification that includes names and addresses, birth certificates, drivers' licenses, a state identification card, Social Security numbers or cards, proof of income (pay stubs, W2 forms, copies of tax returns, monthly banking statements, proof of place of residency, proof of citizenship or acceptable immigration status, vehicle registration, verification of child care, educational expenses, health insurance premiums, and court order child support payments). Single parents, as well as single pregnant women after the birth of their baby, must often cooperate with welfare programs to document whether an absent parent can provide their children with medical insurance.

As this list demonstrates, application and renewals of eligibility are time-consuming and arduous—leading many eligible persons not to apply or renew their eligibility.

They are often written at a 10th-grade reading level. Some eligibility staff may treat them in demeaning ways. They may feel stigmatized by application processes. They must often complete many forms totaling 19 pages (as in Wisconsin) or more. They may be confused by technical, ambiguous, or ominous language on forms, such as on a Medicaid application form for elderly, blind, and disabled applicants in Wisconsin that states "Also, if you reside in a nursing home or are institutionalized in a hospital, and are not expected to return home to live, a lien may be placed on your home if you, your spouse, or certain other family members reside in the home" (Marsh, 2005).

States have different procedures for obtaining Medicaid application forms. In California, for example, forms can be obtained by calling a toll-free number, at a local welfare office, or at many hospitals and clinics including public and private ones. Some schools have children apply for Medicaid at the same time they apply for Free and Reduced-Cost Lunch programs. A separate application is used for children under age 19 with expedited review (Los Angeles Coalition to End Hunger and Homelessness, 2008).

Advocates can help consumers facing these applicant procedures by:

- Providing them with relevant information.
- Helping them obtain an appointment with an eligibility worker.
- Monitoring whether they persisted in gaining eligibility.
- Notifying them of their right to contest adverse eligibility decisions by asking for a fair hearing.
- Giving them numbers and web sites of specific advocacy groups that might help them.
- Providing information about web sites with Medicaid information, such as www .benefits.gov with links to Medicaid programs in all states or National Health Law Program, which has excellent resources about Medicaid programs at www .healthlaw.org.

Post-Obama Plan

I have discussed how the Medicaid program will be greatly expanded by 2014. Even in 2010, states will receive additional federal matching funds for covering some additional low-income individuals and families for whom federal funds were not previously available.

It is unclear if application procedures will be streamlined and made more consumer-friendly. It is unclear how states will change their Medicaid programs as millions of additional consumers join them during 2014 and succeeding years. Medicaid programs in the various states will be required to insure single persons, as well as childless couples, who earn less than 133% of FPL—rather than, as in 2010, many of their enrollees were parents and children, often on welfare rolls.

Scenario 9.6: Advocacy to Help Consumers Contest Medicaid Decisions

Pre-Obama Plan

Federal legislation requires each state to provide fair hearings for consumers who wish to contest specific Medicaid decisions over eligibility, services, and reimbursements. Impartial referees oversee these hearings and make final decisions.

- Consumers often prevail merely by asking for a fair hearing. Consumers should not be intimidated if Medicaid staff tell them that they do not have a case—and should not decide not to proceed until they receive legal advice (Los Angeles Coalition to End Hunger and Homelessness, 2008). Consumers should retain copies of records and documents, as well as names and dates of contacts with Medicaid personnel. They can request a copy of their records and copy them. They can see any regulations that apply to them. Medicaid officials are required to send a notice to consumers 10 days prior to reducing or stopping their benefits.

Post-Obama Plan

These procedures to safeguard consumers' rights will remain intact.

Scenario 9.7: Advocacy to Help Consumers Gain Access to Medicare

Pre-Obama Plan

Medicare is a federal program administered by the Centers on Medical Services (CMS). Eligibility is handled by the Social Security Administration, which typically sends a letter to persons nearing age 65 to enable them to become members when they receive an identification card. Consumers may obtain access to Parts A (hospital benefits), B (physician benefits), and D (pharmaceutical benefits) (Los Angeles Coalition to End Hunger and Homelessness, 2008).

Consumers are automatically eligible for Part A if they are 65 or older, a federal employee who retired after 1982 with enough quarters of coverage, have received SSDI for 24 consecutive months, are a disabled widow or widower age 50 years or older who has received Social Security through their spouse for at least 2 years, has end-stage kidney disease regardless of age with enough quarters, or has Lou Gehrig's of any age but with enough quarters. Other persons age 65 or older and who are U.S. citizens or legal aliens who have resided in the U.S. for at least 5 years continuously may voluntarily purchase both Parts A and B or just Part B. (These consumers pay monthly premiums whose amount depends on how many work quarters they have on record with Social Security.)

Under Part A, Medicare funds up to 60 days of hospital coverage in a benefit period with a deductible of $1,024 (all figures for 2008). Medicare members pay $256 per day for days 61 through 90 with Medicare paying the balance.

Consumers eligible for Part A are also eligible for Part B, which covers 80% of "allowable" charges for a variety of outpatient care, including doctor services, physical therapy, outpatient hospital services, medical equipment, and ambulance services (Los Angeles Coalition to End Hunger and Homelessness, 2008, p. 53). Consumers pay the remaining amount, an annual deductible of $135, and a 15% excess charge if the provider does not take the Medicare assignment, which is an agreement between Medicare and their health provider where Part B providers agree only to charge the Medicare approved rate. Some consumers who continue to receive insurance benefits from their employer because they work past age 65 often participate only in Part A until they retire.

Consumers must enroll into a Medicare Part D drug plan to obtain Part D coverage. They must choose a PDP plan that only provides Medicare drug coverage or an MA-PD plan that provides Medicare Part A, B, and D benefits. Each plan has its own drug formulary, cost-sharing requirements, and restrictions on coverage even though there is a standard Part D benefit package. This part of Medicare is controversial because of its complexity, including a complex formula for determining when consumers qualify for coverage and when they do not—even when they are members of Part D.

Many consumers have selected Medicare Advantage Plans that are offered by many private insurance companies and that are widely viewed as offering some enrollees a larger array of benefits. They provide fee-for-service reimbursement to private providers often with relatively low premiums because of subsidies from the federal government. These plans offer a confusing array of benefits often not well understood by consumers, so they may need to find a new one. Consumers are sometimes lured into purchasing a plan due to low premiums, but they do not realize that some of the plans do not have caps on out-of-pocket maximums. Some private insurance companies are closing their Advantage Plans.

Consumers should realize that Medicare recently expanded its coverage of drugs for cancer treatments not yet approved by the Food and Drug Administration for so-called off-label use—in other words, for drugs prescribed by physicians for uses for which they have not been specifically approved. The drug Gemzar has been approved for four kinds of cancer, for example, but could be used for roughly a dozen additional ones under this Medicare policy. This policy is controversial. Some physicians contend that unproven therapies are often the only hope for some patients, while others see Medicare as using patients as guinea pigs at great expense to the government (Abelson & Pollack, 2009).

Consumers can also enroll in a Medicare Advantage HMO that enrolls Medicare beneficiaries who have both Medicare Parts A and B where Medicare pays their HMO a fixed monthly amount for each enrollee. (They cannot enroll if they have Medicare end-stage renal disease.) They must use the HMO for all of their medical care except for emergencies and urgent care when they are outside of the HMO's service area. Medicare Advantage HMO plans are controversial: They cost the government more per person than traditional Medicare and have higher mortality rates than such groups as elderly veterans—so consumers should see if evaluations exist of plans they consider by state or federal agencies. The Patient Protection and Affordable Healthcare Act of 2010 will change policies in 2011 regarding Medicare Advantage Plans, including prohibiting them from imposing higher cost-sharing requirements than are required by traditional fee-for-service Medicare.

Advocates can help consumers:

- Use the general information line for Medicare: (800) 633-4227.
- Obtain information from the Center for Healthcare Rights (800) 824-0780 or (800) 434-0222.
- Contact the New York–based Medicare Rights Center at www.medicarerights .org or the Connecticut-based Center for Medicare Advocacy at www.medicare advocacy.org.
- Use the web site of Medicare at the Centers for Medicare and Medicaid Services (CMS) at www.medicare.gov or www.mymedicare.gov.
- Consult the web page of the Kaiser Family Foundation to identify specific changes in Medicare eligibility and services made by the Patient Protection and Affordable Care Act of 2010 at www.kff.org.

Post-Obama Plan

Medicare's eligibility and applications procedures, as well as fair hearing processes, will likely remain intact. The donut hole will be phased out by 2020 as discussed earlier. Medicaid Advantage Plans will likely be greatly reduced in number. New prevention services will be funded by Medicare.

Scenario 9.8: Advocacy to Help Consumers Contest Specific Decisions by SSI and Medicare

Pre-Obama Plan

The Social Security Administration is required to mail enrollees a notice of any changes in their benefits for SSI or Medicare. Consumers should request a "Reconsideration" by filling out the appropriate form at a Social Security office if they disagree with these changes, but they should fill out this form within 10 days so that their current benefits remain intact until a decision is made. Consumers can request a waiver if they are told they owe the government money that will be taken out of their check if it will pose a hardship. Consumers can appeal benefits cuts in SSDI by filling out a form that asks for their aid to continue, but must then request a Reconsideration to get lost benefits repaid to them (Los Angeles Coalition to End Hunger and Homelessness, 2008).

Consumers can ask for three kinds of Reconsiderations: case review, informal, or formal conference. Informal conferences usually suffice, but the staff usually requires a case review if the application for SSDI or SSI is denied for medical reasons.

Consumers can request a hearing before an Administrative Law Judge with the Office of Hearing and Appeals if their reconsideration or waiver is denied. The judge makes a decision after holding the hearing or after examining evidence.

Consumers often find their SSI or SSDI benefits to be cut or terminated when they begin working and earn too much. Consumers should request reconsideration at once and file a new application. Working people have rights that may allow them to continue receiving benefits.

Advocates can:

- Make certain that consumers understand that they can question decisions of SSI, SSDI, and Medicare officials and programs.
- Use specific procedures for appealing adverse decisions.
- Understand that they must immediately take action to achieve optimal results.

Post-Obama Plan

These consumer safeguards will likely remain intact.

Scenario 9.9: Advocacy to Help Consumers Obtain Medicare Supplemental Insurance

Pre-Obama Plan

The same strategies should be used for private insurance that supplements Medicare as for private insurance generally (see above). Consumers should not automatically assume that the American Association of Retired Persons (AARP, 2008a) provides the supplemental insurance that best meets their needs because some critics contend that its policies charge excessive fees and are costlier than competing plans (Cohn & Preston, 2008; Drinkard & Welsh 2003).

Web sites and additional information about supplemental insurance are:

- Medicare web site at http://www.medicare.gov/medigap/Default.asp.

Post-Obama Plan

Many consumers will still need supplemental insurance because the Medicare program will likely retain its current configuration.

Scenario 9.10: Advocacy to Help Consumers Who Are Dually Eligible for Medicare and Medicaid

Pre-Obama Plan

Consumers who are eligible for both programs do not usually have to pay Medicare's monthly premiums, deductibles, or co-payments. They must use healthcare providers that take both Medicare and Medicaid. They will have some of their benefits paid by

Medicare and some paid by Medicaid. They can appeal incorrect or unfair decisions about Medicaid by requesting a fair hearing at the toll-free number established by the state agency that administers their Medicaid program.

Post-Obama Plan

Consumers will continue to be dually eligible.

Scenario 9.11: Advocacy for Consumers Who Are Immigrants

Pre-Obama Plan

States vary in their policies regarding health benefits for specific kinds of immigrants. In one state (California), for example, undocumented immigrants can obtain a "restricted" Medicaid card making them eligible for Medicaid-financed emergency services, pregnancy-related care and long-term care services (Los Angeles Coalition to End Hunger and Homelessness, 2008). Persons defined as "refugees" by the federal government qualify for Medicaid if they meet income requirements. Most legal immigrants can get Medicaid for all medically necessary health needs including green-card holders and immigrants lacking green cards but who are victims of domestic violence or those applying for Legal Permanent Residency. Many immigrants are eligible for public health programs geared to preventing and treating tuberculosis and HIV/AIDS, as well as some prenatal and postnatal health programs.

Periodic efforts by Congress to insist that immigrants submit birth certificates and passports rather than simply declaring in writing, under penalty of perjury, that they are citizens or qualified immigrants, have often led to many eligible persons not getting healthcare because they often cannot find these documents (*New York Times* editorial, 2007). Others fear that health staff may report them to immigration authorities.

Advocates can:

- Distribute information to immigrants about their healthcare rights.
- Inform all immigrants that they are eligible for emergency services.
- Refer them to immigrant-rights groups when their health rights are violated such as legal aid offices and ones in Los Angeles County like the Asian Pacific American Legal Center, the Center for Human Rights and Constitutional Law, and the Coalition for Humane Immigrant Rights of Los Angeles.

Post-Obama Plan

The Obama Plan does not fundamentally change policies for undocumented persons. Many members of the House and the Senate insisted that its benefits not go to this population.

Scenario 9.12: Advocacy for Consumers to Obtain SCHIP

Pre-Obama Plan

SCHIP—the State Children's Health Insurance Program—is a federal-state program that provides medical benefits to children in families that have too much income to qualify for Medicaid. Some states implement this program through their Medicaid programs, while others established separate programs specifically for this population. States that select the Medicaid option must provide all Medicaid mandatory benefits as well as all optional services offered under their Medicaid state plan, while separate state programs must follow specific coverage and benefit options outlined in the SCHIP law. Total annual aggregate cost-sharing cannot exceed 5% of total income per year—and preventive programs are exempt from cost-sharing. Great variation exists in SCHIP programs among states with one state offering the highest upper-income eligibility at 350% of FPL in 2007 (Herz, Peterson, & Baumrucker, 2008). Enrollment in SCHIP was slowed in the years after its enactment in 1997 by complex application procedures in most states, but many states have simplified them, as well as received cooperation of schools, the media, and others in disseminating information about it. In one state (California), for example, Medicaid and SCHIP established a joint application and mail-in form and a telephone number with multilingual staff. SCHIP staff, known as the Healthy Families program in California, respond within 10 days to applications (Los Angeles Coalition to End Hunger and Homelessness, 2008).

Efforts to allow specific states to expand eligibility for SCHIP markedly were vetoed by President George W. Bush in 2007, but Congress enacted this policy in the first year of the Obama presidency so that 4 million additional children would be covered and states would be permitted to use federal money to cover children and pregnant women who are legal immigrants. Some states cut eligibility for SCHIP, however, when they developed large budget deficits in the recession from 2007 to 2009—and even considered terminating the program

Advocates can:

- Direct consumers to SCHIP officials to gain eligibility.
- Visit www.insurekidsnow.gov for more information about SCHIP eligibility.

Post-Obama Plan

It is not clear how the size of this program will be affected by the Obama Plan.

Scenario 9.13: Advocacy for Consumers for Safety-Net Health Systems in Cities and Counties

Pre-Obama Plan

Cities and counties often operate safety-net health systems for consumers who do not qualify for public or private insurance and medical programs. They sometimes fund these programs with their own funds or draw as well, or instead, on state and federal funds. These consumers include immigrants and uninsured persons. Benefits vary widely between these local jurisdictions. Public systems of care are often encumbered by long waits and difficulties in obtaining appointment from specialists. Many of them are closely linked to medical schools, which gives consumers medical care that is often supervised by medical-school faculty.

Most urban areas possess an array of free clinics that strive to provide free or low-cost outpatient care to uninsured consumers, immigrants, and others. They depend upon local, state, and federal funding; contracts with public systems of care; and charitable contributions. Many of them rely extensively on volunteer help from healthcare professionals. Advocates can:

- Link consumers with specific services and programs in safety-net health systems that are accessible to them.
- Seek expedited or better service for specific consumers by contacting health authorities charged with implementing safety-net services in their jurisdiction, local public officials, or the state agency charged with overseeing them, including state Medicaid officials.

Post-Obama Plan

Safety-net health programs will remain intact, but probably with even greater focus on undocumented immigrants, as well as the roughly 23 million persons that will be uninsured in 2019.

Scenario 9.14: Advocacy for Consumers Who Seek Disability Health Benefits

Pre-Obama Plan

Persons who believe they are disabled have recourse to several programs. They can obtain disability benefits, including income and health coverage, from Social Security Disability Insurance (SSDI).

Consumers who do not qualify for SSDI can seek income and health coverage by gaining eligibility to the Supplemental Security Income Program (SSI), which makes them eligible for Medicaid. This is a means-tested program administered by the Social Security Administration.

SSI and SSDI provide income and health benefits to consumers with ongoing disabilities that preclude them from working. Workmen's compensation gives consumers who have suffered job-related injuries income and health benefits during the period when they obtain medical treatment for them.

Advocates can:

- Discuss these different ways of obtaining income and medical benefits for disabilities.
- Direct consumers to relevant agencies and technical resources.
- Refer consumers to the Social Security Administration web site at www.ssa.gov.

Post-Obama Plan

No changes are anticipated in policies of SSI and SSDI.

Scenario 9.15: Advocacy for Consumers Who Seek In-Home Supportive Services

Pre-Obama Plan

States offer in-home supportive services for persons who cannot perform some or many daily activities through their Medicaid programs. The nature and scope of these services varies considerably among states. They are typically accessed through local welfare offices, which are required to provide assistance to disabled applicants, such as helping them write and complete applications if necessary or help them if they cannot come to an office due to their disability. Consumers can ask for a fair hearing if they believe they are unfairly denied services (see the discussion of fair hearings under advocacy for consumers contesting decisions by Medicaid officials). Disabled consumers who believe they are treated unfairly can contact the Civil Rights Division of the U.S. Department of Justice, P.O. Box 66118, Washington, D.C. 20035-6118.

Consumers can also obtain in-home supportive services from Medicare. These services can include intermittent (and not full-time) skilled nursing care, or physical therapy or speech language pathology services, or a continued need for occupational therapy. Medicare provides benefits for consumers during acute bouts of illness rather than for chronic conditions, including in-home services. Consumers can receive them only if physicians request them as needed to promote consumers' recoveries from acute bouts of illness—and only as long as physicians attest that their health is continuing to improve. Consumers have to self-fund these in-home services once their eligibility for them has lapsed—or get them covered with supplemental insurance or the means-tested Medicaid program.

Many consumers who need in-home supportive services are not covered by Medicaid or Medicare.

Post-Obama Plan

The Obama Plan will fund some demonstration projects for innovative approaches to helping elderly and disabled persons who need in-home assistance—with the goal of prevention institutionalization of these consumers. It will provide incentives to keep elderly persons in community rather than institutional settings.

MOVING FROM CASE ADVOCACY TO POLICY ADVOCACY

The Obama Plan will greatly reduce the likelihood of some of the scenarios discussed in this chapter and may even eliminate some of them—while having little or no impact on others as discussed throughout this chapter. As an exercise in moving from case advocacy to policy advocacy, take any of the scenarios and discuss the likely effect of the Obama Plan on them. Identify some policy reforms that advocates might consider to make the Obama Plan even more responsive to consumers' financial problems in negotiating the U.S. health system.

FIFTEEN SCENARIOS PRESENTED IN THIS BOOK

- Advocacy to Help Consumers Select a Health Insurance Policy
- Advocacy to Help Uninsured Consumers Get Health Insurance
- Advocacy to Help Consumers Gain Access to Charitable Funds of Hospitals and Clinics
- Advocacy to Help Uninsured Consumers Obtain Medical Services
- Advocacy to Help Consumers Gain Access to Medicaid
- Advocacy to Help Consumers Contest Medicaid Decisions
- Advocacy to Help Consumers Gain Access to Medicare
- Advocacy to Help Consumers Contest Specific Decisions by SSI and Medicare
- Advocacy to Help Consumers Obtain Medicare Supplemental Insurance
- Advocacy to Help Consumers Who Are Dually Eligible for Medicaid and Medicare
- Advocacy for Consumers Who Are Immigrants
- Advocacy for Consumers to Obtain SCHIP
- Advocacy for Consumers for Safety-Net Health Systems in Cities and Counties
- Advocacy for Consumers Who Seek Disability Health Benefits
- Advocacy for Consumers Who Seek In-Home Supportive Services

ONLINE MATERIALS RELEVANT TO THIS CHAPTER

Access five additional scenarios relevant to helping consumers obtain benefits and services at the web site of John Wiley & Sons at www.wiley.com/go/jansson.

- Advocacy to Help Consumers Contest Denials of Costs by Insurance Companies
- Advocacy to Help Consumers Contest Service Decisions by Their Managed Care Plan

- Advocacy for Consumers to Obtain Long-Term Care Insurance or Reverse Mortgages
- Advocacy for Consumers to Finance Their Medications
- Advocacy for Consumers to Avert Medical Bankruptcy and Avoidance of Care

SUMMARY

As this chapter suggests, the Obama Plan both reforms the U.S. health system and retains many of its characteristics. Advocates will need to help many consumers who will be largely unaffected by the Obama Plan while helping others take advantage of its many benefits. As discussed in Chapter 14, healthcare professionals need to become policy advocates to make certain their states implement the provisions of the Patient Protection and Affordable Care Act in a timely and effective way.

10

Advocacy for Healthcare Consumers Needing Mental Health Services

COAUTHORED WITH JENNIFER PAEK, MSW AND DOCTORAL STUDENT; AND MIN AH KIM, MSW AND DOCTORAL STUDENT

Clinics and hospitals attract many numbers of consumers with varying types and levels of psychological distress, but they often do not diagnose or treat mental conditions because they often focus on physiological issues. I identify psychological distress experienced by some consumers. I identify factors in the policy and regulatory thicket that promote and discourage provision of services to persons with such diagnoses or challenges. I provide 26 scenarios encountered by case advocates when they discover consumers who are not receiving help for mental distress. (Eighteen are presented in this book and eight are accessed in online materials for this chapter.) To illustrate different levels of rigor in existing research, I place asterisks by many articles in this chapter including four asterisks (****) next to cited research that are review articles and meta-analysis, three asterisks (***) next to experimental studies, two asterisks (**) next to quasi-experimental or correlational studies, and one asterisk (*) next to case or other kinds of studies.

WHY MANY CONSUMERS TURN TO HEALTH SETTINGS FOR HELP WITH MENTAL CONDITIONS

Many consumers have mental distress in health settings for a number of reasons. Consumers often need mental health interventions because their physical and mental conditions are entwined. Many medical conditions cause mental distress such as depression and anxiety, including many chronic diseases, as well as serious acute conditions like cancer (Browne, 2006). Consumers with these health problems often experience losses, such as in physical abilities and appearances that exacerbate mental distress. They may confront the end of their lives. Health problems can upset family and personal relationships. They can cause loss of status, such as when they require consumers to end their careers or leave their work.

Mental health conditions, in turn, cause or exacerbate some chronic and acute health problems (Browne, 2006). Some problems cause physiological changes, such as weakening consumers' immune systems, causing increases in blood pressure, or platelet formation. Some conditions may accelerate the accumulation of plaque in blood vessels. Some cause or exacerbate illnesses whether by causing consumers to make lifestyle choices, such as poor diets and lack of exercise, that exacerbate their health conditions.

Many consumers' health problems are caused or exacerbated by toxic relationships that cause physiological and mental distress. Women and children often suffer injuries when they are physically or sexually assaulted. Low-income persons are often victims of gang warfare, gun shootings, or other injuries stemming from life in communities afflicted with high levels of violence.

Consumers with substance abuse often experience physiological and mental problems. The abuse can cause cirrhosis of the liver, esophageal injuries, accidents from falling, and car accidents in the case of alcoholics; neurological and physical injuries from excess use of drugs and alcohol; and premature deaths from excess levels of toxins in their bodies from substance abuse. It can cause loss of employment and promotions, divorce, and family violence (Caulkins, Reuter, Iguchi, & Chiesa, 2005).

Many consumers with mental and substance abuse problems turn to primary-care physicians who are the largest providers of mental health and substance abuse services in the United States for several reasons. Consumers often view mental healthcare from these physicians as less stigmatizing than care from mental health clinics or mental health professionals. They may believe that they will be more likely to have their mental healthcare covered by health insurance if they seek it from physicians. They may believe that physicians will be less likely to engage them in discussions that probe highly personal issues than mental health professionals. They may have long-standing relationships with specific primary-care physicians rather than with specific mental health practitioners. They may doubt that mental health clinicians have the skills to help them. They may believe that medications will cure their mental or substance abuse conditions, such as antidepressants and antianxiety medications.

Reliance on primary-care physicians and ERs have some shortcomings (Institute of Medicine, 2006a; Kessler et al., 2005). Mental problems of many consumers are concealed because most of them present physical rather than mental problems (Browne, 2006a). Many primary-care physicians lack mental-health clinical skills to identify mental health problems. Many physicians rely excessively on medications. They often limit the time that they spend with consumers who need mental interventions because they are not reimbursed at all or at low levels. They are sometimes reluctant to ask probing questions because they do not wish to embarrass their patients (Institute of Medicine, 2006a).

Consumers seek help for mental conditions from hospitals for many reasons. Some of them are brought to health settings involuntarily by paramedics, the police, or relatives because these consumers have attempted or threatened suicide, assaulted other persons, or created a public disturbance. They can be unconscious, semi-conscious, or delirious from high levels of alcohol or drugs.

Many consumers voluntarily come to emergency departments when they experience acute mental distress. They know that they will see a mental health specialist rapidly and receive medications. They find emergency departments (EDs) accessible around the clock unlike many mental health clinics.

Many consumers who come to emergency rooms have attempted suicide. They seek help for their injuries, as well as their mental problems.

Hospitals are places of refuge for persons who have been raped or assaulted, including women, children, and victims of hate crimes. They may come to hospitals primarily for help with their physical injuries, only to realize that they often need help for the mental trauma that accompanies rapes and assaults. Some of these consumers will develop posttraumatic stress disorder.

Screening questions that are routinely used in many outpatient and inpatient settings often detect mental distress even when consumers do not come to these settings for it. Social workers, nurses, and physicians sometimes detect mental distress through their observations of consumers who have been admitted to hospitals for other medical services. Notes in the medical record may refer to affect, insomnia, general appearance, or other indicators of depression, anxiety, psychoses, manic depression, or other mental conditions. Mental distress can sometimes be detected when consumers do not adhere to recommended treatments. Persons with clinical depression are far less likely, for example, to keep appointments or take medications than other consumers. Mental distress can sometimes be detected, as well, when consumers do not recover from surgeries or other medical procedures at customary rates.

Many consumers come to outpatient clinics and ERs with neurological problems such as dementia, Alzheimer's disease, epilepsy, amnesia, and Parkinson's disease. Some consumers experience short- and long-term cognitive problems in the wake of heart surgeries.

Consumers with substance abuse problems are often brought to ERs when they are unconscious or semi-conscious. They may have been discovered in public places, fraternity houses, or private homes. They may have suffered trauma in automobile accidents as reflected by the fact that roughly 50,000 deaths occur each year due to driving under the influence of alcohol or other drugs.

Some consumers have been called the "worried well" because they use health systems with greater frequency than others, such as frequent visitors to ERs, outpatient clinics, and specialists. Many of them appear not to have important physical problems, but their compulsive use of health services may be driven by psychosomatic illness, somatization, depression, anxiety, and loneliness that require mental health interventions.

Some consumers use health services to get respite from the streets and short-term housing, such as some homeless persons. They seek help, as well, for health problems stemming from exposure, malnutrition, and assaults.

Consumers who use ERs often reflect social and economic problems of the broader society. Visits increase during recessions when rates of depression, substance abuse, and suicide escalate. Unemployed consumers have higher rates of depression, anxiety, and substance abuse than employed persons. Consumers who lose their homes to foreclosure are more likely than others to have mental and substance abuse problems.

KINDS OF MENTAL DISTRESS OFTEN EXPERIENCED BY CONSUMERS

Healthcare consumers often experience many kinds of mental distress such as ones defined by the *Diagnostic and Statistical Manual of Mental Disorders*, 4th edition (*DSM-IV*) of the American Psychiatric Association (1994). These include Clinical Disorders on Axis I, including adjustment disorders, anxiety disorders, cognitive disorders, dissociative disorders, eating disorders, factitious disorders, impulse-control disorders, mental disorders due to a general medical condition, mood disorders, schizophrenia and other psychotic disorders, sexual and gender identity disorders, paraphilias, sexual dysfunction, sexual pain disorders, sleep disorders, somatoform disorders, and substance-related disorders. Consumers must experience more than one symptom from a cluster of symptoms for some of these clinical disorders. To be diagnosed with Major Depressive Episode, for example, they need to be diagnosed with depressed mood (or irritable mood for children and adolescents) or loss of pleasure or interest in activities and (at least) four of the following symptoms: significant change in weight or appetite; insomnia or hypersomnia; psychomotor agitation or retardation; fatigue or loss of energy; feelings of worthlessness or excessive or inappropriate guilt; impaired concentration or indecision; and recurrent thoughts of death, suicidal ideation, or suicide attempt (American Psychiatric Association, 2003, p. 327). Persons who are diagnosed for General Anxiety Disorders and Posttraumatic Stress Disorders must have conditions with "intensity, duration, and impact on daily functioning" (Engstrom, 2006, p. 223).

Mental distress includes Personality Disorders and mental retardation on Axis II. Personality disorders are defined as "an enduring pattern of inner experience and behavior that deviates markedly from the expectations of the individual's culture, is pervasive and inflexible, has an onset in adolescence or early childhood, is stable over time, and leads to distress or impairment." (Engstrom, 2006). Personality disorders include Paranoid Personality Disorder, Schizoid Personality Disorder, and Borderline Personality Disorder.

Axis III discusses general medical conditions that may be relevant to the understanding or management of consumers' mental disorders, whether because it relates to the development or worsening of the disorders or allows understanding or treatment.

Axis IV describes specific psychosocial and environmental stressors that may influence the diagnosis, treatment, and prognosis of mental disorders. These include stressors like negative life events, environmental deficiencies or difficulties, and inadequate social supports. They also include positive stressors like job promotions. *DSM-IV* identifies nine categories of stressors including problems with the primary support group, problems related to the social environment, educational problems, occupational problems, housing problems, economic problems, problems with accessing healthcare services, problems related to interactions with the legal system and crime, and other psychosocial and environmental problems.

A Global Assessment of Functioning (GAF) is described on Axis V based on psychological, social, and occupational factors. Low scores, such as 10, are interpreted to mean a person is in "persistent danger of hurting self or others"; a moderate score, such as 50, is interpreted as meaning someone has serious symptoms such as suicidal ideation or serious impairment in social, occupational, or school functioning; a relatively high score, such as 91, indicates superior functioning in a wide range of activities (Browne, 2006a). *DSM-IV* acknowledges that many persons possess more than one mental condition. Someone may be homeless, suffer from substance abuse, and have a personality disorder. They can move between different conditions, such as between anxiety and depression. Many mental conditions do not reach a threshold sufficient to be included in Clinical Disorders in the *DSM-IV*. Persons with fewer of the symptoms associated with Major Depressive Episode and with less impact on their functioning may be diagnosed, for example, with "minor depression," which is under consideration for the fifth edition of *DSM*, or dysthmia, a diagnosis in which people report having a depressed mood and two additional symptoms of depression for more than two years with notable distress or impaired functioning, or adjustment disorder with depressed mood with symptoms of depression following a stressful life event in conjunction with significant distress or impaired functioning (American Psychiatric Association, 1994). Persons who are merely "worried" do not qualify for a diagnosis of Generalized Anxiety Disorder or Posttraumatic Stress Disorder (American Psychiatric Association, p. 223).

Consumers possess the various mental conditions described by *DSM-IV* when they visit health clinics and hospitals. They can be the presenting condition. Conditions can be discovered when consumers use these facilities for physical illnesses.

The usefulness of *DSM-IV* to health staff should not be overstated. We have already noted that many mental health conditions, such as minor depression, are not included in *DSM-IV*, yet many healthcare consumers possess and need treatment for them. Critics contend that some mental conditions in *DSM-IV* have not been empirically verified but are "social constructs." *DSM-IV* fails to place many mental conditions in an ecological context, save for psychosocial and environmental conditions described on Axis IV.

When *DSM-V* is released in 2013, some of the diagnoses and symptoms in preceding discussion may be changed—and additional ones may be added.

Healthcare consumers often require interventions that include family, economic, and community dimensions. Family roles are often reversed as heads of household become patients who need help from others. Partners often must cope with interruption of sexual intimacy. Households must often be reconfigured to accommodate the needs of persons who no longer can cope with prior arrangements. Families must often accommodate in-home staff for brief or long periods or move to new locations. Disruptions of prior family patterns can, in turn, produce resentments, anger, and blaming behaviors. Families and partners must deal with stigmatized health conditions, such as addictions, disability, and HIV.

It is not possible to divorce many health problems from economic factors. Some families are thrown into poverty or economic uncertainty when they make significant out-of-pocket payments or when persons can no longer work. These economic uncertainties may spawn mental distress, family conflict, and feelings of inadequacy—and require some families to relocate.

Medical conditions and their treatments may interfere with sexual functioning from medications, surgeries, or stress emanating from illness and disability. They may impact careers. They may require early retirements. They may harm self-image. They may cause some consumers to contemplate suicide. They may cause medical bankruptcy.

Health staff must often be educators as they explain the biological bases of specific medical conditions, as well as proposed treatments. They inform consumers of their prognoses in a way that does not demoralize them even when they confront serious illnesses. They explain what consumers need to do in order to adhere to medical regiments—and monitor them to ascertain why they do not adhere so that corrective measures are taken. They help them deal with side effects from medications and surgeries.

Health staff often work to empower consumers in their everyday lives as they contend with their medical conditions. They refer them to support groups to help them obtain advice from others with the same ones—and often staff these groups. They refer them to web sites where they can obtain important information. They encourage them to resume normal life activities as soon as possible. They help them surmount learned helplessness, that is, excessive dependence on the medical system that may impede them from other activities like employment and volunteering.

Consumers from many vulnerable populations particularly need psychosocial services. Many elderly consumers need help with their living situations, with physical limitations, and with neurological problems. Disabled consumers have to negotiate myriad occupational, welfare, housing, and legal issues. Women need help in juggling family and occupational roles with their medical conditions. Adolescents need help in surmounting mental distress, substance abuse, and education issues.

Low-income and poorly educated consumers are more likely than others to experience depression and other kinds of mental distress (Barr, 2008). Health conditions often expose them to devastating economic problems that cause other problems, such as loss of housing and inadequate nutrition. Uncertain living arrangements and poverty, when combined with low education, can lead to lack of adherence, which can spawn additional medical problems.

Table 10.1   Mental Health Interventions in Healthcare

- Diagnose psychosocial factors that contribute to mental problems (*differential assessment*).
- Help consumers resolve their internal conflicts and uncertainties (*counseling*).
- Help consumers cope with adverse news (*supportive counseling*).
- Provide consumers with medical assistance, including medications (*psychiatric or medical interventions*).
- Facilitate the diagnosis of specific mental health conditions that might otherwise not be detected (*screening*).
- Help consumers resolve familial tensions and conflicts (*family counseling*).
- Help consumers resolve tensions and conflicts within their social networks (*social network counseling*).
- Help consumers find meaning and dignity when they confront disabilities, chronic diseases, and terminal illness (*existential counseling*).
- Help consumers deal with grief, bereavement, and trauma (*grief, bereavement, and trauma counseling*).
- Help consumers deal with persisting psychological and social effects of trauma (*post-traumatic stress counseling*).
- Gauge the cognitive competence of specific persons to determine if they can make decisions about their healthcare (*assessing competence*).
- Diagnose why specific consumers do not adhere to treatment recommendations and develop interventions to improve adherence (*adherence counseling*).
- Help stabilize persons with psychotic and other disorders who are disruptive in health settings (*stabilizing services*).
- Help consumers deal with specific crises (*crisis intervention services*).
- Help consumers with specific mental health interventions (cognitive, behavioral, psychosocial, and other therapeutic strategies).
- Provide social service and mental health interventions as part of a healthcare team to achieve specific health objectives like weight loss, including psychosocial and behavioral counseling (*adjunctive counseling in a health team*).
- Educate physicians and other health staff about the mental health problems (*mental health education for professionals*).
- Use yoga, meditation, biofeedback, and other interventions (*nontraditional interventions*).
- Help consumers avoid learned helplessness (*empowerment strategies*).
- Help consumers surmount environmental stressors, such as economic, housing, and community ones (*coping with environmental stressors*).
- Help consumers obtain knowledge about psychological conditions that often accompany physical illness—and how to address these psychological conditions (*psychoeducation*).

Our discussion suggests, then, that consumers need many kinds of mental health interventions (see Table 10.1).

WHO ATTENDS TO CONSUMERS' MENTAL HEALTH NEEDS?

All health staff should engage in case finding to identify consumers who possess mental conditions that may harm their well-being, contribute to physical illness, or slow recovery from physical illnesses. They engage in case finding through conversations and observations.

Primary-care physicians have considerable discretion in treating mental conditions. They sometimes give brief counseling. They sometimes combine brief counseling with prescriptions of specific medications, such as antidepressant medications. They sometimes seek consultations from psychiatrists or psychologists or refer consumers to them. They may refer consumers to social workers.

Social workers and psychiatric nurses may refer consumers with serious mental conditions to psychologists or psychiatrists for diagnosis and treatment or to community-based mental health practitioners. These psychologists and psychiatrists are often reimbursed by consumers' insurances, Medicare, or Medicaid.

Sibling rivalry sometimes exists between different kinds of mental health practitioners. Counseling psychologists sometimes contend that they are better trained to provide culturally sensitive services, empowerment of consumers, and use of evidence-based practices than clinical psychologists. Physicians often refer patients to consultation-liaison psychiatrists due to their expertise and skill in ethically complex situations in life-threatening, life-ending, and life-restoring situations. Social workers "address social, behavioral, and emotional concerns of individuals and their social support network(s)" (Browne, 2006a, p. 24). Physicians and nurses bring technical information.

Social workers and psychiatric nurses provide psychosocial services to healthcare consumers related to their coping with specific health conditions, end-of-life care, deaths, and environmental factors. They provide skilled differential assessment where they analyze how ecological factors (such as race, ethnicity, cultural background, socio-economic status, employment status, sexual orientation, spiritual background, family, social support, gender, and age), health conditions, substance use, co-occurring psychiatric disorders, medications, and medical treatment contribute to mental health symptoms (Engstrom, 2006). Unless they work as members of multiprofessional teams with consumers with chronic diseases, such as kidney failure, they usually provide relatively short-term mental health services. They are usually salaried employees of clinics and hospitals.

SOME LIABILITIES IN THE POLICY AND REGULATORY THICKET

I discuss some shortcomings in existing policies and regulations.

Stereotypes About Mental Health Services

Discrimination against mental health problems by insurance companies, Medicaid, and Medicaid has often stemmed from the belief that more extensive coverage would be inordinately expensive. Would not mental health professionals, critics asked, resort to expensive long-term therapy at great cost to insurers? Would not many consumers seek help for many mental health problems if they were fully covered? These misgivings often prove to be incorrect. Many mental health interventions are relatively brief in duration. Consumers who use them usually have serious mental health conditions. Treatment often decreases other costs to the medical system, such as curtailing inappropriate use of health services, preventing illnesses, or speeding recovery from them. This discrimination has been partly corrected by state and federal mental health parity statutes that are discussed subsequently.

Some health staff harbors negative stereotypes about mental health services or lacks knowledge of them. They may view these services as less scientific than traditional medical services. They may be unaware that the evidence-based practice extends to mental health interventions with proven effectiveness for some of them. They may not realize that social workers and psychiatric nurses can provide effective mental health interventions.

Some health staff may have negative stereotypes about consumers with serious mental health conditions. They may believe that persons with schizophrenia are usually disruptive in waiting rooms and clinics (Brekke Interview, 2009).

Perhaps reflecting the schism between services for physiological problems and mental problems, the Patient Protection and Affordable Care Act of 2010 as amended by Congress provides scant financial support for mental health services, even within clinics and hospitals. It provides Medicaid payments to "institutions of mental disease" for adult Medicaid enrollees who require stabilization of emergency conditions from October, 2011 through December 31, 2015.

Lack of Sufficient Training in Mental Health Services

Consumers often receive low-quality mental health services in health settings. Many primary-care physicians are poorly trained in mental health diagnosis or interventions (Reiss-Brennan, 2006). Some of them prescribe antidepressants to consumers, for example, rather than interviewing them to gain a better understanding of their mental condition or referring them to mental health practitioners. Some consumers who visit ERs with suicidal ideation or attempted suicide are medically stabilized, but not referred to mental health providers for more extended treatment or given follow-up services to ascertain if they received treatment. Some consumers do not receive mental health interventions when screening instruments suggest that they possess serious mental health conditions.

Declining Length of Stays in Hospitals

Provision of mental health services is impeded by the inability of hospital and clinic mental health staff to establish clinical relationships with consumers due to the short-term nature of medical care as average hospital stays have declined. Many hospital-based mental health professionals do not have ongoing contact with consumers once they are discharged, requiring them to depend on referrals to community-based clinics and professionals who may require long waits.

Inadequate Accreditation Standards

Insufficient numbers of social workers and psychiatric nurses are employed by clinics and hospitals to provide case-finding and biopsychosocial services. These staff often find their time for counseling and mental health triage to be severely limited due to other tasks that they must perform, such as discharge planning. I discuss the inadequacy of Joint Commission standards for numbers of social workers and psychiatric nurses in health settings subsequently.

ASSETS IN THE POLICY AND REGULATORY THICKET

I now discuss some policies and regulations that encourage or promote mental health interventions.

Protections for Vulnerable Populations in States

To introduce readers to these protections, I focus on those in California because it is not possible to review those in every state. Because of their sheer number and complexity, it is impossible to describe relevant statutes, regulations, and court rulings in great detail in a publication that is not exclusively devoted to them. I want to sensitize health staff to some legal issues that they might encounter in their work so that they will recognize them and seek legal advice from their supervisors, health administrators, or attorneys who work for their health organizations. Three limitations should be noted. By discussing merely a portion of existing legal requirements, I may simplify some specific legal issues, so I provide merely an introduction to select legal issues. Relevant legal requirements are different in various states, so health professionals should always consult persons and materials relevant to their states. Laws, court rulings, and regulations are constantly changing, so the discussion is outdated in some respects. This book does not offer legal advice, but is merely an introduction to some legal issues. It does not cover all relevant laws, court rulings, and regulations due to space limitations.

I have relied heavily upon the 35th edition of the *Consent Manual* published by the California Hospital Association in 2008 in this section. This manual has already been updated in 2009 and 2010 at the time of this publication. Advocates using this book should always consult similar publications made by their state's Hospital Association or other relevant sources germane to their individual states—and should consult an attorney when they need legal advice. Comparisons of many relevant statutes and regulations of different states can be found at the web site of the National Conference of State Legislatures at www.ncsl.org.

Some Regulations Pertaining to Law Enforcement Officials

Health professionals and law enforcement officials often interact with one another in the course of their professional duties. Health professionals should ask and seek legal answers to questions such as, but not limited to, the following:

- When can they legally comply with requests from law enforcement for blood, urine, and breath tests for persons brought to hospitals by law enforcement officers and who they suspect may have been driving under the influence of alcohol (DUI) or to have used specific drugs?

- When should hospital professionals require law enforcement to present a written request when a particular patient does not consent to their request for blood and other medical tests?
- When can hospital staff perform specific medical tests on a consumer at the request of law enforcement when that patient does not consent?
- When should hospital staff allow law enforcement to interrogate a patient on hospital premises when the patient does not consent, and under what conditions?
- When and under what circumstances should hospital staff comply with a request from law enforcement to contact them when a specific patient is discharged?
- When should health staff require law enforcement to possess a court-ordered warrant or a subpoena or summons from a judicial officer, grand jury, or appropriate government agency?
- When law enforcement personnel request patient information, if HIPAA regulations conflict with state laws regarding the confidentiality of a patient's personal health information, which regulations take precedence?
- When can (and should) health professionals not honor requests for specific information about a patient—and when should they honor these requests?

Vignette 10.1 Advocacy for a Consumer with Mental Distress by a Police Officer and a Social Worker

Our police department and the local community hospital are tightly linked. Fortunately, this makes our job and services to citizens better. This particular night I was dispatched to the home of a young, 19-year-old woman who claimed that she wanted to commit suicide. Upon interviewing the citizen, I found that this woman was depressed, experiencing multiple stressors, and needing further mental health evaluation. Unfortunately she had no health insurance. Feeling sympathetic toward her case, I called the emergency department social worker to get a sense of whether they could take another patient tonight. Lately, patients had been waiting six hours a night in the waiting room there. However, looking at this young woman, I also felt that she would be horrified by the conditions in the county emergency department and may experience an even longer wait there for a mental health evaluation.

The emergency department social worker was not pleased. I waited on hold while she checked with the charge nurse about bed availability. The social worker said that because the patient had no insurance that I should consider taking her to the county emergency department. I pleaded for this patient, and promised that when I brought her, that the social worker would understand why I insisted. She did.

(*continued*)

(*continued*)

I waited with the patient and reassured her that she was in a good hospital where she would get help for her depression. I told her that she had made the right decision in calling instead of attempting to overdose on pills. She was grateful. The social worker agreed that the patient was young, inexperienced, and going through a hard time, leading to a lapse in judgment tonight. She agreed that the community hospital would be a better place for the patient to receive treatment, allowing the patient to feel perhaps a little more secure with a smaller patient population than county facilities. As I left that night, I felt grateful for our connections to the hospital, and for the benefit of the doubt for the patient, and my judgment as an officer.

Learning Exercise

- How does this case illustrate the need for cooperative relationships between law enforcement officers and hospital staff?
- Does this case suggest that law enforcement officers themselves advocate for specific consumers?
- Do note that the community hospital could not transfer her, even if it had wished to do so, until the patient was medically stabilized.

Regulations Regarding Consumers With Mental Health and Substance Abuse Conditions

Many regulations govern actions of health staff with respect to persons with mental health conditions.

Some Regulations Regarding Consumers Who Threaten Other People

Health providers usually keep medical information confidential as HIPAA and ethical norms require. Specific patients sometimes disclose to them that they intend to harm, even kill, someone. In some cases, a family member or acquaintance may reveal this information to health providers. Psychotherapists must warn or otherwise protect possible victims if they possess a professional relationship with the patient and believe the patient to be dangerous (CHA, 2008, p. 13.12). The psychotherapist may warn the intended victim or others who can warn him or her. The psychotherapist may be required to warn both the intended victim and law enforcement. "Psychotherapists" may include physicians, licensed psychologists, licensed clinical social workers, credentialed school psychologists, licensed marriage and family counselors, and nurses with expertise and credentials in mental health counseling and persons they supervise, including interns (CHA, 2008, p. 13.13).

In making these disclosures, the health provider violates confidentiality on the grounds that the risk of injury to the intended victim outweighs the right to confidentiality, but provides only the information the intended victim needs in order to recognize the danger and to take necessary precautions (CHA, 2008, p. 13.14).

Health staff needs to document the disclosures about intended or possible violent acts from persons who make these threats and why they believe they constitute serious threats. *They should consult legal staff of their health organization, and possible personal legal counsel, to be certain they have acted appropriately.* They should realize that they could face fines, lawsuits, and possible loss of licenses if they fail to act appropriately (CHA, 2008, p. 13.13).

Some Regulations Regarding the Confidentiality of Consumers' Mental Health Information

State laws, such as the Lanterman-Petris-Short Act in California, protect information in medical records and in other communications with health staff, regarding mental problems and developmental disability. (Health staff includes staff in a broad array of hospital, clinic, skilled nursing facilities, and community programs.) HIPAA also protects the confidentiality of mental health information in ways that are sometimes more stringent or less stringent than the laws of specific states (CHA, 2008, p. 17.2). Health providers in each state must determine what specific regulations govern whether and when they may disclose a person's specific mental health information and what to do if HIPAA conflicts with state laws. In some states, for example, mental health information can be released that is germane to workers' compensation, but not in others. HIPAA has specific provisions that govern release of psychotherapy notes with specific consumers covering private counseling or group, joint, or family counseling sessions—and requires them to be separated from the rest of the individual's medical record. Separate authorizations are often needed for these notes, which exclude medication prescriptions, details of treatment, results of clinical tests, and summaries of the treatment plan, symptoms, prognosis, and progress to date (CHA, 2008, p. 17.3). HIPAA allows some disclosures for purposes of healthcare oversight, such as to a department of mental health, for law enforcement purposes, and for judicial and administrative proceedings with documents sometimes filed under seal. (Health staff should consult legal staff to determine when they can release this information and to whom because of the high sensitivity of mental health information.) Hospitals often have HIPAA-compliant authorization forms for disclosures. These include disclosures to patients' attorneys, probation offices, physicians or administrators who work for employers where a patient seeks employment, administrator of programs where a patient appeals specific benefits or eligibility decisions, and county patients' rights advocates.

Disclosures of patient information for treatment purposes may be made by a patient letter or authorization or at the discretion of the provider, such as by the treating psychotherapist with disclosures documented in consumers' charts (CHA, 2008,

p. 17.7). Mental health information to third parties not having responsibility for their medical or psychological care, such as a board and care home, can be released only with the authorization of patients or their guardians or conservators (CHA, 2008, p. 17.4).

Some mental health information can be disclosed to law enforcement, but only in special cases and with a HIPAA-compliant authorization form or a court order (CHA, 2008, p. 17.6). This may include information for persons who are, or have been, incarcerated as mentally disordered sex offenders. (These persons can themselves disclose their psychotherapy notes under a specific authorization.)

Authorizations describe precisely what information is to be disclosed. When information is disclosed without authorizations, it should be limited to only what is necessary for the purpose of the disclosure. Mental health information sometimes can be released without authorization during conservatorship proceedings, for treatment purposes outside a facility that has medical or psychological responsibility for caring for a patient, for certain payment and insurance purposes, for courts as needed for the administration of justice, and to some researchers who have approval from appropriate institutional review boards (IRBs). It can be released to law enforcement agencies, while consumers are hospitalized, by physicians or administrators when probable causes exist that they committed or were victims of an array of specific crimes, including ones committed at the hospital, as well as persons committed by courts to hospitals for various offenses or for insanity but who escape from them (CHA, 2008, pp. 17.7–17.10).

Mental health information can be disclosed in some states to law enforcement officials for consumers who are involuntarily admitted to a hospital for mental disorders, but who disappear from it to unknown locations. Mental health records can be released to various public agencies that inspect health facilities or investigate them, as well as licensing boards. A HIPAA-compliant authorization must be obtained for disclosures to probation officers who evaluate a person after a crime (CHA, 2008, p. 17.5). Legal advice should be sought from legal officials of a health organization about disclosure of mental health information.

Regulations Regarding Substance Abuse

Various state and federal regulations often prohibit disclosure of information about the diagnosis and treatment of substance abuse by health providers, including statutes and federal regulations in the "Confidentiality of Alcohol and Drug Abuse Patient Records Regulations" and the "HIPAA Privacy Rule," which can be found on the web site of the federal Substance Abuse and Mental Health Services Administration at http://www .hipaa.samhsa.gov/Part2ComparisonCleared.htm (CHA, 2008, p. 18.1). Federal substance abuse confidentiality regulations apply to any federally assisted program that provides specialized diagnostic, treatment, or referral services for substance abuse, including general medical care facilities if they have specialized substance abuse centers that receive federal funds. (Federal assistance includes federal licenses, contracts,

Medicare certification, and federal funds.) Privacy extends to the PHI of patients under HIPAA. Staff and administrators that operate facilities that treat substance abusers are not allowed even to acknowledge that a specific person has been or is an alcohol or drug abuse patient (CHA, 2008, pp. 18.2, 18.4).

The intent of privacy regulations is partly to prevent substance abusers from being stigmatized by release of their diagnoses and treatments and to avoid inherent conflict with law enforcement. Because it is illegal under federal law to use many drugs, if substance abusers knew they would be identified and their identity would be given to law enforcement, many of them would not seek treatment. Federal regulations sometimes permit rather than require the disclosure of information to law enforcement authorities. However, health officials should seek legal advice before they share diagnostic or other information with law enforcement and the courts, or if they are asked by law enforcement to provide PHI for investigation of criminal conduct. They should realize, too, that many states possess their own privacy laws and regulations.

Other regulations may allow certain breaches of confidentiality for minor children, for persons in grave danger from substance abuse, for persons that are incompetent, for medical emergencies, and for suspected child abusers. Even here, state or federal laws and statutes often limit information that can be divulged to others without consumers' consent, so again, health professionals should seek advice from an attorney in their health organization (CHA, 2008).

Some Regulations Governing Voluntary Admission of Persons With Mental Health and Substance Abuse Conditions

Consumers with mental disorders, alcoholism, and drug abuse, including persons under conservatorship, can seek voluntary admittance. Attending physicians have to certify that they are sufficiently mentally competent to understand the nature of their admissions and the treatments they will receive (CHA, 2008, p. 12.2).

Some Regulations Governing Involuntary Admissions and Detention of Consumers With Mental Health and Substance Abuse Conditions

Each state has its own procedures for the involuntary detaining of persons dangerous to themselves or others or gravely disabled as result of mental disorder, inebriation, use of narcotics or restricted dangerous drugs (CHA, 2008, p. 12.6). These procedures usually include an initial holding period for evaluation and treatment, such as 72 hours, an additional intensive treatment period, such as 14 days, an additional period of intensive treatment, such as 30 days, and further confinement depending on the person's condition. Other intensive treatment periods and confinement periods exist for persons who are imminently suicidal or present a demonstrated danger of substantial physical harm to others. California makes no distinction between mental disorders of organic and inorganic origin, including Alzheimer's disease, brain injuries, and other organic brain disorders (CHA, 2008, p. 12.6). Specific procedural safeguards exist in each state to protect the rights of consumers who are involuntarily committed can be accessed at http://www.ncsl.org or in publications of various state hospital associations. In California, involuntary treatment must take place in a facility designated for such purposes by relevant local and state public agencies (CHA, 2008, p. 12.6).

Some Regulations Governing Involuntary Outpatient Treatment

Some states allow courts to order consumers to participate in outpatient mental health treatment. A petition must be filed with the court in California to initiate this process and specific processes must be followed (CHA, 2008, pp. 12.28–12.29).

Some Regulations Governing Conservatorships for Persons With Mental Health and Substance Abuse Conditions

Conservators can be appointed for persons who are gravely disabled by mental disorders or impairment by chronic alcoholism through special proceedings. Criteria used by courts may include: inability to provide for basic personal needs for food and clothing; unwillingness of a person to engage in treatment voluntarily; and disorders sufficient in magnitude to make the person gravely disabled (CHA, 2008, pp. 12.26–12.27). Some patients can be detained by acute care hospitals if medical staff cannot identify destinations where their personal needs, including food, clothing or shelter, can be met, or if medical staff have not been able to locate appropriate mental health treatment. State laws often establish limits on such detention, such as 24 hours (CHA, 2008, pp. 12.27–12.28). Responsible family members, friends, or others can sometimes help to provide for the basic personal needs, allowing the patient to survive safely without involuntary detention, but those persons must specifically indicate in writing that they can and will provide this assistance (CHA, 2008, p. 12.6). Gravely disabled minors are minors whose mental disorders make them unable to use the elements of life necessary for their health, safety, and development, including food, clothing, and shelter, even though it is provided to them by others (CHA, 2008, p. 12.6). Minors' mental retardation, epilepsy, alcoholism, other drug use, or repeated antisocial behavior do not, by themselves, constitute a mental disorder in California (CHA, 2008, p. 12.6). Conservatorships can be appointed under Welfare and Institutions Codes or under Probate Codes, so hospital staff must realize that significant differences in roles of conservators under these two codes in California. Conservators place them in the least restrictive alternative placement without court order or proceeding, but have to find placements that meet their needs and protect the public. They have to provide written notification to the court of the impending transfer.

Some Federal and State Laws Regarding Use of Illegal and Other Substances

Many laws and regulations exist at federal and state levels that govern use of specific drugs. Federal drug laws are discussed in Chapters 5 and 8. Advocates need to research laws and regulations in their own states because they vary considerably, including whether and to what extent specific drugs like marijuana are available under physicians' prescriptions for nausea and pain. States and localities vary considerably, as well, in the number of legal marijuana dispensaries in those states where state laws allow physicians to write prescriptions for this drug.

Some Regulations Governing Maternal Substance Abuse

Health staff do not have to report findings that a mother has tested positively for substance abuse at the time of the birth of her child, but such a finding precipitates a required assessment of the child and mother. If *other* factors indicate risk to the child, then a report must be made to child welfare or probation departments, not to law enforcement in California (CHA, 2008, p. 10.2).

Some Regulations Requiring Notifying Next of Kin and Others About Admissions, Releases, Transfers, Illness, or Death

States, as well as HIPAA, sometimes allow certain kinds of information to be released to next of kin or other designated persons when consumers are admitted for inpatient services, such as when they cannot communicate. Hospitals must also make reasonable attempts to inform such persons designated by patients of their release, transfer, serious illness, injury, death, diagnosis, prognosis, prescribed medications, side effects of medications unless consumers do not want this information divulged. (The patient's consent form should state what information should be disclosed.) The law does not define who "next of kin" is, but health facilities often seek to reach spouses or partners followed by adult children, adult grandchildren, either parent, adult brothers and sisters, and adult nephews and nieces.

Restrictions on Release of HIV Test Results

Physicians, hospitals, and other healthcare providers must report all AIDS cases, HIV infections, and viral hepatitis infections to the local health officer or other designated agency within specific time frames. In many states, this includes ones caused by transfusions (CHA, 2008, p. 20.4). Conflicting regulations and statutes exist throughout the United States: though some states require patient consent for an HIV test, others give the physician the right to administer that test (CHA, 2008, pp. 10.1, 23.4–23.12). The medical provider must note in consumers' medical records if they decline the HIV test (in some states). Consult a legal officer in your health organization to discover the policies of your state. Different procedures exist for minors 12 years and older and persons under age 12, as well as criminal defendants and inmates. Physicians who order HIV tests in California may, but are not required to, disclose positive results of specific patients with their spouses, persons reasonably believed to be sexual partners, and persons who shared use of hypodermic needles, but without identifying the infected person (CHA, 2008, p. 23.8). They should first discuss the results with the consumer, counsel them, and attempt to obtain their voluntary consent to notifying their contacts. (Their physician should refer notified contacts to appropriate care.) Improper disclosures can bring civil penalties, including fines (CHA, 2008).

First responders and healthcare personnel who have experienced significant exposure to patients' blood or other potentially infectious materials can ask for HIV testing of them under certain conditions (CHA, 2008, p. 23.9).

Some Regulations Dealing With Victims and Perpetrators of Family Violence

Consumers who have been subject to sexual and other assaults often visit ERs, clinics, and other health providers.

Some Regulations for Possible Victims of Family Violence

Health practitioners are required to make reports to local law enforcement when they treat injured victims of rape, child abuse, elder abuse, and neglect or abuse suffered during transfers from another health facility (CHA, 2008, pp. 19.1–19.2). They must make the telephone report immediately, or as soon as practically possible—and the written report within two working days (in California, even if victims object) (CHA, 2008, p. 19.3). Health practitioners include physicians, psychologists, residents, interns, licensed nurses, marriage and family therapists, clinical social workers, and others (CHA, 2008, p. 19.3). Reports can be submitted by individual health practitioners or by a team of them (CHA, 2008, p. 19.2). Supervisors or administrators cannot block or inhibit the filing of these reports nor sanction a person or team who makes the report (CHA, 2008, p. 19.2). Reporting persons are not required to disclose their identities to supervisors (CHA, 2008, p. 19.2). Reports are required for wounds caused by firearms, whether inflicted by a patient or by other persons, as well as any wound or other physical injury from assaultive or abusive conduct (CHA, 2008, p. 19.2). Persons who are victims of abuse or domestic violence must be informed that a report has been or will be made unless the providers fear a report could place them in danger of serious harm (CHA, 2008, p. 19.3). Health practitioners often enter into the medical record comments by the injured person regarding past domestic violence or the name of the person(s) suspected of inflicting injuries or engaging in assaultive or abusive conduct, as well as a map of the injured person's body showing where wounds were inflicted and a copy of the law enforcement reporting form (CHA, 2008, p. 19.4). Failure to report is a misdemeanor punishable by fines, imprisonment, or both. Health practitioners who make reports are immune from civil or criminal liability as a result of their reports and, in California, they can make claims to the state for attorneys' fees for any legal action against them on the basis of their report. Health practitioners and health organizations must keep reports confidential. Nor can they inform the person suspected of causing the injury or divulge the location of the injured person (CHA, 2008, p. 19.4).

Assaultive or abusive conduct includes a wide range of offenses, including murder; manslaughter; mayhem; aggregative mayhem; torture; assault with intent to commit mayhem, rape, sodomy, or oral copulation; administering controlled substances or anesthetic to aid in commission of a felony; battery; sexual battery; incest; throwing corrosive materials with intent to injure or disfigure; assault with a deadly weapon; rape, spousal rape; procuring any female to have sex with another man; child abuse and endangerment; abuse of a spouse or cohabitant; sodomy; lewd and lascivious acts with a child; oral copulation; sexual penetration by a foreign object; and elder abuse. (CHA, 2008, p. 19.3).

Health facilities must establish written policies and procedures for routine screenings of patients to detect spousal or partner abuse, including identifying victims, document-ing them, and educating staff about criteria for identifying them, as well as referring victims to crisis intervention or counseling agencies whether in the hospital or in the community (CHA, 2008, p. 19.4).

Some Regulations Germane to Alleged Rape

Hospitals are required to report sexual assaults to law enforcement by telephone and in writing. They must notify them by telephone before beginning a required medical examination. Failure to report is a misdemeanor (in California) punishable by fine, imprisonment, or both (CHA, 2008, p. 19.5).

All hospitals must comply with standards, protocols, and guidelines in examining or treating victims of sexual assault and attempted sexual assault including child molestation—or refer these patients to a local hospital that does comply with them (CHA, 2008, p. 19.6). Physicians who examine victims must use the standard form developed by State Departments of Justice and Public Health in California and must make such observations and perform such tests as may be required for recording of the data required by the form if the patient consents to be so examined (CHA, 2008, p. 19.6). Consent must be obtained from victims to collect and preserve evidence of the assault, including examination of injuries from the assault, collection of physical evidence of sexual assault, and photographs of injuries (CHA, 2008, p. 19.6). Victims must be informed that failure to consent will not result in denial of treatment for injuries, possible pregnancy and sexually transmitted diseases, as well as postcoital contraception. They have the right to have a sexual assault counselor (in California) or at least one other support person of their choosing at any medical evidentiary or physical examination (CHA, 2008, p. 19.7)—and must be informed of this right orally or in writing, prior to the examination. Suspected sexual assault forms are confidential except as permitted or required by another law, such as in response to a court order or pursuant to child abuse reporting laws (CHA, 2008, p. 19.7).

Suspects of sexual assault who are in custody of law enforcement can be physically examined by health practitioners, who must prepare a written report that is confidential, but may be released on request to any person or agency involved in any related investigation or prosecution of a criminal case (CHA, 2008, p. 19.7).

Some Regulations Germane to Elder Abuse and Neglect

Providers are required to report suspected elder abuse to law enforcement authorities as soon as possible. Failure to report is a misdemeanor (in California), punishable by fine, imprisonment, or both. Abuse of an older person includes physical abuse, abandonment, isolation, abduction, or the deprivation by a care custodian of goods or services that are necessary to avoid physical harm or mental suffering (CHA, 2008, p. 19.17).

Some Regulations Germane to Alleged Child Abuse and Neglect

Health practitioners who reasonably suspect that specific children have been victims of child abuse or neglect must report such suspected instances to a designated agency in an initial report (CHA, 2008, p. 19.7). When two or more health practitioners jointly become aware of child abuse or neglect, they can decide which one makes the report. Mandated reporters include many other professions including school teachers and the clergy (CHA, 2008, p. 19.10). The report must be made immediately or as soon as possible by telephone with a follow-up written report within 36 hours (in California) (CHA, 2008, p. 19.7). It must include specific information including the identity of the mandated reporter, information that gave rise of reasonable suspicion, identifying information of the child and the child's parents or guardians, and identifying information of the suspected persons who abused or neglected the child (CHA, 2008, pp. 19.10–19.11). They must report at the same time if they know or reasonably suspect that homes or institutions where these children reside are unsuitable because of the abuse or neglect (CHA, 2008, p. 19.7). If they have knowledge that a child has serious emotional damage or is at risk for it, as evidenced by "states of being or behaviors including, but not limited to, severe anxiety, depression, withdrawal, or untoward aggressive behaviors toward self or others," they may, but are not required to, make a report to the appropriate agency (CHA, 2008, p. 19.7).

Medical professionals who examine children for physical injury or for sexual assault must also submit a report within 36 hours of receiving information about the incident in California (CHA, 2008, p. 19.11). Physicians or dentists can take X-rays of children where reasonable cause exists for abuse or neglect without the permission of parents or guardians. Minor children can give consent for diagnosis and treatment, but consent from parents or guardians is not necessary (CHA, 2008, pp. 19.11–19.12).

Providers must also submit a report for pregnant minors or minors with sexually transmitted diseases if reasonable suspicion exists that these conditions were caused by sexual assault. Child abuse reports are not needed if minors under age 14 have consensual sex and are of similar age, but is required if a minor has sex with a person of disparate age even if it is consensual (CHA, 2008, p. 19.12).

Providers who fail to report suspected child abuse or neglect are guilty of a misdemeanor (in California) punishable by fine, imprisonment, or both. Some court rulings, such as in *Landeros v. Flood* by the California Supreme Court, hold that abused children can recover damages for subsequent injuries if it can be shown that the physician or hospital knew or should have known about their abuse or neglect and that the hospital failed to report it (CHA, 2008, p. 19.2).

Child abuse or neglect can occur within a child's home or in out-of-home care including a child care center, school, facility licensed to care for children, or other institution. It includes "physical injury or death, sexual abuse, neglect, willful harming or injuring of a child or endangering of the person or health of a child, or unlawful corporal punishment or injury" (CHA, 2008, p. 19.8). Neglect means the negligent treatment or maltreatment of a child by a person responsible for the child's welfare and includes both acts and omissions on their part, including failure to protect the child from severe malnutrition, or willfully causing or permitting a child to be placed in a situation such that their health is endangered, including the intentional failure to provide adequate food, clothing, shelter, or medical care (CHA, 2008, p. 19.8). It also includes general neglect, including lack of supervision where no physical injury to the child has occurred. Parents or guardians who make an informed and appropriate medical decision about treatment with their physicians cannot be considered neglectful. A physician or other health practitioner may file a report if they believe a medical decision was not made in the child's best interest (CHA, 2008, p. 19.8).

Other reportable conditions for children include sexual assault, which includes rape, incest, sodomy, any penetration of the vagina or anal opening, any sexual contact between the genitals or anal opening and the mouth or tongue of another person; any intrusion with objects into the genitals or anal opening; intentional touching of genitals and intimate parts; and intentional masturbation in the presence of a child (CHA, 2008, p. 19.9). Sexual exploitation includes a range of actions including preparation or sale of matter depicting minors engaged in sexual acts; or encouraging children to engage in prostitution. Unlawful corporal punishment or injury means infliction of cruel or inhuman corporal punishment on children. Willful harming or endangering of a child occurs when someone causes or permits the child to suffer or inflicts "unjustifiable physical pain or mental suffering on him or her" (CHA, 2008, p. 19.9).

Regulations Pertaining to Women Who "Surrender" Newborns

Some women decide not to keep newborns. Rather than giving them up for adoption through child welfare agencies, they "surrender" them to hospitals and other sites such as police stations. They cannot be reported for child abuse in California, where safe-surrender laws allow them to legally give newborns to police and health facilities (CHA, 2008, p. 19.13).

Some Regulations Regarding Treatment Choices With Infants With Serious Medical Conditions

Physicians must sometimes decide whether to discontinue treatment to infants in the context of specific court decisions, state statutes and regulations, and the federal Child Abuse Amendments of 1984. In these situations, these and other questions may arise:

- Is medical care futile, such as when an infant is chronically and irreversibly comatose or when treatment will merely prolong dying—and when can physicians discontinue treatment under these circumstances?
- Are specific parents competent to make medical decisions about their infant based on information that the infant's physician gives them about the infant's diagnosis, prognosis, and available treatment?
- What remedies or solutions are available when parents have an irreconcilable disagreement between themselves—or if the physician and health team disagree with the parents?
- What remedies or solutions exist when a physician decides that parents favor a choice of action that is not in the infant's best interest?
- Can the physician attempt to resolve a disagreement between parents about treatment before resorting to the courts?
- Can qualified resource persons, such as a multidisciplinary hospital ethics committee, help to resolve differences between parents and members of the healthcare team—while recognizing that the committee does not make treatment decisions, but facilitates communication and provides advisory guidance (CHA, 2008, p. 5.14)?
- Under what circumstances, if ever, can hydration and nutrition be withheld from an infant with serious health conditions?

Parents face difficult choices when they have infants who have serious medical conditions that may terminate their lives. Using information from their physicians, parents usually make final decisions unless they are incompetent or cannot agree with one another. Nonetheless, various court rulings state that physicians should always act in the best interests of the child and presume life-sustaining treatment should be provided unless and until a court resolves the dispute. In general, withdrawal or withholding of life-sustaining treatment for newborns should not occur merely because they have a disability such as Down's syndrome or because their medical care will be costly.

Substantial differences exist between abuse and neglect statutes and regulations of many states and the Federal Child Abuse Amendments of 1984. Some states do not regard parents' decisions to withhold or withdraw treatment to newborns as abuse or neglect if they make these decisions in consultation with physicians. This federal legislation recommends that state child protective agencies require reports for "withholding of medically indicated treatment" from disabled infants with life-threatening conditions. The federal legislation only allows withholding of life-sustaining treatment if infants are comatose and if treatment merely prolongs dying and would be medically futile. Yet the federal legislation does not require a mandatory reporting obligation. Hospital legal counsel should be consulted when federal conditions are not met and whenever treatment is withheld (CHA, 2008, p. 5.15).

THE POLICY AND REGULATORY THICKET: LAWS, REGULATIONS, AND STAFF THAT FACILITATE SOCIAL AND MENTAL HEALTH SERVICES

Provisions That Support Mental Health Services

Consumers with mental health conditions can often receive coverage for their conditions.

Regulations Requiring Private Insurance Companies to Cover Mental Illness

Many private health insurance companies failed to cover mental illness prior to 2009 partly because they feared that it would be excessively costly, particularly when consumers encountered long-term health problems like schizophrenia and manic-depressive conditions. This lack of coverage had devastating economic effects on many consumers who lacked coverage. After some states had taken the lead, Congress finally enacted the Mental Health Parity and Addiction Equity Act in 2008 to take effect in January 2010. It required employers offering group plans to employees not to restrict access to mental health services by limiting benefits or requiring higher patient costs than apply to general medical and surgical coverage.

Coverage of Some Mental Health Conditions by Medicare and Medicaid

Medicare provides relatively brief treatments and some medications for mental health problems among elderly persons. Oriented toward acute rather than chronic care, however, it does not provide long-term coverage for seniors' mental problems or for Alzheimer's disease or dementia. Some seniors with supplemental health insurance are able to obtain medications for long-term mental conditions, however, if their policies cover them. Seniors with chronic mental conditions, Alzheimer's disease, or dementia often "spend down" to become eligible for Medicaid, which does fund long-term treatment for these conditions, including nursing home and assisted-living coverage for those facilities and programs willing to accept Medicaid enrollees. The extent of mental health coverage by Medicaid varies between states, however, with some states providing less generous coverage than others.

Case-Finding Regulations for Social Workers in Some States

Some states have enacted regulations that give social workers the right to approach any patient in hospitals to discover if they need their help as is currently contained in Section 22 of the Health and Welfare Code of California. This provision enhances their role because it allows them to take the initiative in providing social and mental health services to specific consumers—or to engage in case advocacy, referrals, or case management—rather than waiting until they receive referrals from specific physicians.

Federal Requirements for Social Workers in Nephrology

End-stage renal disease (ESRD) is the only disease or treatment regimen with a public policy requirement that master's level social workers be included on health teams. Medicare, which funds dialysis and kidney transplants for persons of all ages, mandates that they be on the staff for every dialysis and kidney transplant program (Browne, 2006b, p. 481).

The Family and Medical Leave Act

Congress enacted this legislation in 1993 to give employees the right to take a medical leave when they experienced a family medical or social crisis, such as the death of a family member or the birth of a child. Unlike most European nations, however, the legislation does not apply to small employers, and does not require employers to give paid leaves, and requires these leaves to last only to 12 weeks.

Employment of Social Workers in Healthcare

Accreditation standards of the Joint Commission require hospitals to have a social worker on their staff, but do not require a master's degree or stipulate that the social worker should be a full-time employee. Twenty-two percent of all social workers were employed in medical and public health settings in 2004, but many hospitals only meet the minimum Joint Commission requirement or have only a few social workers (Department of Labor, 2010b).

The Growth of Multidisciplinary Health Teams That Include Social Workers

Social workers and nurses are often members of multiprofessional teams that provide care to seniors, consumers with chronic diseases, consumers receiving dialysis, consumers with kidney and other transplanted organs, and others. They provide supportive, psychosocial, and behavioral services to these consumers as members of these teams. These teams are not legally required, however, except in nephrology services and hospice services. Considerable research suggests that persons with chronic diseases, obesity, end-of-life, and some other health conditions benefit from care from multidisciplinary teams (Brumley et al., 2007; Lin et al., 2000***). Many health providers who are used to solo practice need to be retrained to view new practitioner roles that facilitate partnerships, such as the mental health integration model (MHI) developed for helping persons with depression (Reiss-Brennan, 2006). Chronic disease management models (CDM) have widely evolved in health settings, even if many health providers still rely on solo-based care (Bower & Gask, 2002*).

Positive Evaluations of Mental Health Services

A growing body of research suggests that psychosocial services provided by frontline workers improves consumers' physiological health, including morbidity, recovery rates, and mortality; contributes to consumers' adherence to treatment regimens and appropriate use of health systems; improves consumers' mental health; and contributes to the efficiency of the health system. Some research suggests that biopsychosocial services reduce costs because patients with psychiatric co-morbidity have increased lengths of hospital stays in adult nonelderly and elderly populations (Bourgeois, Kremen, Servis, Wegelin, & Hales, 2005*; Katon et al., 2005***). I discuss some of these findings when discussing specific scenarios encountered by case advocates. Not all of these findings emanate from studies with experimental designs and random assignments of participants to experimental and other groups. Some of this research is discussed in the Campbell Collaboration at www.campbellcollaboration.org.

Research Useful in Finding Consumers at Risk of Mental Illness

Considerable research has emerged that identifies consumers with risk of having mental illness, including postpartum women, consumers with various chronic diseases, consumers receiving dialysis, persons with organ transplants, and disabled persons who have relatively high rates of mental illness, for example, as compared to the general population. I discuss some of these findings when discussing specific scenarios encountered by case advocates.

Research Useful in Improving Consumers' Quality of Life

Some interventions are directed toward improving consumers' quality of life rather than specific health or mental health conditions. Membership in support groups do not necessarily lengthen lives of consumers with such diseases as metastatic cancer, as psychiatrist David Siegel discovered in randomized research (2007). Consumers who are highly optimistic even when confronting serious health conditions often report higher quality of life (Ubel, 2001). Prognostic information should include the truth, however, such as "within weeks or months," so that patients can plan their lives and deaths (Ubel, 2001).

TWENTY-SIX SCENARIOS ENCOUNTERED BY CASE ADVOCATES

Scenario 10.1: Advocacy to Help Consumers Receive Clinical Assessments Through Screening Instruments

The Surgeon General estimates that one in five Americans of all ages have psychiatric symptoms that are diagnosable mental health conditions (U.S. Department of Health and Human Services, 1999, p. 207). These include various anxiety disorders (including posttraumatic stress disorder, simple phobia, social phobia, agoraphobia, generalized anxiety disorder, panic disorder, and obsessive-compulsive disorder) and mood disorders (major depressive episode, unipolar major depression, dysthymia, and bipolar disorder), disruptive disorders among children, and many other psychiatric and substance abuse conditions identified by *DSM-IV* (American Psychiatric Association, 1994).

Specific screening instruments can be used of varying length. The U.S. Preventive Services Task Force (2003, p. 760) and presented in Engstrom (2006, p. 213), contends that two questions identify the majority of adults with depression and are probably as effective as longer instruments: "Over the last 2 weeks, have you felt down, depressed, or hopeless; have you felt little interest or pleasure in doing things?" Levinson and Engle (1997, pp. 2–3) suggest eight questions: (1) "Would you describe yourself as a nervous person? Do you feel nervous or tense?" (Generalized Anxiety Disorder); (2) "Have you ever had a sudden attack of rapid heartbeat or rush of intense fear, anxiety or nervousness?" (Panic Disorder); (3) "Have you ever avoided important activities because you were afraid you would have a sudden attack like the one I just asked you about?" (Agoraphobia); (4) "Some people have strong fears of being watched or evaluated by others. For example, some people don't want to eat, speak, or write in front of people for fear of embarrassing themselves. Is anything like this a problem for you?" (Social phobia); (5) Some people have strong fears, or phobias, about heights, flying, bugs, or snakes. Do you have any phobias?" (Specific phobia); (6) Some people are bothered by intrusive, silly, unpleasant, or horrible thoughts that keep repeating over and over. For example, some people have repeated thoughts of hurting someone they love even though they don't want to; that a loved one has been seriously hurt; that they will yell obscenities in public; or that they have been contaminated by germs. Has anything like this troubled you?" (Obsession); (7) "Some people are bothered by doing something over and over. They can't resist the urge, even when they try. They might wash their hands every few minutes, or repeatedly check to see that the stove is off or the door is locked or count things excessively. Has anything like this been a problem for you?" (Compulsion); and (8) "Have you ever seen or experienced a traumatic event when you thought your life was in danger? Have you ever seen someone else in grave danger? What happened?" (Acute Stress and Posttraumatic Stress Disorder [PTSD]).

A mental status exam allows healthcare staff to observe consumers' appearances, attitudes, and activities to elicit consumers' perspectives, make observations about them, and to prompt questions that explore information that emerges (Trzepacz & Baker, 1993). These include observations of the consumer's degree of consciousness (Is the consumer alert and respond to stimuli?); Does the consumer's age and appearance correspond or does this person appear younger or older? Does the consumer's posture and position appear rigid or relaxed and is the consumer able to sit down during the interview? Is the consumer's attire and personal hygiene appropriate for the season and how does the person's personal hygiene appear? Are there any notable physical characteristics in addition to race, ethnicity, and gender? What is the consumer's attitude toward you and toward the interview—and are there changes in this response during the meeting? Is there any significant movement or paralysis, such as does the consumer have difficulty sitting still, move quickly or slowly, appear to have any tremors or involuntary movements? These questions can be followed by questions that probe mood and affect, such as "How have you been feeling lately?" or "How do you feel right now?" (Trzepacz & Baker, 1993). Further questions can probe speech and language, thought processes, thought content, and perception, cognition and insight and judgment (Trzepacz & Baker, 1993).

Screening can sometimes be accomplished over the telephone to monitor consumers for mental health conditions and to give feedback to physicians (Simon, Ludman, & Operskalski, 2006***).

Case advocates can identify consumers who have not been screened for mental conditions or whose mental conditions remain undetected. Many physicians, such as cardiologists, lack sufficient skill in screening for mental conditions like depression that they may fail to identify roughly 25% of cardiac patients with depression. Psychiatrists and other staff skilled in mental health diagnosis and interventions often are not assigned to coronary care and other units because medical and psychiatry departments do not want to pay for liaison mental health staff—and often do not train cardiologists and other medical staff to screen their patients (Strain & Blumenfield, 2008*).

It is beyond the scope of this book to discuss these various mental conditions in detail, because the *DSM-IV*, as well as many educational materials on clinical practice exist. The *DSM-IV* identifies specific criteria that can be used to make specific diagnoses, depending on their symptoms, the frequency of these symptoms, the intensity of the symptoms, and their history or duration. These considerations could lead a clinician to differentiate, for example, between major and minor mental conditions (Engstrom, 2006). *DSM-IV* also discusses how to rank the relative seriousness of mental health conditions when a consumer has several or more of them (Engstrom, 2006).

Advocates need skills in recognizing consumers with undetected and unaddressed mental distress from observations or discussions with them, such as asking the preceding questions, so that they can determine if they need to use case advocacy to help them obtain clinical services that they might otherwise not receive. Advocates may:

- Observe that specific consumers look dejected, anxious, or traumatized.
- Triage them with brief questions like the ones above.
- Examine the medical record to see if they have received mental health services.
- Express their concerns to a consumer's physician.
- Make arrangements for special services for consumers who appear to be at risk of harming themselves or others.
- Empower consumers to seek help for themselves to the extent they view themselves as needing clinical intervention.
- Use *DSM-IV* criteria to make an informed decision about whether a specific consumer needs clinical services for a more definitive diagnosis and possible mental health intervention.

Scenario 10.2: Advocacy to Obtain Brief Mental Health Therapy for Consumers

Staff in many health settings cannot give consumers extended mental health therapy due to insufficient staff, brevity of patient visits, and lack of insurance coverage. They can, however, give short-term therapy such as crisis intervention and time-limited psychosocial services. They can give brief therapy over telephones that monitors consumers and helps them manage their care (Simon, Ludman, & Operskalski, 2006***).

Case advocates can:

- Identify consumers who may benefit from short-term therapy.
- Direct them to health staff skilled in short-term therapy, who can also refer them to other mental health staff if it is not sufficient.

Scenario 10.3: Advocacy to Help Postpartum Mothers to Obtain Mental Health Interventions

Roughly 15% to 20% of women who give birth suffer from significant symptoms of anxiety or depression for varying lengths of time. These include not only postpartum depression, but postpartum anxiety, postpartum obsessive-compulsive behavior, post-partum posttraumatic stress disorder, and postpartum psychosis. Women can be screened by such questions as: Are you feeling sad or depressed? Do you feel more irritable or angry with those around you? Are you having difficulty bonding with your baby? Do you feel anxious or panicky? Are you having problems eating or sleeping? Are you having upsetting thoughts that you can't get out of your mind? Do you feel as if you are "out of control" or "going crazy"? Do you feel like you never should have become a mother? Are you worried you might hurt your baby or yourself? (www.postpartum.net/Get-the-Facts.aspx). Some states mandate mental health screening and care for postpartum mothers.

- Refer consumers to Postpartum Support International web site at www.post partum.net.
- Engage in screening and case-finding with postpartum mothers.

Scenario 10.4: Advocacy for Mental Health Interventions for Children

Healthcare professionals often see children with mental health problems, including autism, attention-deficit/hyperactivity disorder (ADHD), and developmental disabilities. Considerable attention has been given to overmedication of children for some of these disorders. Medication is, for example, often the first intervention to treat ADHD, but lower amounts of medication with fewer side effects can often be used if they are combined with psychosocial interventions that involve teachers and parents; behavioral interventions, and nursing interventions that assess parental knowledge, support parents, and promote partnerships among teachers, parents, and providers (McGuinness,

2009). Considerable controversy exists about how to diagnose and treat children with some mental disorders.

Parents confront many barriers when seeking mental treatments for children. Relatively few schools offer special treatments for children with autism, ADHD, or disorders that lead children to act out—so parents face long waiting lists. Private insurance often does not cover treatment for autism.

Case advocates can:

- Identify children with possible undiagnosed and/or untreated mental conditions.
- Help parents identify treatment resources.
- Refer consumers to the National Alliance on Mental Illness www.nami.org.

Scenario 10.5: Advocacy to Help Consumers with PTSD Receive Mental Health Services

About 61% of men and 51% of women have lifetime exposure to trauma, including seeing others who have been injured or killed; experiencing a natural disaster; having a life-threatening accident; engaging in combat; or experiencing a physical or sexual assault (Kessler, Sonnega, Bromet, Hughes, & Nelson, 1995).

The National Center for PTSD suggests screening for PTSD, a relatively common condition often not identified in health settings, with the following paper and pencil questions that ask, "In your life, have you ever had any experience that was so frightening, horrible, or upsetting that, *in the past month*, you . . . 1. Have had nightmares about it or thought about it when you did not want to? 2. Tried hard not to think about it or went out of your way to avoid situations that reminded you of it? 3. Were you constantly on guard, watchful, or easily startled? 4. Felt numb or detached from others, activities, or your surroundings?" (http://www.depression.abut.com/library/quizzes/ptsdquiz/blptsdscreening.htm).

Certain populations are most likely to experience PTSD, including refugees from war-torn areas, combat veterans, and persons who have been assaulted sexually or physically even when significant time has elapsed between their experiences with violence (Marshall, Schell, Elliott, Berthold, & Chun, 2005).

Case advocates can:

- Identify persons with possible PTSD and seek mental health assistance for them.
- Refer patients to web sites of the Anxiety Disorders Association of America www.adaa.org or the Department of Veterans Affairs National Center for PTSD http://www.ptsd.va.gov/.

Scenario 10.6: Advocacy to Help Consumers With Terminal Conditions Obtain Mental Health Interventions

Many consumers experience mental distress when they are informed that they have a terminal condition. Some persons respond with stoicism and realism while others become disoriented (Brooks, 2005). Some persons do not accept negative prognoses because they are convinced they can surmount their health condition by aggressively accepting treatments and clinical trials (Henig, 2005). If a minority of consumers are predisposed to be relatively pessimistic or optimistic, most take cues from their physicians by accepting their optimism or pessimism (Henig, 2005).

Some mental health practitioners recommend that a comprehensive psychosocial and spiritual assessment accompany physical evaluations through the use of screening questions (Block, 2001). Consumers can be asked question like: How have you made sense of why this is happening to you (and) what do you think is ahead? (*to understand the meaning of illness*). How have you coped with hard times in the past (and) What have been the major challenges you have confronted in your life? (*to understand coping style*). Who are the important people in your life now? On whom do you depend and in whom do you confide about your illness? How are the important people in your life coping with your illness? (*to understand their social support network*). What are the biggest stressors you are dealing with now? Do you have concerns about pain or other kinds of physical suffering—and about your and your family's emotional coping? (*to understand their stressors*). What role does faith or spirituality play in your life? What role has it taken in facing difficult times in the past? Now? (*to understand their spiritual resources*). Have you experienced periods of significant depression, anxiety, drug, or alcohol use or other difficulties in coping? What kinds of treatment have you had and which have you found helpful? (*to understand their psychiatric vulnerabilities*). How much of a concern are financial issues for you? (*to understand their economic circumstances*). How do you want me to help you in this situation? How can we best work together? (*to assess the patient-physician relationship*).

Psychosocial and spiritual assessments help advocates decide whether consumers needs a mental health intervention to cope with their terminal conditions by using screening questions like ones discussed above or in *DSM-IV* criteria. Roughly 47% of cancer patients in varying stages of illness suffer from psychiatric conditions—and roughly 68% of these consumers had anxious or depressed mood, 13% had major depression, and 9% had organic mental disorders (delirium). Significant anxiety occurs in about 25% of patients with life-threatening illness. Roughly 85% of patients with very advanced disease experience delirium as a terminal event (Block, 2001).

Block (2001) contends that healthcare professionals can help specific consumers "achieve their unique vision of a 'good' death" by optimizing their physical comfort (such as managing their pain), maintaining a sense of continuity with their own selves, maintaining and enhancing relationships, helping them decipher the meaning of their life and death, achieve a sense of control, and confront and prepare for death. They achieve these goals by asking questions that mobilize consumers' coping strengths and inner resources such as "What could you do that would help you feel that this has been a meaningful time for you and the people you care about?" (for other questions, see Block, 2001, p. 2902). They can ask questions that elicit a consumer's goals for health and strengthening relationships like, "Are there important relationships in your life, including relationships from the past, that need healing or strengthening?" (for other questions, see Block, 2001, p. 2902).

Case advocates need to help consumers decide what setting and what kind of professional help will help them die with dignity. These could include: at home care with hospice care, palliative care at home or in a hospital, care from a multidisciplinary team that provides considerable in-home care, residence in an assisted-living facility, and residence in a nursing home. They need to be certain that consumers know about these options so that they can make informed choices.

Case advocates can:

- Help consumers obtain clinical and medical services if they appear to suffer from serious mental distress during a terminal illness.
- Be certain that consumers have discussed various options for end-of-life care so that they can make informed choices.

Vignette 10.3 When Can We Go Home?

Richard asked me every time he saw me when he and his wife, Nida, could go home from the ICU. She had been hospitalized two weeks ago due to complications with her breathing and pneumonia and was not intubated. Over time, we had built a rapport, but he seemed to be avoiding the idea that his wife may not be able to go home.

After being married for 52 years, they had no children, but a limited social network through church. Their few friends were in their eighties, and compassionate, but reluctant to step in, from what they told me. We would never want to take Richard's hope away, Cindy, an 80-year-old friend of his, told me one afternoon. The pulmonologist says they can wean her off the ventilator more and that she may be able to eventually return home after some rehab.

Nida died one week later. Richard was angry. Richard felt traumatized that the doctors had told him she might eventually return home.

Learning Exercise

- Did Richard receive sufficient communication from ICU staff about his wife's condition?
- Would fuller, and possibly more accurate, information have possibly helped Richard respond to his wife's death with less trauma?
- Could the frontline staff have engaged in case advocacy to help him get more information?

Scenario 10.7: Advocacy for Consumers at Risk of Suicide to Obtain Mental Health Services

Specific populations are at higher risk of suicide than the general population, including men, persons over age 65, Caucasian men over age 85, and young adults between ages 15 and 24—and particularly among youth exposed to domestic violence, rejection, disciplinary stress, and incarceration (Engstrom, 2006, pp. 224, 226). (Suicide in elderly consumers is discussed in a subsequent scenario.) The suicide rate of African-American male adolescents has significantly increased. Among ethnic and racial populations, suicide was the 8th leading cause of death among Native Americans and among Asian or Pacific Islanders, 10th among Caucasian Americans, 11th among Latinos, and 16th among African Americans—although some researchers question the accuracy of this data. If women are more likely to attempt suicide, males are more likely to commit suicide (Engstrom, 2006). Single or divorced people are more likely to commit suicide than married persons (Moscicki, 1997).

Gay, lesbian, and bisexual youth are more likely than other youth to attempt suicide (Engstrom, 2006). Persons with specific medical conditions have elevated risk of suicide, including persons with HIV/AIDS, Huntington's disease, malignant neoplasms, multiple sclerosis, peptic ulcer, renal disease, spinal cord injuries, and systemic lupus erythematosus—as well as consumers with cancer including oral, pharyngeal, and lung cancers, advanced stage cancer and poor prognosis, confusion/delirium, inadequately controlled pain, and presence of deficit symptoms like loss of mobility, loss of bowel and bladder control, amputation, sensory loss, parapalegia, inability to eat and to swallow, exhaustion, and fatigue. Consumers with a psychiatric or substance abuse disorder and with co-occuring psychiatric and substance use disorders have higher suicide risk (Engstrom, 2006, pp. 225–226). Consumers are at higher risk of suicide if they are hopeless; have attempted suicide previously; have firearms; have experienced recent losses; have stressful legal, financial, and employment stress; have limited social support; are socially isolated; live alone; have a family history of mood or substance abuse disorders; have a family history of suicide; have familial stress; were physically or sexually abused in childhood; have seen suicide in their family or peer group; have a history of impulsive behavior; and have experienced stigma or other obstacles to seeking help (list presented in Engstrom, 2006, pp. 225–226, drawing on many research sources). Consumers with several or many of the preceding risk factors are at particularly risk of suicide.

Case advocates need skills in triaging consumers to locate ones who are at risk of suicide and who are not receiving psychosocial services or medical care. Many consumers who commit suicide had seen a physician within several months, but their physicians were not aware of their suicide risk (Murphy, 1975a, 1975b). Fifty-five percent of persons with a history of suicidality favored inquiry about their mental health at each visit (Zimmerman et al., 1995), although many persons at risk of suicide do not reveal themselves or may indirectly communicate through "expressions of hopelessness, an inability to see a problem, a feeling that others might be better off without them, a desire to give up, or a feeling that current problems are insurmountable (Ivanoff & Smyth, 1992*). Health staff do not increase the likelihood of suicide by asking about suicidal ideation such as whether consumers have considering hurting themselves as part of broader discussions or routine questions (Williams, Hitchcock, Cordes, Ramirez, & Pignone, 2002*). The likelihood of suicide increases as consumers have developed plans, have access to the means of implementing them, intend to carry out the plan, consider ways to hide the plan, have written or plan to write suicide notes, have substance abuse, possess psychotic symptoms, and disclose hopelessness (Ivanoff & Smyth, 1992*).

Once case advocates have decided that specific consumers are at risk of committing suicide and that they are not receiving needed diagnosis and treatment, they need to talk with a supervisor, follow all laws of their state germane to suicidal patients as well as rules of their health institution, and never allow them to leave their offices "until (they) have used all necessary resources to satisfy (themselves) that (they) are not at imminent risk of trying to kill themselves" (Lukas, 1993*). (Using California as an example, I discussed its regulations regarding suicidal patients earlier in this chapter while recognizing state regulations may be different in other states.) They should stay on the phone with persons at risk of suicide and not place them on hold; sometimes involve a supportive person to stay with them; seek to have them dispose or put aside medications or firearms they contemplate using; and contact police or emergency medical services if suicide has been attempted or is in process of occurring (Ivanoff & Smyth, 1992). (Consumers needing evaluation for inpatient hospitalization should not drive themselves.) They should contact family members in the case of children and adolescent.

I do not discuss actual mental health interventions because I focus on the case advocates' roles in getting diagnostic and treatment services for suicidal consumers. They may include inpatient hospitalization, as well as specific mental health interventions, including ones supported by evidence-based medicine while recognizing that only limited research exists.

Advocates can:

- Identify consumers who are in groups at risk of suicide who also present specific symptoms that place specific consumers at possible risk, while recognizing that considerable numbers of them do not disclose information.
- Make certain that state and institutional rules are followed carefully.
- Stay with persons at risk of suicide until their safety is assured.
- Be alert to consumers who have discontinued care for possible suicide.
- Inform consumers they can talk to a trained counselor at the National Suicide Prevention Lifeline at 1-800-273-TALK (8255); TTY: 1-800-799-4TTY (4889). Spanish hotline 1-888-628-9454 or visit web site at www.suicideprevention lifeline.org/.

Scenario 10.8: Advocacy to Help Consumers Whose Mental State Has Been Adversely Affected by Environmental Factors

Many environmental factors can cause consumers to have mental distress, such as depression or anxiety, as they deal with their health problems, including housing, nutrition, economic, and employment factors. Certain populations, such as homeless persons, often have mental health and substance abuse problems (Kushel, Vittinghoff, & Hass, 2001). Single mothers often hold two or more jobs, lack health insurance, and cannot afford sufficient food for their families. Many women on welfare suffer from depression and substance abuse, as well as economic stress (Siefert, Bowman, Heflin, Danziger, & Williams, 2000).

Advocates can:

- Engage in case advocacy by helping these population gain access to healthcare programs and resources.
- Intercede with specific persons or institutions that stress consumers with health problems.
- Empower consumers to become their own advocates with respect to environmental stressors.

Scenario 10.9: Advocacy to Help Consumers With Family Problems That Intersect With Health Problems

Health problems of family members often create problems within their families, including role confusion and tension, economic issues, housing problems, guilt, parenting issues, and mental distress among family members (Rolland & Werner-Lin, 2006). Wiehs, et al., (2002, p. 8, cited in Rolland & Werner-Lin, p. 306) define families to be "groups of intimates with strong emotional bonds . . . and with a history and a future as a group."

Rolland and Werner-Lin discuss the Family Systems-Illness Model that examines in the family context as distinct from the ill individual of the medical model (Rolland & Werner-Lin, 2006, p. 306). They contend that family members need to understand the impact that different kinds of illness and disability can have on families, such as how illnesses with acute onset impact families differently than ones with gradual onset, like Alzheimer's disease; how progressive diseases, like Alzheimer's disease or Parkinson's disease, affect families as compared to constant or relapsing/episodic diseases, like back pain and asthma; and how the extent, kind, and timing of disability may lead to different kinds of family stress. They may have difficulty responding to family members with strokes, but adjust to this disability in time, but have greater long-term and ongoing difficulties in coping with family members with progressive cognitive disorders like Alzheimer's disease. They analyze development tasks of families during crisis, chronic, and terminal phases of illness. In the crisis phase, for example, families have to understand themselves in systems terms, understand an illness in practical and emotional terms, create meaning that promotes family mastery and competence, accept permanence of illness and disability, learn to live with symptoms, adapt to treatments and healthcare settings, and establish functional collaborative relationships with health providers. In the chronic phase, they have to maximize autonomy for all family members given the constraints of the illness, balance connectedness with separateness, and minimize relationship skews. In the terminal phase, they have to complete the process of anticipatory grief and unresolved family issues, support the terminally ill person, help survivors and the dying member live as fully as possible, and begin the family reorganization process (Rolland & Werner-Lin, 2006, p. 311).

The extent and nature of the family's strengths and weaknesses powerfully influence how its members respond to a family member's illness. Illnesses may bring family members together or exacerbate long-standing disagreements or role conflict. Some families can engage in frank discussion but others find this difficult.

Rolland and Werner-Lin discuss how psychotherapists can create a psychosocial map of specific families and develop specific goals linked to their Family-Systems Illness Model. They can assess specific families, such as analyzing their histories and how they responded to past stresses. They can use a psychoeducational approach to help families work together early in the illness process and even bring together different families facing similar demands (Rolland & Werner-Lin, 2006, p. 315). They can help specific families understand how their culture and family development shape their individual and collective responses to a family member's illness.

Multifamily discussion groups and collaborative family-oriented primary and tertiary care have demonstrated multiple positive outcomes, including promoting patient family coping and adaptation, reducing medical- and psychiatric morbidity for all family members, containing healthcare costs, and enhancing adherence (McDaniel, Campbell, Hepworth, & Lorenz, 2005; McFarlane, 2002; Weihs, Fisher, & Baird, 2002).

Case advocates can help consumers obtain help with disruptive children. Roughly 1 out of 10 children are likely to experience disruptive behaviors each year. These behaviors can include attention/hyperactivity disorder, conduct disorder, or oppositional deficit disorder (DHHS, 1999). Some of these children also have health problems, but their mental conditions may inhibit adherence or be disruptive during medical care. Patient-child interaction therapy (PCIT) is a promising mental-health intervention, which is a two-phase intervention that attempts to give the child better relations with the parent through play therapy in phase 1 and improving parents' parenting skills in phase 2 (Bagner, Fernandez, & Eyberg, 2004*).

Scenario 10.10: Advocacy to Help Consumers at Risk of Family Violence

The World Health Organization (WHO) declared violence to be a major public health issue in 1996, including child abuse and neglect, youth violence, intimate partner violence, sexual violence, elder abuse, self-directed violence, and collective violence (Krug, Dahlberg, & Zwi, 2002*). The United States spends $300 billion per year on violence-related problems when health, child welfare, and mental health, productivity, and other costs are aggregated (Khan, 2004). Violence is pronounced among inner-city youth, with a recurrence rate of between 6% and 44% and with a 5-year mortality rate of 20% (Zun, Downey, & Rosen, 2005).

Health staff encounters consumers who have been victims of intimate partner violence in primary care and hospital settings, as well as children who have been assaulted or neglected. Health staff must follow specific regulations in helping and reporting persons suspected to have been sexually or physically assaulted, so they must know the specific regulations of their state and health institution.

Some women who enter hospitals or clinics have been sexually or physically assaulted with injuries, but do not divulge their experiences. Rather than asking these women whether they have been victims of domestic violence, health staff are advised to ask specific questions about behavior, such as, "In the last year, were you hit, slapped, kicked, or otherwise physically hurt by someone?" (Soeken, McFarlane, Parker, & Lominack, 2003). They can use other questions drawn from the Abuse Assessment Screen (Soeken, McFarlane, Parker, & Lominack, 2003). These questions can be used, as well, with seniors and with children. If consumers are identified who have been victims of sexual or physical assaults, health staff need to follow specific procedures in their state laws and regulations for reporting their conditions. In a survey of an ethnically diverse population of adolescent and young adult women, researchers found that almost all of them supported universal screening for intimate partner violence—and more than 90% of them believed a healthcare provider should assume this role (Zeitler et al., 2006).

Some research suggests that specific interventions can reduce revictimization of consumers who have been subjected to violence. Assessment and case-management services somewhat reduced revictimization of youth victims of violence in a hospital's ED as compared to a control group (Zun, Downey, & Rosen, 2006)—but existing research on secondary prevention of youth violence is insufficiently rigorous or numerous (Fields & McNamara, 2003****).

Low-income women have the highest incidence of intimate partner violence. One study found that African-American females who came to the ED for treatment of injuries suffered high rates of depression, PTSD, and suicidality when they had suffered recent physical abuse, sexual abuse, or mental abuse (Houry, Kemball, Rhodes, & Kaslow, 2006).

Case advocates can:

- Engage in case-finding to identify consumers who may have been subjected to sexual or physical violence.
- Direct these consumers to health staff skilled in dealing with these situations.
- Refer consumers to the National Domestic Violence Hotline www.ndvh.org, 1–800–799–SAFE (7233), TTY 1–800–787–3224.

Scenario 10.11: Advocacy for Consumers With Chronic Diseases Who Need Mental Health Interventions

Growing numbers of Americans possess chronic diseases due to aging of the population, poor lifestyle choices, and medicine's inability to cure or prevent infectious diseases. Heart disease is the leading cause of death and afflicted 18 million Americans in 2000. Diabetes is the sixth leading cause of death and afflicted between 13.4 million to 16.7 million Americans in 2000—with an additional 5.2 million Americans believed to possess it but not aware of their condition (National Institute of Diabetes and Digestive and Kidney Diseases, 2004). HIV/AIDS is the 19th leading cause of death and afflicted 1.163 million Americans in 2002. Consumers with chronic diseases often possess mental health conditions that are linked to the long duration of their health conditions, their progressive nature, and mounting challenges in dealing with them as they become more serious, including major depression (Chapman, Perry, & Strine, 2005). They also face the challenge of adhering to treatments and lifestyle recommendations over an extended period. Many of them confront serious financial and housing problems. Some research indicates that depression increases medical costs of chronic illness by about 50% even after controlling for severity of physical illness by stimulating poor health habits as well as direct adverse physiologic effects (Chapman, Perry, & Strine, 2005).

Persons with diabetes often have co-morbidities that are linked to their disease, such as heart disease, kidney failure, amputations, and vision problems. Consumers with type 1 or type 2 diabetes have risk of depression that is twice that of consumers without diabetes in women, men, children, and adults, leading roughly 11% of diabetics in a large sample to have depression (R. Anderson, Freedland, Clouse & Lustman, 2001). Twenty-eight percent of children with type 1 diabetes developed depression in a 10-year period (Kovacs, Goldston, Obrosky, & Boner, 1997). Depression, in turn, causes dietary habits that exacerbate the disease and interferes with adherence. Diabetics are more likely than other persons to have anxiety disorders and psychological distress (Grigsby, Anderson, Freedland, Clouse, & Lustman, 2002). Diabetics who received care management that offered education, problem-solving treatment, and support for antidepressant care by their primary care physicians had improved affective and functional status, particularly for those persons with poor glycemic control (Katon et al., 2004). Diabetics with depression who received a 12-month stepped-care intervention accumulated an average of 61 additional days free of depression and required significantly reduced outpatient costs compared with diabetics in usual care (Simon et al., 2007).

About 15% to 20% of consumers with heart disease have depression compared to 4% to 7% in the general population (Auslander & Freedenthal, 2006; Lett et al., 2004). Not only can depression aggravate heart disease, such as by increasing platelet activity, but it can shorten lives of persons with heart disease as much as 15 years and cause lifestyle choices that cause and exacerbate heart disease such as poor eating and lack of exercise (Barth, Schumacher, & Herrmann-Lingren, 2004).

The so-called drug cocktail known as highly active antiretroviral therapy (HAART) has dramatically slowed death rates from AIDS since 1996, allowing many persons to have normal or nearly normal life spans. Many of them, however, suffer serious physical and psychological side effects from these medications. Many persons with AIDS are unable to work. Distressingly, the rate of HIV infections continues to rise even as death rates from AIDS plummet. Consumers with HIV/AIDS have a suicide rate twice as high as other persons (Dannenberg, McNeil, Brudage, & Brookmeyer, 1996; Marzuk et al., 1997). Other research not using control groups or random samples suggests that between 4% and 19% of them have serious mental illness (Lyon, 2001). The disease can cause dementia and cognitive disorders (Forstein & McDaniel, 2001). Women with HIV with chronic depression are twice as likely to die as other women, whether because depression affects their neuroendocrine and immunological functioning, contributes to smoking and other adverse lifestyle choices, or lowers adherence (Engstrom, 2006). Consumers with HIV who receive medical care have a prevalence of 47.9% of psychiatric disorders—with 21% of them experiencing both major depression and dysthymia—and many others with generalized anxiety disorders and panic attacks (Bing et al., 2001).

It is likely that depression and other mental disorders cause chronic diseases and result from it. Considerable research suggests that they cause these diseases through biological mechanisms or by causing harmful lifestyle choices (Auslander & Freedenthal, 2006). In turn, these chronic diseases may trigger biological processes that contribute to mental disorders, as well as by exposing consumers to the trauma, life restrictions, treatment regimens, and poor prognoses often associated with them (Auslander & Freedenthal, 2006, pp. 554–556).

COPD consumers may experience mental problems such as depression and anxiety, insomnia, low levels of social interaction, lack of exercise, financial problems, and inability to perform daily activities. They are often stigmatized by healthcare professionals and others who blame them for contracting their disease, such as from smoking. Higher levels of positive social support are linked to lower levels of depression and anxiety. Psychological problems often need to be addressed for them to improve the quality of their lives (McCathie, Spence, & Tate, 2002).

Many persons with multiple sclerosis (MS) suffer from major depressive disorder (MDD)—or 26% in one sample. Roughly two-thirds of them receive no treatment for their depression. One study found that a two-question screening instrument accurately identified MS consumers with MDD (Mohr, Hart, Julian, & Tasch, 2007).

Healthcare professionals should seek and provide interventions to address mental health needs of consumers with these chronic diseases. These can include psychotherapy, medical crisis counseling, and relaxation training (Auslander & Freedenthal, 2006). Existing research does not confirm the effectiveness of psychotherapy with specific illnesses, but cognitive-behavioral therapy has been shown to reduce depression among consumers with type 2 diabetes (Lustman, Griffith, Freedland, Kissel, & Clouse, 1998), as well as consumers with heart disease, even if death rates were not decreased (L. Berkman, 2003). Medical crisis counseling, which is counseling that addresses various fears of persons with chronic diseases not to last more than 10 sessions, may help decrease social support for patients with diabetes and heart disease (Koocher, Curtiss, Pallin, & Patton, 2001). Relaxation training diminishes fear and anxiety of children and adolescents with type 1 diabetes (Lammers, Naliboff, & Straatmeyer, 1984; Surwit & Schneider, 1993) and can lower blood pressure and heart rate for diabetics and persons with other chronic health conditions (Benson, 1976). More evaluations of mental health interventions are needed to ascertain their effectiveness and to see if they cut health costs.

Case advocates can:

- Promote screening and triage of consumers with these diseases to ascertain kinds and levels of mental distress that they possess.
- Develop mental health interventions for ones with serious mental conditions.
- Refer consumers to Medline Plus Coping with Chronic Illness web site at http://www.nlm.nih.gov/medlineplus/copingwithchronicillness.html.
- For an excellent overview of mental conditions of persons with chronic disease, see Wendy Auslander and Stacey Freedenthal, "Social Work and Chronic Disease: Diabetes, Heart Disease, and HIV/AIDS, in Sarah Gehlert and Teri Arthur Brown, eds., *Handbook of Health Social Work* (Hoboken, NJ: John Wiley & Sons, 2006), pp. 532–567.

Scenario 10.12: Advocacy for Consumers With Cancer Who Need Mental Health Interventions

Cancer is currently the second leading cause of death. Roughly one in two men and one in three women will develop it during their life spans (Ries et al., 2003). The top five kinds of cancers in 2002 were ones of the digestive tract (251,000), breast cancer (205,000), prostate cancer (189,000), cancer of the lung and bronchus (169,000), and cancer of the urinary system (90,700).

Consumers with aggressive cancers, advanced cancers, and certain types of cancer have short survival rates, such as persons with specific kinds of pancreatic cancer, some forms of lung cancer, and some kinds of brain cancers. Yet many persons who develop cancer are either cured or live for relatively long periods even with several recurrences, radiation, and extended chemotherapy. Roughly 9 million persons have survived it with marked decreases in deaths from lung, breast, prostate, and colorectal cancers in recent decades.

Even though many consumers survive cancer or are cured, the diagnosis of cancer is traumatizing for most people because of the widespread perception that it is usually lethal. Consumers need help in surmounting trauma associated with this diagnosis, including help with guilt from the belief that they caused their cancer, shock, and anxiety. They need psychoeducation as they learn to deal with surviving this disease including accurate information about their prognosis and treatment options.

Many consumers benefit from membership in support groups, as well as contact with advocacy groups dedicated to helping persons with specific kinds of cancer. They often need family counseling to help families cope with this disease and its effects on family functioning. Social workers can form cancer support teams for specific consumers that bring together friends, neighbors, and community members to help specific consumers cope with the disease, help with food and household chores, and helping to research treatment options (Werner-Lin & Biank, 2006).

Existing research estimates wide ranges of depressive symptoms and major depression to persons with cancer from 1% to 42% (Patrick et al., 2003) and from 10% to 30% for anxiety disorders (Stark et al., 2002) possibly due to methodological limitations (Engstrom, 2006, p. 208). Consumers with extended survival with cancer sometimes need mental health services associated with chronic health conditions, which is discussed in Scenario 10.17.

Consumers with cancer from specific age groups need specific kinds of services. Children need help with coping anxiety, depression, isolation, and regression (Zebrack & Chesler, 2001). They need help in adjusting to school after extended absences and from being teased. Adolescents need help with changed appearances, interference with sexual functioning, and relations with peers, as well as depression and anxiety. Elderly consumers need help in coping with economic, social, and physical losses.

Case advocates can:

- Identify consumers with cancer with specific mental health conditions.
- Direct them to professionals with expertise in helping them with biopsychosocial services.
- Use a wide array of Internet sites germane to mental health services including www.apos.org (American Psychosocial Oncology Society), www.aosw.org (Association of Oncology Social Work), and www.ipos.org (International Psycho-Oncology Society).

Scenario 10.13: Advocacy for Consumers With Chronic Neurological Diseases Who Need Mental Health Interventions

Consumers with chronic neurological disorders often require mental health interventions. These disorders include Parkinson's disease, Alzheimer's disease, and dementia. As many as 50% of consumers with Parkinson's Disease experience depression—and some of them have hallucinations, delusions, and paranoia (www.benefits-snow.co.uk/health/pdmental.asp and http://my.clevelandclinic.org/disorders/Parkinsons_Disease/hic_mental-distrubances_associated-with-parkinsons-disease.aspx). Epileptics have suicide rates five times greater than others—and 25 times if seizures from the temporal limbic system of the brain are involved (Gehlert, 2006b, p. 181).

- Advocates can engage in case-finding for mental health conditions in consumers with neurological disorders.
- Advocates can help consumers with neurological disorders obtain mental health services.

Scenario 10.14: Advocacy for Disabled Consumers Who Need Mental Health Interventions

Disabled consumers are consumers who meet at least one of three criteria: have a physical or mental impairment that substantially limits their ability to perform one or more life activities; have a record of this impairment; and are regarded as having it (National Council of Disability, 1997). Impairments can include mobility, cognitive, and sensory ones—and can range from mild to severe (Brashler, 2006).

Disabled consumers were traditionally treated as relatively dependent patients in the health system, relying on medications, surgeries, and relatively confined settings. A powerful disability-rights movement emerged in the early 1970s that secured enactment of the Rehabilitation Act of 1973 building on a growing movement that sought community-based independent living centers as places for disabled persons to live and to obtain services. Advocates also secured enactment of the means-tested Supplemental Security Insurance Program (SSI) to provide resources to low-income disabled persons as a supplement to Social Security insurance (SSDI). While the Rehabilitation Act prohibited job discrimination by public agencies, advocates obtained more sweeping legislation when they enacted the Americans with Disabilities Act of 1990 that required many private corporations also to put in place many work accommodations for disabled persons and to hire more of them.

Advocates for disabled consumers realized that many of them possess mind-sets that can negatively impact their lives. Attribution theory analyzes how persons view the world when they face a world over which they have little control, such as when persons have illness or disability (Abramson, Seligman, & Teasdale, 1978). It "predicts depression for persons who attribute negative events in their lives, such as not being able to get or keep a job, to their own doing, and positive events, such as being given a compliment, to an outside source, e.g., other persons, fate, or luck" (Gehlert, 2006b). Persons with negative attributional styles are relatively pessimistic, becoming passive when faced with illness, having relatively few supportive social networks, and being less able to solve problems. Such consumers are more likely than others to be sick between ages 45 and 60 than others according to one study (Peterson, Seligman, & Vaillant, 1988).

Persons with disabilities often need medical care, including medications, surgeries, and an array of electronic and mechanical aids that include state-of-art computer assists. Healthcare professionals face the challenge, however, of moving beyond this "medical model" to ones that empower consumers, such as consumers with disabilities who do not seek employment, are content to watch television during their waking hours in relatively confined settings, and are depressed. Gehlert (1995) helped a small group of epileptics identify and stop negative thoughts and substitute more realistic ones and found that she reduced their depression and pessimism. Other successful interventions seek to shift the focus of treatment to psychological and family issues without succumbing to pathologizing consumers (Brashler, 2006). They can use a "social model" that "shifts the focus from the impairment within an individual or family system" to emphasis on social, institutional, and physical-world realities that constrain disabled consumers (Asch, 2001).

Disabled persons with four or more persistent major depressive symptoms who receive augmented care for their depression with on-site psychiatric care that is linked to care from primary care physicians receive small to moderate functional improvements (Lin et al., 2000***).

Advocates need to:

- Identify consumers with disabilities who receive medical care, but not psychosocial or empowerment services that supplements it or replaces it.
- Be certain that consumers with disabilities are aware of many community and support-group agencies and resources.
- Be certain consumers with disabilities are aware of their rights under the ADA— and that they know how to access these rights online.
- Help consumers who want health staff to use an empowerment rather than a medical model to find staff, support groups, and advocacy groups with this orientation.

Scenario 10.15: Advocacy to Help Consumers With Substance Abuse Obtain Mental Health Services

It is beyond the scope of this book to discuss services for consumers with substance abuse problems in light of the sheer number of substances that can be addictive and that can produce mental and physical problems. I have discussed how the federal government categorizes drugs, including ones that are declared "illegal." States differ widely in their laws concerning specific substances, such as marijuana. Consumers often need assistance with addictions to legal substances, including alcohol and cigarettes.

Two e-books are offered by the Partnership for a Drug Free American that discuss, respectively, how to assess persons with possible addictions and how to treat them, as well as other informative information about resources in specific locations (see below). They are written in consumer-accessible language.

- Refer consumers to Partnership for a Drug Free America Intervention web site at www.drugfree.org/Intervention/.

Scenario 10.16: Advocacy to Help Consumers With Sleep Disorders Obtain Mental Health Services

Sleep disorders are experienced by a considerable percentage of the adult population in the United States. Insomnia is associated with general physical and some mental health problems, PTSD, schizophrenia, as well as accidents linked to drowsiness (Benca, 2005; Bixler, Keles, Soldatos, Keles, & Healey, 1979; Brunello et. al, 2000; Marcks & Weisbert,

2009). Roughly half of children referred to a sleep clinic had a co-morbid medical diagnosis and 31% had a co-morbid psychiatric diagnosis in one study by psychologist Lisa Meltzer (www.medicalnewstoday.com/articles/111026.php.). Treatment should be individualized based on medical and psychiatric history, medication use, sleep history, family history, and substance abuse history (H. Lynch, Mathes, & Sawicki, 2007). Many consumers with sleep disorders receive physiological screening (such as polysomnographies) with observations during the night in medical settings, such as to ascertain if they have sleep apnea (Hilty, Young, Bourgeois, Klein, & Hardin, 2009). Some consumers receive pharmacological interventions but often with side effects. Some nonpharmacological interventions produce significant and durable changes in sleep patterns of consumers with chronic insomnia (Morin, Culbert, & Schwartz, 1994). No conclusive evidence exists to favor either pharmacologic or behavioral therapies (Benca, 2005).

Case advocates can:

- Identify persons who have problems with chronic insomnia.
- Work to help them receive diagnostic and treatment services.
- Refer consumers to American Academy of Sleep Medicine at www.sleepeducation .com.

Scenario 10.17: Advocacy for Consumers With End-Stage Renal Disease to Obtain Mental Health Services

I have discussed how end-stage renal disease (ESRD) is the only disease category or treatment regimen with a public policy requirement that MSW social workers be included on health teams (Browne, 2006b). ESRD requires highly intrusive treatments, including dialysis, that lead 89% of consumers with it to experience significant lifestyle changes as they contend with medical complications and side effects including pain. Significant numbers of them have problems adhering to recommended treatments. Persons with ESRD often have co-morbidities like hypertension and diabetes. They have high rates of suicide. About 52% of them have significant anxiety (G. Auslander, Dobrof, & Epstein, 2001) and about 49% are depressed (Wuerth et al., 2001.). These mental conditions are strongly associated with poor nutrition, mortality rate, extent of adherence, diminished quality of life, insomnia, diminished sexual functioning, and high hospitalization rates (DeOreo, 1997; Frank, 2003; Kimmel, Auslander, & Weissgarten et al., 2000; Paniagua, Amato, Guo, & Mujais, 2005; Valdez, 1997; Wu et al., 2001), Many persons with ESRD need psychosocial services to help them cope with end-of-life issues, hospice, and palliative care. Some of them decide to terminate dialysis due to diminished quality of life knowing that this will lead to death. They often need help with family stress, role conflicts, and financial issues.

Social workers conduct comprehensive individual psychosocial assessment of persons with ESRD and assess consumers' suitabilities for transplant (Browne, 2006b). Research confirms that cognitive therapy effectively reduces depression among persons with ESRD disease (Beder, 1999; Cabness, 2005). Most depressed dialysis patients preferred counseling from social workers on their treatment team rather than from outside mental health practitioners (Johnstone & LeSage, 1998). Social workers' interventions increase adherence and reduced fluid weight gains (G. Auslander & Buchs, 2002; Johnstone & Halshaw, 2003; Root, 2005). Social workers provide end-of-life counseling, rehabilitation assistance, team collaboration, and case advocacy (Browne, 2006b). Many ESRD units hire insufficient numbers of social workers, however, to provide these various services, particularly because they are burdened by considerable paper work (Browne, 2006b, p. 485).

Case advocates can:

- Conduct need assessments for mental health services in specific ESRD and compare the needs to the number of staff.
- Use existing literature to justify biopsychosocial services in ESRD units.
- Use web sites for more information, including www.aakp.org (American Association of Kidney Patients); www.asn-online.org (American Society of Nephrology); (www.cms.gov/providers/esrd.asp (Centers for Medicare and Medicaid Services); www.renalnet.org/renalnet/renalnet.cfm (Kidney Information Clearinghouse); www.renalweb.com (RenalWeb: vortex web site of the Dialysis World).

Scenario 10.18: Advocacy for Independent Case-Finding and Augmentation of Mental Health Staff

I have discussed advocacy to help consumers obtain mental health services, but staff with skills in mental health services often have to advocate for themselves to make this feasible. Provision of mental health services is often compromised in health settings due to lack of sufficient staff, including social workers and psychiatric nurses. These services are not required at any specific threshold by Joint Commission accreditation standards or by external regulations—except for Medicare-funded dialysis and end-stage renal disease. These services can be slashed when hospitals experience budget deficits because they are mostly funded internally rather than through specific Medicare or insurance reimbursements.

Many consumers do not divulge specific mental health conditions that they possess. They may be ashamed of them. They may assume that healthcare professionals cannot help them cope with them. Many health staff lack skills in screening for them or detecting these conditions through observations of consumers.

Hospitals and clinics need to employ sufficient numbers of staff with training in mental health services, then, to locate, refer, and help consumers who need mental health services. They also need sufficient latitude to engage in independent case-finding that they can identify consumers with undetected mental health conditions—whether through informal understandings, protocols of specific hospitals and clinics, or public regulations. In California, for example, Section 22 of the State Health and Welfare Code gives hospital social workers the right to engage in independent case-finding.

Staff with training in mental health services can:

- Compare themselves with comparable health institutions to ascertain if they are relatively understaffed.
- Document specific instances where they could not engage in case-finding or service provision due to insufficient staff.
- Conduct need assessment studies by using research literature, as well as screening instruments, to document the kinds of consumers that need mental health services—and compare this literature and these findings with actual staff to ascertain if more staff are needed.
- Determine if staff with training in mental health services have sufficient latitude to engage in independent case-finding, and, if not, identify ways to increase it in specific units or departments, the overall institution, or in public regulations. The need for staff who are skilled in mental health assessments and interventions is illustrated by Vignette 10.5.

Vignette 10.5 Hiding From the Truth—"I am suicidal."

My order from the emergency department doctor to see this 52-year-old male Caucasian patient read "overdose on pain medication, rule out suicide." My second possible suicidal case of the night. I was not excited. We were running low on beds for psychiatric patients and I was worried about the four-hour wait in the waiting room. I sighed and went to the patient Mark's bedside.

He was calm and seemed unsurprised to see me. Mark gave me his particulars: worked as a manager at a supermarket for 30 years. He had hurt his back on the job 20 years ago, and was taking opiates for pain management since. He denied suicidal ideation at first. However, as I spent more time with him and began probing to get the more intimate details of his life, which would add up to a more accurate biopsychosocial assessment, the depression and anxiety that had been plaguing him for past few years broke through his placid facade.

He began disclosing to me his struggle with alcohol and his pain medication, though he functioned despite his addictions and depression. Mark reported that he and his partner were more distant as of late. He was growing more depressed, had been drinking more, and what he first reported as his "accidentally" taking too many pills since he was in pain and "forgot" how many he took initially, turned into a confession that he was hoping he would overdose and die.

I got a call on my emergency department cell phone that his partner had arrived at the emergency department and wished to see Mark. With the patient's permission, his partner, Jared, entered and sat with us as we continued the

(continued)

(*continued*)

discussion. As Jared realized that Mark was being truthful about his addiction and depression, and that Mark was reaching out for help tonight, Jared's eyes filled with tears. Jared held Mark's hands, and stated, "I feel like I'll get you back now that you're going to get the help you need." Mark admitted that this was the first time he had admitted to anyone publicly that he had a problem with substance abuse; he had been held captive to these problems for nearly 20 years.

I discussed with them the process of psychiatric admissions to the hospital. After my assessment, the physician would have to "medically clear" the patient after all the clinical exams and lab tests. Then, a psychiatric nurse would come and assess Mark further for placement. Finally, we would seek the most suitable placement for him, by working with his insurance company and providing our recommendations for treatment.

When Martha, the psychiatric nurse came, I gave her a verbal report of my assessment. She reviewed his medical record, went and spoke with him, and agreed with me; he needed to be admitted for psychiatric treatment. I breathed a sigh of relief. Martha and I had not always seen eye to eye in the past. Furthermore, patients like Mark sometimes changed their story depending on the practitioners they were seeing. After a patient divulges details of an addiction she has been struggling with for years, she may have a cathartic experience, and believe that rather than inpatient treatment, she has the motivation to deal with it on her own. Unfortunately, such instances are often unsuccessful, because attempting to recover from substance abuse without appropriate support is quite difficult.

The next hurdle emerged. Our hospital had no more availability for male patients. However, Martha, the nurse reported that she knew that a nearby substance abuse/psychiatric facility, with which our hospital had good relations, had a bed. Martha also informed me that Mark's primary-care doctor dealt with substance abuse patients often, and that getting an information release from Mark, allowing us to inform his doctor, could benefit Mark's medical and psychiatric treatment. Mark had suffered alone all these years, when his doctor specialized in helping people with his types of illnesses.

Mark willingly signed the release and I informed him that in the next few hours, we would arrange for his transfer by ambulance to the other facility. Due to his expression of suicidal ideation, the psychiatric nurse decided he should be psychiatrically hospitalized. He was willing to go voluntarily, thus, an involuntary hospitalization (5150), was not necessary in this case. As I informed Mark and Jared about what the next days would look like, Mark and Jared looked thoughtfully at me. Mark uttered words that make me proud to be in my profession, "Thank you for saving my life." I told him then, "Thank you for having the courage to understand you need help." I did not see patients like Mark often in the emergency department. Seeing him wanting to get help was a gift to me and a reminder why I chose social work as a profession.

Learning Exercise

- How does this case illustrate how frontline staff often partner to provide case advocacy?
- How does this case illustrate the need for psychiatric nurses and social workers in hospitals?

ONLINE MATERIALS RELEVANT TO THIS CHAPTER

We have discussed eighteen scenarios. Another eight scenarios can be found in the online materials.

The eighteen scenarios in this book include:

- Scenario 10.1   Advocacy to Help Consumers Receive Clinical Assessment Through Screening Instruments
- Scenario 10.2   Advocacy to Obtain Brief Mental Health Therapy for Consumers
- Scenario 10.3   Advocacy to Help Postpartum Mothers Obtain Mental Health Interventions
- Scenario 10.4   Advocacy for Mental Health Interventions for Children
- Scenario 10.5   Advocacy to Help Consumers With PTSD Receive Mental Health Services
- Scenario 10.6   Advocacy to Help Consumers With Terminal Conditions Receive Mental Health Services
- Scenario 10.7   Advocacy for Consumers at Risk of Suicide to Obtain Mental Health Services
- Scenario 10.8   Advocacy to Help Consumers Whose Mental State Has Been Adversely Affected by Environmental Factors
- Scenario 10.9   Advocacy to Help Consumers With Family Problems That Intersect With Health Problems
- Scenario 10.10   Advocacy to Help Consumers at Risk of Family Violence
- Scenario 10.11   Advocacy for Consumers With Chronic Diseases Who Need Mental Health Interventions
- Scenario 10.12   Advocacy for Consumers With Cancer Who Need Mental Health Interventions
- Scenario 10.13   Advocacy for Consumers With Chronic Neurological Diseases Who Need Mental Health Interventions
- Scenario 10.14   Advocacy for Disabled Consumers Who Need Mental Health Interventions
- Scenario 10.15   Advocacy to Help Consumers With Substance Abuse Obtain Mental Health Services

(*continued*)

(*continued*)

- Scenario 10.16   Advocacy to Help Consumers With Sleep Disorders Obtain Mental Health Services
- Scenario 10.17   Advocacy for Consumers With End-Stage Renal Disease to Obtain Mental Health Services
- Scenario 10.18   Advocacy for Independent Case-Finding and Augmentation of Mental Health Staff

We discuss an additional eight scenarios that can be accessed at the web site of John Wiley & Sons at www.wiley.com/go/jansson. They include:

- Scenario 10.19   Advocacy to Help Consumers Receive Mental Healthcare in Primary Settings
- Scenario 10.20   Advocacy to Help Consumers Manage Stress That Accompanies Physical Illness
- Scenario 10.21   Advocacy to Help Consumers With Mental Conditions Caused by Illness
- Scenario 10.22   Advocacy to Help Consumers Who Somatize Mental Conditions or Imagine They Are Ill
- Scenario 10.23   Advocacy for Consumers With Loss of Sexuality and Physical Intimacy
- Scenario 10.24   Advocacy for Older Adults Who Need Mental Health Interventions
- Scenario 10.25   Advocacy to Help Consumers With Grief or Bereavement Obtain Mental Health Services
- Scenario 10.26   Advocacy to Help Consumers With Genetic Information

MOVING FROM CASE ADVOCACY TO POLICY ADVOCACY

Take any of the 18 scenarios presented in this chapter or the 8 scenarios in the online materials related to this chapter. Identify specific policies in organizational, community, or governmental settings that might lead consumers to need case advocacy in the first instance when confronting one of them.

Advocacy to Help Consumers
Receive Community-Based Care

M any healthcare consumers need community-based care, but receive "insular care," which I define as healthcare that fails to link consumers to their communities. I discuss why many consumers need community-based care by drawing on existing research and theory. I discuss how the policy and regulatory thicket, as well as medical culture, both discourages and promotes community-based care. I provide 14 scenarios (12 are in this book and 2 are online) as well as some vignettes. I discuss some provisions of the Patient Protection and Affordable Care Act of 2010 as amended by the Congress that may increase community-based healthcare.

CONSUMERS' HEALTH ECOSYSTEMS

Healthcare consumers live in ecosystems that profoundly shape their health, as well as their use of health systems (DuBois & Miley, 2002). They may live in housing that causes or exacerbates asthma (Bell & Standish, 2005). They may live in neighborhoods with relatively spartan health services so that they are less likely to use them. They may be unable or unwilling to become reenrolled in public programs like Medicaid with arduous eligibility renewals (Perez-Pena, 2005). They may lack transportation services to health programs. They may reside in housing that is not designed for persons with disabilities. They may be deterred from seeking and using health services by family members. They may be unaware of the need for specific kinds of services, such as prenatal services, or the existence of specific programs like the Women's, Infant, and Children program (WIC) or the Children's Health Insurance Program (SCHIP).

Low-income consumers and consumers with low levels of education have higher rates of morbidity and shorter lives than other people (Kawachi, Daniels, & Robinson, 2005). Health disparities are caused by a combination of economic and social factors including lack of nutrition and adequate housing; lack of stable employment; lack of health knowledge; community violence; fatalism; mental disorders linked to poverty; in-accessible healthcare; inability to finance healthcare; substance abuse; and unstable support systems (Jacobs, Kohrman, Lemon, & Vickers, 2003).

The impact of these community factors on specific consumers can often be detected by health staff and primary-care physicians during medical visits—provided they are sensitized to them, discuss them, and have knowledge needed to be helpful. In some cases, they can fully understand them only by visits to consumers in their homes and neighborhoods. If they cannot make these visits, they should try to identify community agencies that can perform this function.

Many consumers cannot easily access health services because of physical limitations, such as ones with disabilities, consumers with age-related physical impairments, and consumers who lack transportation. Health organizations and plans need outreach workers, vans, and accessible clinics, as well as outreach staff and teams, to reach these consumers. The term, "hard to reach," is used in the disability literature to define disabled consumers who will not typically be reached unless a dedicated effort is made to engage with them, such as women whose visual, auditory or mobility limitations make it difficult for them to leave their homes. (Hughes, Robinson-Wheelen, Taylor, Petersen, & Nasek, 2005; Smeltzer, Sharts-Hopko, Ott, Zimmerman, & Duffin, 2007).

Many consumers do not return for appointments even when they imperil their well-being, such as returning for results of biopsies and returning for medical care after they have been given a serious diagnosis (see Vignette 11.1). Often lacking outreach workers, however, many disappear, sometimes with fatal consequences.

Vignette 11.1 A Good Samaritan Nurse

A nurse in a health clinic used primarily by low-income consumers in the Bronx decided to follow up on consumers who had received biopsies that indicated they had cancer at relatively advanced stages, but who failed to keep appointments to receive their biopsy results. She often assumed the role of a detective because many of them lacked telephones and frequently changed addresses. She was not asked to undertake this assignment by clinic staff, but felt ethically impelled to locate these fugitive consumers in after-work hours. She was able to locate many of them and to convince them come to the clinic so that they could begin treatments.

Learning Assignment

- How does this vignette illustrate a tendency to define medical practice as confined to the four walls of specific clinics and hospitals?
- Why does this clinic rely on a good Samaritan nurse to perform this life-preserving function—and what are some disadvantages of this informal practice?
- Could this frontline nurse have engaged in policy advocacy to persuade clinic administrators to hire an outreach worker to engage in this assignment?

Lack of outreach is linked, as well, to bifurcation of public health programs and traditional medical care. Public health staff is often out-stationed in STD, TB, HIV-AIDS, WIC, and prenatal clinics that are scattered throughout urban and some rural areas, but that often are not closely linked with primary-care clinics or hospitals. These clinics often lose contact with their clientele when they refer them to health clinics and hospitals when they could usefully follow and assist their care as they return to their neighborhoods.

Lifestyle choices are ultimately made in home and community settings where many factors shape whether consumers make healthy choices regarding diet, smoking, substance abuse, and exercise, as well as reducing stress in their lives in personal and work relationships.

Disabled and elderly consumers, as well as ones with chronic diseases, often have to receive help in their homes because they cannot travel to distant clinics or hospitals where healthcare professionals assist them to receive help from family members and friends, contend with financial barriers, deal with logistical issues, negotiate specific barriers to healthy lifestyle choices in their homes and communities, such as educating family members with unhealthy dietary preferences; find ways to purchase healthy food; and develop strategies for exercise in neighborhoods ridden with violence (Glasgow et al., 1999).

It is often useful to develop community-based health education and support groups that meet in local churches or other locations. Consumers may be more amenable to advice, instruction, and support from community-based initiatives than ones located in formal health settings. Even in these cases, however, consumers often need assistance in attending them. Many women with severe disabilities find attending informational sessions difficult, for example.

Many consumers find transitions between different locations to be traumatic, whether from hospitals to community living situations, from homes to long-term care institutions, from homes to retirement homes, and from homes to assisted-living apartments. These transitions are often accompanied by high levels of stress, as well as increased morbidity and mortality (Forster, Murff, Peterson, Gandhi, & Bates, 2003).

Healthcare professionals also need skill in working with caregivers because they often experience financial and mental hardships. Many of them leave their jobs to care for their relatives, often placing them in or near poverty. They often suffer mental distress, including depression and anxiety, as well as fatigue from around-the-clock care from the amount of time they devote to caregiving, as well as the onerous tasks they often undertake. Consumers often lack in-home supportive help because it is not well covered by health plans and insurance programs and because it often is not available in specific geographic areas (Schultz et al., 2003).

Health staff should provide follow-up care to some consumers who are admitted to institutions and discharged from them, such as mental institutions and prisons. Many of these consumers possess health, mental health, and substance abuse problems partly because they often do not receive sufficient healthcare in institutions; have limited financial resources; and lack supportive relationships. Margaret O'Kane, the president of the National Committee for Quality Assurance, calls the performance of most medical plans as "pitiful" in following up with consumers after hospitalization for mental illness (Comarow, 2009). Released prisoners, who often have not had adequate medical or dental care within prisons, often do not receive follow-up medical care so that important health conditions are not diagnosed or treated (Mallik-Kane & Visher, 2008).

The health of many consumers is shaped by their occupational settings. Some consumers work in toxic settings because work-safety standards are not sufficiently monitored by public authorities or because inadequate standards exist. Some consumers experience job-related stress, such as from tyrannical supervisors, unrealistic production demands, and hostile relations with other workers—stress that can lead to cardiac and other disorders (Orth-Gomer, 2007). Many employers do not promote exercise, diet, and other wellness programs.

A COMPENDIUM OF COMMUNITY-BASED HEALTH SERVICES

This discussion suggests that at least 13 community-based health services are needed in healthcare. (See Table 11.1.)

Table 11.1   Community-Based Health Services at the Case Level

- Connecting consumers to other persons, networks, or institutions by sending them to them for services or benefits (*referral services*).
- Helping consumers making transitions between institutions and programs (*transition or discharge services*).
- Negotiating service arrangements between consumers and other professionals within a specific health setting or between them and other institutions such as home health agencies, convalescent homes, nursing homes, schools, mental health agencies, rehabilitation agencies, and outpatient clinics (*brokerage services*).
- Developing or using integrated care (*linking systems of care*).
- Helping consumers develop and implement preventive health strategies in home and community settings (*home-based and community-based prevention*).
- Helping consumers manage chronic health conditions in home-based and community settings (*community-based management of chronic conditions*).
- Helping consumers use technology to discover community-based resources and manage their health conditions (*technology-assisted community-oriented care*).
- Helping consumers gain concessions, services, or accommodations from employers and to provide health prevention at worksites (*occupational advocacy services*).
- Improving community health conditions for specific consumers (*public health advocacy*).
- Helping consumers develop supportive family and social networks (*family and social-network counseling*).
- Linking consumers to legal or advocacy services that will protect their rights with respect to financing of medical services, as well as services that they have received (*protecting consumers' rights to financing and receipt of medical care*).
  - ○ Including access to SCHIP, Medicaid, and other public programs.
  - ○ Including insurance companies.

(continued)

- ○ Including coverage of hospital charges.
- ○ Including poor services and poor service providers.
- Protecting consumers' rights with law enforcement agencies, schools, child welfare departments, disease control, and other external agencies that can direct or control consumers (*protection of consumers' rights*).
- Linking consumers in hospitals and clinics with dental services (*linking medical and dental services*).

ASSETS AND LIABILITIES IN THE POLICY AND REGULATORY THICKET

Many policies and regulations impede community-based care by healthcare professionals including medical culture, a schism between medical and dental care, insufficiency of staff with broader ecological perspectives and knowledge, lack of access, beleaguered free clinics and other primary clinics, substitution of ERs for community care, lack of partnerships between health institutions and community agencies, and the state of research on the impact of community-based care on health outcomes.

Medical Culture

Community health has been a long-standing specialty in medicine that aims to prevent illness, facilitate community services including rehabilitative services for consumers with disabilities, mental illness, and chronic diseases; promote public health services; and integrate community, primary care, and hospital services. This branch of medicine has embraced community services for elderly, homeless, low-income, and HIV/AIDS populations. Many physicians have degrees or specializations in public health and rehabilitation as do some nurses and social workers, including many with dual degrees (Hernandez & Munthali, 2007; Reardon, 2009). Public health has deep roots in the United States as reflected by remarkable health advancements from the late eighteenth century, when epidemics were common, through the Great Depression (Weinstein, 2000).

Many physicians view health as mostly confined to the physiological realm, however, failing to factor culture, social class, community realities, fiscal constraints, family dynamics, emotions, and consumers' mental conditions into diagnoses and treatments (Glasgow et al., 1999). Many physicians assume, as well, that most consumers will adhere to treatment regimens rather than exploring financial, family, mental, cultural, and community factors that might contravene them (Glasgow et al., 1999).

Many critics of U.S. medicine note, as well, that specialists often do not converse with one another about the medical care of specific consumers unless they work in health systems that emphasize collaboration, such as the Mayo Clinic (Berry & Seltman, 2008). Used to diagnosing and treating problems within their own specialty, they often do not recognize that many consumers have co-morbidities that have to be diagnosed and treated in tandem. Healthcare professionals often focus on consumers with severe problems while ignoring less serious ones, such as giving attention to a consumer's psychosis while ignoring a substance abuse problem.

Dental Care

Millions of Americans do not receive adequate dental care. This omission partly stems from a long-standing separation of healthcare from dental care in existing literature, professional training, and insurance plans that places dental care in an inferior position as compared to medical care or do not cover it at all. Medicaid and SCHIP provide some dental benefits as do some Medicare supplemental policies that are purchased by seniors, but Medicaid's dental benefit often covers only emergency dental care such as extractions. Dental care is rarely provided in health clinics or hospitals.

Consumers often do not receive dental coverage from their employers at all—or receive coverage with low annual ceilings on benefits and high out-of-pocket costs. State Medicaid plans and SCHIP often provide negligible dental benefits, such as limiting them to extractions and other emergency procedures—and often cut dental benefits when states experience budget deficits (Varner, 2010).

Dental services often are not accessible to specific populations, such as disabled and elderly consumers who are confined to their homes, homeless consumers in portions of urban areas where they reside, and low-income populations. Low-income persons must often rely on not-for-profit clinics, such as ones run by dental schools, that provide free or low-cost dental care to many consumers, often from volunteer dentists or supervised dental students.

Hiring Health Staff with Training in Community Services

Some professionals are trained to provide consumers with multifaceted care that addresses their community-based needs including public health workers, social workers, community-oriented nurses, and case managers.

Increasing numbers of case managers have been hired in the health system in the last decade often with social work or nursing backgrounds. They are variously hired by health plans, insurance companies, clinics, and hospitals to oversee the care of consumers who have complex problems or costly problems.

Yet the health system lacks sufficient numbers of staff with training in community services. Accreditation standards allow hospitals only to hire social work consultants or part-time social work staff rather than full-time social workers. Relatively few social workers are hired in health clinics or by private-practice physicians. Nor do hospitals hire many nurses with rehabilitation, case-manager, psychiatric, or community specializations. Nor are sufficient numbers of social workers hired by hospitals and clinics that primarily serve low-income consumers even though community-oriented care is needed by many of them. The numbers of community-oriented staff often are cut when hospitals and clinics suffer budget shortfalls because they are often funded not by billable hours, but from administrative budgets of health institutions.

Relatively few public healthcare professionals are employed by primary-care clinics and hospitals, although many of them work in public health clinics devoted to prevention of STDs, TB, HIV/AIDS, and premature births. They work, as well, in local, state, and federal public health agencies that inspect health facilities, markets, and restaurants; engage in pest and rodent control; and prevent the transmission of infectious diseases.

Many physicians have inadequate knowledge about services provided by these community-oriented staff, often not making sufficient referrals to them. This lack of collaboration between health plans, health providers, and community agencies can adversely impact the well-being of consumers. Physicians often cannot provide community-oriented care to consumers because they lack sufficient training in it, lack the time to give it, and are not reimbursed by insurance and health plans to devote sufficient time to it. They find it hard to serve the expanding populations of mentally ill, disabled consumers, and chronically ill consumers.

Increasing Access to Care

Efforts to improve access of consumers to healthcare are an essential component of community-based care. Access is determined by geographic proximity of services to consumers, the affordability of healthcare, and outreach programs to community, schools, child-care programs, and places of work.

Each of these different dimensions of access can improve the healthcare of consumers. Bindman et al. (1995) discovered an inverse relation between access to care and preventable hospitalization rates for all five chronic medical conditions in a survey of low-income California residents with asthma, hypertension, congestive heart failure, chronic obstructive pulmonary disease, and diabetes. Hwang, Johnston, Dyson-Hudson, & Komaroff, (2009) found that consumers' perception of their access to and coordination of care is a significant predictor of health outcomes.

Some progress has been made in improving access. An initial network of community clinics, often with community outreach workers and multidisciplinary teams, was established in the 1960s with funding from the War on Poverty in underserved areas (K. Davis & Schoen, 1978). This network never grew to major size, however, because of funding cuts in the 1970s, as well as federal policies that required them to revert to staff and service requirements of traditional medical clinics. The failure to develop sufficient numbers of clinics in underserved areas forced many uninsured and Medicaid recipients to travel considerable distances to receive medical care in public clinics and hospitals and led some to receive their medical care in ERs rather than primary-care clinics.

The Patient Protection and Affordable Care Act of 2010 as amended by Congress creates a Prevention and Public Health Fund to modernize disease prevention and improve access to clinical preventive services in schools, as well as Medicare annual wellness programs. It will provide $15 billion to community health centers beginning in 2010. It will fund health prevention programs in occupational settings. It contains substantial subsidies for not-for-profit community-based clinics.

Financial accessibility to services has been greatly increased by Medicare, Medicaid, and SCHIP programs. Medicaid provides Disproportionate Share (DSH) payments to hospitals with a relatively high percentage of uninsured and Medicaid consumers, but these payments will be decreased as the Patient Protection and Affordable Care Act of 2010 reduces the number of uninsured Americans significantly during and after 2014 with the expansion of Medicaid and mandates for employers and individuals to obtain private health insurance and insurance from Co-ops.

Research on Community-Based Services

Most medical care is delivered in clinics and hospitals, as well as convalescent- and nursing homes. A substantial research agenda needs to be established and implemented that examines whether and to what extent care that extends into the community improves health outcomes and is cost-effective. To what extent, for example, are health outcomes of consumers with chronic illness improved when they receive coordinated care from mental health, primary care, medical care from several specialists, dietary, physical therapy, and other providers? To what extent do community outreach workers prevent illness when they visit homes and dispense advice and referrals for at-risk consumers (Israel, Schulz, Parker, & Becker, 1998; Levine et al., 2003)? To what extent does the training of physicians and other health staff about familial, community, social, and economic realities confronted by many consumers lead to better medical care and better outcomes (Jacobs, Kohrman, Lemon, & Vickers, 2003)?

Community-based services for terminally ill persons can reduce the cost of their services, such as by curtailing ER visits and visits with specialists. Disabled consumers who do not receive physical therapy in a timely and effective way, such as while receiving primary care, often experience physical consequences, compromised independence, and psychological consequences that, in turn, can have adverse consequences for their disabilities (Neri & Kroll, 2009).

Community Roles of Primary Care Health Staff

Primary healthcare is a medical beachhead or way station between communities and hospitals. Primary-care physicians are not reimbursed by public or private insurance programs to discuss or address community dimensions of consumers' care or to make home visits. They often do not have access to social workers, community-oriented nurses, or case managers because few of them work in primary-care settings. Their encounters with consumers are often brief and focused on interpreting results from lab tests with selective referrals to specialists or with dispensing of medications. They are often inundated, as well, with paperwork, interpreting diagnostic tests, and communications with specialists as they encounter large caseloads.

The Patient Protection and Affordable Care Act of 2010 will increase the number of primary-care physicians in underserved areas with financial incentives for ones who work there. It will increase Medicaid funding of primary care physicians so that they are commensurate with Medicare rates (beginning in 2013). It will improve care for seniors after they leave hospitals by establishing a Community Care Transitions Program (2011) that decreases unnecessary readmissions by coordinating care and connecting patients to services in their communities.

The Patient Protection and Affordable Care Act of 2010 as amended by Congress promises other innovations that will increase community-based care. It establishes a Community-based Collaborative Care Network Program to support consortia of healthcare providers to coordinate and integrate healthcare services for low-income uninsured and underinsured populations. It provides $15 billion for community health centers, including free clinics. It establishes new programs to support school-based health programs and nurse-managed health clinics.

The role of primary-care physicians may be enhanced by the Act, as well, by its creation of "bundled payments for episodes of care" that fund pediatric providers, safety net health systems, and Medicaid providers for the primary and specialty care given to specific consumers. This bundled approach aims to decrease fragmentation between primary care physicians and specialists.

Research suggests that many primary-care physicians do not give multifaceted care to consumers with disabilities. Many consumers with schizophrenia do not receive statins, for example, even when they have high cholesterol and blood pressure (Newcomer & Hennekens, 2007). Jansen, Krol, Groothoff, and Post (2006) contend that consumers with intellectual disability often do not receive care for hearing and vision impairments, thyroid disorders, and high blood pressure. More research is needed to examine to what extent primary-care physicians refer disabled consumers, elderly persons, and consumers with chronic diseases to community-based services.

Some experts in chronic care contend that diabetics and others with chronic conditions should receive "proactive" care that emphasizes education, intensive follow-up with practice-initiated phone calls, referrals to professionals with clinical and behavioral skills, and troubleshooting when consumers do not adhere to treatments (Glasgow et al. 1999).

As we have discussed, the Patient Protection and Affordable Care Act of 2010 will establish a national Medicare pilot program to develop and evaluate a bundled payment for acute inpatient hospital services, primary-care services, outpatient hospital services, and postacute care services for an episode of care. It will evaluate whether this approach will decrease medical silos and improve outcomes.

Community Roles of Emergency-Room Staff

The medical problems of consumers who come to ERs are often linked to mental trauma, family violence, malnutrition, exposure, drug overdoses, gang violence, homelessness and other social and economic problems that cause or exacerbate their medical problems. Many ER physicians, nurses, and social workers engage in referral, brokerage, and liaison services, including with law enforcement, mental health, child welfare, substance abuse, assisted-living, and nursing home agencies, as well as shelters. They often help consumers gain eligibility to specific safety-net programs such as Medicaid, SCHIP, Food Stamps, and Section-8. Some hospitals and health systems have established primary-care clinics in close proximity to ERs so that consumers who do not need urgent care can receive services from them.

Many ERs do not provide community-oriented care, however, because of the sheer volume and speed of their work. The staff is often preoccupied with following procedures prescribed by laws, regulations, and litigation that define their relationships with law enforcement and external agencies. I discussed policies and regulations that protect vulnerable populations in Chapter 10. ERs need to be linked more closely with primary-care clinics so that consumers with complex problems receive ongoing care from them as well as community-based services.

Transition Planning

Many consumers need help in transition planning as they move from health institutions and their homes, convalescent homes, nursing homes, assisted-living homes, and retirement homes. Staff in hospitals are required to provide such planning by federal and state statutes; Medicare, Medicaid, and state regulations; and Joint Commission accreditation standards.

The federal Emergency Medical Treatment and Active Labor Act (EMTALA) established procedures that apply not only to consumers who are transferred from ERs to other locations, but to all transfer cases (CHA, 2008, p. 9.1). Consumers need to be transferred from ERs and hospitals for many reasons, such as when they need specialized services that are not offered or available, a shortage of hospital beds such as in a psychiatric unit, requests of consumers or their legal representatives, when they no longer need acute care, when their health insurance plan funds nonemergency care only at other facilities, and when consumers cannot pay for their medical services. *They cannot seek transfer of specific patients, however, until they are medically stabilized.* Hospitals are legally responsible "for the safety, appropriateness, and monitoring of the transfer process and protocol" (CHA, 2008, p. 9.1). Medicare, Medicaid, and the Joint Commission add additional requirements.

Both transferring hospitals and receiving health facilities need articulated transfer procedures that describe administrative and professional responsibilities that insure that transfers do not create medical hazards, consumers receive appropriate medical care throughout the transfer process, transfers are implemented safely, transfers occur expeditiously, consumers' consents are obtained and documented, and administrative tasks are accomplished like billing, transfer of medical records, and documentation (CHA, 2008, p. 9.2). Medical responsibility for the consumer must be provided at all times by either the transferring or the receiving agency. Transferring hospitals and physicians must use "due care" in overseeing the transportation process to insure consumers' safety, including use of paramedics and ambulances when consumers medically require them (CHA, 2008, p. 9.2).

The transferring hospital should determine that consumers are medically fit to transfer, that is, are medically stabilized. The receiving physician and health facility must consent to the transfer and accept responsibility for the consumer's care and this agreement must be documented in the consumer's medical record. A consumer's consent must be obtained after they have been informed of risks and benefits of transfers related to his or her condition, whether transit will aggravate his or her medical condition, and why physicians have chosen the specific mode of transportation, such as use of paramedics instead of ambulance attendants (CHA, 2008, p. 9.3).

Consumers can both refuse to leave acute care when healthcare professionals believe they no longer need care—and can leave acute care even when healthcare professionals believe their departure could endanger their health. They may refuse to leave from their own decision or because family members insist that they not be discharged. Although each case is different, healthcare professionals must be certain that all medical and legal requirements for transfer or discharge have been met and documented. They must follow all requirements of Medicare and other payers that give consumers the right to appeal medical decisions. They should ask consumers to express their wishes not to be discharged or transferred on a signed document, but only after they have been informed of possible consequences of this choice. They should identify all possible options with resort to legal solutions as only a last resort (CHA, 2008, p. 9.3).

Consumers sometimes want to leave acute care despite medical advice that they could endanger themselves. Health staff should follow procedures in their organizations established for such consumers. When consumers want to use transportation procedures other than ones recommended by medical staff, such as driving themselves or taking public transportation rather than transportation in hospital vehicles or ambulances, hospitals should follow their procedures for such situations, such as asking them to sign documents that they have declined medical advice (CHA, 2008, p. 9.3).

Receiving institutions should receive relevant portions of medical records with consumers, with other materials transmitted if required by state law. Consumers' consents may not be needed if medical information is transmitted for purposes of diagnosis and treatment, but the sending institution can choose to secure consent on a specific form (CHA, 2008, p. 9.5). Special forms and procedures are needed for release of psychiatric information, treatment for drug or alcohol abuse, and HIV test results (CHA, 2008, p. 9.8). Consumers' consent should be obtained in advance if they are transferred to another institution to receive a specific medical treatment or procedure there.

Transfer summaries should be provided to consumers transferred to nursing or inter- mediate care facilities that discuss essential information, such as consumers' medical care, diagnoses, dietary requirements, rehabilitation potentials, and a treatment plan signed by their physicians (CHA, 2008, p. 9.4). (Such transfer summaries should also be provided to other acute care facilities.) Some states, such as California, require consumers who need long-term care after discharge to receive contact information for one or more public or nonprofit agencies that provide information and referral services relating to local long-term care options as well as the area agency on aging (CHA, 2008, p. 9.5).

Transfers of consumers often occur for financial reasons when consumers lack health insurance. EMTALA prohibits transfers before consumers are medically stabilized. Some states prohibit transfers of consumers for financial reasons from specific vulnerable populations, such as race, disability, or sexual orientation, because they are *suspected* of lacking resources to fund their medical care without determining that they are actually medically indigent (CHA, 2008, p. 9.8). California requires emergency services to be given to consumers without *first* investigating to see if they can fund them even though payment can be sought *after* they have been treated (CHA, 2008, p. 9.8). These laws also prohibit discrimination in providing emergency services on the basis of race, gender, and other characteristics. While healthcare professionals can transfer consumers for financial reasons, they should realize that patient transfers based on medical indigency may raise questions about the hospital's Medicare or Medicaid status, so hospital staff should have their organization's legal counsel examine their policies regarding transfer of medically indigent patients (CHA, 2008, p. 9.8).

California enacted a law regarding the discharge of homeless persons, who have been inappropriately transported by some hospitals to skid row areas in such cities as Los Angeles, sometimes even in their hospital gowns, and without ensuring they receive a place in shelters. It requires hospitals to notify and obtain authorization from specific social service agencies, health providers, or nonprofit social service providers. It is recommended that hospitals obtain documentation from the receiving agency or provider and place it in the medical record (CHA, 2008, p. 9.22). A severe shortage of beds exists to serve homeless persons who need nonemergency medical care on their release from hospitals, because most shelters do not provide medical services—a shortage that can only be remedied by policy advocacy at local, state, and federal levels.

Hospitals can incur stiff penalties for violation of transfer rules, including fines, exclusion from Medicare and Medicaid programs, and loss of accreditation.

Transition planning is often inadequate, however, because hospitals and clinics do not hire sufficient social workers and discharge nurses to provide effective interventions. These professionals can be pressured to speed up the release of consumers from hospitals to save them resources when they are reimbursed with capitation or with prospective payments such as Medicare's DRGs.

Links Between Health Institutions and Community Agencies

Healthcare professionals can promote community-oriented care for consumers by establishing links among community agencies that can include mental health, family, substance abuse, shelter, income assistance, health insurance, public health, housing, employment, physical therapy, speech and language, and other health-related problems. These links can take place among autonomous agencies (linkage), can include more systematic relationships (coordination), or can involve "joint goals, very close and highly connected networks . . . and high degrees of mutual trust and respect" (integration) as discussed by Glendinning (2002).

These links involve two-way agreements between staff in different organizations. Staff in two agencies may informally and mutually agree to prioritize services for consumers referred to them by staff in the other agency in a bootstrap arrangement. Or administrators of a unit, such as a psychiatric unit of a hospital, may meet with administrators of a community-based mental health agency to orchestrate mutual support and assistance agreements for specific kinds of consumers, such as ones with specific mental conditions. More ambitiously, separate agencies can establish a hybrid entity that pools new benefits and services and possess common information services (Leutz, 1999).

Hospitals or health plans sometimes contract with a community-based agency to provide specific services to some of their clientele. In the case of "carve-out" arrangements, for example, health plans contract with mental health organizations to treat persons with specific mental conditions or substance abuse problems through capitation payments—contracting arrangements established by high-level administrators in both organizations (Ray, Daugherty, & Meador, 2003).

Links among separate agencies often founder on specific obstacles including lack of communication across disciplines, competitive relationships, lack of contracting resources, and logistical barriers (Lasker, Weiss, & Miller, 2001). It is difficult even within health systems to obtain coordination between different specialties, as well as between primary care and acute care. HIPAA and other confidentiality policies can sometimes make collaborative care difficult as health, mental health, child welfare, substance abuse, and other agencies do not divulge information to other professionals. Staff can be disinclined to engage in time-consuming case conferences.

Consumers ultimately bear the cost of insufficient links between health and related organizations and programs. Parents with autistic children or children with attention deficit and hyperactivity disorder (ADHD) have to negotiate arrangements with health staff, schools, mental health agencies, psychiatric units and hospitals, and the police (Lantos, 2007). Parents with diabetic children have to deal with outpatient medical care, inpatient care, schools, and insurance companies (Clark et al., 1995).

Organized Systems of Community-Based Care

Organized systems of community-based care allow some consumers to receive multifaceted services from them for an extended period, such as hospice, some health programs for elderly persons, and some programs for disabled consumers. (Hospice is discussed in Chapter 5.)

Community-based care for elderly consumers has increasingly relied on multiprofessional teams in health organizations that include case managers (also called care managers) who, in turn, help orchestrate in-home care that includes health aides, visiting nurses, physical therapists, and others. These elderly consumers may use, as well, programs funded by regional agencies established by the Older Americans Act, such as meals on wheels or congregate eating arrangements.

Various models of community care have evolved, such as the ON LOK approach, where elderly persons enroll in programs that give them care in a community program during the day that includes congregate eating, physical therapy, social activities, and healthcare with funding with Medicare and out-of-pocket fees (Bodenheimer, 1999). (ON LOK does not provide nursing home care or hospice.)

The federal government has funded demonstration programs that use community-based services to keep elderly consumers in their homes rather than institutions. The Social Health Maintenance Organization (S/HMO) demonstrations, which began with four sites in 1985 but expanded to 10 sites by 1995, enrolled seniors who are eligible for nursing home care but living in their homes. They gave them acute and ambulatory services, as well as preventive services. Seniors attend day-centers where they receive regular healthcare, as well as socialization with other seniors. They can receive in-home supportive care. When they are assessed as eligible for long-term care, they receive long-term care services. The organizations administering these demonstrations are financed from Medicare payments for services and capitation payments from state Medicaid programs. Other demonstrations funded with Medicare and Medicaid funds have been initiated with promising results, but evaluations are still inconclusive (Geron, 2001).

The Patient Protection and Affordable Care Act of 2010 as amended by Congress will create the State Balancing Incentive Program in Medicaid to provide enhanced federal matching payments to increase noninstitutionally based long-term care services. It will establish the Community First Choice Option in Medicaid to provide community-based attendant support services to certain people with disabilities.

Community-based programs for disabled consumers exist in many communities with funding from public and private sources. Often using an empowerment approach that aims to diminish stigma and reliance on traditional rehabilitative and medical models of care, these programs provide an array of health, job, recreational, and case advocacy services to disabled persons with strong emphasis on helping them obtain civil rights established in the Americans with Disabilities Act 1990.

Community-based programs exist for many persons with chronic diseases. Healthcare professionals increasingly offer dietary, exercise, and other programs to help diabetics manage their weight and intake of sugar in community settings that include support groups. Consumers with HIV-AIDS sometimes reside in housing that provides social programs and healthcare with some funding from the Ryan White Act.

Many retirement homes that cater to relatively affluent Americans exist in the United States, such as the Quaker-sponsored Kendal retirement homes. Consumers pay a considerable fee to enter these homes, such as $175,000, as well as a monthly fee. They live in independent apartments or town houses at the outset, move to intermediary units where they need assisted care, and move to nursing facilities when they have disabling illnesses. These homes offer many services and activities to their residents. Some of them allow seniors to purchase apartments or town houses, which are often sold by their estates when they die.

Some experts who contend that nursing homes are dehumanizing have developed innovative programs geared to helping seniors avoid nursing homes. They provide seniors with relatively small congregate residences that house five to 20 seniors, as well as medical and social services including care when they are no longer ambulatory.

Other community alternatives to retirement homes and nursing homes have developed in recent years. Seniors in some communities remain in their homes, but contribute a fee to a community organization that provides them with in-home care when they might need it, congregate meals, and an array of education and socializing activities.

Community-based services have been developed, as well, for persons with mental illness as illustrated by the Village in Los Angeles that provides housing, social services, psychiatric services, and employment services for persistent and chronic mental conditions.

Organized systems of care must surmount specific obstacles, however. They often need to convince insurance plans, Medicare, Medicaid, and other sources to give them pooled or capitation funds for enrollees. They need skilled administrators to manage their systems. They need to recruit consumers who would otherwise use fee-for-service or managed-care health systems. Public officials, employers, and other funders of healthcare will fund community-based care only if they believe it is less expensive than traditional medical care (Scheid, 2004). Research is needed, as well, to establish if organized systems of care produce better health outcomes and consumer satisfaction than service alternatives.

Information Technology

Emerging technology allows providers to link providers with consumers in their homes and communities. Physicians and other health staff increasingly communicate with consumers through video conferencing where they enter their homes electronically. They communicate with family members and in-home supportive staff who assume important roles in caring for elderly, disabled, and other consumers. They monitor consumers' vital signs electronically so that they can dispatch healthcare professionals to their homes to troubleshoot specific health conditions. They use video cameras to observe health-related activities of consumers in their homes, such as whether elderly persons adhere to recommended treatments.

The promise of technology has not been realized, however, in many health settings. Only 8.1% of hospitals and 17% of physicians use electronic health records

(DesRoches et al., 2008; Jha et al., 2009). Many consumers do not receive care from multiprofessional teams even when they have complex or chronic health conditions. Few consumers engage in video conferencing with health staff.

Many factors have slowed the dissemination of information technology. It requires considerable investments of resources and time to install it and to educate healthcare professionals about its use. It has to surmount HIPAA regulations. It requires IT staff to troubleshoot it. It requires the electronic systems of different providers to be compatible. Costs of adoption are high (Shea & Hripcsak, 2010).

In-Home Supportive Services and Long-Term Care

Many consumers receive in-home supportive care that is funded by Medicare, Medicaid, long-term care insurance, managed-care plans, and some private insurance plans. It includes short-term in-home care in the wake of acute illness that is funded by Medicare when consumers return home from hospitals or convalescent homes. It must be ordered by consumers' physicians for a specified period and can include visiting nurses, social workers, speech and language services, and OT/PT services. (Some of these services can be obtained outside of the home, such as PT services.) Physicians can request an extension of these services beyond the specified period if they document that consumers are making continuing improvement.

Medicaid provides ongoing in-home supportive services without time limit as long as consumers' physicians order them for persons with disabilities, chronic illness, and other illnesses. The quality of in-home supportive staff varies widely, however. Because Medicaid often funds these services at low levels, in-home staff may have limited education and training. These services may be cut, moreover, during states' budget deficits.

Informal caregivers provide the most common form of in-home care, such as adult children for their parents, parents for their children, or spouses for their spouses. They provide in-home supportive care to elderly, disabled, chronically ill, acutely ill, and mentally ill consumers, as well as to children with extended illnesses, mental conditions, or disabilities. Most of these caregivers are women who often endure considerable hardships to provide free assistance to relatives, including poverty or significant loss of income, mental distress, health problems, and family problems. They must often negotiate complex relationships with the consumers that they help, such as persons with dementia, Alzheimer's disease, and physical disabilities—relationships that often include tensions and hostility. Some informal caregivers help relatives only for brief periods, many of them give care for many years (Schultz et al., 2003).

Their ranks have been expanded by the Family and Medical Leave Act of 1993 that allows workers to obtain leaves from their employment to care for relatives with medical problems or for care of a newborn child. Because the leaves are unpaid, they are disproportionately used by relatively affluent people who can afford them. It also exempts small employers from granting these leaves.

Some innovative programs give support to informal caregivers, such as giving them respite through day services to their relatives; giving them educational supports so that they can provide assistance more effectively; giving them financial assistance; and providing them with counseling to deal with stress and mental conditions often linked to their help with their relatives. Relatively few informal caregivers benefit from these programs, however, because they are not usually funded by Medicare, Medicaid, or private insurance programs, relying instead on private funding and regional programs established by the Older Americans Act.

Occupational Factors

Many corporations have instituted wellness programs in their work sites, such as rail company CSX Transportation, Johnson & Johnson, and Coors Brewing (Brink, 2008; CSX, 2005). Many technology companies, such as Google and Microsoft, have wellness programs, as well as exercise facilities at their work sites.

Few safeguards prevent employers from making massive lay-offs such as when companies relocate operations abroad. Many U.S. corporations give their employees no vacations or only brief ones. Workers are not protected from abusive treatment from employers unless it violates civil rights protections for persons of color, women, the disabled, and other populations protected by specific state and federal laws. Work-related stress causes heart disease, insomnia, and other health problems (Orth-Gomer, 2007).

FIFTEEN ADVOCACY SCENARIOS FOR CONSUMERS NEEDING COMMUNITY-BASED CARE

I present 13 scenarios encountered by case advocates who need community-based care in this book, as well as two scenarios online.

Scenario 11.1: Advocacy for Consumers Needing Community Referrals

Case advocates often give consumers referrals to a wide array of community resources to give them assistance not available from clinics and hospitals (Samet, Friedmann, & Saitz, 2001). Referral assistance may be ineffective, however, if case advocates are not familiar with the network of community resources that exists because they may refer consumers to nonexistent ones, ones not appropriate for specific consumers, or ones that provide inferior services. They need to know, as well, how accessible specific community resources are, because they may otherwise refer consumers to ones that require such lengthy waits that most of them will not access them at all—or too late to help them with their needs.

As Leutz, Greenlick, and Nonnenkamp (2003) contend: "Knowing more about community agencies helps the medical system make more referrals and better referrals, and this translates directly into more help for members with disabilities and for their families. By keeping up on what's offered and who qualifies, better fits can be made, and this in turn increases the likelihood that the member will actually get help . . . By developing personal relationships with community agency staff and by establishing more explicit linkage arrangements and follow up systems, hooking up is not left to the member. Closer relationships also hold promise of improving the quality and efficiency of care on both sides of the system."

Case advocates must devote considerable time to intelligence gathering in the community if they wish to make effective referrals. The nurses and social workers who staffed Kaiser Permanente's San Francisco's community-based medicine program had long-standing difficulties making successful referrals to community agencies. They increased their successes by relying on social workers and caseworkers to collect current information and establish personal contacts—strategies that led to increasing referrals to participating community agencies despite financial barriers (Leutz et al., 2003).

Case advocates need, as well, not to be satisfied with "passive referrals" when consumers urgently need assistance or if they have reason to believe that they will not make connections. When they make passive referrals, they point consumers in specific directions, but make no effort to see if they made contact and began to use specific community resources. They make follow-up contacts with consumers and referral sites when they use "active referrals" and may even personally intervene with consumers, such as accompanying them to a referral site. Active referrals should be strongly considered with consumers at risk of suicide, substance abuse overdoses, family violence, advanced chronic diseases, malnutrition, and poverty. They need to use active referrals, too, with consumers who lack the ability to use needed resources, such as consumers with cognitive impairments or poorly educated consumers. Consumers' prior histories of making and keeping appointments may sometimes signal whether they need active referrals.

Referrers can track referrals through telephone calls, e-mail, or social Internet contacts with specific consumers, as well as with those professionals or agencies to which they are sent.

Case advocates should:

- Be familiar with the community-based network to know what services or benefits are available by spending considerable time researching it online, through personal contacts, or through conversations with other professionals.
- Have knowledge of the relative quality of services provided by specific professionals and agencies through feedback from consumers or other professionals, by observations, or by evaluations of their services when they exist.
- Know specific staff in various agencies who become "inside contacts" that can provide accurate information about their services and who can expedite entrée for consumers who have been referred to them. Referrals to specific professionals and agency staff can be more effective than blind referrals.

- Provide active referrals to those consumers who have urgent and important needs.
- Be familiar with Internet sites that list and describe specific services in their communities, such as ones provided by United Way, the Jewish Federation, and specific advocacy groups, as well as use i-phones, i-pads and similar technology from other sources to link consumers with relevant resources.

Scenario 11.2: Advocacy to Help Consumers Make Transitions

I have already discussed how healthcare professionals must meet specific requirements of local, state, and federal authorities when providing assistance to consumers such as when they move from hospitals to homes, from skilled nursing facilities to hospitals, and between other locations. E. Coleman, Parry, Chalmers, and Min (2006) created the care transitions model to provide guidance to healthcare professionals that was developed from feedback from qualitative interviews with patients and caregivers about elements needed for successful transitions. The model centers on four pillars or conceptual domains, which include medication self-management, a patient-centered record, follow-up, and use of "red flags" to understand when the patient may be having a change in condition requiring medical attention (E. Coleman et al., 2006). An important aspect of this intervention is the goal of empowering the patient and/or caregiver to play a more active role during transitions to be assured that consumers' needs are met regardless of setting. Coleman contends that a transitions coach be assigned to consumers to teach them how to maneuver safely between whatever settings may be encountered in a patient's journey through the healthcare maze. The transitions coach needs medical knowledge, such as to help consumers avoid adverse medication interactions and to help consumers maintain a personal medical record to be used by providers during and after the transition.

If consumers move from hospitals to nursing homes, convalescent homes, or assisted living, case advocates must help them evaluate them. They can refer them to local, state and federal rating systems that often provide on-line data. They can determine which of them have been cited or fined or lost accreditation from local and state agencies. They can make visits to them or have relatives or friends visit them with recommended lists of questions to ask.

I discuss some difficulties in finding quality nursing homes in Chapters 6 and 9. Nursing home regulations are often insufficient. For example, federal regulations require facilities with more than 120 beds to employ one full-time "qualified social worker" defined as someone with a college degree in social work or a related field and at least one year of experience in a health setting. Yet some studies show that "a full-time social worker can handle only 60 or fewer long-term residents and only 20 or fewer subacute care residents" (Bern-Klug, Kramer, Sharr, & Cruz, 2010).

Consumers should be assessed for their relative comfort or distress before and as they make transitions.

Case advocates can:

- Empower consumers by giving them choices about transition strategy.
- Provide consumers with clear plans for managing their care in the new setting.
- Identify family relatives or others who can help consumers adhere to treatments, including medications, physical therapy, and nutritional recommendations—with education so that they can fill these functions.
- Make arrangements to obtain needed medical equipment.
- Implement and monitor strategies for reducing pain.
- Help consumers find needed in-home supportive care.
- Clarify what portions of recommended care are covered by consumers' insurances, as well as strategies for obtaining important noncovered items.
- Make referrals to relevant community agencies and professionals.
- Establish dates and places of medical follow-up services.
- Inform consumers of an array of in-home services and web sites where they can learn about them, their locations, and their costs, as well as programs that might help finance them.

Scenario 11.3: Advocacy for Home Healthcare

Many consumers who are not in hospice or palliative care programs, often persons with chronic diseases, must organize their own home healthcare, often over a period of years. If they do not qualify for Medicaid, which funds in-home supportive services such as aides in many states, and if they do not have insurance policies that cover home healthcare, they often run into huge costs that may drive them into medical bankruptcy to enable them to qualify for Medicaid. They confront logistical challenges in a society that lacks a trained cadre of home health workers. They encounter these challenges at the very time that they are feeling sick, fear loss of control to these workers, and deal with their impending deaths. Some home health workers are highly skilled, but others are less reliable and may even steal property from elderly persons. High turnover often occurs in these home health teams. If they can afford it, consumers can purchase home healthcare from for-profit agencies that provide home health services, as well as from not-for-profit visiting nurses associations.

Advocates should help consumers consider the following:

- Help consumers gain access to home health services from Medicaid if they qualify.
- Help consumers gain technical advice from not-for-profit Visiting Nurse Associations in their jurisdiction, as well as possible consultants.
- Advise consumers to explore the Visiting Nurse Association of America web site at http://vnaa.org.

Scenario 11.4: Advocacy with Students in Schools

Many schools lack sufficient health personnel to assist students with substance abuse problems, mental health issues, unsafe sex, diabetes and other chronic diseases, as well as students who commit violence or are subject to bullying (Delisio, 2009).

Schools sometimes violate rules that protect rights of students with specific health, cognitive, or mental health problems. They may fail to follow state and federal regulations that protect disabled students (Hansen, 2009). They may fail to mainstream students with cognitive problems. They may place pregnant students in special schools even when regulations require them to let them decide if they wish to remain in regular classrooms (Pillow, 2004).

Case advocates can:

- Protect the rights of specific students by educating school personnel about them in liaison with specific students.
- Discover local regulations and programs regarding safe sex and birth control so that students have access to them.
- Inform school administrators and teachers about health resources for specific kinds of problems whether in a school district, from community agencies, or from clinics.
- Empower parents to become advocates for the rights and healthcare of their children.

Scenario 11.5: Advocacy to Help Consumers Become Less Dependent on the Health System

As discussed in Chapters 7 and 8, some consumers may benefit from alternative medical providers that provide yoga, meditation, and exercise that not only provide them with psychological and physiological benefits, but make them less dependent on traditional medicine.

Other consumers, too, can become excessively dependent on the medical system. Many elderly consumers devote extraordinary time, for example, to visits to medical specialists to the point that they dominate their lives (Wartman, 2006). (See Vignette 11.3.)

🖎 Vignette 11.3 A Frustrated Elderly Person

An elderly person with congestive heart failure devoted much of her time to visits to physicians as she dealt with her chronic disease. She consulted many specialists who sometimes gave her conflicting advice. She experienced adverse interactions among some of the medications that she received. When discussing her situation

(continued)

(*continued*)

with a frontline worker in a local hospital, she came to realize that her life had become so dominated by the medical system that she had ceased participating in many community activities that had given meaning to her life before she developed congestive heart failure. She gradually resumed her volunteering with local environmental groups. She volunteered at a local public library. As she engaged in these activities, her use of the medical system declined even as she still needed medications and other medical help.

Learning Exercise

- Discuss why some consumers become excessively absorbed with the medical system. How do medical providers sometimes encourage excessive dependence? How does excessive use of medical care often create such dependence?
- How can health professionals help consumers resume or begin activities that give their lives meaning?

Some consumers identify activities in their communities or in their personal lives that can give them a purpose for living beyond merely receiving medical care. Health professionals can explore ways that some of these consumers can make greater use of community resources. They can volunteer in schools, local charities, or hospice. They can attend local cultural events. They can become docents. They can join support groups.

Case advocates can:

- Examine medical records to identify consumers who make frequent visits to health facilities out of proportion to diagnosed health conditions.
- Engage them in discussion to understand why they are such frequent users of health services (Diamond, 2003).
- Help them identify some nonmedical activities that might make their lives meaningful.

Scenario 11.6: Advocacy to Obtain Community-Based Preventive Services

As discussed in Chapter 8, health is powerfully shaped by an array of factors that must be addressed in home and community environments. These include poverty, low levels of education, smoking, poor diet, lack of exercise, stress, and isolation. Research implicates other factors, such as divorce or deaths of spouses, depression, and psychoses. Home environments contribute to health outcomes including trauma from falls, and exposure to toxic chemicals, as well as exposure to family violence.

Unless frontline staff visit consumers in their homes, or find community-based agencies that can provide these services, these threats to well-being will not be mitigated. Some consumers' well-being is compromised, as well, by systemic community factors, such as community violence, toxic chemicals, and other kinds of pollution—particularly in low-income communities.

Residents in affluent communities also confront threats to their health, such as an elderly person who is abused by his child. When the CDC investigated high rates of teenage STDs in an affluent suburb of Atlanta, it discovered that teenagers left unsupervised by parents who worked long hours engaged in sexual orgies on a daily basis in their homes (California Newsreel, 2008).

It is usually not possible for specific health organizations or plans to provide services to address environmental factors that may impact the health of their consumers adversely. They can, however, notify public health authorities and advocacy groups that some of their consumers' health problems may stem from environmental conditions. They can obtain epidemiological data that suggests that consumers from specific geographic areas have higher rates of specific diseases, particularly if they serve these areas.

Health organizations and plans should encourage and promote community organizations and activities that foster health prevention, particularly in the geographic areas served by them. These include health fairs, mobile units, provision of diagnostic tests at community sites, out-stationing of health personnel in community agencies, sponsoring of athletic teams for youth, sponsoring of athletic contests and running events, educational programs in schools, and other activities. These activities not only help consumers, but market services of health plans to the communities where potential clientele reside.

Case advocates can:

- Encourage administrators of health organizations and plans to participate in a wide array of community-based health education programs and activities.
- Create a calendar of existing prevention programs in specific geographic areas where their consumers reside—and notify them of these events as they are relevant to them.
- Empower consumers to contact public health and other public authorities when they fear that environmental conditions in their communities threaten their health.

Scenario 11.7: Advocacy for Low-Income Consumers

Poverty is the best predictor of poor health and relatively short life expectancy. Consumers in the lower one-third of the nation's income distribution (or less than 200% of the federal poverty line) lose an estimated 8.2 years of perfect health—or far more than the 6.6 years from smoking, 5.1 years from dropping out of high school,

4.2 years from obesity, and even fewer years from being uninsured or being a binge drinker (J. Stein, 2009). I noted in Chapter 8 that the CDC (2002) estimated, instead, that persons who smoke lose 14 years of life rather than 6 years, but the CDC focused on years of life rather than lost years of good health.

Health staff cannot elevate many poor persons from poverty because they lack the resources, expertise, or programs. It is tempting to contend that poverty reduction falls outside the purview of the health system. Many poor persons, however, fail to use resources that are open to them, such as the roughly 50% of eligible persons who do not use Food Stamps and the Earned Income Tax Credit. Many other eligible consumers have not applied for Section 8 housing, Medicaid, SCHIP, Temporary Assistance for Needy Families (TANF), refugee assistance programs, One-Stop Centers funded by the federal Department of Labor, shelter programs for homeless persons, and many other programs that can increase consumers' incomes in the short- and long-term.

Many health programs that target low-income persons are also underused, including Medicaid, SCHIP, Women, Infant, and Children Program (WIC), lead paint abatement programs, and housing inspection programs that cite landlords for dangerous conditions including for rodents and lack of heat. Hospitals and clinics should discuss possible out-stationing of staff from programs in their facilities to expedite application procedures and developing procedures for implementing medical treatment for consumers pending enrollment in these programs.

Case advocates can:

- Develop lists of resources in several or more languages that include where to go to obtain eligibility to many safety-net programs and distribute them widely.
- Refer low-income consumers to one or more of these programs.
- Prioritize active referrals as discussed in Scenario 11.1 for consumers whose health is jeopardized by *not* receiving assistance from one or more of these programs, such as families with malnourished children that stems from their poverty, families living in dangerous housing conditions, and consumers living on the streets.
- Discuss whether representatives of some of these agencies, such as Medicaid eligibility staff, can co-locate on the premises of health facilities when a large percentage of their consumers experience poverty.

Scenario 11.8: Advocacy to Enhance Community-Based Care With Technology

Technology can be used to link hospitals and clinics with consumers' homes and communities. Current technology allows, for example, home-bound consumers to converse with health staff in clinics and hospitals; transmission of video data from homes to clinics and hospitals to check adherence and consumers' health; and family members and caregivers to converse with health staff in distant locations (C. Miller, 2009). It allows consumers to obtain second opinions from distant health staff through video-conferencing that is preceded by electronic transmission of diagnostic data. Electronic medical records (EMRs) allow health staff in many locations to view consumers' health information, whether they are stored by specific providers or placed "on the cloud" by specific consumers (Lohr, 2009). Geographic positioning technology, such as Google Earth, can help health staff gain information about specific communities that is germane to the health of specific consumers. Personal health records (PHRs) let patients converse online with their physicians, enter health data, and let them access their medical record. They should advance the goal of making healthcare more patient-centered (Reti, Feldman, Ross, & Safran, 2010).

The stimulus plan of the Obama Administration earmarked considerable resources for the development of electronic records, and well as other IT innovations. Medicare and Medicaid will give bonus payments to hospitals that implement EMR.

The Internet is a vast resource for consumers. It contains research and advice about the prevention of specific diseases, how to manage chronic illnesses, advocacy groups, and support groups. It helps consumers locate accessible health services. It describes services of community-based agencies that are relevant to consumers' health problems.

It may facilitate the exchange of medical information among physicians, consumers, in-home supportive staff, family caregivers, and community agencies subject to HIPAA regulations. Medical staff at a central location can link consumers with advanced diabetes, for example, to community-based rehabilitation services, agencies that provide meals on wheels, agencies that provide in-home supportive services, visiting nurses, and relatives in another city.

Information technology has greatly facilitated the work of multiprofessional teams that include members who help consumers in their homes and communities. It provides centralized records that include the periodic comments of team members as they interact with specific consumers. A visiting nurse may, for example, comment on the diet of a consumer that is accessed by the consumer's physician at a regular appointment, as well as other lifestyle habits. The visiting nurse monitors whether the consumer adheres to her physician's recommended medications and other treatments that she obtains from the consumer's EMR.

Significant barriers must still be surmounted when using technology, such as confidentiality issues, incompatible electronic systems, lack of sufficient IT support in some facilities, and reluctance of some health staff to use EMRs.

Case advocates can:

- Inquire whether technology can usefully link the homes and communities with health staff.
- Consult IT staff and other health staff to see if it is feasible to use it in specific situations.

Scenario 11.9: Advocacy to Improve Consumers' Work Environments

Special accommodations are required by law and regulations for specific populations, including pregnant women, disabled consumers, and youth. Regulations regarding pregnant women include the Family and Medical Leave Act. This act required employers to give 12 weeks of unpaid medical leave after birth of adoption and for complications of pregnancy (Department of Labor, 2010a). Individual states also have laws protecting pregnant women at work. Regulations regarding disabled consumers are defined by various federal and state statutes and regulations, including ones established by the federal Americans with Disabilities Act of 1990. They require work accommodations for consumers with physical and mental disabilities and prohibit discrimination against disabled persons. Work regulations for youth include the Fair Labor Standards Act, which restricts the hours that youth under 16 years of age can work and lists hazardous occupations too dangerous for young workers to perform (Department of Labor, 2010b).

The federal Occupational Safety and Health Administration (OSHA), as well as state OSHA departments, inspect work sites to determine if they meet health standards regarding levels of toxicity, whether in the air, in work procedures and equipment, or in materials to which workers are exposed. Hotlines exist at both federal and state levels.

An array of antidiscrimination statutes and regulations exist with respect to specific populations in hiring, dismissal, and promotion policies. Discrimination can be considered a health issue because consumers who have been treated unfairly in work settings may develop stress-related health problems, not to mention economic hardship. Discrimination can deprive some consumers of health insurance. Federal antidiscrimination policies protect persons of color, women, persons with disabilities, and persons with genetic propensity to specific health conditions. Many state laws also protect these populations, as well as gay, lesbian, and transgender persons, and prohibit discrimination based on national origin, ancestry, marital status, age (over 40), or request for family leave (California Department of Industrial Relations, 2010).

Some health plans provide interventions to reduce stress in occupational settings, such as Kaiser Permanente in Los Angeles, which uses interactional exercises to teach employees and managers how to reduce excessive conflict and tension (Orth-Gomer, 2007).

Workmen's compensation laws give leaves and benefits to employees who are injured at their places of employment if they meet specific medical criteria. Considerable research indicates that many workers suffer mental, physical, and financial consequences from excessive absences from work once they have recovered from their injuries, partly because their primary-care physicians lack sufficient knowledge about disabilities and because they believe that encouraging them to return to work is "contrary to their role as patient advocates" (McGrail et al., 2002).

Case advocates can:

- Empower consumers to call hotlines, make complaints, or seek investigations of possible violations of state or federal policies with respect to work conditions, hiring, dismissal, and promotions.
- Encourage injured workers to obtain accurate information about whether and when they can return to work.
- Establish health education programs in work places.

Scenario 11.10: Advocacy to Give Consumers Public Health Interventions

Public health programs are an important resource for frontline health staff because they are situated in communities across the nation, as well as in state, local, and federal government. Public health departments and programs in federal, state, county, municipal, and rural locations inspect food products and preparation, long-term care facilities, hospitals, clinics, and research laboratories to ascertain if they meet sanitary requirements. They are often linked to local housing agencies that inspect rental apartments and other living units for safety standards. They inspect residential and commercial sites for cleanliness and infestation by rodents. They inspect facilities that manufacture, prepare, and sell food. They inspect schools and other public facilities to see if they meet sanitary requirements.

Public health agencies and departments oversee a national network of clinics that prevent and detect HIV/AIDS, STDs, tuberculosis, and other communicable diseases. They operate many prenatal clinics particularly in underserved areas. They sometimes operate primary-care clinics in underserved areas. These various programs often offer services for free or at minimal charge.

Case advocates can:

- Familiarize themselves with the network of public health programs, services, and regulations in their geographic areas.
- Refer consumers to relevant programs and services.
- Empower or partner with consumers to make complaints about sanitation in their apartments, homes, communities, or places of employment.

Scenario 11.11: Advocacy to Help Incarcerated or Institutionalized Consumers Transition to the Community

The majority of inmates are eventually released back to their communities, so public health officials have begun to recognize the tremendous public health opportunity within corrections and the potential to benefit the community with reduced illness rates, financial savings, improved public safety, and better use of the existing healthcare system and resources (Travis, Solomon, & Waul, 2001). From a policy perspective, inmates' healthcare and their reintegration back into the community began to take on new importance with the increasing number of HIV/AIDS cases identified in correctional settings (Conklin, Lincoln, & Flanigan, 1998). Collaborations among corrections, community, and public health programs at federal and state levels have increasingly been developed to take advantage of the incarceration episode to decrease the burden of illness on those incarcerated and the greater community (Community Health and Public Health Collaborations).

Innovative programs are needed, such as Project Bridge, a federally funded demonstration project that provides intensive case management for HIV-positive ex-offenders being released from the Rhode Island state prison to the community. The program is based on collaboration between co-located medical and social work staff. The primary goal of the program is to increase continuity of medical care through social stabilization; it follows a harm reduction philosophy in addressing substance use. Program participants are provided with assistance in accessing a variety of medical and social services. The treatment plan may include the following: mental illness triage and referral, substance abuse assessment and treatment, appointments for HIV and other medical conditions, and referral for assistance to community programs that address basic survival needs. Project Bridge has demonstrated that it is possible to maintain HIV-positive ex-offenders in medical care through the provision of ongoing case management services following prison release (Rich et al., 2001).

Many ex-prisoners who are released from prison have medical and dental problems stemming from the lack of appropriate care within prisons. Some of them need plastic surgery to remove tattoos. Many need to gain eligibility to safety-net programs including Medicaid. Some benefit from halfway houses or other programs to help them transition to the community.

Consumers who have been released from mental institutions also need help in transitioning to their communities.

Case advocates can:

- Identify possible unaddressed dental, medical, or other needs of released prisoners, as well as consumers who transition from mental institutions to the community.
- Refer them to special programs, halfway houses, counseling, and vocational services that may be helpful to them.
- Locate advocacy programs that might help them.

Scenario 11.12: Advocacy to Enhance Consumers' Social Networks

Increasing attention is now being given to consumers' social networks, which can include relatives, friends, neighbors, fellow employees, and schoolmates. Promising research implicates family members and members from social networks in causing or sustaining consumers' obesity, substance abuse, failure to engage in safe sex, depression, and other health conditions (Christakis & Fowler, 2007; Gould, Wallenstein, & Kleinman, 1987; Phillips & Carstensen, 1986). Considerable research indicates that isolated consumers who lack social networks have enhanced health risks, such as some single males, as well as elderly consumers (Cornwell & Waite, 2009). Some home-bound disabled consumers spend most of their time watching television with little contact with others.

Many problems confront researchers when analyzing social networks. It is difficult to decide who to include or to exclude from analysis. Some research suggests, for example, that women's social networks prevent disease and even extend their lives, but include not only persons in their communities but persons who live at great distance and who they infrequently see. Some research connects the size of social networks with positive health benefits, but other researchers contend that some social networks can be harmful, such as when they contain abusive or hostile persons (Hoch & Hemmons, 1987). Consumers who lack substantial networks may be unable to establish and sustain friendships, so they cannot easily increase their networks. Some healthcare consumers may not want to divulge health information to other people, making it difficult to convince others to help them contend with them.

Case advocates can:

- Empower isolated consumers, such as elderly persons, to join day treatment programs or to transition to assisted living or congregate living arrangements.
- Organize a meeting of family members and relatives to discuss how they can help a consumer cope with a health condition and to address sources of stress and conflict within a consumer's social network.
- Link a consumer to a community resource skilled in working with consumers' social networks.
- Link some consumers to occupational and vocational therapists and programs that will help them obtain employment.
- Link some consumers to volunteer roles.
- Empower consumers to discuss how they can develop supportive networks.

Scenario 11.13: Advocacy to Link Consumers to Dental Care

An unfortunate chasm often exists between traditional medical care and dental care in the health sciences. Health professionals who observe that specific consumers cannot chew their food, have extensive tooth decay, or complain of pain from their teeth probably need dental care.

Low-income persons are particularly unlikely to have sufficient dental care. If about 40% of families with incomes at or below $21,200 per family of four lacked dental care in 2008, only a fourth of people earning four times the poverty level lacked dental care (Felland, Lauer, & Cunningham, 2008). Other research demonstrates that persons with mental disability have higher rates of poor dental care and have more periodontal disease than the general population (Department of Health and Human Services, 2000). Persons with disabilities have higher numbers of cavities. About 27% of adults with cerebral palsy, 14% with spinal cord injuries, 30% with head injuries, and 17% of deaf persons have dental problems (Arnett, 1994). The Obama Plan did not expand dental coverage, unless it is included in required insurance coverage in 2014.

Advocates can:

- Gain knowledge of dental clinics that provide care for consumers who lack coverage and cannot afford it.
- Empower consumers to seek dental care.
- Help home-bound consumers find dental resources that can help them in their homes.

MOVING FROM CASE ADVOCACY TO POLICY ADVOCACY

As an exercise, discuss how health staff can move from case advocacy to policy advocacy when confronting the scenarios in this chapter. Select any of the scenarios discussed in this chapter and identify how health staff might seek changes in policies within specific units of a clinic, hospital, or health plan; within specific communities; by specific funders of health services; or in public policies at local, state, or federal levels.

ONLINE MATERIALS RELEVANT TO THIS CHAPTER

We have provided 13 scenarios in this book that include:

Scenario 11.1 Advocacy for Consumers Needing Community Referrals

Scenario 11.2 Advocacy to Help Consumers Make Transitions

Scenario 11.3 Advocacy to Help Consumers Obtain Home Health Services

Scenario 11.4 Advocacy for Students

Scenario 11.5 Advocacy to Help Consumers Become Less Dependent on the Health System

Scenario 11.6 Advocacy to Help Consumers Obtain Community-Based Preventive Services

Scenario 11.7 Advocacy for Low-Income Consumers

Scenario 11.8 Advocacy to Enhance Community-Based Care With Technology

Scenario 11.9 Advocacy to Improve Consumers' Work Environments

Scenario 11.10 Advocacy to Give Consumers Public Health Interventions

Scenario 11.11 Advocacy to Help Institutionalized or Incarcerated Consumers Transition to the Community

Scenario 11.12 Advocacy to Enhance Consumers' Social Networks

Scenario 11.13 Advocacy to Link Consumers to Dental Care

We provide two additional scenarios in online materials that accompany this chapter that can be accessed at the web site of John Wiley & Sons at www.wiley.com/go/jansson. They are:

Scenario 11.14 Advocacy to Help Consumers Find Case Managers, Multi-Professional Teams and Care Managers

Scenario 11.15 Advocacy to Help Consumers Obtain Integrated Services

SUMMARY

I have identified 15 case-advocacy scenarios (both in this book and online) where health professionals and consumers engage in advocacy to obtain community-based care, as well as two scenarios in online materials for this chapter. I have discussed barriers to factors that promote community-based healthcare. Healthcare professionals need to move healthcare from inside the walls of clinics and hospitals into communities where consumers live.

A Framework for Policy Advocacy by Healthcare Professionals

U p to this point, case advocacy has been the focus, but I will now shift direction and discuss how healthcare professionals can engage in policy advocacy. The policy-advocacy framework presented in this chapter identifies specific tasks, skills, and strategies needed by policy advocates. Like case advocacy, policy advocacy is a practice intervention that requires tasks, skills, and strategy (Jansson, 2011). If case advocacy aims to "help specific consumers obtain services and rights that would (likely) not otherwise be given to them and that would advance their personal well-being," policy advocacy "develops interventions to change protocols, budgets, procedures, regulations, missions, organizational culture, and statutes that guide health services in specific settings and jurisdictions." Both of these practice interventions require their practitioners to undertake specific tasks and use specific skills. I present a policy advocacy framework in this chapter that complements the case advocacy framework that is discussed in Chapters 3 and 4.

THE IMPORTANCE OF POLICY ADVOCACY

Although case advocacy helps consumers one-by-one, it does not address systemic factors that often lead consumers to need case advocacy in the first instance. Assume, for example, that a hospital or clinic fails to deliver culturally competent care to members of an ethnic group that comprise more than 10% of their clientele. Also assume that significant numbers of these ethnic consumers have limited English proficiency (LEP). Assume, as well, that healthcare professionals must repeatedly seek translation services for members of this group because the hospital or clinic has hired no personnel from this ethnic group and has failed to make translation services available to its members. Healthcare professionals in this hospital or clinic should ask whether this problem stems from:

- Specific administrative, budget, personnel, and staff training decisions, policies, and regulations in the clinic or hospital—or some combination of them.
- Defective government policies in their state, such as failure of their states to help health organizations fund translation services, whether they are provided in person, by telephone, or by video conferencing.
- Failure of Medicare and Medicaid to fund translation services, as well as staff-recruitment and staff training to promote culturally competent care.
- Failure of private insurance companies to reimburse clinics and hospitals for translation services as well as other culturally competent services.
- An absence of community-based programs, such as support groups for specific ethnic groups, to give consumers information and skills to navigate the health system when they have limited English proficiency (LEP).

Scenarios discussed in Chapters 5 through 11 can help healthcare professionals to move from case advocacy to policy advocacy by identifying when consumers' needs and wishes are not met. Take, for example, Scenario 7.2 in Chapter 7 that discusses when specific consumers need translation services. Assume that your health organization does not provide adequate translation services for LEPs as required by federal law, Joint Commission accreditation standards, and many state laws. Healthcare professionals could engage in policy advocacy to identify and reform policies, procedures, staff training, organizational culture, or other factors within their health organizations that lead to this result. They could work to increase subsidies to their hospitals or clinics from Medicare or Medicaid to offset the cost of translation services. They could work with community-based agencies to provide educational services about healthcare to LEPs. They could seek reimbursement from private insurance companies for translation services.

Healthcare professionals can use any of the scenarios discussed in this book to identify dysfunctional policies in organizational, community, and government settings. They can identify, as well, new scenarios that are not discussed in this book. Assume, for example, that President Barack Obama had not issued a federal executive order in mid-April 2010 to require hospitals receiving Medicare and Medicaid funds to allow gay partners of specific patients to visit them when they were hospitalized. Assume that healthcare professionals worked in a hospital where visitation rights were not given to these gay partners on grounds they were not legally married to hospitalized partners or related to them by family lineage. They could have initiated policy advocacy within their institutions or in government settings to secure rules or laws to correct this situation.

If case advocates often deal with errors, omissions, poor ethical reasoning, hostility, narrow mind-sets, incompetent staff, and prejudice of specific health staff as they help consumers, policy advocates address five systemic factors that can spur policy advocacy (see Figure 12.1).

I have already discussed four of these systemic factors with respect to securing culturally competent services for LEPs. Do not ignore, however, societal inequalities

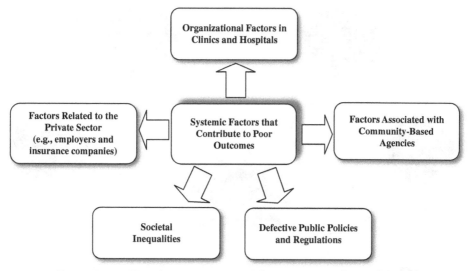

Figure 12.1   Five Systemic Factors That Require Policy Advocacy

because they powerfully shape health access, services, and outcomes in the United States. Persons in poverty suffer greater illness and have shorter life expectancies than relatively affluent persons (Kawachi, Daniels, & Robinson, 2005), as do African Americans and Native Americans (Satcher et al., 2005), and persons with only high school education or less (Kawachi, Daniels, & Robinson, 2005). Persons with disabilities possess less income than other people, including ones with schizophrenia (Newcomer & Hennekens, 2007) and diabetes (Kleinfeld, 2006).

Healthcare professionals need to be cognizant of social inequalities and try to decrease them because of their potent effects on health outcomes as is discussed in Chapter 11.

A POLICY ADVOCACY FRAMEWORK

Policy advocates encounter eight challenges when they launch policy advocacy interventions in organizational, community, and legislative settings. See Figure 12.2, which combines some features from two existing ones (Dorfman, Sorenson, & Wallack, 2009; Jansson, 2011). They decide whether to proceed with policy advocacy in a specific situation (challenge 1), determine where to focus, in other words, what policy they wish to change and in what location (challenge 2), secure decision makers' attention, (challenge 3), develop a base of support (challenge 4), develop a proposal (challenge 5), secure the enactment or approval of the proposal (challenge 6), secure implementation (challenge 7), and assess or evaluate the implemented policy (challenge 8).

Policy advocates use the same four skills as case advocates when they engage in these eight tasks, but they use them for different purposes. They use value-clarifying skills to help them determine whether to proceed with policy advocacy and develop a principled

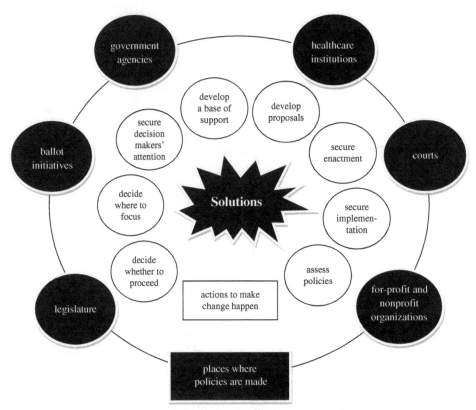

Figure 12.2   Policy Advocacy Framework

intervention. They use influence-using skills to develop and use influence resources effectively. They use analytic skills to develop strategy and policy proposals. They use interactional skills to communicate effectively; develop task groups and coalitions; enlist allies; and manage conflict.

Challenge 1: Deciding Whether to Proceed

Policy advocates initiate a policy-advocacy intervention when they decide that an existing policy is flawed. It may be ethically flawed, whether because it violates ethical first-order principles or because it leads to adverse outcomes for consumers as is discussed in Chapter 5. It may be incongruent with evidence-based practices as is discussed in Chapters 6 through 11. Policy advocates sometimes initiate policy advocacy to advance the well-being of their organizations, such as preserving revenues essential to their operations as well as consumers' needs, such as opposing cuts in a state's Medicaid program.

Advocates often consider practical factors. They may gauge the relative difficulty of changing a specific policy, sometimes deciding that it is futile to change a policy that is supported by powerful persons and interests even when they believe the policy is flawed. Their decisions may be influenced by their perceptions of the relative ease of locating allies. They may estimate how long it might take to change a specific policy.

When deciding whether to proceed with policy advocacy, policy advocates use value-clarifying skills to determine whether and to what extent they are ethically obliged to engage in policy advocacy. They need to beware of rationalizations for *not* engaging in it, such as finding excuses that distract them from engaging in policy advocacy when it is important to consumers' well-being.

Challenge 2: Deciding Where to Focus

Policy advocates have to decide where to focus their work in the complex medical system. Assume, for example, that a case advocate discovers that many diabetic Latinos did not receive preventive services in a particular clinic or hospital even when they were diagnosed in a timely manner. She has to decide whether to develop prevention programs in a specific clinic or hospital, develop prevention programs in schools, liaison with public health authorities to develop outreach services to the Latino community, or seek enhancements of her state's Medicaid program to allow it to fund preventive programs for diabetics. Or she might focus on a combination of these settings.

Once she has prioritized one or more settings, she decides what policies, procedures, budget items, or other policies that she wants to change within those settings. Would enhanced preventive services to early-stage diabetics best be enhanced, she might wonder, by convincing her managed-care plan to allocate more funds to them, hiring public health staff with expertise in health education and lifestyle modification, or hiring outreach workers who would visit the homes of Latinos diagnosed with early-stage diabetes—or a combination of these policies?

Challenge 3: Securing Decision Makers' Attention

Policy advocates must often obtain the attention of decision makers if they wish to be effective, such as supervisors, mid-level managers, specific physicians, or high-level administrators in clinic or hospital settings; directors of community-based agencies; elected officials in legislative settings; civil servants or political appointees in government agencies; or elected public officials.

These decision makers sometimes serve as "policy entrepreneurs" in advocating for a specific policy reform (Jansson, 2011). They may help to give it a title that is appealing to others. They may couple or link it with another policy or program such as a program geared to preventing obesity among Latinos who have recently moved from normal-weight to early-stage obesity levels. They may negotiate and bargain with clinic program and budget officials to see if they can find resources and office space for the new program. They may assemble other sponsors and supporters of the program from within the clinic and from the surrounding community—or within a legislature in the case of proposed legislation. They may seek key endorsements, such as from the

American Diabetes Association or public agencies that would implement or oversee a proposed policy.

Policy advocates sometimes persevere even when they discover opposition to specific policy reforms, such as by taking an "outside-in" approach where they exert pressure on one or more decision makers. Perhaps they gain the attention of one or more advocacy groups that places external pressure on decision makers in organizational or legislative settings, such as the American Diabetes Association, which pressured principals and superintendents of public schools to provide on-site medical care for diabetic children in many states.

Policy advocates work closely with decision makers in framing policy proposals so that they attract support. Imagine, for example, how less appealing the preschool program known as Head Start would have been to many legislators had it been called "Kindergarten for Low-Income Children"—or had Medicare been called "the Medical Program for Retirees." New initiatives need to be presented in ways that appeal to top managers, boards of directors, and funders in organizational settings.

Policy advocates sometimes rely on advocacy groups to sponsor and run with an issue, such as the National Association of Social Workers, the American Nursing Association, the American Public Health Association, the American Diabetes Association, the American Cancer Association, or many other interest groups in the health field. (Each of these groups has national associations located in or near Washington, DC, as well as state chapters.) They have lobbyists, researchers, media officials, and others with skills and experience in advocating for legislation and regulations in legislatures and government agencies. Some unions assume important roles in securing policy reforms or in blocking proposals.

Policy advocates use their communication skills to persuade specific decision makers, legislators, or advocacy groups to assume leadership with respect to a specific issue. They use organizing skills to develop coalitions. They use influence-using skills to assess the feasibility of getting support for a specific policy initiative and to assess the likelihood and power of potential opponents.

Challenge 4: Developing a Base of Support

Policy advocates develop a base of support as they seek policy changes such as several people or a network of staff in a specific organization; a community-based coalition; lobbyists from one or more advocacy groups; or a group of legislators.

The base of support can change through time. It may grow in size. It may meet more frequently. It may change its leadership. It may engage in fund raising. Policy advocates decide how heterogeneous to make their base of support and help to find its leaders. Effective leaders are not only committed to their cause, but can listen to different points of view, enlist new members, develop and implement effective strategy, make mid-course corrections, and compromise when necessary.

Table 12.1　Using Policy Analysis to Develop Policy Proposals

Option	Consumer Satisfaction (0.3)	Cost per Consumer (0.3)	Service Effectiveness (0.4)	Total Score
1. Make next-day appointments in outpatient clinics	3.0 0.9	8.0 2.4	7.0 2.8	6.1
2. Add primary care capabilities to the ER	8.0 2.4	6.0 1.8	8.0 3.2	7.4
3. Establish out-patient clinic, 24/7, next to the ER	8.0 2.4	7.0 2.1	10.0 4.0	8.5

Challenge 5: Developing Proposals

Policy advocates develop proposals to reform specific policies. They sometimes use a policy-analysis matrix (Francoeur, 1983). Assume that policy advocates in a managed-care system develop a proposal to divert consumers with nonurgent problems from their ERs. Not only will this strategy save resources, they believe, but give these consumers more effective services for their nonurgent problems (see Table 12.1). They develop three policy options: (1) make next-day appointments for most nonurgent consumers in outpatient clinics; (2) add primary-care capabilities to the ER so that most nonurgent consumers can be treated without long delays in the ER; and (3) establish a 24/7 outpatient clinic next to the ER that is widely advertised to the managed-care plan's clientele as, "The place you go if you think you need rapid care, but don't have a full-fledged emergency." They identify criteria to evaluate the options, including consumer satisfaction, cost, and the effectiveness of services in addressing consumers' problems. They rank the relative importance or weight of each criterion from 0.1 to 0.9 with the proviso that the weights for the three criteria add up to 1.0. They give the highest weight to service effectiveness (0.4), while giving client satisfaction and cost weights of 0.3 as can be seen at the top of Table 12.1. They rank each option from 1 (lowest score) to 10 (highest score) in the upper left-hand corner of each cell in the table, such as giving option 1 rankings of 3, 8, and 7 respectively on the three criteria. They multiply these scores in the upper side of each cell by the weight of the criterion at the top of the column to obtain an overall rating of each option in the lower side of each of its three cells—and then sum these scores across the rows to reach total scores for each option. The third option received the highest overall score when its scores of 2.4, 2.1, and 4.0 are summed for a total score of 8.5 compared to only 6.1 and 7.4 for the first two options.

Policy analysis relies on step-by-step reasoning to develop policy proposals. It is not a panacea because policy advocates can differ about the selection of criteria and options, as well as how to rank the options. A chief financial officer (CFO) of this hospital might, for example, have given greater weight—say 0.5 instead of 0.3—to the cost criterion.

Options that receive the highest score are not always the ones that are selected because they are not politically feasible or are difficult to implement. Assume, for example, that the administrator of ERs in this health plan was adamantly opposed to developing a 24/7 primary-care clinic because she believed that they would decrease the ER's revenues.

Policy advocates do not have to use policy matrices like the one in Table 12.1 to develop policy proposals. Proposals sometimes emerge from the deliberations of several persons or a group. They may emerge from brainstorming by a group. They may emerge from observing innovations in other health settings.

Policy advocates present their proposals to decision makers in organizational, community, or government settings. They use communication skills to present them in ways that will build support for them.

Challenge 6: Securing the Approval or Enactment of the Proposal

Policy advocates have to develop effective strategy if they wish to secure policy reforms. They have to establish policy goals, hone their proposal, establish a style, and select and use influence resources.

Developing Policy Goals

Policy advocates have to decide whether they want incremental change or basic change. They often have to downsize a proposal in the give-and-take of the political process. Policy advocates sometimes decide they want basic (or major) policy changes even if they encounter substantial opposition. They often develop fall-back strategies if they cannot obtain fundamental changes.

Honing Their Proposal

Policy advocates often develop an initial proposal, but have to fine-tune it as they proceed. When asked to identify his most difficult challenge, a top aide to President Bill Clinton said that he and the President constantly had to decide when to hold fast to specific policy proposals and when to accept compromises in them in the push-and-pull of the political process.

Developing a Style

Policy advocates sometimes use high-conflict strategy that may include emotion-laden language and use of the mass media. They may use low-conflict strategy that emphasizes the technical details of their proposals and shared goals. They select a style that they believe will be most effective in a specific situation. They may change their style as deliberations proceed. Stylistic options include:

- Focusing on technical details versus underlying principles.
- Inviting substantive changes in the proposal versus resisting changes.

- Expanding the number of persons who participate versus limiting participation.
- Seeking rapid resolution versus encouraging an extended process.

Selecting and Using Influence Resources

I discussed the nature of influence in Chapter 4, where 20 resources were identified, including:

- Networking
- Use of influence in interpersonal exchanges
- Using ethical arguments
- Using medical culture
- Employing power dependency
- Taking initiative and responsibility
- Developing a positive track record
- Using process skills
- Managing conflict
- Using intermediaries
- Bypassing specific professionals
- Navigating regulations
- Gaining entrée
- Interpreting a professional role
- Appropriate assertiveness
- Designing communication strategy
- Using group skills
- Citing collective self-interest
- Using peer pressure
- Using influence resources in tandem and sequentially

If case advocates use these sources of influence to help consumers obtain services and benefits that they need, policy advocates use them to obtain policy reforms in organizational, community, governmental, and legislative settings.

Implementing and Assessing Their Strategy

Even wise strategy choices are undermined, however, if advocates do not implement them skillfully. They need to be flexible, such as revising their strategies as events change.

Challenge 7: Secure Implementation of a Policy Reform

Enacted policies sometimes come to naught because they are not implemented at all, such as when they fail to receive needed budgetary resources, or are poorly implemented,

Vignette 12.1 Revising Strategy: The Case of Policy Advocacy by President Barack Obama

President Barack Obama knew that he would encounter headwinds when he decided to initiate healthcare reform during the first year of his presidency. He knew, for example, that presidents Harry Truman, Richard Nixon, Jimmy Carter, and Bill Clinton had failed to achieve ambitious proposals to overhaul the American health system. Many of his top aides, including Rahm Emanuel, had lived through Clinton's failed attempt in 1994 when he failed to get reforms through both houses of Congress. Obama and his staff decided to let the Congress develop its own national health plan, but sharply revised his strategy at a strategic moment. The Senate and the House had each enacted their version of health reform, but the chances of its enactment by the Congress plunged in the wake of the election of Republican Scott Brown to the Senate to the seat that had been held by Democratic Senator Ted Kennedy before his death. Brown's election meant that Democrats lost the ability to muster a two-thirds vote to overcome a likely Republican filibuster in the Senate, which would defeat Democratic legislation. Working in tandem with Democratic House Speaker Nancy Pelosi, the President and his staff orchestrated a strategy that included House passage of the more conservative Senate version of health reform, as well as Senate passage of a so-called Reconciliation Bill that included some provisions favored by the House. (The Reconciliation Bill only require a majority vote in the Senate to be enacted.)

Learning Exercise

- Would this legislation have been enacted had the President, as well as Nancy Pelosi, not shifted their strategies?
- What groups within the proreform coalition objected to this change in strategy?

---

such as when executives and staff are not committed to them (Berwick, 2003). Assume, for example, that healthcare professionals in a specific hospital succeeded in getting approval of the use of so-called checklists in its ICUs that prescribed specific steps to be used by physicians before and as they launched specific surgical and other medical interventions—as supported by evidence-based research that documented that checklists could save tens of thousands of lives (Gawande, 2010a). They discovered to their chagrin that many physicians did not implement this new protocol, whether because they were still committed to older practices, viewed checklists as infringing on their autonomy, believed they lacked the time to implement them, or lacked sufficient support or direction from top administrators and senior physicians. As Berwick (2003) contends, many innovations are not implemented in medical settings, even when they have been approved.

Policy advocates use their analytic skills to identify factors that prevent implementation of new policies. They use their influence-using skills to identify those staff and administrators who are likely to support and oppose them, as well as ones who may be undecided but could be persuaded to be supporters. They use interactional skills to frame innovations in ways that make it appealing to health staff.

Challenge 8: Assessing Implemented Policies

Policy innovations have to be evaluated to ascertain if they improve consumers' well-being (effectiveness) and if they achieve these gains at acceptable costs (cost-effectiveness) as is discussed in Chapter 6, preferably with gold-standard research that uses experimental designs. Rigorous evaluations are often not conducted, however. They take considerable expertise to conduct, as well as considerable resources—and their findings may not emerge for several years.

Improvising When Engaging in the Eight Tasks

Policy advocates rarely engage in the eight policy-advocacy tasks in a sequential process. They may bypass a task. They may engage in a task only to return to it at a later point. They improvise as events change.

SURMOUNTING FATALISM, CONTROVERSY, AND VESTED INTERESTS

Healthcare professionals have to surmount fatalism, controversy, and vested interests to become effective policy advocates in organizations, communities, and government settings.

Fatalism

Excessive fatalism impedes involvement in policy advocacy by undercutting a sense that it is even possible. Fatalists sometimes believe that they confront an intractable power structure such as the credentials, status, and power of many physicians and administrators in health settings (MacNeilage & Adams, 1982). They can be intimidated, as well, by their lack of access to decision-making bodies in health settings, such as physicians' committees and some top administrative committees, as well as governing boards that are discussed in Chapter 4. Fatalism can be fed, as well, by hierarchical arrangements in many health institutions extending from senior physicians and administrators down to janitorial staff. Social workers, OT/PT staff, and speech language pathologists may be intimidated by use of the term, "ancillary staff" to describe them. Nurses are often viewed as implementers of physicians' orders.

Fatalism is sometimes fostered, too, by status differentials linked to economic realities. Clinics and hospitals can only operate in the U.S. health system if they attract sufficient numbers of paying consumers that they can fund their physical structures, equipment, administrative staff, overhead costs, marketing costs, and other staff. These resources mostly derive from those physicians who bring or attract consumers to clinics and hospitals that fund part or most of their own care from reimbursements from private insurance companies, public programs, and employers' contributions to managed-care plans—as well as consumers' or out-of-pocket payments. Physicians' economic power contributes to their status. Many social workers and nurses are funded from their institutions' central budgets even if some of them can bill some insurance companies and public programs for their services.

Fatalism can be accentuated by personal experiences of frontline staff. Some medical staff does not respond favorably to them when they view them as intruding on their work such as offering medical advice to consumers, questioning medical decisions, or prompting consumers to ask questions about their work. They realize that some physicians do not understand what they do, sometimes viewing them as primarily performing specific tasks required by regulations and funders such as discharge planning and implementing physicians' treatments.

Frontline staff has to surmount fatalism not only when providing case- and policy advocacy. They have to initiate suggestions, ideas, and proposals in ways that will attract the support of influential administrators and physicians. They have to enlist support from others through creative strategy. They will not take any of these actions, however, if they succumb to fatalism.

They possess considerable influence resources stemming from their sheer numbers, as well as the logistical, counseling, case advocacy, public relations, and other services they provide.

They possess knowledge about family and personal dynamics, community factors, economic factors, mental distress, cultural factors, family violence, ethical issues, and substance abuse that is required to help many healthcare consumers who confront the 118 scenarios discussed in this book.

As constituents of elected officials in local, state, and federal governments, healthcare professionals possess considerable power in government settings because of their sheer numbers, as well as the power of the professional associations and trade unions that represent them in state capitols and in Washington, D.C.

The Controversial Nature of Some Health Policies

Health policies are often controversial because they bind or commit providers, consumers, healthcare professionals, interest groups, administrators, insurance companies, unions, politicians and others to specific courses of action that they may, or may not, like or desire.

Ideology often shapes the policy preferences of participants. Conservatives often want to minimize the role of the federal government, the level of taxes and spending, and regulations, but want to maximize free markets, roles of state and local governments, and use of private savings to fund healthcare. Liberals often want relatively large roles for the federal government and relatively robust regulations, place less emphasis on free markets, and are less likely to seek cuts in taxes and spending. Republicans, corporate officials, and the American Medical Association (AMA) have traditionally favored relatively conservative positions as compared to relatively liberal positions of Democrats and relatively liberal professional associations like the American Public Health Association, the American Nurse Association, and the National Association of Social Workers.

Ideology powerfully shaped perspectives of public officials toward the Patient Protection and Affordable Care Act of 2010 (Stolberg, 2009). If Democrats favored legislation that would cover 32 million uninsured persons, Republican Representative John Boehner supported a proposal that would extend coverage only to 3 million uninsured persons. If Democrats favored a plan that greatly increased roles of the federal government, Republicans supported tax incentives to allow uninsured persons to develop medical savings accounts. Ideology does not always predict who will support specific policy proposals, however. Conservative politicians sometimes support relatively liberal policies because they believe many of their constituents favor them. So-called "blue dog Democrats" often oppose increased government spending.

Traditions

Traditions often influence how persons and interests respond to specific policy proposals as illustrated by an aversion to European- or Canadian-style universal coverage on grounds that it is not compatible with U.S. traditions. Electoral interests often shape the policy preferences of specific public officials and administrators as their constituencies include relatively liberal, moderate, or conservative voters.

Vested Interests

Healthcare professionals may sometimes be deterred from participating in policy advocacy because they believe that decisions are driven by the clout of special interests, such as pharmaceutical companies, medical-device companies, private insurance companies, and trade associations of managed-care plans and other health plans—as well as the American Medical Association (Steinbrook, 2008). Special interests have often blocked national policy reforms. The AMA blocked enactment of national health insurance in the Truman Administration—and rallied opposition to health reforms proposed by presidents Nixon and Clinton. Pharmaceutical companies and private insurance companies funded televised advertisements against Clinton's proposed health legislation in 1994 that assumed a pivotal role in defeating it.

It should be remembered, however, that many of these groups came to support the Patient Protection and Affordable Care Act of 2010. Their support was sometimes contingent, however, on key concessions given to them, such as agreements by pharmaceutical companies, physicians, and hospitals to decrease revenues coming to them from the Act in coming years.

POLICY ADVOCACY IN FOUR SETTINGS

Policy advocates work in organizational, community, government, and electoral settings. They have to adapt their strategy to the unique requirements of each of these settings. Policy advocacy in organizational and community settings is discussed in Chapter 13, while Chapter 14 focuses on policy advocacy in communities, government, and electoral settings.

Using Policy Advocacy to Embed Advocacy in Healthcare Organizations

THIS CHAPTER IS COAUTHORED WITH ERICA LIZANO, MSW, MPA, AND DOCTORAL CANDIDATE AT THE SCHOOL OF SOCIAL WORK OF THE UNIVERSITY OF SOUTHERN CALIFORNIA

Policy advocacy in organizational settings is discussed in general terms in the early part of this chapter before illustrating it with ways that healthcare professionals can use it to embed advocacy in their healthcare organizations. We provide some examples of hospitals and health plans where advocacy is viewed as a professional responsibility. We discuss how advocates address the eight policy-advocacy challenges identified in Figure 12.2 when seeking reforms within specific clinics and hospitals. (Policy advocacy in community, electoral, and government settings are discussed in Chapter 14.)

WHAT ADVOCATES SEEK TO CHANGE IN HEALTH ORGANIZATIONS

Policy advocates can change many kinds of policies and procedures in health organizations. They can write or change protocols, which are written statements that require or recommend that health staff follow specific procedures when confronting specific situations whether in specific units or departments or at the level of the organization itself. Many of them are discussed in Chapters 5 through 11, including the recommendations of the Joint Commission; and regulations established by city, county, state, and federal authorities. Some protocols are established by health staff in specific units or departments or committees, such as a rule that social workers should participate in end-of-life discussions.

Policy advocates can try to change organizational culture so that it supports specific activities, such as case- and policy advocacy, involvement of several kinds of professionals in ethical deliberations, and use of a biopsychosocial framework when helping consumers whose health problems have mental health, familial, and economic components.

Policy advocates can change budgetary priorities in specific clinics and hospitals. Do specific organizations hire, for example, sufficient numbers of frontline staff to complete specific tasks? Are preventive programs sufficiently funded as compared to curative ones? Does staff receive sufficient training in cultural competence?

Policy advocates can participate in the strategic planning process in health organizations to develop specific directions to guide the future activities of their institutions. Their strategic plan might, for example, seek greater linkages with the communities where their clientele reside.

Policy advocates can try to change personnel policies to enable the staff of health facilities and plans to engage in specific activities. They might want to include case advocacy, for example, in job descriptions of their health organizations.

Policy advocates can increase professional training to enhance healthcare professionals' knowledge, for example, of any of the seven problems of consumers discussed in this book, as well as to give them skills to engage in advocacy.

They can propose changes in the design of their programs, such as placing a 24/7 primary clinic in close proximity to the ER to enhance services to consumers needing outpatient care.

Policy advocates can propose or change policies relevant to the collection and use of data. A specific health organization might want to gather additional data about mental-health needs of some of their clientele through new screening instruments or make better use of screening information that it already collects. We argue in this chapter that health organizations should gather data to determine the extent their clientele possess the seven consumer problems we discuss throughout this book so that they can devise strategies to address them.

Policy advocates can propose additional program monitoring to ascertain if specific policies are implemented, such as informing terminally ill consumers of the hospice or palliative-care option as required by the Joint Commission and federal law.

Some Strategy Options in Organizational Settings

Healthcare professionals undertake the eight tasks when they engage in policy advocacy in organizational settings (see Figure 12.2). They decide whether to proceed (challenge #1) in light of the importance of the issue, the feasibility of getting support for change, and time commitments that may be involved. They have to be aware of excessive fatalism when making this decision. They should ask themselves if they can secure support for this change from other health staff, their supervisors, and hospital administrators as well as specific physicians. They can ask if negligible or considerable resources might be needed.

Advocates decide where to focus (challenge #2) by deciding what specific policy, organizational norm, protocol, budget item, or procedure that they want to change or propose. They decide whether they want to change one or more of these entities in a specific unit of the organization or at a system level.

Policy advocates ask how to obtain decision makers' attention to this issue or problem (challenge #3). They can identify strategic goals of the clinic or hospital that their policy initiative might advance, such as improving consumers' well-being, cutting costs, averting litigation, increasing revenues, improving staff morale, and improving consumers' satisfaction with services. They can develop effective verbal and written persuasive tactics.

Advocates can develop a base of support (challenge #4) where they enlist specific frontline staff, supervisors, physicians, and administrators to participate whether as leaders or members of an action system such as a task force. They might want to draw support primarily from healthcare professionals in a specific unit or department—or to span several or more of them.

Policy advocates develop an initial proposal or concept for the policy advocacy project that discusses the rationale for the policy advocacy project, as well as suggested reforms (challenge #5). It may include a discussion section that presents alternatives that were considered as the proposal was developed to demonstrate that they have developed their proposals in a thoughtful way.

Advocates gain the approval or enactment of the proposal by developing and implementing strategy (challenge #6). They decide whether to seek incremental or major change as measured by budget resources, extent of departure from existing policies, and number of staff and consumers to be affected by it. They hone their proposal in the give-and-take of discussions with other staff, such as modifying it or considering different options. They decide how to initiate an action system, such as:

Option 1. A healthcare professional can initiate a new policy on her own in light of the considerable autonomy that is given to frontline workers. She might, for example, initiate a protocol for managing transitions of homeless persons from the hospital to the community in her own practice in the ER—with the intention of moving it to other units of the hospital at a later point in time.

Option 2. With the support of her supervisor, a healthcare professional initiates a pilot project, such as establishing referrals of suicidal consumers to a community-based agency—intending subsequently to expand the program with funding from a foundation.

Option 3. A healthcare professional decides to develop a grant proposal to a foundation or government agency for a new health program in a hospital to help children with behavioral disorders—thus developing new budget resources for it.

Option 4. A healthcare professional organizes a broad-based coalition in a health setting to make a specific policy change that is described in a document.

Option 5. A healthcare professional decides to seek multidisciplinary training about a specific issue she has seen in her work to promote evidence-based care.

Option 6. A healthcare professional establishes a task force that will use a collaborative planning style to develop a policy proposal.

Option 7. A healthcare professional informs her supervisor about a problem in existing services and persuades her to take this issue to a high-level administrator for consultation and for recommended action.

Option 8. A healthcare professional uses a staff meeting to obtain support for a specific proposal to enhance existing services.

Option 9. A healthcare professional discusses with union personnel some strategies for obtaining greater protections for personnel who engage in case advocacy.

Option 10. A healthcare professional encourages a consumer to seek specific policy changes from specific hospital administrators.

Option 11. A healthcare professional develops a proposal for initiating a new program in a clinic with her clinic—and receives support for it from high-level nurses after discussing it with her supervisor.

Option 12. A healthcare professional persuades an expert or official who is external to her health organization to consult with high-level staff in her health organization about whether it complies with existing local, state, or federal regulations.

Policy advocates develop, and work with, their base of support as they proceed with their interventions. The base of support may be small or large. It may be homogeneous or heterogeneous in its composition. It may have a single leader or rotating leaders. Its leader or leaders need to rejigger their strategies as time and events evolve. Members assume specific roles, such as researching the issue, drafting a proposal, making contact with administrators, or drafting a grant.

Unless policy advocates win quick concessions or policy changes, they persist in their efforts. They may experience setbacks. They may lose momentum only to have to regain it.

Policy advocates secure the implementation of enacted policies (challenge #7). Many policies and procedures come to naught if they are not actually implemented as is discussed in Chapters 5 through 11. Many hospitals still fail, for example, to have consumers complete advance directives, despite federal law, state laws, and Joint Commission accreditation standards that require it. A new field of "translational medicine" has emerged that focuses upon securing implementation of evidence-based practices (Berwick, 2003).

Policy advocates assess implemented policies in clinic and hospital settings (challenge #8). As we discuss subsequently in this chapter, for example, they assess the extent case advocacy cuts the cost of healthcare, improves consumers' satisfaction with services, and curtails litigation.

USING POLICY ADVOCACY TO EMBED ADVOCACY IN HEALTH ORGANIZATIONS

We discuss how healthcare professionals might work to embed advocacy in their health organizations as they address the eight challenges in the Policy Advocacy Framework in Figure 12.2. They can embed advocacy in their organizations only by engaging in policy advocacy over an extended period of time. (We will identify some health organizations and health plans where healthcare professionals have made considerable progress already.)

Challenge 1: Deciding Whether to Proceed

We have made an ethical case that health organizations should work to promote advocacy by their staff at both case- and policy advocacy levels. We have argued that consumers' seven problems will often remain unaddressed if healthcare professionals do not come to their assistance when their needs and rights are not met.

Some healthcare professionals may wonder if it is even feasible to embed advocacy in their organizations in light of possible obstacles. Exemplars suggest that they should not prematurely succumb to fatalism as is discussed in Chapter 12. The Planetree hospital model is undergirded, for example, by three fundamental principles: allowing consumers broad access to medical information; encouraging patients to be active participants in the decision-making process related to their health and medical care; and allowing patient's friends and family to actively participate in patient care (Mycek, 2007). Angelica Theirot, a native of Argentina, was admitted to a large San Francisco hospital in 1978 due to illness from a rare virus that had nearly killed her a number of times (Logan, King, Fischer-Wright, 2008). Although she was impressed by the medical technology of U.S. hospitals, she came to believe that she would have been treated more humanely had she been in the Argentinean medical care system with which she was familiar. She opened a small medical library staffed by volunteers and available to patients to empower patients by educating them about their medical conditions so that they could participate in decision making that would ultimately impact their health. When the medical library attracted the attention of the hospital's CEO who asked her to expand the model, she and some advisors developed the Planetree Model, which now exists in 112 affiliate hospitals in Canada, the United States and Europe with roughly 600,000 patient admissions, 10 million out-patient admissions, and 90,000 births annually, as well as 80,000 healthcare professionals (Logan, King, & Fischer-Wright, 2008; Planetree, 2009).

Susan Frampton, the current president of Planetree, as well as Laura Gilpin have identified some strategies to develop patient-centered culture in hospitals, by shifting hospitals from authoritarian to collaborative approaches. This culture asks all members of hospitals and clinics to become advocates, including housekeepers who some patients cite as offering them critical support during difficult times. Physicians are also asked to become patient advocates. Patients are given the tools and the knowledge necessary to learn about their medical conditions and to be able to collaborate with hospital staff in decision making, including ready access to medical information. Frontline staff and consumers educate medical staff about alternative medicine as one option for some health conditions.

The Planetree Model builds an organizational culture that makes extensive use of social supports for patients from family members and social networks. Frampton and Gilpin (2008) contend that traditional medical institutions establish arbitrary rules, such as limits on the amount of time and the precise time that patients can have visitors that emanate from the convenience of hospital staff rather than patients' needs.

They maintain that it is critical to distinguish between necessary and unnecessary standardization. Medical settings should, they argue, retain needed standardization, while shedding unnecessary standardization that reduces patient comfort, such as standards that excessively limit or disrupt consumers' eating and sleeping habits. They advocate personalizing healthcare to the extent possible, such as extending visiting hours and allowing patients to see their pets.

They support open lines of communication between staff and administrators as these rules are evaluated and changed. They support work norms that encourage staff to serve as patient advocates, as well as patients (Frampton & Gilpin, 2008). Specific interventions favored by Planetree underscore its commitment to open communication and advocacy by consumers and by staff include:

- Encouraging stakeholders to adopt and embrace a new set of values that are clearly communicated to all staff in the organization.
- Using these values to guide the development of policies by administrators in the organization.
- Requiring that individual-level advocacy by patients and their families be promoted and supported throughout the organization.
- Evaluating all policies and practices in the hospital setting from patients' perspectives.
- Educating and training staff around patient-centered care.
- Facilitating patient empowerment by making user-friendly material readily available to patients, family members, and the community.
- Facilitating more positive interactions between hospital staff, patients, and family members by adopting consumer-friendly policies (Frampton & Gilpin, 2008).

Frampton and Gilpin (2008, p. 299) make clear that the Planetree Model emphasizes not only advocacy by patients but by frontline staff. They note that:

Many hospitals support task or procedure specific training for frontline staff, but this more extensive approach to understanding of advocating for the individual patient's perspective has traditionally been viewed as an unacceptable expense. The Planetree model, however, underscores the long-term value of personalization and *encourages staff to question all hospital routines from a patient perspective, in an atmosphere of acceptance and openness to looking at things differently.* (emphasis added, p. 299)

Some evidence supports the cost-effectiveness of the Planetree Model. Charmel (2009) points to positive marketing outcomes associated with patient-centered care in a competitive medical marketplace, as well as effects in reducing adverse events, malpractice claims, and operating costs (Charmel & Frampton, 2008). Consumers want consumer-friendly care in addition to clinical excellence. They want "market differentiation" that gives them choices between different models of care—and many of them will gravitate toward models that emphasize collaborative systems of care that allow input from consumers and staff. A retrospective quasi-experimental evaluation of the Planetree Model conducted by S. Stone (2007) compares patient satisfaction, clinical outcomes, and the cost of providing care of two comparable hospital units. The patient-centered unit was associated with such positive outcomes as higher levels of patient satisfaction, improved clinical outcomes, and lower patient-care costs. Other evaluations of the Planetree Model have consistently discovered significantly higher patient satisfaction, as well as higher employee satisfaction in the workplace (Frampton & Gilpin, 2008). Planetree advocates not only evaluate its programs, but monitor them, such as through "cultural audits" to see if they adhere to its patient-centered and empowerment approach.

Geary (2003) delineates the successes, challenges, and lessons learned from the process of adopting the Planetree tenets at a large tertiary hospital in an urban setting. Banner Health's Samaritan Medical Center, a 652-bed hospital in Phoenix, Arizona, began initial efforts to adopt the Planetree Model in 1995. Visits by its administrators and managers to Planetree affiliated institutions served as a preliminary step to organizational change. The formation of the Service Excellence/Healing Environment committee and the building of a healing garden served as the nascent steps in adoption, as well as the initiation of many programs and services designed to promote a patient-centered healing environment. In addition to the healing garden, massage therapy, dog therapy, housing accommodations for relatives and loved ones, aesthetic restoration of the facilities, live music (e.g., harp and piano), and an employee-wellness program to minimize work-related stress for staff were adopted.

A challenge faced by the hospital was its setting. As a large urban medical institution, it differed greatly from the smaller medical institutions in rural areas that had more commonly utilized the Planetree Model. Physicians and staff opposed flexible visiting hours so the hospital retained a traditional visiting schedule. The hospital locked down some of its units because of its urban setting to ensure patient safety such as its ICU. Medical staff strongly opposed implementation of alternative and complimentary healing services, such as massage therapy except for staff as part of the hospital's wellness program. As staff used this low-cost massage therapy, they eventually came to see it as an adequate form of treatment for consumers.

Economic constraints posed a barrier to the renovation and aesthetic revamping of the medical facilities. Employees were encouraged and empowered to undertake restoration and enhancement efforts, such as the remodeling of nursing lounges through partnership efforts between management and staff. With an allocation of just $1,800 per lounge for all 26 nurse lounges in the hospital, the project of renewing the nursing quarters began. Unit-based Healing Environment Committees were formed to organize, decorate, and furnish nursing lounges during personal time rather than during work and were left solely in the hands of staff but with support from managers. The project successfully beautified the nursing facilities and was extended into other areas of the hospital. Banner Health's Samaritan was able to effectively adopt the Planetree Model and continues to be part of the Planetree Alliance (Banners Health's Samaritan Medical Center, 2010).

The Geisinger health system, ranked among the top 6 health systems in the United States (*U.S. News & World Report*, 2010), serves as an exemplary model of a healthcare system that holds advocacy at its core. Patient advocacy is fundamental to the Geisinger health system's stated organizational vision (Geisinger Health System, 2009). It is not merely given lip service, but is manifested in service provision, selection of staff, and the system's medical training program. It is not only encouraged among staff but is a stipulated job duty (Geisinger Health System, 2010).

Some health plans provide advocacy-training programs for healthcare professionals such as the Advocating for Clinical Excellence (ACE) Project of the City of Hope Comprehensive Cancer Center in Duarte, California. This training is given to social workers, psychologists, and spiritual care professionals working in palliative care settings in a 30-hour program of intensive training (City of Hope, 2009). Curriculum topics include advocacy and ethics, trans-disciplinary team collaboration, interprofessional communication, and strategies for systems changes.

Training programs for professionals similar to the ACE Project are found in other institutions like John's Hopkins Hospital. A Patient Advocacy Seminar is open to all healthcare professionals where the employees are taught about the patient's bill of rights, patient education, and navigation across the continuum of care, and elements of quality care (Institute for John's Hopkins Nursing, 2010). This seminar also prepares attendees to develop advocacy programs for specific consumer population groups.

Children's Hospital of Philadelphia has committed itself to promoting advocacy practice in medicine. The hospital's Community Pediatrics and Advocacy Program (CPAP) integrates community-based pediatrics and advocacy in its residency programs (Children's Hospital of Philadelphia, 2010). Advocacy training is considered to be an integral part of the residency training and is incorporated into the residents' rotations. Advocacy training for residents includes workshops, lectures, and hands-on development of advocacy programs.

Advocacy training in pediatric residency programs can be found in training hospitals across the United States. The American Academy of Pediatrics (2010) lists more than a dozen such programs at various training hospitals such as Phoenix Children's/Maricopa Medical Center, University of California San Francisco, University of Florida-Gainsville, Mount Sinai Hospital, Chicago, Carolinas Medical Center (Levine Children's Hospital), and Columbia University Medical Center.

The Mayo Clinic launched a 4-year clinical trial of the Midwest Advocacy (MAP) project to study consumer empowerment of consumers with traumatic brain injury, as well as their family members. This innovative and community-based project is a randomized clinical trial to engender self- and system-advocacy skills among consumers and their family members to allow them to advocate for themselves and their loved ones, as well as to make their communities more responsive to their needs (Mayo Clinic, 2010; U.S. National Institutes of Health, 2010).

The Denver Children's Hospital, ranked as the top children's hospital in the U.S. in 2009–2010, is known for its advocacy efforts (Showalter, 2008) that include online resources, advocacy events, and a strong advocacy network. Empowerment of patients to participate in case- and cause advocacy led to the development of the "Be a Champ for Children 365" program, which provides advocacy tools, resources, and tips for individuals who have the desire to advocate for the health and well-being of children (Children's Hospital, Denver, 2010). The program was developed out of a desire to have advocacy resources available at all times through the hospital's web site. Equipped with literature and "how-to" videos, it provides individuals with the tools necessary for case and cause advocacy. It developed a 4,000-member grassroots advocacy network comprised of parents, educators, leaders, healthcare professionals, and hospital staff, which recently persuaded the Colorado state legislature to increase funding for child immunizations and for community health outreach targeting child immunizations (Showalter, 2008). The organization has three full-time staff that organizes the network; keeps the network informed through newsletters and events, and infuses the network with resources and tools (Showalter, 2008).

Many Free Clinics around the nation invest themselves in advocacy. In Los Angeles County, for example, directors and staff of Free Clinics have made numerous trips to Sacramento and Washington, D.C., to seek policy reforms, including helping to obtain considerable resources for outpatient ambulatory clinics from the Patient Protection and Affordable Care Act of 2010.

Many more hospitals and clinics have moved toward patient-centered care and away from a "traditional, paternalistic approach to medicine" (Commonwealth Fund, 2010), including the Dana-Farber Cancer Institute in Boston, the Vanderbilt University Medical Center in Nashville, the Southcentral Foundation in Anchorage, and the Lucile Packard Children's Hospital at Stanford University. The Agency for Healthcare Research and Quality (AHRQ) and the Centers for Medicare and Medicaid Services (CMS) are creating a Hospital Consumer Assessment of Healthcare Providers and Systems survey that will provide data in 2010 about patient-provider communication.

These many examples suggest, then, that healthcare professionals *can* secure policies, procedures, and organizational culture that promote advocacy interventions at both case-advocacy and policy-advocacy levels. This is not a comprehensive list, but one that suggests that considerable progress has been made by health plans, hospitals, and clinics toward embedding advocacy within their mission, job descriptions, and organizational practices.

Challenge 2: Deciding Where to Focus

Healthcare professionals have several options. They can focus on changing the culture and practices of specific work units or programs within their health organizations to place greater emphasis on advocacy. They can simultaneously seek policy changes at higher levels, such as by discussing ways to encourage case- and policy advocacy with top administrators and physicians in their health organizations. They can brainstorm reforms of organizational policies that might increase the use of advocacy.

Challenge 3: Securing Decision Makers' Attention

Advocacy cannot become embedded in health organizations without support from top administrators. To obtain their support, advocates need to make a case that case advocacy serves the needs and wishes of consumers while also advancing organizational goals. They face several obstacles in securing their attention: lack of data about the extent consumers experience the seven problems in specific health settings, as well as lack of data about the extent frontline and other healthcare professionals currently engage in case- and policy advocacy.

Lack of Data About Consumers' Seven Problems

Clinics and hospitals collect substantial information about consumers' health histories and problems at intake and during their health transactions—information likely to markedly increase with increased use of electronic medical records. Clinics and hospitals collect considerable data about consumers' diagnoses and tests, surgeries, lengths of stay, medications, and discharge destinations. They collect information about client satisfaction as required by accreditation teams as well as Medicare and Medicaid.

Most of clinics and hospitals *do not* collect information, however, about most or any of the seven problems that consumers often confront as discussed in Chapters 5 through 11 of this book—whether from consumers themselves or from the frontline staff who help them. Health administrators and professional staff do not know to what extent, for example, consumers in their institutions experience the 118 scenarios discussed in Chapters 5 through 11 in this book. They do not know which of these scenarios negatively impact the healthcare of their clientele. Health professionals in most clinics and hospitals do not know, for example, how many consumers do not receive:

- Second opinions for complex medical procedures as currently recommended by many health experts.
- Specific kinds of primary preventive services.
- Services that slow the progress of an array of chronic diseases.
- Health insurance, Medicaid, or SCHIP to which they are eligible.
- Information about end-of-life options when they have been given a terminal diagnosis.
- Follow-up care for serious mental disorders.
- Adequate translation services.

Data could be collected by surveys about consumers' seven problems in specific settings, much as considerable information is already obtained at intake or as they exit a hospital. It can be collected from surveys of healthcare professionals who can report the frequency they have observed consumers to have unresolved problems as defined by the various scenarios discussed in this book. They can be asked if they provided case advocacy to consumers with these problems, particularly ones who they believed could be harmed if they did not receive it as is discussed in Chapter 3. They can indicate which scenarios cannot be resolved to consumers' satisfactions to enhance planning to improve outcomes.

This information could be collected from samples of consumers rather than from all of them to provide an estimate of the prevalence of problems and case advocacy in specific settings. It can be used to identify problems in current programs and services and to devise strategies for reaching some consumers with case advocacy services.

Lack of Data About How Often Healthcare Professionals Currently Engage in Advocacy

Data is not usually available in healthcare organizations about the extent that their healthcare professionals engage in case- or policy advocacy. Existing health literature is not helpful because health researchers have not studied the extent that healthcare professionals provide these interventions.

The paucity of information about case advocacy extends to professional research aside from a few studies in Canada, as well as research by Epstein (1981), Jansson and Dodd (2002), and Dodd and Jansson (2004). Herbert and Levin (1996) analyzed advocacy practice among frontline social workers in 96 Canadian hospitals. They measured the relative amount of time dedicated to five work-related tasks traditionally carried out by frontline hospital social workers, including assessment, counseling, locating and arranging resources, consultation and collaboration, and advocacy. They discovered that although staff members expressed an interest in providing client advocacy, they gave it less time than the other tasks. More than two-thirds of the social workers either ranked advocacy as the task allotted the least amount of time or did not rank it at all. Nelson (1999) had similar findings in a study of social workers in 19 hospitals. They attributed their lack of case advocacy to the pressure to meet other work-related responsibilities.

If the preceding studies provide quantifiable measures of time devoted to case advocacy, Gosselin-Acomb, Schneider, Clough, and Veenstra (2007) measured nurses' reports of the relative frequency of case advocacy in their work. Forty-three percent of 142 nurses recruited from the Oncology Nursing Society reported frequently engaging in case advocacy—a remarkably high number that suggests that case advocacy is integral to their work.

In his exploratory study of self-identified social work advocates, Epstein (1981) discovered a high level of commitment to advocacy by frontline social workers. He found that more than two-thirds of 105 of them spent 50% or more of their work hours on advocacy-related tasks. Almost two-thirds of the social work advocates reported spending time outside of the workplace engaged in advocacy efforts. Epstein's study (1981) points to the role of one's position in an organization and case advocacy practice since two thirds (64%) of the advocates were in direct service provision positions and only 34% were in management positions. The nonprobability sampling utilized in Epstein's (1981) study limits generalizability of the study's findings through the author's own admission. Nevertheless, his study and those previously cited suggest that case advocacy is widely practiced in human service and health settings, including by nurses and social workers.

The need to collect data is made more urgent by speculation by many experts and researchers that case advocacy often does not take place in hospitals and clinics even when consumers possess serious problems. Considerable literature suggests that many physicians do not invite or encourage social workers' or nurses' participation in ethical deliberations even though many of these decisions require knowledge of patients and their families and caregivers (Csikai, 1997; Reckling, 1997; S. Roberts, 2004). Waz and Henkind (1995) found that most pediatric residents believed they could not participate in physicians' ethical decisions. Social workers were more likely to defer to physicians' authority according to Walden, Wolock, and Demone (1990) than to supervisors' and administrators' authority in nonmedical settings. Although nurses have long subscribed to the caring approach to patient care, which emphasizes the inclusion of consumers and their surrogates in ethical deliberations, they often are not included in ethical deliberations (McCurdy, 1996).

Exploratory research demonstrates that it is feasible to collect data from frontline staff about specific scenarios confronted by consumers in hospitals. Dodd, Jansson, Brown-Saltzman, Shirk, and Wunch (2004) defined case advocacy used to help consumers resolve ethical issues as "ethical assertiveness," which they defined as "actions to enter or facilitate ethics deliberations in which social workers or nurses have not been included, whether through personal initiative, coaching of patients, advocating patients' wishes to others, or ethical case finding." They gathered data from 162 hospital social workers from 37 hospitals in Los Angeles County, as well as from 165 nurses from three major hospitals in Los Angeles for a total of 327 health staff. They developed a questionnaire that identified 28 ethical issues experienced by patients and medical staff from the literature and from interviews with nurses and social workers—and were asked to

Table 13.1   Extent Nurses and Social Workers Reported They Were Aware of, Became Involved in, and Wanted Greater Participation in Ethical Deliberations

	Aware	Involved	Want More Involvement
Discussing advance directives	1,343	1,095	142
Providing heroic treatment to terminally ill patients	1,239	742	149
Premature discharge	1,010	784	148
Inadequate discharge destination	679	633	150
Determining incompetent	828	554	135
Increasing pain medication	1,591	1,134	166
Not providing treatment for poor prognosis patients	654	427	137
Informed consent for treatment	811	487	138
Providing treatment for poor prognosis patients	617	374	133
Appointing a guardian	438	289	99
Forgoing ventilation	444	291	108
Withholding treatment from terminally ill patients	503	303	110
Withholding information due to family pressure	504	313	143
Self determination vs. patient self-interest	573	437	131
Honoring advance directives	456	313	133
Rationing healthcare	437	259	107
Breaching confidentiality	308	189	90
Reporting professional incompetence	560	335	130
Organ donation	327	221	108
Decreasing pain medication	654	404	125
Forgoing artificial nutrition	314	223	96
Referrals to specialists	333	237	109
Informed consent for research	478	251	112
Staff performing tasks beyond their expertise	336	201	88
Pressure to accept home care	322	199	102
Forgoing artificial hydration	267	185	101
Ignoring advance directives	183	104	98
Pain medication that may lead to death	369	260	91

indicate whether they were aware of ethical deliberations involving their patients with respect to each of these issues during the past two months. Collected responses reveal that these frontline staff often see ethical deliberations among their patients (see column 1 in Table 13.1), including many of them that are discussed in Chapter 5. They were most likely to report that they were aware of ethical deliberations among their patients about discussing advance directives, whether to provide heroic treatment to terminally ill persons, whether to increase pain medication, and discharges that they believed to be premature. They were least likely to report they were aware of ethical deliberations among their patients about whether to ignore advance directives, forego artificial hydration, pressure persons to accept home care, and forego artificial nutrition. These 327 frontline staff were surrounded by ethical issues, reporting that they observed 16,582 ethical deliberations during the past two months.

These researchers also asked respondents to indicate the number of ethical deliberations that they had personally joined with respect to these 28 ethical scenarios during the past two months (see column 2 in Table 13.1). Data suggest that they had often been involved in these ethical deliberations particularly with respect as to whether to increase pain medication, discuss advance directives, provide heroic treatment to terminally ill patients, and avert premature discharge. They were least likely to participate in ethical deliberations about whether to ignore advance directives, what to do about staff performing tasks beyond their expertise, ethical issues regarding organ donation, and whether patients should forego artificial hydration. Here, too, these frontline staff appeared to engage in ethical deliberations frequently—a total of 11,244 ethical deliberations during the past two months. They participated in 68% of the 16,582 ethical deliberations that they had observed.

This descriptive data underscores the sheer extent of professional involvement in ethical issues by frontline staff. It conflicts with the assertion by some researchers and theorists that frontline staff lacks the time to engage in it—or that they do not participate in it due to other obstacles, such as fear of reprisals.

The researchers also asked respondents to indicate whether they believed they *should* have been involved in even more ethical deliberations with respect to each of the 28 ethical scenarios (see column 3 in Table 13.1). Many of them answered "yes," particularly with respect to advance directives, providing heroic treatment to terminally ill patients, preventing premature discharge, preventing inadequate discharge destinations, determining the competence of specific patients, increasing pain medication, not providing treatment for patients with poor prognosis, providing informed consent to patients, reporting professional incompetence, honoring advance directives, withholding information from patients due to family pressure, and decreasing pain medication. We can reasonably assume that respondents who answered "yes" regretted *not* participating in ethical deliberations because they believed that consumers would have benefited from it. Hard-pressed frontline staff wants, in other words, to engage in ethical deliberations even more than currently.

The data from this research strengthens the likelihood that frontline workers also engage in interventions to help consumers with the other six problems discussed in this book including how to help consumers obtain quality services, culturally competent services, preventive services, help in financing their healthcare, assistance with mental health or substance abuse problems, and assistance in obtaining community-based care. Further research is needed, however, to confirm this possibility.

Jansson and Dodd (2002, 2004) also asked frontline staff to respond to three questions that probed the extent they engage in case advocacy with respect to ethical issues, using a scale extending from 1 (never), 2 (occasionally), 3 (sometimes), 4 (often), 5,

Table 13.2   Questions Probing Extent of Case Advocacy Regarding Consumers' Ethical Issues By % Choosing Specific Answers

	1	2	3	4	5	6
1. Extent they coach patients about questions to ask physicians regarding ethical choices or dilemmas						
A. SOCIAL WORKERS	15.6	24.5	27.2	13.6	11.6	7.5
B. NURSES	21	23	17	17	13	9
2. Extent they advocate patients' wishes with physicians ethical issues or dilemmas						
A. SOCIAL WORKERS	29.8	26.5	23.2	13.2	7.3	0
B. NURSES	10	16	19	23	14	19
3. Extent they call ethical issues to the attention of physicians, i.e., act as ethical case finders						
A. SOCIAL WORKERS	18.5	19.2	21.9	21.9	15.9	2.6
B. NURSES	19	22	19	19	10	10

frequently, to 6 (always): the extent they coach patients about questions to ask physicians regarding ethical choices or dilemmas, advocate patients' wishes with physicians regarding ethical issues, and call ethical issues to the attention of physicians, in other words, act as ethical case finders. As can be seen in Table 13.2, many of them selected "always," "frequently," and "often" to each of the three measures of case advocacy. Sixty-seven percent of the social workers and 61% of nurses chose these three responses with respect to coaching patients to ask physician about ethical issues or dilemma. Eighty percent of social workers chose these three response and 45% of nurses selected these responses to characterize the extent they advocate patients' wishes with physicians regarding ethical issues or dilemmas. Sixty percent of social workers and 60% of nurses chose these responses to characterize the extent they call ethical issues to the attention of physicians, that is, act as case finders. In other words, solid majorities of social workers and nurses chose relatively high ratings of their case advocacy with regard to these three questions—leaving only minorities of them choosing "never," "occasionally," and "sometimes" to them.

Even less information exists about the extent healthcare professionals engage in policy advocacy within their organizations or in the external world. Jansson and Dodd (2002, 2004) also collected data from their sample of nurses and social workers about the extent they engaged in policy advocacy within their organizations to increase staff participation in ethical decision making. Respondents were asked to rate the extent they engaged in four activities on a 6-point scale extending from "never" to "always": seeking written protocols to promote social work (or nurse) participation in ethical deliberations in their settings, seeking multidisciplinary training sessions in ethics that include social

Table 13.3 Social Workers and Nurses Involvement in Policy Advocacy to Create Policies and Practices to Enhance Involvement in Ethical Deliberations

	Never	Occasionally	Sometimes	Often	Frequently	Always
Extent respondents seek written protocols to promote social work (or nurse) participation in ethical deliberations in specific settings						
Social Workers	83 (55%)	24 (16%)	14 (9%)	13 (8%)	9 (6%)	7 (5%)
Nurses	85 (56%)	30 (20%)	18 (12%)	10 (7%)	7 (5%)	2 (1%)
Extent respondents seek multidisciplinary training sessions in ethics that include social workers (or nurses)						
Social Workers	63 (42%)	34 (23%)	18 (12%)	16 (11%)	9 (6%)	10 (7%)
Nurses	75 (49%)	35 (23%)	20 (13%)	13 (9%)	5 (3%)	4 (3%)
Extent respondents promote norms that encourage social work (or nurse) participation in multidisciplinary ethical deliberations						
Social Workers	35 (23%)	33 (22%)	13 (9%)	27 (18%)	14 (19%)	29 (19%)
Nurses	57 (38%)	37 (25%)	23 (16%)	16 (11%)	10 (7%)	5 (3%)
Extent respondents educate physicians about social work (or nurse) roles in ethics						
Social Workers	29 (19%)	40 (27%)	27 (18%)	19 (13%)	16 (11%)	20 (13%)
Nurses	80 (53%)	38 (25%)	14 (9%)	10 (7%)	4 (3%)	5 (3%)

workers (or nurses), promoting norms that encourage social work (or nurse) participation in multidisciplinary ethical deliberations, and educating physicians about social work (or nurse) roles in ethics.

As can be seen in Table 13.3, considerable numbers of social workers and nurses *do* engage in policy advocacy in their organizations to make them more supportive of their inclusion in ethical deliberations about consumers. Many social workers responded "sometimes," "often," "frequently," or "always" to the four questions— or 29%, 35%, 55%, and 54% respectively indicating considerable involvement in policy advocacy. (Nurses reported considerably less involvement in policy advocacy, but 25%, 28%, 37%, and 22% of them still reported "sometimes" or more frequently to these four questions.) These data are important because they suggest that it is feasible for frontline staff to be policy advocates, even if there is data for only one of the seven problems discussed in Chapters 5 through 11.

These data also suggest, however, that many social workers and nurses do not engage in policy advocacy to obtain policies likely to increase their participation in ethical deliberations. A considerable number of them indicated they "never" or only "occasionally" engaged in each of the four types of policy advocacy, such as 71% with respect to seeking written protocols, 65% with respect to seeking multidisciplinary training sessions in ethics that included social workers, 45% with respect to promoting norms to encourage social work participation in multidisciplinary ethical deliberations, and 46% with respect to educating physicians about social work roles in ethics (see Table 13.3).

Considerably larger numbers of nurses reported no or only occasional involvement, such as 76% with respect to seeking written protocols and 75% with respect to educating physicians with respect to social work roles in ethics.

These data are important because they suggest that many frontline staff work to create a culture and environment that encourages their participation in ethical deliberations. We can hypothesize that many of them may also seek institutional reforms, changes in organization culture, and multidisciplinary training with respect to the six consumer problems discussed in Chapters 6 through 11.

Lack of Research About the Extent Advocacy Addresses Health Organizations' Needs

Risk managers and administrators should obtain data to analyze whether and to what extent the timely and effective provision of case advocacy provides secondary gains for their institutions and health plans. We can hypothesize that case advocacy sometimes cuts the cost of healthcare by preventing some problems or situations that could later require expensive healthcare. Some data suggests, for example, that receipt of second opinions cuts health costs by leading some consumers not to obtain unnecessary diagnostic tests, medications, surgeries, or other medical procedures (Kronz, Westra, & Epstein, 1999). Consumers who enroll in hospice or palliative care sometimes do not obtain costly heroic and futile medical care (Vermeire, Hearnshaw, Van Royen, & Denekens, 2001). Consumers who receive certain kinds of preventive care often avoid or delay the emergence of serious health conditions (P. Stone et al., 2000). Consumers who enroll in Medicaid, SCHIP, SSI, and SSDI may not need uncompensated care and may bring additional revenues into health systems. Case advocates that increase adherence to treatments recommended by their physicians may slow the progression of, or cure, illnesses that would otherwise be costly to treat. All case-advocacy interventions do not bring cost savings, so research is needed to identify ones that produce these secondary outcomes. We have cited research that advocacy helps increase client satisfaction and cuts costs in some Planetree-affiliated hospitals.

We can hypothesize, as well, that some case-advocacy interventions increase consumers' satisfaction with services, which, in turn, could decrease disenrollments as well as lead to some of their acquaintances to enroll in a health plan or to use a health facility or program. Satisfied consumers are more likely than other consumers to adhere to treatments and to decrease the time required by risk managers and others to handle consumers' complaints.

Case advocacy may increase consumer satisfaction in two ways. Many consumers may appreciate efforts of frontline staff to empower them to engage specific issues or problems even before they arise or become serious, such as by referring them to a web site or support- or advocacy group. This assistance would likely be viewed as consumer-friendly because it demonstrates that health staff cares about them, while also empowering them. Consumers' satisfaction may be enhanced when they receive help that allows them to address or resolve important problems or issues that they currently confront. Assume, for example, that a consumer is discontented with the quality of services she receives when she is recovering from a hysterectomy as a result of uterine cancer. She may view a case-advocacy intervention, even a simple one, from a frontline staff member positively (see Vignette 13.1).

Vignette 13.1 An Appreciated Intervention by a Social Worker

A Caucasian woman in her late sixties was hospitalized after having a hysterectomy for early-state uterine cancer. She viewed most of the care that she received in the hospital as substandard. Tubes in her wrist were linked to a bedside stand, so she could use the bathroom in the semi-private room only if she was assisted by a nurse or orderly, but none of them offered this help so she had to urinate in a container. The registry nurse bungled the placing of a tube in her wrist so badly that extensive bleeding took place—and another nurse who later viewed this injury could not believe that a nurse had inserted it so ineptly. The nurse did not remove from her wrist a tube that was no longer needed. She frequently commented to the woman that she found her work to be onerous. She did not know how to operate the drip line on the bedside stand that gave the patient nutrients and medications, requiring frequent visits from other nurses to help her. When the patient became flushed, causing her to perspire and to have mild tremors, none of the staff knew what to do nor did they summon help from others. Another nurse placed medication for diabetes before her even though she was not diabetic after she had mistaken her for another patient. One aide stated to another aide that "the patient threw the towel on the floor" when, in fact, the woman had dropped it and was unable to reach it.

In the middle of her stay, a social worker entered the room and asked if she needed help. When viewing the woman's perspiration and tremors, she offered to place a cold towel on her head and to bring ice chips. She helped move her bedside stand so that she could use the bathroom. She helped her wash her face.

This case advocacy greatly improved the woman's morale, even if it did not change her view that she had received substandard care in a hospital that widely advertised itself as consumer-friendly—a view she presented to a Medicare surveyor who asked her if she had been satisfied with her care at this hospital.

Learning Exercise

- How does this case illustrate how case advocacy can serve the interests of hospitals as well as consumers?
- How could this case have led to institutional reforms?

Staff at the Consumer Reports National Research Center conducted a survey of 731 nurses who cared directly for patients in ERs, critical-care units, operations rooms, and other areas of the hospital—and surveyed 13,540 readers about their own or a family member's hospital stay during the previous year. The nurses were far more critical of services than patients, citing the following problems: lack of coordinated care (38% versus 13%), and hospital cleanliness (28% versus 4%). Nurses were then asked to indicate steps they would recommend to patients to help them get better hospital care. Fifty-two percent of them recommended that a consumer should work "closely with health advocate, social worker, or case manager to coordinate care." In other words, staff nurses in the trenches of hospitals made this recommendation as their lead suggestion for receiving quality healthcare, tied only with "checking to ensure that staff routinely washes hands before treatment." Unfortunately, however, the survey of readers found that only 12% of patients took this step (Consumer Reports National Research Center, *Consumer Reports*, September 2009, pp. 18–19).

Embedding advocacy in health organizations may also increase the morale of healthcare professionals. Some frontline staff may experience considerable guilt or remorse for not engaging in case advocacy more frequently or in specific situations, particularly in health organizations that do not support or value it. The ethical code of nurses, social workers, OT/PT staff, and speech pathologists, as well as residents and senior physicians, requires them to promote the well-being of consumers. Social workers' Code of Ethics states, for example, that they "should advocate for living conditions conducive to the fulfillment of basic human needs and should promote social, economic, political, and cultural values and institutions that are compatible with the realization of social justice." Ones that do not engage in case advocacy may experience postdecisional regret when they believe their failure to act may have been inimical to a person's well-being.

We can hypothesize that case advocacy decreases litigation in some cases, as well as formal complaints from consumers to hospital risk managers or to administrators of health plans. When consumers believe that healthcare professionals are concerned about them, they may be less likely to litigate against them as has been discovered when health providers admit errors (Delbanco & Bell, 2007). Case advocates bring possible issues or problems into the open rather than allowing them to fester and take positive steps to empower consumers to address them or partner with them or take action themselves when consumers are unable to do so.

Case advocacy may help some clinics and hospitals receive higher evaluations from accrediting officials by alerting other staff to violations of statutory and regulatory requirements. The federal Patient Self-Determination Act of 1990, Medicare and Medicaid regulations, and some state regulations require hospital staff, for example, to provide patients with advance directives when they are admitted to their hospitals and to discuss these directives with them. If this policy is not honored by specific hospitals and if staff fails to record in medical records that they followed it with specific consumers, hospitals can be cited by accreditation teams—an outcome possibly less likely had case advocates brought this omission to the attention of medical staff and hospital administrators. Case advocates who intervene to prevent ER staff from prematurely discharging nonstabilized homeless persons may help their hospitals not only to protect consumers' well-beings, but to avert negative publicity that has sometimes been given to specific hospitals.

Case advocacy may help discover dishonest or unethical professionals who work in their facilities. Some professionals practice even when they have been cited for poor performance in prior jobs and even had criminal records, sometimes in other states. Some professionals abuse substances with adverse consequences for their on-job effectiveness. Some professionals have conflicts of interest that lead them to refer consumers to institutions and services in which they have a fiduciary interest. Some physicians fail to give some consumers needed services in order to curb costs in their managed-care plans (Levey & Hill, 1988).

Proceeding With Available Information

With even the information presented in this book, healthcare professionals can make an initial case that their organizations should consider embedding advocacy in them. They can argue:

- Some leading health organizations have already made progress toward this outcome.
- Considerable research suggests the strong likelihood that many of their clientele experience the seven problems discussed throughout this book.
- Exploratory research strongly suggests that frontline staff engages in case advocacy extensively with respect to ethical issues even if data does not exist from a cross-section of U.S. clinics and hospitals with respect to extent of their case advocacy.
- Some data from surveys of nurses, as well as from several hospitals, suggests that case advocacy addresses some organizational goals like reducing costs, reducing litigation, and increasing client satisfaction—even though far more data needs to be collected.

Healthcare professionals who wish to embed advocacy in their organizations can make an initial and strong case to decision makers to initiate policies and procedures to advance it.

Challenge 4: Developing a Base of Support

Healthcare professionals who want to embed advocacy in their health organizations encounter a challenge in gaining the support of their colleagues, particularly in those health organizations that do not currently value it or who even discourage it.

How Support for Advocacy Is Strongly Linked to Organizational Culture

The extent that healthcare professionals provide case advocacy is shaped by subtle and direct cues from their organizational setting. It is a relatively public intervention because case advocates come to the defense of specific consumers who have experienced errors of commission and omission in their healthcare. They move beyond their comfort zone as they empower consumers to self-advocate, partner with them, or help them directly when they cannot advocate for themselves. They sometimes cross professional and hierarchical boundaries, such as when frontline nurses and social workers advocate for consumers with hospital administrators or physicians. Even when it is done tactfully, case advocacy can elevate conflict between professionals and between consumers and professionals. Case advocacy sometimes exposes fault lines in health settings, such as tensions between members of different professions, between residents and senior physicians, or between health staff and administrators. It can incite defensive behaviors by persons who believe they are criticized by consumers or case advocates.

We can hypothesize, then, that healthcare professionals' propensities to engage in case advocacy—both generally and in specific situations—is shaped by contextual factors, such as organizational culture, professional culture, institutional arrangements, views and skills of frontline staff, personal relationships, and characteristics of specific consumers. Any one of these can cause healthcare professionals to refrain from providing case advocacy in specific situations. We hypothesize that these and other factors sometimes cumulatively influence the extent and nature of case advocacy of frontline staff as well as healthcare professionals in general.

Dodd and Jansson (2002, 2004) discovered strong relationships between the organizational context and the extent nurses and social workers engaged in case advocacy with respect to patients' ethical issues in hospitals. They developed several scales to measure setting receptivity to case advocacy among hospitals' healthcare professionals. One of them (MD Collaboration) asked frontline staff to indicate the extent that physicians informed them when they were aware of specific ethical issues or dilemmas; asked them to gather information from family members, friends, or significant others; and asked them confidentially to discuss ethical dilemmas with them. They asked respondents to indicate the extent that they received a mandate from their hospital to participate in ethical deliberations (Mandate) by asking them questions to probe the extent that they were encouraged to become involved in ethical issues, to participate as co-equals in ethical deliberations with members of other disciplines; to be involved in a range of ethical issues; to be involved in ongoing discussions of ethical issues after being initially consulted; to have their views solicited by an ethics committee; to be considered an integral member of ethics deliberations; and to be encouraged to make referrals to an ethics committee when they encounter difficult ethical issues. They asked frontline staff to rank the extent that ethical dilemmas were discussed by multiprofessional teams and the extent that multiprofessional training sessions had been developed on ethical reasoning (Collegiality). They asked frontline staff to rank the extent that an atmosphere existed in their hospitals that allowed them to question the resolution of ethical issues or dilemmas and the extent sufficient time was devoted to discussion of ethical issues with patients (Climate).

The likelihood that frontline staff participated in case advocacy in ethics was powerfully linked to respondents' scores on *each* of these scales for both social workers and nurses ($p = 0.0001$). These findings strongly suggest that hospital administrators and physicians must give positive encouragement and feedback to frontline staff if they are to participate extensively in case advocacy.

These same organizational variables were strongly associated, as well, with the propensity of social workers and nurses to engage in policy advocacy as reflected by their responses to questions in Table 13.3, such as the extent that they had sought multidisciplinary training sessions in ethics or protocols that promote their participation in ethical deliberations.

When building support for embedding advocacy in health organizations, then, healthcare professionals encounter a dilemma. They are more likely to gain support for it among those healthcare professionals that work in organizations that already provide a supportive environment for it—and least likely to gain support for it in settings that do not support advocacy at case- or policy-advocacy levels. They have to surmount fatalism in ones that do not provide a supportive environment.

Developing Coalitions of Supportive Professionals

Healthcare professionals need support from their supervisors and department directors to engage in advocacy because of their vulnerability to adverse repercussions from engaging in it in some settings. They need their help in developing strategy in specific situations. They need their informed advice about how to proceed. They need their backup support in those situations where they might or do confront hostility from other healthcare professionals or administrators.

Support for advocacy needs to span different professions in healthcare organizations, including frontline staff, residents, and physicians.

Engaging Leadership

High-level leadership is needed to move healthcare organizations toward advocacy. High-level leaders have to view it as not only helping consumers, but advancing organizational goals like cutting costs, reducing litigation, increasing consumer satisfaction, increasing staff morale, and enhancing accreditation and legal requirements.

Challenges 5 and 6: Developing Proposals and Securing Enactment

We combine Challenges 5 and 6 because they are often linked. Healthcare professionals can consider nine strategies for embedding advocacy in health organizations. These strategies include disaggregating perceptions; obtaining support of physicians; using scenarios, gaining support from supervisors; solving logistical problems; making case advocacy more feasible for frontline staff; developing support systems for advocates; phasing case advocacy into place; and obtaining high-level protections.

Disaggregating Perceptions

Healthcare professionals can and should analyze their host institutions to ascertain to what extent they provide a supportive context for case advocacy. They may need to be more deliberate about providing it in nonsupportive settings than supportive ones.

At the same time, however, all health institutions are ultimately comprised of an array of professionals, as well as other staff. Even in supportive settings, healthcare professionals encounter specific professionals who are relatively supportive or unsupportive of case advocacy.

It is useful to view case advocacy as a series of one-on-one encounters, whether they empower consumers to self-advocate or partner with them or provide case advocacy through their own interventions. They must convince physicians and administrators that case advocacy is needed for some consumers by demonstrating to them that it advances their well-being and provides secondary benefits to specific health organizations. They have to do this even in health settings that they believe are relatively supportive of advocacy such as one that ascribes to the Planetree Model. They do not have to transform the culture of the entire institution to make progress to embedding advocacy in their organizations, but can begin by making specific professionals with whom they work more receptive to it. This may give them more confidence to proceed to more ambitious reforms even in unsupportive environments.

Using Scenarios

Specific scenarios, such as the ones discussed in Chapters 5 through 11, may be useful in securing the support of those supervisors who do not see the need for case advocacy. They describe concrete situations rather than abstract ideology. They pose tangible questions about consumers' well-being. They promote discussion of evidence-based findings and ethical considerations that are relevant to specific scenarios. They require supervisors and frontline staff alike to ask:

- Is this consumer seriously endangered if she doesn't receive case advocacy and why might this be the case?
- How do we develop an effective case-advocacy intervention under the specific circumstances that frontline staff and consumers encounter?

Producing Data for Administrators and Health Staff

Healthcare professionals and their supervisors should document their work in ways that are understandable to them. They could be informed, for example, how many consumers in specific time periods were directed to Internet sites; helped to gain eligibility to Medicaid and SCHIP; referred to a community-based agency; helped to obtain services for a mental health or substance abuse condition; given copies of the institution's publication on consumers' ethical rights; referred to a multiprofessional team; given an advance directive as well as discussion about it; and referred to the risk manager. These are reportable case-advocacy events. They can be linked to possible positive outcomes for the hospital or health plan, such as cutting costs, increasing revenue, improving quality outcomes, increasing client satisfaction, helping the hospital meet its legal and regulatory obligations; and helping the institution meet specific accreditation standards.

Considerable data exists about the prevalence of the seven problems discussed in this book in the general population, such as the numbers of consumers who have become medically bankrupted, the consumers who are not given evidence-based interventions for asthma, and the numbers of children who do not receive any dental care. Although this information is useful and can sometimes be used to estimate how prevalent specific problems are in specific health plans, it is more abstract than information collected from consumers that use specific clinics, hospitals, or health plans. Were a managed-care plan to discover, for example, that half of asthmatic children under its care did not receive evidence-based care, its risk managers, compliance officers, high-level physicians, and administrators would probably be more likely to take ameliorative action than if they learned that half of asthmatic children do not receive this care in a national sample of children.

Data collected from frontline staff could also help to embed case advocacy in specific institutions, whether their perceptions of the extent that consumers' possess the seven problems, the extent that they engage in case advocacy with respect to these problems, and the extent that they wish to engage in greater case advocacy. Data could identify obstacles to case advocacy, as well as factors that promote its use.

Data should relate to the purpose of the organization, such as analyzing if best practices are followed in it, including practices required by accreditation standards; by state or federal regulations; and by evidence-based research. It should analyze the extent that some consumers do not reimburse the organization because staff does not bill for services, such as in a psych setting, that are covered by insurances or public programs.

The gathering of data is not a panacea, but could alert health providers to consumers' problems; promote discourse about how best to address them, including greater use of case advocacy; trigger discourse about the role of case advocacy in healthcare; and stimulate in-service training. Perhaps data could promote not only case advocacy, but policy advocacy to modify policies and regulations in health institutions, funders of healthcare, communities, legislatures, and government agencies.

Some data could be gathered from all consumers, while other data could be gathered from samples of consumers or from specific units.

Research is needed that documents outcomes of advocacy such as improved patient empowerment (Rafael, 1995) improved patient survival (Long, 2002), and healthcare cost savings (Rydholm, 1997).

Solving Logistical Problems

Some logistical problems need to be solved to promote case advocacy in health settings. Someone or some department has to be vested with a lead role in promoting it, writing it into job descriptions, monitoring it, and providing frontline and other staff with training in it. This could be an existing department such as social work. A new unit could be created to be the lead entity and given a name, such as "the patient advocacy department" to contain some staff dedicated to case advocacy.

Case-finding needs to be established as an accepted intervention for frontline staff in health settings. Social workers and nurses need to be able to talk with consumers without waiting for referrals so that they can discover when specific consumers need case-advocacy assistance.

Consumers need to be informed that they can talk with a case advocate when they have problems with their care, treatment, finances, or any other aspect of their service-seeking behavior. They need to be told that frontline staff is always willing to talk with them about their care. They should be given printed materials about the accessibility of frontline staff to them.

Internet sites should be available to consumers in clinics and hospitals in highly visible places and at many sites. They should be able to access technical support if they need it to locate information relevant to their condition.

Consumers should be told that their clinic or hospital is linked to surrounding communities and that staff are able to connect them to community agencies and programs that are relevant to their health needs.

Making Case Advocacy More Feasible for Frontline Workers

Some researchers report that nurses have cited lack of time as one of the primary reasons why case advocacy is one of the least frequently practiced work tasks (Gosselin-Acomb et al., 2007; Hanks, 2007). The nursing literature suggests that high case- and workloads, understaffing, and feelings of powerlessness in health institutions are key reasons that nurses do not provide advocacy (Boswell, Cannon, & Miller 2005).

We have discussed, as well, how many frontline staff do not receive materials about case advocacy in their professional curriculum. Lack of educational training that prepares employees to practice case advocacy is not unique to the healthcare setting. Previous studies of social work advocacy practice in the field of child welfare found that one of the primary deterrents to case-advocacy practice was a lack of knowledge or training on how to advocate (Herbert & Mould, 1992). Lack of knowledge regarding insurance-related matters such as coverage, reimbursement, and other related issues was cited as a limitation to a nurse's ability to advocate on behalf of clients facing challenges in these areas (Gosselin-Acomb et al., 2007). Among a sample of oncology nurses that were asked about the use of patient advocacy, 97% of them reported that they believed that nurses should advocate for their patients, but only 81% believed they had the appropriate skills and knowledge to do so (Herbert & Levin, 1996).

Case advocacy should become part of official job descriptions so that it is not viewed as a distraction from other official duties. Not only should it take place, but a method recording case-advocacy interventions and how they link to desired outcomes of the institution should be developed so that administrators and supervisors better understand consumers' needs.

Many healthcare professionals are unlikely to make advocacy a central part of their work unless it is part of their official duties—and unless they are given sufficient time to provide it.

Developing Support Systems for Case Advocates

Informal systems can promote case advocacy in health settings. M. Nelson contends (1999) that the likelihood that frontline employees' propensities to provide advocacy increases as they are supported and encouraged by colleagues, are connected to colleagues and peers outside of their institution, and are part of an external network of advocates outside of their institution. They should discuss case advocacy with one another including its challenges and dilemmas. They should discuss how to elevate its importance in their health organizations. They should socialize staff to their ethical and evidence-based commitments to provide it.

Phasing Case Advocacy Into Place

Chapters 3 and 4 discussed how case advocates triage consumers to locate ones with pressing unaddressed problems that could harm their well-being. Specific clinics and hospitals should identify those scenarios that may rise to this standard—and initiate training and planning to increase the likelihood that frontline staff, as well as physicians, will be attentive to them. They should also identify kinds of case advocacy that would advance goals of the institution, thus increasing the status of advocates.

Obtaining High-Level Protections

Fear of reprisal in the workplace deters use of advocacy in many healthcare settings when it is viewed as a deviation from organizational policies and culture (Hardina, 1995) or when advocates fear loss in job status (Vaartio & Leino-Kilpi, 2005).

To diminish this obstacle, hospitals, clinics, and health plans should develop clear statements that make clear that advocacy to promote the well-being of consumers is a professional duty and is a protected activity. This statement should be disseminated to all employees.

Health organizations should recognize that case- and policy advocates sometimes support causes or issues that conflict with organizational economic interests as illustrated in Vignette 13.2, including physicians (Levey & Hill, 1988) and nurses (Hanks, 2007). Professionals often have conflicts between economic imperatives, professional core values, patient needs, and loyalty to the organizations where they work (Hanks, 2007; Levey & Hill, 1988; M. Mallik, 2000; Swick, 2000).

Vignette 13.2 Conflicts of Interest in a Major Hospital

(Case is drawn from Atul Gwande, "Now What?" *New Yorker*, April 5, 2010, p. 22)

Clinicians at Children's Hospital, Boston, were concerned about the sheer number of asthma attacks among low-income youth in Boston's inner city. They developed an innovative prevention strategy that included:

- Having nurses visit parents after their children's discharge to educate them about adherence to medications and follow-up visits to their pediatricians.
- Home inspections for mold and pests.
- Provision of free vacuum cleaners to parents who lacked them.
- Funding costs of these interventions from the hospital's budget because insurance covered only the cost of a prescribed inhaler.

This strategy was so successful that hospital readmissions of these children dropped by more than 80%—and costs of treating dropped precipitously. This intervention threatened to bankrupt the hospital, however, because it had depended on revenues from public and private insurances and programs for the many beds that had been occupied by these children.

Learning Exercise

- If you worked in this hospital and wanted to be an advocate for this creative program, what conflict of interest would you confront?
- What ethical issues would you face?
- What kinds of policy advocacy might the hospital staff, its board, its community supporters, and its clientele undertake to ease this conflict?

These stated protections within health organizations would complement whistle-blowing protections in statutes of many states, as well as federal protections. If case advocates seek improvements in services, benefits, and ethical rights of consumers *within* health and other organizations, whistle-blowers inform *external* public authorities that specific providers or staff have provided inferior or dangerous services, have committed fraud, or have engaged in criminal conduct. Protections for whistle-blowers sometimes do not suffice as illustrated by the prosecution of two nurses in 2010 in Texas for "defaming" a physician when they reported alleged substandard care (Sack, 2010). Whistle-blowing statutes do not protect frontline staff, as well from unofficial reprisals in the workplace, such as threats, isolation, and ostracism; attacks on their credibility; and attacks on their emotional stability—and some have even been advised to seek psychiatric help (McDonald & Ahern, 1999). McDonald and Ahern also discovered that nurses who decided not to blow the whistle because they feared reprisals experienced high levels of stress resulting in feelings of fatigue, depression, and a depletion of energy.

Healthcare professionals also need backing from their supervisors as well as directors of their units or departments when their case advocacy incites adverse repercussions. When her nursing staff faced repercussions when they were seeking to advance consumers' well-being through their advocacy, a legendary head of nursing for a major public hospital system of healthcare defended them before the personnel board when physicians or other staff sought their dismissal or wanted them to be reprimanded. She only hired nurses who were committed to case advocacy as part of their job descriptions—and only if she believed that they valued it. She trained them to provide it.

Some consumers refrain from self-advocacy for fear that their medical care will be compromised or withdrawn by their providers. Consumers sometimes hear stories from other consumers such as: "When I complained about my physician's treatment of my shoulder pain, he entered my complaint in my medical record and other physicians in the same plan shunned me." Health plans and hospitals should issue statements that protect consumers from reprisals for registering complaints or questions about the services they receive, including claims that they made medical errors. Organizational leaders must "advocate for staff so that staff can fill the role of patient advocate" (Frampton & Gilpin, 2008, p. 309). They must make clear that well-intentioned and skilled advocacy is a professional and valued activity.

Involving High-Level Administrators

We have already discussed how high-level administrators must be integral to efforts to embed advocacy in their health organizations. Risk managers, marketing staff, personnel managers, legal staff, and finance officers need to examine the extent that advocacy advances organizational goals like cutting costs, decreasing litigation, decreasing adverse publicity, and enhancing staff morale—not to mention improving the quality of healthcare. They need to recognize that cuts in numbers of frontline staff, such as social workers and nurses, depletes their ability of their staff to provide case- and policy advocacy that could enhance these organizational goals.

Assume, for example, that a hospital has been sued for poor management of transitions of some consumers to the community. Legal staff might develop guidelines to promote improved management of transitions and ask frontline staff vested with transitions to provide case advocacy if they observe that the guidelines are not implemented in specific cases. A hospital's CFO might discover that consumers who are eligible for, but do not enroll in, Medicaid or SCHIP are likely not to pay hospital fees. She might orchestrate some training sessions not only for intake and discharge staff, but for frontline staff so they provide case advocacy to some of these uninsured consumers to help them get enrolled in these programs. A hospital's marketing staff might ask frontline staff to be on the alert for dissatisfied consumers in the wake of mediocre client-satisfaction data from Medicare enrollees that has been published online.

Healthcare professionals need to educate top administrators about their important roles in addressing these organizational goals and needs. They need to help them to see them as important allies rather than mostly a fiscal expenditure with no fiscal contributions to the organization. They need also to educate them about how they improve consumers' well-being by addressing their seven problems (see Vignette 13.3). Subject to approval from them, they might themselves launch some surveys to samples of consumers to identify how their services would have been improved. Ask them whether and to what extent the experienced the seven problems and whether they received, or would have liked to receive assistance with them.

In taking these initiatives, frontline staff makes clear to high-level administrators that they are team players who are problem solvers, not only for consumers but for health organizations.

Vignette 13.3 Not Making False Assumptions About High-Level Administrators

The CFO of a major hospital was widely perceived by frontline staff as interested only in enhancing its surpluses. She had, in fact, eliminated or pruned frontline staff. A social work director discovered, however, that she was deeply committed to finding resources for consumers who lacked any or adequate insurance. As the director and her staff successfully persuaded her to tap the hospital's charitable fund for these persons, they made some headway in educating her about how frontline staff addressed other organizational goals, such as enhancing their satisfaction with the hospital's services.

Learning Experience

- To what extent can frontline staff advance organizations' interests by addressing consumers' seven problems?
- How can they persuade top administrators that they are team players?

Challenge 7: Securing Implementation

As discussed in Chapters 5 through 11, policies come to naught if they are not implemented. Advocacy needs to be viewed as an organized activity of healthcare professionals. It needs to be monitored and supported. It requires ongoing attention from high-level administrations, supervisors, senior physicians, attending physicians, residents, and frontline staff.

Challenge 8: Assessing Policies

As we have discussed but wish to emphasize again, it is important to collect data about the extent advocacy produces positive outcomes **for consumers, health professionals, and health organizations**.

SUMMARY

We have discussed some strategies for embedding case advocacy within health organizations and empowering frontline staff, as well as other staff, to provide it. The next chapter discusses policy advocacy in community and government settings, which seeks to change systemic factors in organizations, communities, government, and legislative setting that will encourage case advocacy, as well as make case advocacy less necessary for consumers by redressing basic causes of healthcare that does not meet their needs or preserve their ethical rights.

Policy Advocacy in Community, Electoral, and Government Settings

Healthcare professionals should venture into their communities to advance the well-being of consumers through policy advocacy. They should seek reforms, as well, in government settings at local, state, and federal levels, whether through coalitions that they initiate or in liaison with advocacy groups. As they take these initiatives, they follow in the tradition of health reformers in fields of public health, social work, and nursing that go back to the nineteenth century, as well as those physicians who battled for policy reforms as we discussed in the online materials for Chapter 2.

HEALTH ADVOCACY IN COMMUNITIES

Consumers' health is profoundly influenced by communities where they reside as comparisons of relatively affluent and relatively impoverished communities reveal (Barr, 2008). Affluent residents do not have to worry about violent encounters on their streets; have relatively safe places to engage in recreation; possess "full-service" grocery stores with a wide range of products at relatively low prices; live in homes or apartments not plagued by lead paint, vermin, or crowding; and live relatively near their jobs or have access to convenient transportation. They have a modicum of economic security; they are not plagued by frequent bouts of unemployment, do not have to work multiple jobs to make ends meet; take periodic vacations; and do not have to contend with demeaning welfare agencies. Their neighborhoods are not as inundated with bars and fast-food restaurants. They are likely to have better schools than counterparts in relatively impoverished neighborhoods. They are likely to have more knowledge of health and medical issues. They are more likely to have decent health insurance—and to be less worried that they will lose it. They are far less likely to have to make difficult choices, such as whether to pay the rent on the one hand or buy food, purchase medications, or seek medical care on the other hand.

Relatively poor residents are, moreover, far more likely than affluent ones to view themselves as marginal members of society. They know affluent persons live in larger homes, do not have as much graffiti and broken windows in their neighborhoods, purchase more expensive cars, eat in better restaurants, and send their children to high-priced colleges and universities. Their perceived (and actual) marginal status degrades their sense of well-being and exposes them to greater uncertainty and fears than more affluent persons, particularly as it exists for long periods of time (Barr, 2008). Marginal status has been demonstrated to induce adverse physiological responses, such as higher stress-response hormones, elevated blood pressure, progressive damage to organs, and compromised immune systems (Barr, 2008). Considerable research implicates inequality, itself, as a predictor of disparities in health outcomes (Kawachi, Subramanian, & Almeida-Filho, 2002, with online update).

All of these factors, singly and in tandem, can influence the health of residents in these contrasting communities, mostly to the detriment of less affluent persons as is reflected in health statistics. It is reflected not only in lower life expectancies, but greater rates of chronic diseases. It manifests itself in poor lifestyle choices, such as higher rates of cigarette smoking, obesity, and lack of exercise. It results in less ability to engage in one or more activities of daily living (Barr, 2008).

Because healthcare professionals are committed by their ethical codes to advancing the health of consumers, they should engage in policy advocacy to improve the health of consumers who live under these adverse conditions.

They can seek to change health programs in specific community institutions, such as persuading schools to hire school nurses or develop education programs. They can work to establish health partnerships between different community-based agencies, such as linking schools and hospitals with community-based mental health agencies to provide care for autistic children or children with behavioral problems. They can pressure local welfare officials to expedite eligibility of low-income persons to Medicaid and SCHIP so they do not have to endure excessive paperwork and delays. They can pressure local authorities to augment resources for health and health-related programs, such as including allocations from city, county, or state budgets for specific health programs. They can pressure local authorities to modify zoning requirements to disallow or limit construction of facilities that harm health (such as fast-food establishments or bars) or promote the construction of ones that promote health (such as parks, exercise areas, health clinics, and full-service grocery stores). They can pressure city and county officials to improve public health programs, such as constructing or developing more primary-care clinics, special clinics to provide prenatal and family planning services. They can pressure city, county, state, and federal authorities to mitigate toxic chemicals whether from airborne sources or from ground sources. They can pressure local agencies to enforce laws that prevent violent trauma such as family violence, driving while intoxicated, gang violence, and excessive sales and distribution of handguns. They can support social programs that avert violence, such as after-school programs and job-training programs for youth. They can urge the development of new for-profit companies in specific communities, such as working to obtain full-service grocery stores in low-income areas or persuading a for-profit health agency to locate a rehabilitation hospital in a community lacking these services. They can seek to fill gaps in the social service network, such as persuading a mental health agency to provide services for children with autism and behavior disorders near a local school with many children with these problems.

They can pressure local and state agencies to develop and enforce public health regulations such as ones that forbid vending machines in schools that sell unhealthy products, sales of tobacco products to minors, and sale and use of dangerous illicit drugs to minors and adults such as methamphetamines. Policy advocates can help change community habits that contribute to poor health, such as failure to use condoms, poor dietary choices, and sedentary lifestyles—such as through outreach public health programs to community groups, places of worship, and places of employment. They can seek to change policies that govern access to specific agencies so that specific kinds of consumers can receive faster access to services. They might persuade a shelter for women who have experienced family violence to give higher priority to women who have been determined to be at particular risk of serious injuries.

Establishing, Partnering with, or Volunteering in Free Clinics

Free clinics exist in many low-income urban areas, such as the St. John's Well Child and Family Center in South Los Angeles. Funded by a combination of government and nonprofit public health grants with a budget of $20 million, it provides about 150,000 yearly patient visits to a low-income community where 80% of residents live in substandard housing, 54% of children tested by its clinics have excessive lead in their blood, 40% of its adult patients have diabetes, and 10% of its child patients are homeless. Inundated with liquor stores, residents lack full-service grocery stores. It offers an array of preventive programs, such as podiatrists who inspect feet of diabetics to avert amputations, dance classes, outreach workers called *promotoras* who make home visits to diagnose "everything in patients' lives that is harming their health," giving free mattress covers and lending vacuum cleaners to prevent asthma, teaching parents how to reduce rats and roaches with boric acid, pressuring landlords to cover up lead paint, giving obese patients dietary assistance, providing yoga classes to pregnant women, and finding rent-subsidized apartments for homeless people or persons living in substandard housing (go to www.scpr.org/patt-morrison/2010/02/10/st-johns-clinic-from-the-front-lines-of-health-care/).

Barriers to, and Opportunities for, Community-Based Policy Advocacy

A schism exists in many communities between public health services, such as the St. John's Well Child and Family Center, and traditional medical services with little integration, joint programs, and cross-fertilization between these two branches of medicine. Many healthcare professionals in clinics and hospitals rarely venture into the communities where at-risk consumers reside.

Most of the trillions of dollars of monies spent on health in the United States are used for traditional health services. Public health expenditures are mostly devoted, moreover, to a national network of small clinics that prevent TB, HIV/AIDS, STDs, and smoking, free clinics, and pre- and postnatal clinics—as well as to licensing of health providers, inspection of restaurants and other public facilities, and cooperation with the CDC to prevent epidemics and the spread of other infectious diseases.

Health providers might consider the following options to make themselves more relevant to the needs of their consumers:

- Expand mission statements to include commitment to working to change community factors that harm consumers' well-being.
- Pressure foundations to fund projects that establish community coalitions to engage in community-based health advocacy.
- Hire one or more community organizers to establish and work with community institutions and coalitions to establish innovative health programs.
- Conduct focus groups in specific communities to identify factors that community residents believe are harmful to their health.
- Contribute resources and volunteers to community-based free clinics.
- Develop multidisciplinary training sessions for health staff to sensitize them to economic, social, and other factors that adversely affect the health of consumers in specific neighborhoods near clinics and hospitals.
- Donate resources and staff volunteers to advocacy groups. Zavis (2010) discusses recent research by the National Committee for Responsive Philanthropy that shows that donations to advocacy groups engaged in fighting poverty, as well as improving health and education, returned $91 in benefits to local residents for every donated dollar in Los Angeles County. Clinics, hospitals, and health plans should consider making donations to these advocacy groups through donations of resources, in-kind benefits, and volunteers.

When engaging in policy advocacy, hospitals and clinics need to honor the autonomy of community-based coalitions and organizations. They should encourage community residents to take leadership roles in them, whether on their boards or as staff. They should honor priorities that are established by them.

Strategy in Community-Based Policy Advocacy

Many kinds of communities exist. Some of them are relatively heterogeneous containing an array of ethnic groups, social classes, businesses, and neighborhoods. Others are relatively homogeneous such as relatively affluent ones or ones containing primarily low-income populations. Communities have a vertical dimension that describes economic and social factors that descend on them from the outside, such as corporations, the media, and social movements. They have a horizontal dimension that describes community groups, local businesses, religious institutions, and other organizations.

Most communities possess an array of community organizations that focus on specific issues. Some of them may be long-lived while others are newer or relatively transient. They often possess coalitions and task forces.

Each community has an array of elected officials in local, state, and federal venues that provide important support to specific health programs and advocacy projects. They possess local governance bodies, such as city councils, county boards of supervisors, school boards, municipal and county departments, and task forces.

Policy advocates must be familiar with the fabric of those communities where they engage in community-based work. They can provide staff functions to community-based groups and coalitions, helping them gain members, obtain resources, obtain necessary technical information, and develop effective strategy.

They have to be versed in developing and maintaining coalitions, which are often necessary to secure policy reforms in communities. They also need skills in working with the mass media, often coaching community members in organizing press conferences, writing press releases, and talking with reporters.

If changes within health organizations are usually obtained by "working within the system" and avoiding open conflict, community-based advocates sometimes escalate conflict to draw attention to specific issues and to pressure local officials and organizations and to get coverage from the mass media. On other occasions, however, they rely on behind-the-scenes negotiations.

Health administrators can:

- Hire community-based advocates or fund them.
- Link these advocates to their healthcare professionals so that the latter can volunteer, offer expert information, or otherwise participate in community health events.

POLICY ADVOCACY IN ELECTORAL SETTINGS

Policies and regulations established by government profoundly influence the U.S health system as recently illustrated by enactment of the Patient Protection and Affordable Care Act in March, 2010. It will lead to billions of dollars of additional expenditures on community-based prevention programs, as we discussed in Chapter 8. Federal and state governments fund more than half of health services in the United States with Medicare, Medicaid, SCHIP, and tax deductions—to be augmented by tax credits, expansion of Medicare's drug benefit, and expansion of Medicaid in coming years in response to the aforementioned Act, rapid increases in health costs, and the aging of the baby-boomer generation.

Public policies and regulations are often controversial, but no one can deny their importance to the U.S. healthcare. They are fashioned by elected officials, as well as political appointees made by elected officials, such as top staff of the federal Department of Health and Human Services, NIH, and the CDC.

Public agencies and not-for-profit agencies must adhere to laws that state how and when they can participate in electoral politics, as well as propositions and initiatives placed directly on ballots. They are more restricted than employees of for-profit organizations, as well as trade unions and corporations, partly because a Supreme Court ruling in early 2010 gave corporations and trade unions even broader latitude in elections, such as by allowing them to endorse specific candidates and fund political advertisements for them. These corporations and unions can also fund advertisements and organizing of campaigns for and against specific propositions or initiatives that are placed on ballots by procedures in each state, such as by obtained signed petitions with specified minimum numbers of signatures. They may now be able to fund specific candidates and support them with advertisements. Not-for-profit agencies cannot keep their tax-exempt status if they directly engage in partisan politics—and state laws prohibit public agencies, as well, from engaging in partisan politics.

Yet not-for-profit agencies often *can* take positions on ballot-based propositions and initiatives without jeopardizing the tax-exempt status—subject to specific laws in their states. They can organize forums to discuss issues, as well as debates between candidates. They can distribute information about ballot-based initiatives. They can encourage citizens to vote. They can allow voting to occur on their premises.

Healthcare professionals can participate in and make donations to campaigns to support and oppose specific candidates and ballot-based measures as private citizens, even if they cannot engage in them as representatives of specific hospitals, clinics, or health plans.

POLICY ADVOCACY IN LEGISLATIVE AND REGULATORY SETTINGS

The policy and regulatory thicket greatly influences the nature and quality of health services in the United States as discussed in Chapters 5 through 11. Statutes established Medicare, Medicaid, the Patient Self-Determination Act, COBRA, HIPAA, and many other programs in federal, state, and local legislatures. Myriad regulations have been established by the Department of Health and Human Services at the federal level, as well as by public agencies at state and local levels of government that determine how specific programs are implemented such as thousands of pages of Medicare and Medicaid regulations. I discuss barriers and opportunities for policy advocacy in these venues and policy-advocacy strategies.

Barriers and Opportunities for Policy Advocacy in Government Settings

Health organizations often delegate policy advocacy in government associations to trade associations that represent them in state and federal capitols, as well as with city and county governments, including the American Hospital Association, the American Medical Association, the American Public Health Association, the American Nurse Association, and the National Association of Social Workers.

It is understandable that healthcare professionals often rely on their trade associations, trade unions, and professional associations to represent them in government settings in cities, counties, states, and the federal government. It is difficult for them to travel to some of these locations. They often lack the expertise to develop proposals or to lobby for them unlike trade associations, professional organizations and trade unions that usually hire lobbyists and researchers with expertise, time, and resources to be effective advocates in government settings. It takes time, expertise, and persistence to convince elected officials to support specific proposals, as well as to shepherd them through the political process.

Healthcare professionals ought not entirely to cede advocacy, however, to professional lobbyists. These lobbyists may not be aware of consumers' needs. They do not participate directly in the 118 scenarios discussed in this book. They do not experience consumers' angst as they find it difficult to access services and entitlements, as well as honoring their ethical rights.

Healthcare professionals are situated, moreover, to empower consumers to become policy advocates. Elected officials are particularly impressed when consumers make presentations to them at hearings or in delegations, not only because they are constituents, but because they speak from the heart. As one advocate recently noted in a public forum, "Politicians take note when the 'usual suspects' (advocates who they habitually see) aren't present, but community residents make presentations to them." Frontline staff can be particularly adept at finding these consumers and helping them reach elected officials in their district offices or in their offices in state capitols or Washington, D.C.

Health organizations should consider:

- Collecting information from staff about specific gaps or problems in existing statutes and regulations that they experience in their work with consumers, that is, that contribute to one or more of the seven problems discussed in Chapters 5 through 11—and forwarding these to their professional associations, as well as to specific elected officials.
- Pressuring trade associations, professional associations, and trade unions to prioritize specific policy and regulatory changes—and assign specific health staff to monitor their work on these changes to be more certain that they will prioritize them.
- Holding public meetings with elected officials and government officials that focus on specific policy and regulatory issues germane to the well-being of consumers.

- Organizing visits to local, state, and federal legislatures during nonworking hours in behalf of specific policy and regulatory changes—where they also bring consumers.
- Organizing a policy-advocacy group among health staff and consumers to monitor legislative and regulatory activities of local, state, and federal governments and to prioritize policy changes with most significance to consumers that they serve.
- Assigning credit to healthcare professionals for membership in professional associations, coalitions, and campaigns for ballot-based initiatives, as well as visits to public officials.

Strategy in Government Settings

Statutes should be distinguished from regulations because they require different strategies. Statutes are enacted by legislatures and usually signed by chief executives, such as governors and presidents, unless legislatures override their vetoes. Regulations are established by government agencies to prescribe how specific programs or policies will be implemented because the statutes that authorize programs are vague or silent on many issues. Both statutes and regulations have the force of law.

Advocates who seek statutory changes confront specific challenges. They have to fashion an initial proposal that defines what they want, often in cooperation with one or more specific legislators or their staff. They must decide if they want new legislation or want to amend existing legislation and what funding they seek. They must address technical issues in their proposals, such as legal ones, by securing consultation from legislatures or from specific sources available to them from state governments, professional associations, or trade associations.

They must produce a concise statement of their proposal, called a policy brief (deKieffer, 1997). It discusses why existing policy is insufficient or how a gap exists within it. It discusses alternative options for correcting existing policy. It describes a policy proposal.

Every policy proposal must pass a feasibility test. In an era of budget deficits in many states and in the federal government, legislators are certain to ask how much it will cost and where these resources can be found. The Congress requires that policy proposals recommend cuts in other programs to free up resources for new policies—as do many states. Legislators will want to know, too, how a policy proposal will be implemented and how snafus will be averted.

Legislators will want to know about the political feasibility of a proposal. They will want to know whether sufficient support can be mustered for it to make it a worthwhile investment of their time.

Advocates often develop a confidential strategy book where they develop an overview of their political strategy (deKieffer, 1997). It discusses how advocates will liaison with the mass media, which legislators will be contacted, who will oversee letter-writing and sending e-mail, and when they might schedule a "blitz" of the legislature where a delegation contacts an array of legislators.

They often seek an initial sponsor or sponsors at the outset, preferably elected officials with solid reputations. To secure these sponsors, they usually follow a specific protocol where they make an appointment with legislators through their appointment secretaries at least a week in advance and for no more than 15 minutes. They ask legislative assistants who are versed in the issue to be present—and brief them before the meeting. They give the legislator a one- or two-page summary of the proposal and go briefly over its central points—while also stressing how it will help them politically. They speak respectfully and do not overstate claims for the legislation. They send thank-you notes after the meeting.

They have to find additional supporters of their proposal, including relevant public agencies that possess programs and expertise related to their proposal, important interest groups, and possibly the head elected official such as a mayor, governor, or the president. They need help in writing legislation from experts affixed to legislative committees that will consider the proposal. They need help from the Chair and staff of the legislative committees to schedule hearings on the proposal relatively early in a legislative session. They need to monitor the proposal to see that it progresses through the legislative process in a timely way.

Securing enactment of proposals through legislation is not an easy process. Many unforeseen events can sidetrack a proposal, such as opposition, competition with other legislative proposals for legislators' scarce time, and budget shortfalls. Legislation requires many sequential actions in a relatively constricted time period, such as approvals of committees in both chambers, approval of a consolidated bill to the extent the two chambers pass different versions, and approval of the mayor, governor, or president. If it fails to be enacted in a specific time period, it "dies" and must be reactivated from the start in another legislative session.

Advocates can alternatively work through existing advocacy groups or professional associations if they can persuade them to give priority to their proposal from myriad proposals that come before them. They can rely on their lobbyists, while backstopping them with delegations, testimony, and consumers' participation. Vignette 14.1 in the online materials for this chapter discusses how Vivian Sarubbi, RN, sought legislation to help obtain funding to help children with a rare disease, Eosophilic Gastrointestinal Disorder. To access this vignette, go to the web site of John Wiley & Sons at www.wiley .com/go/jansson and view the materials relevant to this chapter.

ADVOCATING FOR REGULATORY CHANGES

Policy advocates can propose or amend regulations that are established by government agencies charged with administering specific statutes, such as ones governing Medicare and Medicaid programs; defining procedures for discharging homeless persons; and determining the kinds of information that can be given to law enforcement personnel.

Government regulations have the force of law so providers or professionals who fail to implement them can face fines, penalties, loss of licenses or accreditation, or even prosecution in a court of law. Legislatures delegate rule-making authority to government agencies that implement specific programs in federal, state, and local levels.

Advocates can operate on four fronts (Loue, Lloyd, & O'Shea, 2003). They can review relevant regulations that will be revised by a specific government agency, such as in the *Federal Register* or equivalent publications in specific states. Or they can approach a government agency and request it to approve a proposed regulation that addresses a specific concern. Or they can draft proposed regulations themselves and ask the government agency to consider and approve them. Or they can make comments on final rules of the government agency in the minimum specified time period required by law, such as 30 days.

This is a relatively technical process, but regulations can have considerable impact on providers and consumers. Perhaps a healthcare professional or consumer discovers that specific regulations are misdirected or harmful in a specific medical program. Or perhaps they want regulations to protect consumers' health, such as one secured by advocates from the Maryland Occupational Health and Safety Board that banned smoking in the workplace (Loue, Lloyd, & O'Shea, 2003).

ESTABLISHING A POLICY AGENDA
IN SPECIFIC HEALTH SETTINGS

The discussion of seven problems of healthcare consumers in Chapters 5 through 11 can establish a way for healthcare professionals to establish a policy agenda on which they can work. This agenda might flow from feedback from consumers about issues or problems they confront with respect to their ethical rights, securing quality care, obtaining culturally competent care, getting preventive care, financing their care, having mental problems addressed, or receiving community-based care. Any of the 118 scenarios can help advocates identify policies and procedures in organizational, community, and government settings that detract from ethical, evidence-based, and needs-addressing care of consumers. So also can new or additional scenarios that consumers, frontline staff, other healthcare professionals, or administrators identify.

Healthcare professionals can peruse the policy agendas of advocacy groups and professional associations to identify reforms that they, too, wish to support. They can examine the web site of the National Conference of State Legislatures (www.ncsl.org) that identifies policy reforms underway in different states.

Advocates should be alert, too, to issues or problems that may arise during the implementation of the Patient Protection and Affordable Care Act of 2010 as amended by Congress. This historic legislation promises to greatly ease financing problems of many consumers and to enhance preventive services. Healthcare professionals are well-situated to identify changes that will be needed in this legislation, as well as changes in regulations promulgated by the Department of Health and Human Services as it is implemented.

This Act gives extraordinary roles to the different states in implementing many of its provisions, including expansion of Medicaid, insurance exchanges, funding community clinics, and regulating insurance companies. They will have to enroll consumers in these programs. They will have to integrate Medicaid with the new exchanges. They will have to monitor insurance companies so they do not violate provisions of the Act. They will have to urge providers to participate in many demonstration programs to be funded by the Act (Stewart Altman, Kaiser Family Foundation, http://healthreform.kff.org, accessed 4/30/10).

I can anticipate, however, that many states will be remiss in implementing the Act because they have many problems of their own. Many of them have large deficits because states will have deficits totaling $375 billion from 2010 to 2012. Many states have fluid political arrangements, with 37 governorships being contested in 2010 and 2012. Top leaders in many states opposed the Patient Protection and Affordable Care Act of 2010 as amended by Congress on ideological grounds, as witnessed by lawsuits filed by many state attorney generals to block the mandate in the Act to citizens to obtain health insurance.

Advocates will need, then, to monitor the actions of officials in their states—and take action when they find them remiss in implementing this legislation. Its promise to improve healthcare will be realized only when its benefits trickle down to healthcare consumers—and this will be far more likely if healthcare professionals assume advocacy roles in coming years.

ONLINE MATERIALS RELEVANT TO THIS CHAPTER

To access Vignette 14.1 by Vivian Sarubbi, RN, BSN, PHN, "Child Advocacy in the Healthcare Maze," please go to the web site of John Wiley & Sons at www.wiley.com/go/jansson.

SUMMARY

I hope that this book will inspire healthcare professionals to add an advocacy dimension to their work at both case-advocacy and policy-advocacy levels. If so, they will join forces with legions of healthcare professionals who infuse their work with determination to help consumers receive services and rights that might otherwise have been denied them (case advocacy) and to help entire populations or groups of consumers gain new rights and services (policy advocacy). They will not be successful in some of these advocacy interventions, but they will succeed in some or many of them if they assume leadership in advancing consumers' needs.

References

AARP. (2008a). *Affordable healthcare.* Retrieved on April 20, 2010 from http://www.aarp.org/issues/dividedwefail/about_issues/divided_we_fail_platform_affordable_health_care.html

AARP. (2008b). *Big thinkers think 50+.* Retrieved on April 20, 2010 from http://www.aarpmedia.org/.

Abelson, R., & Pollack, A. (2009, January 27). Medicare widens drugs it accepts for cancer. *New York Times,* p. A1.

Abramson, L., Seligman, M., & Teasdale, J. (1978). Learned helplessness in humans: Critique and reformulation. *Journal of Abnormal Psychology, 87,* 49–74.

Adamek, M. E. (2003). Late-life depression in nursing home residents: Opportunities to prevent, educate and alleviate. In B. Berkman & L. Harootyan (Eds.), *Social work and healthcare in an aging society: Education, policy, practice and research* (pp. 15–48). New York, NY: Springer.

Adams, J., Asch, S. M., DeCristofaro, A., Hicks, J., Keesey, J., Kerr, E. A., & McGlynn, E. A. (2003). The quality of healthcare delivered to adults in the United States. *New England Journal of Medicine, 348*(26).

Agatston, A. (2003). *The South Beach diet: The delicious, doctor-designed, foolproof plan for fast and healthy weight loss.* New York, NY: Random House.

Agency for Healthcare Research and Quality. (2009, March). *National healthcare disparities report 2008* (AHRQ Publication No. 09-0002). Rockville, MD: Agency for Healthcare Research and Quality, United States Department of Health and Human Services.

Alle-Corliss, L., & Alle-Corliss, R. (1998). *Advanced practice in human service agencies.* Pacific Grove, CA: Brooks-Cole.

Alper, B. S., Epstein, R. M., & Quill, T. E. (2004). Communicating evidence for participatory decision making. *Journal of the American Medical Association, 291*(1).

American Academy of Pediatrics. (2010). *Community pediatrics: Advocacy education at pediatric residency programs.* Retrieved on March 18, 2010, from http://www.aap.org/commpeds/cpti/advocacyprogram info.html

American Cancer Society. (2009, December). *Tobacco-related cancers fact sheet.* Retrieved on February 25, 2010, from http://www.cancer.org/docroot/PED/content/PED_10_2x_Tobacco-Related_Cancers_Fact_Sheet.asp?sitearea=PED

American Heart Association. (2010, March). *Cardiovascular disease cost.* Retrieved from http://www.americanheart.org/presenter.jhtml?identifier=4475

American Lung Association. (2010, February). *Trends in tobacco use.* Retrieved from http://www.lungusa.org/assets/documents/publications/tobacco-policy-trend-alerts/Tobacco-Trend-Report.pdf

American Psychiatric Association. (2003). *Practice guideline for the assessment and treatment of patients with suicidal behaviors.* National Guideline Clearinghouse. Retrieved February 3, 2010, from http://www.psychiatryonline.com/pracGuide/pracGuideTopic_14.aspx. DOI: 10.1176/appi.books.9780890423363.56008.

Anda, R. F., Remington, P. L., Sienko, D. G., & Davis, R. M. (1987). Are physicians advising smokers to quit? The patient's perspective. *Journal of the American Medical Association, 257,* 1916–1919.

Anderson, B. (2007, December 12). Fresno is state's asthma capital. *Fresno Bee.* Retrieved from http://www.fresnobee.com/2007/12/12/263218/fresno-is-states-asthma-capital.html

Anderson, G. F., & Frogner, B. K. (2008). Health spending in OECD Countries: Obtaining value per dollar. *Health Affairs, 27,* 1718–1727.

Anderson, G. F., Hussey, P. S., Frogner, B. K., Waters, H. R. (2005). Health spending in the United States and the rest of the industrialized world. *Health Affairs,* vol. 24, 903–914.

Anderson, L. M., Scrimshaw, S. C., Fullilove, M. T., Fielding, J. E., Normand, J., & the Taskforce on Community Preventive Services (2003). Cultural competent healthcare systems: A systematic review. *American Journal of Preventive Medicine, 24*(3S), 68–79.

Anderson, R. (1995). Revisiting the behavioral model and access to medical care: Does it matter? *Journal of Health and Social Behavior, 36,* 1–10.

Anderson, R. J., Freedland, K.E., Clouse, R. E., & Lustman, P. J. (2001). The prevalence of comorbid depression in adults with diabetes: A meta-analysis. *Diabetes Care, 24,* 1069–1078.

Anderson, R. M., & Funnell, M. M. (2005). Patient empowerment: Reflections on the challenge of fostering the adoption of a new paradigm. *Patient Education and Counseling, 57*(2), 153–157.

Anderson, R., Grigsby, A., Freedland, K., de Groot, M., McGill, J., & Clouse, R. (2002). Anxiety and poor glycemic control: A meta-analytic review of the literature. *International Journal of Psychiatry in Medicine, 32,* 235–247.

Annas, G. (2003). HIPAA regulations—a new era of medical-record privacy? *New England Journal of Medicine, 348,* 1486–1490.

Applebaum, P. (2007). Assessment of patients' competence to consent to treatment. *New England Journal of Medicine, 357*(18), 1834–1840.

Aragón, T. A., Lichtensztajn, D. Y., Katcher, B. S., Reiter, R., & Katz, M. H. (2008). Calculating expected years of life lost for assessing local ethnic disparities in causes of premature death. *BMC Public Health, 8:* 116, doi: 10.1186/1471-2458-8116.

Arendt, K. W., Sadosty, A. T., Weaver, A. L., Brent, C. R., & Boie, E. T. (2003). The left-without-being-seen patients: What would keep them from leaving? *Annals of Emergency Medicine, 42,* 317–323.

Arnett, H. (1994). First round results of the access to health survey for selected disabilities and secondary conditions. Boston, MA: Independent Living Centers.

Asch, A. (2001). Disability, bioethics and human rights. In G. Albrecht, K. Seelman, & M. Bury (Eds.), *Handbook of disability studies* (pp. 297–326). Thousand Oaks, CA: Sage.

Associated Press. (2007, April 6). Women's health plan cost is higher. *Los Angeles Times,* p. C2.

Associated Press. (2009, May 6.) Health insurers offer to lower rates for women. *Los Angeles Times,* p. B7.

Atkins, R. C. (1992). *Dr. Atkins new diet revolution.* New York, NY: M. Evans.

Auslander, G. K., & Buchs, A. (2002). Evaluating an activity intervention with hemodialysis patients in Israel. *Social Work in Healthcare, 35*(1/2), 407–423.

Auslander, G., Dobrof, J., & Epstein, I. (2001). Comparing social work's role in renal dialysis in Israel and the United States: The practice-based research potential of available clinical information. *Social Work in Healthcare, 33*(3/4), 129–151.

Auslander, W. (1993). Brief family interventions to improve family communication and cooperation regarding diabetes management. *Spectrum, 6*(5), 330–333.

Auslander, W., Anderson, B., Bubb, J., Jung, K., & Santiago, J. (1990). Risk factors to health in diabetic children: A prospective study from diagnosis. *Health and Social Work, 15,* 133–142.

Auslander, W., & Freedenthal, S. (2006). Social work and chronic disease: Diabetes, heart disease, and HIV/AIDS. In S. Gehlert & T. Browne (Eds.) (2006), *Handbook of health social work* (pp. 532–567). Hoboken, NJ: John Wiley & Sons.

Austin, J. C., & Honer, W. G. (2007). The genomic era and serious mental illness: A potential application for psychiatric genetic counseling. *Psychiatric Services, 58,* 254–261.

Austin, M., & Pecora, P. (1987). *Managing human services personnel.* Newbury Park, CA: Sage.

Awe, C., & Lin, S-J. A. (2003). Patient empowerment model to prevent medication errors. *Journal of Medical Systems, 27,* 502–517.

Azoulay, E., Pochard, F., Kentish-Barnes, N., Chevret, S., Aboab, J., Adrie, C., & Schleemer, B. (2005). Risk of post-traumatic stress symptoms in family members of intensive care unit patients. *American Journal of Respiratory Critical Care Medicine, 171,* 987–994.

Bagner, D., Fernandez, M., & Eyberg, S. (2004). Parent-child interaction therapy and chronic illness: A case study. *Journal of Clinical Psychology in Medical Settings, 11*(1), 1–6.

Baker, D. W., Stevens, C. D., & Brook, R. H. (1991). Patients who leave a public hospital emergency department without being seen by a physician. Causes and consequences. *Journal of the American Medical Association, 266,* 1085–1090.

Bal, D. G. (2001). Cancer statistics, 2001: Quo vadis or whither goest thou? *Ca: A Cancer Journal for Clinicians, 51,* 11–14.

Ball, D. (2008). Addiction science and its genetics. *Addiction, 103,* 360.

Banners Health's Samaritan Medical Center. (2010). *About Banner Good Samaritan.* Retrieved on February 27, 2010, from http://www.bannerhealth.com/Locations/Arizona/

Banners Health's Samaritan Medical Center. (2010). *About Banner Good Samaritan.* Retrieved on February 27, 2010, from http://www.bannerhealth.com/About+Us/_About+Banner+Health.htm

Barnes, P. M., Bloom, B., & Nahin, R. (2008). *Complementary and alternative medicine use among adults and children: United States, 2007* (CDC National Health Statistics Report #12). Bethesda, MD: National Center for Complementary and Alternative Medicine.

Barr, D. (2008). *Health disparities in the United States: Social class, race, ethnicity, and health.* Baltimore, MD: Johns Hopkins University Press.

Barth, J., Schumacher, M., & Herrmann-Lingen, C. (2004). Depression as a risk factor for mortality in patients with coronary heart disease: A meta-analysis. *Psychosomatic Medicine, 66,* 802–813.

Beach, M. C., Gary, T. L., Price, E. G., Robinson, K., Gozu, A., Palacio, A., & Cooper, L. A. (2006). Improving healthcare quality for racial/ethnic minorities: A systematic review. *BioMed Central Public Health, 6,* 104. Retrieved on April 10, 2010 from http://www.biomedcentral.com/1471-2458/6/104

Beach, M. C., Price, E. G., Gary, T. L., Robinson, K. A., Gozu, A., Palacio, A., Smarth, C., et al. (2005). Cultural competence: A systematic review of healthcare provider educational interventions. *Medical Care, 43,* 356–373.

Beal, A. (2005). Policies to reduce racial and ethnic disparities in child health and healthcare. *Health Affairs 23*(5), 171–179.

Beauchamp, T., & Childress, J. (1994). *Principles of biomedical ethics* (4th ed.). New York, NY: Oxford University Press.

Beder, J. (1999). Evaluation research on the effectiveness of social work intervention on dialysis patients: The first 3 months. *Social Work in Healthcare, 30*(1), 15–30.

Beitz, K., Forcehimes, A., Levensky, E. R., & O'Donohue, W. T. (2007). Motivational interviewing. *American Journal of Nursing,* vol. 107(10).

Bell, J., & Standish, M. (2005). Communities and health policy: A pathway for change. *Health Affairs, 24,* 339–342.

Benca, R. M. (2005). Diagnosis and treatment of chronic insomnia: A review. *Psychiatric Services, 56,* 332–343.

Benson, H. (1976). *The relaxation response.* New York, NY: HarperTorch.

Berkman, L., Blumenthal, J., Burg, M., Carney, R., Catellier, D., Cowan, M., Czajkowski, S. et al. (2003). Effects of treating depression and low perceived social support on clinical events after myocardial infarction: The Enhancing Recovery in Coronary Heart Disease Patients (ENRICHD) randomized trial. *Journal of the American Medical Association, 289,* 3106–3116.

Berkman, N. D., DeWalt, D. A., Pignone, M. P., Sheridan, S. L., Lohr, K. N., Lux, L., Sutton, S. F., et al. (2004, January). *Literacy and health outcomes. Summary.* (Evidence Report/Technology Assessment No. 87, AHRQ Publication No. 04-E007-1). Rockville, MD: Agency for Healthcare Research and Quality.

Bern-Klug, M., Kramer, K. W. O. Sharr, P., & Cruz, I. (2010). Nursing home social services director's opinions of residents they can serve. *Journal of Aging & Social Policy, 22*(1) 33–52.

Berry, L. L., & Seltman, K. D. (2008). *Management lessons from the Mayo Clinic: Inside one of the world's most admired service organizations.* New York, NY: McGraw-Hill.

Berwick, D. (2003). Disseminating innovations in healthcare. *Journal of the American Medical Association, 289,* 1969–1975.

Betancourt, J., Green, A. R., Carrillo, E., & Park, E. R. (2005). Cultural competence and healthcare disparities: Key perspectives and trends. *Health Affairs, 24,* 499–505.

Betancourt, J., Blumenthal, D., Campbell, E. G., Clarridge, B., Kim, M., Lee, K. C., & Weissman, J. S. (2005). Resident physicians' preparedness to provide cross-cultural care. *Journal of the American Medical Association, 294*(9).

Biesecker, B. B., & Peters, K. F. (2001). Process studies in genetic counseling: Peering into the black box. *American Journal of Medical Genetics, 106,* 191–198.

Bindman, A. B., Grumbach, K., Keane, D., Rauch, L., & Luce, J. M. (1991). Consequences of queuing for care at a public hospital emergency department. *Journal of the American Medical Association, 266,* 1091–1096.

Bindman, A. B., Grumbach, K., Osmond, D., Komaromy, M., Vranzian, M. A., Lurie, N., Billings, J., et al. (1995). Preventable hospitalizations and access to healthcare. *Journal of the American Medical Association, 274,* 305.

Bing, E., Burnam, A., Longshore, D., Fleishman, J., Sherbourne, C., London, A., & Turner, B. J., et al., (2001). Psychiatric disorders and drug use among human immunodeficiency virus-infected adults in the United States. *Archives of General Psychiatry, 58,* 721–728.

Bixler, E. O., Kales, A., Soldatos, C. R., Kales, J. D., & Healey, S. (1979). Prevalence of sleep disorders in the Los Angeles metropolitan area. *American Journal of Psychiatry, 136,* 1257–1262.

Blair, S. N. (1993). Evidence for success of exercise in weight loss and control. *Annals of Internal Medicine, 119,* 702–706.

Block, S. (2001). Psychological considerations. Growth and transcendence at the end of life the art of possible. *Journal of the American Medical Association. 285,* 2898–2905.

Bodenheimer, T. (1999). Long term care for frail elderly people—on the Lok model. *New England Journal of Medicine, 341,* 1324–1328.

Bodenheimer, T. (2006). Primary care—Will it survive? *New England Journal of Medicine, 355,* 861–864.

Boswell, C., Cannon, S., & Miller, J. (2005). Nurses' political involvement: Responsibility versus privilege. *Journal of Professional Nursing, 21,* 5–8.

Boult, C., Boult, L., Boyd, C. M., Darer, J., Fried, L. P., & Wu, A. W. (2005). Clinical practice guidelines and quality of care for older patients with multiple comorbid diseases. *Journal of the American Medical Association, 294,* 6.

Bourgeois, F. T., Shannon, M. W., & Stack, A. M. (2008). "Left without being seen": A national profile of children who leave the emergency department before evaluation. *Annals of Emergency Medicine, 52*(6), 599–605.

Bourgeois, J. A., Kremen, W. S., Servis, M. E., Wegelin, J. A., & Hales, R. E. (2005). The impact of psychiatric diagnosis on length of stay in a university medical center in the managed care era. *Psychosomatics, 46*(5), 431–439. DOI: 10.1176/appi.psy.46.5.431.

Bower, P., & Gask, L. (2002). The changing nature of consultation-liaison in primary care: Bridging the gap between research and practice. *General Hospital Psychiatry, 24,* 63–70.

Boyer, A., & Indyk, D. (2006). Shaping garments of care: Tools for maximizing adherence potential. *Social Work in Healthcare, 42*(3/4), 151–166.

Brach, C., & Fraserirector, I. (2000). Can cultural competency reduce racial and ethnic health disparities? A review and conceptual model. *Medical Care Research and Review, 57,* 181–217.

Brashler, R. (2006). Social work practice and disability issues. In S. Gehlert, & T. Browne (Eds.), *Handbook of health social work* (pp. 448–470). Hoboken, NJ: John Wiley & Sons.

Breast Cancer Action. (2008). *Mammography screening and new technologies,* 6.4.08, C2000–2008, Breast Cancer Action. Retrived June 4, 2008, from http://bcaction.org/index.php?page=mammography-and-new-tech

Brekke, J. Interview with B. Jansson in December 2009.

Brink, K. (2008, April 29). *Wellness programs at work.* Retrieved from http://www.associatedcontent.com/article/724387/wellness_programs_at_work_pg3.html?cat=5

Brislin, R. (2000). *Understanding culture's influence on behavior* (2nd ed.). Belmont, CA: Wadsworth.

Brody, J. E. (2009, April 27). Paying a price for loving red meat. *New York Times,* p. D7.

Brooks, D. (2005, November 6). Courage in cancerland. *New York Times,* p. 30.

Brown, E. R., Wyn, R., Yu, H., Valenzuela, A., & Dong, L. (1999). Access to health insurance and healthcare for children in immigrant families. In D. J. Hernandez (Ed.), *Children of immigrants: Health, adjustment, and public assistance* (pp. 126–186). Washington, DC: National Academy Press.

Brown, R. P., & Gerbarg, P. L. (2005). Sudarshan Kriya yogic breathing in the treatment of stress, anxiety, and depression: Part II—Clinical applications and guidelines. *The Journal of Alternative and Complementary Medicine, 11*, 711–717.

Browne, T. (2006a). Nephrology social work. In S. Gehlert & T. Browne (Eds.) (2006), *Handbook of health social work* (pp. 471–506). Hoboken, NJ: John Wiley & Sons.

Browne, T. (2006b). Social work roles and healthcare settings. In S. Gehlert, & T. Browne (Eds.) (2006), *Handbook of health social work* (pp. 23–42). Hoboken, NJ: John Wiley & Sons.

Brumley, R., Enguidanos, S., Jamison, P., Seetz, R., Morganstern, N., Saito, S., McIlvaine, J. et al. (2007). Increased satisfaction with care and lower costs: Results from a randomized trial of in-home palliative care. *Journal of American Geriatric Society*, in press.

Brunello, N., Armitaged, R., Feinberge, I., Holsboer-Trachsleri, E., Légerj, D., Linkowskik, P., & Mendlewiczk, J. (2000). Depression and sleep disorders: Clinical relevance, economic burden and pharmacological treatment. *Neuropsychobiology, 42*, 107–119.

Buist, A. S., McBurnie, M. A., Vollmer, W. M., Gillespie, S, Burney, P., Mannino, D. M., Menenzes, A. M., et al., (2007, September 1–7). International variation in the prevalence of COPD (The BOLD Study): A population-based prevalence study. *The Lancet, 370*, 741–750.

Bureau of Labor Statistics. (2009, October). *Consumer expenditure survey*. Retrieved February 20, 2010, from http://www.bls.gov/cex/tables.htm

Bureau of Labor Statistics. (2010, (January). *Union members summary*. Retrieved from http://www.bls.gov/news.release/union2.nr0.htm

Burkhauser, R. V., & Cawley, J. (2008). Beyond BMI: The value of more accurate measures of fatness and obesity in social science research. *Journal of Health Economics, 27*, 519–529.

Burrow, J. (1977). *Organized medicine in the progressive era*. Baltimore, HD: Johns Hopkins University Press.

Butow, P., Coates, A., & Dunn, S. (1999). Psychosocial predictors of survival in metastatic melanoma. *Journal of Clinical Oncology, 17*(7), 2256–2263.

Cabness, J. (2005). *National Kidney Foundation second quarter research progress report*. New York: National Kidney Foundation.

California Department of Industrial Relations. (2010). *Labor law: Retaliation/discrimination*. Retrieved from http://www.dir.ca.gov/dlse/FAQ_Discrimination.htm

California Health Interview Survey. (2007). *Type of current health insurance—All ages*. Los Angeles: UCLA Center for Health Policy Research. Retrieved from http://www.chis.ucla.edu/

California Hospital Association. (2008). *Consent manual—A reference for consent and related healthcare law*. Sacramento, CA.

California Newsreel (Producer). (2008). *Unnatural causes . . . Is inequality making us sick? [Television series]*. Washington, DC: Public Broadcasting Service.

Campaign for Tobacco-Free Kids. (2010, January). *Toll of tobacco in the United States of America*. Retrieved from http://www.tobaccofreekids.org/research/factsheets/pdf/0072.pdf

Campinha-Bacote, J. (2002). The process of cultural competence in the delivery of healthcare services. *Journal of Transcultural Nursing, 13*(3), 181–184.

Carbone, E. J., Gorrie, J. J., & Oliver, R. (2003, May). Without proper language interpretation, sight is lost in Oregon and a $350,000 verdict is reached. *Healthcare Risk Management*, 1–3.

Carrasquillo, O., Orav, J., Brennan, T.A., & Burstin, H.R. (1999). Impact of language barriers on patient satisfaction in an emergency department. *Journal of General Internal Medicine, 14*, 82–87.

Casperson, C. J., & Merritt, R. K. (1995). Physical activity trends among 26 states, 1986–1990. *Medicine & Science in Sports & Exercise, 27*, 713–720.

Castilla, J., Sobrino, P., de la Fuente, L., Noguera, I., Guerra, L., & Parrasa, F. (2002). Late diagnosis of HIV infection in the era of highly active antiretroviral therapy: Consequences for AIDS incidence. *AIDS, 16*, 1945–1951.

Caulkins, J., Reuter, P., Iguchi, M., & Chiesa, J. (2005). *How goes the "war on drugs?"* Santa Monica, CA: Rand Corporation.

CCTV. (2009, August 31). *Voter turnout hits record 69% in Japan's lower house election*. Retrieved from http://english.cctv.com/20090831/111318.shtml

Census Bureau. (2009, July). *Voter turnout increases by 5 million in 2008 presidential election, U.S. Census Bureau reports*. Retrieved from http://www.census.gov/PressRelease/www/releases/archives/voting/013995.html

Center for American Progress. (2009, February). *Health care in crisis: 14,000 losing coverage each day*. Retrieved from http://www.americanprogressaction.org/issues/2009/02/health_in_crisis.html

Center for Children and Families. (2008, May). *Medicaid and state budgets: Looking at the facts*. Retrieved from http://ccf.georgetown.edu/index/medicaid-and-state-budgets-looking-at-the-facts

Center for Healthcare Research and Transformation. (2010). *Cover Michigan survey 2010*. Retrieved from http://www.chrt.org/assets/cover-michigan/CHRT-Cover-Michigan-Survey-2010.pdf

Centers for Disease Control and Prevention. (1995). Missed opportunities in preventive counseling for cardiovascular disease—United States, 1995. *Journal of the American Medical Association, 279*, 741–742.

Centers for Disease Control and Prevention. (1996). State-specific prevalence of participation in physical activity—1994. *Morbidity and Mortality Weekly Report, 45*, 673–675.

Centers for Disease Control and Prevention. (1998). Missed opportunities in preventive counseling for cardiovascular disease—United States, 1995. *Journal of the American Medical Association, 279*, 741–742.

Centers for Disease Control and Prevention. (1999). Achievements in public health, 1900–1999: Decline in deaths from heart disease and stroke—United States, 1900–1999. *Morbidity and Mortality Weekly Report, 48,* 649–656.

Centers for Disease Control and Prevention. (2002a). Annual smoking-attributable mortality, years of potential life lost, and economic costs—United States, 1995–1999. *Morbidity and Mortality Weekly Report, 51,* 300–303.

Centers for Disease Control and Prevention. (2002b). Recommended adult immunization schedule—United States, 2002–2003. *Morbidity and Mortality Weekly Report, 51,* 904–905.

Centers for Disease Control and Prevention. (2004). Alcohol-attributable deaths and years of potential life lost—United States, 2001. *Morbidity and Mortality Weekly Report, 53,* 866–870.

Centers for Disease Control and Prevention. (2009a, October). *Healthy people.* Retrieved from http://www.cdc.gov/nchs/healthy_people.htm

Centers for Disease Control and Prevention. (2009b, May). *Herpes zoster—Vaccine Q&As for providers (shingles).* Retrieved from http://www.cdc.gov/vaccines/vpd-vac/shingles/vac-faqs-hcp.htm

Centers for Disease Control and Prevention. (2009c). National, state, and local area vaccination coverage among children aged 19–35 months—United States, 2008. *Morbidity and Mortality Weekly Report, 58,* 921–926.

Centers for Disease Control and Prevention. (2010a, February). *Immunization faststats.* Retrieved from http://www.cdc.gov/nchs/fastats/immunize.htm

Centers for Disease Control and Prevention. (2010b, February 4). *Pneumonia FastStats.* Retrieved from http://www.cdc.gov/nchs/fastats/pneumonia.htm

Centers for Medicare & Medicaid Services. (n.d.). *NHE Web Tables.* Retrieved February 9, 2010, from http://www.cms.hhs.gov/NationalHealthExpendData/02_NationalHealthAccountsHistorical.asp

Central Intelligence Agency. (2009). Country comparison: Infant mortality rate. *The World Factbook.* Retrieved March 1, 2010, from https://www.cia.gov/library/publications/the-world-factbook/rankorder/2091rank.html

CHA (2008). See California Hospital Association (2008)

Chapman, D., Perry, G., & Strine, T. (2005). The vital link between chronic disease and depressive disorders. *Preventing chronic disease, 2*(1), 14–25.

Chapple, A., Dumelow, C., Evans, J., Prinjha, S., Rozmovits, L., & Ziebland, S. (2004). How the Internet affects patient's experience of cancer. *BMJ,* vol. 328, (564).

Charmel, P., & Frampton, S. (2008, March). Building the business case for patient-centered care: Patient-centered care has the potential to reduce adverse events, malpractice claims, and operating costs while improving market share. *Healthcare Financial Management.*

Chen, P. (2008a, November 13). Confronting the racial barriers between doctors and patients. *New York Times,* Health Section.

Chen, P. (2008b, October 23). Stories in the service of making a better doctor. *New York Times,* Health Section.

Chen, W. S., Leong, K. C., Leong, K. W., Mastura, I., Mimi, O., Ng, C. J., & Zailinawati, A. H. (2006). *The use of text messaging to improve attendance in primary care.* Oxford, UK: Oxford University Press.

Chesney, M. (2003). Adherence to HAART regimens. *AIDS Patient Care and STDs, 17,* 169–177.

Chew, L. D., Bradley, K. A., & Boyko, E. J. (2004). Brief questions to identify patients with inadequate health literacy. *Family Medicine, 36,* 588–594.

Children's Hospital of Philadelphia. (2008). *Economic impact report 2007–2008.* Retrieved on March 18, 2010, from www.chop.edu/export/download/pdfs/ . . . / economic_impact_2008.pdf

Children's Hospital of Philadelphia. (2010). *Pediatric residency program: Community pediatrics and advocacy (CPAP).* Retrieved on March 18, 2010, from http://www.chop.edu/professionals/pediatric-residency-program/residency-program/curriculum-rotations-and-responsibilities.html

Christakis, N. A., & Fowler, J. H. (2007). The spread of obesity in a large social network over 32 years. *New England Journal of Medicine, 357,* 370–379

City of Hope. (2009). *Advocating for excellence: ACE project.* Retrieved on February 20, 2010, from http://www.Cityofhope.org/education/health-professional-education/nursing-education/ACE-project/Pages/default.aspx

Clark, N. M., Norhwehr, F., Gong, M., Evans, D., Maiman, L. A., Hurwitz, M. E., & Mellins, R. B. (1995). Physician-patient partnership in managing chronic illness. *Academic Medicine, 70,* 957–959.

Cohn, G., & Preston, D. (2008). AARP's stealth fees often sting seniors with costlier insurance. Retrieved from http://www.bloomberg.com/apps/news?pid=20601109 & sid=a4OkPQIPF6Kg

Coleman, E. A., Parry, C., Chalmers, S., & Min, S. J. (2006). The care transitions intervention: Results of a randomized controlled trial. *Archives of Internal Medicine, 166,* 1822–1828.

Coleman, M. (2005, August 29). High-deductible health plans loom. *Investor's Business Daily,* p. A12.

Coleman, S. K. (2009). Rethinking AARP as an "Advocate," *NASW California News, 35*(6), 14.

Colker, D. (2009, June 21). Resources for those without insurance. *Los Angeles Times,* pp. B1, B5.

Collins, J. L., Marks, J. S., Koplan, J. P. (2009). Chronic disease prevention and control: Coming of age at the Centers for Disease Control. *Prevention of Chronic Diseases, 6*(3), A81.

Comarow, A. (2009, November 11). America's best health insurance plans: How they were ranked: Data from 135 measures showed how well plans satisfy their members and prevent and treat illness. *U.S. News & World Report.* Retrieved from http://health.usnews.com/health-news/health-plans/articles/2009/11/11/americas-best-health-insurance-plans-how-they-were-ranked.html

Comarow, A. (2009, June). Best children's hospitals honor roll. *U.S. News & World Report*. Retrieved on March 17, 2010, from http://health.usnews.com/articles/health/best-childrens-hospitals/2009/06/17/best-childrens-hospitals-honor-roll.html

Commonwealth Fund. (2010). Quality matters. Online newsletter. February-March. Accessed at www.commonwealthfund.org/Content/Newletters/Quality-Matters/2010/February-March, 2010.

Congressional Budget Office. (2009, February). *Monthly budget review fiscal year 2010: A Congressional Budget Office analysis*. Retrieved from http://www.cbo.gov/doc.cfm?index=11041

Conklin T. J., Lincoln T., & Flanigan T. P. (1998). A public health model to connect correctional healthcare with communities. *American Journal of Public Health*, 88, 1249–1250.

Consumer Reports National Research Center. (2009, September). *Consumer Reports*, 18–19.

Conwell, Y. (2009). Suicide prevention in later life: A glass half full, or half empty? *American Journal of Psychiatry*, 166(8), 845–848. doi: 10.1176/appi.ajp.2009.09060780.

Cooper, C., Inskip, H., Croft, P., Campbell, L., Smith, G., Mclearn, M., & Coggon, D. (1998). Individual risk factors for hip osteoarthritis: Obesity, hip injury and physical activity. *American Journal of Epidemiology*, 147, 516–522.

Cooper, M. (1999). Quality assurance and improvement. In L. Wolder (Ed.), *Healthcare Administration* (3rd ed., pp. 545–573) Great Neck, NY: Aspen Publishers.

Cooper-Patrick, L., Gallo, J. J., Gonzales, J. J., Vu, H. T., Powe, N. R., Nelson, C., & Ford, D. E., (1999). Race, gender, and partnership in the patient-physician relationship. *Journal of the American Medical Association*, 282(6), 583–589. doi: 10.1001/Journal of the American Medical Association.282.6.583.

Cornwell, E., & Waite, L. (2009). Social disconnectedness, perceived isolation, and health among older adults. *Journal of Health and Social Behavior*, 50(1), 31–48.

Council on Ethical and Judicial Affairs. (1990). Black-white disparities in healthcare. *Journal of the American Medical Association*, 263, 2344–2346.

Cowles, L. (2003). Social work in the health field: A care perspective. New York, NY: Hawworth.

Cox, C. (2007). Grandparent-headed families: Needs and implications for social work interventions and advocacy. *Families in Society*, 88(4), 561–566.

Csikai, E. (2007). Social workers' participation on hospital ethics committees: An assessment of involvement and satisfaction. *Aret*, 22, 1–13.

CSX. (2005). *Safety is a way of life*. Retrieved April 26, 2010, from http://www.csx.com/?fuseaction=about.safety

Cummings, S., & Jackson, D. (2000). Hospital discharge planning. In R. L. Schneider, N. P. Kropf, & A. J. Kisor (Eds.), *Gerontological social work: Knowledge, service settings, and special populations* (2nd ed., pp. 191–224). Belmont, CA: Brooks/Cole.

Daley, J. (2001). A 58 year old woman dissatisfied with her care. *Journal of the American Medical Association*, 285, 2629–2635.

Dance, A. (2009, May 18). Wise at heart. *Los Angeles Times*. Retrieved from http://www.latimes.com/news/health/heartawareness/la-he-framingham18,0,4198236,full.story

Dannenberg, A., McNeil, J., Brudage, J., & Brookmeyer, R. (1996). Suicide and HIV infection: Mortality follow-up of 4147 HIV seropositive military service applicants. *Journal of the American Medical Association*, 276, 1743–1746.

Darnell, J. (2007). Patient navigation: A call to action. *Social Work* 52(1), 81–83.

Davenport-Ennis, N., Cover, M., Ades, T. B., & Stovall, E. (2002). An analysis of advocacy: A collaborative essay. *Essays in Oncology Nursing*, 18(4), 290–296.

Davis, A., & Konishi, E. (2007). Whistleblowing in Japan. *Nursing Ethics*, 14(2), 194–204.

Davis, J. W., Ross, P. D., Preston, S. D., Nevitt, M. C., & Wasnick, R. D. (1998). Strength, physical activity and body mass index: Relationship to performance-based measures and activities of daily living among older Japanese women in Hawaii. *Journal of the American Geriatrics Society*, 46, 274–279.

Davis, K., & Schoen, C. (1978). *Health and the war on poverty: A ten-year appraisal*. Washington, DC: Brookings Institution.

Davis, N., Pohlman, A., Gehlbach, B., Kress, J. P., McAtee, J., Herlitz, J., & Hall, J. (2003). Improving the process of informed consent in the critically ill. *Journal of the American Medical Association*, 289, 1963–1968.

Debusk, R. (2000). Evaluating the cardiovascular tolerance for sex. *American Journal of Cardiology*, 86(Suppl. 2A), F51–56.

DeKieffer, D. (1997). *The citizen's guide to lobbying congress*. Chicago: Chicago Review Press.

Delbanco, T., & Bell, S. (2007). Guilty, afraid, and alive—struggling with medical error. *New England Journal of Medicine*, 22, 2, 1682–1683.

Delisio, E. R. (2009, January 21). *Lack of school nurses impacts students' health, academics*. Retrieved from http://www.educationworld.com/a_issues/issues/issues430.shtml

de Lorgeril, M., Renaud, S., Salen, P., Monjaud, I., Mamelle, N., Martin, J. L., & Delaye, J. (1994). Mediterranean alphalinolenic acid-rich diet in secondary prevention of coronary heart disease. *Lancet*, 343, 1454–1459.

de Lorgeril, M., Renaud, S., Mamelle, M., Salen, P., Martin, J. L., Monjaud, I., Guidollet, J., et al. (1994). Mediterranean dietary pattern in a randomized trial: Prolonged survival and possible reduced cancer rate. *Archives of Internal Medicine*, 158, 1191–1187.

De Navas-Salt, C., Proctor, B. D., & Smith J. C. (2009, September). *Income, poverty, and health insurance coverage in the United States: 2008*. Retrieved from http://www.census.gov/hhes/www/hlthins/hlthin08.html

Denekens, J., Hearnshaw, H., Van Royen, P., & Vermeire, E. (2001). Patient adherence to treatment: Three decades of research. *Journal of Clinical Pharmacy and Therapeutics, 26,* 331–342.

DeOreo, P. B. (1997). Hemodialysis patient-assessed functional health status predicts continued survival, hospitalization, and dialysis-attendance compliance. *American Journal of Kidney Diseases, 30*(2), 204–212.

Department of Agriculture, Foreign Agricultural Service. (2006). *Beef: Per capita consumption summary selected countries.* Retrieved from http://www.fas.usda.gov/dlp/circular/2006/06-03LP/bpppcc.pdf

Department of Agriculture. (2010, February). *My pyramid.gov: Steps to a healthier you.* Retrieved from http://www.mypyramid.gov/

Department of Health and Human Services. (1990). *The health benefits of smoking cessation: A report of the surgeon general.* Washington, DC: Government Printing Office.

Department of Health and Human Services. (1999). *Mental health: A report of the surgeon general.* Rockville, MD: Author.

Department of Health and Human Services. (2000). *Oral health in America: A Report of the Surgeon General,* Rockville, MD., U.S. Department of Health and Human Services, National Institute of Craniofacial Research, National Institutes of Health.

Department of Health and Human Services. (2001). *Mental health: Culture, race, and ethnicity—A supplement to mental health: A report of the surgeon general.* Rockville, MD: Author.

Department of Health and Human Services. (2003, August 8). *Guidance to federal financial assistance recipients regarding Title VI prohibition against national origin discrimination affecting limited English proficient persons.* Federal Register, 68(153), 47311–47323.

Department of Health and Human Services Office of Minority Health. (2001). *National standards for cultural and linguistically appropriate services in healthcare: Executive summary.* Washington, DC: Department of Health and Human Services.

Department of Health and Human Services Office of Minority Health. (2005, October 19). *What is cultural competency?* Retrieved April 28, 2009, from http://www.omhrc.gov

Department of Health and Human Services Office of Minority Health. (2007). *National standards on culturally and linguistically appropriate services (CLAS).* Retrieved May 12, 2009 from http://www.omhrc.gov

Department of Labor. (2010a). *Family & medical leave.* Retrieved from http://www.dol.gov/dol/topic/benefits-leave/fmla.htm

Department of Labor. (2010b). *Occupational outlook handbook 2010–2011Edition: Social workers.* Retrieved January 19, 2010, from http://www.bls.gov/oco/ocos060.htm

Department of Labor. (2010c). *Youth and labor.* Retrieved from http://www.dol.gov/dol/topic/youthlabor/

DesRoches, C. M., Campbell, E. G., Rao, S. R., Donelan, K., Ferris, T. G., Jha, A., & Blumenthal, D. (2008). Electronic health records in ambulatory care—A National survey of physicians. *New England Journal of Medicine, 359,* 50–60.

Diamond, F. (2003, June). How to manage the worried well. *Managed Care.* Retrieved from http://www.managedcaremag.com/archives/0306/0306.worriedwell.html

Dickens, W. T., & Leonard, J. S. (1985). Accounting for the decline in union membership, 1950–1980. *Industrial & Labor Relations Review, 38,* 323–334.

DiMatteo, M. (2004). Social support and patient adherence to medical treatment: A meta analysis. *Health Psychology, 23*(2), 207–218.

Divi, C., Koss, R. G., Schmaltz, S. P., & Loeb, J. M. (2007). Language proficiency and adverse events in US hospitals: A pilot study. *International Journal for Quality in Healthcare, 19*(2), 60–67.

Diwan, S., & Balaswamy, S. (2006). Social work with older adults in healthcare settings. In S. Gehlert & T. Browne (Eds.), *Handbook of health social work* (pp. 417–447). Hoboken, NJ: John Wiley & Sons.

Dlugacz, Y., Restifo, A., & Greenwood, A. *The quality handbook for healthcare organizations.* San Francisco: Jossey-Bass.

Dodd, S. J., Jansson, B., Brown-Saltzman, K., Shirk, M., & Wunch, K. (2004). Expanding nurses' participation in ethics: An empirical examination of ethical activism and ethical assertiveness. *Nursing Ethics, 11*(15), 15–27.

Dodd, S. J., & Jansson, B. (2004). Expanding the boundaries of ethics education: Preparing social workers for ethical advocacy in hospital and other settings. *Journal of Social Work Education, 40,* 3, 455–465.

Dohan, D., & Levintova, M. (2007). Barriers beyond words: Cancer, culture, and translation in a community of Russian speakers. *Journal of General Internal Medicine, 22*(Suppl. 2), 300–305.

Doorenbos, A. Z., & Schim, S. M. (2004). Cultural competence in hospice. *American Journal of Hospice and Palliative Care, 21*(1), 28–32.

Dorfman, L., Sorenson, S., & Wallack, L. (2009). *Working upstream.* Berkeley, CA: Berkeley Media Studies Group.

Dorr, D. A., Wilcox, A., Donnelly, S. M., Burns, L., & Clayton, P. D. (2005). "Impact of generalist care managers on patients with diabetes," *Health Services Research, 40,* 1400–1421.

dos Santos, L. M., Stewart, G., & Rosenberg, N. M. (1994). Pediatric emergency department walk-outs. *Pediatric Emergency Care, 10,* 76–78.

Dreifus, C. D. (2009, April 21). A conversation with Richard Wrangham: From studying chimps, a theory on cooking. *New York Times,* p. D2.

Drinkard, J., & Welch, W. M. (2003, November 20). AARP accused of conflict of interest. *USA Today.* Retrieved from http://www.usatoday.com/news/Washington/2003-11-20-aarp-protest_x.htm

DuBois, B., & Miley, K. K. (2002). *Social work: An empowering profession* (4th ed.). Boston, HA: Allyn and Bacon.

Dunton G. F., Kaplan J., Wolch J., Jerrett M., & Reynolds, K. D. (2009). Physical environmental correlates of childhood obesity: a systematic review. *Obesity Reviews, 10*(4), 393–402.

Dusseldorp, E., van Elderen, T., Maes, S., Meulman, J., & Kraaij, V. (1999). A meta-analysis of psychoeducational programs for coronary heart disease patients. *Health Psychology, 18*(5), 506–519.

Dziegielewski, S. (2004). *The changing face of health social work: Professional practice in managed behavioral healthcare* (2nd ed.). New York, NY: Springer.

Earp, J., French, E., & Gilkey, M. (Eds.) (2008) *Patient advocacy for healthcare quality.* Sudbury, MA: Jones and Bartlett.

Economist. (2009). *The Economist pocket world in figures 2010 edition.* London, UK: Profile Books.

Editorial (2010, April 25). *New York Times*, p. 11.

Edward, B. (1993, September). When the physician won't give up. *American Journal of Nursing*, 34–37.

Ehrenreich, B. (1973). *Complaints and disorders: The sexual politics of sickness.* Old Westbury, NY: Feminist Press.

Ehrlich, S. F., Quesenberry, Jr., C. P., Van Den Eeden, S. K., Shan, J., & Ferrara, A. (2010). Patients diagnosed with diabetes are at increased risk for asthma, chronic obstructive pulmonary disease, pulmonary fibrosis, and pneumonia but not lung cancer. *Diabetes Care, 33*(1), 55–60.

Elections Canada. (2009, December). *Voter turnout at federal elections and referendums, 1867–2008.* Retrieved from http://www.elections.ca/content.asp?section=pas&document=turnout&lang=e&textonly=false

Engstrom, M. (2006). Physical and mental health: Interactions, assessment, and intervention. In S. Gehlert & T. Browne (Eds.), *Handbook of health social work* (pp. 194–251). Hoboken, NJ: John Wiley & Sons.

Enthoven, A. (1980). *Health plan: The only practical solution to the soaring cost of medical care.* Reading MA: Addison-Wesley.

Epstein, I. (1981). Advocates on advocacy: An exploratory study. *Social Work Research and Abstracts, 17*(2), 5–12.

Expedia.com. (2009). *2009 international vacation deprivation survey results.* Retrieved from http://media.expedia.com/media/content/expus/graphics/promos/vacations/Expedia_International_Vacation_Deprivation_Survey_2009.pdf

Ezell, M. (1991). Administrators as advocates. *Administration in Social Work, 15*(4), 1–8.

Ezell, M. (2001). *Advocacy in the human services.* Belmont, CA: Brooks/Cole.

Felland, L. E., Lauer, J. R., & Cunningham, P. J. (2008). *Community efforts to expand dental services for low-income people issue: Brief no. 122.* Center for Studying Health System Change. Retrieved from http://www.hschange.com/CONTENT/1000/?words=dental

Fellows, J. L., Bush, T., McAfee, T., & Dickerson, J. (2007). Cost effectiveness of the Oregon quitline "free patch initiative." *Tobacco Control, 16*, i47–i52. doi: 10.1136/tc.2007.019943.

Fields, S. A., & McNamara, J. R. (2003). The prevention of child and adolescent violence: A review. *Aggression and Violent Behavior, 8*(1), 61–91. DOI: 10.1016/S1359-1789(01)00054-4.

Fincher, C., Williams, J. E., MacLean, V., Allison, J. J., Kiefe, C. I., & Canto, J. (2004). Racial disparities in coronary heart disease: A sociological view of the medical literature on physician bias. *Ethnicity & Disease, 14*, 360–371.

Finkelstein, E. A., Trogdon, J. G., Cohen, J. W., & Dietz, W. (2009). Annual medical spending attributable to obesity: Payer- and service-specific estimates. *Health Affairs, 28*(5), w822–w831 doi: 10.1377/hlthaff.28.5.w822.

Finucane, T. E., & Carrese, J. A. (1990). Racial bias in presentation of cases. *Journal of General Internal Medicine, 5*, 120–121.

Flegal, K. M., Graubard, B. I., Williamson, D. F., & Gail, M. H. (2005). Excess deaths associated with underweight, overweight, and obesity. *Journal of the American Medical Association, 293*, 1861–1867.

Flores, G. (2005). The impact of medical interpreter services on the quality of healthcare: A systematic review. *Medical Care Research and Review, 62*(3), 255–299.

Folkman, S., & Greer, S. (2000). Promoting psychological well-being in the face of serious illness: When theory, research and practice inform each other. *Psycho-oncology, 9*, 11–19.

Fontaine, K. R., Redden, D. T., Wang, C., Westfall, A. O., & Allison, D. B. (2003). Years of life lost due to obesity. *Journal of the American Medical Association, 289*, 187–193.

Forstein, M., & McDaniel, J. (2001). Medical overview of HIV infection and AIDS. *Psychiatric Annals, 31*, 16–20.

Forster, A. J., Murff, H. J., Peterson, J. F., Gandhi, T. K., & Bates, D. W. (2003). The incidence and severity of adverse events affecting patients after discharge from the hospital. *Annals of Internal Medicine, 138*, 161–167.

Francoeur, R. (1983). *Biomedical ethics: A guide to decision making.* New York, NY: John Wiley & Sons.

Frampton, S. B., & Gilpin, L. (2008). Planetree, a hospital model for patient-centered care. In: J. A. Earp, E. A. French, & M. B. Gilkey (Eds.), *Patient advocacy for healthcare quality: Strategies for achieving patient-centered care* (pp. 289–311). Sudbury, MA: Jones and Bartlett.

Frank, A., Auslander, G. K., & Weissgarten, J. (2003). Quality of life of patients with end-stage renal disease at various stages of the illness. *Social Work in Healthcare, 38*(2), 1–27.

Freedman, R. (2005). The choice of antipsychotic drugs for schizophrenia. *New England Journal of Medicine, 353*(12), 1286–1288.

Freedman, V. A., Martin, L. G., & Schoeni, R. F. (2002). Recent trends in disability and functioning among older adults in the United States: A systematic review. *Journal of the American Medical Association, 288*, 3137–3146.

Freeman, H., Muth, B., & Kerner, J. (1995). Expanding access to cancer screening and clinical follow-up among the medically underserved. *Cancer Practice, 3,* 19–30.

Freudenheim, M. (2007, April 6). New urgency in debating healthcare. *New York Times,* pp. C1, C4.

Freudenheim, M. (2005, May 27). Other perils of overweight. *New York Times.* Retrieved from http://www.nytimes.com/2005/05/27/business/27bariatric.html?_r=1#

Frick, K. D., & Lantz, P. M. (1999). How well do we understand the relationship between prenatal care and birth weight? *Health Services Research, 34,* 1063–1082.

Frolkis, J. P., Zyzanski, S. J., Schwartz, J. M., & Suhan, P. S. (1998). Physician noncompliance with the 1993 national cholesterol education program (NCEP-ATPH) guidelines. *Circulation, 98,* 851–855.

Froman, L. (1967). *The congressional process: Strategies, rules, and procedures.* Boston, MA: Little, Brown.

Gabel, J. R., McDevitt, R., Lore, R., Pickreign, J. Whitmore, H., & Ding, T. (2009). Trends in underinsurance and the affordability of employer coverage, 2004–2007. *Health Affairs, 28,* w595–w606. doi: 10.1377/hlthaff.28.4.w595.

Galanti, G. A. (2008). *Caring for patients from different cultures* (4th ed.). Philadelphia, PA: University of Pennsylvania Press.

Gallagher, T.H., Waterman, A.D., Ebers, A.G., Fraser, V. J., Levinson, W. (2003). Patients' and physicians' attitudes regarding the disclosure of medical errors. *Journal of the American Medical Association, 289*(8), 1001–1007.

Gallo-Silver, L., & Weiner, M. (2005, May). *Survivors of childhood sexual abuse with cancer: Managing early trauma and the impact on adjustment to illness.* Paper and workshop presented at the 21st Annual Association of Oncology Social Work Conference, Austin, TX.

Galuska, D. A., Will, J. C., Serdula, M. K., & Ford, E. S. (1999). Are healthcare professionals advising obese patients to lose weight? *Journal of the American Medical Association, 282,* 1576–1578.

Gambrill, E. (1983). *Casework, a competency-based approach.* Englewood Cliffs, NJ: Prentice-Hall.

Gatrad, A. (2008). Palliative care needs of minorities: Understanding their needs is the key. *British Medical Journal, 327,* 176–177.

Gawande, A. (2010). *The checklist manifesto: How to get things right.* New York, Henry Holt, NY.

Gawande, A. (2010, April 5). "What Now?" *New Yorker,* p. 22.

Gazelle, G. (2007). Understanding hospice, an underutilized option for life's final chapter. *New England Journal of Medicine, 357,* 321–324.

Geary, H. (2003). Facilitating an organizational culture of healing in an urban medical center. *Nursing Administration Quarterly, 27,* 231–239.

Gehlert, S. (1995). Cognitive restructuring for psychosocial problems in epilepsy. *Epilepsia, 36*(Suppl. 3), S190.

Gehlert, S. (2006a). The conceptual underpinnings of social work in healthcare. In S. Gehlert & T. Browne (Eds.), *Handbook of health social work* (pp. 3–22). Hoboken, NJ: John Wiley & Sons, 3–22.

Gehlert, S. (2006b). Theories of health behavior. In S. Gehlert & T. Browne (Eds.), *Handbook of health social work* (pp. 179–193). Hoboken, NJ: John Wiley & Sons.

Geisinger Health System. (2009). *Geisinger: 2009 system report.* Danville, PA: Author.

Geisinger Health System. (2010). *Careers.* Retrieved on February 26, 2010, from http://www.geisinger.org/professionals/careers/index.html.

Geithner, T. F., Solis, H. L., Sebelius, K., & Astrue, M. J. (2009). *Status of the Social Security and Medicare programs.* Retrieved from http://www.ssa.gov/OACT/TRSUM/index.html

Geng, D. (2005, December 19). GM *vs.* Toyota: By the numbers. Retrieved from www.npr.org/news/specials/gmvstoyota/

Geron, S. M. (2001). Managed care and care management for older adults. In N. W. Veeder & W. C. Peebles-Wilkins (Eds.), *Managed care services: Policy, programs, and research.* (pp. 150–162). New York, NY: Oxford University.

Gibson, S., & Weinder, D. (Eds.) (2005). *Pain in older persons: Progress in pain research and management,* Seattle, WA: IASP.

Gilkey, M., Earp, J., & French, E. (2008). What is patient advocacy? In J. Earp, E. French, & M. Gilkey (Eds.), *Patient advocacy for healthcare quality* (pp. 3–28). Sudbury, MA: Jones and Bartlett.

Girion, L. (2008a, June 17). Doctors call pay method flawed. *Los Angeles Times,* pp. C1, C7.

Girion, L. (2008b, February 14). Heat is on health insurers. *Los Angeles Times,* pp. A1, A23.

Girion, L. (2008c, February 23). Insurer loses, alters course. *Los Angeles Times,* pp. A1, A21.

Girion, L. (2008d, June 8). Untangling health insurance troubles. *Los Angeles Times,* pp. C1, C8.

Girion, L. (2009, June 17). Insurers refuse to limit policy cancellations. *Los Angeles Times,* pp. B1, B5.

Glasgow, R. E., Wagner, E. H., Kaplan, R. M., Vinicor, F., Smith, L., & Norman, R. D. (1999). If diabetes is a public health problem, why not treat it as one? A population-based approach to chronic illness. *Annals of Behavioral Medicine, 21,* 159–170.

Glassner, B. (1999). *The culture of fear: Why Americans are afraid of the wrong things.* New York, NY: Basic Books.

Glassner, B. (2007). *The gospel of food: Everything you think you know about food is wrong.* New York, NY: Ecco.

Glendinning, C. (2002). Breaking down barriers: integrating health and care services for older people in England. *Health Policy, 65,* 139–151.

Goode, T. D., Dunne, C., & Bronheim, S. M. (2006). *The evidence base for cultural and linguistic competency in healthcare* (Publication no. 962). New York, NY: Commonwealth Fund.

Goode, T. D., & Jones, W. (2006). *A definition of linguistic competence.* Washington, DC: National Center for Cultural Competence, Georgetown University Center for Child and Human Development.

Goodwin, J. S. (1989). Social, psychological and physical factors affecting the nutritional status of elderly subjects separating cause and effect. *American Journal of Clinical Nutrition, 50,* 1201–1209.

Gordon, R. G. (Ed.). (2005). *Ethnologue: Languages of the world* (15th ed.). Dallas, TX: SIL International.

Gosselin-Acomb, T. K., Schneider, S. M., Clough, R. W., & Veenstra, B. A. (2007). Nursing advocacy in North Carolina. *Oncology Nursing Forum, 34,* 1070–1074.

Gouging women on health insurance [Editorial]. (2008, November 3). *New York Times,* p. A26.

Gould, M. S., Wallenstein, S., & Kleinman, M. (1987). *A study of time-space clustering of suicide: Final report.* Atlanta, GA: Centers for Disease Control.

Govaert, T.M.E., Thijs, C.T.M., Masurel, N., Sprenger, M. J. W., Diant, G. T., & Knotnerus, J. A. (1994). The efficacy of influenza vaccination in elderly individuals: A randomized double-blind pacebo-contolled trial. *Journal of the American Medical Association, 272,* 1661–1665.

Green, A. R., Ngo-Metzger, Q., Legedza, A.T.R., Massagli, M., Phillips, R. S., & Iezzoni, L. I. (2005). Interpreter services, language concordance, and healthcare quality: Experiences of Asian American with limited English proficiency. *Journal of General Internal Medicine, 20,* 1050–1056.

Greenhouse, L. (2005, October 6). Justices explore U.S. authority over states on assisted suicide. *New York Times,* p. 1.

Gregory, K., Wells, K. B., & Leake, B. (1987). Medical students' expectations for encounters with minority and non-minority patients. *Journal of the National Medical Association, 79,* 403–408.

Grigsby, A., Anderson, R., Freedland, K., Clouse, R., & Lustman, P. (2002). Prevalence of anxiety in adults with diabetes: A systematic review. *Journal of Psychosomatic Research, 53,* 1053–1060.

Grogan, C. & Gusmano, M. (2007). *Healthy voices, unhealthy silence: Advocacy and health policy for the poor.* Washington, DC: Georgetown University Press.

Groopman, J. (2000). *Second opinions: Stories of intuition and choice in a changing world of medicine.* New York, Viking.

Guyer, B., Freedman, M. A., Strobino, D. M., & Sondik, E. J. (2000). Annual survey of vital statistics: Trends in the health of Americans during the 20th century. *Pediatrics 106,* 1307–1317.

Hacker, J. (2002). *The divided welfare state: The battle over public and private social benefits in the U.S.* Cambridge: Cambridge University Press.

Hadley, J., Holohan, H., Coughlin, T., & Miller, D. (2008). Covering the uninsured in 2008: Current costs, sources of payment and incremental costs. *Health Affairs, 27,* w399–w415.

Halbert, C. H., Armstrong, K., Gandy, Jr., O. H., & Shaker, L. (2006). Racial differences in trust in healthcare providers. *Archives of Internal Medicine, 166*(8), 896–901.

Halper, E. (2007, June 10). Public sector reels at retiree healthcare tab. *Los Angeles Times,* pp. A1, A32.

Halper, E., & Saillant, C. (2007, June 10). Daunting outlook, diverse actions. *Los Angeles Times,* p. A33.

Halverson, D. (2008). *Healthcare tsunami: The wave of consumerism that will change U.S. business.* Madison, WI: Glowac, Harris, Madison, Inc.

Halvorsen, G. (2007). *Healthcare reform now.* San Francisco: Jossey-Bass.

Hamilton. G. (1940). *The theory and practice of social case work.* New York, NY: Columbia University.

Hamric, A., Spross, J., Hanson, C. M., & Spross, J. (1996) *Advanced practice nursing: An integrative approach.* Philadelphia: W. B. Saunders.

Hanks, R. G. (2007). Barriers to nursing advocacy: A concept analysis. *Nursing Forum, 42,* 171.

Hansen, R. (2009, August 20). Discrimination alive and well against children with disabilities this month. *Examiner.com.* Retrieved from http://www .examiner.com/x-/x-4959-Special-Education-Examiner~ y2009m8d20-Discrimination-alive-and-well-against-children-with-disabilities

Hardina, D. (1995). Do Canadian social workers practice advocacy? *Journal of Community Practice, 2,* 97–121.

Harper, J. (2008, December 2). Medical security tops urgency list. *Washington Times.* Retrieved from http://www.washingtontimes.com/news/2008/dec/02/ medical-security-tops-urgency-list/

Harris, M. I., Klein R., Welborn, T. A., & Knuiman, M. W. (1992). Onset of NIDDM occurs at least 4–7 years before clinical diagnosis. *Diabetes Care 15,* 815–819.

Hartman, A. (1972). *Readings for social work practice.* New York, NY: MSS Information.

Hasnain-Wynia, R., Yonek, J., Pierce, D., Kang, R., & Greising, C. H. (2006). *Hospital language services for patients with limited English proficiency: Results from a national survey.* Chicago: Health Research and Educational Trust.

Hauser, W., & Hesdorffer, D. (1990). *Epilepsy: Frequency, causes and consequences.* New York, NY: Demos.

Haynes, R. B., McDonald, H. D., & Garg, A. X. (2002). Helping patients follow prescribed treatment. *Journal of the American Medical Association, 288,* 2880–2883.

Health Grades Inc. (2005). *The health grades quality study: Second annual patient safety in American hospitals report.* Retrieved on April 10, 2010 from http://www.health-grades.com/media/dms/pdf/patientsafetyinamerican-hospitalsreportfinal42905post.pdf

Healy, M. (2009, July 13). If red wine's good, are resveratrol pills even better? *Los Angeles Times.* Retrieved on April 10, 2010 from http://articles.latimes.com/2009/ jul/13/health/he-resveratrol13 p

Helfand, D. (2010, February 19). Consumers who buy individual health policies feel trapped. *Los Angeles Times.* Retrieved on April 10, 2010 from http://www .latimes.com/business/la-fi-insurance-trap20-2010feb 20,0,3448202.story

Helman, C. G. (2007). *Culture, health, and illness.* London, UK: Hodder Arnold.

Henig, R. (2005, August 7). Will we ever arrive at the good death? *New York Times,* p. 1.

Hepworth, D. H., Rooney, R. H., & Larsen, J. A. *Direct Social Work Practice: Theory and Skills,* (6th ed.). Pacific Grove, CA: Brooks/Cole.

Herbert, M., & Levin, R. (1996). The advocacy role in hospital social work. *Social Work in Healthcare, 22,* 71–83.

Herbert, M., & Mould, J. (1992). The advocacy role in hospital social work. *Child Welfare, 71,* 114–130.

Hernandez, L. M., & Munthali, A. W. (Eds). (2007). *Training physicians for public healthcareers.* Washington: National Academies.

Herz, E. J., Peterson, C. L., & Baumrucker, E. P. (2008). State Children's Health Insurance Program (SCHIP): A brief overview. In M. T. Ewing (Ed.), *State Children's Health Insurance Program (SCHIP)* (pp. 99–128). New York, NY: Nova Science.

Hilty, D., Young, J. S., Bourgeois, J. A., Klein, S., & Hardin, K. A. (2009). Algorithms for the assessment and management of insomnia in primary care. *Patient Preference and Adherence, 3,* 9–20.

Himmelstein, D., Thorne, D., Warren, E., & Woolhandler, S. (2009). Medical bankruptcy in the United States, 2007: Results of a national study. *American Journal of Medicine, 122,* 741–746.

HM Revenue and Customs. (2007). *Child poverty statistics: National indicator 116: The proportion of children in poverty.* Retrieved March 2, 2010, from http://www.hmrc.gov.uk/stats/personal-tax-credits/child_poverty.htm

Hobbs, D., Kunzman, S. C., Tandberg, D., & Sklar, D. (2000). Hospital factors associated with emergency center patients leaving without being seen. *American Journal of Emergency Medicine, 18,* 767–772.

Hoch, C., & Hemmons, G. (1987). Linking informal and formal help during the continuum of care. *Social Service Review, 9,* 434–445

Hogan, C. H., Lynn, J., Gabel, J., Lunney, J., O'Mara, A., & Wilkinson, A. (2000, May). *Medicare beneficiaries' costs and use of care in the last year of life. Final Report.* Retrieved from http://www.medicaring.org/educate/download/medpac.doc

Hook, J. (2009, November 4). Insurance discounts for healthy habits spur debate in Washington. *Los Angeles Times.* Retrieved from http://articles.latimes.com/2009/nov/04/nation/na-wellness4

Hooper, E. M., Comstock, L. M., Goodwin, J. M., & Goodwin, J. S. (1982). Patient characteristics that influence physician behavior. *Medical Care, 20,* 630–638.

Houry, D., Kemball, R., Rhodes, K. V., & Kaslow, N. J. (2006). Intimate partner violence and mental health symptoms in African American female ED patients. *American Journal of Emergency Medicine, 24*(4), 444–450. DOI: 10.1016/j.ajem.2005.12.026.

Hoyert, D. L., Freedman, M. A., Strobino, D. M., & Guyer, B. (2001). Annual summary of vital statistics: 2000. *Pediatrics, 108,* 1241–1255.

Hu, F. B., Stampfer, M. J., Colditz, G. A., Ascherio, A., Rexrode, K. M. Willett, W. C., & Manson, J. E. (2000). Physical activity and risk of stroke in women. *Journal of the American Medical Association, 283,* 2961–2967.

Huang, Z. J., Yu, S. M., & Ledsky, R. (2006). Health status and health service access and use among children in US immigrant families. *American Journal of Public Health, 96*(4), 634–640.

Hughes, R. B., Robinson-Wheeler, S., Taylor, H. B., Petersen, N., & Nasek, M. A. (2005). Characteristics of depressed and non-depressed women with physical disabilities. *Archives of Physical Medical Rehabilitation, 80,* 473–479.

Hummer, R. A., Ellison, C. G., Rogers, R. G., Moulton, B. E., & Romero, R. R. (2004). Religious involvement and adult mortality in the United States: Review and perspective. *Southern Medical Journal, 97,* 1223–1230.

Hurst, M., Gaines, M., Grob, R., Weil, L., & Davis, S. (2008). Educating for health advocacy in settings of higher learning. In J. Earp, E. French, & M. Gilkey (Eds.), *Patient Advocacy for Healthcare Quality* (pp. 481–506). Sudbury, MA: Jones and Bartlett.

Hwang, K., Johnston, M., Dyson-Hudson, T., & Komaroff, E. (2009). Access and coordination of healthcare service for people with disabilities. *Journal of Disability Policy Studies, 20*(1), 28–34.

Infoplease. (2007). *Paid vacation around the world.* Retrieved March 2, 2010, from http://www.infoplease.com/ipa/A0922052.html

Institute for John's Hopkins Nursing. (2010). *Continuing education: Patient advocacy seminar.* Retrieved on February 21, 2010, http://www.ijhn.jhmi.edu/programDetail_Class.asp?id=1019

Institute of Medicine. (2000). *To err is human: Building a safer health system.* Washington, DC: National Academy Press.

Institute of Medicine. (2001). *Crossing the quality chasm: A new health system for the 21st century.* Washington, DC: National Academies of Science.

Institute of Medicine. (2003). *Unequal treatment: Confronting racial and ethnic disparities in healthcare.* Washington, DC: National Academy Press.

Institute of Medicine. (2004). *Health literacy: A prescription to end confusion.* Washington, DC: National Academy Press.

Institute of Medicine. (2006a). *Emergency care for children: Growing pains.* Washington, DC: National Academy Press.

Institute of Medicine. (2006b). *Quality chasm series.* Washington, DC. National Academy Press.

Institute of Medicine. (2008). *Knowing what works in healthcare.* Washington, DC: National Academy Press.

Institute of Medicine. (2009). *America's uninsured crisis: Consequences for health and healthcare.* Washington, DC: National Academy Press.

Insurance company schemes [Editorial]. (2009, June 28). *New York Times,* p. A20.

International Diabetes Federation. (2010). *IDF Diabetes Atlas.* Retrieved April 22, 2010, from http://www.diabetesatlas.org/content/regional-data

Israel, B. A., Schulz, A. J., Parker, E. A., & Becker, A. B. (1998). Review of community based research: Assessing partnership approaches to improve public health. *Annual Review of Public Health, 19,* 173–202.

Ivanoff, A., & Smyth, N. (1992). Intervention with suicidal individuals. In K. Corcoran (Ed.), *Structuring* change: *Effective practice for common client problems* (pp. 111–137). Chicago: Lyceum Books.

Jackson, A. (2002). *Canada beats USA—But loses gold to Sweden.* Canadian Council on Social Development. Retrieved November 15, 2007, from http://www.ccsd.ca/pubs/2002/olympic/indicators.htm

Jackson, J. C., Rhodes, L. A., Inui, T. S., & Buchwald, D. (1997). Hepatitis B among the Khmer: Issues of translation and concepts of illness. *Journal of Internal General Medicine, 12,* 292–298.

Jacobs, E. A., Kohrman, C., Lemon, M., & Vickers, D. L. (2003). Teaching physicians-in-training to address racial disparities in health: A hospital-community partnership. *Public Health Reports, 118,* 349–355.

James, C., Thomas, M., Lillie-Blanton, M., & Garfield, R. (2007). *Key facts: Race ethnicity and medical care.* Retrieved from http://www.kff.org

Jansen, D., Krol, B., Groothoff, J. W., & Post, D. (2006). Towards improving medical care for people with intellectual disability living in the community: Possibilities of integrated care. *Journal of Applied Research in Intellectual Disabilities, 19,* 214–218.

Jansson, B. (1994). *Theory and practice of social welfare policy.* Belmont, CA: Wadsworth.

Jansson, B. (1995). *Theory and practice of social welfare policy.* Belmont, CA: Wadsworth.

Jansson, B. (2001). *The sixteen-trillion-dollar mistake: How the U.S. bungled its national priorities from the New Deal to Clinton.* New York, NY: Columbia University Press.

Jansson, B. (2004). *Becoming an effective policy advocate: From policy practice to social justice* (4th ed.). Belmont, CA: Brooks/Cole.

Jansson, B. (2008). *The reluctant welfare state: Engaging history to advance social work practice in contemporary society* (6th ed.). Belmont, CA: Brooks/Cole.

Jansson, B. (2011). *Becoming an effective policy advocate: From policy practice to social justice* (6th ed.). Belmont, CA: Brooks/Cole.

Jansson, B., & Dodd, S. J. (2002). Ethical activism: Strategies for empowering medical social workers. *Social Work in Healthcare, 36*(1), 11–28.

Jansson, B., & Simmons, J. (1985). The ecology of social work departments: Empirical findings and strategy implications. *Social Work in Healthcare 11,* 1–16.

Jansson, B., & Simmons, J. (1986). The survival of social work units in host organizations. *Social Work 31,* 336–345.

Jansson, R. (2003). Researcher liability for negligence in human subject research: Informed consent and researcher malpractice actions. *Washington Law Review Association, 78*(1), 229–263.

Jemal, A. (2008). Annual report to the nation on the status of cancer, 1975–2005, featuring trends in lung cancer, tobacco use and tobacco control. *Journal of the National Cancer Institute, 100,* 1672–1694.

Jensen, (1986). Consumers who are weighing surgery are likely to seek second opinions. *Modern Healthcare, 24* (925), 14–16.

Jezewski, M. A., & Sotnik, P. (2005). Disability service providers as culture brokers. In J. H. Stone (Ed.), *Culture and disability: Providing culturally competent services* (Multicultural Aspects of Counseling Series, No. 21). Thousand Oaks, CA: Sage.

Jha, A. K., DesRoches, C. M., Campbell, E. G., Donelan, K., Sowmya, R., Ferris, T. G., & Blumenthal, D. (2009). Use of electronic health records in U.S. Hospitals. *New England Journal of Medicine, 360,* 1629–1638.

Johnson, P. A., Lee, T. H., Cook, E. F., Rouan, G. W., & Goldman, L. (1993). Effect of race on the presentation and management of patients with acute chest pain. *Annals of Internal Medicine, 188,* 593–601.

Johnstone, S., & Halshaw, D. (2003). Making peace with fluid social workers lead cognitive behavioral intervention to reduce health-risk behavior. *Nephrology News and Issues, 17*(13), 20–27, 31.

Johnstone, S., & LeSage, L. (1998). *The key role of the nephrology social worker in treating the depressed ESRD patient: Patient utilization preferences and implications for on-site staffing practices.* Unpublished manuscript.

Joint Commission. (2008). *Office of Minority Health Culturally and Linguistically Appropriate Services (CLAS) Standards crosswalked with the Joint Commission 2008 Standards for Hospitals, Ambulatory, Behavioral Health, Long Term Care, and Home Care.* Retrieved May 7, 2009, from http://www.jointcommission.org

Joint Commission. (2009a). *Comprehensive accreditation manual for hospitals: The official handbook: Refreshed core.* Oakbrook Terrace, ILL.: Joint Commission Resources.

Joint Commission. (2009b). *Developing proposed requirements to advance effective communication, cultural competence, and patient-centered care for the hospital accreditation program.* Oakbrook Terrace, IL: Joint Commission. Retrieved on April 10, 2010 from http://www.jointcommission.org

Kabat-Zinn, J. (2003). Mindfulness-based interventions in context: Past, present, and future. *Clinical Psychology: Science and Practice, 10*(2), 144–156.

Kabat-Zinn, J., Massion, A., Kristeller, J., Peterson, L., Fletcher, K., Pbert, L., & Santorelli, S. (1992). Effectiveness of a meditation-based stress reduction program. *American Journal of Psychiatry, 149*(7), 936–943.

Kahn, J. G., Kronick, R., Kreger, M., & Gans, D. N. (2005). The cost of health insurance administration in California: Estimates for insurers, physicians, and hospitals. *Health Affairs, 24,* 1629–1639. doi: 10.1377/hlthaff.24.6.1629.

Kahn, K. L, Pearson, M. L., Harrison, E. R., Desmond, M. S., Rogers, W. H., Rubenstein, L. V., Brook, R. H., et al. (1994). Healthcare for black and poor hospitalized Medicare patients. *Journal of the American Medical Association, 271,* 1169–1174.

Kaiser Family Foundation. (2007, January). *Healthcare spending in the United States and OECD countries.* Retrieved from http://www.kff.org/insurance/snapshot/chcm010307oth.cfm

Kaiser Family Foundation. (2008a, February). *Fact sheet: The Medicare prescription drug benefit.* Retrieved from http://www.kff.org/medicare/7044.cfm

Kaiser Family Foundation. (2008b). *United States: Non-federal primary care physicians as a percent of total physicians,* 2008. Retrieved from http://www.state-healthfacts.org/profileind.jsp?ind=432&cat=8&rgn=1

Kaiser Family Foundation. (2009, February). *Kaiser health tracking poll: Public opinion on healthcare issues.* Retrieved from http://www.kff.org/kaiserpolls/upload/7866.pdf

Kaiser Family Foundation. (2010, January). *Medicare at a glance fact sheet.* Retrieved from http://www.kff.org/medicare/1066.cfm

Kaiser Family Foundation and Health Research and Education Trust. (2009, September). *Employer health benefits 2009 annual survey.* Retrieved from http://ehbs.kff.org/

Kane, R. L. (2000a). Choosing and using an assessment tool. In R. L. Kane & R. A. Kane (Eds.), *Assessing older persons: Measures, meanings, and practical applications* (pp. 237–260). New York, NY: Oxford University Press.

Kane, R. L. (2000b). Physiological well-being and health. In R. L. Kane & R. A. Kane (Eds.), *Assessing older persons: Measures, meanings, and practical applications* (pp. 237–260). New York, NY: Oxford University Press.

Kane, R. L. (2000c). Mandated assessments. In R. L. Kane & R. A. Kane (Eds.), *Assessing older persons: Measures, meanings, and practical applications* (pp. 458–482). New York, NY: Oxford University Press.

Kanter, R. (1977). *Men and women of the corporation.* New York, NY: Basic Books.

Kaplan, K., & Gellene, D. (2007, November 29). Waistlines in U.S. are expanding no more. *Los Angeles Times,* pp. A1, A21.

Karliner, L. S., Jacobs, E. A., Chen, A. H., & Mutha, S. (2007). Do professional interpreters improve clinical care for patients with limited English proficiency? A systematic review of the literature. *Health Services Research, 42*(2), 727–754.

Katon, W., Van Korff, M., Ciechanowski, P., Russo, J., Lin, E., Simon, G. et al. (2004). Behavioral and clinical factors associated with depression among individuals with diabetes. *Diabetes Care, 27,* 914–920.

Katon, W. J., Schoenbaum, M., Fan, M. Y., Callahan, C. M., Williams, J., Jr., Hunkeler, E., Harpole, L. et al. (2005). Cost-effectiveness of improving primary care treatment of late-life depression. *Archives of General Psychiatry, 62*(12), 1313–1320. doi: 10.1001/archpsyc.62.12.1313.

Katz, A. (1990). *Helping one another: Self-help in a changing world.* New York, NY: Third Party.

Kawachi, I., Daniels, N., & Robinson, D. E. (2005). Health disparities by race and class: Why both matter. *Health Affairs, 24*(2), 343–352.

Kawachi, I., Subramanian, S. V., & Almeida-Filho, N. (2008). A glossary of health inequalities. *Journal of Epidemiology and Community Health, 56,* 647–652 (updated online at http://jech.bmj.com/content/full/56/9/647)

Kelley, G. A., & Kelley, K. S. (2000). Progressive resistance exercise and resting blood pressure: A meta-analysis of randomized controlled trials. *Hypertension,* 2000, 838–843.

Kelly, R. B. (2009). Acupuncture for pain. *American Family Physician, 80,* 481–484.

Kessler, R., Demler, O., Frank, R., Olfson, M., Pincus, H., Walters, E., Wang, P., et al. (2005). *New England Journal of Medicine, 352*(25), 15–23.

Kessler, R., Sonnega, A., Bromet, E., Hughes, M., & Nelson, C. (1995). Posttraumatic stress disorder in the National Comorbidity Survey. *Archives of General Psychiatry, 52*(12), 1048–1060.

Khan, A. (2004). WHO argues the economic case for tackling violence. *The Lancet, 363*(9426), 2058–2058. DOI: 10.1016/S0140-6736(04)16490-8.

Kilbridge, P. (2003). The cost of HIPAA compliance. *New England Journal of Medicine 348,* 1423–1424.

Kim, M., Van Wye, G., Kerker, B., Thorpe, L., & Frieden, T. R. (2006). *The health of immigrants in New York City.* New York, NY: New York City Department of Health and Mental Hygiene.

Kimmel, P., Peterson, R., Weihs, K., Simmens, S., Allegne, S., & Cruz, I. (2000). Multiple measurements of depression predict mortality in a longitudinal study of chronic hemodialysis outpatients. *Kidney International, 5*(10), 2093–2098.

Kim-Rupnow, W. S. (2005). Disability and Korean culture. In J. H. Stone (Ed.), *Culture and disability: Providing culturally competent services* (pp. 115–138). Thousand Oaks, CA: Sage.

Klein, A., & Cnaan, R. (1995). Practice with high risk clients. *Families in Society, 76,* 203–212.

Kleinfeld, N. (2006, January 9). Diabetes and its awful toll quietly emerge as a crisis. *New York Times,* p. 1.

Knight, J. A. (2004). *A crisis call for new preventive medicine: Emerging effects of lifestyle on morbidity and mortality.* Singapore: World Scientific.

Knopp, R. H., Walden, C. E., Retzlaff, B. M., McCann, B. S., Dowdy A. A., Albers, J. J, & Cooper, M. N. (1997). Long-term cholesterol-lowering effect of 4 fat-restricted diets in hypercholesterolemic and combined hyperlipidemic men: The dietary alternatives study. *Journal of the American Medical Association,* 1997, 1509–1515.

Koerbel, L. S., & Zucker, D. M. (2007). The suitability of mindfulness-based stress reduction for chronic Hepatitis C. *Journal of Holistic Nursing, 25,* 265.

Koffman, J. & Higginson, J. (2001). Accounts of caregivers' satisfaction with healthcare at end of life: A comparison of first generation Caribbeans and white patients with advanced disease. *Palliative Medicine, 15,* 337–345.

Kolata, G. (2005, November 29). Does stress cause cancer? Probably not, research finds. *New York Times.* Retrieved from http://www.nytimes.com/2005/11/29/health/29canc.html?_r=1&scp=1&sq=&st=nyt

Kolata, G. (2007, May 8). Title genes take charge, and diets fall by the wayside. *New York Times.* Retrieved from http://www.nytimes.com/2007/05/08/health/08fat.html?pagewanted=1&_r=1&sq=hirsch&st=nyt&scp=3

Koocher, G., Curtiss, E., Pollin, I., & Patton, K. (2001). Medical crisis counseling in a health maintenance organization: Preventive Intervention. *Professional Psychology: Research and Practice, 32,* 52–58.

Kovacs, M., Goldston, D., Obrosky, D., & Bonar, L. (1997). Psychiatric Disorders in youth with IDDM: Rates and risk factors. *Diabetes Care, 20,* 36–44.

Kraus, W. E., Houmard, J. A., Duscha, B. D., Knetzger, K. J., Wharton, M. B., McCartney, J. S., & Slentz, C. A. (2002). Effects of the amount and intensity of exercise on plasma lipoproteins. *New England Journal of Medicine, 347,* 1483–1492.

Kristof, K. M. (2009, June 21). Finding the right health plan doesn't have to make you ill. *Los Angeles Times,* pp. B1, B4.

Kritz, F. L. (2009a, June 22). Grads, are you covered? *Los Angeles Times,* pp. E1, E6.

Kritz, F. L. (2009b, January 26). New job? Pick your best plan. *Los Angeles Times,* p. F3.

Kronfol, R. N., Childers, K., & Caviness, A. C. (2006). Patients who leave our emergency department without being seen: The Texas Children's hospital experience. *Pediatric Emergency Care, 22,* 550–554.

Kronz, J. D., Westra, W. H., & Epstein, J. I. (1999). Mandatory second opinion surgical pathology at a large referral hospital. *Cancer, 86,* 2426–2435.

Krueger, P. M., & Scholl, T. O. (2000). Adequacy of prenatal care and pregnancy outcome. *Journal of the American Osteopathic Association, 100,* 485–492.

Krug, E. G., Mercy, J. A., Dahlberg, L. L., & Zwi, A. B. (2002). The world report on violence and health. *The Lancet, 360*(9339), 1083–1088. DOI: 10.1016/S0140-6736(02)11133-0.

Krugman, P. (2007, February 16). The healthcare racket. *New York Times,* p. A19.

Krugman, P. (2009a, May 11). Harry, Louise and Barack. *New York Times,* p. A21.

Krugman, P. (2009b, June 5). Keeping them honest. *New York Times,* p. A21.

Ku, L., & Matani, S. (2001). Left out: Immigrants' access to healthcare and insurance. *Health Affairs, 20*(1), 247–256.

Kuehn, B. (2007). Hospitals embrace palliative care. *Journal of the American Medical Association, 298*(11), 1263–1265.

Kushel, M., Vittinghoff, E., & Hass, J. (2001). Factors associated with the healthcare utilization of homeless persons. *Journal of the American Medical Association, 285*(2), 200–206.

Kutner, M., Greenberg, E., & Baer, J. (2006). *National Assessment of Adult Literacy (NAAL): A first look at the literacy of America's adults in the 21st century* (Report no. NCES 2006-470). Washington, DC: National Center for Education Statistics, Institute of Education Sciences, U.S. Department of Education.

Kutner, M., Greenberg, E., Jin, Y., Paulsen, C., & White, S. (2006). *The health literacy of America's adults: Results from the 2003 National Assessment of Adult Literacy* (Report no. NCES 2006-483). Washington, DC: National Center for Education Statistics, Institute of Education Sciences, U.S. Department of Education.

La Ganga, M. L. (2009, July 13). They're doing a feel-good thing. *Los Angeles Times.* Retrieved from http://articles.latimes.com/2009/jul/13/local/me-sisters13

Lammers, C., Naliboff, B., & Straatmeyer, A. (1984). The effectives of progressive relaxation on stress and diabetic control. *Behavior Research and Therapy, 22,* 641–650.

Lantos, J. (2007). The edge of the known world. *Health Affairs, 26,* 510–514.

Lasker, R. D., Weiss, E. S., & Miller, R. (2001). Partnership synergy: A practical framework for studying and strengthening the collaborative advantage. *Milbank Quarterly, 79*(2), 179–205.

Last Acts Report. (2002). C Means to a better end: A report on dying in America today. Washington, DC. Retrieved December 10, 2008, from http://www.lastacts.org

Lautrette, A., Ciroldi, M., Ksibi, H., & Azoulay, E. (2006). End-of-life family conferences: Rooted in the evidence. *Critical Care Medicine, 34*(11), S364–S372.

Lawrence, D. (2003). My mother and the medical care ad-hoc-racy. *Health Affairs, 22*(2), 238–242.

Lazarus, D. (2009a, June 14). Feeling sick over sky-high rate hike. *Los Angeles Times,* pp. B1, B8.

Lazarus, D. (2009b, June 24). Going broke for health coverage. *Los Angeles Times,* pp. B1, B6.

Lazarus, D. (2009c, February 4). Health savings accounts are ill advised. *Los Angeles Times.* Retrieved from http://articles.latimes.com/2009/feb/04/business/fi-lazarus4

Lazarus, D. (2009d, July 5). Wal-Mart taking a good-guy stance. *Los Angeles Times,* pp. B1, B3.

Lazebnik, R., & O'Brien, G. (1998). Telephone call reminders and attendance in an adolescent clinic. *Pediatrics, 101*(e6).

Leape, L. (Ed.). (2006). *When things go wrong: Responding to adverse events.* Burlington, MA: Massachusetts Coalition for the Prevention of Medical Errors.

LeClere, F. B., Jensen, L., & Biddlecom, A. E. (1994). Healthcare utilization, family context, and adaptation among immigrants to the United States. *Journal of Health and Social Behavior, 35*(4), 370–384.

Lee, H., & McConville, S. (2007). Death in the Golden State: Why do some Californians live longer? *California counts: Population trends and profiles, 9:1.* Retrieved from http://www.ppic.org/content/pubs/cacounts/CC_807HLCC.pdf

Lee, I-M., & Paffenbarger, R. S. (1998). Physical activity and stroke incidence: The Harvard alumni health study. *Stroke, 29,* 2049–2054.

Lefton, R. (2008). Reducing variation in healthcare delivery. *Healthcare Finance Management, 62*(7), 42–44.

Lett, H., Blumenthal, J., Babyak, M., Sherwood, A., Strauman, T., Robins, C., & Newman, M. F. (2004). Depression as a risk factor for coronary artery disease: Evidence, mechanisms and treatment. *Psychosomatic Medicine, 66*(3), 305–315.

Leuck, T. J., & Severson, K. (2006, December 6). New York bans most trans fats in restaurants. *New York Times.* Retrieved from http://www.nytimes.com/2006/12/06/nyregion/06fat.html

Leutz, W. (1999). Five laws for integrating medical and social services: Lessons from the United States and the United Kingdom. *The Milbank Quarterly, 77*(1), 77–110.

Leutz, W., Greenlick, M. R., & Nonnenkamp, L. (2003). *Linking medical care and community services: Practical models for bridging the gap.* New York, NY: Springer.

Levey, S., & Hill, J. (1988). Advocacy reconsidered: Progress and prospects. *Hospital & Health Services Administration, 33,* 467–479.

Levine, D. M., Bone, L. R., Hill, M. N., Stallings, R., Gelber, A. C., Barker, A. & Clark, J. M. (2003). The effectiveness of a community/academic health center partnership in decreasing the level of blood pressure in an urban African-American population. *Ethnicity & Disease,* vol. *13,* 354–361.

Levinson, W., & Engel, C. (1997). Anxiety. In M. D. Feldman & J. F. Christensen (Eds.), *Behavioral medicine in primary care: A practical guide* (pp. 193–211). Stamford, CT: Appleton & Lange.

Lichtenstein, A. H., Appel, L. J., Brands, M., Carnethon, M., Daniels, S., Franch, H. A., & Wylie-Rosett, J. (2006). Diet and lifestyle recommendations revision 2006: A scientific statement from the American Heart Association Nutrition Committee. *Circulation, 114,* 82–96.

Lin, E.H.B., VonKorff, M., Russo, J., Katon, W., Simon, G. E., Unutzer, J., Bush, T., et al. (2000). Can depression treatment in primary care reduce disability?: A stepped care approach. *Archives of Family Medicine,* 9(10), 1052–1058. doi: 10.1001/archfami.9.10.1052.

Link, C. L., & McKinlay, J. B. (2009). Disparities in the prevalence of diabetes: It is race/ethnicity or socioeconomic status? Results from the Boston area community health (BACH survey). *Ethnicity & Disease, 19,* 288–292.

Lipsky, M. (1980). *Street-level bureaucracy: Dilemmas of the individual in public services.* New York, NY: Sage.

Liu, G. Z. (2005). Best practices: Developing cross-cultural competence from a Chinese perspective. In J. H. Stone (Ed.), *Culture and disability: Providing culturally competent services* (pp. 65–85). Thousand Oaks, CA: Sage.

Liu, S., Manson, J. E., Stampfer, M. J., Hu, F. B., Giovannucci, E., Colditz, G. A., Hennekens, C. H., et al. (2000). A prospective study of whole-grain intake and risk of type 2 diabetes mellitus in US women. *American Journal of Public Health,* 90(9), 1409–1415.

Liu, S., Stampfer, M. J., Hu, F. B., Giovannucci, E., Colditz, G. A., Hennekens, C. H., & Willett, W. C. (1999). Whole-grain consumption and risk of coronary heart disease: Results from the Nurses' Health Study. *American Journal of Clinical Nutrition, 70,* 412–419.

Logan, D., King, J., & Fischer-Wright, H. (2008). *Tribal leadership: Leveraging natural groups to build a thriving organization.* New York, NY: HarperCollins.

Lohr, S. (2009, July 13). Electronic health records: A Texas model. *New York Times.* Retrieved from http://bits.blogs.nytimes.com/2009/07/13/electronic-health-records-a-texas-model/?scp=2&sq=electronic%20health%20records&st=Search

Long, M. J. (2002). Case management model or case manager type? That is the question. *Healthcare Manager, 20* (4), 53–65.

Los Angeles Coalition to End Hunger and Homelessness. (2008). *The peoples guide to welfare, health and other services,* (32nd ed.). Retrieved from http://www.lacehh.org/tpg/documents/english08PeoplesGuide.pdf

Los Angeles County Department of Health Services (2003). *Cultural and linguistic competency standards (developed by the DHS cultural and linguistic competency standards workgroup).* Los Angeles, CA: Los Angeles County Department of Health Services.

Loue, S., Lloyd, L., & O'Shea, D. (2003). *Community health advocacy.* New York, NY: Kluwer Academic/Plenum.

Loyola University Health System (2004). Umbilical Cord Blood Transplants, Bone Marrow Transplants Save Lives. *ScienceDaily.* From http://www.sciencedaily.com–/releases/2004/06/040602060912.htm

Lukas, S. (1993). *Where to start and what to ask: An assessment handbook.* New York, NY: Norton.

Lustman, P., Griffith, L., Freedland, K., Kissel, S., & Clouse, R. (1998). Cognitive behavior therapy for depression in type 2 diabetes mellitus: A randomized, controlled trial. *Annals of Internal Medicine, 129,* 613–621.

Lynch, A. M., Jarvis, C. I., DeBellis, R. J., & Morin, A. K. (2007). State of the art reviews: Nonpharmacologic approaches for the treatment of insomnia. *American Journal of Lifestyle Medicine, 1,* 274.

Lynch, H., Mathes, M., & Sawicki, N. (2008). Compliance with advance directives: Wrongful living and tort law incentives. *Journal of Legal Medicine 29,* 133–178.

Lyon, D. (2001). Human immunodeficiency virus (HIV) disease in persons with severe mental illness. *Issues in Mental Health Nursing, 22,* 109–119.

Mackie, J. (1977). *Inventing right and wrong.* London: Penguin.

MacNeilage, L., & Adams, K. (1982). *Assertiveness at work.* Englewood Cliffs, NJ: Prentice Hall.

Mallik, M. (2000). Advocacy in nursing—A review of literature. *Journal of Advanced Nursing, 25,* 1, 130–138.

Mallik-Kane, K., & Visher, C.A. (2008). *Health and prisoner reentry: How physical, mental, and substance abuse conditions shape the process of reintegration.* Washington, DC: Urban Institute. Retrieved from http://www.urban.org/UploadedPDF/411617_health_prisoner_reentry.pdf

Maltz, W. (2001). *The sexual healing journey: A guide for survivors of sexual abuse.* New York, NY: HarperCollins.

Maltz, W. (2003). Treating the sexual intimacy concerns of sexual abuse survivors. *Contemporary Sexuality, 37* (7), i–viii.

Management Sciences in Health. (2004). *The provider's guide to quality & culture (web-based).* Retrieved from http://erc.msh.org

Mangione-Smith, R., DeCristofaro, A., Setodji, C., Keesen, J., Klein, D., Adams, J., Schuster, M., Glynn, Glynn, F. (2007). Quality of ambulatory care delivered to children in the U.S. *New England Journal of Medicine,* 357(15), 1515–1523.

March of Dimes. (2009, October). *PeriStats: Born too soon and too small in the United States.* Retrieved from http://www.marchofdimes.com/peristats/pdflib/195/99.pdf

Marcks, B. A., & Weisberg, R. B. (2009). Co-occurrence of insomnia and anxiety disorders: A review of the literature. *American Journal of Lifestyle Medicine, 3,* 300.

Markel, H., & Golden, J. (2005). Children's public health policy in the United States: How the past can inform the future. *Health Affairs, 23*(5), 147–152.

Marmot, M. G., & Smith, G. D. (1989). Why are the Japanese living longer? *British Medical Journal, 299,* 1547–1551.

Marsh, B. (2005, April 10). The nation: The story of government forms, a real page-turner. *New York Times,* p. 9.

Marshall, G., Schell, T. L., Elliott, M. N., Berthold, S. M., & Chun, C. (2005). Mental health of Cambodian refugees two decades after resettlement in the United States. *Journal of the American Medical Society, 294*(5), 571–579.

Martin, S. (1982). The sentinel effect in Second Opinion Programs. *Employee Benefit Plan Review, 36*(8), 24, 26.

Marzuk, P., Tardiff, K., Leon, A., Hirsch, C., Hartwell, N., Portera, L., & Iqbal, M. (1997). HIV seroprevalence among suicide victims in New York City, 1991–1993. *American Journal of Psychiatry, 154,* 1720–1725.

Matthews, C. (1988). *Hardball: How politics is played.* New York, NY: Summit.

Mayo Clinic. (2010). *Education and research: Midwest advocacy project.* Retrieved on February 27, 2010, from http://mayoresearch.mayo.edu/tbims/midwest.cfm

Mayo, N., Nasmith, L., & Tannenbaum, C. B. (2003) Understanding older women's healthcare concerns: A qualitative study. *Journal of Aging & Women, 15*(4).

Mazel, J. (1981). *The Beverly Hills diet.* New York, NY: Macmillan.

McBean, A. M., & Gornick, M. (1994). Differences by race in the rates of procedures performed in hospitals for Medicare beneficiaries. *Healthcare Financial Review, 15,* 77–90.

McCathie, H.C.F., Spence, S. H., & Tate, R. L. (2002). Adjustment to chronic obstructive pulmonary disease: The importance of psychological factors. *European Respiratory Journal, 18*(1), 47–53.

McCurdy, D. (1996). Nurses and euthanasia: Supposing it's so. *Making the rounds in health, faith, and ethics, 12* (1), 1–3.

McDaniel, S., Campbell, T., Hepworth, J., & Lorenz, A. (2005). *Family-oriented primary care* (2nd ed.). New York, NY: Springer.

McDonald, S., & Ahern, K. (1999). Whistle-blowing: Effective and ineffective coping responses. *Nursing Forum, 34*(4), 5–13.

McFarlane, W. (Ed.). (2002). *Multifamily groups in the treatment of severe psychiatric disorders.* New York, NY: Guilford.

McGlynn, Eq.A., Asch, S. M., Adams, J., Keesey, J., Hicks, J., DeCristofaro, A., & Kerr, E. A. (2003). The quality of healthcare delivered to adults in the United States. *New England Journal of Medicine, 348,* 2635–2645.

McGrail, M. P., Calasanz, M., Christianson, J., Cortez, C, Dows, B., Gorman, R., & Westman, G. (2002). The Minnesota Health Partnership and coordinated healthcare and disability prevention: The implementation of an integrated benefits and medical care model. *Journal of Occupational Rehabilitation, 12,* 43–54.

McGuinness, T. (2009). Helping parents decide on ADHD treatment for their children. *Journal of psychosocial nursing mental health services, 47*(2), 13–20.

McKinlay, J. B., Potter, D. A., & Feldman, H. A. (1996). Non-medical influences on medical decision-making. *Social Science and Medicine, 24,* 769–776.

Meert, K. L., Thurston, C. S., & Briller, S. H. (2005). The spiritual needs of parents at the time of their child's death in the pediatric intensive care unit and during bereavement: A qualitative study. *Pediatric Critical Care Medicine, 6*(4), 420–427.

Mehta, D., & McCarthy, E. (2009). Complementary and alternative medicines. In C. Trinh-Shevrin, N. S. Islam & M. J. Rey (Eds.), *Asian American communities and health: Context, research, policy and action* (pp. 285–322). San Francisco, CA: John Wiley & Sons.

Meier, B. (1997, August 8). For-profit's care's human cost. *New York Times,* pp. C1, C4.

Mestel, R. (2003, December 29). Round and round we go. *Los Angeles Times,* p. F1, F5.

Military Health System. (2010, January). *Tricare: Your military health plan. Eligibility.* Retrieved March 10, 2010, from http://www.tricare.mil/mybenefit/home/overview/Eligibility

Miller, C. C. (2009, December 20). The virtual visit may expand access to doctors. *New York Times,* p. B4.

Miller, D. (2005). An introduction to Jamaican culture for rehabilitation service providers. In J. H. Stone (Ed.), *Culture and disability: Providing culturally competent services* (pp. 87–113). Thousand Oaks, CA: Sage.

Miller, S. M., Roussi, P., Daly, M. B., Buzaglo, J. S., Sherman, K., Godwin, A. K., Balshem, A., & Atchison, M. E. (2005). Enhanced counseling for women undergoing BRCA1/2 Testing: Impact on subsequent decision making about risk reduction behaviors. *Health Education & Behavior, 32,* 654.

Miller, W., & Rollnick, S. (2002). *Motivational interviewing: Preparing people for change* (2nd ed.). New York, NY: Guilford.

Mohr, D., Hart, S., Julian, L., & Tasch, E. (2007). Screening for depression among patients with multiple sclerosis, two questions may be enough. *Multiple Sclerosis, 13*(2), 215–219.

Mojon, P., Budtz-Jorgensen, E., & Rapin, C-H. (2000). Relationship between oral health and nutrition in very old people. *Age and Aging, 28,* 463–468.

Montori, V., Gafni, A., & Charles, C. (2006). A shared treatment decision-making approach between patients with chronic conditions and their clinicians: The case of diabetes. *Health Expectations, 9,* 25–36.

Morin, C. L., Culbert, J. P., & Schwartz, S. M. (1994). Nonpharmacological interventions for insomnia: A meta-analysis of treatment efficacy. *American Journal of Psychiatry, 151,*8, 1172.

Morris, N. S., MacLean, C. D., Chew, L. D., & Littenberg, B. (2006). The single item literacy screener: Evaluation of a brief instrument to identify limited reading ability. *BMC Medical Practice, 7*(21).

Moscicki, E. (1997). Identification of suicide risk factors using epidemiologic studies. *Psychiatric Clinics of North America, 20*(3), 499–517.

Mullahy, C. (1995). *The case manager's handbook.* Gaithersburg, MD: Aspen.

Murphy, G. (1975a). The physician's responsibility for suicide: Pt. 1. An error of commission. *Annals of Internal Medicine, 82*(3), 301–304.

Murphy, G. (1975b). The physician's responsibility for suicide: Pt. 2. Errors of omission. *Annals of Internal Medicine, 82*(3), 305–309.

Murphy, S. P., Davis, M. A., Neuhaus, J. M., & Lein, D. (1990). Factors influencing the dietary adequacy and energy intake of older Americans. *Journal of Nutrition Education, 22,* 224–291.

Murray, C.J.L., & Lopez, A. D. (1996). Evidence-based health policy—Lessons from the global burden of disease study. *Science, 274,* 740–743.

Mycek, S. (2007). Under the spreading planetree. *Trustee, 60,* 22–25.

National Alliance to End Homelessness. (2010). *2007 Homelessness counts.* Retrieved on March 2, 2010, from http://www.endhomelessness.org/section/data/homelessmap#

National Association of Home Care. (2001). *Basic statistics about home care.* Retrieved February 10, 2010, from http://www.nahc.org/consumer/hcstats.html

National Association of Social Workers. (Approved 1996, revised 1999). *Code of ethics of the National Association of Social Workers.* Washington, DC: Author.

National Cancer Institute. (2005). *Fact sheet: Magnetic field exposure and cancer: Questions and answers.* Retrieved on April 10, 2010 from http://www.cancer.gov/cancertopics/factsheet/Risk/magnetic-fields

National Center for Chronic Disease Prevention and Health Promotion, Office on Smoking and Health. (1998). *Tobacco use Among U.S. Racial/Ethnic minority groups—African Americans, American Indians and Alaska Natives, Asian Americans and Pacific Islanders, and Hispanics: A report of the surgeon general.* Atlanta, GA: Centers for Disease Control and Prevention.

National Center for Education Statistics. (n.d.). *National assessment of adult literacy 2003: Demographics—Overall.* Retrieved March 3, 2010, from http://nces.ed.gov/naal/kf_demographics.asp

National Center for Health Statistics. (1999). *National nursing home survey: Trends from 1973 to 1999.* Retrieved February 10, 2010, from http://www.cdc.gov/nchs/data/nnhsd/NNHSTrends1973to1999.pdf

National Center for Immunization and Respiratory Diseases. (2008, June). *Childcare and school immunization requirements.* Retrieved from http://www2a.cdc.gov/nip/schoolsurv/immunizationRqmts.htm

National Center for Posttraumatic Stress Disorder. (n.d.). *Screening for PTSD in a primary care setting.* Retrieved January 30, 2010, from http://www.ptsd.va.gov/professional/pages/assessments/pc-ptsd.asp

National Center for Veterans Analysis and Statistics. (2010, February). *VA benefits and healthcare utilization.* Retrieved from http://www1.va.gov/VETDATA/Pocket-Card/4X6_winter10_sharepoint.pdf

National Council of Disability. (1997). *Equality of opportunity: The making of the Americans with disabilities act.* Washington, DC: Author.

National Diabetes Information Clearinghouse. (2008, June). *National diabetes statistics, 2007.* NIH Publication No. 08-3892. Retrieved from http://diabetes.niddk.nih.gov/DM/PUBS/statistics/#costs

National Highway Traffic Safety Administration. (2009, December). *Lives saved FAQS.* Retrieved from http://www-nrd.nhtsa.dot.gov/Pubs/811105.PDF

National Institute of Diabetes and Digestive and Kidney Diseases. (2004). *National diabetes statistics fact sheet: General information and national estimates on diabetes in the United States, 2003.* Betheseda, MD: National Institutes of Health.

National Institute on Aging. (2004). *General information: How many Americans have AD?* (Alzheimer's Diesease Education and Referral Center). Retrieved February 10, 2010, from http://www.nia.nih.gov/Alzheimers/AlzheimersInformation/GeneralInfo/

National Institutes of Health. (2010). *Behavioral trial studying programmed training to improve advocacy skills for individuals with traumatic brain injury (MAP).* Retrieved on February 27, 2010, from http://clinicaltrials.gov/ct2/show/NCT01002677

National Network of Libraries of Medicine. (2008). *Health literacy.* Retrieved June 2, 2009, from http://nnlm.gov/outreach/consumer/hlthlit.html

National Quality Forum. (2009). *A comprehensive framework and preferred practices for measuring and reporting cultural competency: A consensus report.* Washington, DC: National Quality Forum.

Neergaard, L. (2009, July 1). Obesity study lean on positives. *AP Features.* Retrieved July 8, 2010, from http://www.onlineathens.com/stories/070209/new_458011024.shtml

Nelson, K., Brown, M. E., & Lurie, N. (1998). Hunger in an adult patient population. *Journal of the American Medical Association, 279,* 1211–1214.

Nelson, M. (1999). A view of social work advocacy in hospitals in eastern Ontario. *Social Work in Healthcare, 29,* 69–92.

Neri, M. T., & Kroll, T. (2009). Understanding the consequences of access barriers to healthcare: experiences of adults with disabilities. *Disability and Rehabilitation, 25*(2), 85–96.

New York Times Editorial (2009, September 11). Immigrants, healthcare, and lies, p. A 26.

Newcomer, J. W., & Hennekens, C. H. (2007). Severe mental illness and risk of cardiovascular disease.

Journal of the American Medical Association, 298, 15, pp. 1794–1796.

Ngo-Metzger, Q., Massagli, M., Clarridge, B. R., Manocchia, M., Davis, R. B., Iezzoni, L. I., & Phillips, R.S., (2003). Linguistic and cultural barriers to care: Perspectives of Chinese and Vietnamese immigrants. *Journal of General Internal Medicine, 18,* 44–52.

Nielsen Company. (2009, December). *A2/M2 Three screen report. V.5 second quarter 2009.* Retrieved from http://blog.nielsen.com/nielsenwire/wp-content/uploads/2009/09/ThreeScreenReport_US_2Q09 REV.pdf

Obama, Barack (2010). *The Patient's Bill of Rights* (Organizing for America). Retrieved on July 10, 2010 at www.barackobama.com

Ockene, I. D., & Houston, N. (1997). Cigarette smoking, cardiovscular disease and stroke: A statement for healthcare professionals from the American Heart Association. *Circulation, 96,* 3243–3247.

Office of Management and Budget. (2010). *Budget of the United States Government.* Retrieved February 20, 2010, from http://www.whitehouse.gov/omb/rewrite/budget/fy2008/summarytables.html

Office of Minority Health. (2009, December). *Diabetes and Hispanic Americans.* Retrieved from http://minorityhealth.hhs.gov/templates/content.aspx?ID= 3324

Office of National Drug Control Policy. (2004). *The economic costs of drug abuse in the United States, 1992–2002.* Washington, DC: Executive Office of the President (Publication No. 207303)

Olshinski, A. (1999). Risk management in healthcare. In A. Kilpatrick & J. Johnson (Eds.), *Handbook of health administration and policy* (pp. 421–438). New York: Marcel Dekker.

Organisation for Economic Cooperation and Development. (2006, October). *OECD health data 2006.* Retrieved from http://www.oecd.org/health/healthdata

Organisation for Economic Cooperation and Development. (2010). Social expedition: Aggregated data. *OECD Stat Extracts.* Retrieved from http://oecd.org

Orth-Gomer, K. (2007). Job strain and the risk of recurrent coronary events. *Journal of the American Medical Association, 298,* 1693–1694.

Osmond, D. H. (2003). *Epidemiology of HIV/AIDS in the United States: Table 3. AIDS cases and deaths, by year and age group, through December 2001, United States.* Retrieved from http://hivinsite.ucsf.edu/InSite-KB-ref.jsp?page=kb-01-03&ref=kb-01-03-tb-03&no=3

Padre Contra Costa website (2008). Retrieved on March 30, 2008 from http://www.iamhope.org.

Pagán, J., & Pauly, M. (2005). Access to conventional medical care and the use of complementary and alternative medicine. *Health Affairs, 24*(1), 255–262.

Paniagua, R., Amato, D., Guo, A., & Mujais, S. (2005). Health-related quality of life predicts outcomes but is not affected by peritoneal clearance: The ADEMEX trial. *Kidney International, 67*(3), 1093–2005.

Pashos, C. L., Normand, S. L., Garfinkle, J. B., Newhouse, J. P., Epstein, A. M., & McNeil, B. J. (1994). Trends in the use of drug therapies in patients with acute myocardial infarction: 1988 to 1992. *Journal of the American College of Cardiology, 23,* 1023–1030.

Passel, J. S., & Cohn, D. (2008). *U.S. population projections: 2005–2050.* Washington, DC: Pew Research Center.

Passel, J. S., & Suro, R. (2005). *Rise, peak, and decline: Trends in U.S. immigration, 1992–2004.* Washington, DC: Pew Hispanic Center.

Patrick, D., Ferketich, S. L., Frame, P. S., Harris, J. J., Hendricks, C. B., Levin, B., Link, M. P., et al. (2003). National Institutes of health state-of-the-science conference statement: Symptom management in cancer: Pain, depression, and fatigue, July 15-17, 2002. *Journal of the National Cancer Institute, 95*(15), 1110–1117.

Pear, R. (2008, February 24). Governors of both parties oppose Medicaid rules. *New York Times.* Retrieved from http://www.nytimes.com/2008/02/24/washington/24medicaid.html?_r=1&scp=1&sq=medicaid++robert+pear&st=nyt

Pear, R. (2010, April 5). New health initiatives put spotlight on prevention. *New York Times,* p. A10.

Perez-Pena, R. (2005, October 15). At a Bronx clinic, high hurdles for Medicaid Care. *New York Times,* p. A1.

Perkins, J., & Youdelman, M. (2008). *Summary of state law requirements: Addressing language needs in healthcare.* Los Angeles: National Health Law Program.

Perkins, J., Youdelman, M., & Wong, D. (2003). *Ensuring linguistic access in healthcare settings: Legal rights and responsibilities.* Los Angeles: National Health Law Program.

Perlman, H. (1957). *Social casework, a problem-solving process.* Chicago, IL: University of Chicago.

Peterson, C., Seligman, M., & Vaillant, G. (1988). Pessimistic explanatory style is a risk factor for physical illness: A thirty-five-year longitudinal study. *Journal of Personality and Social Psychology, 55,* 23–27.

Pew Research Center. (2006, April). *Eating more, enjoying less.* Retrieved from http://pewresearch.org/pubs/309/eating-more-enjoying-less

Pham, H. H., Schrag, D., Hargraves, J. L., & Bach, P. B. (2005). Delivery of preventive services to older adults by primary care physicians. *Journal of the American Medical Association, 294,* 473–481.

Phillips, D. P., & Carstensen, L. L. (1986). Clustering of teenage suicides after television news stories about suicide. *New England Journal of Medicine, 315,* 685–689.

Pillow, W. S. (2004). *Unfit subjects: Educational policy and the teen mother.* New York, NY: RoutledgeFalmer.

Planetree. (2009). *About planetree.* Retrieved on November 20, 2009, from http://www.planetree.org/about.html

Poen, M. (1979). *Harry S. Truman versus the medical lobby: The genesis of Medicare.* Columbia, MS: University of Missouri Press.

Ponce, N. A., Ku, L., Cunningham, W. E., & Brown, E. R. (2006). Language barriers to healthcare access among Medicare beneficiaries. *Inquiry, 43,* 66–76.

Preston, J. (2007, November 29). US immigrant population is highest since the 1920s. *New York Times,* p. A15.

Price, G. M., Uauy, R., Breeze, E., Bulpitt, C. J., Fletcher, A. E. (2006). Weight, shape, and mortality risk in older persons: Elevated waist-hip ratio, not high body mass index, is associated with a greater risk of death. *American Journal of Clinical Nutrition*, 84(2), 449–460.

Prigerson, H. G., & Jacobs, S. C. (2001). Caring for bereaved patients: "All the doctors just suddenly go." *Journal of the American Medical Association*, 286 (11), 1369–1376. doi: 10.1001/Journal of the American Medical Association.286.11.1369.

Pritikin, N. (1979). *The Pritikin program for diet & exercise*. New York, NY: Bantam.

Prochaska, J., & DiClemente, C. (1983). Stages and processes of self-change of smoking: Toward and integrative model of change. *Journal of Consulting and Clinical Psychology*, 51, 390–395.

Purnell, L. D., & Paulanka, B. J. (2008). *Transcultural healthcare: A culturally competent approach* (3rd ed.). Philadelphia: F.A. Davis.

Rabow, M. W., Hauser, J. M., & Adams, J. (2004). Supporting family caregivers at the end of life: "They don't know what they don't know." *Journal of the American Medical Association*, 291(4), 483–491. doi: 10.1001/Journal of the American Medical Association.291.4.483.

Rafael, A.R.F. (1995). Advocacy and empowerment: Dichotomous or synchronous concepts? *Advanced Nursing Science*, 18, 25–32.

Rafferty, M. (1998). Prevention services in primary care: Taking time, setting priorities. *Western Journal of Medicine*, 98, 851–855.

Rainbow Heights Club (2009). *5 steps towards effective and culturally competent treatment with lesbian, gay, bisexual and transgender people living with mental illness*. Retrieved March 20, 2010 from http://www.rainbowheights.org

Ramsay, N. (2008, May 24). *TV viewing figures vs. IQ ranking by country*. [Web log post]. Retrieved from http://www.longcountdown.com/2008/05/24/tv-viewing-figures-vs-iq-ranking-by-country/

Ransdell, L. B., & Wells, C. L. (1998). Physical activity in urban white, African-American, and Mexican-American women. *Medicine & Science in Sports & Exercise*, 30, 1608–1615.

Ratcliffe. J., Thomas, K. J., MacPherson, H., & Brazier, J. (2006). A randomised controlled trial of acupuncture care for persistent low back pain: Cost effectiveness analysis. *British Medical Journal*, 333(7569), 626–628.

Ravn, K. (2009, April 6). Habits can be broken, but not forgotten. *Los Angeles Times*. Retrieved from http://articles.latimes.com/2009/apr/06/health/he-badhabits6

Ray, W., Daugherty, M. S., & Meador, K. G. (2003). Effect of a mental health "carve-out" program on the continuity of antipsychotic therapy. *New England Journal of Medicine*, 348, 1885–1894.

Reardon, C. (2009). Dual degree programs—Connecting social work with other disciplines. *Social Work Today*, 9(5), 16.

Reckling, J. (1997). Who plays what role in decisions and withholding and withdrawing life-sustaining treatment? *Journal of Clinical Ethics*, 8(1), 39–45.

Red Meat Industry Forum. (2007, May). *Beef and veal consumption and choosing the right cut*. Retrieved from http://redmeatindustryforum.org.uk/supplychain/BVConsumption.htm

Reede, J. Y. (2003). A recurring theme: The need for minority physicians. *Health Affairs*, 22(4), 91–93.

Reese, D. J., Ahern, E., O'Faire, J.D., & Warren, C. (1999). Hospice access and use by African Americans: Addressing cultural and institutional barriers through participatory action research. *Social Work*, 44(6), 549–559.

Reilly, J. J., Hull, S. F., Albert, N., Waller, A., & Bringardener, S. (1988). Economic impact of malnutrition: A model system for hospitalized patients. *Journal of Parenteral and Enteral Nutrition*, 12, 371–376.

Reiss-Brennan, B. (2006). Can mental health integration in a primary care setting improve quality and lower costs? A case study. *Journal Managed Care Pharmacy*, 12(Suppl. 2), 14–20.

Reti, S. R., Feldman, H. J., Ross, S. E., & Safran, C. (2010). Improving personal health records for patient-centered care. *Journal of the American Medical Information Association*, 17, 192–195.

Rich, J. D., Holmes, L., Salsa, C., Macalino, G., Davis, D., Ryczek, J., & Flanigan, T. (2001). Successful linkage of medical care and community services for HIV-positive offenders being released from prison. *Journal of Urban Health*, 78(2), 279–289.

Ries, L., Eisner, M., Kosary, C., Hankey, B., Miller, B., Clegg, L., Weir, HK, et al. (2003). (Eds.), *SEER cancer statistics review, 1975–2000*. Bethesda, MD: National Cancer Institute. Available from http://seer.cancer.gov/csr/1975_2000/

Roberts C. (1989). Conflicting professional values in social work and medicine. *Health & Social Work*, 14, 211–218.

Roberts, S. (2004, January). Advocacy firms help cure benefit troubles. *Business Insurance*, 38, 32.

Rogers S., & Komisar, H. (2003). *Who needs long-term care?* Retrieved from http://ltc.georgetown.edu/pdfs/whois.pdf

Rogers, S., & Shirey, L. (2002, November). Chronic obstructive pulmonary disease: A chronic condition that limits activities. *Center on an Aging Society Data Profiles Series 2: Challenges for the 21st Century: Chronic and Disabling Conditions*. Retrieved from http://ihcrp.georgetown.edu/agingsociety/profiles.html

Rolland, J., & Werner-Lin, A. (2006). Families, health, and illness. In S. Gehlert & T. Browne (Eds.), *Handbook of Health Social Work* (pp. 305–344). Hoboken, NJ: John Wiley & Sons.

Rolland, J. (1994). *Families, illness, and disability*. New York: Basic Books.

Root, L., (2005). Our social work group's process of conducting an outcomes-driven project. *Journal of Nephrology Social Work*, 24, 9–13.

Rothman, J., & Sager, J. (1998). *Case management: Integrating individuals and communities.* Boston: Allyn & Bacon.

Ryan, J. G., Leguen, F., Weiss, B. D., Albury, S., Jennings, T., Velez, F., & Salibi, N. (2008). Will patients agree to have their literacy skills assessed in clinical practice? *Health Education Research, 23*(4), 603–611.

Rydholm, L. (1997). Patient-focused care in parish nursing. *Holistic Nursing Practice, 11,* 47–60.

Saad, L. (2008, July). *U.S. smoking rate still coming down: About one in five American adults now smoke.* Retrieved from http://www.gallup.com/poll/109048/us-smoking-rate-still-coming-down.aspx

Sack, K. (2010, February 7). Texas nurse faces trial and possibly 10 years in prison for reporting a doctor. *New York Times,* p. 14.

Sacks, F. M., Bray, G. A., Carey, V. J., Smith, S. R., Ryan, D. H., Anton, S. D., McManus, et al., Williamson, D. A. (2009). Comparison of weight-loss diets with different compositions of fat, protein, and carbohydrates. *New England Journal of Medicine 360*(9), 859–873.

Samet, J. H., Friedmann, P., & Saitz, R. (2001). Benefits of linking primary medical care and substance abuse services: Patient, provider, and societal perspectives. *Archives of Internal Medicine. 161*(1), 85–91.

Santana-Martin, S., & Santana, F. O. (2005). An introduction to Mexican culture for service providers. In J. H. Stone (Ed.), *Culture and disability: Providing culturally competent services* (pp. 161–186). Thousand Oaks, CA: Sage.

Satcher, D., Fryer, G. E., McCann, J., Troutman, H., Woolf, S. H., & Rust, G. (2005). What if we were equal? A comparison of the black-white mortality gap in 1960 and 2000. *Health Affairs 24*(3), 459–464.

Schattschneider, E. (1980). *The Semi-Sovereign People.* New York: Holt, Rinehart, & Winston.

Scheid, T. L. (2004). Service system integration: Panacea for chronic care populations. In J. J. Kronenfeld (Ed.), *Chronic care, healthcare systems and services integration* (pp. 141–158). Oxford, UK: Elsevier.

Schild, D. R., & Sable, M. R. (2006). Public health and social work. In S. Gehlert & T. A. Browne (Eds.), *Handbook of Health Social Work* (pp. 70–122). Hoboken, NJ: John Wiley & Sons.

Schild, D. R., Taylor-Brown, S., & Djurdjinovic, L. (2006). Social work and genetics. In S. Gehlert, & T. Browne, (Eds.), *Handbook of health social work* (pp. 568–614). Hoboken, NJ: John Wiley & Sons.

Schneider, R. L., & Lester, L. (2001). *Social work advocacy: A new framework for action.* Belmont, CA: Brooks/Cole.

Schover, L. (2000). Sexual problems in chronic illness. In S. R. Leiblum & R. C. Rosen (Eds.), *Principles and practice of sex therapy* (pp. 57–81). New York: Guilford.

Schulman, K. A., Berlin, J. A., Harless, W., Kerner, J., Sistrunck, S., Gersh, B., Dube, R., et al. (1999). The effect of race and sex on physicians' recommendations for cardiac catheterization. *New England Journal of Medicine, 340,* 618–626.

Schultz, R., Mendelson, A. B., Haley, W. E., Mahoney, D., Allen, R. S., Zhang, S., & Thompson, L. (2003). End-of-life care and the effects of bereavement on family caregivers of persons with dementia. *New England Journal of Medicine, 349,* 1936–1942.

Schwartz, J. (2005, July 4). A team effort to resolve family bedside conflicts. *New York Times,* p. 1.

Sczezepura, A. (2004). Healthcare access for minorities. *Postgraduate Medical Journal, 81,* 141–147.

Seal, M. (2007). Patient advocacy and advance care planning in the acute hospital setting. *Australian Journal of Advanced Nursing, 4,* 29–36.

Segal, U. (2002). *A framework for immigration: Asians in the United States.* New York: Columbia University Press.

Shea, S., & Hripcsak, G. (2010). Accelerating the use of electronic health records in physician practices. *New England Journal of Medicine. 362,* 192–195.

Shenker, F., Wang, F., Selig, S. J., Ng, R., & Fernandez, A. (2007). The impact of language barriers on documentation of informed consent at a hospital with on-site interpreter services. *Journal of General Internal Medicine, 22*(Supplement 2), 259–299.

Showalter, A. (2008, January). Can you influence laws to benefit your organization? *Nonprofit World, 26*(1), 29.

Shumer, F. (2009, September 29). After a death, the pain that doesn't go away. *New York Times,* pp. D1, D6.

Siefert, K., Bowman, P., Heflin, C., Danziger, S., & Williams, D. (2000). Social and environmental predictors of maternal depression in current and recent welfare recipients. *American Journal of Orthopsychiatry, 70*(4), 510–522.

Simon, G. E., Ludman, E. J., & Operskalski, B. H. (2006). Randomized trial of a telephone care management program for outpatients starting antidepressant treatment. *Psychiatric Services, 57,* 1441–1445.

Simon, G. E., Katon, W. J., Lin, E. H. B., Rutter, C., Manning, W. G., Von Korff, M., Ciechanowski, P. et al. (2007). *Archives of General Psychiatry, 64*(1): 65–72.

Singer, P. (2007, January 3). Early births fade to grey. *The Australian,* p. 10.

Skenker, Y., Wang, F., Selig, S. J., Ng, R., & Fernandez, A. (2007). The impact of language barriers on documentation of informed consent at a hospital with on-site interpreter services. *Journal of General Internal Medicine, 22*(Suppl. 2), 295–299.

Smeltzer, S. C., Sharts-Hopko, N. C., Ott, B. B., Zimmerman, V., & Duffin, J. (2007). Perspectives of women with disabilities on reaching those who are hard to reach. *Journal of Neuroscience Nursing, 39*(3), 163–171.

Smerd, J. (2007). The silent treatment: "Just be quiet about it." *Workforce Management, 1,* 16–20.

Smith, M., & Mason, M. (1995). Developmental disability services to Caribbean Americans in New York City. *Journal of Community Practice, 2,* 87–106.

Soeken, K. L., McFarlane, J., Parker, B., & Lominack, M. (2003). *The abuse assessment screen.* Retrieved January 19, 2010, from http://chipts.ucla.edu/assessment/IB/List_Scales/Abuse%20Assessment%20Screen.htm

Sohn, E. (2009, February 23). The power of potassium. *Los Angeles Times.* Retrieved from http://www.latimes

.com/news/health/heartawareness/la-he-sodium23,0,
6956422.story

Solomon, B. (1976). *Black Empowerment*. New York, NY:
Columbia University Press.

Sosin, M., & Caulum, S. (1983). Advocacy: A concep-
tualization for social work practice. *Social Work, 28*
(1), 12–17.

Sotnik, P., & Jezewski, M. A. (2005). Culture and the
disability services. In J. H. Stone (Ed.), *Culture and
disability: Providing culturally competent services* (pp. 15–
36). Thousand Oaks, CA: Sage.

Spiegel, D., Butler, L. D., Giese-Davis, J., Koopman, C.,
Miller, E., DiMiceli, S., & Kraemer, H. C. (2007).
Effects of supportive-expressive group therapy on survival of patients with metastatic breast cancer: A
randomized prospective trial. *Cancer, 110*, 1130–1138.

Sporn, M. B. (1996). The war on cancer. *Lancet, 347*,
1377–1381.

Sprenger, M. J., Mulder, P. G., Beyer, W. E., Van Strik, R.,
& Masurel, N. (1993). Impact of influenza on mortality in relation to age and underlying disease, 1967–
1989. *International Journal of Epidemiology, 22*,
334–340.

Stark, D., Kiely, M., Smith, A., Velikova, G., House, A., &
Selby, P. (2002). Anxiety disorders in cancer patients:
Their nature, association, and relation to quality of life.
Journal of Clinical Oncology, 20(14), 3137–3148.

Starr, P. (1982). *The social transformation of American
medicine*. New York, NY: Basic Books.

Statistics Canada. (2009, June). *Income in Canada 2007.
Catalogue no. 75–202-X*. Retrieved from www.statcan
.gc.ca

Stein, J. (2009, December 22). Being poor could be the
greatest health burden. *Los Angeles Times*. Retrieved
from http://latimesblogs.latimes.com/booster_shots/
2009/12/being-poor-could-could-be-the-greatest-health-
burden.html

Stein, T. (2004). *Role of law in social work practice and
administration*. New York: Columbia University Press.

Steinbrook, R. (2005). Wall street and clinical trials.
New England Journal of Medicine, 353(11), 1091–
1093.

Steinbrook, R. (2008). Campaign contributions, lobbying, and the U.S. health sector. *New England Journal of
Medicine, 359*(13), 1313–1315.

Steiner, J. F. (2005). The use of stories in clinical research
and health policy. *Journal of the American Medical
Association*, vol. 294(22).

Stevens, R., & Stevens R. (1974). *Welfare medicine in America: A case study of Medicaid*. New York, NY: Free Press.

Steward, J. K. (2009, May 24). Medicare benefits slated to
change. *Los Angeles Times*, p. B3.

Stolberg, S. (2009, September 27). Taking healthcare
courtship up another notch. *New York Times*, p. 20.

Stone, J. H. (Ed.). (2005). *Culture and disability: Providing
culturally competent services*. Thousand Oaks, CA: Sage.

Stone, P. W., Teutsch, S., Chapman, R. H., Bell, C.,
Goldie, S. J., & Neumann, P. J. (2000). Cost-utility
analyses of clinical preventive services published ratios, 1976–1997. *American Journal of Preventive Medicine, 19*(1), 15–23.

Stone, S. (2007). *Retrospective evaluation of the Planetree
patient-centered model of care program's impact on inpatient quality outcomes*. PhD Dissertation, Hahn School
of Nursing and Health Science, University of San
Diego.

Strain, J. J., & Blumenfield, M. (2008). Challenges for
Consultation-Liaison Psychiatry in the 21st Century,
Psychosomatics 49(2), 93–96.

Street, R. L., O'Malley, K. J., Cooper, L. A., & Haidet, P.
(2008). Understanding concordance in patient-
physician relationships: Personal and ethnic dimensions of shared identify. *Annals of Family Medicine, 6*
(3), 198–205.

Substance Abuse and Mental Health Services Adminis-
tration. (2006). *Drug abuse warning network, 2006:
National estimates of drug-related emergency room visits*.
Retrieved from https://dawninfo.samhsa.gov/files/
ED2006/DAWN2k6ED.pdf

Substance Abuse and Mental Health Services Administration. (2008). *Drug abuse warning network, 2006:
National estimates of drug-related emergency department
visits*. Retrieved from https://dawninfo.samhsa.gov/
files/ED2006/DAWN2k6ED.pdf

Substance Abuse and Mental Health Services Administration. (2009). *Results from the 2008 national survey on
drug use and health: National findings*. Rockville, MD:
Office of Applied Studies.

Sullivan, D. H., Sun, S., & Walls, R. C. (1999). Protein-
energy undernutrition among elderly hospitalized
patients: A prospective study. *Journal of the American
Medical Association, 28*(1), 2013–2019.

Sumner, J. (2001). Caring in nursing: A different interpretation. *Journal of Advanced Nursing, 35*(6), 926–932.

Sunley, R. (1983). *Advocating today: A human service
practitioner's handbook*. New York, NY: Family Services America.

Sunley, R. (1997). Advocacy in the new world of managed care. *Families in Society, 78*(1), 84–94.

Sunley, R. (2008). *Righting wrongs: Advocacy principles,
methods & practice*. Victoria, BC: Trafford.

Surwit, R., & Schneider, M. (1993). Role of stress in the
etiology and treatment of diabetes mellitus. *Psychosomatic Medicine, 55*, 380–393.

Swendiman, K. S., & Jones, N. L. (2007). *Extensively drug-
resistant tuberculosis (XDR-TB): Quarantine and isolation*. Congressional Research Service Report for Congress. Retrieved from http://fpc.state.gov/documents/
organization/86251.pdf

Swick, H. M. (2000). Toward a normative definition of
medical professionalism. *Academic Medicine, 75*(6),
612–616.

Syrjala, K. L., Langer, S. L., Abrams, J. R., Storer, B.,
Sanders, J. E., Flowers, M.E.D., & Martin, P. J. (2004).
Recovery and long-term function after hematopoietic
cell transplantation for leukemia or lymphoma. *Journal of the American Medical Association, 291*, 2335–
2343.

Tamayo-Sarver, J. H., Hinze, S. W., Cydulka, R. K., &
Baker, D.W. (2003). Racial and ethnic disparities in
emergency department analgesic prescription. *American Journal of Public Health, 93*, 2067–2073.

Tarkan, L. (2008, December 2). Arrogant, abusive, and disruptive—And a doctor. *New York Times*, p. D1.

Tarnower, H. (1978). *The complete Scarsdale medical diet plus Dr. Tarnower's lifetime keep-slim program*. New York: Rawson, Wade.

Taylor, H. A., Jr., Cano, J. G., Sanderson, B., Rogers, W. J., & Hilbe, J. (1998). Management and outcomes for black patients with acute myocardial infarction in the reperfusion era. National Registry of Myocardial Infarction 2 Investigators. *American Journal of Cardiology, 82*, 1019–1023.

Thacker, K. S. (2008). Nurses' advocacy behaviors in end-of-life nursing care. *Nursing Ethics, 15*(2), 174–175.

Thom, D. H., Hall, M. A., & Pawlson, L. G. (2004). Measuring patients' trust in physicians when assessing quality of care. *Health Affairs, 23*(4), 124–132.

Timmermans, S., & Mauck, M. (2005). Promises and pitfalls of evidence-based medicine. *Health Affairs, 24*(1), 18–28.

Touvier, M., Kesse, E., Clavel-Chapelon, F., & Boutron-Ruault, M. (2005). Dual association of beta-carotene with risk of tobacco-related cancers in a cohort of French women. *Journal of the National Cancer Institute, 97*, 1338–1344.

Trattner, W. (1974). *From poor law to welfare state: A history of social welfare in America*. New York, NY: Free Press.

Travis, J., Solomon, A. L., & Waul, M. (2001). *From prison to home: The dimensions and consequences of prisoner reentry*. Washington, DC: Urban Institute.

Trumbo, P., Yates, A. A., Schlicker, S., & Poos, M. (2001). Dietary reference intakes. *Journal of the American Dietetic Association, 200*, 294–301.

Trzepacz, P., & Baker, R. (1993). *The psychiatric mental status examination*. New York, NY: Oxford University Press.

Turk, D., & Melzack. (2001). *Handbook of Pain Assessment*. New York, NY: Guilford.

Ubel, P. A. (2001). Truth in the most optimistic way. *Annals of Internal Medicine, 134*(12), 1142–1143.

UKpolitical.info. (2010). *General election turnout 1945–2005*. Retrieved March 2, 2010, from http://www.ukpolitical.info/Turnout45.htm

United Nations Office on Drugs and Crime. (2010). *Homicide statistics, criminal justice and public health sources—Trends 2003–2008*. Retrieved from http://www.unodc.org/unodc/en/data-and-analysis/homicide.html

Urban-Brookings Tax Policy Center. (2009, May). *Table T09–0228: Various reforms of the ESI exclusion impact on tax revenues ($ billions), 2010–2019*. Retrieved from http://www.taxpolicycenter.org/numbers/displayatab.cfm?DocID=2302

U.S. Department of Veterans Affairs. (2010, February). *CHAMPVA*. Retrieved March 10, 2010, from http://www4.va.gov/hac/forbeneficiaries/champva/champva.asp

U.S. News & World Report. (2010). *Rankings of health Plans*. Retrieved November 15, 2010, from http://health.usnews.com/health-plans (see "Best Commercial Plans").

U.S. Preventive Services Task Force. (2003, June). *Routine vitamin supplementation to prevent cancer and cardiovascular disease: Recommendations and rationale*. Agency for Healthcare Research and Quality, Rockville, MD. Retrieved from http://www.ahrq.gov/clinic/3rduspstf/vitamins/vitaminsrr.htm

Vaartio, H., & Leino-Kilpi, H. (2005). Nursing advocacy—A review of the empirical research 1990–2003. *International Journal of Nursing Studies, 42*, 705–714.

Valdez, R. (1997). A comparison of sleep patterns among compliant and noncompliant chronic hemodialysis patients. *Journal of Nephrology Social Work, 17*, 28–36.

Van Ryn, M., & Burke, J. (2000). The effect of patient race and socioeconomic status on physicians' perceptions of patients. *Social Science and Medicine, 50*, 813–828.

Varner, S. (Writer). (2010, February 21). Dental coverage cuts leave California's poor in pain [Radio Broadcast Episode]. In *Weekend Edition Saturday*. Washington, DC: National Public Radio.

Vastag, B. (2009). Nutrients for prevention: Negative trials send researchers back to drawing board. *Journal of the National Cancer Institute. 101*, 446–451.

Veatch, R. (1981). *A theory of medical ethics*. New York: Basic Books.

Veatch, R. M. (2009). Patient, heal thyself: How the new medicine puts the patient in charge. *Journal of the American Medical Association, 301*(13), 1388–1389.

Vermeire, E., Hearnshaw, H., Van Royen, P., & Denekens, J. (2001). Patient adherence to treatment: Three decades of research. A comprehensive review. *Journal of Clinical Pharmacy and Therapeutics, 26*, 331–342.

Wadden, T. A., West, D. S., Neiberg, R. H., Wing, R. R., Ryan, D. H., Johnson, K. C., & Look AHEAD Research Group. (2009). One-year weight losses in the Look AHEAD study: Factors associated with success. *Obesity, 17*(4), 713–722.

Walden, T., Woloch, I., & Demone, H. (1990). Ethical decision-making in human services: A comparative study. *Families in Society: Journal of Contemporary Human Services, 71*, 67–75.

Walker, C. (2008). Antioxidant supplements do not improve mortality and may cause harm. *American Family Physician 78*, 1079–1080.

Walsh, P. (2001). *Guide to surviving prostate cancer*. New York: Warner.

Wang, C., Gonzalezb, R., & Merajverc, S. D. (2004). Assessment of genetic testing and related counseling services: Current research and future directions. *Social Science & Medicine, 58*(7), 1427–1442.

Wang, P. S., Lane, M., Olfson, M., Pincus, H. A., Wells, K. B., & Kessler, R. C. (2005). Twelve-month use of mental health services in the United States. *Archives of General Psychiatry, 62*, 629–640.

Warkentien, S., Clark, M., & Jacinto, B. (2009). *English iteracy of foreign-born adults in the United States: 2003* (Issue Brief no. NCES 2009–034). Washington, DC: National Center for Education Statistics, Institute of Education Sciences, U.S. Department of Education.

Warren, E. (2005, February 9). "Sick and Broke." *Washington Post*, p. A 23.

Wartik, N. (2002, June 23). Hurting more, helped less? *New York Times*, pp. 1, 6.

Wartman, S. (2006). My mother, a professional patient. *Health Affairs, 25*, 1407–1411.

Waz, W., & Henkind, J. (1995). The adequacy of medical ethics education in a pediatrics training program. *Academic Medicine, 70*, 1041–1043.

Webb, A., & Zhivan, N. (2010). *How much is enough? The distribution of lifetime healthcare costs*. Chestnut Hill, MA: Center for Retirement Research at Boston College.

Wechsler, H., Levin S., & Idelson, R. K. (1996). The physician's role in health promotion revisited—A survey of primary care practitioners. *New England Journal of Medicine, 334*, 996–998.

Wee, C. C., McCarthy, E. P., Davis, R. B., & Phillips, R. S. (1999). Physician counseling about exercise. *Journal of the American Medical Association, 282*, 1583–1587.

Weihs, K., Fisher, L., & Baird, M. (2002). Families and the management of chronic disease. Report for the Committee on Health and Behavior. Institute of Medicine, National Academy of Sciences, Families, Systems, and Health. *Families, Systems, and Health, 20*(1), 7–47.

Weinstein, I. (2000). Eighty years of public health in New York City. *Journal of Urban Health: Bulletin of the New York Academy of Medicine, 77*, 121–136.

Weiss, B. D. (2007). *Health literacy and patient safety: Help patients understand. Manual for clinicians*. Chicago: American Medical Association Foundation.

Weissman, J. et al. (2005). Resident physicians preparedness to provide cross-cultural care. *Journal of the American Medical Association, 294*(9), 1058–1067.

Wells, K. B., Sherbourne, C., Schoenbaum, M., Duan, N., Meredith, L., Unutzer, J., Miranda, J., et al. (2000). Impact of disseminating quality improvement programs for depression in managed primary care: A randomized controlled trial. *Journal of the American Medical Association, 283*, 212–220.

Werner-Lin, A., & Biank, N. (2006). Oncology social work. In S. Gehlert & T. Browne (Eds.), *Handbook of health social work* (pp. 507–531). Hoboken, NJ: John Wiley & Sons.

Wiecha, J. L., Dwyer J. T., & Dunn-Strohecker, M. (1991). Nutrition and health services needs among the homeless. *Public Health Reports, 106*, 364–374.

Wieland, D., & Hirth, V. (2003). Comprehensive geriatric assessment. *Cancer Control, 10*(6), 454–462.

Williams, D. R., & Mohammed, S. A. (2009). Discrimination and racial disparities in health: Evidence and needed research. *Journal of Behavioral Medicine, 32*(1), 20–47.

Williams, J., Hitchcock, P., Cordes, J., Ramirez, G., & Pignone, M. (2002). Is this patient clinically depressed? *Journal of the American Medical Association, 287*(9), 1160–1170.

Williams, J., Katon, W., Lin, E. H. B., Noel, P. H, Worchel, J., Cornell, J., Harpole, L., et al. (2004). Effectiveness of depression care management on diabetics. *Annals of Internal Medicine, 140*(12), 1015–1024.

Willingham, S., & Kilpatrick, E. (2005). Evidence of gender bias when applying the new diagnostic criteria for myocardial infarction. *Heart 91*, 237–238.

Wilper, A., Woolhandler, S., Lasser, K., McCormick, D., Bor, D., & Himmelstein, D. (2009). Health insurance and mortality in US adults. *American Journal of Public Health, 99*(12), 2289–2295.

Wolf, S. L., Barnhart, H. X., Kutner, N. G., & McNeely, E. (1996). Reducing frailty and falls in older persons: An investigation of Tai Chi and computerized balance training. *Journal of the American Geriatrics Society 1996, 44*, 489–491

Wolfberg, A. (2007). The patient as ally—Learning the pelvic exam. *New England Journal of Medicine, 356*(9), 495–500.

Woods, M., & Hollis, F. (2000). *Casework: A psychosocial therapy*. Boston: McGraw-Hill.

Woolf, S. H. (1999). The need for perspective in evidence-based medicine. *Journal of the American Medical Association, 282*, 2358–2365.

Woolf, S. H., Johnson, R. E., Fryer, G. E., Rust, G., & Satcher, D. (2004). The health impact of resolving racial disparities: An analysis of U.S. mortality data. *American Journal of Public Health, 94*, 2078–2081.

Woolhandler, S., Campbell, T., & Himmelstein, D. (2003). Costs of healthcare administration in the United States and Canada. *New England Journal of Medicine, 349*, 768–775.

World Health Organization. (2009). Table 7: Health expenditure. *World health statistics*. Retrieved from http://www.who.int/whosis/whostat/EN_WHS09_Table7 .pdf

Worth, T. (2009, September 28). Reliable nursing home information can be difficult to get. *Los Angeles Times*, p. E3.

Worth, T., (2009, September 28). How to decide whether a nursing home is the right fit. *Los Angeles Times*, p. E3.

Wu, A., Fink, N., Cagney, K., Bass, E., Rubin, H., Meyer, K., Sadler, et al. (2001). Developing a health related quality-of-life measure for end-stage renal disease: The CHOICE health experience questionnaire. *American Journal of Kidney Diseases, 37*, 11–21.

Wuerth, D., Finkelstein, S., Ciarcia, J., Peterson, R., Kliger, A., & Finkelstein, F. (2001). Identification and treatment of depression in a cohort of patients maintained on chronic peritoneal dialysis. *American Journal of Kidney Diseases, 37*(5), 1011–1017.

Youdelman, M. K. (2007). *Medicaid and SCHIP reimbursement models for language services*. Washington, DC: National Health Law Program.

Youdelman, M. K. (2008). The medical tongue: U.S. laws and policies on language access. *Health Affairs, 27*(2), 424–433.

Zavis, A. (2010, March 2). *Los Angeles Times*, p. AA3.

Zavis, A., & Mutert, E. (2010, March 21). California's food stamp participation rate is nation's second-lowest. *Los Angeles Times*. Retrieved from http://www.latimes.com/news/local/la-me-food-stamps21-2010mar21,0,3183867,full.story

Zebrack, B., & Chesler, M. (2001). Health-related worries, self-image, and life outlooks of long term childhood cancer survivors. *Health and Social Work, 26* (4), 245–256.

Zeitler, M. S., Paine, A. D., Breitbart, V., Rickert, C. O., Stevens, L., Rottenbert, L., Davidson, L. L. et al. (2006). Attitudes about intimate partner violence screening among an ethnically diverse sample of young women. *Journal of Adolescent Health, 39*(1), 119.e1–119.e8. doi: 10.1016/j.jadohealth.2005.09.004.

Zimmerman, M., Lish, J., Lush, D., Farber, N., Plescia, G., & Kuzma, M. (1995). Suicidal ideation among urban medical outpatients. *Journal of General Internal Medicine, 10*(10), 573–576.

Zun, L. S., Downey, L., & Rosen, J. (2006). The effectiveness of an ED-based violence prevention program. *The American Journal of Emergency Medicine, 24*(1), 8–13. doi: 10.1016/j.ajem.2005.05.009.

Author Index

Subject Index